OXFORD **READERS**

Sexuality

Edited by Robert A. Nye

OXFORD
UNIVERSITY PRESS
1999

philosophical discussions of western sexuality, this reader is obviously an essential resource for any serious investigation of one of our culture's central concerns.'

Angus McClaren
Department of History
University of Victoria, Canada

'Robert Nye has compiled a fascinating, wide-ranging and thought-provoking anthology. It will provide an important introduction to a notoriously difficult topic. His insistence on historicising sexuality is especially significant. The lucid introductory material helps to set the extracts in context, making the reader useful for a wide range of teaching and accessible to the general reader. Nye draws on an impressive variety of times, places and approaches to an elusive human phenomenon in selecting his texts, and he rightly keeps reminding reader how "sexuality" is an invention, moulded afresh in new circumstances. He emphasises the complex ways in which people experience and think about those tricky phenomena that, since the nineteenth century, have been called "sexuality".'

Ludmilla Jordanova
School of World Art Studies and Museology
University of East Anglia

'Foucault, "essentialists", "constructionists", the nineteenth-century "discovery" of sex and perversion, the modern sense of sexual identity, and the current understanding of AIDS, along with a host of other topics, all gain a rich and nuanced treatment here that will make this volume invaluable both in the classroom and for a general public that wants to have a deeper understanding of what the current "sex wars" are all about. ... Nye's extensive and thoughtful introduction provides an excellent "stand alone" introduction to the hottest issues of current debate; it is at once moderate, judicious and challenging—no small feat in an area where debate has been so intense and acrimonious.'

Guido Ruggiero
Josephine Barry Weiss Chair in the Humanities and Professor of Renaissance History
Pennsylvania State University

'I doubt if any field of study within the Anglo-American academic humanities of the past fifteen years has been livelier, faster growing, more revealing, or had greater contemporary resonances than the history of sexuality. Robert Nye's Oxford Reader *Sexuality* is an admirably comprehensive anthology of this work. It gathers together historical texts and scholarly commentaries from the ancient, medieval, and modern periods under chronological and thematic headings while Professor Nye's selection introductions compactly and intelligently place the readings in historical and theoretical context.'

Mark S. Micale
Department of History
University of Manchester

OXFORD **READERS**

The Oxford Readers series represents a unique interdisciplinary resource, offering authoritative collections of primary and secondary sources on the core issues which have shaped history and continue to affect current events.

Available

Aesthetics
Edited by Patrick Maynard and Susan Feagin

Class
Edited by Patrick Joyce

Classical Philosophy
Edited by Terence Irwin

Ethics
Edited by Peter Singer

Ethnicity
Edited by John Hutchinson and Anthony D. Smith

Evolution
Edited by Mark Ridley

Faith and Reason
Edited by Paul Helm

Fascism
Edited by Roger Griffin

Feminisms
Edited by Sandra Kemp and Judith Squires

The Mind
Edited by Daniel Robinson

Nationalism
Edited by John Hutchinson and Anthony D. Smith

Sexuality
Edited by Robert A. Nye

War
Edited by Lawrence Freedman

Forthcoming

Anit-Semitism
Edited by Paul Lawrence Rose

The British Empire
Edited by Jane Samson

Consciousness
Edited by Geoffrey Underwood

Nazism
Edited by Neil Gregor

Political Thought
Edited by Jonathan Wolff and Michael Rosen

Racism
Edited by Martin Bulmer and John Solomos

Revolution
Edited by Jack Goldstone

Slavery
Edited by Stanley Engerman, Seymour Drescher, and Robert Paquette

OXFORD
UNIVERSITY PRESS

Great Clarendon Street, Oxford OX2 6DP

Oxford University Press is a department of the University of Oxford.
It furthers the University's objective of excellence in research, scholarship,
and education by publishing worldwide in

Oxford New York

Athens Auckland Bangkok Bogotá Buenos Aires Calcutta
Cape Town Chennai Dar es Salaam Delhi Florence Hong Kong Istanbul
Karachi Kuala Lumpur Madrid Melbourne Mexico City Mumbai
Nairobi Paris São Paulo Singapore Taipei Tokyo Toronto Warsaw

with associated companies in Berlin Ibadan

Oxford is a registered trade mark of Oxford University Press
in the UK and in certain other countries

Published in the United States
by Oxford University Press Inc., New York

British Library Cataloguing in Publication Data
Data available

Library of Congress Cataloging in Publication Data
Sexuality / edited by Robert A. Nye.
(Oxford readers)
Includes bibliographical references and index.
1. Sex—History.   2. Sex customs—History.   3. Sex (Psychology—
History.   I. Nye, Robert A.   II. Series.
HQ21.S4752   1999   306.7'09—dc21   98-31709
ISBN 0-19-288019-5

10 9 8 7 6 5 4 3 2 1

Typeset in Dante
by Cambrian Typesetters, Frimley, Surrey
Printed in Great Britain
on acid-free paper by
Biddles Ltd
Guildford and King's Lynn

To the Oyster and Other Aphrodisiacs

Acknowledgements

I would like to thank the staffs of the Valley Library at Oregon State University, Widener Library at Harvard, and the Cambridge University Library. Marilyn Bethman and Ginny Domka were very gracious in helping me bundle packages off to the UK. I was very fortunate in having Nick Leggatt as a research assistant throughout most of this project. He was reliable, meticulous, and resourceful and retained his inimitable sense of humour throughout. I would also like to thank Kathy Greaves. Mary Jo Nye, Matt Reed, a group of anonymous reviewers, and George Miller at Oxford University Press read and criticized portions of the manuscript. Elinor Accampo read most of the introductory material and improved it; I am in her debt. I would also like to thank the students to whom I have taught the history of sexuality at the University of Oklahoma, Harvard University, and Oregon State University. They taught me that it is not always easy to know where to draw the line between the present and the past.

Contents

Sexuality

Introduction

On Why History is so Important to an Understanding of Human Sexuality

Historicizing Sexuality

The search for 'true' sexuality or for the 'truth' of sexuality has occupied humankind from ancient times. The word itself, as we shall see, did not come into being until the modern era, but that has not prevented students of human nature, moralists, or the custodians of power from attempting to locate and define this aspect of humanity that seems to link us variously to animals and to gods. The ancient Greeks and other peoples believed *eros* to be of divine inspiration; medieval Christianity celebrated the human sexuality of Christ incarnate; mainstream and sectarian religions alike have been animated by devotional practices imbued with erotic symbolism. But the animal features of sexuality have been equally noted and investigated. The connection it indicates of our relation to 'lesser' species has been celebrated and deplored: praised as a universal bond of organic nature and damned as a degrading and unworthy vestige of our primitive past.

Whether animal or divine, sexuality in the West has usually been portrayed in an antagonistic relationship to society. The most common characterization of sexuality has been as a corruptor or enemy of human culture, an unruly impulse that needs regulation or ritual to contain it. But this perspective has coexisted, paradoxically, alongside one that holds sexuality to have an emancipatory and liberating potential for individuals, couples, even whole communities thwarted by repressive social restraints. Nowadays these two contrary relations of sexuality and society seem more in balance with one another than in the distant past, but they both continue to tap into social ideals that arouse profoundly utopian expectations.

Given the protean and paradoxical qualities of sexuality, how should it be studied? There is no easy answer to this question. As an object of disciplinary knowledge, sexuality has never been the monopoly of any single field. It has been a principal subject for ethicists, philosophers, theologians, anthropologists, sociologists, historians, creative artists, medical professionals, psychologists, and psychoanalysts. Each perspective has contributed something to our grasp of it, but none can claim anything approaching full understanding.

I propose in this reader a *historical* approach that draws upon all the disciplines which have made sexuality an object of study or concern. This may be the best way to track a phenomenon whose outward manifestations in behaviour have changed dramatically over time but which are always expressed in and through bodies that appear to be, in R.W. Connell's phrase, 'a domain of eternal repetition'.[1] As we shall learn, however, the universality and timelessness of the body's sexuality is more apparent than real. Bodies, too, have changed, together with our understandings of them and our awareness of their potentials and functions. Paradoxically, the fact that the sexual body has always been embedded deeply in social and cultural processes has given sexuality whatever stability it has had over the centuries. Societies have always grounded sexuality in bodies that are gendered male or female; this is a theme, as we shall see, that reappears constantly throughout the history of the West.

Treating sexuality historically does not resolve our epistemological dilemma; it simply defers to the past the requirement that we provide a direct and unambiguous answer to queries about its 'truth'. We still must ask the question the eminent social historian Jeffrey Weeks poses: 'So what is a history of sexuality a history of?'[2] Once we have asked this question we are obliged to look at the myriad answers provided by past societies and individuals who thought about and lived their sexual lives in ways unique to them. We discover that the past is like a foreign country and a historian is like an ethnographer who collects catalogues of curious habits and beliefs and seeks to find in them some common pattern of resemblance. In this contest between unity and diversity, the historian / ethnographer who looks for general laws about sexuality and its historical evolution will be defeated by the sheer variety of past thought and behaviour, but the effort to ponder the historic spectrum of human sexual expression in order to reveal some underlying truth has been a regular activity of naturalists and ethicists since Greek times; it deserves our careful consideration.

Outside academic history itself, sexuality is seldom treated in a systematically historical way. Contemporary social science textbooks on sexuality often pay brief lip-service to the history of sexuality before making it clear that only in recent years have Western societies reached a level of enlightenment about sexual matters that allows them to understand the 'facts' about sexuality revealed by current sexological research. Most such texts have liberal and tolerant views of past sexual beliefs and practices. They invoke history for two purposes: first, to remind readers that because history reveals a diversity of past beliefs and practices, our present beliefs are not necessarily 'natural' or 'correct', but, secondly, to identify 'which contemporary beliefs are based more on the traditions and mythology developed by our ancestors than on current factual knowledge'.[3]

The contradictory outlook embodied in these statements suggests the presence of a selective application of the denaturalizing and deconstructive features

[1] R.W. Connell, 'Sexual Revolution', in Lynne Segal (ed.), New Sexual Agendas (New York: New York University Press, 1997), 64.

[2] Jeffrey Weeks, Sexuality (London: Routledge, 1986), 21.

[3] Albert R. Allgeier and Elizabeth R. Allgeier, Sexual Interactions, 4th edn. (Lexington, Mass.: D.C. Heath, 1995), 3–4.

of historical analysis. In this perspective history is useful because it helps us target the misguided views and actions of our ancestors that have survived into our more enlightened era, and, inversely, because it helps us locate the heroic pioneers who first recognized an ethical or scientific 'truth' of sexuality in some otherwise benighted time.

There is much to recommend such a position; the idea that knowledge is cumulative and produces greater and greater degrees of certainty is a venerable aspect of the human relationship to nature and society. However, the weakness of this assumption lies in the ease with which we allow ourselves to be persuaded that the kind of critical historical analysis we use to undermine past and present 'falsehoods' is somehow not applicable to knowledge we believe to be currently 'true'. In this reader I hope to avoid the kind of historical selectivity that merely acts to confirm present certainties, and instead to historicize the whole of human sexuality: the praised and the despised, scientific norms and the charlatan fringe, mainstream and periphery.

There is certainly considerable tension between the search for universal and timeless laws of sexuality and a historicizing approach that seeks to explain sexual ideals and behaviour as a product of changing historical circumstances. In a form appropriate to the field, these different epistemological approaches have played an important role in the methodological debates within the history of sexuality itself. Sex and sexual morality have been a subject of historical writing for centuries, but as a serious field of academic study the history of sexuality is only a few decades old. It has grown out of the recent interest in gender studies, the history of the body, and from the important work of a generation of philosophers and of feminist, gay, and lesbian theorists who have found it useful to explain social arrangements—including norms governing sex and reproduction—as cultural products amenable to change.

The universalist/historicist debate in the history of sexuality has most often been characterized as one between the 'essentialists' and the 'social construc-tionists', a distinction first systematically explored in a celebrated essay by the historian John Boswell in 1982.[4] As Boswell himself pointed out, the 'debate' was in reality not equally joined within the historical community itself. Though historians occasionally have claimed they are looking for general laws, the vast majority of historical research and writing assumes, with the social construc-tionists, that institutions, customs, social practices, and legal systems are created and shaped by men and women in particular historical circumstances. The debate has been concerned with just how much about bodies, sex differ-ence, sexual practices, and the gender arrangements of society can be explained on constructionist principles alone, or whether there is not some 'essential' and

[4] John Boswell, 'Revolutions, Universals and Sexual Categories', reprinted in Martin Duberman, Martha Vicinus, and George Chauncey (eds.), *Hidden from History: Reclaiming the Gay and Lesbian Past* (New York: NAL, 1989), 17–36.

unchanging sexual nature that persists in spite of cultural and linguistic changes no one would deny.

Despite the apparent one-sidedness of this 'debate', what is at stake is nothing less than an important epistemological purchase on the question about the 'truth' of sexuality with which this introduction began. If history could demonstrate that there is some unchanging substratum of human sexual nature that has persisted throughout the ages, it might permit us to make judgements on some of the controversial sex and gender arrangements in contemporary society. If, for example, one could demonstrate that homosexual orientation has always existed in more or less its present form, this might lend more plausibility to the current biological arguments about the existence of a 'gay gene'. This greater certainty might in turn permit us to consider sexual orientation in the same deterministic frame of reference that we have become accustomed to use for race and make it subject to the same legal discriminations and protections that race has always enjoined. The same kinds of historical 'truths' might be found for heterosexuality or for the incommensurability and permanence of sexual difference, from which we might then be encouraged to draw particular conclusions about marriage, reproduction, transsexual operations, or the gendering of the workplace.

If, on the other hand, it could be demonstrated that all sexual 'essentials' may be historically deconstructed into more or less unique phenomena that take their meanings and significance from their social and historical context, then we could not so easily appeal to the 'truth' of history to privilege one set of our contemporary sexual values or practices over another. The spectre of relativism raised by this prospect has encouraged some thinkers to worry about how we would ever be able to distinguish between 'good' or 'bad' sexual behaviour, but a truly radical historicization would also destabilize our ability to decide about the 'typical' or 'unusual' in sexuality, or draw conclusions about frequent or infrequent phenomena. If sexuality and its meaning is entirely dependent on the context in which it occurs, so the argument might go, what significance can we attach to its rarity or commonality?

Indeed, what may be most at stake are the different prospects a constructionist method raises for innovation and tradition in sexual matters. Michel Foucault, one of the most influential anti-essentialist theorists of recent times, wrote that good critical-historical method involves 'making visible a *singularity* at places where there is a temptation to invoke a historical constant', so that 'what reason perceives as *its* necessity, or, rather, what different forms of rationality offer as their necessary being can perfectly well be shown to have a history; and the network of contingencies from which it emerges can be traced. ... It means that they reside on a base of human practice and human history; and that since these things have been made, they can be unmade, as long as we know how it was that they were made.'[5]

---

[5] Michel Foucault, 'Critical Theory/Intellectual History', in Lawrence Kritzman (ed.), *Michel Foucault: Politics, Philosophy, Culture: Interviews and Other Writings* (New York: Routledge, 1988), 37.

Constructionism, then, implicitly offers the possibility of reconstruction. It appears to presume the inescapability of choice and voluntarism and to insist that politics and power have been and are inseparable from sexual thought and practice. But the reality of the 'constructionist/essentialist' debate is far more complex. As Edward Stein has pointed out, social constructionism and essentialism are often conflated with the so-called 'nature/nurture' debate and with the distinction between voluntarism/determinism. In practice any number of possible combinations might arise from these binaries. A social constructionist might be a determinist with respect to sexual orientation, for instance, and it is possible to conceive of an essentialist who believes that nurture can powerfully offset our 'natural' sexuality and who is therefore a voluntarist with respect to sexual orientation.[6]

Many scholars agree that there is little to be gained by caricaturing either position in this debate. Perhaps the most useful thing to do is to stake out terrain that can accommodate all but the most extreme epistemological positions. In recent years some creative ways of thinking about sexual categories and sexual identity have been advanced that explore this middle ground. These approaches attempt to amalgamate a 'nominalist' and constructionist analysis that emphasizes language with a 'realist' assessment of lived bodily experience. Most of the debates about method in the history of sexuality are about the extent to which language and linguistic categories are capable of shaping sexual behaviour and identity. The question is, are bodies and their pleasures independent of the ways that language characterizes them, or do we require linguistic and cultural representations to prompt and interpret bodily experience? Can the experience or the identity of homosexuality exist, for instance, if the concept 'homosexuality' has not yet appeared or the word not yet been coined?

David Halperin, a distinguished classical scholar who has written extensively on these issues, argues that sexual categories like homosexuality are indispensable to the experience of 'being' homosexual. Such categories, he writes, are 'objectivated fictions', cultural constructions that have real presence in the world. He wants to make clear that such categories do not exist 'outside of history and culture', nor are they some form of 'false consciousness'. Instead he argues that there is a sense in which culture sediments 'categories of thought' into 'categories of erotic response', which, he explains, 'have a claim on my belief that's stronger than intellectual allegiance. That, after all, is what it means to be acculturated into a sexual system: the conventions of the system acquire the self-confirming inner truth of "nature". If one could simply think oneself out of one's acculturation, it wouldn't be acculturation in the first place.'[7]

[6] Edward Stein, 'Conclusion', in Edward Stein (ed.), *Forms of Desire: Sexual Orientation and the Social Constructionist Controversy* (London: Routledge, 1992), 327–31.

[7] David Halperin, *One Hundred Years of Homosexuality and Other Essays on Greek Love* (London: Routledge, 1990), 28, 53.

Halperin is arguing here for a form of cultural determinism strong enough to influence the desire and orientation of individuals.

From a related philosophical perspective, Ian Hacking has suggested that questions of sexual category and identity might be best approached using a method he calls 'dynamic nominalism' that seeks to explain the historical convergence of people's behaviour and the linguistic classification that evolves to explain it: 'The claim of dynamic nominalism is not that there was a kind of person who came increasingly to be recognized by bureaucrats or by students of human nature but rather that a kind of person came into being at the same time as the kind itself was being invented. In some cases, that is, our classifications and our classes conspire to emerge hand in hand, each egging the other on.'[8] Hacking makes use of the notion of human 'action under a description' to remind us that how we describe what we do when we do it literally constitutes the meaning of the act itself, for ourselves of course, but also for those observing us operating under the same description. Thus, he concludes, 'if new modes of description come into being, new possibilities for action come into being in consequence'.[9] The puzzle this kind of approach poses for the historian is the difficulty of identifying and explaining the moment in this social process when behaviour and classification merge, when the body and its desire fit, happily or less so, into a socially produced description.

Some theorists argue that this process is altogether linguistic, holding that we cannot approach the truths of desire or the material body directly, but must do so through the mediations of the discourse we inherit as language users. According to Judith Butler, to posit the existence of a material body that stands 'outside of language is still to posit that materiality, and the materiality so posited will retain that positing as its constitutive condition'. There is a certain sense, Butler argues, in which we can never escape the constraints of linguistic signifiers when we describe or conceptualize the body and its (sexual) functions. Butler denies she is arguing that 'everything, including materiality, is always already language', but her strong constructionist position makes it difficult to understand the body other than as a referent of language.[10]

Some scholars have suggested that such one-sided linguistic approaches would profit from being better grounded on a foundation of social events. As Carole S. Vance has asked, 'If sexuality is constructed, what is the site of the construction?'[11] The sexual body may be an elusive and changing object, but if the practitioners of much recent social constructionism have failed it is because, as R. W. Connell writes, 'it is not social enough'. It is the history of social relations, he writes, that will deepen and materialize our understandings of bodies

---

[8] Ian Hacking, 'Making up People', in Stein (ed.), *Forms of Desire*, 78.

[9] Ibid. 81.

[10] Judith Butler, *Bodies that Matter: On the Discursive Limits of 'Sex'* (London: Routledge, 1993), 67–8.

[11] Carole S. Vance, 'Pleasure and Danger: Toward a Politics of Sexuality', in Carole S. Vance (ed.), *Pleasure and Danger: Exploring Female Sexuality* (London: Routledge, 1984), 10.

engaged in social practices of a sexual kind.[12] What is more, Connell suggests, there may be and have been in the past situations in which social relations are constructed on the basis of antecedent 'sexual social relations' that are in some sense embodied in individuals' sexual practices. As he writes, 'Sexuality involves bodily arousal and pleasure, bodily processes such as pregnancy and childbirth, bodies as objects of desire. Sexual practice, then, is body-reflexive practice, even in its most refined cultural forms.'[13]

The originator of this notion of embodied practice is the ethnologist-sociologist Pierre Bourdieu. Bourdieu has argued in his book *The Logic of Practice* in favour of a notion he calls a 'practical belief'. This form of knowledge is not based on formal rationality, but is virtually *embodied* as a kind of 'social necessity turned into nature', a form of tacit knowledge that exists 'below the level of conscious expression, and the reflexive distance which these presuppose. The body believes in what it plays at; it weeps if it mimes grief. ... What is "learned by the body" is not something that one has, like knowledge that can be brandished, but something that one is.'[14] Bourdieu suggests here that there is a level of emotional or gestural expressiveness in bodies that language or discourse cannot fully grasp. It is at the very core of body experience but may be shown to have been culturally acquired.

The historian and anthropologist William M. Reddy has recently proposed a way for better understanding the history of emotions in modern societies that builds upon but moves beyond notions of Bourdieuian social practice. Like Bourdieu's, Reddy's work has important implications for the history of sexuality. Reddy argues that efforts to present emotions and emotional experience as discursive constructions empty individuals of content. He presents the evidence for the presence in individuals of a substratum of generalized emotional states such as grief, fear, and anger, and he coins the term 'emotive' to describe the language we use to explain or present these emotions to ourselves and others. Emotives are anchored directly to the feelings they describe; they possess the unique capacity to intensify, diminish, or deny those feelings in the very process of characterizing them. When we discourse on our anger we may deepen, mitigate, or otherwise enrich that feeling, and in doing so leave traces that permit historians to do a 'historical ethnography' of these emotional states in so far as they survive in speech, literature, or other cultural representations. We may thereby, Reddy suggests, deepen our understanding of the way that communities establish and maintain conventions for 'stipulating styles of emotional control that exploit the capacity of emotives to shape emotions'.[15]

[12] R. W. Connell, 'Sexual Revolution', 64–5.

[13] Ibid. 69.

[14] Pierre Bourdieu, *The Logic of Practice*, trans. Richard Nice (Stanford, Calif.: Stanford University Press, 1990), 68–73.

[15] William M. Reddy, 'Against Constructionism: The Historical Ethnography of Emotions', *Current Anthropology* 38/3 (June 1997), 335.

Migration toward an epistemological middle ground has also occurred within psychoanalysis, which was at one time a profoundly 'Darwinian' and ahistorical enterprise. In certain hands psychoanalysis has developed a highly sensitive historical and constructionist perspective on sexuality. Though Sigmund Freud admitted the bisexual nature of all human beings, in his system the 'normal' mode of sexual development was heterosexual; explanations were required only when sexual object choices or aims other than reproductive activity with the 'opposite' sex occurred. As Nancy J. Chodorow has argued, if this were true then '*any* man would suit a heterosexual woman's sexual or relational object need and vice-versa, whereas in fact there is a great cultural and individual psychological specificity to sexual object choice, erotic attraction, and fantasy. Any *particular* heterosexual man or woman chooses *particular* objects of desire (or types of objects), and in each case we probably need a cultural and individual developmental story to account for these choices.'[16] All cultures, and all the individuals within them, Chodorow suggests, have a 'history' that explains their sexuality.

The foregoing approaches to the study of sexuality and sexual desire might be grouped loosely under the heading 'moderate social constructionism'. To paraphrase Marx, and to give history a purposive, teleological nature it does not possess, one might say that this means history makes sexuality in certain ways, but not exactly as it chooses. There are certain things about bodies and the ways they have taken pleasure that are contained within the physiological and anatomical horizons of the material body itself, though even these horizons have receded or advanced with changes in nourishment, medical technologies, and life expectancy. But within these horizons a bewildering array of expressions have appeared that we include conventionally under the heading 'sexuality'. History provides the best approach for appreciating the extraordinary diversity of these expressions, the limits within which they have occurred, and the differing and recurrent ways societies have identified, regulated, channelled, and sought to contain them.

Sexuality in the West

It would be an impossibly daunting task to include in a reader of this sort extracts that treated the entire human history of sexuality, not to mention the range of sexual beliefs and practices that one finds spread across the globe today. I have limited the coverage, therefore, to sexuality in the West, which I follow chronologically through the traditional trajectory of the ancient world, Europe, and the New World of North America. Western contacts with other

---

[16] Nancy J. Chodorow, *Femininities, Masculinities, Sexualities* (Lexington: University Press of Kentucky, 1994), 37.

cultures have enriched and complicated the sexualities of the West in important ways; immigrant cultures in the nineteenth and twentieth centuries are topics of intense scholarly interest to students of sexuality. In the interests of adequate coverage, however, I have attempted to limit this reader to Western sexualities. There is a sense in which the 'otherness' of race and ethnicity is fundamental to our thinking about all forms of human 'otherness' including sexualities, but readers will find in the extracts I have chosen a substantial number of examples of this phenomenon drawn from Western sexuality alone which operate to exclude and include individuals and groups in many of the same ways.

If there is a story line in the narratives that unfold here, it is that thinking about sexuality in the West has oscillated between two fundamental questions since ancient times: 'What should I do?' and 'Who am I?'[17] Sexuality has been crucially involved in the history of ethics and the history of selfhood since Greek times. Far the older of these two queries is that of ethical reflection on the theory and practice of sexual conduct. The Greeks thought deeply about such problems as did the early Christians and their heirs in the medieval and early modern churches. Proper sexual conduct has always been regulated in criminal and civil law, and of course sexual ethics is still relevant today, judging from the recent introduction of codes of sexual conduct on university campuses and in the workplace.

As we shall see, the ethical outlook on sexual conduct—most conventionally expressed as religious morality—has infused virtually all observations on Western sexuality. The temptation to draw conclusions about proper conduct has proven irresistible for even the most secular and scientific students of sex, including those whose philosophical credos have explicitly deplored a moralizing approach. Ethical recommendations are smuggled into modern sexual commentary and research in the form of behavioural, evolutionary, or social 'norms' that become, willy-nilly, more natural, 'healthy', or reassuring guides to how we should behave. Even libertarians who refuse to condemn any form of sexual behaviour are, in effect, aligning themselves to an ethic of sexual freedom by default.

The second question, 'Who am I?', is arguably of more recent vintage. It was not unknown to ancient cultures, but its modern form dates from the rise of widespread property ownership and the emergence of civil individualism in the late Middle Ages. Westerners have experienced a gradual expansion of a sense of autonomous selfhood since that time, although these personal selves have remained deeply rooted in religious, clan, class, geographical, linguistic, or national identities. It was probably some time in the eighteenth century that a coherent notion of a sexual self and its significance for individual identity was first articulated. This era marks the beginning of the application to sexuality of

[17] See the general discussion in John H. Gagnon and Richard G. Parker, 'Conceiving Sexuality', in Richard G. Parker and John H. Gagnon, *Conceiving Sexuality* (New York: Routledge, 1995), 12–14.

what philosophers have called the 'search for natural kinds'.[18] During the Enlightenment the interest in finding recurrent examples in nature of natural kinds turned inward toward the psyche and the successive stages of personal development. What emerged by 1800 or so was a rich naturalistic discourse that regarded sexual passion as a force of nature akin to gravity or the cycle of the seasons.

The early romantics and their realist successors were intensely interested in what they called the 'physiology of love'. The more scientifically minded among them, such as the founders and practitioners of phrenology, carried their investigations into the domain of anatomy itself, claiming to locate a protuberance on the skull that varied according to the strength of an individual's 'amorous' impulses. At the beginning of the nineteenth century, the greatest interest in sexuality as a natural kind was in the quantitative differences in the sexual passions of individuals. The sinister Don Juan, immortalized in Mozart's opera *Don Giovanni*, was a monster of sexual excess and violence, but the objects and aims of his sexual tastes were the same as other men. The gendered version of this schema portrayed the sexual passions of women as gentle and slow to arouse, and those of men as more insistent and difficult to curb, though prostitutes and saintly men strained the limits of these stereotypes.

In the course of the nineteenth century more qualitative distinctions emerged in scientific, medical, and popular thinking about sexuality. Individuals were understood to differ not only in the strength and endurance of their sexual appetites but also with respect to the objects they preferred and the fashion in which they took their sexual pleasure. It seems likely that by the 1890s these preferences had become forms of personal identity that corresponded roughly to the clinical descriptions that had evolved in the psychiatric and sexological writings of the era. The answer to the question 'Who am I?' at the beginning of the twentieth century would now probably include some reference to one of these new sexual categories: heterosexual, homosexual, masochist, sadist, or fetishist. Thus constituted, sexual identity became, and remains, an integral part of our modern sense of self.

Audience and Themes

This reader is designed to stand on its own as a history of sexuality in the West or as a companion for historical or social science coursework. About three-quarters of the volume deals with the period since 1880 when the foundations for the modern medical, scientific, developmental, and social survey

---

[18] Noretta Koertge, 'Constructing Concepts of Sexuality: A Philosophical Commentary', in David P. McWhirter, Stephanie A. Sanders, and June Reinisch (eds.), *Homosexuality/Heterosexuality: Concepts of Sexual Orientation* (New York: Oxford University Press, 1990), 389.

approaches of the study of sexuality were laid. I have selected a mix of primary and secondary texts in these latter sections that include the voices of pioneer sexologists, endocrinologists, psychiatrists, and geneticists together with extracts from secondary sources that place these figures and their findings in historical context. The extracts are generally short; I have provided narrative transitions and introductions in order to give readers a sense of historical and topical continuity. This will, I hope, make the volume more accessible to the general reader who wishes to obtain a broad perspective on Western sexuality.

The reader is organized chronologically. The sections of Part I are organized to correspond to a conventional periodization through the nineteenth century. The title 'Before Sexuality' refers to the theme, discussed briefly in the previous sections of the introduction, that our modern concept of sexuality as a natural and integral aspect of modern selfhood did not fully emerge in the West until the nineteenth century. The Greeks and Romans organized their erotic lives to correspond to the gendered distribution of power that prevailed in their societies: property-owning citizens in active sexual roles, women in passive ones, adolescent boys occupying a liminal status of their own.

The early Christians deeply distrusted their sexual impulses because they bound them to the earthly, human sphere. The most devout attempted to purge themselves altogether of desire; the married majority were enjoined to restrict sexual desire to procreative coupling. In the Middle Ages a revival of Greek medical learning elevated discussions of sexual matters into a topic for theological disputations. The medieval church acknowledged the necessity of pleasure in marital, procreative sex, but forbade all other carnal contact, warning believers in particular about the dangers of loose women. The growth of stronger state authority in the period after 1500 provided religious elites with more power to regulate sexuality closely and greater reason for princes—in the name of public order—to see danger in forms of sexual expression that violated patriarchal and procreative norms.

In the course of the eighteenth and nineteenth centuries, a more secular and middle-class conception of sexuality established itself. Members of the urban bourgeoisie were engaged in an effort to define and valorize their self-disciplined and abstemious habits in contrast to the perceived disorders and excesses of peasant and working-class life. In doing so they sought to internalize the mechanism for sexual regulation that had been enforced externally by religious and moral authorities. They also began the process of naturalizing sexual impulses, gendering them and ascribing them to distinctively male and female bodies. Perhaps because sexual self-governance required the application of conscious will, sexuality became in this period a metaphor and a marker for public and private power. Women, whose sexuality was contradictorily regarded by scientific and political authorities as both disorderly and reassuringly maternal, were excluded from public life and confined to a domestic regime under masculine protection.

The spatial segregation of the sexes characteristic of nineteenth-century society permitted, perhaps encouraged, some otherwise forbidden forms of love to thrive by default. However, in Part II of the reader we investigate the systematic efforts of doctors and public health authorities to study the forms of sexual behaviour they deemed most dangerous to morality, health, and public order. The medical man replaced the priest in this era as the arbiter and expert on sexual desire, and medical discourse gradually became the form in which the pathologies and norms of sexual health were publically discussed. Hysteria, a nervous condition that afflicted women in particular, prostitution, another female pathology, and masturbation, an evil that beset both sexes, were the characteristic sexual disorders of the nineteenth century. As we shall see, in their various ways all of them dramatized the contradictions of that deeply gendered time. The medical practitioners who specialized in their study and treatment gradually concluded that these and many related sexual problems were not the consequence of simple wilful 'perversity', as they had been regarded since the early Christian era, but true 'perversions' deeply rooted in the organism over which individuals had little control. The 'discovery' that these perversions seemed to fall more or less neatly into certain categories corresponding to deviations of sexual aim and object encouraged experts in thinking they were natural kinds. This is the historical moment when 'sexuality' achieved a phenomenological status that made it a possible and therefore appropriate object of scientific study. It is also the moment, as we have discussed above, when these disparate 'sexualities' could crystallize into personal identities. These identities included heterosexuality itself, which only came into existence as a concept after the classical perversions—inversion, sadism, masochism, fetishism—had been studied and classified.

In Part III we follow the deepening and expanding scientific and medical investigations of the modern sexual body. In the course of the twentieth century biologists have used evolutionary theory to try to explain the specialized sexual structures and processes of the human body, including the sexual gametes themselves. Embryologists have tried to explain the failed developmental mechanisms that produce intersexual individuals, historically called 'hermaphrodites', and psychiatrists and surgeons have developed techniques for normalizing their appearance and behaviour. Human sex hormones were 'discovered' between the late 1880s and about 1910. The role that these substances play in sexual growth and development has preoccupied endocrinologists throughout the century and has provided the scientific foundations of modern developmental biology and psychology. Knowledge of hormonal function, together with the surgical techniques developed to address intersexuality, now permit transsexual operations to transform individuals who claim that their biological sex is not their 'true' gender.

The most extraordinary thing about the scientific investigation of the modern sexual body is that each new discovery reveals the extent to which sex and sexuality are dependent on developmental and evolutionary processes or medical and surgical interventions. That is, they demonstrate that sex has been and is remarkably malleable. Yet in the very discourse in which these discoveries are announced a counter-discourse may be found that re-establishes a gendered version of the sexual body and operates to anchor protean sexuality in a stabilizing social and epistemological matrix. To the same end, the search for 'true' sex has continued in the form of claims about the existence of gay genes and brain structures that explain homosexual sex orientation.

In Part IV we explore the history of the twentieth-century sexual revolution, beginning with the turn-of-the-century sex 'radicals' and 'reformers' who promoted birth control, sex hygiene, and sexual enlightenment. The ideological aim of these reformers and progressive sexologists was clearly directed at a loosening or dismantling of traditional sexual morality; there is little doubt their efforts helped bring about this effect. But sexual 'enlightenment' was achieved at the price of substituting 'modern' sexual and moral norms that may be, in practice, as hard to live up to as the old ones.

The utopian component in the Western outlook on sexuality is most completely revealed in the liberationist ideals that undergirded the 'sexual revolution' of the 1970s, the process of 'coming out', and the vast expansion of pornography. All these movements enjoined great expectations; all of them have reaped a measure of disappointment and experienced unintended consequences, as utopian expectations generally do. Sexual liberation in general and gay and lesbian liberation in particular have stimulated an influential neo-conservative discourse in matters of sex and reproduction. This includes an invidious association of gay liberation with the terrible epidemic of HIV/AIDS, and criticism of pornography by a coalition of conservative and feminist activists.

Despite these setbacks to the liberationist outlook, something has changed in the late twentieth century that is probably irreversible. Sexuality has always been an obsessive human concern; it has often been the 'real' subject of cultural, religious, and political discourses that did not dare to mention it or did not have the language for addressing it directly. We now possess both the language and the cultural temerity to discuss sexuality as straightforwardly as we like and with a frankness that would have shocked people a few decades ago. It now seems impossible to contemplate human happiness without some measure of sexual fulfilment, although that remains a notoriously exclusive and negotiable ideal. Nor is it possible now to think about our identities or the identities of others without factoring in sexual tastes and orientation. The idea that tastes and identities appear in particular historical circumstances means that we are unlikely to understand the promise or the limits of our contemporary sexualities unless we understand those of the past.

Section I

Before 'Sexuality'

I.a. The Ancient World

For a number of reasons the ancient world has played an important role in much recent thinking and writing about sexuality. First, we have reason to believe that public and private sexual behaviour were very different from the modern era, enough so that those who favour the idea that sexuality has been socially and culturally variable may strengthen their case by referring to classical Greece or Rome or to even older ancient cultures. By the same token, authors wishing to stress the continuities and timelessness of human sexuality can make their best case for the most remote period of Western history, where one might reasonably expect to find the greatest contrast with our own era. Finally, sexuality in the ancient world figured prominently in the birth-pangs of our modern notions of sexuality in the nineteenth century as a kind of historical exemplar for radical sexual reform and greater tolerance for diversity, a role it still plays today.

It might seem obvious or trivial to say, but the most important thing to note about the thousand years or so of human history prior to the birth of Christ is precisely that it was pre-Christian. Christianity etched its concepts of the body, the good life, and the road to salvation deeply into Western culture and law, a development we take up in the next section. However, in keeping with our theme of continuity within change, some selections in this and the following section will stress the way that ancient cultures themselves provided some of the inspiration for Christian sexual teachings, in much the same way that Graeco-Roman temples sometimes served as the foundations for later Christian churches. Whether one prefers to see the later Christian era as a reaction against pagan sexual excess or a synthesis of earlier practices and beliefs, there is no doubting the importance of ancient sexuality for any full understanding of either the history and nature of sexuality or modern sexual politics.

The first thing we note is the embeddedness of sexuality. Sexual acts were invariably discussed or represented as part of a larger theological, metaphysical, or ethical context. Ancient civilizations owed their survival to their ability to wrest a living from the soil. It is not surprising that they associated sexuality with reproduction and with the general fertility of nature. Cuneiform tablets from third-millennium Mesopotamia reveal the male god Enki displaying the inseminating and irrigational power of virility, while the goddess Inanna, in a variety of 'bridal songs', celebrates the well-watered fertility of her vulva

(Extract 1). Much later, in first-century AD Graeco-Roman Egypt, the Nile delta town of Canopus was the site of a religious festival and cultic fertility rites associated with the annual inundation of the Nile. As in ancient Mesopotamia, sexual pleasure is openly celebrated, but it is yoked to profound sexual and religious requirements (Extract 2).

Similar examples linking penetration, procreation, and the fertility of nature may be found in classical Greece and Rome. From the earlier example it should be clear that there was something highly symbolic about the act of penetration itself; it represented a genuinely unequal ethical and power valuation between the penetrator and the penetrated. This judgement, which comes remarkably close to universality in human cultures, was originally produced in these patriarchal and largely agricultural societies, but, as we shall see, it continued to thrive well into modern times (Extract 3).

In classical Greece, sexual behaviour and values owed much of their orientation to a code of honour and shame that regulated relations between members of the male elite in the Greek city-states that flourished between the sixth and fourth centuries BC. Women were only a part of this system of honour as possessions of their fathers or husbands, who, in order to guarantee an undisputed blood-heir and the smooth succession of their property, were obliged to protect their womenfolk from other men. The hard business of producing an heir did not prevent men from visiting prostitutes, taking mistresses, cultivating pederastic relations with young boys, or increasing the measure of their own honour by having illegal, adulterous relations with the wives of other men, as numerous texts and vast paintings of the time reveal (Extract 4).

It was certainly a man's world, and one that was in its essence hierarchical and keenly conscious of power. However, if we can credit Pausanias's speech in Plato's dialogue The Symposium, within the slave-holding upper classes an ethic flourished that distinguished between vulgar and ennobling forms of love and scorned those who only cared about 'completing the sexual act' (Extract 5).

This and similar passages in Greek texts celebrating pederastic love are the subject of considerable interpretative disagreement among contemporary scholars. The late French philosopher Michel Foucault stressed the importance to the Greeks of the beauty of the love object (whether male or female) and the great value attached to the condition of being in love over sexual consummation (Extract 6).

However, in a study of Greek law, David Cohen doubts the extent of tolerance for male–male sexual relations generally. He prefers to link ancient Greek society to its modern Mediterranean heirs, which are practically as patriarchal, but deeply committed, in theory and in practice, to heterosexual sexual relations (Extract 7).

GWENDOLYN LEICK

1   Inanna Rejoicing in her Vulva

In the Bridal Songs Inanna represents the voice of the adolescent girl. She expresses her longing to be in the presence of the beloved:

> 'I am the girl, the lady, where are you, my man?'

and

> 'Me, the lady, let me go, let me go to the garden! In the garden
> dwells the man of my heart.'[1]

These romantic sentiments imply the temporary separation of the lovers before their wedding. We also found a certain amount of imaginary intimacy in anticipation of time spent together. The bride is shown as looking forward to her married state, not least because she will enjoy then full adult sexual relations:

> 'Going to the lap of the groom—let us rejoice,
> Let us dance, let us dance,
> O Bau, let us rejoice over my vulva!
> Let us dance, let us dance,
> (until) the end it will please him, it will please him!'[2]

Intercourse with full penetration was the traditional consummation of the marriage. It allowed the 'fertilising sperm to be deposited in the woman's womb'[3] and thus induce pregnancy. It seems that it was also the form of sexual act which was forbidden to the unmarried girl.[4]

Another poem focuses on Inanna's anticipation of sexual relations within marriage.[5] In preparation for the wedding bed Inanna bathes and dresses in her grand robe:

> 'The lady started to sing in praise of herself,[6]
> The *gala*[7] will sing of it,
> Inanna started to sing a song of praise of herself;
> She sang a song of her vulva.'[8]

In this song she implies that:

> 'My bridegroom will rejoice in me; the shepherd, Dumuzi,
> will rejoice in me.'

She then embarks on a highly evocative eulogy of her vulva (*gal-la*), which is unfortunately obscure in some parts.[9] She compares it among others to a horn:

> 'The heavenly barge of the moon (with its) mooring ropes,
> The lovely crescent of the new moon,

> A fallow plot in the desert, a field of ducks, full of ducks,
> Well-watered hilly land'

and asks rhetorically

> 'For me, open my vulva—for me!
> For me, the maiden, who is its ploughman?
> My vulva, a wet place, for me—
> For me, the lady, who will provide the bull?'[10]

To which the audience replies:

> 'Oh, lady, the king will plough it for you,'

and she urges him herself:

> 'Plough my vulva, man of my heart.'

The ploughing metaphor, which we often find in the Bridal Songs, is then not just a general euphemism for sexual intercourse, but applied more specifically to the first penetration of the vagina. The young woman is compared to a field waiting to be rendered fertile, by the plough (i.e. the penis) driven by the bull (i.e. the man). It is in the context of marital intercourse that the male sexual role defines itself as the provider of fertility. The woman joyfully participates and declares her readiness 'to be ploughed'. It is hardly a coincidence that the description of the vulva in the text above captures the stages of sexual excitement in the woman. At the beginning her vulva resembles the narrow curve of the new moon until it opens 'like a boat with its mooring ropes' (more likely to refer to the labia minora than pubic hair). Then there are several references to the transudation of the mucous membranes ('well-watered low land', 'my vulva, a wet place'), at which point she cries out for the 'plough'.

If one takes the setting of these lines within the context of a marriage ceremony into account, one could say that Inanna stands for the Bride, who rejoices in her vulva because it symbolizes and contains her new identity as a sexually active and hence reproductive woman. The transitional process is only completed when she gives birth to the first child.[11] The Sumerian songs are phrased in such a manner as to emphasize the sensual pleasure the bride is to experience. In contrast to contemporary Bedouin societies of the Middle East, there seems to have been little value put on reticence and modesty in sexual matters.[12] The bride flaunts the evidence of maturity ('our parts have grown hair', 'our breasts are now standing out') and takes an interest in amatory arts (see the erotic fantasies in the Bridal Songs). She is portrayed as keenly anticipating the sensual experience of the marital bed. But we have to remember that Inanna's role as the goddess of sexual love might also have influenced the explicit nature of these references.

[*Sex and Eroticism in Mesopotamian Literature* (London: Routledge, 1994), 90–2.]

2 Festivals of Licence

The 'Canopic life' was proverbial in antiquity for being consumption run amok:[1] it was thought to be a delirious orgy of drinking, dancing, music and sex indulged in by wealthy Alexandrians against the spectacular lush landscape of the Nile Delta. Read *in vacuo* ancient accounts of the 'Canopic life' sound suspiciously like sex holidays on Phuket Island, and indeed people did anticipate finding sex at Canopus; but a crucial element is different. As well as being a smart holiday resort, Canopus was one of the major cult centres of the god Sarapis. Strabo's account of the place makes clear the links between religion, festivals and sex, conjuring up a dizzy combination of Lourdes and St Tropez:

In the town is the sanctuary of Sarapis, who is worshipped with great reverence and brings about such cures that even the most famous people believe in them and sleep in his sanctuary, whether on their own behalf, or with others standing proxy. Some sources record the cures, others the excellence of the oracles there. Opposite to all this is the throng of festival-goers (*panêgyristôn*) who travel down from Alexandria by canal; every day and every night Canopus is crowded with people on the boats who play the flute and dance unrestrainedly, with the greatest licentiousness (*akolasia*), both men and women, and also with the people of Canopus itself, who have places to stay close to the canal for the purpose of the same kind of relaxation and merry-making.

So the town of Canopus, according to Strabo, is geared up to facilitate sex, even to the extent of the local people providing places of assignation in suitable locations. But the point of Strabo's account is the way that it juxtaposes religion and festival observance with collective sexual release. The encounters one might expect at Canopus are transient, taking place in little gazebos by the canal, and are marked by excess, untramelled by the normal constraints of domestic space. Strabo's vocabulary reflects this: he talks of *akolasia* and *lamyria*, licentiousness and excess, both opposites of the control that characterised Greek ideals of sexual behaviour. But all this sexual activity takes place in a strongly sacral context. The participants are festival-goers making a religious observance; the acts take place in a town dominated by one of the holiest and most numinous religious buildings in Egypt. To me, Strabo paints a vivid picture of the erotic effect of an emotionally-charged religious atmosphere on the collective mind. The pretty physical setting—the boats bobbing about on the canal, and their lights reflected in the water—conspires with the ecstatic elements of communal festive music, the singing, the dancing, the liberation from home, the relief of devotional duties fulfilled or cures received and, no doubt, the drink, to make Canopus *the* place to find sexual release within the parameters of cultic action. [...]

However, it is one thing for individuals to get carried away with the freely-flowing drink in the relaxed festival atmosphere and have sex; sexual meanings being deeply embedded in the structure of religion and religious observance is quite another. Egyptian cosmogonies and myths about regeneration stressed the centrality of the sexual act. The annual inundation, honoured by the festival-goers in Aristaenetus' account, was metaphorised by Egyptian theologians as a human copulation on a grand scale. The Nile bursting its banks and pouring over the fields was compared to a lover mounting a woman and impregnating her. One personification of the fertility goddess Hathor was as the divine hand which masturbated the god Re-Atum, who emerged from the primordial mound. The semen spilt in this act engendered the gods who enabled life to come about on earth.[2] At Edfu in the Ptolemaic period, a festival was held during which Hathor was presented with 'the phallus that caused to flourish what has been brought into being'. And actual sexual unions between gods, so-called hierogamies, lay at the heart of religious celebrations such as the Radiant Festival of the Wadi at Thebes. This was an extended festival when the cult image of Amun-Re from the great temple at Karnak crossed the Nile in his sacred barque to visit the deities in their shrines on the west bank. Among the ritual visits he paid was one to Hathor in her temple at Deir el-Bahri, with whose cult image the ithyphallic Amun-Re 'slept' in a sexual union. It seems probable that couples came and slept in or near the shrine of Hathor on the festival night, hoping to share in the heightened sexual potency of the divine couple. Graffiti show that all classes of people, from priests to artisans, visited Hathor's temple during the Radiant Festival of the Wadi to pray and sacrifice to the goddess at this spiritually and sexually charged time.[3]

[*Sex and Society in Graeco-Roman Egypt* (London: Kegan Paul International, 1996), 163–6.]

HELEN KING

3 Sowing the Field

Myth may thus provide a language in which to speak of sexual variations, but the characters of myth are far from being models for mortals. Artemidoros here raises two further themes relevant to ancient sexology: the image of woman as earth, and the relationship between pleasure and labour. The dominant image of woman in classical culture is that of the field to be ploughed and sown. This combines the features of inequity, penetration and the objectification of women, and is explicit in many of the texts already discussed in this chapter. In the Hippocratic medical works, 'the young girl's flesh had to become porous and spongy, like earth that had been plowed for planting'; subsequent sexual ploughing promoted good drainage of the menstrual fluids.[1] The imagery of 'breaking up the earth' is used on Daphnis and Chloe's wedding night,[2] and

Ovid's 'the wheat | Grows tallest in well-dug fields' suggests that frequent ploughing leads to healthy offspring.[3] The Roman agricultural manuals show a similar concern for ensuring that the soil is suitable for planting, while Cato advises that, having chosen a good farm, 'In his youth the owner should devote his attention to planting. He should think a long time about building, but planting is a thing not to be thought about, but done.'[4] Is one objection to the sex manuals that, in women as well as in fields, planting is a thing not to be thought about, but done?

['Sowing the Field', in Roy Porter and Mikuláš Teich (eds.), *Sexual Knowledge, Sexual Science: The History of Attitudes to Sexuality* (Cambridge: Cambridge University Press, 1994), 38.]

DAVID M. HALPERIN

4 Active and Passive Sexuality

Let me begin by observing that the attitudes and behaviors publicly displayed by the citizens of Athens (to whom the surviving evidence for the classical period effectively restricts our power to generalize) tend to portray sex not as a collective enterprise in which two or more persons jointly engage but rather as an action performed by one person upon another.[1] I hasten to emphasize that this formulation does not purport to describe positively what the experience of sex was 'really' like for all members of Athenian society but to indicate how sex is *represented* by those utterances and actions of free adult males that were intended to be overheard and witnessed by other free adult males.[2] Sex, as it is constituted by this public, masculine discourse, is either act or impact (according to one's point of view): it is not knit up in a web of mutuality, not something one invariably has *with* someone. Even the verb *aphrodisiazein*, meaning 'to have sex' or 'to take active sexual pleasure,' is carefully differentiated into an active and a passive form; the active form occurs, tellingly, in a late antique list (that we nonetheless have good reason to consider representative for ancient Mediterranean culture, rather than eccentric to it)[3] of acts that 'do not regard one's neighbors but only the subjects themselves and are not done in regard to or through others: namely, speaking, singing, dancing, fist-fighting, competing, hanging oneself, dying, being crucified, diving, finding a treasure, having sex, vomiting, moving one's bowels, sleeping, laughing, crying, talking to the gods, and the like.'[4] As John J. Winkler, in a commentary on this passage, observes, 'It is not that second parties are not present at some of these events (speaking, boxing, competing, having sex, being crucified, flattering one's favorite divinity), but that their successful achievement does not depend on the cooperation, much less the benefit, of a second party.'[5]

Not only is sex in classical Athens not intrinsically relational or collaborative in character; it is, further, a deeply polarizing experience: it effectively divides, classifies, and distributes its participants into distinct and radically opposed categories. Sex possesses this valence, apparently, because it is conceived to center essentially on, and to define itself around, an asymmetrical gesture, that of the penetration of the body of one person by the body—and, specifically, by the phallus[6]—of another. Sex is not only polarizing, however; it is also hierarchical. For the insertive partner is construed as a sexual agent, whose phallic penetration of another person's body expresses sexual 'activity,' whereas the receptive partner is construed as a sexual patient, whose submission to phallic penetration expresses sexual 'passivity.' Sexual 'activity,' moreover, is thematized as domination: the relation between the 'active' and the 'passive' sexual partner is thought of as the same kind of relation as that obtaining between social superior and social inferior.[7] 'Active' and 'passive' sexual roles are therefore necessarily isomorphic with superordinate and subordinate social status; hence, an adult, male citizen of Athens can have legitimate sexual relations only with statutory minors (his inferiors not in age but in social and political status): the proper targets of his sexual desire include, specifically, women, boys, foreigners, and slaves—all of them persons who do not enjoy the same legal and political rights and privileges that he does.[8] Furthermore, what a citizen does in bed reflects the differential in status that distinguishes him from his sexual partner: the citizen's superior prestige and authority express themselves in his sexual precedence—in his power to initiate a sexual act, his right to obtain pleasure from it, and his assumption of an insertive rather than a receptive sexual role. (Even if a sexual act does not involve physical penetration, it still remains hierarchically polarized by the distribution of phallic pleasure: the partner whose pleasure is promoted is considered 'active,' while the partner who puts his or her body *at the service* of another's pleasure is deemed 'passive'—read 'penetrated,' in the culture's unselfconscious ideological shorthand.) What Paul Veyne has said about the Romans can apply equally well to the classical Athenians: they were indeed puritans when it came to sex, but (unlike modern bourgeois Westerners) they were not puritans about conjugality and reproduction; rather, like many Mediterranean peoples, they were puritans about virility.[9]

When the sexual system of the classical Athenians is described in that fashion, as though it constituted a separate sphere of life governed by its own internal laws, it appears merely exotic or bizarre, one of the many curiosities recorded in the annals of ethnography. But, if, instead of treating Athenian sexual attitudes and practices as expressions of ancient Greek 'sexuality' (conceived, in modern terms, as an autonomous domain), we situate them in the larger social context in which they were embedded, they will at once disclose their systematic coherence. For the 'sexuality' of the classical Athenians, far from being independent and detached from 'politics' (as we conceive sexuality to be), was constituted by the very principles on which Athenian public life was organized. In fact, the correspondences in classical Athens between sexual norms and social practices were so strict that an inquiry into Athenian 'sexuality' *per se* would be nonsensical: such an inquiry could only obscure the phenomenon it was intended to elucidate, for by isolating sexual norms from social practices it would conceal the sole context in which the sexual protocols of the classical Athenians make any sense—namely, the structure of the Athenian polity.

In classical Athens a relatively small group made up of the adult male citizens held a virtual monopoly of social power and constituted a clearly defined élite within the political and social life of the city-state. The extraordinary polarization of sexual roles in classical Athens merely reflects the marked division in the Athenian polity between this socially superordinate group, composed of citizens, and various subordinate groups (all lacking full civil rights, though not all equally subordinate), composed respectively of women, foreigners, slaves, and children (the latter three groups comprising persons of both sexes). Sex between members of the superordinate group was virtually inconceivable, whereas sex between a member of the superordinate group and a member of any one of the subordinate groups mirrored in the minute details of its hierarchical arrangement, as we have seen, the relation of structured inequality that governed the lovers' wider social interaction.

Sex in classical Athens, then, was not simply a collaboration in some private quest for mutual pleasure that absorbed or obscured, if only temporarily, the social identities of its participants. On the contrary, sex was a manifestation of personal status, a declaration of social identity; sexual behaviour did not so much express inward disposition or inclinations (although, of course, it did also do that) as it served to position social actors in the places assigned to them, by virtue of their political standing, in the hierarchical structure of the Athenian polity. Far from being interpreted as an expression of commonality, as a sign of some shared sexual status or identity, sex between social superior and social inferior was a miniature drama of polarization which served to measure and to define the social distance between them. To assimilate both the senior and the junior partner in a paederastic relationship to the same '(homo)sexuality,' for example, would have struck a classical Athenian as no less bizarre than to classify a burglar as an 'active criminal,' his victim as a 'passive criminal,' and the two of them alike as partners in crime:[10] burglary—like sex, as the Greeks understood it—is, after all, a 'non-relational' act. Each act of sex in classical Athens was no doubt an expression of real, personal desire on the part of the sexual actors involved, but their very desires had already been shaped by the shared cultural definition of sex as an activity that generally occurred only between a citizen and a non-citizen, between a person invested with full civil status and a statutory minor.

The social articulation of sexual desire in classical Athens furnishes a telling illustration of the interdependence in culture of social practices and subjective experiences. It thereby casts a strong and revealing light on the ideological dimension—the purely conventional and arbitrary character—of our own conceptions of sex and sexuality. The Greek record suggests that sexual choices do not always express the agent's individual essence or reveal the profound orientation of the inner life of a person, independent of social and political life. Quite the contrary: the sexual identities of the classical Athenians—their experiences of themselves as sexual actors and as desiring human beings—seem to have been inseparable from, if not determined by, the social identities, their public standing.[11] If the Greeks thought sex was 'non-relational' in character, for example, that is because sex was so closely tied to differentials in their personal status of the sexual actors rather than to the expressive capacities of individual human subjects. Thus, the classical Greek record strongly supports the conclusion drawn (from a quite different body of evidence) by the French anthropologist Maurice Godelier: 'it is not sexuality which haunts society, but society which haunts the body's sexuality.'[12]

Even the relevant features of a sexual object in classical Athens were not so much determined by a physical typology of sexes as by the social articulation of power.[13] Sexual partners came in two significantly different kinds—not male and female but 'active' and 'passive,' dominant and submissive.[14] That is why the currently fashionable distinction between homosexuality and heterosexuality (and, similarly, between 'homosexuals' and 'heterosexuals' as individual types) had no meaning for the classical Athenians: there were not, so far as they knew, two different kinds of 'sexuality,' who differently structured psychosexual states or modes of affective orientation, corresponding to the sameness or difference of the anatomical sexes of the persons engaged in a sexual act; there was, rather, but a single form of sexual experience which all free adult males shared[15]— making due allowance for variations in individual tastes, as one might make for individual palates. This 'universal' form of sexual experience could be looked at differently, to be sure, according to whether one viewed it from the perspective of the 'active' or the 'passive' sexual partner, but its essential nature did not change with such shifts in point of view.

[*One Hundred Years of Homosexuality and Other Essays on Greek Love* (New York: Routledge, 1990), 29–33.]

PLATO

5 The Speech of Pausanias[1]

It is a well-known fact that Love and Aphrodite are inseparable. If, therefore, Aphrodite were a single goddess, there could also be a single Love; but, since there are actually two goddesses of that name, there also are two kinds of Love. I don't expect you'll disagree with me about the two goddesses, will you? One is an older deity, the motherless daughter of Uranus, the god of heaven: she is known as Urania, or Heavenly Aphrodite. The other goddess is younger, the daughter of Zeus and Dione: her name is Pandemos, or Common Aphrodite. It follows, therefore, that there is a Common as well as a Heavenly Love, depending on which goddess is Love's partner. And although, of course, all the gods must be praised, we must still make an effort to keep these two gods apart.

The reason for this applies in the same way to every type of action: considered in itself, no action is either good or bad, honorable or shameful. Take, for example, our own case. We had a choice between drinking, singing, or having a conversation. Now, in itself none of these is better than any other: how it comes out depends entirely on how it is performed. If it is done honorably and properly, it turns out to be honorable; if it is done improperly, it is disgraceful. And my point is that exactly this principle applies to being in love: Love is not in himself noble and worthy of praise; that depends on whether the sentiments he produces in us are themselves noble.

Now the Common Aphrodite's Love is himself truly common. As such, he strikes wherever he gets a chance. This, of course, is the love felt by the vulgar, who are attached to women no less than to boys, to the body more than to the soul, and to the least intelligent partners, since all they care about is completing the sexual act. Whether they do it honorably or not is of no concern. That is why they do whatever comes their way, sometimes good, sometimes bad; and which one it is is incidental to their purpose. For the Love who moves them belongs to a much younger goddess, who, through her parentage, partakes of the nature both of the female and the male.

Contrast this with the Love of Heavenly Aphrodite. This goddess, whose descent is purely male (hence this love is for boys), is considerably older and therefore free from the lewdness of youth. That's why those who are inspired by her Love are attracted to the male: they find pleasure in what is by nature stronger and more intelligent. But, even within the group that is attracted to handsome boys, some are not moved purely by this Heavenly Love; those who are do not fall in love with little boys; they prefer older ones whose cheeks are showing the first traces of a beard—a sign that they have begun to form minds of their own. I am convinced that a man who falls in love with a young man of this age is generally prepared to share everything with the one he loves—he is eager, in fact, to spend the rest of his own life with him. He certainly does not aim to deceive him—to take advantage of him while he is still young and inexperienced and then, after exposing him to ridicule, to move quickly on to someone else.

As a matter of fact, there should be a law forbidding affairs with young boys. If nothing else, all this time and effort would not be wasted on such an uncertain pursuit—and what is more uncertain than whether a particular boy will eventually make something of himself, physically or mentally? Good men, of course, are willing to make a law like this for themselves, but those other lovers, the vulgar ones, need external restraint. For just this reason we have placed every possible legal obstacle to their seducing our own wives and daughters. These vulgar lovers are the people who have given love such a bad reputation that some have gone so far as to claim that taking *any* man as a lover is in itself disgraceful. Would anyone make this claim if he weren't thinking of how hasty vulgar lovers are, and therefore how unfair to their loved ones? For nothing done properly and in accordance with our customs would ever have provoked such righteous disapproval.

[*Symposium*, trans. with intro. and notes, by Alexander Nehamas and Paul Woodruff
(Indianapolis: Hackett, 1989), 13–15.]

MICHEL FOUCAULT

6   Were the Greeks Bisexual?

Were the Greeks bisexual, then? Yes, if we mean by this that a Greek could, simultaneously or in turn, be enamored of a boy or a girl; that a married man could have *paidika*; that it was common for a male to change to a preference for women after 'boy-loving' inclinations in his youth. But if we wish to turn our attention to the way in which they conceived of this dual practice, we need to take note of the fact that they did not recognize two kinds of 'desire,' two different or competing 'drives,' each claiming a share of men's hearts or appetites. We can talk about their 'bisexuality,' thinking of the free choice they allowed themselves between the two sexes, but for them this option was not referred to as a dual, ambivalent, and 'bisexual' structure of desire. To their way of thinking, what made it possible to desire a man or a woman was simply the appetite that nature had implanted in man's heart for 'beautiful' human beings, whatever their sex might be.[1] [...]

To be sure, the preference for boys or girls was easily recognized as a character trait: men could be distinguished by the pleasure they were most fond of;[2] a matter of taste that could lend itself to humorous treatment, not a matter of topology involving the individuals's very nature, the truth of his desire, or the natural legitimacy of his predilection. People did not have the notion of two distinct appetites allotted to different individuals or at odds with each other in the same soul; rather, they saw two ways of enjoying one's pleasure, one of which was more suited to certain individuals or certain periods of existence. The enjoyment of boys and of women did not constitute two classificatory categories between which individuals could be distributed; a man who preferred *paidika* did not think of himself as being 'different' from those who pursued women.

[*The Use of Pleasure*, vol. ii of *The History of Sexuality*, trans. Robert Hurley (New York:
Vintage, 1990), 188, 190.]

7 Honourable Sexuality

Having briefly surveyed this wide range of legislation pertaining to homoerotic behavior it is easy to understand why Plato made Pausanias characterize Athenian law as many-hued, intricate, and difficult to understand in contrast with other Greek cities which either prohibited or permitted paederasty in a straightforward way. Now, if legal norms are one reflection or embodiment of the values, attitudes and ideology of a society (or parts of a society), what do these Athenian laws reveal about the values and beliefs of the social order which they defined and regulated? Scholars have not addressed this question despite its crucial importance in unraveling the way in which homoeroticism was regarded at Athens.

The set of legal norms embodied in these statutes reflects a social order which encompassed a profound ambivalence and anxiety in regard to male–male sexuality; a social order which recognized the existence and persistence of such behavior but was deeply concerned about the dangers which it represented. The chief of these dangers was the corruption of the future of the polis, represented by the male children of citizen families. Boys who, under certain circumstances, participated in sexual intercourse with men were believed to have acted for gain and to have adopted a submissive role which disqualified them as potential citizens.[1] Likewise, adult citizens who prostituted themselves were subject to the same civic disabilities and opprobrium. These laws represented one of the severest sanctions which such a society could impose, and reflect the high level of concern for the preservation of the citizen body. [...]

Indeed, that honor and shame define the normative boundaries of homoeroticism (and sexuality in general) is implicit, and often explicit, in all our sources from Plato, Aristotle, and Xenophon to the orators and drama.[2] Sexual submission is shameful and slavish; it dishonors and humiliates a free male.[3] Thus, as it constitutes public slander to say that a man's mother was a whore, the same is true of saying that his father or his son prostituted himself.[4] Similarly, Aristotle[5] depicts the plot of Aristogeiton and Harmodius against the Athenian tyrant, Hippias, as arising out of an insult about the effeminacy of Harmodius; or, as Isocrates comments, those boys who preserve their youth untrodden (*abaton*) by the base are honored greatly.[6]

Though scholars have recognized the importance of honor and shame as dominant values in Greek society, some of the consequences which arise through their operation according to a 'zero-sum' rule in the area of homoeroticism deserve elaboration. Indeed, such an elaboration permits a clearer understanding of the divergent attitudes and practices in Athenian homosexuality. As was shown above, honor is largely defined by reference to sexuality, both for men and for women. The honor of a man is measured through the sexual purity of his wife, mother, sisters, and daughters, and likewise through the virility to which his public behavior gives testimony. Thus, in the Andalusian communities studied by Pitt-Rivers and Brandes, a man of honor is a man who has *cojones* (testicles); a man without honor is *manso*—tame, castrated, woman-like.[7] For men and women, 'The natural qualities of sexual potency or purity and the moral qualities associated with them provide the conceptual framework on which the system [of honor and shame] is constructed.'[8] Thus the politics of reputation overlap with the politics of gender, for a male can become, morally speaking, a female (according to Aristotle, in the case of a eunuch also physiologically). This is most readily accomplished by acquiring the reputation of adopting the submissive, passive role that, ideologically speaking, characterizes women. The man who submits is a victim of *hubris*; he becomes woman-like, and hence dishonored, or even disenfranchised.[9]

[*Law, Sexuality, and Society: The Enforcement of Morals in Classical Athens* (Cambridge: Cambridge University Press, 1991), 180–1 , 183–4.]

I.b. Early Christianity

Early Christian societies and the beliefs and practices born among them did not arise in a vacuum. Christian writers and saints borrowed important medical and cultural traditions from the Roman and Jewish world in which they lived, adapting them to their own purposes. However, these purposes were sufficiently revolutionary to provoke a decisive break between Christianity and the syncretic pagan culture around it and to lay the foundations for the next thousand years of Western history. As we shall see, a characteristic notion of sexuality and of the body was central, perhaps indispensable, to this emergent Christian world view, providing unity and coherence to fledgling Christian sects scattered throughout the vast Roman world.

Christian doctrines on sex, marriage, and family were an important component of the preaching of the first generation of disciples, particularly the Pauline Epistles, when the Church sought to spread its gospel through established pagan households, as well as in the writings and commentaries of the early church fathers from Tertullian, who flourished around the beginning of the second century AD, to Augustine of Hippo, who lived in North Africa at the end of the fourth century. Some Christian sects were persecuted and lived in isolation and poverty, others lived respectable and prosperous lives in the midst of the decaying and disparaged Roman *polis*, but they were remarkably agreed on a set of disciplinary tenets that could be practised in varying degrees of rigour on the bodies of Christian believers.

In the selections that follow, the principal developments in this new synthesis of sexual ideals are discussed in the works of recent scholars. Uta Ranke-Heinemann points out the classical Greek and Roman antecedants of Christian sexual asceticism in ancient medicine and philosophy, themes that remained important throughout the Middle Ages and, in the case of Hippocratic medicine, nearly up to modern times (Extract 8).

Paul, writing to Christians from the mid-first-century Corinth, favoured and practised sexual abstinence but he sanctioned marriage and procreation as a way of maintaining existing lines of authority in patriarchal households. In doing so, as Peter Brown argued, he helped shape an essentially negative notion of marriage that haunted Christianity for the next millennium (Extract 9).

Meanwhile, beginning at the start of the second century AD, an enthusiastic minority of Christian militants formed associations and a doctrinal unanimity around rituals of abstinence that included fasting and sleep deprivation but whose core belief was a rejection of marriage and the practice of celibacy (Extract 10).

Though some of these early groups lived in sex-segregated monastic communities, many male anchorites acknowledged women's ability to resist sexual temptation by living in egalitarian but celibate relations with them. This practice was contrary to the interests of male-dominated families and the newly emergent church hierarchy, and provoked a long debate within the church that eventually resolved itself into the characteristic Western Catholic bifurcation between a celibate male clergy and sex-segregated monastic orders on the one hand and a patriarchal marital order on the other (Extract 11).

By the end of the third century, though female celibacy and women's monastic orders were tolerated, the tone of Christian sexual asceticism was set by male hermits and desert monastics, whose exploits of self-denial and renunciation reverberated down the centuries in the form of a misogynistic distrust of woman the temptress. As Peter Brown tells it, Clement of Alexandria, a second-century church father, understood that the ideal of continence originated with the Greek philosophers, who taught their students to resist passions in order to '"train the instincts to pursue rational goals." But Christians, he added, went further: "Our ideal is not to experience desire at all."'[1] As Aline Rousselle shows in this account of the 'six degrees of chastity' in an early monastic brotherhood, sexual desire was treated as the deepest and most intractable of the body's cravings, requiring the extension of discipline even into dreams and the control of nocturnal emissions (Extract 12).

[1] Peter Brown, *The Body and Society: Men, Women and Sexual Renunciation in Early Christianity* (New York: Columbia University Press, 1988), 31.

8 Non-Christian Roots of Christian Sexual Pessimism

It is not true that Christianity brought self-control and asceticism to a pagan world that delighted in pleasure and the body. Rather, hostility to pleasure and the body are a legacy of Antiquity that has been singularly preserved to this day in Christianity. Christians did not teach licentious, dissolute pagans to hate pleasure and control themselves; instead, the pagans had to acknowledge that the Christians were almost as advanced as they were [. . .]

Sexual pessimism in Antiquity is derived, not, as it would be later in Christianity, from the curse of sin and punishment for it, but predominantly from medical considerations. Pythagoras (sixth century B.C.) is reported as saying that one should indulge in sex in the winter, but not in the summer, make moderate use of it in the spring and fall, but that it was harmful to health in every season. To the question of what was the best time for love, he answered: When you want to weaken yourself. The ancients, by the way, believed that women are not harmed by sexual intercourse, since unlike men they are not affected by the loss of energy through the loss of semen. The sexual act is presented as dangerous, hard to control, harmful to health, and draining. Xenophon, Plato, Aristotle, and the physician Hippocrates (fourth century B.C.) all look on it in this way. Plato (d. 348 / 47 B.C.) writes in the *Laws* about the Olympic victor Issos of Tarentum: He was ambitious and 'possessed in his soul the technique and the power of restraint.' Once he began devoting himself to his training, 'it was said that he never touched a woman or a boy.' Hippocrates describes the fate of a young man who died insane after a twenty-four-day illness that began with a simple upset stomach. Previously he had overindulged in sexual pleasure. Hippocrates thought that man (the male) gave the body the greatest amount of energy by withholding his semen, because excessive loss of semen led to tabes dorsalis and death. Sexual activity was a dangerous drain on one's energy. Soranus of Ephesus (second century A.D.), personal physician of Emperor Hadrian, considered continual virginity salubrious. The only justification for sexual activity was the begetting of posterity. Soranus describes the harmful effects of going beyond the bounds of procreation [. . .]

This increasingly stern and reductive assessment of sex was shaped by the Stoa, the greatest school of ancient philosophy, which lasted from about 300 B.C. to 250 A.D. To this day the word 'Stoic' stands for stolid, passionless behavior. While Greek philosophers in general accorded pleasure-seeking considerable importance for the humane ideal of life, the Stoics, especially during the first two centuries of the Christian era, changed all that. They rejected the quest for pleasure. The positive effect of this rejection was the concentration of sexual activity on marriage. But to the extent that carnal pleasure became suspect, marriage was also called into question and celibacy was valued more highly. [. . .]

In Seneca we find an idea that would later disastrously prompt Christian morality to concentrate on sex. Seneca is writing to his mother Helvia: 'If you reflect that sexual pleasure has been given to man not for enjoyment, but for the propagation of his race, then if lust has not touched you with its poisoned breath, that other desire will also pass you by without touching you. Reason strikes down not only the individual vices, but all of them together. The victory takes place only once and in all respects.' That means that morality is essentially sexual morality. To be vigilant here is to be vigilant, period.

[*Eunuchs for the Kingdom of Heaven: Women, Sexuality and the Catholic Church*, trans. Peter
Heinegg (New York: Doubleday, 1990), 9–10, 11, 13.]

PETER BROWN

9 Paul and Christian Marriage

Paul was, indeed, determined that his own state of celibacy should not be adopted by the church of Corinth as a whole. To have done so would have been to sweep away the structures of the pious household. And to abolish the household would have undermined Paul's own authority in the distant city. It would have broken the subtle chain of command by which his own teachings were passed on to each local community through the authority of local householders.[1] A community of total celibates, and especially if it were a community in which women and slaves realized a little of the equality promised them, in ritual terms, at their baptism, would have been a community effectively sealed off against the outside world. But Paul had hoped to gather the gentiles into Israel in large numbers before Jesus returned from heaven. A community rendered starkly separate from its neighbors by group-celibacy would hardly have attracted many pagans into its midst. In coming down firmly on the side of allowing marriage to continue within the Church, Paul acted as he usually did whenever his converts were tempted to erect excessively rigid barriers between themselves and the outside world. As in his tolerant attitude to the eating of 'polluted' pagan foods, so in his attitude to marriage, Paul sided with the well-to-do householders who had most to lose from total separation from the pagan world.[2] For it was they who would support his ambitious mission to the gentiles most effectively.

Paul, therefore, needed to deter his correspondents from so radical a remedy for their ills. Hence the distinctly lopsided quality of the one chapter that was to determine all Christian thought on marriage and celibacy for well over a millennium. It had not been Paul's concern to praise marriage; he strove, rather, to point out that marriage was safer than unconsidered celibacy. Much of the letter, therefore, consisted of blocking moves. Married couples should not renounce intercourse for fear that worse might happen—'because of the temptation of immorality' that abstinence might provoke.[3] After protracted bouts of abstinence, like those with which contemporary Jewish prophets prepared themselves to receive their visions, husbands and wives must resume intercourse, 'lest Satan tempt you through lack of self-control.'[4] It was no sin for the hot young to marry: 'for it is better to marry than to be aflame with passion.'[5] These remarks were supposed to carry the leaden weight of the obvious. Parallels to every one of them recur in the plentiful folklore invoked by the rabbis in favor of early marriage.[6] What was notably lacking, in Paul's letter, was the warm faith shown by contemporary pagans and Jews that the sexual urge, although disorderly, was capable of socialization and of ordered, even warm, expression within marriage. The dangers of *porneia*, of potential immorality brought about by sexual frustration, were allowed to hold the center of the stage. By this essentially negative, even alarmist, strategy, Paul left a fatal legacy to future ages. An argument against abandoning sexual intercourse within marriage and in favor of allowing the younger generation to continue to have children slid imperceptibly into an attitude that viewed marriage itself as no more than a defense against desire. In the future, a sense of the presence of 'Satan,' in the form of a constant and ill-defined risk of lust, lay like a heavy shadow in the corner of every Christian church.

[*The Body and Society: Men, Women and Sexual Renunciation in Early Christianity* (New York, Columbia University Press, 1988), 54–5.]

PETER BROWN

10   The Earliest Christian Ascetics

The question which had preoccupied many Christian groups in the second century was embarrassingly simple:

What new things did the Lord bring by coming down to earth?[1]

The answer was clear:

One mighty deed alone was sufficient for our God—to bring freedom to the human person.[2]

It was as to how this had happened, and, above all, as to how it could be seen to have happened, in their own community, in their own time, that many Christian teachers and their disciples came to startlingly radical conclusions.

It was believed that the coming of Christ to earth had brought 'the present age' to an end. The duty of every Christian was to make His victory plain and to hasten the collapse of the power of the 'Rulers of the present age.' The 'present age' was the product of an overriding demonic tyranny, to which human beings and, indeed, the universe as a whole, had come to be subjected. Christ's victory over death had brought about a stunning reversal of the crushing flow of irreversible negative processes that made the tyranny of the demons seemingly irresistible on earth. The problem, then, was where precisely to locate the outward visible sign of the huge, inward mutation that had brought freedom to a humanity locked in the grip of gigantic forces of evil. Tertullian put the question to the radicals with his accustomed brutal clarity. How could ordinary human beings, men and women 'subject still to doctors and to debt,'[3] dare to claim to have achieved, in the narrow compass of their cramped lives, the new freedom which, so they said, had become available to them with the coming of Christ? 'How can you possibly think that you are freed from the Ruler of this Age, when even his flies still crawl all over you?'[4]

Yet there was one potentially reversible process shared by all human beings. Sexuality was based on a drive that was widely spoken of as irresistible—a current Greek euphemism for the penis was 'The Necessity.'[5] This drive, furthermore, was the known cause of the one irrefutably unidirectional process to which human beings freely contributed—procreation. Without human collaboration, that layer, at least, of the somber landslip of the 'present age' would not continue. If sexual activity could cease among human beings, the tumultuous cascade of the human race from copulation, through birth to the grave, would come to a halt: 'Jordan' would 'roll backwards.'[6] To give up sexual joining (even, some thought, to transcend the sexual urge) was known to be humanly possible. Given the manner in which freedom from the 'present age' was posed—in terms of the halting of one-way processes—to halt sexual activity could be regarded as a symbolically stunning gesture.

It was the perfect answer to Tertullian's question. The 'present age' might be a vast engine, too large to be seen. Its faceless energy was too dangerously impalpable to the average person, its tyranny too intricate to trace in all its ramifications. But at least one part of that mighty current could be symbolically condensed in the sexual urge and in its manifest consequences, the endlessly repeated cycle of birth and death. In a world seemingly governed by iron constraints, the human body could stand out as a clearly marked locus of free choice. To renounce sexual intercourse was to throw a switch located in the human person; and, by throwing that precise switch, it was believed possible to cut the current that sustained the sinister *perpetuum mobile* of life in 'the present age.'

From the second century onward, and almost certainly from an earlier, less well-documented period, little groups of men and women, scattered among the Christian communities throughout the eastern Mediterranean and in the Near East, as far as the foothills of Iran, strove to render almost audible, by their 'singleness,' their studied isolation from marriage, the vast hush of the imminent end of the age. It was for this reason, they claimed, that Christ had come to earth. He came to

deliver us from error and from this use of the generative organs.[7]

When Salome asked the Lord: 'How long shall death hold sway?' He answered: 'As long as you women bear children. . . .'

They say that the Savior himself said: 'I came to undo the works of women', meaning by this 'female,' sexual desire, and by 'work,' birth and the corruption of death.

[*The Body and Society: Men, Women and Sexual Renunciation in Early Christianity* (New York: Columbia University Press, 1988), 83–5.]

DAVID F. NOBLE

11 Celibacy vs. the Family

In their conservative defense of the Christian patriarchal household, the orthodox bishops condemned the male heretical teachers not only for their ascetic ways and their eschatological excesses, but also for their iconoclastic relations with women. The close companionship of men and women in these groups and the active participation of women in their religious practice, in defiance of the norms of both church and society, aroused the concern and wrath of orthodox leadership. As Elizabeth Clark observed, 'since the "mainstream" church was in competition with these sects for adherents, it distressed orthodox churchmen that women found these groups appealing.' Indeed, from the earliest times the idea of heresy and the independence of women were inextricably linked. The generally prominent role of women in these otherwise disparate groups became, in the eyes of the orthodox leadership, their chief identifying characteristic, from which the orthodox church had to distinguish itself. 'In the second and third centuries,' Clark explains, 'the Christian church was engaged in the quest for its own self-definition. Striving to define itself over against non-Christians without and dissenters within, the church drew firm lines, precise boundaries, between itself and these heretical . . . movements.' Moreover, in order

to demarcate the boundaries between 'us and them,' the church fathers singled out for attack various features of the sects' allegedly misguided teaching and practice, such as the leadership roles of Gnostic women. Over against the blasphemies and permissiveness of the sects, no orthodox Catholic woman should teach, preach, baptize, exorcise, offer the Eucharist, or prophesy. Thus the mainstream church's limitation of women's roles can be understood in part as an aspect of its quest for self-definition—that is, for an identity that clearly distinguished it from rival movements.[1]

'In the light of the emergency caused by the persecutions,' JoAnn McNamara noted, 'Clement of Alexandria viewed the independent Christian women of his city with dismay,' fearing that the women might be the 'weak link in the chain of resistance to the persecutors.' He attacked the heretical preachers, prophets, and sects and sought 'to bring women back under the . . . instruction of approved representatives of the church.' Bishop Irenaeus likewise thought it seriously divisive 'that women especially [were] attracted to heretical groups' which 'accorded to their women members respect and participation increasingly denied to women' in the patriarchal-household-based orthodox churches.[2]

[*A World without Women: The Christian Clerical Culture of Western Science* (New York: Oxford University Press, 1993), 46–7.]

ALINE ROUSSELLE

12   The Six Degrees of Chastity

But although all opportunities for physical contact were removed by the organization of the monasteries, the monk still had to contend with his own body, without any direct external stimulation, and he thus relived the experiences of the pioneers who had tried to resist desire in total isolation in the desert.

If monks were forbidden to lock their cell doors in an attempt to prevent masturbation, although one was supposed to knock before entering into another monk's cell, and if we assume that the monks came with the sincere intention of living a life of abstinence, the only genital manifestation left these men was ejaculation during sleep.

We have seen how the doctors replied to those who were worried by the fact that they ejaculated. There the concern was above all the man's health. In the desert the question was entirely different [. . .] John Cassian is the most explicit on this point which is clearly related to his theology of man's merit which opposed the theology of grace which Augustine imposed on the Church. Cassian devotes one entire dialogue[1] in a collection of twenty-four 'Conferences' to 'illusions of the night', and he deals with ejaculation in sleep in his dialogue on concupiscence and chastity, and in relation to other questions.[2] We also have a saying by Antony on this subject,[3] and a discourse by Dioscorus.[4] In order to define and elucidate the problem, the monks must have compared experiences. The frequency with which some of the older monks ejaculated was known and presented in order to show that they had won the struggle. Thus of Abba Serenus it was said: 'He was very privileged to receive the gift of chastity to such a high degree that he was no longer disturbed, even during sleep, by the natural arousal of the flesh'.[5] Evagrius died at the age of fifty-four, stating that he had known no lust for three years. The Fathers concluded that if one observed a truly ascetic lifestyle one should not ejaculate in one's sleep more than once every two months[6] or even every four months.[7] In this period of seeking one's goal, visible signs of sexual activity were not seen as bad in themselves, but as harmful to the goal one had set oneself. John Cassian distinguishes six degrees of chastity.[8] The first consists of not succumbing to the assaults of the flesh while conscious and awake. In the second degree, the monk rejects voluptuous thoughts. In the third, the sight of a woman does not move him any more. In the fourth, he no longer has erections while awake; in the fifth, no reference to the sexual act in the holy texts affects him 'any more than if he was thinking about the process of making bricks', and in the sixth and final degree of chastity 'the seduction of female fantasies does not delude him while he sleeps. Even though we do not believe this fantasy to be a sin,' says Cassian, 'it is nevertheless an indication that lust is still hiding in the marrow'.

Thus these genital manifestations were considered as signs of the stage the individual had reached in his pursuit of a life directed constantly towards God.

In affirming that the monk is responsible for his thoughts and his dreams and even for the 'natural movements of his body', Cassian, who is here doubtless reproducing the conviction held by numerous Fathers of the desert, is proclaiming the unity of the body and the mind:

Indeed, the quality of one's thoughts, which requires less care during the day because one has many distractions, is tested when one rests at night. So when an illusion of this sort occurs to one, one must not blame sleep but one's own negligence in the time before sleep. This is the sign of evil hiding within, to which night has not given birth, but which, buried deep in the soul, has risen to the surface in sleep, revealing the hidden fever of the passions with which we have been infected by thinking unhealthy thoughts all day long.[9]

[*Porneia: On Desire and the Body in Antiquity*, trans. Felicia Pheasant (Oxford: Basil Blackwell, 1988), 156–8.]

I.c. The Middle Ages

The period from roughly 900 to 1300, the so-called 'Middle Ages', was important in the history of sexuality for two principle reasons. First, it was in this era that the blend of medical and theological (moral) knowledge characteristic of Western discourses on sexuality became firmly established. Second, it was in the middle ages that the Church was finally able to establish the legitimacy of marriage and make the marital relationship the single acceptable one for sexual activity. However, the extension of clerical authority over the theory and practice of sexuality in this era was neither monolithic nor universal. As we shall see, debates among theological and scholastic experts on issues related to sex and reproduction never achieved anything like unanimity, and the strengthening of the marital bond, still a dangerous concession in the eyes of many clerical ascetics, proved to be an imperfect foundation for the reliable regulation of sexuality.

The intellectual legacy of Greece and Rome to the medieval West in the area of sexuality was crucial and complex. At least three related traditions of medical knowledge bearing on sex and reproduction circulated in the academic and theological culture of the era. Scholastic philosophers, whose aim it was to square scripture and the writings of the church fathers with other forms of knowledge, were deeply respectful of the extant writings of the ancients. They did not always see fit to privilege one classical authority over another, but typically considered their respective positions in the form of disputations and debates. This argumentative style lent their writings a notably eclectic, open-ended character which makes generalization about trends difficult. It was scholastic disputation, however, that constituted the mental furniture of the literate elites of the era and that informed their interventions in the social order.

In point of time, the first body of expert knowledge about sex and reproduction to gain influence in medieval Europe was the Hippocratic corpus, a body of Greek medical texts that was often used by scholars in an edition and commentary by the second-century AD Greek physician Galen. Galen's work in general provided a related but distinct position on themes crucial to sexuality. By the end of the twelfth century the writings of Aristotle, particularly his *Generation of Animals*, were more widely circulated, and these in turn provided a contrasting position to the earlier two schools.

Hippocratic writers tended to imagine women's sex organs as functional inverted homologies of men's (ovaries are female testes, the vagina and clitoris are the penis); both produced the seed required for generation and experienced pleasure at doing so; differences between men and women were accounted for by a system of balanced 'humours' wherein men were relatively hotter and drier, women cooler and wetter. Though he also subscribed to the system of dynamic humours, Aristotle denied that women produced seed, emphasized the differences between the sexes, and pronounced women to be imperfect and passive versions of men. The historian Joan Cadden summarizes one of the principal debates—on the existence and nature of male and female 'seed'—engaged in by medieval scholastics and considers its implications (Extract 13).

Scholastics and theologians did not concede much to asceticism in these discussions. Following the ancient texts, many medieval commentators accepted the notion that pleasure, including simultaneous orgasm, was a necessary ingredient of reproductive success for both sexes, as we see in the next extract (Extract 14).

However, without denying that women experienced pleasure in coitus, authors who relied on the Aristotelian tradition tended to dissociate women's pleasure from the emission of seed, ensuring that this conceptual point of view would persist in Catholic dogma (Extract 15).

This distinction left women's sexual desire unmoored from the godly purpose for which it was intended, and it allowed medieval preachers to dwell on the dangers of female lust, particularly that of the 'common woman' or prostitute (Extract 16).

Indeed, as we see in the next extract, the deep suspicion churchmen had of desire in general and that of women in particular allowed them to move from a condemnation of particular forms of lustful sex to open disapproval of any sexual activity that was not directly related to procreation (Extract 17).

13 Do Women Produce 'Seed'?

Do women produce something which might properly be called a 'seed' or 'sperm'? Medieval answers range from 'no, but ...' to 'yes, but. ...' They reflect the conflict between what were understood to be the philosophical (Aristotelian) and medical (Galenic) opinions and a pervasive unwillingness to choose sides unequivocally. In spite of his expressing different views elsewhere, in his set of *questiones* on Aristotle's *On Animals*, Albertus Magnus makes the strongest case for the Aristotelian position that women do not produce sperm properly speaking. First, he argues, sperm is to a man as menstruum is to a woman. A man produces sperm because he does not menstruate; a woman menstruates because she does not produce sperm. This symmetrical picture arises from the asymmetry of heat: sperm is the final form of completely digested food, and women lack the heat to complete the digestion and therefore produce only menstruum. Second, argues Albertus, moving to a higher level of abstraction and citing Aristotle's *Physics*, matter and agent cannot coincide. That which effects a result, that which is the efficient or moving cause, cannot also be the material which is affected, in which the result resides. And since the woman supplies the matter for reproduction and sperm is the agent, the woman cannot produce sperm. Albertus gives only cursory consideration to the contrary position, omitting to deal with what Aristotle himself had treated as among the most serious challenges to his account of reproduction: children's resemblance to their mothers. To the argument that the greatest pleasure occurs as a result of the emission of semen, that women experience the greatest pleasure in intercourse, and that therefore women must emit seed, Albertus replies that this pleasure comes not from sperm produced by the woman but from the touch either of the man's sperm in the womb or of the penis against her sexual part.[1] [. . .]

The question, first posed by Aristotle, whether the male semen persists materially in the fetus was, to judge from the frequency of its occurrence in commentaries and *questiones*, much less interesting to scholastic writers than the questions surrounding the female seed. In some respects what was at stake was equivalent to what was at stake in discussions about the female seed: admitting an active role for the female or a passive (material) role for the male erodes the strict Aristotelian distinction between the efficient, agent cause and the material cause, and thus between the sexes. In addition, the question involved the medium by which life was conveyed to the offspring. But the ontological parity of the two questions did not make them equally compelling for medieval authors, for whom the attribution of activity and power to the female was the subject of greater concern and therefore of more extensive discussion. Although keeping women in their place was hardly the main goal of scholastic treatments of the sexual division of labor, the tendency to give more attention to the problem of female activity than to the problem of male materiality may well suggest which case would be more disturbing within late medieval culture and society. [. . .]

In spite of their differences on what lines to draw where, scholastic authors generally agreed that the role of the female seed—if such a thing existed at all—was very limited. Thus, although they might occasionally and momentarily seem to subscribe to some version of the Hippocratic opinion that the male and the female seeds compete to determine the offspring's sex,[2] in their serious discussions of the subject they had to take their conclusions about the female semen into account. Taddeo Alderotti argued, for example, that no matter how great a female's physiological power, no matter how strong her animal, natural, or spiritual virtues, *with respect to sperm* she cannot be stronger than a male. Even when commenting on a medical text, Taddeo took what was probably the simplest course: he supported the Aristotelian position that the father's heart, as the source of greater or lesser warmth, is the ultimate cause of the offspring's sex. The heart determines the heating and refinement of the male semen, which in turn gives the seed its strength, its virtue. 'The strength of virtue of the male's sperm over the woman's sperm produces a male; and its weakness over it makes a female.'[3] The phrasing here, emphasizing the strength or weakness of the male component, rather than the relative strength of female and male, stresses the Aristotelian passivity of the female contribution, the matter. [. . .]

The premise that sex determination originates with the father's semen (or, ultimately, with the father's capacity to concoct semen, which resides in his heart) is also the basis of the Aristotelian notion that every female child is a failed male child. If taken to mean that girls are essentially birth defects or monstrosities, the employment of the phrase *mas occasionatus*—a ruined or defective male—would seem less an incidental implication of ideas about reproductive roles and more a salvo of medieval misogyny. But the scholastic philosophers who employed the term thus translated from Aristotle's *Genera-tion of Animals* invoked it in an explicitly limited sense and with larger principles of natural philosophy in mind.[4] According to Albertus Magnus, since the father's sperm is determinative, and since whatever reproduces seeks as much as possible to create a likeness of itself, the goal of the male sperm is to produce sons. But the father's heat is not always sufficient to prepare the sperm adequately for the task, and thus females are frequently born.[5] Speaking of the blindness of moles, Albertus insists that such regular deficiencies cannot be treated as 'failures' in the strict sense. Although ordinarily eyes are for seeing and thus blindness is a defect, in moles, which hunt for food in the darkness underground, sight would be superfluous.[6] There is thus a reason for the mole's apparent deficiency, the failure of its eyes to be realized and perfected. The medieval natural world encompassed varying degrees of perfection, including defects which occurred with some persistence. Female offspring, although the result of some material necessity, such as a lack of seminal warmth, had, nevertheless, their own purpose, their own final cause. [. . .]

These views on the way sex is determined resonate with values—active and passive, strong and deficient. But in the context of academic teaching and scholarship they were not consciously, much less willfully, chosen to denigrate women. Rather, they formed part of a coherent system of reproductive theory, which, in spite of differences between the 'medical' and 'philosophical' versions, provided a common ground for scholastic authors. Abstract considerations, such as form and matter or activity and passivity, and concrete considerations, such as the regular occurrence of male and female children or the resemblance of offspring to their parents, all fit more or less comfortably into the framework that thirteenth- and fourteenth-century authors constructed in the course of answering questions on the female seed and related subjects.

[*Meanings of Sex Difference in the Middle Ages: Medicine, Science, and Culture* (Cambridge: Cambridge University Press, 1993), 121, 127, 131–2, 133, 134.]

JOHN W. BALDWIN

14   Sex and Pleasure

If the conjugal obligation is joined to the observation that women are the usual petitioners, and reinforced by medical theory, that women's sexual appetites exceed those of men, we have precisely the situation that was exploited in the fabliau, *La dame qui aveine demanoit pour Morel sa provende avoir* (The lady who asked for Dobbin to be fed his oats). This lady and a *vallet* loved each other with great abandon of heart and body. Even after marriage each continues, according to the biblical command, to love the other equally as one is loyally obligated. More than Tristan and Iseut, they make love without cease, day and night, in bed and on the ground. In order to respond to his wife, the husband asks her to signal her desires with the euphemism 'Let Dobbin have his oats'. Finding the expression crude and offensive, the wife refuses, but after a few days of abstinence, relents and employs it with abandon. Thereafter Dobbin's hunger persists unabated by the week, day, hour. ... Unable to extinguish the devouring flame—like Gilles de Corbeil's Greek fire—the husband falls sick, his bones drained of their marrow. After a short convalescence revives him, the wife recalls him once more to his duty (*devoir*). Reduced to desperation at this point, the *vallet* turns his backside to her lap and discharges his bowels. 'Here, take the bran; the barn has been emptied of oats.' Thereafter the wife accepts what she can have without forcing the rest, whereas the husband serves her as he can whenever he pleases. 'I do not say,' interposed the narrator, 'at her wish but at the will of her husband.' The moral for the married, he concluded, 'is to do it in measure whenever you see the time and place'. Fully comprehending the terms and implications of the theological principle, the fableor, not without malicious humor, uncovered the latent conflict between the unqualified marital obligation between spouses and the female reputation for sexual voracity. Contrary to theological teaching, however, his conclusion was to subordinate the wife's appetite to the husband's will.

Like the theologians, the physicians were less interested in specific sexual techniques than in general principles of human behavior and physiology. Only the *Liber minor de coitu*, which concentrated on therapeutics, considered the question of coital positions. The safest and most natural is the man lying prone on a supine woman with her head raised for greater pleasure. If the woman, however, assumes the male position, performs from either side, or sits, the man risks abscess of the loins, eruptions in the bladder and penis, and hernia.[1] We have seen that it was axiomatic in twelfth-century physiology that sexual desire was necessary for emitting sperm. Since the *Prose Salernitan Questions* remained faithful to the Galenic doctrine of the two seeds, both men and women had to experience desire to produce seed and bring about conception. Although the Salernitans had also argued that feminine desire could exceed masculine, conception nonetheless required reciprocity between men and women; both partners had to garner sufficient desire to emit their respective seed. Implicit in the theory, therefore, was the simultaneous emission of both seeds. The *Prose Salernitan Questions* did not treat this assumption in their discussion of conception, but they did note the advantages of simultaneous climaxes in coitus as they dealt with the variety of female complexions discovered among prostitutes. After discussing how women with cold and moist complexions needed to be warmed by vigorous lovemaking, the discussion then turned to coital techniques. If the duties of both partners are exercised and completed at the same time (*simul*) so that neither anticipates or delays the climax (*celebratio*), then such great delight follows that sex is repeatedly and frequently sought. Because prostitutes find so much pleasure in men experienced in these techniques, they embrace them more ardently and fervently than others.[2]

[*The Language of Sex: Five Voices from Northern France around 1200* (Chicago: University of Chicago Press, 1994), 194–5.]

JOAN CADDEN

15 Is Female Pleasure Necessary for Conception?

Because pleasure and the emission of seed were so closely associated, the role of pleasure in conception was more controversial with respect to women than with respect to men: it raised, in another way, the problem of the female seed. William of Conches had explained prostitutes' infertility in terms of their lack of pleasure in intercourse and had gone so far as to insist that raped women, all appearances to the contrary, must experience some pleasure, since they sometimes conceive.

This position was repeated in later compilations that carry on the earlier traditions. As scholastic authors placed limits and qualifications on the character and
function of female 'seed,' they tended to take the position that women could
indeed conceive without experiencing pleasure.[1] At the turn of the thirteenth
century, even before Aristotle's *Generation of Animals* had been translated in full,
David of Dinant was paraphrasing this aspect of the Philosopher's argument
against female semen: not only do women frequently conceive without experiencing pleasure, but the sexual pleasure which (some) women do experience is
like that of boys before they become fertile, that is, unassociated with true seed.[2]
The concept of female pleasure dissociated from the emission of seed solved
several problems at once: it disqualified female pleasure as evidence for female
seed; it absolved men of a reproductive interest in women's sexual satisfaction;
and at the same time it permitted emphasis upon women's strong sexual
impulses. Albertus Magnus suggested that 'woman does not always have intercourse with emission, but she also has other pleasures in intercourse and is always
prepared for intercourse.'[3] Other scholastic authors treated a woman's pleasure as
inessential to reproduction, although it might be usual and helpful.[4] For these
authors female pleasure was, therefore, a part of the divine plan insofar as it
promoted coitus and thereby reproduction. It did not, however, serve in any way
as a necessary efficient cause in conception. This understanding represents a mild
contrast with views on the efficacy of male pleasure. For although there was not
complete agreement on the absolute necessity of male pleasure, most authors
implicitly or explicitly associated it with the emission of active seed, which is
indeed required for conception.

[*Meanings of Sex Difference in the Middle Ages: Medicine, Science and Culture* (Cambridge:
Cambridge University Press, 1993), 142–3.]

RUTH MAZO KARRAS

16 The Dangers of Female Lust

The important question here, though, is not whether medieval preaching, and
thus the teaching of the church as it reached the general public, was misogynist
overall—surely everyone can agree that it included misogynistic elements—but
rather what particular negative views of women it presented. In late medieval
England those negative views primarily concerned sexuality. Women were
lustful and therefore dangerous to men. All the other criticism of women ultimately came down to the sexual threat that they presented, and even good
women presented that threat, despite their intentions.

Of all the deadly sins (sloth, avarice, gluttony, envy, wrath, lust, and pride), that
of lust was most closely connected with women.[1] A list of twelve abuses of the
age included 'a wise man without works, an old man without religion; an adoles-

cent without obedience, a rich man without alms, a woman without modesty, a lord without virtue; a contentious Christian, a proud pauper, a wicked king, a negligent bishop, the masses without discipline, a people without law.'² The abuse to which women were particularly susceptible was specifically sexual. When works of art depicted sinners, lust was exemplified by a woman more frequently than were the other sins (although it also was sometimes represented as a pair of lovers). Often lust appeared as a woman with her breasts gnawed by serpents.³

One way to determine the association of particular sins with women is simply by counting examples, and here lust clearly predominates. John of Bromyard's *Summa Praedicantium*, compiled around the middle of the four-teenth century, is a good choice for such a count because it is the most compre-hensive encyclopedia of exempla and other sermon material, unoriginal but widely used.⁴ Out of the 1,300 exempla, about 14 percent include female charac-ters. Women make up 13 percent of the avaricious characters, about the same as their percentage of total vicious characters; this is also true of the other sins to which Bromyard devotes fewer exempla. In the case of lust, however, women make up fully half the sinners, despite the fact that so few total exempla include them. This overrepresentation may not be surprising, since lust so often involves two people; but even in the exempla that mention only one sinner, women make up half the examples.

Lust, then, was the woman's sin par excellence, not only in Bromyard's work but in other sources as well. Women did not figure as importantly in most texts as did men, but when they did, they were disproportionately lustful. Even when it was men who committed the sin of lust, they were frequently tempted by women or demons in the shape of women; and though these tales may not have explicitly shown women sinning, they reinforced the medieval tendency to blame women for tempting men rather than men for lusting after women.⁵ These tales may originally have been intended for the monastery, to make the monks understand that threats to chastity come from the devil, but they were being told to the laity in the late Middle Ages.

The particular attribution of lust to women was in part an effort to displace onto them the responsibility for the sins of men who could not control their own temptations. The placing of blame also indicated a real fear of women—that they would disrupt the established order of things by leading men astray, by causing bastards to inherit, by destroying clerical celibacy, by polluting the nunnery. The arena of sexuality was the only one in which women could compete with men in importance—their degree of control over money, for example, was so much less than men's that it is not surprising they did not appear as disproportionately sinful in regard to the getting and hoarding of wealth—and it was the one in which men most feared they would not be able to control them. The treatment of prostitutes in the Middle Ages must be seen in this context.

[*Common Women: Prostitution and Sexuality in Medieval England* (Oxford: Oxford University Press, 1996), 107–8.]

17   The Manner of Intercourse

Implicit in all medieval discussions of intercourse is the understanding that there is a natural and morally correct way to have sex. There are two dimensions to this natural way that might be called the basic form, on the one hand, and the position, on the other. The fundamental requirement of the basic form is that intercourse must be vaginal intercourse. This is a necessary condition of all morally correct sexual relations, since only in this way can coitus respect the natural procreative finality of sex. The natural position is what is sometimes referred to today as the missionary position, the woman lying on her back with the man lying on top, facing her.[1]

The sketch of such an account was already in Augustine, who distinguishes between acting contrary to nature and acting in line with the natural use but slipping in regard to the manner of its execution (defective in its mode). To act contrary to nature is described in a formula adopted in the later Middle Ages— to use a bodily member (or vessel) not granted by nature for such use. I assume this is a reference to oral and anal sex.[2] Augustine does not expand on what he means by natural use that is defective in its mode, but he was understood to refer to sexual positions.[3]

Various distinctions were made in an attempt to capture the difference between infringements against the basic form and those against the natural position or manner. One of the clearest was made by William Peraldus, who distinguished between acting against nature in terms of the substance of the act (non-vaginal intercourse) and in terms of the manner of the act (intercourse not in the missionary position):

The fifth species [of lechery] is the sin against nature, which occurs in two ways. For sometimes it is against nature in terms of the manner as when a woman mounts or when this act is done in a bestial manner but in the correct vessel. But sometimes it is against nature in terms of the substance when someone procures and consents to semen being spilled elsewhere than in the place deputed by nature.[4]

Mention of the proper form and position for sexual relations is encountered frequently in the later Middle Ages; Albert the Great raises the issue explicitly in a separate question. Although the text of Peter Lombard provides grounds for introducing the question, Albert's reason for dealing with the matter is quite practical. Before offering his account he excuses himself on the grounds that he is compelled to treat such 'foul questions' because of his confessional experience.[5] Confessors were forced to touch on the question of proper sexual behaviour because of the requirement that each mortal sin was to be confessed in its full specification. Priests were caught in a dilemma of needing to know whether married people observed the correct forms, on the one hand, and of wanting to avoid informing penitents of novel ways to have sex, on the other. The passage just cited from Peraldus continues: 'There is to be great caution in speaking and preaching about this vice and in asking questions about it in confession so that nothing is revealed to men that might provide them an occasion for sinning.'[6] Manuals of penance attempted to chart a middle course by advising confessors to be cautious in inquiring about the issue, but, if the evidence suggested they should, to pursue the questioning to determine whether there was an infringement of the correct form.

Albert first approaches the question from the point of view of the possibility of acting against nature with one's own spouse. His concern is whether any form of behaviour is intrinsically a mortal sin. As long as the proper vessel is respected then nothing that a husband does with his wife is in and of itself a mortal sin. The implication is that non-vaginal intercourse is against nature and intrinsically mortal. That matter is disposed of rather swiftly. Albert's principal interest is in the subject of sexual positions, which he introduces in this way: 'it seems that none of the things a husband does with his wife, as long as the proper body or vessel is respected, is in and of itself a mortal sin. But there can be a sign of deadly concupiscence when, for instance, the manner that nature determines through the arrangement of the members is not enough for them and they engage in the ways of brute animals.'[7] The correct sexual position is known from the placement of the sexual organs, and in this way nature itself teaches the proper manner so as to ensure conception.[8]

The importance of Albert's formulation of the first question becomes clear in his discussion of sexual positions. As long as there is vaginal intercourse, deviations from the natural position are not intrinsically mortal sins. Consequently, there should be reasons to justify positions other than the missionary position. Such deviations are graded from the least serious (couples on their side) through sitting and standing, to the most serious that Albert describes as being done *retrorsum*, in the manner of mules. This latter is intercourse from the rear, described in the older penitential literature as being *retro*, in a doglike fashion.[9]

It goes without saying that deviations from the norm were believed to be wrong, particularly when used to achieve variety or novel pleasures in intercourse. By the time of Albert's writing, however, the view had been well established that in some circumstances necessity might require couples to take sexual positions other than the one taught by nature. The two most frequently discussed cases were when physical obesity did not allow the natural position and when there was danger of smothering the fetus in the advanced stages of pregnancy. The received view, with which Albert agrees, allowed deviations in such cases.[10]

Curiously, in his grading of deviations from the natural position Albert does not mention one that seemed to have been viewed with particular horror—the reversal of the missionary position. For Peraldus such reversal is not conducive to the proper emission and reception of semen.[11] This reason does not explain the particular animus with which the position was viewed. That explanation (referred to by Peraldus in the passage just mentioned) is found in Peter Comestor's account of the Flood. Peter cites a work attributed to Methodius in which the Flood is said to be sent by God in response to increasingly serious sexual offences. One of those offences was that women were so crazed that they misused men by mounting them.[12]

Aquinas, echoing Albert, summarizes the matter:

Use of a spouse is against nature when it bypasses the proper vessel, or the proper manner instituted by nature in terms of the position. The first case is always a mortal sin because offspring cannot result and so the intention of nature is totally frustrated. In the second case it is not always a mortal sin, as some say, but can be a sign of deadly concupiscence. Sometimes it can even be without sin when the disposition of the body does not allow the other way [the position instituted by nature]. Otherwise, the gravity is in proportion to the distance from the natural manner.[13]

[*The Bridling of Desire: Views of Sex in the Later Middle Ages* (Toronto: University of Toronto Press, 1993), 76–9.]

I.d. The Renaissance and Religious Reform

Toward the end of the Middle Ages, new instruments and institutions for containing sexual activity emerged, for individuals both within marriage and without. This was so in Catholic countries policed by the Inquisition, and in Protestant communities ruled by pious elites. The end of the fifteenth century coincided with a period of dramatic growth in royal authority and state power throughout Europe. England, Spain, France, the Habsburg domains of central and eastern Europe, and smaller entities like the prosperous city-states of Venice and Geneva, began a process of rationalization and centralization that continued into the nineteenth century. In seeking to expand their power over citizens, monarchs and princes often allied with churches in order to permit the state easier entry into the domain of families. In practice, this meant strengthening the legal and moral authority of fathers and condemning forms of sexual expression and behaviour that seemed to run against the grain of patriarchy. In the eyes of monarchs interested in extending control in their domains, strong fathers were reliable domestic allies.

After centuries of hesitation about the acceptability of sex even in holy matrimony, the Catholic church settled for tightening the bonds of marriage, requiring yearly confessions of the faithful in order to be certain that sexual activity—of the right kind—was restricted to wedded couples, and punishing individuals who committed fornication (sexual relations out of wedlock). Until this era it was possible nearly everywhere in the West to contract a marriage and set up a household by exchanging private vows and commencing conjugal relations by mutual consent. Families cared more about dowries and the exchange of property than the sanction of the Church, which was often bestowed, but after the fact. Because sexual relations could produce a child, and therefore an heir, popular belief held that consummation of sexual relations, not some deeper spiritual or personal bond, made a marriage, even when a woman was violated against her will.

In Renaissance Venice, for instance, in the interests of general order, the state's prosecutor (Avogadori) could bring charges against a man for fornication for failing to carry through on a promise of marriage and try him before a court called the Council of Forty (Extract 18).

Though a man had brute force on his side, contemporaries did not think women were entirely without resources. Indeed, the courts recognized their ability to put a spell on a man to enslave his passion, which was another way of acknowledging the possibility that sexual love could be mutually pleasurable (Extract 19).

In the sixteenth-century German city of Augsburg, the evangelical Protestant elite of the town followed literally Luther's injunction to close the whorehouses and the monastic houses and make marriage, so far as possible, the unique setting for sexual relations. Men called 'Discipline Lords' and 'Marriage

Judges' ruled over courts that tried offences against public order and the stern new civic morality. In attempting to eliminate premarital sex, prostitution, and adultery through repression, zealous religious reformers contributed to three distinct developments: they came perilously close to conflating prostitution with adultery, they treated sexual sin as a particularly feminine crime, and they justified legal and administrative intervention in family affairs in the name of both piety and sexual orthodoxy (Extract 20).

As a response to the challenge of the Protestant Reformation, the Council of Trent (1545–63) put in place a series of measures designed to advance the cause of Catholicism by repressing heresy and immorality. These measures included the founding of the Spanish and Roman Inquisitions, strengthening of Ecclesiastical Courts in Catholic lands, and the intensified use of the confessional as a mode of personal discipline. Though the policing of sexual aberrations became an important part of the machinery of post-Tridentine Catholicism, Catholic moral reforms shared with their Protestant rivals the aim of inspiring a new and purified sexual morality in their flock, especially amongst women, who might be tempted, or tempt others into adultery (Extract 21).

The rigorous demands of these puritanical standards severely tested the resolve of both confessors and penitents; numerous inquisitional proceedings were brought in early modern Spain against priests who succumbed to the intense intimacies of the confession box (Extract 22).

Perhaps the greatest irony of Protestant and Counter-Reformation Catholic efforts to confine the sexuality of their adherents to a procreative, marital expression was a relative diminution of the spiritual side of sexual love and the appearance of a standard of marital legitimacy that was, in effect, wholly sexual in nature. The most extreme example of this utterly physicalistic notion of the marital relationship was the trials that were held in French Ecclesiastical Courts in connection with a married woman's request for an annulment on the grounds of her husband's impotence. The very fact that a handful of such trials took place is testimony to the extreme importance reproductive sexuality and heirship had attained in early modern Europe and the extent to which marital sexual activity had become literally saturated with religious meaning. The excerpt reprinted below concerns one notorious 'trial by congress' held near the end of the sixteenth century involving a certain Etienne De Bray whose wife wished an annulment of their childless marriage, and who did not scruple to make the 'trial' as hard as possible for her husband (Extract 23).

However, the greatest horror in the eyes of secular and church authorities in this period was sodomy. The term derived from the passage in Genesis in which the male inhabitants of the town of Sodom force Lot to surrender his male house guests to their evil passions, despite Lot's willingness to yield up instead his own virginal daughters. The destruction of Sodom by a vengeful God only partly explains the medieval and early modern abomination of 'unnatural' sex; the term remained vague in the law and there was extraordinary variation in the application of punishments for sodomy throughout Europe and North America. The broadest possible meaning of the term was non-reproductive sex, which included masturbation, anal intercourse (with a man or a woman), bestiality, 'unfertile' and therefore 'unnatural' sexual positions, oral sex, and even coitus interruptus, the sterile spilling of seed destined by nature for the womb. Although all varieties of the crime were punished in the era (as they are still), the first and most vigorous efforts to repress sodomy were directed at same-sex monastic communities in the Middle Ages, and the greatest animus against 'sodomites' was expressed against male–male sexual relations, particularly anal intercourse.

The punishment for this kind of sodomy almost everywhere in late medieval and early modern Europe was death, often by burning accompanied by torture. However, though the crime aroused great storms of sulphurous rhetoric, the punishment was usually applied only in times of social, economic, or political upheaval or in situations of great danger. The English 'Buggery' law of 1533 criminalizing sodomy was an aspect of Henry VIII's effort to promote English Protestantism by punishing the 'sodomitical' sins infecting the monastic domains he coveted for the crown. The punishment of death by burning was seldom exacted; when it was applied it was in connection with secular develop-ments that spread misery or fear (Extract 24).

In a similar manner the harsh and uncertain conditions of life in colonial New England helped make sodomy the worst of a series of sexual offences that the early puritans believed vitiated the community's ability to put down roots and grow (Extract 25).

There were, however, instances of waves of executions for sodomy that were initially provoked by economic or social crises but that subsequently fed on the panic aroused by the discovery of groups of sodomites scattered throughout society. In the Low Countries during the early modern period, for example, sodomy cases spiked up in the last quarter of the seventeenth century, culmin-ating in a full-fledged moral panic between 1730 and 1732. The fact that there appear to have been networks of men practising sodomy indicates that in certain places in early modern Europe there were mechanisms in place allowing men with similar sexual interests to identify and communicate with one another, a social situation lying somewhere between individual isolation and our modern notion of the gay 'community' (Extract 26).

18 Fornication and then Marriage

A promise of marriage was not always a peaceful step on the road to fornication. Courtship and sexuality still retained a considerable level of the brutal directness traditionally associated with feudal mores. It was not atypical to begin a relationship with rape, move on to a promise of marriage, and continue with an affair. One assumes that marriage was, in fact, often the end result of such brutal directness; occasionally when it was not, as in the case of Giacomello Zaratino's violent wooing of Maria di Martino in 1424, the event was recorded. The Avogadori reported that 'the said Giacomello Zaratino with a naked blade in hand crossed the little bridge and grabbed this Maria by her arm. He then dragged her under a pomegranate tree and beneath the tree raped her twice taking her virginity. While accepting her flower [of virginity] he promised to take her as his wife.'[1] Knife, rape, and a promise of marriage apparently seemed less daunting to Maria and many other young women than one might expect. In her case an affair ensued: 'After [the rape] he regularly entered the house of the said Nicolò [Nicolò Contarini, the noble in whose house Maria lived], knowing her carnally in bed and on a chest.'[2]

In a similar case from 1455 a certain Blasio raped Maria, the young daughter of a boatman. Although she was only ten years old, Blasio's promise of marriage secured a continuation of their relationship without further violence, until Blasio disappeared. At that point the government stepped in to prosecute fornication, once more with the primary goal of promoting the institution of marriage. Blasio's crime was more serious than most because it involved a child (*puella*), so he was sentenced by the Forty to be beaten from San Marco to the Rialto and to serve a year in jail. In addition, he was ordered to provide 200 *lire de piccoli* for the girl's dowry. But they gave Blasio an option—eight days to decide to marry Maria and credit her with a 50-ducat dowry. If he accepted, he would be spared his other penalties. Apparently Blasio found it an easy decision, for the Avogadori noted in the margin of their register: 'The same day after lunch the said Blasio ... indicated that he was content to accept this Maria as [his] wife and dictated a dowry contract of 50 gold ducats for Maria and thus in accordance with the terms of the condemnation, he was freed.'[3] From rape to fornication to marriage appears to have been a relatively common progression—one that was occasionally aided by a fornication case heard by the Forty.

[*The Boundaries of Eros: Sex Crime and Sexuality in Renaissance Venice* (Oxford: Oxford University Press, 1985), 31.]

Reasoned crimes were seen as more dangerous and crimes based on emotions, less so. The criminal records imply, in fact, that love could push a person beyond reason to madness—a state of lack of legal responsibility for one's actions. The strange case of Domenico Contarini, a noble of important family caught in a love that became a mad passion, illustrates how uncontrollable love might become in the eyes of the Venetian nobility. A Greek woman named Gratiosa, it seems, was most eager in the early 1480s to keep the love of young Contarini, for she banded together with Menega di Modon and Maria Greca to brew several potions and perform a number of magical operations to win and hold his love, with amazing success. According to the Avogadori, a confection composed of the heart of a rooster, wine, water, and menstrual blood mixed with flour and cooked to a powder, when administered by Gratiosa to her unwitting admirer, 'rendered him insane and wild to such an extent that the said Domenico committed the most diverse and sad stupidities … and moreover diverse bestial and wild acts coerced in the end by an unbreakable bond of love.'[1] Love, helped by Gratiosa's potion, was a force that was thought to have destroyed Domenico's rational self-control. Not only did he fall madly in love, he 'committed the most diverse and sad stupidities.' Significantly, however, his insane love rendered him not culpable. It appears the Avogadori and the Forty were eager to accept the unusual effectiveness of Gratiosa's potion, at least in part, to explain and devaluate those 'wild' and 'bestial' deeds of Contarini left intentionally vague.[2] The potion also excused Domenico of responsibility for his 'frequent and diligent copulation' with Gratiosa; thus, the Forty could punish Gratiosa for her magic while allowing Domenico to go free and recover from the havoc wreaked on his psyche by love, spells, and potions.

Suggestive of a darker vision of Renaissance love is the fear that Gratiosa's womanly wiles provoked in the Venetian nobility. We seem to be already on the road to the witch craze that later swept Europe. Yet, at the same time it is interesting to note that Gratiosa and her advisers believed they had a wide range of weapons in their arsenal. In addition to the potion noted above, the Avogadori reported that 'one day when she was in bed with Domenico and they were playing together, Gratiosa took from his navel some of that dust or material that collects there and mixed it with some of her own. Part of it she gave to him in a drink and part of it she drank herself.'[3] The results of this strategy were not so dramatic as those of the earlier potion, but the mix of sympathetic magic and potion making is reminiscent of much magic. The virility of a rooster's heart and the 'centralness' of menstrual blood and the navel all pooled the love of the lovers, reinforced it, and created an intense, ultimately uncontrollable emotion.[4] Similar magic can be found in apparently unrelated cultures (for example, among the American Indians), implying that here at the most intense levels of human emotions we may be touching groups of perceptions and associations that have come together quite independently to form similar cultural patterns.

One is caught also by aspects of this affair that go beyond magic. The Avogadori innocently report the couple 'playing' (*luderent simul*) in bed together when she was harvesting her navel lint. Or again they note their playing and fooling in bed when Gratiosa measured his *membrum virile* against a candle that had been blessed previously and that ultimately would be lighted at Mass in the name of their love.[5] This was a far cry from the direct brutality of courtship punctuated by violence and rape noted earlier. It would be too simplistic to picture Renaissance sexuality as male-dominated with little room for affection expressed between partners. Of course, that was often the case, but Gratiosa and Domenico could play in bed together and enjoy each other. Perhaps that explains to a degree the success of Gratiosa's magic.

[*The Boundaries of Eros: Sex Crime and Sexuality in Renaissance Venice* (Oxford: Oxford University Press, 1985), 33–5.]

LYNDAL ROPER

20 Protestant Sexual Discipline

The Discipline Ordinance of 1537 was the principal marker of change here, as it was in the organization of human relationships in general, now to be ordered in accordance with the principles of civic righteousness. But the manner in which it deals with prostitution is distinct. The ordinance does not mention prostitution by name, but speaks instead of those who commit fornication and adultery. No longer a clearly identifiable trade, prostitution was subsumed under these sins; and the prostitute was not addressed as a separate class of woman. The sexual discipline which the whole citizenry was to adopt was both more all-embracing and less well defined than it had been before the Reformation. Now any sexual relationship outside marriage was counted sinful and any occasion on which the sexes mingled, such as dances, might lead to sin. So absolute were the demands of the ideal that the Council was drawn inevitably to define marriage and the relations which ought to hold between husband and wife, parents and children, masters and servants as it articulated the concept of discipline. Indeed, the ordinance amounted to an attempt to order the household, to emphasize the distances which ought to exist between its members, and to define the rights and duties of each. The same ordinance also included an admonition to all citizens to wear clothing appropriate to their social position, so that each may 'be recognized for whom he or she is'.[1]

Prostitution had previously been regarded as the cure for the dangers of male lust, protecting (as all who favoured its existence insisted) the honour of women within the household. The wives, daughters, and maids for whom they feared were their own; and the sexual threat derived from the young men of the house. Once the brothel was abolished, and prostitutes were considered either as fornicators or adulteresses like other women, it is not surprising that such care should have been devoted to redrawing the boundaries within the household. Nor is it difficult to see why one of the Reformation's major concerns should have been the reworking of the concept of incest, making it both a narrower but a far more strictly held set of rules.[2] [. . .]

But it was in the interrogations of the prostitutes themselves that the Council most explicitly developed its language of sexuality, crime, and sin. Using the religious rhetoric of sin, it attempted to arouse a sense of guilt in the women, while at the same time robbing them of their own words to define what happened. Let us return to the interrogation of Appolonia Strobel. The first question she was asked was prefaced with: 'Since it is well known that for some time past she has led an undisciplined and ungodly life ...', and asked her to name who had first involved her.[3] These words were new: until the 1530s a neutral word like 'trade', or the term *Buberei*, villainy, a word so broad as to cover any sort of misbehaviour and lacking religious connotations, would have been used to refer to prostitution.[4] The force of the world *unzuchtig* can hardly be caught in the English word 'undisciplined'. In essence a civil, moral term—the series of ordinances regulating citizens' moral behaviour were *Zuchtordnungen*—*unzuchtig* carried implications of disorder as well as of sexual misbehaviour, and it represented the antithesis of the *Zucht*, the moral order, which the Council wished to inculcate. The word 'ungodly' added an explicitly religious dimension, echoing the injunction that no fornicator shall enter the Kingdom of Heaven.

The questioning centred on the occasion on which she had lost her virginity. 'Who was the first?', the interrogators asked Appolonia Strobel; and, doubting her answer, they tried to shake her statement at the second interrogation. The very expressions they used to refer to this first intercourse—'robbed her of honour', 'brought her to fall', 'felled her', 'weakened her'—imply corruption and the destruction of her integrity. By extracting a response to the question 'Who had first brought her to fall?', the woman was made to participate in her own condemnation.

'Because she is robbed of her virginity,' the Council told Catharina Ziegler, 'it is not to be supposed that she has remained pious since.'[5] Once fallen, promiscuity was inevitable, the Council believed. Prostitution was described as 'unchaste acts', 'sinful acts', 'the undisciplined life', 'dishonourable doings'. The central words from which these expressions derive are honour, discipline, and sin. Good women were 'honourable', 'disciplined', 'chaste', or 'pious', *fromm*. *Fromm*, as the Council used the word, meant right living, obeying the sexual code; but it also meant pious, right believing. Piety began to merge with sexually orthodox behaviour.

The techniques involved derived from those of the confessional; but now it was the Council who required details of the events. The object of the interrogation was a complete revelation of the woman's sexual history, a kind of verbal undressing of the prostitute, leading to an acknowledgement, from her, of her sinfulness. The new moralism made a very sharp distinction between married women and single women working as prostitutes. Married women were found guilty and punished for 'having committed adultery many times', as the placard read out and displayed at their punishment put it. Single women were accused of multiple fornication. The moralization of the offence had the effect of denying the existence of prostitution as a trade—instead, two quite separate types of immorality were distinguished. And, conversely, there was now no clear distinction between prostitutes and adulteresses or fornicators.

The logical consequence of this redefinition was that the women's clients were equally sinners; and indeed, the Council did begin to take note of the names of all customers. In the 1540s it proceeded to punish a number of men, including some quite prominent civic figures. It even maintained, consistently, that men who knowingly visited married prostitutes were guilty of adultery even if they were bachelors.

[*The Holy Household: Women and Morals in Reformation Augsburg* (Oxford: Clarendon Press, 1989), 112, 123–5.]

JAMES R. FARR

21   Catholic Sexual Discipline

This inward turn toward asexual, self-disciplined purification, so prominent in the very influential Salesian spirituality, reflected the new 'incentive for the systematic interior monitoring by the individual of his own life,' which was, according to Bossy, a hallmark of the Catholic Reformation. Since the fifteenth century, spiritual handbooks on the examination of conscience, like *The Imitation of Christ*, had heralded the shift of 'emphasis in sacramental penance from satisfaction following confession to interior discipline preceding it.' The difference after Trent (1545–1563) was that the examination of conscience 'grew into a general programme of devout self-consciousness and a model of the Christian life.' This more systematic examination of conscience was marked by a trend toward more regular and frequent confession and communion than had been common in the late middle ages. Cajoling the faithful to a new conception of penance required continued and watchful external disciplinary systems, and moralists, bishops, and judges all 'conspired to enforce the conception that the proper description of sin was disobedience—disobedience to God, Church, king, to parents, teachers and authorities in general.' The body, disciplined and purified by the examination of conscience, thus became sacred space suitable for the temple of the holy ghost.[1] [...]

Marriage was a social and economic institution, but in the seventeenth century the moralistic program was broad-based, and reformers also perceived

the pure marriage as the centerpiece of the purified Christian society. Furthermore, the ethic of the new pastoral of the Catholic Reform and that of the patriarchal family shared the assumption that obedience, discipline, and purity in
females were needed, and associated these qualities with honor. Adultery
embodied all that was anathema to this ethic. Typically, Boileau wrote of the
sanctity of the patriarchal family in terms of its desecration by adultery. He
argued that virgin maids were the spouses of Christ, so any maids appearing in
public with partially exposed breasts and necks were, by their enticing evil
thoughts in and actions from men, 'unfaithful to God.' He shifted smoothly
from God to husband, and continued that 'a husband is not less jealous of the
purity of his wife, than of his own honor; and as, if he be prudent, he does never
indanger himself to lose his honour, so there is not any likelyhood that he
should desire his wife to rune the risque of losing her innocence. A husband is
always interested for the reputation for his wife. ...' Bishop Godeau gives an
explanation of why husbands must feel this way, and in the process reveals how
closely intertwined political, social, and religious ideologies had become. He
asserted in his book on penitence that the sin of adultery is abhored by nature
because it ruins the natural basis of society (marriage), and is condemned by *la
politique* because it disrupts the order of legitimate succession by 'putting in
families those who have dishonoured them' and giving the fruit of the labor of
fathers to those offspring to whom it does not belong. It is thus commonplace
in moralistic literature from the late sixteenth through the early eighteenth
century to find portraits of the ideal woman painted in terms of chastity, disciplined humility, and fidelity as essential to a certain hierarchical order.[2]

['The Pure and Disciplined Body: Hierarchy, Morality and Symbolism in France during the
Catholic Reformation', *Journal of Interdisciplinary History* (1991), 399, 400–1.]

STEPHEN HALICZER

22   Sexuality in the Confessional

Even more fundamental to the failure of so many marriages were the feelings of
sexual dissatisfaction and frustration that were an almost inevitable consequence
of the traditional Catholic conception of nuptial relations. The earliest Church
fathers were highly suspicious of sex, viewing it as a powerful impulse that could
overcome human reason. Premarital sex was a mortal sin, but sexual relations in
marriage were also suspect. For St Augustine, any marital sex designed to avoid
procreation was sinful and even married couples who behaved properly were
enjoined to cease having sexual relations after having one or two children. St
Jerome took an even more negative view of sex in marriage, which he saw
as having no value except as a way of avoiding illicit extramarital fornication.
Consequently, he and other writers said that a man who had sex with his wife too

frequently was an adulterer. Sex in marriage should be undertaken rarely and in a spirit of moderation instead of lust since 'nothing is filthier than to have sex with your wife as you might do with another woman.'[1] This famous phrase inspired much of the medieval thinking about the purpose of marital sex and gave rise to a number of opinions, some highly pessimistic and others more reasonable.[2] The fact that proper or licit marital sex was so hard to define created enormous confusion and insecurity and made each conjugal act a cause for anxiety. In spite of the fact that later theologians like the Spanish Jesuit Thomás Sánchez tried to moderate Church teaching on marital sex, the idea that there was something sinful about it had penetrated deeply into the popular imagination. Pedro Galindo alludes to this in his discussion of popular misconceptions about mortal and venial sins when he tells us that some individuals wrongly confess as a mortal sin sexual relations in marriage designed to secure or heighten arousal. Such popular misconceptions were reinforced by priests who continued in the old rigorist tradition. In a visitation carried out in 1585, Inquisitor Fernando Martínez received a deposition from a witness who declared that Dr. Francisco Bezerria, a canon in the collegiate church of Antequera, had declared in several sermons that 'the sex act in marriage is always sinful' and that 'Our Lord can no longer tolerate the sinfulness of coitus in marriage.'[3]

Even though Thomás Sánchez and other post-Tridentine theologians took a somewhat more liberal attitude toward marital sex, they still left a cloud of suspicion over anything that did not lead to 'natural' intercourse, which was carefully defined as coitus in the missionary position. Other positions were seen as making conception less likely and therefore subverting the proper goal of all sexual relations. Other sexual practices were permitted if they led to 'natural' intercourse, but were venially sinful if they were done merely for pleasure. If orgasm resulted from foreplay, the sin was considered mortal.[4]

Apart from the strictures placed on foreplay, coital positions, and orgasm, moralists felt that women should play an entirely passive role in sexual relations. According to Juan Luis Vives, women should never be aggressive in seeking sex from their husbands. Instead, married women should follow the example of Zenobia, the ancient queen of Palmyra, who never allowed her husband to have sex with her unless she wished to become pregnant and 'had no more sensitivity in her sexual parts than in her feet or hands.'[5]

Confronted with a society that systematically ignored their sexual needs, condemned all forms of sexual experimentation and sharply restricted the frequency of coitus, many women felt a profound sense of sexual dissatisfaction. These feelings were reflected in Pedro de Luxán's *Coloquios matrimoniales*, in which Eulalia, one of the women involved in the dialogue, declares that she would 'sometimes rather sleep next to a pregnant pig' than share her husband's bed.[6] Sexual dissatisfaction was certainly one of the reasons for the remarkable string of successes that the Franciscan, Francisco de las Llagas, had with married women. His relationship with Victoria Casas began in the confessional when she complained about her sexual relationship with her husband. Carried away, as he later told Toledo's inquisitors, by 'his desire' and 'ensnared by the wiles of the devil,' he asked her if she would like it better if he took her husband's place in bed. She agreed that she would and the next time she came to confess, told Llagas that she was feeling much better because every time she had sex with her husband she thought of him. As their relationship developed, it was marked by the breaking of numerous sexual taboos, including foreplay in the confessional box and mutual masturbation, which Victoria told him she enjoyed more than having intercourse with her husband.[7] Something very similar happened with twenty-five-year-old Isabel de Tena, who began her affair with Llagas by offering him flowers that she drew from between her breasts during confession. He responded by offering her almonds, which she took from his mouth through a hole in the confessional screen. She became obsessed with Llagas, thought about him every night, and had coitus with him in her home on more than twenty occasions. They also engaged in untraditional forms of sex, including oral stimulation and mutual masturbation in the confessional and in her home.[8]

At forty-three, when Francisco de las Llagas was brought before the Toledo tribunal, he had a long history of affairs, mainly with married women, that had been carried on both inside and outside the confessional. As an unusually sensitive and imaginative lover in an age of stultifying conformity, anxiety, and negativism about sex, he could offer the kind of sensual joy so often missing in the marriages of the period. For Isabel de Tena, who was described by inquisitorial notary Bartolomé Sánchez Plaza as 'devout' and 'extremely modest,' his blend of gentle sensuality and daring sexual practices was simply overwhelming. She became so obsessed with him that she began confessing with him three times a week just to be near him.

But Llagas, too, was a victim of the Counter-Reformation's negative view of sex. He kept a scourge by his bedside and used it frequently on himself and was constantly feeling the shafts of God's anger entering his breast to alert him to change his life and resist temptation. Unfortunately for Llagas, but perhaps fortunately for some of his married penitents, he was unable to do this and therefore provided them with a degree of sensual pleasure sorely lacking at home.

[*Sexuality in the Confessional: A Sacrament Profaned* (Oxford: Oxford University Press, 1996), 127–9.]

PIERRE DARMON

23 Trial by Sexual Congress

The experts who were in attendance on these occasions would insist upon a long rigmarole of precautions to exclude the possibility of fraud. Tagereau, who left a particularly faithful account of trial by congress, explains the procedure as follows:

Both parties are examined all naked, from the crown of the head to the soles of the feet and in all parts of their bodies—*etiam in podice*—to find if there be any thing upon their person as might assist or harm the congress.

[To prevent the use of astringents] the woman is put in a shallow bath where she does remain some period of time.

[Next is examined] the state of the privy parts, by such means to establish the difference betwixt their extent of expansion and distention before and after the congress, and if intromission hath occurred or no.

After this the trial proper could commence.

This being done, the man and wife do betake them to bed in broad day, and the experts that are present do either remain in the bedchamber or retire away (if the parties or one of the parties require this) to some garderobe or gallery close by, the door remaining however at jar, and as for the matrons they do stay around the bed. And the curtains of which then being drawn, it is the duty of the man to set to making proof of his potency, whence often there arise nonsensical disputes and altercations, the husband complaining that his partner will not permit him to perform and does hinder intromission, his wife the while denying the charge and claiming that he would put his finger therein and dilate and open her by such means alone . . .

[Tagereau reckons that it would take] a marvellous determined man and even brutish not to turn flaccid, assuming him to be already in a state of excitation. And if nonobstant such indignities and obstacles he carry on even unto intromission, this were impossible unless the legs and arms of his partner were to be held down . . .

At the last, the parties having passed some time abed, like one hour or two, the experts being called or, weary of waiting, do of their own accord approach and open the curtains, to discover what hath taken place between the couple. The woman is examined close up, to discover if she be more dilated than on the last inspection before her retiring to bed, and whether intromission has occurred (and if there be an emission, and where, and of what nature). This is conducted without the use of candles or those spectacles worn by people advanced in age, though not without exceedingly profane and shameful inspection and argumentation. And they do make up their reports which they deliver to the judge that is in the same house, installed in a separate room or chamber together with the prosecutors and patricians of the ecclesiastic courts that do await the end and issue of the act, which report always disadvantages the man, unless he hath achieved intromission.

In accordance with the same scenario, De Bray was subjected to three trials in succession. According to his lawyer, the situation was made even more unbearable by the flagrantly indelicate behaviour of his wife, the youthful Mademoiselle de Corbie. The second trial, at which the experts were present, took place under particularly dramatic circumstances:

The man De Bray was examined from the soles of his feet to the crown of his head, including all the concavities and secret parts of his body, this being done much less to determine if he had anything hid about his person that might assist him in performing the said act of congress, than to vex him in order that he might leave the field.

Moreover, Mademoiselle de Corbie provoked an absurd argument concerning 'the bonnets that they would wear upon their heads, so that some of these had to be sent out for from the Petit Pont.' Meanwhile, the time allotted for De Bray to accomplish his task was running out, his chances of success were diminishing, and his virile ardour was flagging. To add insult to injury 'the plaintiff [his wife] did give vent to an infinity of scandalous and injurious expressions for to anger him and distract him from his undertaking.' De Bray's nerves had already been shattered by the postponement of several previous trials at the insistence of his shrewish wife, who claimed either to be 'having her months' or that 'the sheets of the bed were poisoned . . .' In the end, however, Dr Bray seemed to triumph over all the odds: 'the doctors and matrons do all report having seen and touched his member, that it was big, stiff, red and long, and that it was in place and in good order to perform the said congress.' And yet he subsequently lost the case, on the grounds that he had superfluously scattered a 'too aqueous and serous' seed around the edges of the appropriate orifice.

[*Damning the Innocent: A History of the Persecution of the Impotent in Pre-Revolutionary France*, trans. Paul Keegan (New York, Viking Press, 1986), 193–5.]

ALAN BRAY

24   Sodomy and its Punishment

That is a conclusion borne out by an analysis of the prosecutions that do occur, for they fall into a limited number of clearly recognisable classes. One of these are those which occur in times of social upheaval. A likely response to the suffering this brings is to seek a scapegoat, and in the mentality of seventeenth-century England a sodomite was a likely candidate for that role: it was exactly at such times that fear crystallised around those customary figures of evil which in more normal times were kept at a distance from everyday life, figures such as the trio of the Papist, the witch and the sodomite. One victim of this seems to have been the Domingo Cassedon Drago mentioned in the last chapter, who was recorded as being in the Hampshire county gaol in 1647 awaiting return to Essex to face trial for 'a buggery' he was supposed to have committed. His arrest came in the wake of just such a period of dislocation produced by the ravages of the Civil War, and coincided with the presence of the witch-craze in Essex, in the person of Matthew Hopkins the witch-finder. What marked Drago out for such treatment? There is good reason to think that it was the colour of his skin. A member of a non-European race was more than a merely unusual sight in mid seventeenth-century England: he specifically brought to mind the image of the sodomite, which was linked in the literature of the time with non-European races.[1] Drago's homosexuality was all too likely to attract attention. The word 'negar' (negro) is used four times in the short entry in the Order Book concerning him. It is not surprising that he should have been singled out. A similar period of social upheaval surrounded the trial and execution of John

Swan and John Litster for sodomy in Edinburgh in 1570. Their arrest coincided with the social tensions brought about by the coming of the Reformation to Scotland and the return of the Calvinist exiles; and as with Drago in 1647 it was accompanied by the arrival of the witch craze.[2] In each case similar pressures were at work; in times of social disturbance like these people are apt to see in the world about them the image of the figures they fear: a 'sodomite' in seventeenth-century England as much as a 'communist' or 'zionist' today.

[*Homosexuality in Renaissance England* (New York: Columbia University Press, 1995), 71–2.]

JONATHAN NED KATZ

25   Sodomy and Sin in New England

In the early colonies, the term and concept 'sodomy' had connotations that they do not generally have for present-day Americans. For the colonists struggling to survive in the wilderness, the word 'sodomy,' no doubt, evoked the destruction of Sodom and Gomorrah, as much or more than illicit sex. For those early settlers perched precariously on the edge of a hostile continent, the term 'sodomy' provoked thoughts of Sodom, that archtypal settlement destroyed for sin. Living from day to day with the threat of social dissolution, the early colonists no doubt felt a special kinship with that particular ancient city.

The early colonists found themselves at the mercy of natural, life-threatening forces which, personified as 'God,' seemed angry, vengeful and punishing. The biblical Sodom and Gomorrah story likewise reflected an era of social development in which natural disasters were seen as God's punishment for human moral error. Inhabited by a vindictive God, the early Puritan universe also included an active, malicious Devil, an often-evoked hell, and occasional malevolent witches. Early colonial lists of capital crimes included both sodomy and witchcraft. [. . .]

In early New England, sodomitical sinners were not thought of as differing in their essential natures from Puritan saints. All persons' 'cursed Natures' inclined them to every variety of wickedness—the 'holiest man hath as vile and filthy a Nature, as the Sodomites,' said Reverend Danforth in 1674. Even the most outwardly respectable Puritan might be inwardly guilty of 'heart sodomy' or 'heart buggery'—as well as 'heart whoredom,' 'heart blasphemy' and 'heart drunkenness'—warned Reverend Shepard in 1641. No Puritan was perfectly pure. Only a deep faith in God distinguished the saved from the damned; both were equally corrupted by 'original sin,' both were potential committers of sodomy—and other sins. In today's terms, original sin was 'normal', not 'deviant.'

The Puritans did not punish sodomitical sinners because they were 'deviant,' 'different,' 'abnormal' or a 'minority.' As sinners, committers of sodomy belonged to the Puritan majority. Those graced by faith and salvation were the minority. Given this social situation, the idea of a 'sodomitical minority' would have made no sense to the early settlers. In a society in which an elite few were the 'elect,' and the many were the damned, no democratic political ideology had yet influenced the social response to carnal intercourse. For the Puritans the numbers of persons who performed certain numbers of acts had no bearing on those acts' 'naturalness' or 'unnaturalness.' An absolute, qualitative, procreative standard determined what was considered 'natural', not a quantitative norm. It is anachronistic to speak of a 'gay,' 'homosexual,' or even a 'sodomitical minority' as if it existed for the early colonists. Projecting modern concepts on the past prevents us from understanding those settlers' responses to copulation.

['The Age of Sodomitical Sin, 1607–1740', in Jonathan Goldberg (ed.) *Reclaiming Sodom* (New York: Routledge, 1994, 51–2, 52–3.]

THEO VAN DER MEER
....
26   Sodomy and Moral Panic in the Low Countries

It was only after 1675 that sodomy trials were more often held by Dutch courts or that references to sodomy began to show up more or less regularly in Dutch court records. In 1676 three men—including a *burgomaster* (mayor)—were prosecuted on sodomy charges in Utrecht, which resulted in one death penalty.[1] In 1721 a man was also put to death in Utrecht on the same charges and, at the same time, the legal authorities received information about other men.[2] Between 1682 and 1684 four sodomites were executed in Rotterdam, and at least one in the Hague.[3] Several others were sentenced in absentia. In the next few decades, especially in Rotterdam, such trials became recurrent affairs. In 1702 two men were put to death there because they had perpetrated sodomy in an almoner's house.[4] In 1717, eight men who had been arrested at public toilets were sent into permanent exile by the court of Rotterdam.[5] Two men may have been drowned in a barrel because of sodomy in 1686 in Amsterdam, and in 1689 and 1715 the court in this city became aware of same-sex practices at public places through blackmail cases.[6] The same had happened with the Court of Holland in The Hague in 1702. Probably in connection with this last blackmail case, several men were prosecuted by the local court in that city.[7]

From 1730 On

In 1730, 'the most extraordinary and accidental discovery of a tangle of ungodliness'[8]—a nationwide network of sodomites, including men from all social strata—triggered a series of prosecutions of sodomites that was unprecedented in the history of the country. As the provincial Court of Holland expressed that year, it was necessary 'to exterminate this vice to the bottom.'⁹ Indeed, in terms of penalties meted out to the culprits, they were among the harshest of their kind in early modern Europe. Between 1730 and 1732, at least seventy-five men were put to death. Over a hundred men who had fled the country were sentenced in absentia and permanently exiled. Until 1811, the year in which the French penal code was enforced in the Netherlands, a series of such prosecutions as well as incidental sodomy trials occurred, most notoriously in 1764 in Amsterdam, in 1776 in several cities in the province of Holland and in 1797 in the cities of Dordrecht, The Hague and Utrecht. [. . .]

Several other points must be observed as far as sodomite prosecutions are concerned. First, many of the trials before 1675 involved adult men who had had sex with adolescents, while those in later years generally involved adult men who had sex with one another. Second, on rare occasions up to the early seventeenth century when men were found guilty of sodomy, at least those who had been 'agens,' inserters, were usually burned at the stake. Later in that century, until 1730, when they were found guilty of anal intercourse, sodomites were generally garroted, and whereas burning occurred almost by definition in public, garroting was usually carried out in secret in the cellars of city halls, 'so that it might not be known that sodomy was perpetrated in this country.'¹⁰ The year 1730 not only was a watershed in terms of the sheer number of people prosecuted but also was marked because executions—again usually by garroting— were carried out (at least in the province of Holland) at the scaffold in front of large audiences.

['Sodomy and the Pursuit of a Third Sex in the Early Modern Period', in Gilbert Herdt (ed.), *Third Sex, Third Gender: Beyond Sexual Dimorphism in Culture and History* (New York: Zone Books, 1994), 140–1, 148.]

I.e. Enlightenment and Revolution

By 1700 or so the power of religion and religious authority in sexual matters had begun to wane in the most prosperous and enlightened parts of Europe and North America and within the educated classes. Religious surveillance of personal life was not as effective in growing cities like London, Paris, or Philadelphia as it remained in rural parishes and small towns, and the power of the Church was challenged by new elites armed with an authority drawn from the growing prestige of natural science. Although the modern scientific discourse on sex and sexuality did contest some of the positions religious dogmatism had built on a foundation of ancient philosophical authority, a remarkable agreement between them persisted on certain key issues. As we shall see, if anything scientific discoveries reinforced some of the dissolving foundations of traditional patriarchy and the social order with more authoritative arguments.

First, the family unit continued to be recognized as the primordial sexual space, with procreation and child rearing as its principal tasks. Second, the divine ordinance that made all humankind into the sons or daughters of Adam and Eve was firmly sustained by the findings of modern natural science on the differences between the sexes. And third, the newly emergent liberal and democratic order readily embraced this new knowledge and legitimized it in law, much as medieval and early modern polities had used dogma to deepen and extend their power. However, our modern distinction between the public and private spheres culminated during this era in the French Revolution, a development that, in theory, was intended as a way of protecting citizens against the unwarranted interference of Church and state in the personal affairs of citizens. Ironically, however, the growth of a private sphere where men and women could presumably do what they pleased coincided with the triumph of a new form of individualism that fulfilled the dream of sixteenth-century religious reformers to internalize sexual self-discipline. In becoming more private, sexuality was becoming more a part of an individual's personal nature and therefore something for which he or she was responsible. But in becoming more tied to natural biological processes, it also became a more universal human condition, linking both sexes to certain inexorable laws. This paradox is the heritage of the discovery of Enlightenment science of the two sexes.

A more self-conscious notion of the close relationship between character and the control of sexual impulses had already emerged in the early modern era within the educated upper classes. In the complicated intrigues of court life, the successful courtier learned how to master every gesture, gauge the effect of every word, and control every impulse. Since aristocratic women had more personal liberty than women in the rest of the social hierarchy, it was possible for them to think of their sexuality as an asset in courtly politics that they could dispose of or withhold. In a celebrated seventeenth-century novel written by the aristocratic Madame de Lafayette, *La Princesse de Clèves* (1678), the Princess, hopelessly but secretly in love with a man other than her husband, finds that the only constraints on her to refrain from an adulterous affair are her own, but that these are more than sufficient for the task (Extract 27).

According to Norbert Elias, whose trilogy, *The Civilizing Process*, chronicles the inexorable replacement of external with internalized controls on individual impulses, this development laid the foundations of the modern sexual psyche (Extract 28).

In one of the most intimate and frank autobiographies ever written, and certainly the first to deal with sexuality as an aspect of personal identity, the French philosopher Jean-Jacques Rousseau confided many of the details of his sexual life to his *Confessions* (1778). Rousseau was no saint. He worried about the effects on his health of youthful masturbation, dallied with prostitutes, and had an extended affair with an older woman, Madame de Warens, who had acted for many years as his protector and patroness. Exceptionally among secular contemporaries, he persisted in believing that the things that occurred in his sexual life were not incidental matters but profound indications of his character. In this passage he reflects on a visit to a celebrated Venetian courtesan when he was a little over 30 (Extract 29).

Despite all his railings against science and reason, Rousseau's reaction to Giulietta's 'imperfection' was altogether typical of Enlightenment notions of the orderliness and symmetry of the natural world. Scientists and aesthetes alike in the eighteenth century agreed on the merits of the search for the ideal forms and rules governing natural phenomena. The numerous exceptions and deviations from these models that one found in nature tended to prove, to their satisfaction, the great virtues of the patterns and laws that governed both the cosmos and human creation and confirmed the rewards attached to discovering them (Extract 30).

Nowhere was this more evident than in the effort of eighteenth-century anatomists and biologists to sweep away medieval confusions and bring coherence into the study of the human body. What they discovered when they looked deeply into the body were the extraordinary differences between males and females. As the following two extracts demonstrate, experts in such matters had always acknowledged the dissimilarities between the sexes, but Enlightenment thinkers made those unlikenesses into incommensurable entities that extended to the skeletal underpinnings of sex, but especially to the reproductive organs (Extracts 31 and 32).

Though representations of the body stressed the differences between men and women and placed particular emphasis on women's reproductive function in the eighteenth century, an ideology of romantic love and domesticity appeared that integrated these scientific findings with a traditional familial framework. In the following extract we see how scientific and medical writers also helped lay down the discursive foundations for this development (Extract 33).

The triumph—at least within the middle and upper classes—of romantic marriages did not mean an improvement in the status or condition of women; indeed, in those parts of Europe where the new domestic ideals were most widespread, women may have exercised less rather than more control over their own fertility even though, in general, the number of children they had decreased (Extract 34).

Perhaps the greatest irony of the Enlightenment discovery of the sexes was the consequence it appeared to hold for women's sexual pleasure. We have seen that for centuries learned males had been suspicious of women's sexuality, which they generally characterized as voracious and extreme. But neither experts nor popular early modern manuals on sex and reproduction like the oft-reprinted *Aristotle's Master-Piece* had doubted the important role female sexual pleasure played in conception, whether by raising a woman's body heat or causing the release of female 'seed' (Extract 35).

By the turn of the nineteenth century, however, although the physiology of female reproduction was still not much better understood, some medical experts found it possible to minimize if not abandon the female orgasm and female pleasure generally.[1] The reasons for this new construction of the sexual nature of women are inseparable from developments in politics and society. During the French Revolution, radical opponents of the monarchy circulated political pornography blaming the Queen, Marie Antoinette, for assorted crimes against France in terms that were explicitly sexual in nature (Extract 36).

The Queen's sexuality, in this rhetoric, served as a synecdoche for that of women in general; this in turn served as a justification for permitting women to be excluded from the new public sphere as full citizens. Social contract theory, which guided parliamentary reformers in seventeenth-century England in their successful struggle against monarchical absolutism, now undergirded French Revolutionaries attempting democratic reforms of their own. In this arrangement women were excluded from the public sphere and subjected to the tutelage of husbands and fathers, where, as noted above, their sexual appetites underwent a convenient atrophication (Extract 37).

[1] Thomas Laqueur, *Making Sex: Body and Gender from the Greeks to Freud* (Cambridge, Mass.: Harvard University Press, 1990), 150, 182–3, 188–9.

27 Sexual Self-Discipline: The Princess of Clèves

M. de Clèves spoke like the honorable man he was, and worthy of what she had done. I have no misgiving over your conduct, he said. Your character and your virtue are stronger than you think, so it is not any fear of the future that makes me so unhappy, but my failure to arouse a feeling in you where another has succeeded.

She replied, What can I say? I die of shame when I speak with you. Please try and spare me these cruel conversations; tell me what I must do. Arrange matters so that I see nobody—this is all I ask of you—but do not make me talk any more about something which puts me in such a shameful light, unworthy of you and of myself.

You are quite right, he answered. I am taking advantage of your sweetness and your trust in me. All the same you must feel sorry for the state of mind into which you have thrown me, and remember that whatever you may have said, what you have not said is a certain name, and I am dying of curiosity to know it. I am not going to ask, but I cannot help telling you that I believe it is either the Maréchal de Saint André, the Duc de Nemours, or the Chevalier du Guise who I must envy.

She blushed deeply and said, I shall not answer that question or say anything which might increase or decrease your suspicions, and if you try to find out by watching my behavior I shall become so nervous that in the end everybody will notice. For God's sake, therefore, arrange, under some pretext of illness, that I see nobody.

No, Madame, it would soon be known that it was a sham, and furthermore I want to put my trust in you alone; both my heart and my reason approve of this course. In your present state of mind I have you under closer guard by giving you your liberty than in any other way I could imagine.

M. de Clèves was not mistaken. The perfect trust he put in his wife strengthened her defenses against M. de Nemours and made her more strict in her resolutions than any restraint of his could possibly have done.

[*The Princess of Clèves*, trans. Nancy Mitford (Binghamton, NY: New Directions Press, 1951), 129–30.]

28 Civility and Self-Discipline

[*The Princesse de Clèves*] is an example of the pressure toward self-discipline imposed on the sexes by this situation. The husband knows that he cannot hold his wife by force. He does not rant or expostulate because his wife loves another, nor does he appeal to his rights as a husband. Public opinion would support none of this. He restrains himself. But in doing so he expects from her the same self-discipline as he imposes on himself. This is a very characteristic example of the new constellation that comes into being with the diminishment of social inequality between the sexes. Fundamentally, it is not the individual husband who gives his wife this freedom. It is founded in the structure of society itself. But it also demands a new kind of behavior. It produces very specific conflicts. And there are certainly enough women in this society who make use of this freedom. There is plentiful evidence that in this courtly aristocracy the restriction of sexual relationships to marriage was very often regarded as bourgeois and socially unsuitable. Nevertheless, all this gives an idea of how directly a specific kind of freedom corresponds to particular forms and stages of social interdependence among human beings.

The nondynamic linguistic forms to which we are still bound today oppose freedom and constraint like heaven and hell. From a short-term point of view, this thinking in absolute opposites is often reasonably adequate. For someone in prison the world outside the prison walls is a world of freedom. But considered more precisely, there is, contrary to what antitheses such as this one suggest, no such thing as 'absolute' freedom, if this means a total independence and absence of social constraint. There is a liberation from one form of constraint that is oppressive or intolerable to another which is less burdensome. Thus the civilizing process, despite the transformation and increased constraint that it imposes on the emotions, goes hand in hand with liberations of the most diverse kinds. The form of marriage at the absolutist courts, symbolized by the same arrangement of living rooms and bedrooms for men and women in the mansions of the court aristocracy, is one of many examples of this. The woman was more free from external constraints than in feudal society. But the inner constraint which she had to impose on herself in accordance with the form of integration and the code of behavior of court society, and which stemmed from the same structural features of this society as her 'liberation,' had increased for women as for men in comparison to chivalrous society.

[*The History of Manners: The Civilizing Process*, v. i, trans. Edmund Jephcott (New York: Pantheon Books, 1978), 184–5.]

29 Sexuality and Identity

If there is one incident in my life which plainly reveals my character, it is the one I am now going to describe. By forcibly reminding myself at this moment of the purpose of my book, I shall have strength to despise the false modesty which might prevent my fulfilling it. Whoever you may be that wish to know a man, have the courage to read the next two or three pages and you will have complete knowledge of Jean-Jacques Rousseau.

I entered a courtesan's room as if it were the sanctuary of love and beauty; in her person I felt I saw the divinity. I could never have believed it possible to feel anything like the emotion she inspired in me, without my also feeling a respect and esteem for her. No sooner did I recognize from our first familiarities the value of her charms and caresses than, fearing to lose the fruit prematurely, I tried to make haste and pluck it. Suddenly, instead of the fire that devoured me, I felt a deathly cold flow through my veins; my legs trembled; I sat down on the point of fainting, and wept like a child.

Who could guess the cause of my tears, or the thoughts that went through my head at that moment? 'This thing which is at my disposal', I said to myself, 'is Nature's masterpiece and love's. Its mind, its body, every part is perfect. She is not only charming and beautiful, but good also and generous. Great men and princes should be her slaves. Sceptres should lie at her feet. Yet here she is, a wretched street-walker, on sale to the world. The captain of a merchant ship can dispose of her. She comes and throws herself at my head, at mine although she knows I am a nobody, although my merits, which she cannot know, would be nothing in her eyes. There is something incomprehensible about this. Either my heart deceives me, deludes my senses and makes me the dupe of a worthless slut, or some secret flaw that I do not see destroys the value of her charms and makes her repulsive to those who should be quarrelling for possession of her. I began to seek for that flaw with a singular persistence, and it did not so much as occur to me that the pox might have something to do with it. The freshness of her flesh, the brightness of her colouring, the whiteness of her teeth, the sweetness of her breath, the air of cleanliness that pervaded her person, so completely banished that idea from my mind that, being still in doubt about my own health since my visit to the *padoana*, I even felt some qualms about my not being wholesome enough for her, and I am quite convinced that I was not deceived in my confidence.

These well-timed reflections moved me to the point of tears, and Giulietta, for whom this sight was certainly an unusual one in such a situation, was momentarily at a loss. But after walking round the room and passing in front of her glass, she understood—and my eyes confirmed her reason— that repulsion had nothing to do with my freakish behaviour. It was not difficult for her to dispel my melancholy and rid me of my slight sense of shame. But just as I was about to sink upon a breast which seemed to suffer a man's lips and hand for the first time, I perceived that she had a malformed nipple. I beat my brow, looked harder, and made certain that this nipple did not match the other. Then I started wondering about the reason for this malformation. I was struck by the thought that it resulted from some remarkable imperfection of Nature and, after turning this idea over in my head, I saw as clear as daylight that instead of the most charming creature I could possibly imagine I held in my arms some kind of monster, rejected by nature, men, and love. I carried my stupidity so far as to speak to her about her malformed nipple. First she took the matter as a joke and said and did things in her skittish humour that were enough to make me die of love. But as I still felt some remnant of uneasiness, which I could not conceal from her, I finally saw her blush, adjust her clothes, and take her place at the window, without a word. I tried to sit down beside her. She moved and sat down on a couch, then got up next moment and walked about the room, fanning herself. Finally she said to me in a cold and scornful voice: 'Gianetto, lascia le donne, e studia la matematica.[1]

Before leaving, I asked her for another appointment next day, which she put off till the third day, adding with an ironical smile that I must need a rest. I spent the time rather uneasily, with my heart full of her charms and graces, conscious of my strange behaviour and regretting the ill-use I had made of those moments which it had only rested with me to transform into the sweetest in my life. I waited with the liveliest impatience for the moment when I could make good my loss. Nevertheless I could not help uneasily wondering how I could reconcile the perfections of this adorable girl with the unworthiness of her trade. I ran, I flew to her at the hour appointed. I do not know whether her passionate temperament would have been better satisfied by this visit. At least her pride would have been flattered. I looked forward to the delicious pleasure of showing her the manifold ways in which I could repair my mistakes. She spared me the ordeal. The gondolier, whom I had sent to her rooms on landing, brought me the news that she had left the previous evening for Florence. If I had not felt whole-hearted love when she was in my arms, I felt it most cruelly when I lost her. My insane regret has never left me. Pleasant and charming though she was in my eyes, I could console myself for her loss. But what I have never been able to console myself for is, I confess, that she only carried away a scornful memory of me.

[*The Confessions*, trans. J. M. Cohen (Baltimore: Penguin Books, 1963), 300–2.]

BARBARA MARIA STAFFORD

30 Exception and Norm

This chapter, then, is about extremes. It looks at the edges of categories, at the outer margins of the inner brain and body. I examine those foreign or kindred filiations the early modern mentality chose to exclude or include from aesthetic, biological, and cultural discourse. Moreover, I ask by what principles it was done and why. The eighteenth century's notions of what was out or in, lacking or perfect, remain recognizable in the late twentieth century. Monsters and hybrids, exaggeratedly spiritual or material conceptions, all dwelled at the limit of light and dark, at the boundaries of natural viability and social acceptability. Aberrations in language, body, and imagery incarnated unenlightenment in the Age of Enlightenment. [. . .]

For the eighteenth century, looking at monsters developed into an indoor sport. Caricatures were bought or rented, glass slides produced, and friends invited over to gape at the vulgar spectacle of the material body's grossest functions. Eating, drinking, fornicating, defecating needed no translation and were universally understood as aspects of daily life.[1] If lofty allegory magnified the spiritual and the conceptual, the grotesque twisted and minimized those same values through travesty and incongruous contiguity. Poinsinet de Sivry remarked that ridicule was like looking through a telescope. It diminished or exaggerated our esteem for an individual. For Sticotti, this external alteration in perception revolutionized our internal judgment through conversion or perversion. It was a constant refrain in analytical or philosophical criticism that the grotesque was a fault always manifested on the surface or exterior of a body. For the wordsmith guardians of a system of correct art, the grotesque dangerously pictured questionable or equivocal sexual acts and controversial amalgams. Ostentatious structural malformation, and provocative revolt against conventional mores, lay at the heart of its aesthetic operations. Dangerous and uncontrollable expressive freedom constituted its chief formal transgression, irrespective of the genre.[2]

[*Body Criticism: Imaging the Unseen in Enlightenment Art and Medicine* (Cambridge, Mass.: MIT Press, 1993), 212–13, 274.]

LUDMILLA JORDANOVA

31 Sex under the Skin

By the end of the eighteenth century, then, there were a number of ways in which the idea of organic depth manifested itself, through changing practices, ideas and metaphors. This interest in depth was especially significant for the construction of femininity in two distinct although related ways. The first was by promoting the actual unveiling of women's bodies to render visible the emblematic core of their sex in the organs of generation. The second was by giving expression to a model of knowledge, based on looking deeply into and thereby intellectually mastering nature—a model infused with assumptions about gender.

It is fairly easy to see that parts of the body like the breast, uterus, ovaries and so on can provide vehicles through which sex differences of all kinds from the anatomical to the social can be rehearsed. However, organs common to both sexes also carry deeply gendered metaphorical loads. One example of this is the feminization of the nervous system and the masculinization of the musculature in the eighteenth century. Such associations, however, are never historically stable, and their viability particularly depends upon the social and cultural apparatus of class and racial divisions. For example, there are very few female wax anatomical models that are erect. Most of the erect models are male, displaying muscles contracting and relaxing in athletic poses. A rare upright female model displays the nervous system and includes prominent genitals and pubic hair.[1] The idea of the nervous temperament of women and their heightened sensibility was a commonplace in medical writings, which associated hysteria with the nervous system in the eighteenth century.[2] Similarly, such writings abound with assertions of the muscular weakness of women. There is a special kind of 'classism' built into such assertions, which embody a distinctively middle-class notion of femininity as sedentary, domestic and emotional, yet a much more populist image of masculinity as physically active.

[*Sexual Visions: Images of Gender in Science and Medicine between the Eighteenth and Twentieth Centuries* (Madison: University of Wisconsin Press, 1989), 57–8.]

LONDA SCHIEBINGER

32 'Deep Sex' in the Skeleton

A fundamental shift in the definition of sex differences emerged in the course of the eighteenth and early nineteenth century. Beginning in the 1750s, a body of literature appeared in France and Germany calling for a finer delineation of sex differences. In 1750, Edmond Thomas Moreau published a slim book in Paris entitled *A Medical Question: Whether Apart from Genitalia There Is a Difference Between the Sexes?*[1] In 1775, the French physician Pierre Roussel reproached his colleagues for considering woman similar to man except in sexual organs. 'The essence of sex,' he explained, 'is not confined to a single organ but extends, through more or less perceptible nuances, into every part.'[2] In 1788, German anatomist Jakob Ackermann stated that the present definition of sex differences was inadequate. The great physiologists, he complained, have neglected the description of the female body. 'Indeed, sex differences,' he emphasized, 'have always been observed, but their description has been arbitrary.'[3] In his two-hundred-page book on sex differences in bones, hair, mouths, eyes, voices, blood vessels, sweat, and brains, Ackermann called for a 'more essential' description of sex differences and encouraged anatomists to research the most basic parts of the body to discover 'the essential sex difference from which all others flow.'[4] [. . .]

It was as part of this broader investigation of sex differences that drawings of the first female skeletons appeared in England, France, and Germany between 1730 and 1790. The skeleton, as the hardest part of the body, was thought to provide a 'ground plan' upon which muscles, veins, and nerves were to be drawn. In 1749, anatomist Bernhard Siegfried Albinus wrote:

I must pitch upon something . . . as the base or foundation to build my figures upon. And this is the skeleton: which being part of the body, and lying below the muscle, the figures of it ought first to be taken off as certain and natural direction for the others.[5]

If sex differences could be found in the skeleton, then sexual identity would no longer be a matter of sex organs appended to a neutral human body, as Vesalius had thought, but would penetrate every muscle, vein, and organ attached to and molded by the skeleton. [...]

Text and image came together in the French rendering of a female skeleton that made its debut in 1759, capturing the imagination of medical doctors for more than half a century. The skeleton appears to be one of the very few drawn by a woman anatomist. Marie-Geneviève-Charlotte Thiroux d'Arconville, who studied anatomy at the Jardin du Roi, directed the drawing of illustrations from dissections for her French translation of Monro's *Anatomy*.[6] D'Arconville's plates were published under the protection of Jean-J. Sue, member of the Académie royale de Chirurgie. D'Arconville's name does not appear in the volume, and the illustrations were generally attributed to Sue.

In 1796, the German anatomist Samuel Thomas von Soemmerring produced a rival female skeleton.[7] Although d'Arconville's (Sue's) work was known in Germany, Soemmerring's reviewers praised his female skeleton for 'filling a gap which until now remained in all anatomy'.[8] Directly answering Albinus' plea, Soemmerring spent years perfecting his portrayal of the female skeleton, and he considered his female to be of such 'completeness and exactitude' that it made a perfect mate for the great Albinus male. As a model, he selected the skeleton of a twenty-year-old woman from Mayence who had borne a child.[9] Soemmerring also checked his drawing against the classical statues of the Venus di Medici and Venus of Dresden to achieve a universal representation of woman. Soemmerring intended that his skeleton represent not an individual woman but (as Ludwig Choulant put it) 'the most beautiful norm as it was imagined to exist in life, with all the carefully observed minutiae of the differential sexual characters of the entire bony structure of woman.'[10] [. . .]

Great debate erupted over the exact character of the female skeleton. Despite its exaggerations, the d'Arconville/Sue skeleton became the favored drawing in Britain. Soemmerring's skeleton, by contrast, was attacked for its 'inaccuracies.' John Barclay, the Edinburgh physician, wrote, 'although it be more graceful and elegant [than the Sue skeleton] and suggested by men of eminence in modeling, sculpture, and painting, it contributes nothing to the comparison [between male and female skeletons] which is intended.'[11] Soemmerring was attacked, in particular, for showing the incorrect proportions of the ribs to the hips:

Women's rib cage is much smaller than that shown by Soemmerring, because it it well known that women's restricted life style requires that they breathe less vigorously. . . .

The pelvis, and it is here alone that we perceive the strongly-marked and peculiar characters of the female skeleton, is shown by Soemmerring as improperly small.[12] [. . .]

The supposedly 'universal' representations of the human body in eighteenth-century anatomical illustrations were, in fact, laden with cultural values [. . .] For his illustrations, Albinus collected data from 'one body after another.' He then selected one 'perfect' skeleton to serve as his model. Albinus also revealed the criteria by which he 'sifted' nature in the drawing of his male skeleton:

As skeletons differ from one another, not only as to the age, sex, stature and perfection of the bones, but likewise in the marks of strength, beauty and make of the whole; I made choice of one that might discover signs both of strength and agility: the whole of it elegant, and at the same time not too delicate; so as neither to shew a juvenile or feminine roundness and slenderness, nor on the contrary an unpolished roughness and clumsiness.[13]

In his preface to Ackermann's book on sex differences, Joseph Wenzel discussed the difficulties anatomists have in choosing models for their work. He noted that a sharp physiological delineation between the sexes is impossible because the great variation among individual men and women produces continuity between the sexes. In fact, he wrote, one can find skulls, brains, and breast bones of the 'feminine' type in men. Wenzel then defined a standard of femininity that he used as the basis of his own work:

I have always observed that the female body which is the most beautiful and womanly in all its parts, is one in which the pelvis is the largest in relation to the rest of the body.[14]

Soemmerring strived, like Albinus, for exactitude and universality in his illustrations. He made every possible effort to 'approach nature as nearly as possible.' Yet, he stated, the physiologists should always select the most perfect and most beautiful specimen for their models.[15] In identifying and selecting the 'most beautiful specimen,' Soemmerring intended to establish norms of beauty. According to Soemmerring, without having established a norm by means of frequent investigations and abstractions, one is not able to decide which cases deviate from the perfect norm.[16] Soemmerring chose the 'ideal' model for his illustration of the female skeleton with great care:

Above all I was anxious to provide for myself the body of a woman that was suitable not only because of her youth and aptitude for procreation, but also because of the harmony of her limbs, beauty, and elegance, of the kind that the ancients used to ascribe to Venus.[17]

In their illustrations of the female body, anatomists followed the example of those painters who 'draw a handsome face, and if there happens to be any blemish in it, they mend it in the picture.'[18] Anatomists of the eighteenth century 'mended' nature to fit emerging ideals of masculinity and femininity.

['Skeletons in the Closet: The First Illustrations of the Female Skeleton in Eighteenth-Century Anatomy', in Catherine Gallagher and Thomas Laqueur (eds.), *The Making of the Modern Body: Sexuality and Society in the Nineteenth Century* (Berkeley and Los Angeles: University of California Press, 1987), 51, 53, 58, 59, 61–2.]

33 Sexual Complementarity

The new order of separate spheres and sexual segregation was not built wholly out of a discourse of incommensurability. The private realm of the family needed a compatible discursive regime that would acknowledge the difference between the sexes, but justify and reinforce the ideal of domestic happiness and unity. This task required a doctrine of complementarity which could provide a 'harmony of corresponding inequalities.'[1] As we have seen, the medical writings on women and reproduction of the late eighteenth and early nineteenth centuries considered men and women to be different not only in their genital structures, but in every aspect of their physical organizations.[2] The axis on which this difference turned, however, was the singular contribution each sex made to reproduction. In the act of reproduction, sexual distinctiveness was the *premise* of fertility, but the *synthesis* of a new life reconciled these otherwise antithetical principles. Indeed, it was common for medical writers to consider boys and girls sexually indifferent until puberty, when the striking physical changes that made them fertile overcame indifference in all its aspects.

Procreation finally attained from secular medical writers the privileged status it had always merited in the eyes of theologians. In this development, the attraction between the sexes gained, by extension, a new *cachet* it had never before enjoyed. Medical experts characterized the affinities on which fertility depended as an attraction of 'opposite' principle. Since the view of women as 'natural' wives and mothers was already well-developed by 1800 or so, doctors turned their attention to the male role in sexual arousal and fertilization, gradually elaborating a scientific discourse of procreative harmonies. Males were accordingly represented in the medical literature after this date in ways that reflected the criteria of opposition and complementarity. In the process men gained a natural identity as sexual beings that made it increasingly difficult, despite rhetoric to the contrary, for them to be uniquely representative of the human genre 'mankind,' or for women to be the archetypal sexed being, the 'fair sex,' or, simply, the 'sex.'

[*Masculinity and Male Codes of Honor in Modern France* (New York: Oxford University Press, 1993), 57–8.]

34 Romantic Marriage, Women, and Fertility

The evidence suggests that France was the first nation to experience widespread fertility control because of female solidarity. French women might not have had the legal rights of their English counterparts, but they clearly assumed they had a right to control their bodies. Witness the famous letters of Mme de Sévigné to her daughter in 1671 and 1672, warning her not to become pregnant again. 'I beg of you, my dear, do not rely on having two beds; it lends itself to temptation: have someone sleep in your bedroom. Seriously, have pity on yourself, on your health and mine.'[1] [. . .]

The emergence in eighteenth-century France of this new morality that justified fertility control has been attributed to husbands' having a new concern for their wives. Marriages, it is suggested, were now refined and treated with the gallantry previously reserved for liaisons. Husbands sought to protect wives, who faced a 10 per cent chance of death in childbearing.[2] The same is not true in England because, as a result of a decline in infectious diseases and improvements in obstetrical care, maternal mortality was lower.[3] But women's own interests seem oddly absent in such an explanation. It is as likely that a decline in the threat of death in childbed, rather than raising women's confidence, would harden their resolve to avoid such dangers. Moreover, theories that stress male 'gallantry' skate around the evidence that the issue of fertility control could divide couples. A glimpse of such disputes was caught in a 1706 church declaration that a woman had to obey a husband who insisted on employing unnatural means to avoid having children, but that she did not have the right to suggest such means herself.[4]

The stress on the significance of the companionate couple as the key to employment of fertility controls appears unwarranted. Trumbach points out that in England a more 'egalitarian or domestic style of household relationships' in the later eighteen century actually led to larger families. Curiously enough, the 'romantic marriages' of the English aristocracy seemed to limit the freedom of women. Such cloying unions means that English women were less able to move in mixed company than their French counterparts.[5] What Trumbach inadvertently demonstrates is that domesticity, far from laying the basis for an egalitarian relationship, limited the woman's options.

The ideology of domesticity was clearly more successfully rooted in England than in France. But the growing privacy sought by the upper classes in their marriages, the decline of rituals of 'bedding' the couple and offering guests 'favours', did not mean that the needs of the new spouses were placed above those of the family. It meant rather that the upper classes had cut themselves off from the larger community. Presumably this laid the basis, not for a more 'egalitarian' relationship, but for one in which the woman was totally dependent on the man. English upper-class brides of the late eighteenth century, trained to hide any interest in sexuality, warned not to listen to the gossip of servants and cut off from the larger female community, were probably more ignorant of the workings of their bodies than their grandmothers had ever been.

French women enjoyed perhaps a less 'loving' relationship with their husbands, but carved out for themselves a less domestic, less fettered life. Père Féline recognized that French husbands did not impose contraception on their wives; rather they acceded to the latter's demands. 'They [the husbands] become too sensitive to the complaints that the wives make about all that it cost them to bring children into the world. [The husbands] treat kindly their excessive delicacy, they consent to spare them this trouble, without, however, renouncing the right that they believe they have of satisfying themselves.'[6]

Historians of the family always run the risk of mistaking doctrines and practices. A 'love' marriage at the start of the eighteenth century was construed as an unfortunate misalliance; by its end parents were insisting that their children marry for 'love'. The vocabulary had changed; not the concerns of the parents to make a good match. Similarly, the glorification of domesticity indicated that the enriched middle classes of the prosperous eighteenth century were, not more loving parents, but better able to afford such indulgences. The apparent neglect of and lack of interest taken in children in previous centuries were clearly a function of economic deprivation. Likewise the employment of contraception by French couples did not signify that husbands were suddenly overcome by some simple sense of gallantry; a more complicated development took place. Men wanted to maintain their conjugal rights and avoid the division of their property among numerous heirs; women wanted to protect their health and that of their children. Recourse was had to contraception in the light of these practical concerns, not in the rosy glow of romance.

[*A History of Contraception: From Antiquity to the Present Day* (Oxford: Basil Blackwell, 1990), 166, 167–9.]

---

35 The Use of Female Orgasm

The Use of the external Parts, commonly called the Pudenda, are designed to cover the great orifice, or Fissura Magna, and the use of that is to receive the yard in the act of copulation, and to give passage to the child at the birth; and also a passage for the urine: the use of the wings and knobs, like myrtle-berries, are for the security of the internal parts, shutting the orifice and neck of the bladder; and by their swelling up to cause titillation and delight in those parts, and also to hinder the involuntary passage of the urine. The action of the Clytoris in women, is like that of the yard in men, which is erection; and its outer end is like the glans, or the top of the yard, and has the same name, and as the glans in man is the seat of the greatest pleasure in copulation, so is this in women.

The action and use of the neck of the womb, is equal with that of the yard, and is occasioned several ways: for first, it is erected and made strait for the passage of the yard to the womb in the act of copulation; and then whilst the passage is repleted with spirit and vital blood, it becomes more strait for embracing the yard; and as touching the convenience of erection, it is two-fold: first, if the neck of the womb was not erected, the yard could have no convenient passage to the womb: and in second place, it hinders any damage that may happen through the violent concussion of the yard in the time of copulation. [. . .]

Having thus given an account of the use and action of the genitals, in the act of generation, I shall now shew you the opinion of both the ancients and moderns touching the woman's contributing seed for the formation of the child; as well as the man's; which was the opinion of the ancients, but is denied by our modern enquirers into the secrets of nature.

Though it is apparent (say the ancients) that the seed of man is the principal efficient, and beginning of action, motion, and generation, yet that the woman affords seed, and contributes to the procreation of the child, is evident from hence; that the woman has seminal vessels, which had been given her in vain, had she wanted seminal excrescence; but since nature doth nothing in vain, it must be granted they were made for the use of seed and procreation; and fixed in their proper places to operate and contribute virtue and efficacy to the seed; and this, say they, is farther proved from hence, that if women at the years of maturity, use not copulation to eject their seed, they often fall into strange diseases, as appears by young women and virgins, and also it is apparent that women are never better pleased than when they are often satisfied this way; which argues the pleasure and delight they take therein; which pleasure and delight, say they, is double in women to what it is in men; for as the delight in men consists (in copulation) chiefly in the ejection of the seed; so women are delighted both by the ejection of their own, and the reception of man's.

[*Aristotle's Last Legacy*, in the Marriage, Sex and the Family in England 1660–1800 series, ed. Randolph Trumbach (New York: Garland Publishing, 1986), 13, 15.]

LYNN HUNT

36   The Sexuality of the Queen

Explicit in some of the more extreme statements and implicit in many others was a pervasive preoccupation with genealogy. For example, the post-1789 pamphlets constantly raised questions about the paternity of the king's children (they were often attributed to the king's brother, the comte d'Artois). In a fascinating twist on the charge of false genealogy, *Le Père Duchesne* denounced a supposed plot by the queen to raise a young boy who resembled the heir to the throne in order to take the heir's place. The culminating charge, of course, was incest; in the trial, this was limited to the queen's son, but in the pamphlet literature the charges included incest with the king's brother, the king's grandfather Louis XV, and her own father, who taught her 'the passion of incest, the dirtiest of pleasures,' from which followed 'hatred of the French, aversion for the duties

of spouse and mother, in short, all that reduces humanity to the level of ferocious beasts.' The reductio ad absurdum of these charges was the following
verse, which loses most of its effect in translation:

> Ci-gît l'impudique Manon,
> Qui, dans le ventre de sa mère,
> Savait si bien placer son c. . . ,
> Qu'elle f. . . avec son père.[1]

Here lies the lewd Manon | Who, in the belly of her mother | Knew so well how to
place her c. . . | That she f. . . with her father.

Bestialization and accusations of disorderly sexuality and falsification of
genealogy were all linked in the most intimate way.

Promiscuity, incest, poisoning of the heir to the throne, plots to replace the heir
with a pliable substitute—all of these charges reflect a fundamental anxiety about
queenship as the most extreme form of the invasion of the public sphere by
women. Where Rousseau had warned that the salon woman would turn her
'harem of men' into women 'more womanish than she,' the radical militant Louise
de Keralio would warn her readers that 'a woman who becomes queen changes
sex.'[2] The queen, then, was the emblem (and sacrificial victim) for the feared disintegration of gender boundaries that accompanied the Revolution. [. . .]

The charge of incest against the queen was only the most striking example of
the connection of the fear of dedifferentiation with the queen's fate. The charge
of lesbianism (*tribadism* was the term of the time) served the same purpose. In
the pornographic pamphlets written against her, Marie-Antoinette is shown as
a creature whose voracious sexuality knows no limits and no gender differentiation (or, for that matter, class differentiation). She was often denounced as a
whore, that is, as a public woman whose sexuality destroyed any possibility of
tracing paternity. In a violent pamphlet against prostitutes, for example, the
queen was reviled as *la reine des garces*, the queen of whores (and the word *garce*
itself clearly connotes gender blurring, since it has the same root as *garçon*, boy):
'abominable *garce*, execrable model of incurable lewdness . . . you who by your
incestuous examples, your perpetual adulteries, never cease to insult virtue.'[3]

[*The Family Romance of the French Revolution* (Berkeley and Los Angeles: University of
California Press, 1992), 113–14, 115.]

CAROLE PATEMAN

37   The Sexual Contract

Women, their bodies and bodily passions, represent the 'nature' that must be
controlled and transcended if social order is to be created and sustained. In the
state of nature, social order in the family can be maintained only if the husband

is master. Unlimited feminine desire must always be contained by patriarchal right. Women's relations to the social world must always be mediated through men's reason; women's bodies must always be subject to men's reason and judgements if order is not to be threatened. (Mozart's *The Magic Flute* provides a brilliant, dramatic presentation of this claim.) The meaning of the state of nature and civil society can be understood only in conjunction with each other. The 'foundation in nature' for masculine rights is that women cannot develop the political morality required of participants in civil society. 'Femininity' and 'masculinity' in the state of nature are constructed theoretically to reflect women's deficiency so that the Rawlsian 'desired solution' can be obtained in civil society. Women are excluded from the status of free and equal individual because they lack the capacities to undergo that remarkable change that, Rousseau tells us, occurs in men when civil society and 'justice as a rule of conduct' are created.[1] Only men are able to develop the sense of justice required to maintain the civil order and uphold the civil, universal law as citizens. [. . .]

The decision to move from the state of nature to civil society, and to establish the state and its universal laws, is based on a reasoned, rational assessment of the advantages of such a move to all men. Each 'individual' can see that he, along with all other individuals, will benefit if the endemic insecurities of a condition where each man, as master of a family, judges for himself on the basis of particular interests and desires, is replaced by a society in which all individuals are equally bound by universal laws. The making of the original contract thus presupposes that passion and partiality can be constrained by reason. Rousseau is emphatic that women cannot reason in the requisite fashion (and, in any case, they should be prevented from trying). Abstract principles and speculative truths are the preserve of men. Women should study the minds of the men to whom they are subject so that they know how to communicate with their masters. Rousseau was scornful of educated women; 'a brilliant wife is a plague to her husband, her children, her friends, her valets, everyone. ... Outside her home she is always ridiculous ... these women of great talent never impress anyone but fools.'[2] (Kant was even more scathing. He dismissed the woman scholar as follows; 'she uses her *books* in the same way as her *watch*, for example, which she carries so that people will see that she has one, though it is usually not running or set by the sun.')[3]

According to Rousseau and Freud, women are incapable of transcending their sexual passions and particular attachments and directing their reason to the demands of universal order and public advantage. Women, therefore, cannot take part in the original contract. They lack all that is required to create and then protect the protection (as Hobbes puts it) afforded by the state and law to civil individuals. Only 'individuals' can make contracts and uphold the terms of the original contract. Women are 'the opposite' to the civil law; they represent all that men must master to bring civil society into being.

[*The Sexual Contract* (Stanford, Calif.: Stanford University Press, 1988), 100–2.]

I.f. Up from the Beast: The Triumph of Middle-Class Sexuality

The most important social development in the history of modern sexuality is the growth in numbers and influence of a town-dwelling middle class. The urban bourgeoisie inherited the characteristic attitudes and particular kinds of behaviour that had ensured the survival of their hard-working, abstemious ancestors. The members of this class became the wealthiest, the most literate, the most nationalistic, and the most civic-minded group in nineteenth-century states, even though—except in America where the myth was cherished that no one was poor or aristocratic—middle-class merchants, entrepreneurs, rich farmers, and professionals were never more than a tiny minority in societies that were still overwhelmingly rural and working class. However, the bourgeoisie came to exercise an enormous influence in the nineteenth century by means of a cultural hegemony exercised through institutions and networks that had become central to the modern nation state. Thus, churches, medicine, the law, teaching, journalism, and the arts were transformed into powerful and prestigious middle-class domains, ensuring a further expansion and emulation of middle-class values.

A characteristic outlook on sexual matters and a unique set of sexual practices lay at the heart of this system of values. Though they owed something to earlier secular and religious ideals of sexual asceticism and morality, these modern middle-class sexual codes had a far more positive and affirmative orientation than their older, more repressive counterparts. They were not constructed and practised by the middle classes simply as a way to master the sexually dissolute classes beneath them, or for shoring up a sense of moral superiority over their aristocratic betters; they also embodied personal, social, and political ideals that they believed contributed to social hygiene and good citizenship, in short, to both material and spiritual progress.

In the introductory volume to his *History of Sexuality*, Michel Foucault argues that the middle classes began by imposing these sexual codes on themselves, only later presuming that they might apply to others. He emphasizes in his description the way that sexual techniques and attitudes grew directly out of the inheritance and reproductive strategies that had for centuries assured the health and well-being of bourgeois families (Extract 38). In the following extract Isabel Hull indicates how this process played out within the progressive bourgeoisie in the German lands at the turn of the nineteenth century. She stresses the idealistic aspects of middle-class sexual morality, the openness with which the sexual impulses were discussed by reformers, and the relation of healthy sexuality to modern forms of citizenship (Extract 39).

In shaping their own sexuality, however, middle-class individuals invariably compared themselves to those who lacked their own carefully maintained sense of decency and respectability. It is from such invidious comparisons that we learn that the repugnance the middle class felt for the sexual mores of others was inseparable from their deeply felt anxiety about filth and disorder and the threats these appeared to pose to their own health and well-being. In many parts of Europe, the model of sexual disorder most available to the new middle classes was the one presented by the peasantry. Martine Segalen has looked at the descriptions of nineteenth-century French peasants told from the perspective of middle-class folklorists who had undertaken to chronicle rural life. The 'permanent sexuality' of a rural existence centred on the breeding and birth of animals gave rise to exaggerated concerns on the part of these observers (Extract 40).

The Swedish bourgeoisie also constructed its notions of sexual propriety in contrast to peasant life, treating both sex and dirt as things that must be banished from sight. As Frykman and Löfgren explain, the sexual body became a powerful metaphor that was usually discussed, when it was discussed at all, in the abstract rather than in its particularities (Extract 41).

In the most rapidly industrializing parts of Europe, however, middle-class sexuality was constructed in opposition to the imagined sexual irregularities of factory life and the promiscuity of life in the streets and in overcrowded working-class housing. Jeffrey Weeks considers the British example in the early industrial era (Extract 42).

Bourgeois concern about the moral depravity of working-class urban life focused especially on the sleeping arrangements of the poor, whose families often shared one or two small rooms. In Frank Mort's account of the official investigations of working-class dwellings, he draws attention to the way that middle-class concerns about incest and sexual improprieties were confounded with more general hygienic concerns. He concludes that it was in collisions like this between the social realities of lower-class life and middle-class obsessions about the 'other' that modern 'class' sexualities were born (Extract 43).

Hard evidence for sexual promiscuity within working-class families is in fact rather slender, but as Michael Mason has written about this matter, less evidence for sexual dissoluteness is actually more evidence for the adoption of middle-class standards of respectability by the working poor (Extract 44).

With such negative social and moral associations attached to carnal relations, was it possible for bourgeois married couples to experience sexual pleasure without disabling qualms? Yes and no. Most middle-class couples endeavoured to make their own sexual relations into a more refined and spiritualized, and perhaps less frequently practised, version of the reviled sensuality and lack of restraint of 'others'. One widespread device was the elaboration of a cultural projection of women as household angels or nuns whose task it was to exalt and uplift their weary menfolk through selfless and willing devotion, becoming in the process chaste, distant helpmeets. Another way of accomplishing the same thing was by picturing love as a kind of heartless, sexless fusion of two individual 'souls'. This was a common feature of the narrative cultural rhetoric of the early and mid-Victorian era, a way of displacing the sensuality of individual desire onto a bond of greater purity and strength (Extract 45).

While these powerful cultural inhibitions probably discouraged the timid and the ignorant within the bourgeoisie from exploring the sensual possibilities of connubial relations to the fullest, many Victorians managed to conjoin spirituality with sensuality in ways that fulfilled orthodoxy and pleasure alike. The eminent Anglican clergyman Charles Kingsley, later known for his espousal of a manly 'muscular' Christianity, had been attracted as a youth to the asceticism of high-church factions in the Church of England. However, when he met Fanny Grenfall in 1840 the couple fell immediately in love. During an extended period of engagement, and in the early years of their marriage, they endeavoured to experience their deep sexual desire for intimacy within a restraining social and religious framework (Extract 46).

Other documentary evidence for the physical delights of Victorian-era marriage have survived. Mabel Loomis Todd, an upper-class American woman married to a thoroughly respectable astronomer, David Peck Todd, composed a candid journal of their sex life that leaves little doubt about the ardour, the frequency, or the pleasure of their sexual relations. Extract 47 is a version of Mabel's journal as interpreted by the historian Peter Gay.

As industry and urban life spread throughout North America and Europe, the sexual division of labour that had been established in the bourgeois 'separate spheres' of home and work was replicated in the educational and social arrangements established for the young, spreading eventually throughout the social spectrum (Extract 48).

There was no longer a direct transition from childhood to responsible adulthood as there had been in earlier times; an extended period of adolescence was now acknowledged to exist, during which young people spent most waking hours with members of their own sex. It was perhaps inevitable that same-sex erotic attachments developed that sometimes led to active sexual relationships. Such relations proceeded without the benefit of the knowledge of homosexuality, which did not yet exist as a concept. The subjective meanings and the interpretations of same-sex relationships in the nineteenth century were therefore constructed in context. The nineteenth-century American 'female world of love and ritual' is thus a glimpse of same-sex eroticism before it was medicalized into a symptom of deviance (Extract 49). The same might be said for the cities, barracks, prisons, and schools where men were thrown together. In those places relationships developed that combined both romantic and erotic attachments (Extract 50).

It seems that the deployment of sexuality was not established as a principle of limitation of the pleasures of others by what have traditionally been called the 'ruling classes.' Rather it appears to me that they first tried it on themselves. Was this a new avatar of that bourgeois asceticism described so many times in connection with the Reformation, the new work ethic, and the rise of capitalism? It seems in fact that what was involved was not an asceticism, in any case not a renunciation of pleasure or a disqualification of the flesh, but on the contrary an intensification of the body, a problematization of health and its operational terms: it was a question of techniques for maximizing life. The primary concern was not repression of the sex of the classes to be exploited, but rather the body, vigor, longevity, progeniture, and descent of the classes that 'ruled'. This was the purpose for which the deployment of sexuality was first established, as a new distribution of pleasures, discourses, truths, and powers; it has to be seen as the self-affirmation of one class rather than the enslavement of another: a defense, a protection, a strengthening, and an exaltation that were eventually extended to others—at the cost of different transformations—as a means of social control and political subjugation. With this investment of its own sex by a technology of power and knowledge which it had itself invented, the bourgeoisie underscored the high political price of its body, sensations, and pleasures, its well-being and survival. Let us not isolate the restrictions, reticences, evasions, or silences which all these procedures may have manifested, in order to refer them to some constitutive taboo, psychical repression, or death instinct. What was formed was a political ordering of life, not through an enslavement of others, but through an affirmation of self. And this was far from being a matter of the class which in the eighteenth century became hegemonic believing itself obliged to amputate from its body a sex that was useless, expensive, and dangerous as soon as it was no longer given over exclusively to reproduction; we can assert on the contrary that it provided itself with a body to be cared for, protected, cultivated, and preserved from the many dangers and contacts, to be isolated from others so that it would retain its differential value; and this, by equipping itself with—among other resources—a technology of sex.

Sex is not that part of the body which the bourgeoisie was forced to disqualify or nullify in order to put those whom it dominated to work. It is that aspect of itself which troubled and preoccupied it more than any other, begged and obtained its attention, and which it cultivated with a mixture of fear, curiosity, delight, and excitement. The bourgeoisie made this element identical with its body, or at least subordinated the latter to the former by attributing to it a mysterious and undefined power; it staked its life and its death on sex by making it responsible for its future welfare; it placed its hopes for the future in sex by imagining it to have ineluctable effects on generations to come; it subordinated its soul to sex by conceiving of it as what constituted the soul's most secret and determinant part. Let us not picture the bourgeoisie symbolically castrating itself the better to refuse others the right to have a sex and make use of it as they please. This class must be seen rather as being occupied, from the mid-eighteenth century on with creating its own sexuality and forming a specific body based on it, a 'class' body with its health, hygiene, descent, and race: the auto-sexualization of its body, the incarnation of sex in its body, the endogamy of sex and the body.

There were doubtless many reasons for this. First of all, there was a transposition into different forms of the methods employed by the nobility for marking and maintaining its caste distinction; for the aristocracy had also asserted the special character of its body, but this was in the form of blood, that is, in the form of the antiquity of its ancestry and of the value of its alliances; the bourgeoisie on the contrary looked to its progeny and the health of its organism when it laid claim to a specific body. The bourgeoisie's 'blood' was its sex. And this is more than a play on words; many of the themes characteristic of the caste manners of the nobility reappeared in the nineteenth-century bourgeoisie, but in the guise of biological, medical, or eugenic precepts. The concern with genealogy became a preoccupation with heredity; but included in bourgeois marriages were not only economic imperatives and rules of social homogeneity, not only the promises of inheritance, but the menaces of heredity; families wore and concealed a sort of reversed and somber escutcheon whose defamatory quarters were the diseases or defects of the group of relatives—the grandfather's general paralysis, the mother's neurasthenia, the youngest child's phthisis, the hysterical or erotomanic aunts, the cousins with bad morals. But there was more to this concern with the sexual body than the bourgeois transposition of themes of the nobility for the purpose of self-affirmation. A different project was also involved: that of the indefinite extension of strength, vigor, health, and life. The emphasis on the body should undoubtedly be linked to the process of growth and establishment of bourgeois hegemony: not, however, because of the market value assumed by labor capacity, but because of what the 'cultivation' of its own body could represent politically, economically, and historically for the present and the future of the bourgeoisie. Its dominance was in part dependent on that cultivation; but it was not simply a matter of economy or ideology, it was a 'physical' matter as well. The works, published in great numbers at the end of the eighteenth century, on body hygiene, the art of longevity, ways of having healthy children and of keeping them alive as long as possible, and methods for improving the human lineage, bear witness to the fact: they thus attest to the correlation of this concern with the body and sex to a type of 'racism.' But the latter was very different from that manifested by the nobility and organized for basically conservative ends. It was dynamic racism, a racism of expansion, even if it was still in a budding state, awaiting the second half of the nineteenth century to bear the fruits that we have tasted.

[*The History of Sexuality*, vol. i: *An Introduction*, trans. Robert Hurley (New York: Vintage Books, 1980), 122–5.]

ISABEL V. HULL

39 The Middle Class and the State

It is typical of late Enlightened writings that the very strength of a drive should lead in the same breath to the thought of its modification in an institution, in this case the domestication of the sexual drive into marriage. That same thought was behind the criticism of a reviewer leveled at Thomas Abbt's praise of passion in his 'On the determination of the youth as a future useful member of human society' (1794): 'Abbt should not have said, nor should the editor have agreed with him, that passions [*Leidenschaften*] are our benefactors and protectors. One can say that correctly of drives [*Triebe*], but not of the blind outbreak of drives, which is passion.'[1] In short, it was the guided harnessing of drives that made society possible; it was the very development of the sexual drive from nature to society that made it positive. For once confined in marriage, it turned into love, which preserved and ennobled its useful qualities and protected against its destructive potential. As Villaume explained it, 'Love should provide the preservative (*Präservativ*] against excesses; it should be the spur that drives [*antreibt*] a young person to useful striving and noble deeds. But love has even further uses. Strengthening the soul, lifting the heart, directing the drives, education for society, for philanthropy, for courteousness and flexibility—it can do all these things, if one knows how to use it.'[2]

A man without love was a menace to himself and to society. He 'knew no greatness of spirit or excellence [*Volkommenheiten*], nor had he ever felt either the inner worth of such qualities, nor externally [experienced them] for the good of mankind.'[3] In a world in which 'everyone breathes love and sexual attraction [*Wollust*]' such a person remained 'alone and isolated.'[4] Isolation was not only a personal tragedy, but a social one: 'The single man lives for himself; the married man drags throughout his life the heavy burden of being yoked [*Gespannschaft*]:'[5] This burden was, however, his stake in society and society's very lifeblood. In a comparison with the celibate priesthood, one contemporary wrote that 'the citizen [*Bürger*] is tied by marriage to the state [*Staat*] as the clergyman is by celibacy to the church; for the one supports everything concerning the welfare of the state, in which and through which his children find their own welfare, and the other everything concerning the power and majesty of the church.'[6]

This exploration of the sexual drive passed through marriage, love, and altruism to arrive, finally, at the state / society. This analogic slide was something the practitioners of civil society commonly tried in vain to interrupt by distinguishing the sexual drive from love.[7] They never succeeded. The dual usage of 'love' (*Liebe*) to mean both the tender emotion and physical desire was common throughout the period. Even a writer like Villaume, who was intent on distinguishing physical desire from love, nevertheless found himself using a sexual term, 'preservative' or condom, to describe love's function. The point is not that the practitioners of civil society worshiped at the altar of sex, but that, even if they did not want to, they intuited a deep connection between the sexual drive and the foundation of society through the ties it might form via emotional love, marriage, and children.

More than this, however, the mature sexual drive was seen as crucial to the development of the useful citizen. Sexual maturity not only marked the completion of the individual, it actually caused it. The energy the individual inherited through this process was the very motor of productivity and of public life. This argument appeared again and again in the discussion of celibacy; as a contributor to the *Deutsche Monatsschrift* put it:

The creator of nature has not laid this love [*Liebe*, referring to sexual desire] in our hearts for nothing! It is the sun which ripens the fruits of the man! It helps that deeply buried seed of good develop in us; and the unfortunate one whom the law [of celibacy] orders to flee this all-warming sun as if from the very light of day, must not only renounce the most beautiful pleasure of life, but also the great mainspring [*Triebfeder*] of his social perfection/destiny [*gesellschaftlichen Vervollkommung*].[8]

And this argument was repeated again and again in the antimasturbation tracts, for this was the physiological heart of their message. If one squandered sexual energy prematurely, then 'the sexual drive cannot be to people what it is supposed to be,' namely, the finishing school of body and mind: 'All ideas, emotions and desires [*Neigungen*] of people receive [at puberty], if [the sexual drive] ripens at the right time and in the right way, a higher degree of consistency ... it is a certain feeling of inner power and—I would say masculinity, if the observation did not concern both sexes—that fills him.' Those who have interfered with their sexual development 'can never achieve this feeling of a real superfluity of energies'; in Bauer's terms, 'his character can never receive [*empfangen*] solidity through the sexual drive.'[9] [. . .]

The association of sexual maturity, sexual potency, solidity of character, citizenship, marriage, and social stability formed a tightly wound tautology, in which each term flowed ineluctably into the other. Indeed, the very condition of being human was defined in this constellation in which the sexual component was absolutely necessary. Hence, the common descriptions of nuns and monks as 'these unfortunate middle things [*unseeligen Mitteldinger*],' 'these hermaphroditic creatures [*Zwittergeschöpfe*], or of bachelors as 'sick souls.'[10] The free-thinking mayor of Königsberg, Theodor von Hippel, champion of early liberalism and female civil emancipation, made a characteristically pithy summary of this linked chain: 'The word "father" is a great word, the greatest that exists in a state [*Staat*]. Whoever is not [a father] does not deserve the name citizen! and, even being generous, only half deserves the name human!'[11] [. . .]

It has been necessary to describe in some detail the positive views the practitioners of civil society held about the sexual drive in order to counter the widespread belief that the advent of civil society, or bourgeois morality, which is often presented as the shorthand formula for it, inaugurated a regime of sexual repression. After reading umpteen antimasturbation tracts it is in fact easy to forget that it was precisely their almost worshipful attitude toward sexual energy and heterosexual maturity that moved the pamphleteers to such paroxysms of repressive-seeming concern.[12] In fact, the late-eighteenth-century pamphleteers aimed not at repression, but at an ideal of moderate, sensible sexual pleasure. Here the doctors, moralists, pedagogues, state theorists, and philosophers were all of one mind. Furthermore, they applied no different standard to sexual enjoyment than they did to other sorts of consumption (such as food and drink, reading, or emotional indulgence). The moralist Carl Friedrich Bahrdt received a good review in the *Allgemeine Deutsche Bibliothek* for his rules of sexual moderation:

The sexual drive should be satisfied (1) never to the point of destruction, but instead to aid bodily health, and only under conditions of a completely mature body, by means of natural coitus [i.e. man with woman, procreatively], with a naturally aroused drive [i.e., not 'artificially' stimulated], a healthy body and not during digestion or other activities, without vehement passions, but calmly; (2) in marriage . . .,[13] that is, no promiscuous sexual contacts; (3) moderately. Energy determines the amount, of which the sign is that no exhaustion should follow; (4) modestly and cleanly; (5) quietly with the spouse.[14]

[*Sexuality, State, and Civil Society in Germany, 1700–1815* (Ithaca, NY: Cornell University Press, 1996), 239–41, 242, 243–3.]

MARTINE SEGALEN
....

40 Peasant Sexuality

Peasant life is impregnated with sexuality, and there is no problem about education in this area. When they are very young, the children learn about reproduction by observing the farmyard life around them, the cow being taken to the bull, calves and lambs being born. In small houses where old and young all cohabited together, it is likely that sexual relations were more easily known than behind the closed doors of separate rooms. This was certainly something which worried the folklorists. Some of them saw in it a sign of the inferiority and bestiality of the peasant: 'Family life lived entirely in common, with parents and children crammed together in a single room, is, from a moral point of view, a bad thing; the children are made to witness disturbing sights, and it could lead them to a bestial promiscuity.'[1]

The observers feared, as much as an initiation into adult sexuality, the presence of infant sexuality, of incest or homosexuality between brothers and sisters: 'The small number of rooms and the confined space within them, making it necessary to put several beds in a room, and to put them close together, presents serious moral dangers. The parents, as a rule, sleep in the kitchen, while the children and servants of both sexes sleep in other rooms, often in just one room.'[2] On the other hand, peasants are elsewhere presented as being invested with all the sound 'natural' virtues, capable of protecting 'morality': 'Despite the members of the family being crammed together in a small space, there was no falling off in morality. I have lived among them and I never heard even the breath of scandal. An active life, pious habits, a god-fearing father and mother, none of this lent itself to any relaxation in morals.'[3] If peasant sexuality was not seen as bestial, this was because the observer was comparing it with an even more bestial sexuality, that of the 'low', working classes. The remarks made by an observer in the Tarn-et-Garonne show this attitude well:

We do not claim to be sure that our peasants still remain in the innocence of that golden age; but their morality is infinitely greater than that of the workers in the towns. Religious belief and the traditional authority of the father of the family may be held to account for this to a great extent, but equally, it is incontestable that the fact of living in a large room where the whole family sleeps together under the eye of the head of the household, in large beds provided with canopies and generously curtained, does not present the same difficulties as for those crammed together in a narrow garret who have been depraved by immoral example and the lax language of the street, and who are deprived of paternal care.[4]

We do not know whether parents saw their sexuality as something to be hidden from the children; anyway, the bedroom was not the only place in which one could make love. There was the barn, where the men often went in summer while the women invested the house: it was the place for the afternoon rest, and for meetings; and there were the fields. In the Hautes-Alpes, at Saint-Véran, there was an area called the *bois d'Amour*.[5]

Peasant society was imbued with a permanent sexuality, which was related to that of the animals. It is difficult to go beyond that as a statement; to know whether the experience of feminine sexuality was one of frustration or of pleasure; to know whether the husband was concerned for his partner's enjoyment, or whether coitus interruptus had any effect on these relations. Might one suggest that traditional peasant sexuality was less influenced by ecclesiastical repression than earlier writings have implied, that it was a constant theme in peasant life—the pregnant cow, the growing corn, the laying hen—but that it was less fundamental than it is today? The relationship of the nineteenth-century peasant couple was quite different from that of the modern urban couple. Some socio-sexologists claim that, today, a sexual relationship which does not satisfy both partners is an indication of the failure of the marriage and a reason for divorce. That is perhaps an oversimplified view of the modern couple, but it is definitely true that the success of sexual relations is not emphasized to anything like the same extent in the rural couple. Today, and even more so in earlier times, the peasant couple are committed to the same end: the success of the farm. A good harvest, the purchase of land are causes for a deep satisfaction shared by man and wife together. Is it not a proof of ethnocentrism to emphasize sexual relations? Let us leave the *Simple* with the last word on this difficult subject, in which, more than elsewhere, the ethnological approach is insufficient. In *La vie d'un Simple*, bourgeois and peasant behaviour are contrasted. The way in which the bourgeois man and wife exchange tender words is judged by the peasant to be 'a bit stupid. If a married couple talked to each other like that in the country, everyone would be amused by it. Perhaps we love each other as much as they do, but we are not so generous with soft words.'[6]

[*Love and Power in the Peasant Family: Rural France in the Nineteenth Century*, trans. Sarah Matthews (Chicago: University of Chicago Press, 1983), 130–2.]

JONAS FRYKMAN AND ORVAR LÖFGREN

41 From Peasant to Bourgeois

Words that were permitted in the peasant's house were considered embarrassing and unbecoming in the drawing rooms of their betters. Habits of personal hygiene that caused no comment in one environment did not fail to provoke reactions of distaste and repugnance in another.

In the discussion in the preceding chapter on the conditions in which people lived on the quarry island of Tjurkö, an everyday life was portrayed that was permeated with dirt, vermin, odors, and poor bodily hygiene. The carelessness the quarrymen's families showed about this purely physical order also made itself felt in their speech and thoughts. Like the peasants, they called things by their proper names, with no euphemisms or circumlocutions.

A description from a bourgeois home of the same period will show us how practically everything that was permitted and physically present in the working-class home was tabooed and absent here:

We, Father, Mother, and all those we knew, were prudish in a sense that has now become rare. Prudery meant first and foremost the complete prohibition of all talk of physical and sexual matters. We must have learned this taboo so early that I have no recollection of it. I suppose I must at some time have asked my mother why there was a difference between boys and girls, and she must have answered somewhat evasively, and then such questions were forgotten or concealed. But prudery was not just sexual. It affected many things that were considered disquieting or sensitive: people's characters, actions, and feelings: God, love, and death, the meaning of life, or whether there was no meaning. What surprises me about this is that the upbringing, with all its mildness, could be so effective that I failed to question or doubt openly so many things, out of a shyness that felt natural and instinctive. The fear or consideration or shame that more-or-less consciously forced the adults into silence was quickly adopted and practiced by the children, who refrained from embarrassing their parents out of anxiety and concern over their reactions—just as they felt anxiety and concern for the children—and who spared them surprises, pain, and offense. . . .

To take a ridiculous little example: Mother considered the tail end of the pike to be the best part, so she liked to divide it between Father and myself. Occasionally during this operation she would say, proud of her outspokenness, 'Yes, I call it the tail end. Can you imagine, I once had an aunt who always called it the stem, to be really proper.' The story worried me for two reasons. On the one hand I thought that Mother's speech seemed somewhat too free, while on the other I wondered what was so secret and dangerous about the tail end. But I never asked about this; that would have been beyond the bounds of what was permitted. What applied to the tail of the pike also applied to Aunt Lalla's 'accident,' Uncle Salle's suicide, why Uncle Carell's divorce was so terrible, where children came from, why we must die, and the remarkable relationship between God and Jesus.[1]

The prudery described here by Herbert Tingsten took in much more than the human body and its physical processes. For Tingsten the euphemism for the tail end of the pike was condensed information on where to draw the boundaries between what could acceptably be discussed and what could not, between the decent and the indecent. These reflections of his are typical of the children of the Oscarian era. The human body was frequently used as a metaphor for society, the family, the home, and the way people related to one another and to life's great questions. The body has probably never had such a central role as a metaphor and a reference as it had in bourgeois society. The danger that charged the naming of the pike's tail made a whole series of connections clear to the young Tingsten. [. . .]

It could be said as a broad generalization that bourgeois culture was like an organism with a hidden body. The body was there, to be sure but its existence was persistently denied by the head. Bourgeois culture was spiritual, not physical. Even the embarrassing fact that men and women, children and adults possess bodies like other animals—or like people from the lower classes—was concealed as much as language allowed. These remarkable circumstances provide both a challenge and an obstacle for the student of this epoch and its people. When the physical is made private and withdrawn from the public light, the amount of information about it is naturally reduced. The words, or rather circumlocution, that one meets are therefore particularly interesting, valuable, and sometimes also entertaining.

[*Culture Builders: A Historical Anthropology of Middle-Class Life*, trans. Alan Crozier (New Brunswick, NJ: Rutgers University Press, 1987), 221–3.]

42 Middle-Class Views of Working-Class Sexuality

If middle-class moralities invoked peculiar anxieties, the development of a huge working class throughout the nineteenth century posed immense moral problems of its own. The fundamental problem as conceived by the middle-class moralists was the effect of industrialisation and urbanisation, and in particular factory work, on the working-class family and the role of the woman within it. The issue had long exercised the evangelicals but became central in the 1830s and 1840s, coinciding in fact with the crisis of the domestic system in textile areas. Most of the evidence used in the debates of that period relate to this area. The alleged lack of virtues and sense of shame of women cotton operatives was deplored alike in parliamentary debate and government blue books, in contemporary novels and in newspapers. Ashley (later Lord Shaftesbury) wrote with regard to women's labour in the cotton mills:

You are poisoning the very sources of order and happiness and virtue; you are tearing up root and branch all relations of families to each other; you are annulling, as it were, the institution of domestic life decreed by Providence Himself, the wisest and kindest of earthly ordinances, the mainstay of social peace and virtue and therein of national security.[1]

Contemporary observers, including radicals like Friedrich Engels, painted a picture of destruction of working-class family life. Peter Gaskell, in his *Artisans and Machinery: The Moral and Physical Conditions of the Manufacturing Population*, wrote of the family disrupted by machinery and factory working where 'recklessness, improvidence, and unnecessary poverty, starvation, drunkenness, parental cruelty and carelessness, filial disobedience, neglect of conjugal rights, absence of maternal love, destruction of brotherly and sisterly affection, are too often its constituents.'[2] Half a century later Dr Barnardo could write in similar tones: 'The East End of London is a hive of factory life and *factory* means that which is inimical to *home*. . . . There is bred in them (factory women) a spirit of precocious independence which weakens family ties and is highly unfavourable to the growth of domestic virtues.'[3] Many complained of a promiscuous mingling of sexes, and a witness before the Factory Commission in 1833 declared: 'It would be no strain on his conscience to say that three quarters of the girls between fourteen and twenty years of age were unchaste.'[4]

Novels such as Mrs Gaskell's represent the factory girls as too low to be taken into a lady's house as servants and claimed that immoralities were rooted in the conditions of the mills. The lack of sex segregation and the late hours moreover, had bad effect not only on unmarried but also on married women. Peter Gaskell wrote: 'The chastity of marriage is but little known or exercised amongst them: husband and wife sin equally, and an habitual indifference to sexual vice is generated which adds one other item to the destruction of domestic habits.'[5]

It is clear that two factors were of particular symbolic importance and concern to these bourgeois intellectuals, both relating to women: their sexuality and their economic autonomy. Because of the developing ideology of woman's role in the family and her very special responsibility for society's well being, it was women working outside the home who received the most attention from the parliamentary commissioners in the 1830s and 1840s. Moreover, most attention was paid not to the conditions of work as such but to the moral and spiritual degradation said to accompany female employment. Ashley wrote, 'In the male the moral effects of the system are very sad, but in the female they are infinitely worse. . . . It is bad enough if you corrupt the man, but if you corrupt the woman, you poison the waters of life at the very fountain.'[6]

[*Sex, Politics and Society: The Regulation of Sexuality since 1800* (London: Longman, 1989), 57–8.]

FRANK MORT

43 Hygiene, Morality, and Class

These themes were to the fore in all the official inquiries, but they were particularly dominant in the blue books on sanitary reform. The wretchedness of the working-class environment, the state of the dwelling, non-existent sanitation, lack of concern over personal decency and hygiene were seen to encourage irregular sexual conduct. There were constant references to the effects of overcrowding and bad housing on sexual behaviour throughout the official investigations. In the sanitary report it was a sense of horror and ritual denunciation which predominated:

How they lay down to rest, how they sleep, how they can preserve common decency, how unutterable horrors are avoided, is beyond all conception. ... It shocks every feeling of propriety to think that . . . civilized beings should be herding together without a decent separation of age or sex.[1]

Then the narrative moved to a more precise classification of specific immoral acts:

In a cellar in Pendleton I recollect there were three beds in the two apartments . . . in one of which a man and his wife slept; in another, a man, his wife and child; and in the third two unmarried females. . . . I have met with upwards of forty persons sleeping in the same room, married and single, including, of course, children and several young adult persons of either sex. In Manchester . . . I found such promiscuous mixture of the sexes in sleeping-rooms . . . I have met with instances of a man, his wife, and his wife's

sister, sleeping in the same bed together. . . . In Hull . . . I found in one room a prostitute, with whom I remonstrated on the course of her life . . . she stated that she had
lodged with a married sister, and slept in the same bed with her and her husband; that
hence improper intercourse took place, and from that she became more and more
depraved.[2]

Incest was the most common source of moral anxiety, precisely because it
dramatically disrupted middle-class norms of family propriety.[3] But these representations contained rather more than the perception that sexual immorality
resulted from an impoverished and over-crowded environment. Sexual
immorality was defined through the significations of dirt, disease, squalor,
corruption and the political and cultural threat of an urban working class populace. When Chadwick pointed out that the habits of labouring families soon
became 'of a piece' with the dwellings, he evoked precisely that type of conden-
sation.[4] Filthy habits of life were never separated from the moral filthiness for
which they were the type and the representative. [. . .]

In the discourse on the urban poor, reformers constructed the sexual through
the class-related polarities which were central to their programme: physical
health/non-health, virtue/service, cleanliness/filth, morality/depravity, civil-
ization/animality. The binary oppositions were organized in such a way that
each polarity functioned to reinforce the other. Bourgeois cleanliness was
impossible without the image of proletarian filth, middle-class propriety could
not be defined without the corresponding representations of working-class
animality, and so on. All this was not wholly new; as we know it had continuities
with eighteenth-century social medicine and with earlier religious constructions
of sexuality across the spirit/flesh divide. What was new was that these definitions were now incorporated into a variety of official knowledge as part of a
broad programme of state intervention into the culture of the industrial
labouring classes. This discourse on sexuality now had distinctive *class articula-
tions*. Hence, though these representations did not originate in the economic,
political and cultural transformations of early industrial capitalism, in this
period they increasingly became annexed to class-cultural relations.

It is also important to be clear in what sense this configuration around sexuality was a *discursive construction*, a construction within and by very specific sets
of power-knowledge relations, and in what sense it was a product of concrete
environmental conditions. To speak of its discursive formation is not to deny
that this construction of the sexual was grounded in particular historical
conditions and social relations. But discourses did not simply reflect these. We
are not dealing with practices either rendering a 'true picture of reality' (i.e.
sexuality constructed as filthy and diseased because filth and disease were the
realities of the working-class environment) or as neatly representing pre-given
forms of class power and knowledge whose origins lie elsewhere. We are
dealing with specific social practices—religion, medicine and sanitary
science—whose organization was an active force in the production of the

sexual meanings in play. They neither transparently reflected reality nor did they passively represent class relations. They were active in the construction of both.

[*Dangerous Sexualities: Medico-moral Politics in England since 1830* (London: Routledge & Kegan Paul, 1987), 38–9, 41–2.]

MICHAEL MASON

44   Sexual Respectability in the Working Class

The drive to working-class sexual respectability, where it arose, showed a remarkable power to overcome the most important physical constraint in working-class life, namely, domestic crowding. Nineteenth-century middle-class opinion had a strongly environmentalist bias [. . .] and was on the whole incredulous that physical proximity could be other than morally depraving. The belief that individuals who dressed, slept, washed, and excreted very near each other were much more likely to have sexual intercourse seems to have been practically universal. Some otherwise sensible commentators, such as Joseph Kay, dwelt obsessively on the idea of incestuous and freely copulating working-class people in very crowded environments. The proof usually offered of the connection between crowding and sexual licence was simply a kind of thought experiment: high densities of unmarried individuals in beds or bedrooms were alleged, and the reader then invited to draw the supposedly inevitable conclusion about sexual outcomes.

Only occasionally was evidence produced that the worst had happened. Apart from the broad truth of multi-occupied beds and bedrooms the facts mustered by investigators keen to prove the crowding-sexual licence hypothesis now tend to seem strangely feeble. One much cited testimony was that of Riddall Wood, giving evidence in Chadwick's sanitary report. He had visited slum housing in a variety of centres—Manchester, Liverpool, Ashton-under-Lyne, Hull, and Pendelton—and gives several anecdotes of crowding of the sexes, but this was the mouse that emerged when he was asked to summarize his findings on 'persons of different sexes sleeping promiscuously': 'I think I am speaking without bounds when I say I have amongst my memoranda above 100 cases, including, of course, cases of persons of different sexes sleeping in the same room.' Yet these 'memoranda', amounting to very little more than a reiteration of the familiar truth of overcrowding, are endlessly quoted by subsequent commentators as a proof of the fact of general working-class sexual depravity under these conditions.[1]

A modern historian has concluded from a survey of statements made by unmarried mothers applying to London's Foundling Hospital that 'they throw serious doubt on the idea that housing and working conditions at that time gave the popular classes a broad familiarity with sexual matters'. In the last decades of the century parental reticence on sex in front of children was so great that some working-class sons and daughters in London remained ignorant about basic information into adult life.[2] Examples were reported in the literature of illegitimate births to women who had been made pregnant by men in crowded accommodation, but the general statistics of illegitimacy showed no correlation with density in housing; this was carefully demonstrated in 1862. Marriage rates tended to peak in the autumn and early winter, and, for country districts at least, this may be linked to the high known rates of pre-nuptial pregnancy; in other words, according to a modern study, 'in the crowded housing conditions of the period, courtships involving intimacy would be more likely to occur in the summer than in the winter months'. Mothers' depositions concerning illegitimate births in rural Kent often cite sexual encounters at summer festivities.[3]

This puts the relation between crowding and sexual licence in a startling new light—indeed it completely reverses the nineteenth-century wisdom on the question. While it may not have been universally true that courtships were conducted more intensely outdoors [. . .], and while acceptable thresholds of exposure of bodies and bodily functions may have been lower in working-class than in middle-class homes, there is much anecdotal evidence of working-class households trying to mitigate the effects of proximity—so much so that one historian of slum housing has written of her continual surprise at 'the extent to which the poor strove . . . to conform to middle-class standards of morality'.[4]

[*The Making of Victorian Sexuality* (New York: Oxford University Press, 1994), 139–41.]

STEPHEN KERN

45 The Ideal of Transcendent Love

By the mid-nineteenth century the Romantic ideal of a love that unified everything—mind and body, man and woman, rich and poor, sexual desire and love of God—could make lovers hyperventilate. In *Wuthering Heights* Cathy exclaims, 'I *am* Heathcliff—he's always, always in my mind—not as a pleasure, any more than I am always a pleasure to myself—but as my own being'. After her death Heathcliff's own existence, so fused with hers, loses all purpose. He explains how, without her, 'I have to remind myself to breathe—almost to remind my heart to beat!'[1]

In *Jane Eyre* the fusion of Jane's and Rochester's souls in love is symbolized by the chestnut tree, which is split by lightning moments after Rochester first proposes marriage and appeals for divine sanction even though, unknown to Jane, he is already married. Brontë would have us believe that God split only the trunk, for later Jane interprets the tree as a symbol of their underlying union.

Although the tree was split and the branches would soon die, 'the cloven halves were not broken from each other, for the firm base and strong roots kept them unsundered below . . . [and] they might be said to form one tree—a ruin, but an entire ruin'.[2] That invisible root is a symbol of the Victorian ideal of fusion in love. Although the surface structure (and reality) appears sundered, the lovers are organically unified. In fact she and Rochester had very different roots, and love only became possible in the end after those deeply rooted differences were removed *un*organically by her inheritance and by his financial ruin and physical injuries. In the end the lovers do fuse, or so Jane tells her reader in Biblical language: 'I am my husband's life as fully as he is mine. No woman was ever nearer to her mate than I am: ever more absolutely bone of his bone, flesh of his flesh.'[3] This fusion raises questions about the authenticity of their freedom, solitude, and communication. 'To be together,' she proudly proclaims, 'is for us to be at once as free as in solitude.' Their talking is not a struggle between independent selves to communicate but more like a single 'audible thinking'.[4]

The cultural high point of Romantic fusion is the love duet from Wagner's *Tristan and Isolde* (1859).[5] Tristan and Isolde are divided by their different nationalities and, most important, by their different loyalties to King Mark: she is supposed to marry him, while Tristan has sworn to serve him. The real world, symbolized by the light of day, thus forbids their love, which can only come forth in darkness and secrecy, as the couple sings together: 'O sink down upon us, night of love | make me forget I live: | take me into your bosom, | free me from the world!' Their wish for annihilation builds as they yearn to flee the real world and forget their past. They hope to become 'one breath' and to 'die, undivided . . . ever at one in unbounded space.' At the climax they long to fuse, not even separated by names (*ohne Nahmen*), and become 'infinitely, eternally, one consciousness'.[6]

Their words alone do not convey the power of Wagner's music, which evokes a sense of harmonious unity with the magnificently contrasting male and female voices that together span the emotions of lovers attempting to transcend the differences and imperfections of their worldly existence by aspiring to become one if only in death. But their hope to die together, however exquisitely scored, is inauthentic because it seeks to avoid responsibility for their own necessarily separate deaths and spare them from facing up to the everyday problems of living that in fact make fusion impossible. I am not arguing that the opera is inauthentic, only the love it celebrates. Victorian artists, writers, and composers produced numerous masterpieces about inauthentic modes of loving, I would speculate, precisely because the reality of love from which they drew was so constricted by conventions that they were driven to envision the most heroic efforts and sacrifices in order to achieve love. Like Tristan and Isolde, Victorian lovers were forced to flee from seeing one another clearly in the light of day, and in seeking to fuse in secret places of darkness, sometimes even in death, they were seeking ways to escape from themselves as selves.[7]

Victorian novels are full of lovers aspiring or expiring to fuse. Writing to Cosette, Marius praises a love that has 'melted and merged two persons in a sublime and sacred unity'. Hugo adds approvingly, 'love is the melting-pot in which man and woman are fused together'.[8] Flaubert is more cynical about the genuineness of such yearning but includes it in *Sentimental Education*, as Frédéric exclaims to Mme Arnoux, 'I can no more live without you than without the air of heaven. Can't you feel my soul yearning for yours? Don't you feel that they are destined to mingle?'[9] His rhetoric is as excessive as his love is impatient, but both lovers take the rhetoric seriously.

[*The Culture of Love: Victorians to Moderns* (Cambridge, Mass.: Harvard University Press, 1992), 281–3.]

JOHN MAYNARD

46 Spirituality and Sexual Pleasure

As already noted [. . .], sexual paradise of a very brief and post-lapsarian sort was available to university students, despite elaborate regulation by the university, from street-walkers in town and at regular brothels in nearby villages beyond the university's control.[1] Kingsley apparently tried it once, as he later confessed to his bride, and decidedly didn't like it. Or, if he did like it, his intensely guilty reaction didn't allow him to acknowledge it nor, presumably, repeat it. As he spoke of it to her, it was a matter of being spotted, of having sinned and fallen.[2]

It is possible that it was the guilty reaction from first sex that led Kingsley's thinking a distance down the cloister path of celibate Tractarianism. Meeting during a summer vacation with a Fanny Grenfell quickly put him on the more ordinary track of love and sexual interest that would emphatically bring hetero-sexual sexuality back into his religious thinking. Perhaps it was about this time that he drafted a detailed account, now lost or destroyed, of why celibacy was impossible for him.[3] They fell immediately and passionately in love. Even with the rigorous limits on intimacy of his day, he found it practically impossible not to seek a physical side to his relation with Fanny. They found some way at least to kiss passionately. Fanny wrote enthusiastically of 'strong arms' that 'bound me, while my willing limbs were entangled with yours, + my lips clinging to yours, + the warm life flowing into my very soul.' During the four years before they married they devised complicated rituals of sleeping together by imagina-tion as they lay in their distant beds—'feast' or 'festival' times with what Fanny called 'delicious nightery' of 'strange feelings.' 'Never control any desire of pleasure because I am not there to share it with you!' Charles instructed, 'I am there, if *you* are there!'[4] When, after much painful forced separation, they were finally permitted by her family to plan the wedding, they spent a day in the country in which the Victorian equivalent of what in the United States used to be called heavy petting took place rather spontaneously: he writes to celebrate one occasion: 'my hands are all perfumed with her delicious limbs, + I cannot wash off the scent—It has made itself what it should be, a part of myself! And every moment the thought comes across me, of those mysterious recesses of beauty, where my hands have been wandering.'⁵ Their imagination was filled with plans for their first meeting in bed after marriage; Charles imagined that he would 'undress you with my own hands, from head to foot, + cover you all over with burning kisses til you were tired of blushing + struggling, if you *did* struggle, wh I pray you would not.'⁶ Fanny was troubled by 'spasms' for which the pre-Freudian doctor wisely recommended speedy marriage, strongly seconded by her future husband.

A less modern quirk appears as Charles decided to put off full consummation until a month after the wedding—to prove he is capable of 'self-denial,' but perhaps also out of anxiety.⁷ But this was to be no Ruskinian marriage—indeed Kingsley professed contempt for Ruskin on just this point: contempt perhaps especially because he had overcome a similar temptation to evasion.⁸ The delay was in any case even what the sex therapist might have ordered for such an inexperienced couple: a month in bed naked warming to each other before full intercourse. We also may wonder if this planned delay actually took place; Fanny's own letter anticipating marriage shows little bridal hesitation: 'we will kiss + love very much . . . you will take me in your arms, will you not? And lay me down in bed + then you will extinguish our light + *come to me*! How I will open my arms to you, + then sink into yours! + you will kiss me + clasp me + lay blessed [*sic*] body to me.' Man proposes; woman disposes. Later Charles would dream of reenacting 'our marriage night.'⁹ In any event, sooner or later, the result seems to have been a decided success. A child was conceived; as for Kingsley, he found the begetting 'the most delicious moment of my life—*up to that time*—Since then what greater bliss.'¹⁰ It is a pleasure, as it is in reading the Mosher report, to hear such an authentic voice of Victorian sexual gratification to set against the modernist stereotypes of universal sexual blocking and repression in the period—even when we hear it in Kingsley's rather treacly language.¹¹ Here, certainly, is a Victorian who enjoyed sexual intimacy—and did so with enthusiasm. At moments in their letters he even attains an eloquence that we can hear and admire over the passage of time, as in this profession written even after many years of marriage:

I do love you utterly—your image haunts me day + night, just as it used before we married + the thought of that delicious hidden sanctuary of marriage, when we shall clasp + be clasped in blessedness, please God, on Monday night, gives me a proud + yet humbling thrill every time it flashes across me. I cannot believe my own happiness + honour . . . that *you* you, pure + passionate at once, beautiful + wise in my eyes + in the eyes of all who see you, should love *me*! give yourself up to *me*, body + soul! have given me two such children of your own beloved delicious body!—I feel that one gift so great a debt to God.¹²

What is even more interesting is the complicated ways that Kingsley found to justify and rationalize this joyful sex experience against the restraints and conservative ideology—especially religious ideology—that were as much a part of his milieu as they were of Clough's. [. . .]

Against this idea of celibate Christianity he forges not an anti-Christian natur-alism but a pro-sexual Christianity. The enemy is now placed historically and as an ideology: 'the old ascetic,' 'Manichean Popish fancies,' as well as the more recent versions in 'Popery and Puseyism'; Fanny is warned to avoid the later tradition of Church Fathers where Catholic attitudes to sex had taken firm form in favor of celibacy, with marriage seen mainly as a cure for fornication: 'a few self-conceited fools shut themselves up in a state of unnatural celibacy + morbid excitement, in order to *avoid* their duty, instead of *doing* it . . . Avoid the *fathers after Origen*, (including Him).'[13] Against the tendency of ascetic religion to separate body from soul, he boldly asserts to Fanny the holiness of matter, 'God's holy matter awful glorious matter.' 'Let us never,' he proclaims with a boldness equal to a twentieth-century celebrator of the animal in human nature, such as D. H. Lawrence, 'use . . . those words animal, and brutal in a degrading sense.' Unlike Lawrence, Kingsley does not merely transfer religious values to an animal realm, in effect moving away from Western dualism and toward religions that celebrate sex in this world. He attempts to construct a sexual continuum in which there is no essential difference between physical sexuality in this world and spiritual communion in the next. Heaven will be a place of 'resurrection of the flesh, wh is the great promise of Eternity—no miserable fancies about . . . souls escaped from matter, like poor Henry More—but bodies! *our* bodies, beloved, beautiful bodies, ministers to us in all our joys.'[14] Sex becomes a spiritual rite now and gives us a foretaste of the pleasures of interpersonal communication in the hereafter. 'Our toying becomes holy, our "animal" enjoyments religious ceremonies.'[15] Guilt is staved off; sexual needs are rationalized as religious acts; and, because sex is authorized by the highest religious and ethical values, there is no question, as there was in conservative Victorian thinking on sex, that it is a joy in which women indulge as fully and happily as men. Fanny should go to bed, pretend to be naked, open her lips to imagine his kisses, and 'spread out every limb, that I may lie between your breasts all night!' Such a fulfilment, one that few in the twentieth century would say is not devoutly to be desired, is here actually justified devoutly by a parson-ical reference: '(Canticles 1, 13).'[16] In addition he recommends that she say the Te Deum aloud.

[*Victorian Discourses on Sexuality and Religion* (Cambridge: Cambridge University Press, 1993), 90–2, 94–5.]

'David is more passionately my lover than he ever was before our marriage,' Mabel Loomis Todd glowingly recorded in her journal after the first five months, 'and I feel most deeply grateful to God for giving me in my husband a man whose fresh springs of deepest tenderness and love grow fuller & fuller every day, encompassing me with the sweetest life-fountains that a woman's life can ever know.' As so often, so here, Mabel Todd's metaphors were more instructive than she could have guessed. It was not simple brutish sexuality, of course, that swept her away, but the happy combination of sensuality with affection: 'His love for me is so passionate, & yet so pure.'[1] Yet the sensuality was indispensable to her, as it was to her husband.

David Todd, adoring and avid at the same time, doubtless stimulated by his wife's delighted discoveries, generated a steamy domestic atmosphere that Mabel Todd enjoyed and fostered. From the outset of their married life, it seems, the Todds ended their evenings and began their mornings with a sensual routine, preface and postscript to a night spent with their arms around each other. 'Every night,' as Mabel Todd recalled it, 'he undressed me on the bright Turkey rug before the fire, & then wrapped me up to keep warm while he put hot bricks in the bed. Then he took me in his arms and tucked me safely in bed, & kissed me over & over, while he went to his desk & studied an hour, or two longer. And after parties, when I came in cold, he did first the same for me—& loved me so!' Then, in the morning, 'he would get up and brighten the fire, & spread all my clothes around it until they were warm, when he would come for me, & taking me in his arms, set me down on the rug close to the fire, where all my "toasting hot" garments were awaiting me. Then would come the grapes or figs or apples on which he always regaled me before breakfast.'[2] The Todds reveled in the whole menu of married pleasures: working, reading, making music, and taking walks; but their pleasure in marital sexuality transcended and infused all the others.

When they were together, they made love, it would seem, without troubling inhibitions and liked to link their intercourse to other gratifications. There were those figs and grapes in the morning, and, at times, even more suggestive foods. 'Ice cream on the way home—,' Mabel Todd noted in her diary after two months of marriage, 'and the most rapturous & sacred night of all our love.' When they were apart—she visiting her parents, he observing the stars—they could barely contain their hunger for one another's bodies: 'David,' Mabel Todd wrote to her husband, 'it is just dreadful to sleep alone.' And again, three years later, 'I want you very much, dear, very much.' She could almost taste his return: 'The night of the fourth is our time, darling, and

I am anticipating it with joy.' For his part, David Todd would worry just how to contain his appetites alone: 'Can I—Oh! can I, wait so long?' He would scheme to meet her so that they could make love without delay, and manfully tried to control his thoughts and his pen lest, by writing too ardently about love, he inflame himself and his wife too much: 'I have tried to promise myself to write you a dispassionate letter this time, sweet love—' he wrote her after they had been married for almost three years, 'but I've no idea of anything else that I may write, and I love you so that it is hard not to be writing to you all the time about it—but you know I oughtn't to be doing that. If I tell you how intolerably worthless and stupid life seems to me without you here to love me and to be loved, and that two days ago I had fully resolved to be this moment far on my way to Washington, to rest in your arms to-morrow night—notwithstanding that I should have to leave you before twentyfour hours had passed—I shall have said all that you need know, and all that it will be good for me to write.'[3]

Then, when they met again, they made up for wasted time, night after night. 'Tenderest thoughts of my lover-husband.' This is Mabel Todd in her diary late in 1879. '*My own precious David* met me at the Grand Central, having come on by the limited express from Washington for that purpose. Oh joy! Oh! Bliss unutterable—my pure, own husband.' For full measure, she noted the following day: 'Last night was almost too happy for this world.' The years after, her diary shows no slackening in her excitement: 'This night, from 9 p.m. until about 12, was the happiest of my whole happy life, so far.' And again, 'The last was such a happy night! Oh! Oh!' Some of the entries are tantalizingly obscure: 'Oh! my oriental morning,' she writes in 1881, and, the next year, leaving rather less to the imagination, 'We retired at seven & had a magnificent evening, David and I. I shall never forget it, so I'll not write about it.' The entry is followed by two symbols signifying that the couple had intercourse twice that unforgettable night of February 28, 1882. These episodes of what Mabel Todd once called 'a little Heaven just after dinner' are by no means tokens of sexual athleticism: they occur on the average somewhat less than once a week. And there were some disagreeable moments: 'So, dearest,' David Todd wrote to his wife from one of his astronomical expeditions late in 1882, 'I can remain out here quietly away from you until the auspicious occasion arrives when I can come to you as we both desire after such a separation.' He was, he added, inclined to 'save myself and mine own the experiences we have not infrequently had in past time and which are always disastrous & little short of torture'—presumably a reunion while Mabel Todd was menstruating.[4]

But the couple made up in orgasmic intensity what they missed in frequency or spoiled with bad timing. Sightseeing in Europe in the summer of 1885, with some friends but without her husband, Mabel Todd confided the pressures of her sensuality to her travel journal: 'I am longing most uncomfortably for my husband,' she wrote; 'I am counting the days until I get to him for my own satis-faction. I was not made to live alone.'[5] It is true, she was not made to live alone; if she wanted her own satisfaction, she had to get to a man.

[The Bourgeois Experience: Victoria to Freud, vol. 1: Education of the Senses (New York: Oxford University Press, 1984), 81–4.]

JOHN R. GILLIS

48 Sexual Segregation

The expulsion of adolescents from the world of adults had been accompanied and reinforced by the simultaneous segregation of the sexes. Physically separ-ated at school and work, boys and girls had fewer opportunities for the kind of everyday, casual mixing so characteristic of the early industrial period, which had diminished abruptly at the end of the nineteenth century. Not only were male and female roles more strictly defined by 1900, but the world of youth had once again become predominantly homosocial.

The sex and age segregation of the modern adolescent was the invention of the late Victorian era. The middle classes were the first to insist on excluding the teenagers from the adult world of work and leisure, segregating them in same-sex schools and erecting elaborate social barriers reinforced by rigid rules of etiquette. The working classes were slower to adopt the new norms of sexual segregation, in part because crowded housing conditions and overlapping spheres of boy and girl labor made this impracticable. However, as the century progressed, they too began to adopt views on gender similar, if not identical, to those current among the upper classes. A certain amount of heterosociability was acceptable among children, but adolescence now became a phase of compulsory feminization for girls and virilization for boys. Flora Thompson thought it was only in the country where 'a girl who showed any disposition to make friends of, or play games with, the boys was a "tomboy" at best, or at worst, "a fast forward young hussy,"' but, in fact, in towns like Preston the same stigma fell on young ladies who stepped across the gender boundaries.[1] Inhibi-tions that had previously been upper class became part of the working-class code of respectability. Any adolescent who dared show too much interest in the opposite sex felt the displeasure not only of parents but peers.

In the course of the early-twentieth-century sexual taboos multiplied. Among females the onset of menses came to mean withdrawal from all contact with the opposite sex. A Preston woman born just after World War I remem-bered running to tell her mother, who ordered her to 'go home and in my bottom drawer you'll find some cloths. Put them up against you and keep warm, and keep away from lads.' Her sense of vulnerability was further height-ened when girl friends warned her 'Don't let a lad touch you.'[2] Almost total ignorance of anatomy, shared by women of this particular period regardless of class, fostered a fear of all forms of contact, apart from kissing. Sexuality was almost never discussed at home and there was an abhorrence of nakedness, even in the presence of other women. Women could remember learning nothing from their mothers about reproduction: 'Everything was kept hidden from us. We couldn't talk like the . . . mothers and daughters today. . . . Everything was hushed up. You didn't know life as we . . . know it now.'³

As for boys, the beginning of adolescence also marked a significant turning point. Until the end of their schooling boys were, like their sisters, the object of what one contemporary called 'ferocious affection.'⁴ Little distinction was made between male and female children; and at the beginning of the century it was still the habit to keep little boys in long curls and gowns until the age of three or four before 'breeching' them. Even then, they spent their school years in the short trousers known as knickerbockers. When it came, the break with childhood was even sharper for boys than for girls. It usually coincided with leaving school and entering work at fourteen, a point at which the son was also relieved of all household duties and, like his father and older brothers, became a privileged person in the household. One father, who had four daughters but only one son, always took the boy for a walk when there were domestic chores to be done, declaring 'I'm not having him growing up a cissy with all these females.'⁵ As part of his virilization, the boy ceased to attend church, except for social purposes, and gained the freedom of the streets. Gradually, he would acquire masculine dress, language, and that certain swagger that would make him a regular in the local public house: 'The act of "going out with the boys" on Friday night, for the first time, was an initiation into manhood.'⁶

[*For Better, for Worse: British Marriages, 1600 to the Present* (New York: Oxford University Press, 1985), 267–8.]

CARROLL SMITH-ROSENBERG

49 Intimacy between Women

My own research has suggested that the rich world of nineteenth-century female intimacy in fact resulted from an intricate weaving together of psycho-sexual and social-structural forces. At the heart of this world lay intense devotion and identification between mothers and daughters. Mothers and daughters took joy and comfort in one anothers' presence. They often slept with one another throughout the daughters' adolescence, wept unashamedly at separation, and rejoiced at reunions. Mother–daughter bonding served as the model for subsequent relations with other women. [. . .]

The clean lines that distinguish the generations in twentieth-century families, that set apart members of the nuclear household from first cousins, aunts, uncles, even grandparents, were inconceivable in most eighteenth- and nine-teenth-century homes. The ages of biological siblings could span the twenty-odd years of their mother's reproductive life, easily permitting the firstborn daughter to mother the lastborn children, or mothers and daughters to be preg-nant and give birth together.[1] Parents frequently brought their own younger siblings into their households, thus again bridging the gap that separated parents from children. Cousins moved in and out of one another's homes. Conse-quently, a spectrum of alternative maternal figures surrounded the young girl. As the young woman moved toward maturity, aunts, older sisters, and cousins functioned as caretakers, confidantes, playmates, and instructors. This prolifera-tion of maternal figures diffused the intensity of mother–daughter bonding, which has become so psychologically problematic within the isolated nuclear family of the twentieth century. Within the nineteenth-century extended female-kin system, the process of psychological separation developed more gradually and never became as complete as it would in the twentieth century. The overall result was a female adolescence far less fraught with rebellion and crisis.

Biological and psychosexual factors, woven together, constituted the woof and warp of that intricate tapestry. To comprehend the intricacies of the nine-teenth-century world of love and ritual among women is not to explain its end. We must analyze the fears that undercut the intimacy of that world and explore women's response to its loss. Only then will we be prepared to examine women's relations in succeeding worlds, especially our own. [. . .]

Nineteenth- and twentieth-century readers concur about one matter: nine-teenth-century women wrote love letters to one another. But did the word 'love' connote to these women, as it does to us, the recognition of sexual desire? Did nineteenth-century women refer, rather, to a sublimated form of sexual love? Or, alternatively, to feelings rooted not in sexual desire but in experiences of intimacy and affection that grew out of women's shared physical and psycho-logical realities? Their categories and ours differ and thus obscure the meaning. Their words, while graphic, do not illuminate automatically.

To a twentieth-century reader, their words convey erotic, sensual feelings; they speak of physical pleasures. They wrote of longing to be with their loved ones, of bittersweet kisses, of passionate embraces, of nights spent in one another's arms, of dancing together, of burning jealousies. Nearly thirty years after they first met, Molly could still write to Helena: 'It isn't because you are good that I love you—but for the essence of you which is like perfume.'[2] Had these women been writing to men, their letters would clearly fall within one of our post-Freudian conceptual categories—heterosexuality. We would not hesi-tate to deduce sexual desire, if not sexual relations, from their words. If women had written these letters to other women and expressed the need for secrecy, guilt, remorse, a struggle against passion, we could place their passion within a second socially agreed-upon category: self-conscious lesbian deviance. But these women wrote unself-consciously of their passion for other women. They showed their letters to husbands, daughters, and friends. Neither they nor their families defined their emotions as sexually 'unnatural.' Their passion eludes our twentieth-century categories, presenting us with two possible explanations: either these women used words differently than we do, so that their erotic declarations were in fact asexual statements, a natural component of that *rare avis*, the nineteenth-century platonic friendship—or Victorian society did not find erotic passion between married women emotionally unnatural or socially disruptive.

[*Disorderly Conduct: Visions of Gender in Victorian America* (New York: Oxford University Press, 1985), 32, 33–4, 35–6.]

JOHN D'EMILIO AND ESTELLE B. FREEDMAN

50   Intimacy between Men

However difficult it may be to know whether sexual—that is, genital—relations characterized particular same-sex friendships, it is clear that the meaning of same-sex love gradually changed over the course of the nineteenth century. Colonial Americans had no concept of homosexuality as a personal condition or identity. Rather, individual acts of sodomy (anal sex between men) or buggery (sex with animals) were considered sins to be punished and for which a man could repent. The laws almost always applied to men, not women, because they typically referred to the unnatural spilling of seed, the biblical sin of Onan. Nineteenth-century Americans continued to condemn sodomy, a term which they used to refer not only to anal sex between men but also to various nonprocreative sexual acts, including masturbation and oral sex. Over the course of the century, new meanings were attached to these terms. At first, the language of religion remained prominent in discussions of sodomy. For example, an 1810 Maryland court indictment for sodomy stated that the defendant had been 'moved and seduced by the instigation of the Devil.' But gradually legal concerns replaced religious ones. After the American Revolution, the phrase 'crimes against nature' increasingly appeared in statutes, implying that acts of sodomy offended a natural order rather than the will of God. By the end of the century, physicians employed a medical language, referring to sodomy not as a sin or a spiritual failing, but rather as a disease and a manifestation of a bodily or mental condition. During the 1880s, the labels 'congenital inversion' and 'perversion' were applied not only to male sexual acts, but to sexual or romantic unions between women, as well as those between men.[1]

Underlying these redefinitions were growing possibilities for sexual relations between members of the same gender. Within the working class, men and women who lived outside of traditional families formed same-sex partnerships for economic or sexual reasons, or for both. Within the middle class, romantic friendships fostered both spiritual and physical intimacy that might become sexual. For men, more than for women, same-sex relationships often crossed class boundaries. For both sexes, these relationships formed unselfconsciously. Not until the last quarter of the century did those who engaged in same-sex relationships find it necessary to hide or deny their passionate attachments.

The first model of same-sex relationship, that of sexual or romantic partnerships outside the familial model, was most readily available to white wage-earning men. For them, the industrializing economy offered opportunities to explore sexuality outside of marriage, whether on city streets or in the separate sphere of all male activity. The ability to purchase goods and services allowed men to live beyond familial controls, while the city provided anonymity for their actions. Wage-earning men who lived in urban boardinghouses could bring other men to their rooms for the night or longer. In 1846, two New York men who had met in church lived together for three months, engaging in nightly 'carnal intercourse.'[2] During the 1860s, poet Walt Whitman frequently brought home young working-class men whom he met in New York, Brooklyn, and Washington, D.C. 'City of orgies, walks and joys,' he called Manhattan. The city's 'frequent and swift flash of eyes offering me love' repaid the poet's effort:

Saturday night Mike Ellis . . . took him home to 150 37th Street . . . *Dan'l Spencer* . . . slept with me Sept 3d . . . Theodore M. Carr . . . came to the house with me . . . *David Wilson*— night of Oct 11, '62, walking up from Middagh—slept with me . . . October 9, 1863, Jerry Taylor . . . slept with me last night weather soft, cool enough, warm enough, heavenly.[3]

Another writer also benefited from urban anonymity. In 1866, Horatio Alger was run out of his pulpit in a small Massachusetts town for the 'revolting crime of unnatural familiarity with boys.' Alger moved to New York City, where he could avoid censure for his pederastic interest in the young men of the streets, about whom he wrote in his popular novels.[4]

At a time when the state was not heavily involved in the regulation of morality, urban police did not vigorously prosecute consensual sodomy. Between 1796 and 1873, for example, New York City courts issued only twenty-two indictments for sodomy, and these usually involved the use of force or a disparity in the men's ages. Thus in 1857, George Mason was arrested for committing sodomy with boys aged eleven to fourteen. Not until the end of the century did New York law criminalize 'consenting to sodomy.' By then Americans had been alerted to the phenomenon of homosexuality, for as the opportunities for same-sex relationships grew, the first signs of a visible, urban homosexual subculture appeared, along with strong condemnation of homosexuality by medical writers.[5]

In addition to the cities, wherever young, single men congregated—as soldiers, prisoners, or cowboys—the possibility for same-sex relationships increased. During the Civil War, for example, when Walt Whitman served as a nurse, he formed deep attachments to the young Union and rebel soldiers he tended. 'I believe no men ever loved each other as I and some of these poor wounded, sick and dying men love each other,' he wrote. Before he left at night he kissed the 'poor boys.' Of a nineteen-year-old southern captain, he declared 'our affection is quite an affair, quite romantic—sometimes when I lean over to say I am going, he puts his arm round my neck, draws my face down, &c.' Similarly, a Confederate general developed a strong attachment to his adjutant, a young man who shared the officer's 'labours during the day and his blankets at night.' In the navy, accounts of flogging for homosexual activity attest to the opportunities for sex on board ships. After the 1820s, the growth of the American prison system created further possibilities for situational homosexuality. Convicts testified that strong attachments often developed between older and younger prisoners, who shared their possessions, their meals, and their beds. Other prisoners recalled being forced to engage in sex against their will.[6]

[*Intimate Matters: A History of Sexuality in America* (New York: Harper & Row, 1988), 122–4.]

Section II

The Discovery of 'Sexuality' at the Turn of the Century

In the course of the nineteenth century the states of the industrializing West took a keen interest in the health and well-being of populations that were becoming steadily more numerous, more urban, and more 'dangerous' to public order. This was an era of revolutions and civil wars, but also of nation-state formation (Italy, Germany) and nationalist warfare involving virtually all the great powers. There emerged a universal conviction that the foundation of a unified, expanding nation was a healthy and prolific populace. Most states maintained public hygiene establishments and statesmen and the public alike became accustomed to analysing symptoms of national strength or weakness from a medical perspective. Doctors and scientists readily co-operated in this endeavour. They studied organic diseases like tuberculosis, cholera, and smallpox, identified illnesses brought on or worsened by poor nutrition, tainted water, and insalubrious living conditions, and they attempted to expand medical services to the new urban slums and rural backwaters.

In the domain of sex, the attention of health officials was also drawn to certain health concerns that, in one form or another, had long troubled individuals and societies in the West. Hysteria, prostitution and its attendant venereal illnesses, and masturbation had long been thought to fall under the aegis of medical expertise, but until the nineteenth century they had never been grouped together as *sexual* problems worthy of scrutiny by national public health elites. In the process of studying and attempting to cure them, medical experts developed and popularized a set of characteristic theories and treatments and a technical language that situated each one within a larger matrix of national pathologies. As will be discussed in Section II.b, it was while grappling with the classifications, disease nosologies, and clinical evidence arising from the study of prostitution, hysteria, and masturbation that medical experts created our characteristic modern notion of 'sexuality' and its discontents. It is important to remember that in this era sexuality had not reached the status of an autonomous and radically individualized notion of identity and personal behaviour that it appears to have attained today. Sexual concepts and practices were deeply embedded in familial, class, and national contexts and they continued as before to be influenced by traditional discourses of religion and popular morality. However, the development of capitalism and democratizing societies nourished forms of individual behaviour that loosened the bonds of kinship and class and promoted individualism—including erotic innovations—as an ideal.

At the same time, once-dominant religious precepts governing sexual life were challenged increasingly by the growing influence of science and medicine and by a persuasive biomedical discourse of pathology and norm. This discourse resonated powerfully in societies whose citizens had only recently attained elementary literacy. Because the knowledge it conveyed was useful to individuals and the state, the experts who deployed it rapidly gained the authority to pronounce on sexual matters in general. As some of the texts below will argue, the sexual 'perversions' that were produced in the course of the elaboration of this new discourse helped constitute the sexual identity of the individuals whose sexuality they purported to describe. The philosopher Ian Hacking has described this process as a 'feedback effect' linking 'the inter-actions between people, on the one hand, and ways of classifying people and their behaviour on the other. Being seen to be a certain kind of person, or to do a certain kind of act, may affect someone. A new or modified mode of classifi-cation may systematically affect the people who are so classified, or the people themselves may rebel against the knowers, the classifiers, the science that clas-sifies them. Such interactions may lead to changes in the people who are classi-fied and hence in what is known about them.'[1]

When we view this kind of interaction against the background of particular historical and cultural developments, we may employ this 'feedback effect' to help understand the process by which our modern sexual selves have been shaped. We may also better understand why deviations from sexual norms assumed the form of the so-called perversions—homosexuality, fetishism, sadism, masochism—as over against heterosexual, genital relations. The selec-tions in Section II will outline how this system of classification was produced and is maintained in Western societies up to the present day.

[1] Ian Hacking, *Rewriting the Soul: Multiple Personality and the Sciences of Memory* (Princeton: Princeton University Press, 1995), 239.

II.a. Doctors and Sexual Disorders

II.a.i. EXPERTS

In the course of the nineteenth century medicine became both more scientific and more specialized. Psychiatry, sexology, and, eventually, psychoanalysis emerged as branches of medical practice concerned to a great extent with sexuality and its problems. To establish their claims to expertise and carve out a place for themselves in the medical cosmos, these new specialists had to demonstrate that their work was useful and effective. They addressed the 'hot-button' issues of their day and were attracted to theories of human health and illness that were at once grandiose and firmly rooted in scientific materialism. To assure a steady flow of clients, these specialists identified particular symptoms or behaviour and redefined them as medical problems. Abram De Swaan attempts to explain how this process of professional specialization had a corollary public dimension that helped to produce in individuals the 'problems' doctors discovered (Extract 51).

This focus on sexual life and families brought medical experts into direct rivalry with established religion, whose domain this had been for nearly 2,000 years. Their strategy was not so much to contest the moral outlook of Judaeo-Christian religion as incorporate it into a modern scientific world view that in effect preserved the chief elements of sin, discipline, and redemption. The intellectual matrix that served as the basis for this exercise in professional imperialism was the biomedical theory of degeneration, invented in 1857 by a French asylum doctor, Bénédict-Augustin Morel (Extract 52).

Degeneration was the opposite and regressive pole of progressive evolution, with which it was twinned throughout the latter half of the nineteenth century. As employed by doctors in the higher service of the state, degeneration served as a formidable rival to a traditional religious outlook on sexual morality, permitting the substitution of secular for religious authority (Extract 53).

Degeneration also served as the nosological (classification) foundation for understanding hysteria, masturbation, prostitution, and venereal disease, and became in itself, as the following extract shows, an important engine for the generation of stereotypes (Extract 54).

51   Professionalization and Medical Problems

People make trouble with themselves and with others in a family setting, in love relationships, and in their everyday work. In these troubles, psychotherapists recognize psychic problems, they have theories to describe and classify them, methods to treat them, training courses to teach about them, and organizations that regulate collegial co-operation and professional practice in dealing with these problems. And in these respects they are very much like other helping professions.

The professional classifications and conceptions of troubles as problems that may then be categorized and treated by members of a certain profession are next adopted by outsiders; first by people who are socially close to the profession—for example, because they work in adjacent professions, as colleagues, referring clients to members of this profession, as assistants to members of the profession, or next because they have made contact as a client. These insights spread in ever-widening circles of laymen by means of personal conversations, literature, and the media, and also because people pick up such notions in passing in the course of their formal education.

With respect to the various professions, this spreading process is referred to as 'medicalization',[1] 'legalization',[2] 'psychologization', and even as 'professionalization of the client'.[3] In general, these external effects of professionalization upon the conceptualization among laymen may be referred to as their *protoprofessionalization*: in the course of this development, laymen adopt the fundamental stances and basic concepts which are circulating within the profession and, in this way, become 'protoprofessionals' themselves. The process does not take place at the same pace or to an equal degree within all segments of society. On the contrary, it occurs sooner among people who are socially close to the profession or at an intellectual advantage because of their extensive education.

People make troubles with themselves and with one another, and psychotherapists regard these troubles as psychic problems; as this professional concept spreads, people redefine their troubles as psychic problems suitable for treatment by the psychotherapist. But the troubles were already there. The service supply creates the demand, but it doesn't create the misery.

In this way, the division of labour which has evolved among the helping professions also serves as a guideline in the everyday experience of laymen when putting their troubles into words and categorizing them; often there is hardly any other way to talk about these troubles than in the vocabulary that each profession has developed for its problem area and has conveyed to adjacent circles of laymen.

The way these troubles are articulated and the manner in which they are experienced are determined in part by the division of labour and by the treatment claims that have emerged between the various helping professions. In this sense, the very fact that people live in society as potential therapy clients, welfare clients, and patients of one profession or another shapes the troubles they experience.

The entire area of troubled modes of experience and interaction has become the working terrain of the fairly new profession of psychotherapy, and in circles of people who are closely related to it, laymen have begun to recognize their troubles as psychic problems, whereas they were previously accustomed to speaking of bad behaviour and evil moods, of sin and of illness, of deliriums and rage, of bewitchment or destiny, of the usual imperfections of human existence—if they took any note of these troubles and considered them worth discussing at all. Psychotherapy did not exist yet, and psychic problems were not recognized or experienced as such, but in many different ways.

The profession exerts an educating and proselytizing impact on the outside world. The external effect of professionalization is the formation of a clientele: the professionalization process operates in the surrounding society as proto-professionalization. And as people spend a greater part of their lives in circles where it is common practice to label one's everyday experience in accordance with the categories of psychotherapy and to put the basic concepts of the profession of psychotherapy into practice in everyday life, they will be the more likely to seek psychotherapeutic treatment and to benefit from it.

Given this starting point, it follows that what is to be studied first is not the population at large and its suitability or needs, but the professional circles themselves and the way they categorize clients to be treated.

[*The Management of Normality: Critical Essays in Health and Welfare* (London: Routledge, 1990), 100–2.]

DANIEL PICK

52 Degeneration

What conception of *dégénérescence* was produced in Morel's famous *Treatise* of 1857? The term was applied to the patterns of heredity in societies, and specifically to deviations from the 'normal type' of humanity.[1] It did not signify the reproduction of a constant anomaly from one body to another (which was the emphasis in Prosper Lucas' *Treatise*, 1847–1850); it was concerned rather with an infinite network of diseases and disorders, and the patterns of return and transformation between them.[2] Morel pulled together a bewildering array of physical conditions, moral and social habits; from hernias, goitres, pointed ears, absence of secondary teeth, stunted growth, cranial deviations, deaf and dumbness, blindness, albinism, club-feet, elephantitis, scrophula, tuberculosis, rickets and sterility to the effects of toxins like alcohol, tobacco and opium; he explored disturbances of the intellectual faculties and the noxious tendencies of certain forms of romanticism which resulted in languorous desires, effeteness, reveries, impotence, suicidal tendencies, inertia, melancholy and apathy. For Morel, the human being was a unified ensemble, composed of matter and of spirit. Physical degeneration could not but lead to eventual intellectual and moral collapse and vice versa. *Dégénérescence* was the name for a process of pathological change from one condition to another in society and in the body. A vast array of disorders were, as Morel's colleague, Moreau (de Tours) put it, part of the 'empire of the law of inheritance',[3] merely 'different branches of the same trunk'.[4] Madness here could appear partially developed, as for instance 'moral insanity', but it was always part of a deeper and all-encompassing bio-logical process.

[*Faces of Degeneration: A European Disorder, c.1848–c.1918* (Cambridge: Cambridge University Press, 1989), 50–1.]

JACQUES DONZELOT:

53 The Priest and the Doctor

Sexuality, the couple, pedagogy, and social adaptation are brought together in a single mold by the recent appearance of the constellation of counselors and technicians of human relations. But who attended to this kind of problem in the past? The priest and the doctor, the priest *or* the doctor—in any case, they occu-pied two clearly separate registers.

The priest managed sexuality from the angle of family morality. An ancient complicity, consisting of mutual benefits, operated between the system of matrimonial exchanges—the key to the old familial order—and the religious apparatus. The family received the guarantee of its unions through the distri-bution of blessings by the Church. For its part, the clergy received money, for the expenses of celebration and for the exemptions it granted for the contrac-tion of a marriage when the partners had a certain degree of kinship; under the *ancien régime*, this favor was a necessity, for village organization implied a high rate of consanguinity. The convent served the family by preserving those of its offspring whom it destined for marriage and by relieving it of those who were a burden to it. It was just as useful to the Church in recruiting a popula-tion that the Church could employ for its own missionary purposes. The mechanism of confession furnished the family with the means to deal with the inevitable variance between the strategic nature of alliances and sexual attractions. In return, it obtained for the Church a direct hold on individuals, the possibility of a direction of consciences. The Church increased its benefits in money, power, and expansion precisely insofar as it reinforced the family's hegemony over its members: it constituted a veritable Mafia grafted onto the system of alliance.

For a long time, medicine maintained a prudent distance from this social regime of sexual exchanges. In the eighteenth century, it began to take an interest in sexuality from the viewpoint of a specifically corporal as opposed to a spiritual flux. It attached a great importance in the exploration of illnesses to all frauds in the performance of the reproductive functions. The withholding of the mother's milk, the refusal to breast-feed—a tendency commonly found in women who were drawn into the artificial concerns of society life—was designated as the cause of a litany of ills. The dissipation of sperm through onanism could be equally calamitous for the man. We have seen how this type of discourse provided an increasingly important place for doctors during the eighteenth and nineteenth centuries in the activity of family counseling. The family doctor intervened in the domestic organization of the home; through his suggestions concerning hygiene, through his educative advice, he substantially altered its internal arrangement. But he did not dare meddle with the system of alliances, that sacred preserve of the family and the Church. [...]

This restriction of medical intervention in sexuality solely to private hygiene slowly came undone during the nineteenth century. An examination of the popular medical books intended for the use of families reveals an increase in the size and importance of articles devoted to sexual behavior. At the beginning of the nineteenth century, the medical encyclopedias supplemented the standard diatribes concerning onanism and the refusal to breast-feed with rather vague remarks on the greater longevity of married individuals, the doubtful advisability of marriage between persons of widely different ages, and the best compatibility of temperaments. In the middle of the century, the dictionaries of hygiene inserted a few positive considerations regarding nonartificial means of contraception. Starting in 1857, that is, after the publication of Morel's *Traité des dégénérescences*, they grew rich in imperious advice regarding indications and contraindications for matrimony.[1] Eugenism was not far in the future. The end of the century saw the proliferation of a new genre, the medical library, with titles like *Bibliothèque médicale variée*, *Petite bibliothèque médicale*, and so on. In the catalogues of small low-priced books, sexual questions, often dealt with by highly acclaimed physicians, occupied a prominent place. The mandarins of the end of the nineteenth and the beginning of the twentieth century used their pages to wage a campaign of hygienization of sexuality, based on a general mechanism of prevention of the social diseases (venereal disease, alcoholism, tuberculosis). For the doctors, it was a matter of treating sexuality as the business of the state, thus transcending the arbitrariness of families, morality, and the Church. After setting out to rule over bodies, medicine decided the objective could better be reached by legislating on marriages as well.

[*The Policing of Families*, trans. Robert Hurley (New York: Pantheon Books, 1979), 171–3.]

History, sexuality, and degeneracy are inextricably linked in late nineteenth-century thought. Through Hegel's model of history, in which each age succeeds and replaces, on a higher level, the one that preceded it, human sexuality was perceived teleologically. Welded to this movement from the concrete to the abstract is another paradigm. The theological model of the Fall as the wellspring of history and of Christ's sacrifice as mankind's redemption served as an explanation for human degeneration and regeneration. These historical analogies were perceived within the model of human development as understood in the nineteenth century. If the most advanced stage of human sexuality following the redemption of Christ is that of the adult, male European, rather than the child or the Other (woman, black) as child, this is proof that the most primitive sexuality must correspond to the most primitive stage of human history. The Other's sexuality, labeled as perverse because it was seen as retrogressive, was soon identified with all modes of sexuality other than those prescribed for adult Europeans. The child's masturbation is perverse. The Other's sexuality is perverse because it is childlike. Here the linkage among all modes of deviant sexuality can be found. Masturbation, homosexuality, promiscuity (in primitive societies), prostitution (in advanced societies) are all degenerate forms of adult sexual experience, since they are ascribed to the Other.

The projection of deviant sexuality onto the Other during the nineteenth century was understood in theological as well as teleological terms. The aberrant sexuality of the child was proof of humanity's fall from grace. It seldom manifested itself, as humanity had been saved through Christ's sacrifice, but its rare appearance was proof of the potential within each adult of regression to the state before redemption. Here the idea of the degeneracy of the Jew fitted quite nicely. Hegel could not understand the Jews' tenacity at existing following their contribution to a specific stage of Western culture. Nineteenth-century science tried to explain it in terms of medicalization. This categorized the Jews at a stage of sexual development which was understood as primitive and perverse and therefore degenerate. [...]

The city becomes the icon of 'modern life' and the locus of degenerate sexuality. The Rousseauan idea that 'idyllic' life is contaminated by social institutions lasts through the nineteenth century and directs the fear of revolt to one specific locus of 'modern life,' the city.[1] The city, as opposed to the image of the garden, is yet another image of the fall from grace. The city—an icon of the rejection of redemption, of Abraham's failure in Sodom and Gomorrah, of the Jerusalem of Herod—permeates the image of civilization and is represented as the breeding ground of perverse and unnatural sexuality.

Even as medicine during the course of the nineteenth century saw itself more and more as an adjunct to the science of biology, medicine's prime interest in human sexuality remained focused on its pathological aspects. Discussion of normal reproduction and human sexual potential was generally repressed in favor of the protean image of the diseased. The presentation of reproduction, of sexual anatomy, of sexual activity within the medical text-books of the period was in terms of what could and evidently often did go wrong, rather than in terms of what was labeled as 'healthy' or 'normal.' The normal was understood simply as that which was not degenerate, and the sexually normal was defined by the most powerful of contrastive models, that of deviant human sexuality.

Society's power to define the Other was articulated through an explanatory model of human pathology. But all of this distancing reflected only the deep-seated anxiety stemming from the consciousness that power (including the power to stigmatize) can be lost, leaving its erstwhile possessor in danger of becoming the Other. This anxiety affected biologists and physicians as well as the other members of society. The magic of any overarching explanatory model such as degeneracy disguises, but does not eliminate, the potential loss of power. The only buffer 'science' could provide against the anxiety that remained because of this inherent flaw, the fear of oneself eventually being labeled as degenerate, was to create categories that were absolutely self-contained. Thus disease-entities were invented which defined a clearly limited subset of human beings as the group solely at risk. For such diseases were labeled as inherited to one degree or another. The inherited diseases, whether masturbation, hysteria, neurasthenia, congenital syphilis, or even incest, all had one thing in common. In all cases the etiology and the symptomatology are identical. All begin with some type of sexual deviancy and result in sexual perversion. Here we again have the repetition of the Fall. The Fall stems from the sexuality introduced into Eden and is proven by the pains that attend every labor. But also proving the Fall by a necessary, eternal repetition of it is the regular descent into degeneracy of women (and by analogy, Jews). Thus the group at risk was different, inherently, ineluctably separate from the group providing the label (at least in the fantasy of the latter).

[*Difference and Pathology: Stereotypes of Sexuality, Race, and Madness* (Ithaca, NY: Cornell University Press, 1985), 213–14, 214–15.]

II.a.ii. HYSTERIA

First described in ancient Greece, hysteria was perpetuated in Western medicine as a typical female malady associated with the womb. It became a kind of catch-all disease for behaviour in women that either departed from traditional gender roles or that exaggerated them, such as extreme states of emotion. Though hysterical symptoms had always been linked to reproductive disorders, by the eighteenth century doctors began to ascribe such behaviour more generally to sexual or 'genital' abnormalities. In the nineteenth century, debates raged about whether hysteria was a constitutional or a psychological disorder and whether it was caused by too little sexual activity or too much. The fact that hysteria could now be considered a species of sexual illness meant that it could also claim male victims, though women continued to make up the overwhelming majority of hysteria patients in insane asylums. The British alienist (psychiatrist) Robert Brudnell Carter argued in 1853 that hysteria was a psychosexual illness brought on by the repression of sexual thoughts and activity in modern civilization (Extract 55).

But other specialists associated hysteria with sexual excess, so that in midnineteenth-century France it became a classic disorder of prostitutes. It is important to note, however, that doctors believed prostitutes' susceptibility to hysteria was at least in part because genital excitement did not lead to 'normal' orgasm (Extract 56).

Though they disputed the range of symptoms attributable to hysteria, doctors believed the so-called 'genital instincts' were generally involved. The psychiatrist Jules Falret believed hysterical women commonly engaged in the 'most shameful actions' (masturbation) or other domestic peccadilloes, and some of his colleagues regarded nymphomania as the disorder's ultimate endpoint (Extract 57).

The greatest medical impresario of hysteria in the nineteenth century was Jean-Martin Charcot, who presided over a neurology clinic at the Salpêtrière asylum in Paris between 1861 and 1893. Sigmund Freud and other specialists in mental diseases came to witness Charcot and his assistants orchestrate the presentation of hysterical symptoms in his patients. It has been suggested that patients were given subtle cues to make them assume the form of 'typical' hysterical seizures, but, as the case of Charcot's prize pupil Geneviève reveals, the most likely source of the hysterical presentations available to women was the culture in which they lived. As described in Extract 58, in her agony Geneviève oscillated across the whole spectrum of womanhood between madonna and whore.

55 Hysteria and Repression

By hysteria, then, is intended a disease which commences with a convulsive paroxysm, of the kind commonly called 'hysterical'. This paroxysm is witnessed under various aspects, and in various degrees of severity, being limited, in some cases, to a short attack of laughter or sobbing; and in others, producing very energetic involuntary movements, maintained during a considerable time, and occasionally terminating in a period of catalepsy or coma. The diagnosis (in so far as rules for it can be written down,) rests mainly upon the absence of epileptic characteristics, and the existence of some evident exciting cause, such as sudden fright, disappointment, or anger . . . *Simple* hysteria . . . consists in the liability to fits of greater or less severity, either with or without distinct intervals of remission and perfect health, is subject to many complications, which constitute the various disorders known as hysterical spine, hysterical knee, hysterical neuralgia, &c., and may be classified in a way to be considered hereafter. *Complicated* hysteria generally involves much moral and intellectual, as well as physical, derangement, and when it is fully established, the primary convulsion, the 'fons et origo mali,' is sometimes suffered to fall into abeyance, and is lost sight of and forgotten by the friends of the patient, their attention being arrested by the urgency of new maladies . . .

The effect of emotion in producing hysteria has long been a matter of common observation, and is distinctly recognised by many authors on the subject, but they have all regarded it only as an exciting agency, which required for its operation the prior existence of some unknown constitutional state. As a first step in endeavouring to demonstrate the groundlessness of this opinion, it may be well to cite two cases which have fallen under my own observation, and in which the idea of an hysterical diathesis could only be supported by the kind of argument known among logicians as a vicious circle, namely, by inferring its existence from the occurrence of that event which it has been postulated in order to explain . . .

If the relative power of emotion against the sexes be compared in the present day, even without including the erotic passion, it is seen to be considerably greater in the woman than in the man ... But when sexual desire is taken into the account, it will add immensely to the forces bearing upon the female, who is often much under its dominion; and who, if unmarried and chaste, is compelled to restrain every manifestation of its sway ... It may, however, be remarked, that in many cases of hysteria in the male, the sufferers are recorded to have been 'continent', a circumstance which may have assimilated the effects of amativeness upon them to those which are constantly witnessed in the female ... And at the outset of this inquiry, we are ... compelled to investigate the power of the sexual passion, as compared with that of feelings more generally acknowledged ... For while the advance of civilisation and the ever-increasing complications of social intercourse tend to call forth new feelings, and by their means to throw amativeness some-what into the shade, as one powerful emotion among many others, still its absolute intensity is in no way lessened, and from the modern necessity for its entire concealment, it is likely to produce hysteria in a larger number of the women subject to its influence, than it would do if the state of society permitted its free expression. It may, therefore, be inferred, as a matter of reasoning, that the sexual emotions are those most concerned in the production of the disease.

['On the Pathology and Treatment of Hysteria,' in Richard Hunter and Ida Macalpine (eds.), *Three Hundred Years of Psychiatry 1535–1860: A History Presented in Selected English Texts* (London: Oxford University Press, 1963), 1002–3.]

JANN MATLOCK

56 Hysteria and the Prostitute

In place of the specifically sexual desire early nineteenth-century doctors had imagined overloading the hysteric's system, analysts now saw a myriad of desires. Whether they called these desires *causes morales, causes prédisposantes,* or *influences morales,* they repeatedly imagined kinds of emotions and social conditions that harkened back to traditional views of gender, class, and sexu-ality. The stories through which they allowed their hysterics to feel—and thus to become subjects in their own right—remained caught up in masterplots that confined women of all classes. The desires contained in these stories derived from honest attempts on the part of the doctors to hear and report the condi-tions of women's suffering. Yet at a certain point it was hard to know whose desires—those of the women or those of their doctors—had been given narra-tive shape. What was certain, nonetheless, was that these doctors had found ways to formulate their own fears about the working classes, prostitutes, and sexual excess. For despite their attempts to minimize the importance of the sexual in the exegesis of hysteria, they nevertheless remained obsessed with the mental state of prostitutes and, as such, with the relationship of prostitutes' sexuality to hysteria and madness.

Those who worked in the Salpêtrière, like the doctors of the public hospitals, needed only to look around their wards to see whether the sexual activity of prostitutes was a shield against hysteria and other forms of mental illness. Parent had embraced the familiar myth that only upper-class women suffered from the nervous problems of hysteria. Prostitutes were too base, he contended, somehow hardened by their experiences in the streets.[1] Yet prostitutes were omnipresent among the mental patients of the 1830s through 1850s, steadily one of the larger professional groups of inmates in the Salpêtrière. Esquirol had paved the way for views opposed to those of Parent and de Montègre when he declared that nearly all mental problems in women were complicated by hysteria and that five percent of those in the Salpêtrière with mental problems were prostitutes. But the correlation between hysteria and prostitution would not become a widely accepted fact until Briquet brought his skills of observation to the prostitutes in the Hôpital Lourcine. In a flourish meant to end all debate over continence, Briquet used the tools of scientific observation to determine that over half of all prostitutes suffered from hysteria.[2]

By removing hysteria from a direct causal relationship to sexual activity, the Salpêtrière doctors and Briquet made possible a new evaluation of the madness of the prostitute. 'Will people now invoke the overexcitation of the genitals [as the source of hysteria]?' asks Briquet of his astounding findings that 106 out of 197 prostitutes were hysterics and that 28 more were 'impressionable'.[3] According to Briquet, prostitutes avoid orgasms. Should one assume, he asks, that mechanical excitation of the genitals is enough in itself to cause hysteria? His answer would not satisfy those seeking ways to discourage women from clandestine prostitution:

In reflecting on the life led by these women and on the multiplicity of painful experiences and sensations to which they are prey, one will not be surprised that hysteria is so common among them. Poverty, nights spent without sleep, alcohol abuse, constant fears of the demands of the police or of bad treatment by the men with whom they live, the forced imprisonment occasioned by the illnesses they contract, the unbridled jealously and violent passions that animate them—all this explains well enough the frequency of hysterical problems among them.[4]

[*Scenes of Seduction: Prostitution, Hysteria, and Reading Difference in Nineteenth-Century France* (New York: Columbia University Press, 1994), 158–9.]

57 Sexual Hysteria

In his 1866 presentation, Falret described his vision of the hysterical character in detail:

All doctors who have observed many women afflicted with hysteria, all those who have had the misfortunate to share their lives with them, know perfectly that they have, as part of their character and intelligence, a moral physiognomy which is peculiar to them and which allows one to recognize in them the existence of this illness, even before observing the physical symptoms. ... The primary character trait belonging to hysterics is first the great mobility of their psychological temperament at the time one is observing them. They pass alternately and at very frequent intervals from excitation to depression, just as, on a physical level, they shift erratically from an outburst of laughter to one of tears. They become enthusiastic with ardor and passion for a person or object they want to possess at any cost; they stop at nothing, at no sacrifice to achieve their goal. ... This is their character in all things: fantastical and capricious, with an extreme mobility of ideas and sentiments. ... Another equally important characteristic of hysterics is their love of contradiction and argument. ... Obstinacy and passive resistance assume in them a truly sickly quality. ... Another important fact ... is their spirit of duplicity and lying. ... They make up veritable novels in which they intercalate, often cleverly and in an inextricable manner, the true and the false in a way so as to fool even the most perceptive person. ... They affect airs of piety and devotion and succeed in passing themselves off for saints while in secret abandoning themselves to the most shameful actions and at home making the most violent scenes with their husbands and children, scenes in which they make crude and sometimes obscene remarks and engage in the most disruptive acts. ... Finally, hysterical women are generally dreamy and romantic [romanesque], disposed to allow the fantasies of their imagination to predominate over the needs and necessities of real life. They also frequently have pronounced erotic tendencies, although this typical disposition has often been exaggerated, for they are usually coquettes and braggarts rather than truly ardent and sexual.[1]

In the years following Falret's lecture, the clinical portrait of the hysterical temperament was further embroidered within French mental medicine. In 1869, J.-J. Moreau de Tours published his own monograph on hysteria.[2] For him, too, hysteria was a variety of 'neuropathic insanity.' However, Moreau de Tours proposed that hysterical insanity did not affect the intellectual faculties of the patient, which Falret had implicated, but solely the 'moral' sphere. Its symptoms included a high degree of impressionability, 'irresistibility of penchants,' exaggerated erotic impulses, sexual insatiability, and a tendency to suicidal threats or actions.[3] Along the same lines, the internist, pathologist, and former dean of the Paris Medical Faculty, Ambroise Tardieu, proposed in 1872 that hysterical insanity was strictly limited to adult and adolescent females.[4] The victim of hysterical madness, Tardieu held, was not genuinely insane but suffered from 'the perversion of the affective faculties.' He also dissented strongly from Briquet: the hysteric nearly always manifested a certain sexual restlessness, 'the caresses of her husband having failed to satisfy her,' and could collapse at any time into wanton nymphomania.[5]

[*Approaching Hysteria: Disease and its Interpretations* (Princeton: Princeton University Press, 1995), 229–30.]

GEORGE FREDERICK DRINKA

58   Prostitute and Saint

One of the most interesting and significant of the women in the Salpêtrière was Geneviève.[1] Born in Loudon, where the famous 'devils' had been prominent in the time of Richelieu, she was an orphan who went to live on a farm in the country. Fits of anger and a generally temperamental nature led to her early hospitalization. She was soon sent to a second farm. A laborer from an early age, she had no formal education whatsoever. At age twelve, she cut her hand and was left with a slight scar. Then her fits of anger worsened.

At age fifteen, she fell in love with a young man named Camille, to whom she became engaged. Most tragically, Camille died that year of 'cerebral fever.'[2] When her foster father refused to let her go to the funeral for fear of her nervousness, the young Geneviève escaped from home and ran to the cemetery at night. Trying to dig up the remains of Camille, she was overcome with a crisis and was found unconscious by his grave. She remained in this state for twenty-four hours.

For the next year she was sad, withdrawn, refusing to talk, often angry. When her foster mother died she was sent to the hospital in Poitiers, and it was here that she began her career as a professional hysteric. Hospitals were to become her only home.

She was discharged in about a year and established as a chambermaid in Poitiers, where her master seduced her. She returned to the hospital apparently in a pregnant and hysterical state. Her pregnancy, in fact, was a hysterical (imaginary) one. Shortly thereafter Geneviève attempted suicide, first with pills (belladonna) and then with scissors on the left side of her abdomen. From then on, the left side of her body would remain insensible, or anesthetic.

At seventeen, she escaped from the hospital with a medical student, with whom she became sexually entangled. Spending the next two years in and out of this relationship, in and out of mental hospitals, she eventually went to Paris as a chambermaid in 1863. She would often have fits on the street and on one occasion was saved from leaping to her death from a bridge. She was first admitted to the Salpêtrière in 1865.

Her frequent escapes from the Salpêtrière, her fits, her teasing, vain character were described in detail by Charcot's followers Bourneville and Regnard in their book, *Photographic Iconography of the Salpêtrière* (1877–80). Twice she escaped and became pregnant. First she gave birth to a girl, whom she left in the country, and then a boy, who died of exposure.

Charcot appeared in her life from 1874 onward, mostly in order to press the hysterogenic point in the area of her left ovary, which would alternately cause and stop a fit. Charcot's disciples divided her seizures into three parts: tonic, clonic, and delirious. Described most vividly and in greatest detail is the last part—which coincides with Charcot's period of passionate attitudes—in which Geneviève went back and forth between ecstatic and crucified poses. Both poses resembled the dramatic postures of Louise Lateau, a stigmatized saint living in Belgium, who was a current favorite of the Paris newspapers. Intermingled with these poses were a series of erotic gestures in which she would plead for kisses and sexual intimacy from the doctors and attendants in the hospital, uttering such words as 'vagina' and 'penis'. Back and forth, back and forth she would go, saint to prostitute, saint to prostitute, in minutes.

[*The Birth of Neurosis: Myth, Malady, and the Victorians* (New York: Simon & Schuster, 1984), 92–4.]

II.a.iii PROSTITUTION

The 'oldest profession' underwent a similar 'medicalization' in the nineteenth century. Prostitution had always been associated with moral depravity and with poverty, but it fell increasingly under medical surveillance as political elites became concerned about the health of male populations weakened by venereal disease. In Italy and France and some German towns, official regulatory regimes were created that isolated prostitutes in 'closed houses' and subjected them to regular medical inspection. Britain experimented with a similar regulatory regime between 1864 and 1886 by passing and enforcing the Contagious Diseases Acts. Under the Act women could be labelled 'common prostitutes' and confined to 'lock' hospitals to undergo treatment for venereal disease. Women forced into prostitution from sheer poverty thus found themselves marginalized as a class, and, despite their resistance to the medical stereotypes devised to describe them, found it difficult as individuals to escape stigmatization, as Extracts 59 and 60 explain.

Elsewhere, prostitution, like hysteria, was fully assimilated to the medical idea of degeneration. In a study of female criminality, the Italian criminologists Lombroso and Ferrero argued that prostitutes were a species of 'born criminal' identifiable by a set of anatomical and characterological features visible to the medical expert.[1] Lasciviousness, vulgarity, poor personal hygiene, and a complete lack of modesty were the mirror images of 'respectable' women trait for trait.

This Manichaean discourse served as a cultural strategy for segregating the impure prostitute from the putative purity of respectable mothers and wives, but it also inspired fantasies of transgression in middle-class males fascinated by the remarkable frankness of the public debate on the merits of regulationist regimes. As Alain Corbin argues, apart from the occasional courtesan, prostitutes traditionally serviced lower class men, soldiers and sailors, but the very rigidity of a discursive regime of madonna and whore undermined itself by creating new forms of desire in wealthy bourgeois men with time on their hands (Extract 61).

Toward the end of the century public attention shifted increasingly toward the men who frequented prostitutes after publicity surfaced indicating that men were infecting their wives with venereal disease. This seemed to reveal that a 'double standard' of morality did not altogether segregate respectable from non-respectable women. British feminists like Christabel Pankhurst seized on this and on the sensational discovery of a 'white slave trade' in pubescent girls to link women's rights to demands for male chastity. In this book on the 'great scourge', written in 1913, she relies heavily on medical evidence to prove the salubriousness of sexual abstinence. Her tract reveals the graphic bluntness of sexual reform movements, the popularity of biomedical and racialized language, and a lingering suspicion of sensuality inherited from the previous century (Extract 62).

[1] Cesare Lombroso and Gugliemo Ferrero, *La Femme criminelle et la prostituée* (Paris, 1896).

59 **Stigmatization and the Contagious Diseases Act**

In their struggle for survival, the very poor maintained a delicate balance between private interest and public responsibility, between the toleration and the segregation of marginal social behavior. This fragile social equilibrium was upset by the enforcement of the Contagious Diseases Acts. On the one hand, the acts generated an extensive public resistance movement among the women and their community. On the other hand, by forcing prostitutes and their neighbors publicly to acknowledge what had been informally tolerated marginal behavior, they may well have forced a stricter redefinition of permissible behavior, thereby heightening the social isolation of prostitutes.

Among the prostitutes themselves one may observe a shift in attitudes and self-perception, forced upon them by the public exposure of the police registration and examination procedures. This is most plainly seen in the women's reaction to the periodical examination. Their vehement hostility to the internal examination may have partially been a reaction to the brutality of the doctors, as feminists alleged. No more than three minutes was spent on each examination; the instruments may have still been hot from immersion in boiling water (if they were sterilized at all).[1] And of course, a tense, resistant woman could find the examination by speculum painful. Annie Clark found the examination 'painful' and 'disgraceful' and declared, 'I would rather spend fourteen years in prison than submit to it.'[2] Elizabeth Hounsom, who held the record for multiple jailings—five—for refusing to attend examination, also maintained she preferred imprisonment to the 'degradation' of the examination: 'she tore the summons up when it was served upon her and did not appear at her fifth trial.'[3] Another woman who vowed to go to prison rather than to submit to examination told Josephine Butler, 'We ought all to show the officers that we have some respect for our own persons.'[4]

Like the middle-class feminists, registered women regarded the periodic examination as a peculiarly unnatural and degrading experience, a form of 'instrumental' rape.[5] When a repeal agent asked two women the difference 'between exposing themselves to any man who came to have connexion with them and showing themselves to the doctor,' they turned upon him 'fiercely' and replied:

I should have thought you'd have known better nor that. Ain't one in the way of natur', and the other ain't natur' at all. Ain't it a different thing what a woman's obliged to do for a living because she has to keep body and soul together, and going up there to be pulled about by a man as if you was cattle and hadn't no feeling, and to have an instrument pushed up you, not to make you well (because you ain't ill) but just that men may come to you and use you to thersils [sic].[6]

Nonetheless it would be misleading to dwell exclusively upon the brutal and sadistic character of the examination; more subtle means for humiliation were built into the whole procedure. In a society so profoundly class-bound as that of England, an examining physician would have had to do or say very little to make a registered woman feel worthless and degraded. The examination was demeaning because of its public character. Streetwalking at night was one thing; being forced to attend examination during the day, often taunted on the way by young boys who loudly questioned whether the woman were going up to the 'Bougie Fair' or the 'meat market,' was another.[7] One woman confided to a female missionary that 'it was no use trying to reform now, she was registered as a prostitute and everybody would know what she had been doing, and what she was. Going up for examination, she said, was worse than going with 20 men...'[8] The domiciliary visitation by the police and the central location of the examination house made it impossible for a subject woman to keep her private and public worlds apart. This is what destroyed her 'self respect.'

In this way the acts forced prostitutes to adjust their self-images. Repealers complained that the acts hardened the women by forcing many 'who may not have made up their mind to continue as prostitutes' to acknowledge their outcast status. Although women appealing for legal aid to repealers made no attempt to hide the fact that they had been prostitutes, some certainly evidenced a strong ambivalence about their past and even expressed confusion as to what it meant to be a prostitute. Clearly the categories of acceptable social and sexual behavior were not that well defined. Harriet Hicks is a case in point.

When asked at her trial in 1870 whether she was still a prostitute, Hicks responded, 'No, only to the one man.' A sympathetic magistrate then intervened and explained to her, 'You mean that you are not a prostitute, other than as living with one man without marriage?' to which Hicks meekly replied, 'Yes, that's what I mean.'[9] Hicks's confused response that she was a prostitute 'only to the one man' suggests that she many not have understood the question— that the very word 'prostitute' might have been foreign to her general usage. One must question whether a poor woman's testimony before a middle-class audience truly reflected her private self-estimation. It is unlikely that prostitutes fully internalized the notion of being 'fallen' when they knew they could 'rise' again. Moral reformers and rescue agencies appear to have failed to elicit any inner compulsion to be consistent in their public and private lives. Rather, these women seem to have effected a practical and psychological compartmentalization of their lives, except when subjected to concerted public stigmatization.

[*Prostitution and Victorian Society: Women, Class, and the State* (Cambridge: Cambridge University Press, 1980), 201–3.]

In his 1842 *Lectures*, Wardlaw referred to prostitution as 'illicit intercourse' and specified: 'A prostitute is designation of *character* ... To form the character, and to justify the designation, there must be the voluntary *repetition of the act;—the giving up of the person to criminal indulgence.*'[1] Prostitution is thus defined as a pathological condition produced by repeated indulgence in illicit and deviant sex. Wardlaw entirely sidesteps economic and social issues and represents prostitution as a moral state.

This mechanism was also deployed by William Acton in his polemical second edition of *Prostitution* which was published in 1870 to support the Contagious Diseases legislation. Acton defined the prostitute as a perversion of respectable femininity; made impure by her contact with money, she corrupts and infects the rest of society:

What is a prostitute? She is a woman who gives for money that which she ought to give only for love; who ministers to passion and lust alone, to the exclusion and extinction of all the higher qualities ... She is a woman with half the woman gone, and that half containing all that elevates her nature, leaving her a mere instrument of impurity; degraded and fallen she extracts from the sin of others the means of living, corrupt and dependent on corruption, and therefore interested directly in the increase of immorality.[2]

The idea that prostitution was a physical and psychological state which set the prostitute apart from respectable women was also constituted within legal discourse. The Contagious Diseases Acts were framed to control and regulate the 'common prostitute' but there was a great deal of uncertainty about the definition of this group and in the final instance, the category could only be sustained by assuming common knowledge and shared beliefs; as one public inquiry reported:

374. Again, Dr. Brewer asks, What is your definition of a prostitute? To which Mr. Parsons, Visiting Surgeon to the Portsmouth Lock Hospital, replies: Any woman whom there is fair and reasonable ground to believe is, first of all, going to places which are the resorts of prostitutes alone and at times when immoral persons only are usually out. *It is more a question as to mannerism than anything else.*[3] (My italics)

The speaker draws upon dominant beliefs concerning the proper 'sphere' of the respectable woman in order to define the prostitute in terms of her location but, fearing the inadequacy of this definition, Parsons supports this definition in terms of a vague evocation of 'mannerism'. The statement signals a number of the most significant issues raised by the representation of the prostitute in the middle of the nineteenth century. Prostitution was perceived as a threat in terms of its visibility and it was thus the streetwalker who became the symbol for prostitution in general and who was at the centre of the construction of a physical stereotype. This stereotype was circulated and repeated across a wide range of texts; it dominated bourgeois understanding of prostitution.

[*Myths of Sexuality: Representations of Women in Victorian Britain* (Oxford: Basil Blackwell, 1988), 101–3.]

ALAIN CORBIN

61   Prostitution and New Forms of Desire

The increased mobility of bourgeois men and, accordingly, time spent away from their places of work offered ample opportunities for sexual adventure. The development of international tourism, the presence of large numbers of foreigners in Paris and in the watering places, train travel,[1] voyages at sea, holidays by the sea,[2] the new fashion for long pilgrimages, the massive influx of provincials into the capital during the universal expositions,[3] theatrical tours, the density of the network of commercial representation—all these were factors contributing to an increase in the demand for prostitution on the part of bourgeois males. [...]

The blossoming of male sexuality in those bourgeois milieus that tended both to expand and to grow richer was impeded by a number of factors, not all of which (far from it) were related to the obligation to make marriages dictated solely by considerations of fortune. Theodore Zeldin has rightly remarked, in his study of the emotional relations of the bourgeois couple, that the romantic idealization of the wife made prostitution even more necessary: the cult of the purity of the young women of that class made them inaccessible. Freud long ago discerned that the two erotic poles of Victorian man—idealization and degradation[4]—were in fact complementary. This is what Jean Borie describes as 'the cardiac rhythm' of the male sexuality of the time—that is to say, the alternation of 'exploits in brothels' and 'angelic, passionate petitions.' This bipolarity tended finally to be resolved, after the experience of a double failure, in an anesthetizing married life. [...]

It is understandable enough that wives' behavior should have led husbands to seek satisfaction outside marriage and, if necessary, with prostitutes. The unequal frequency of sexual desire in men and women, regarded as a scientific fact, justified the existence of prostitution and led to male adultery being regarded as 'a safety valve.'[5] Furthermore, as Theodore Zeldin notes,[6] the conditions of monogamous marriage did not at this time allow the husband to have regular sexual intercourse with his wife. It was, of course, quite common for women to refuse to fulfil their marital duties. In addition, menstruation, pregnancy, and strictures that sexual intercourse should be moderate, indeed infrequent (nonexistent if possible), during the nursing period, and above all the prevalence of genital diseases in women[7] had the effect of aggravating the supposed difference in frequency of sexual desire between the sexes and led to male frustration. Finally, it goes without saying that for all husbands anxious that their wives avoid an unwanted pregnancy, the prostitute was a partner with whom it was not necessary to practice coitus interruptus. [...]

A bourgeoisie that was expanding and getting richer but whose sexual frustrations were intense, an increase in sexual ghettos in which a growing number of young men found themselves trapped, a rapid increase in the number of urban bachelors—all these things helped create a new demand that, it should be repeated, reinforced the demand already emanating from a proletariat of workers living on the boundaries of the city. It goes without saying that this new demand was different in kind; it no longer involved only lodging-house prostitution, the result of a mere demographic anomaly. The transfer of clientele was accompanied by a mutation in sensibility and, consequently, in behavior where prostitution was concerned. [...]

The client, especially if he was a comfort-loving bourgeois, often wanted his relations with a prostitute to be based on the conjugal model, with, of course, the addition of eroticism. He wanted those relations to form a parallel union if he was married or a substitute for marriage if he was not. This explains the increase in the number of kept women, or at least of prostitutes who were 'seen again,' and also the attraction at the end of the century of the *maison de rendez-vous*, where the client could believe that he was practicing venal adultery or, better still, imagine that he was possessing a woman who belonged to a higher social class than his own, to which he could aspire but could make no claim.[8] It was no longer a matter of giving vent to sudden sexual urges. What a male satisfied when he bought a woman whom, in other circumstances, he could not possibly seduce was fantasy. [...]

To sum up: the circumstances had gradually changed; customs and practices had altered; and, in the years prior to the First World War, this process was reinforced by a campaign of sexual moralization carried out by the military authorities. The period from approximately 1860 to 1914 saw the development, therefore, of a new kind of demand for prostitution. The change was more qualitative than quantitative. It was the demand of a different social and mental nature that was to give rise to more conspicuous forms of consumption, forms that were much more open. It was a demand that now resulted mainly from the frustrations that stemmed from the sexual repression inherent in maintaining and diffusing the bourgeois conjugal model. Naturally enough this demand, and the change in socioeconomic structures that gave rise to it, were to determine in turn a development of a corresponding supply; and this was made easier by the fact that the new needs, which cost more to satisfy, now brought considerably higher profits to those involved. Can it be said, however, that prostitutional activity as a whole had increased, as contemporary observers suggested? Despite the obvious progress of unregistered prostitution, and taking into account the decline of the *maison de tolérance*, it would be difficult to prove that this was the case. In sexual matters, the measure of phenomena depends more on the degree of perception and on the fantasies of the observer than on the reality of the facts.

[*Women for Hire: Prostitution and Sexuality in France after 1850*, trans. Alan Sheridan (Cambridge, Mass: Harvard University Press, 1990) 193–4, 196, 200, 201, 203.]

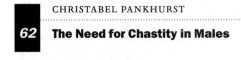

CHRISTABEL PANKHURST

62   The Need for Chastity in Males

This book deals with what is commonly described as the Hidden Scourge, and is written with the intention that this scourge shall be hidden no longer, for if it were to remain hidden, then there would be no hope of abolishing it.

Men writers for the most part refuse to tell what the Hidden Scourge is, and so it becomes the duty of women to do it.

The Hidden Scourge is sexual disease, which takes two chief forms—syphilis and gonorrhœa. These diseases are due to prostitution—they are due, that is to say, to sexual immorality. But they are not confined to those who are immoral. Being contagious, they are communicated to the innocent, and especially to wives. The infection of innocent wives in marriage is justly declared by a man doctor to be 'the crowning infamy of our social life.' [...]

The sexual diseases are the great cause of physical, mental, and moral degeneracy, and of race suicide. As they are very widespread (from 75 to 80 per cent. of men being infected by gonorrhœa, and a considerable percentage, difficult to ascertain precisely, being infected with syphilis), the problem is one of appalling magnitude.

To discuss an evil, and then to run away from it without suggesting how it may be cured, is not the way of Suffragettes, and in the following pages will be found a proposed cure for the great evil in question. That cure, briefly stated, is Votes for Women and Chastity for Men. Quotations and opinions from eminent medical men are given, and these show that chastity for men is healthful for themselves and is imperative in the interests of the race. [...]

The fact is that the sex instinct of these men has become so perverted and corrupted that intercourse with virtuous women does not content them. They crave for intercourse with women whom they feel no obligation to respect. They want to resort to practices which a wife would not tolerate. Lewdness and obscenity is what these men crave, and what they get in houses of ill-fame. Marriage doesn't 'satisfy' them. They fly to women who will not resent foul words and acts, and will even permit unnatural abuse of the sex function. [...]

That immorality causes bodily weakness as well as actual disease is obvious, because the sexual act involves a very great expenditure of a man's energy— energy which can, if it is not expended in that way, be transformed and expended in other ways, either physical or mental.

In support of our contention we may point out that when athletes are in training sexual intercourse, even in the legitimate relation of marriage and in moderation, has to be completely avoided. Considering that a man goes into training with a view to getting himself into a perfect physical condition, the fact to which we have referred is of the very greatest significance. [...]

The doctors inform us that the immorality to which men resort on the pretext of relieving physical distress is, on the contrary, the very cause of that distress.

'Fallen men,' says James Foster Scott, M.D., 'by continual stimulation of their sexual passions with erotic thoughts, sensual conversation and literature, and by the rehearsal of lewd stories, produce in themselves and in others who fall under their noxious influence an uncontrollable passion.' Says the same authority: 'Intercourse with different women is well known morbidly to increase desire.'

Another important statement made by Dr Scott is this:

'The proper subjugation of the sexual impulses and the conservation of the complex seminal fluid, with its wonderfully invigorating influence, develop all that is best and noblest in men.'

'It is incontinent men,' says W. J. Jacobson, Surgeon, Guy's Hospital, 'who are subject to this constant irritability of the sexual organs, and it is they who, from unshunned excitement, must suffer from an excess of seminal secretions and its results. On the other hand, it is the strictly continent men who keep themselves healthily occupied in mind and body, men who, when attacked by imperious sexual desire, simply sally out and seek in exercise a change of surroundings; to such as these the secretion of semen is soon only sufficient to be easily got rid of by an involuntary emission during sleep once or twice a month, a state of things which is perfectly natural.' [...]

To sum up! Chastity for men is not only morally imperative, but is also physiologically imperative. Incontinence on the part of men causes a waste of vital force which impoverishes their moral nature and weakens their body.

Furthermore, the incontinence of men gives rise to terrible sexual diseases, whose victims are not themselves alone and the white slaves whom they destroy, but innocent wives and children.

Chastity for men, far from causing atrophy of men's sexual organs, is the surest guarantee against atrophy. As a high medical authority says: 'No continent man need be deterred by this apocryphal fear of atrophy of the testes from living a chaste life. It is a device of the unchaste—a lame excuse for their incontinence, not founded on any physiological law. The testes will see to it that their action is not interfered with. Physiologically it is not a fact that the power of secreting semen is annihilated in well-formed adults leading a healthy life and yet remaining continent.' Sexuality ought to lie dormant until legitimate occasion arises for its use, when it will be found to exist in full natural vigour.

The sexual power of men has been given to them in trust for the perpetuation of the race, and they have not been faithful to that trust. Says a man who is a doctor: 'The secretion of the testicles is the hope of the future of the race, and yet if wrongfully used it is so potent that it may figuratively be classed with the secretions of the poison fangs of venomous reptiles.'

[*The Great Scourge and How to End it*, in Marie M. Roberts and Tamae Mizua (eds.), *The Campaigners: Women and Sexuality* (London: Routledge/Thoemmes Press, 1994), pp. v–vii, 46, 50–1, 56–8, 59–61.]

II.a.iv MASTURBATION

The third issue that was fully installed in the domain of sexual disorders was masturbation. The first medical tracts relating the grave dangers of masturbation appeared in the eighteenth century. *Onania*, an anonymous British compilation of the lives of men brought low by self-abuse, appeared first in 1710, and the Swiss physician Samuel-Auguste Tissot authored the first medical text on it in 1761, linking it to a host of nervous and organic disorders. The medicalization of masturbation continued throughout the nineteenth century and beyond. The prodigious literature on the subject focused on two chief concerns. First was the fear, based on the lingering influence of humoural medicine, that the body was a self-regulating and closed energy system that could be prematurely exhausted by an excessive loss of bodily fluids. The concept of the male 'spermatic' economy arose from this body of thinking; abuse of this precious resource could lead not only to sexual dysfunction, but more profound psychological and organic problems, including degeneration. Second was the concern, which applied equally to males and females, of a morbid association of sexual excitement with fantasies of an unnatural kind. The danger here was the alienation of the victim from the universe of representations and images that nourished normal family life and civic virtues.

Medical obsessions about masturbation led to intense levels of vigilance and sexual self-observation for the patients of certain doctors, who convinced them that youthful masturbation provoked a vicious cycle of fugitive and partial erections, seminal loss, and impotence. One American physician recorded a patient's record of his seminal ebbs and flows in an anti-masturbationist tract of 1847 (Extract 63).

In the course of the nineteenth century masturbation appeared to pose a threat not only to individuals but to society and even the nation. One French doctor, Dr Claude-François Lallemand, confidently made this connection in 1819, followed later by other specialists whose examination of the problem convinced them of the dangers of fantasy and the unregulated imaginations of children, primitives, and urban crowds (Extract 64).

By the end of the century, though in the name of sexual enlightenment and reform, the neurologist Sigmund Freud was still underlining the public hygiene responsibility of the doctor while repeating the conventional medical pieties about masturbation. In 'Sexuality in the Aetiology of the Neuroses' (1898), Freud confronts directly the growing evidence of birth control (neo-Malthusian) practices amongst the middle classes and expresses a hope that a middle ground between neurosis-inducing abstinence and a wanton spilling of semen might be found (Extract 65).

Bostwick's first supplicant, 'C. R.,' began treatment in December 1845, and, in a remarkable form of those methods of self-surveillance that Foucault described as 'technologies of selfhood', he kept a diary record of his seminal losses, sliding casually in the implied erotic scenarios between the auto- and the alloerotic:

21st. [December]—Excitement—discharge of thin, sticky, transparent, colourless stuff—a few drops.

27th.—Excitement, and drops.

29th.—Excitement and wet shirt—as large round as a half dollar.

5th. [January, 1846]—Dream about daybreak, and loss of semen; excitement during afternoon.

9th.—Met ***. After an hour or so got erection; connexion; she showed every sign of pleasure; I did not appear to discharge, and can't say whether I failed or succeeded, or whether I had pleasure or not.

11th.—Excitement, and drops of semen.

12th.—Excitement in morning; only drops; pain in right groin; it is the left testis that is large; attempt at connexion, and penis got soft under it; a failure. This is the third decided failure, and one doubtful.

14th. Wednesday.—Feel badly; crawling sensation all over me. *** sat on my lap; gave me erections—not firm however—soon subsided; leaked, as usual a few drops; drank brandy.

18th.—Some excitement; felt damp, as usual, about shirt; when I got chance to examine, could see no stain; in fact these drops never leave a stain, or if so, it is very faint.

19th.—… a trace of sticky stuff discharged from penis while at stool. …

25th.—Excitement, and drops.

30th.—Only so-so all day; met ***; a semi-erection; subsided; after an hour or so, by exciting myself got erection; attempt; girl very quick; she gave over, and *then* I had discharge of semen—no jet, more like running from me; saw the semen—looked thick and rich; felt happy, because I can assure myself I have semen.

2d. [February]—… *no discharge* at all; could press out a few drops of thin looking water, semen, or some such stuff as I lose in drops. …

5th.—… no erections; penis a mere pinch—wilted up; after an hour or so tried to excite myself; could not succeed—could only get it a little longer, but not hard; could not get an erection.

6th.—… I now dread I have no semen, and have lost power of erection.

8th, Sunday.—11 o'clock, A.M.; am now writing to Dr. B. I dreamed of many and various subjects last night, or rather since 4 o'clock this morning; on waking, found large and stiff strains of semen; so, thank God, I am not dry entirely, and I may yet hope; parts look small; a half erection on waking; can't call to mind any erection and jet of semen while asleep ... I think both testicles are shrinking and getting smaller ... may they not melt, dissolve, and run from me in drops?[1]

[' "The Roots of the Orchis, the Iuli of Chestnuts": The Odor of Male Solitude', in Paula Bennett and Vernon A. Rosario II (eds.), *Solitary Pleasures: The Historical, Literary, and Artistic Discourses of Autoeroticism* (New York: Routledge, 1995), 176–7.]

VERNON A. ROSARIO

64 Masturbation and Degeneracy

Lallemand had proposed an even more radical intervention—fundamental ideological reform through a return to the 'principles of the Revolution and the Convention': 'It would be necessary to ground the base of a national education on the *duties of the country* towards its citizens, in order to extract from all the *physical, intellectual,* and *moral* dispositions the greatest possible benefit for the prosperity of society, for the happiness of each individual'.[1] Lallemand makes it clear that, by the nineteenth century, the anti-onanism campaign was not simply aimed at preserving the health of individual children but, more important, the health of the state.

The Revolution first made 'social medicine' an institutional reality, and during the Napoleonic period French 'public hygiene' (or public health) rose to world prominence. The new public hygienists argued that the health of the individual body and that of the social body were closely linked.[2] As Dr Julien Joseph Virey stated in his *Philosophical Hygiene, or Health in the Physical, Moral, and Political Regimen of Modern Civilization*: 'We inherit vigor or weakness from the social state; its constitution forms our own, inspires our customs, or deploys our passions.'[3]

It was inevitable that hygienists would also view 'solitary passion' not just as a matter of individual morbidity but, more ominously, as a symptom of social pathology. Alternating their critique between the individual and the social impacts of masturbation, Drs Fournier and Béguin inveighed against juvenile onanism:

Above all it is in young people of one and the other sex that masturbation causes the greatest ravages; it is all the more fatal since it strikes *society* in its element, so to speak, and tends to destroy it by enervating, from their first steps, the subjects who would efficaciously contribute to its preservation and splendor. How often we see these weakened, pallid beings, equally feeble of body and mind, owing only to masturbation, principal object of their thoughts, the state of languor and exhaustion to which they have sunk! Thenceforth, incapable of defending the *nation* or of serving it by honorable or useful work, they lead, in a society that despises them, a life that they have rendered void for others and often onerous to themselves.[4]

No longer was masturbation a devastating disease simply because children were malleable and vulnerable, but, more important, because children were the future wealth of the nation. Fournier and Béguin newly emphasized that self-pollution was not merely a matter of self-destruction but one of social despoliation.

In the nineteenth century, the economy between the individual and the social body was understood to run on the currency of 'heredity'—a biological wealth that was increasingly perceived as a collective endowment.[5] France's vigor seemed particularly threatened given the nation's declining birth rate, which hygienists had noted since 1815.[6] Those who squandered and weakened their seed were therefore viewed as especially noxious to society. Public hygienist Joseph Henri Reveillé-Parise decried the catastrophic effects of 'libertinage of the hand' on social strength:

Masturbation ... is one of those scourges that attack and soundly destroy humanity. ... In my opinion, neither the plague, nor war, nor smallpox, nor innumerable other such evils produce as disastrous results for humanity as this fatal habit. It is the destroyer of civilized societies, and all the more active since it operates continually and saps the generations.[7]

He further warned that pale, nervous women exhausted by manustupration 'could not exercise the functions of maternity,' and likewise, weak, effeminate, corset-wearing men would transmit their masturbatory deterioration to future generations. 'Thus the tree is mutilated right down to its roots,' lamented Reveillé-Parise.[8] Twenty-four years later, he would still be echoed by Dr Debourge, who condemned the 'deplorable solitary maneuver' as a 'potent cause of depopulation, whose effects are all the more fatally disastrous since, although it may not kill, it tends to bastardize, bestialize, degrade, and degenerate the species'.[9]

What emerges from the antimasturbatory literature of the nineteenth century is the perception of 'deviant' individuals as viruses of the social corps—polluting its national strength and purity. Clearly, a profound change had occurred since Rousseau's and Tissot's warnings regarding the corrupting effects of civilization on the innocent, natural bodies of children. By the time of the Restoration (1814–1830), the vector of contagion had been reversed: Reveillé-Parise and other hygienists were denouncing 'mastupratiomaniacs' as the 'destroyers of civilized societies.'

While the condemnation of masturbation had not abated, during the intervening years the dramatic political, social, and ideological conflicts of the Revolution and First Empire had altered the French worldview. Neither the 'state of nature' nor the 'noble savage' were tenable Arcadian fictions any longer. Lallemand, for example, rejected Rousseauvian pastoralism and declared that peasants commonly engaged in onanism as well as sodomy and bestiality.[10] The colonized 'primitives' had also proven far from docile after the Revolution, particularly those of Haiti, where ex-slaves Toussaint-Louverture and Jean-Jacques Dessaline led a revolt that eventually ousted the French in 1803. The Rousseauvian ideal of the Noble Savage, free of civilized, societal constraints, paled further as early-nineteenth-century ethnographers returned from the 'wild' with tales of barbaric 'primitives' who were slaves to violent, natural drives.[11] Closer to home, the once idealized healthy, happy 'productive classes' became the disgruntled industrial workers, and these urban poor, grouped into large crowds, were represented as volatile, rebellious, and primitive masses.[12] Even children, who Rousseau had represented as naturally innocent and good, were increasingly viewed with skepticism and distrust in the nineteenth century. Physicians compared the developing infantile nervous system and moral sense to those of 'primitives'.

[*The Erotic Imagination: French Histories of Perversity* (New York: Oxford University Press, 1997), 38–42.]

SIGMUND FREUD

65 Between Abstinence and Masturbation

Since he has most often to deal with married couples in these instances, he at once finds his efforts confronted by the current malthusian tendencies to limit the offspring of marriage. I have not the least doubt that these principles are gaining ground more and more among our middle classes; I have come across couples who began to practise the prevention of conception as soon as the first child was born, and others who intended that sexual intercourse should accord with these principles from the wedding-night itself. The problem of malthusianism is a far-reaching and complicated one; I have no intention of treating it here in the exhaustive manner which would really be necessary for the therapy of the neuroses. I shall only discuss how a physician who recognizes the importance of sexual aetiology in the neuroses can best face this problem.

Obviously, the worst thing he can do is to ignore it, no matter under what pretence. A thing that is necessary cannot be beneath my professional dignity, and it is necessary to give the assistance of medical advice to a married couple who are planning to limit their offspring, if you wish to prevent one or both of the partners being exposed to a neurosis. It cannot be denied that contraceptive measures become a necessity in married life at some time or other, and theoretically it would be one of the greatest triumphs of mankind, one of the most tangible liberations from the bondage of nature to which we are subject, were it possible to raise the responsible act of procreation to the level of a voluntary and intentional act, and to free it from its entanglement with an indispensable satisfaction of a natural desire.

A clear-sighted physician will therefore take it upon himself to decide under what conditions the use of contraceptive measures is justified, and will require to distinguish between the harmful and the harmless forms among these measures. Everything is harmful that hinders the fulfilment of gratification; it is well-known, however, that at present we possess no method of preventing conception which satisfies all the requirements which may properly be asked of it, that is, which is certain, convenient, does not diminish pleasurable sensation during coitus, nor wound feminine sensibilities. This is a practical problem which physicians might well apply their energy to solve; they would thereby reap great gratitude. Anyone who could fill this gap in our medical technique would be the means of preserving the joy of living and good health for countless men and women, though it is true he would at the same time have initiated a profound change in our social conditions.

This does not exhaust the list of the sources of inspiration which lie in a recognition of the sexual aetiology of the neuroses. The main benefit which we obtain from it for neurasthenia falls in the sphere of prophylaxis. If masturbation is the cause of neurasthenia in youth, and later on also has its aetiological significance in the anxiety-neurosis by its action in reducing potency, then the prevention of masturbation in both sexes is a task that deserves more attention than it has received up to the present time. On considering both the slight and the serious disabilities that have their root in neurasthenia, which is apparently growing more and more prevalent, it becomes evident that it is positively to the public interest *that men should enter upon sexual relations with full potency*. In matters of prophylaxis, however, the individual is almost helpless. The whole community must take an interest in the matter and give its assent to the construction of measures valid for all. At present we are still far removed from a state of things holding out such hope of relief, so that the increase in neurasthenia may quite rightly be accounted to our civilization. There is a great deal which must be changed. The opposition of a generation of physicians who can no longer remember their own youth must be broken down, the pride of fathers who are unwilling to descend to the level of common humanity in the eyes of their children will have to be overcome, the unreasonable prudery of mothers, who at present quite generally regard it as an incomprehensible and also undeserved stroke of fate that 'just their children should be nervous', would have to be met. Above all, popular opinion would have to make room for the discussion of problems of sexual life; it must become possible to speak of such things without being stamped as a disturber of the peace or as a person whose aim is to arouse the lower instincts. And so there still remains plenty of work in this direction for the next century—in which our civilization will have to learn to become compatible with the claims of our sexuality!

['Sexuality in the Aetiology of the Neurosis', in *Collected Papers*, vol. i, authorized translation under the supervision of Joan Riviere (London: The Hogarth Press & the Institute of Psycho-Analysis, 1956), 237–40.]

II.b. The Perversions

The invention of the perversions was not a sudden, but a gradual process that took form over the course of the nineteenth century. By 1890 or so the principal perversions had crystallized into distinct types, each with its own unique symptomatology, archive of clinical cases, and small army of medical and legal specialists devoted to studying, curing, or punishing them. The way in which the perversions assumed their modern forms, and the language in which they were defined, discussed, and circulated in the wider society was deeply indebted to medical terminology and outlook, to clinical standards of pathology and norm, and to a kind of biological determinism characteristic of post-Darwinian evolutionary theory.

However, the society and culture of late 'Victorian' Europe played an equally important role in endowing the perversions with their distinctive features. Although they were regarded as biological anomalies, perverts were also distinctive social and individual 'types' produced in the crucible of urbanizing industrial societies. A dramatic increase in geographical and class mobility had begun to erode traditional class and clan affiliations, and new sprawling cities exposed everyone to tastes, knowledge, and pleasures that were previously unknown or were the preserve of a fortunate few. The consequences of the combination of more individual leisure, the first stirrings of mass culture, and greater personal wealth were discussed passionately by moralists, politicians, and by novelists with a naturalistic bent. Modern individualism was largely constituted in the rich brew of turn-of-the-century culture.

However, the perversions did not have any autonomous meaning until they were compared to the largely unexamined norm of reproductive sexual relations. In itself, any perversion could be considered a 'normal' impulse that, for constitutional or socially determined reasons, was diverted, exaggerated, or weakened in its function. This is why it is possible to speak of the perversions as both social and natural kinds at the turn of the century. Sexologists and psychiatrists described individual behaviour they encountered in their patients and in the society around them, but they used a holistic biomedical language that transformed behaviour into sexualized, natural forms of individuality. The spectra of social and medical variability were thus continuous: abnormality was only a greater or lesser departure from the norm. They were also isomorphic: just as a serious social transgression could spring from a harmless eccentricity, any perversity might become a potential perversion, a perverse individual, a pervert.

However, the ambivalence that contemporary social and cultural elites felt about these developments was expressed in the fascination and horror at individuals who appeared to have wholly succumbed to the polymorphous pleasures of modern life. Egoism was occasionally praised, but most often deplored, and time-worn denunciations of errant individualism took a new turn at the end of the nineteenth century. The sexual nature of individuals was now recognized as a determinative aspect of character, perhaps fundamentally so. This 'sexualization' of individuals was, Lawrence Birken has argued, a new chapter in the history of Western individualism, anchored more in biological science and medicine rather than political economy (Extract 66).

The British sexologist Havelock Ellis underlined both the individuality of human sexuality and its profoundly biological nature in the preface to the first volume of his multi-volume *Studies in the Psychology of Sex* (1899) where he aligns the sexual and the 'nutritive' impulse (Extract 67).

The apparent pluralism and tolerance that seems to be reflected in Ellis's detached and tolerant investigation of human sexual variety must be regarded against the background of what sexual science did *not* discuss at such great length: the norm against which sexual variety was judged abnormal. Arnold Davidson has argued persuasively that the perversions arose as functional deviations from the norm of reproductive sexuality; that is as quantitative and measurable excesses and deficiencies (Extract 68).

The best known of the early sexologists, Richard von Krafft-Ebing, made all the above points in his important book *Psychopathia sexualis* (1886), the first edition of which had all the passages describing genital activity in Latin. In this brief passage Krafft-Ebing distinguishes between (involuntary) perversion and (wilful) perversity, counsels detachment, and makes the point that perversion is an aspect of the 'whole personality of the individual'. As we shall see in what follows, the 'excesses' and 'deficits' of sexual function are transformed into forms of individual perversion that become virtually the 'whole personality' of individuals (Extract 69).

We see how the sexualization of women, children, and perverts appears as the latest step in a long process of democratization which began at the very dawn of Western culture and has been extended by degrees. Sexualization appears apocalyptic because it is symbolic of the extension of the democratic model of society to its furthest limit, a limit that from our perspective appears to be the end of Western civilization.

More specifically, this sexualization takes two specific forms: on the one hand, the recognition of the desires of women and children is symbolic of their emerging individualism; on the other hand, the recognition of the perversions as simple variations is symbolic of the new emphasis on radically idiosyncratic desire which is the basis for that individualism. Something deeply rooted in our culture confers on individuals this right of self-expression. To be sure, in earlier epochs, it was a right restricted to the relatively few. But in succeeding ages, its scope has been extended. Finally, in the course of the twentieth century, desire has begun to replace property as the symbolic badge of individualism. It is in this context that we must perceive a moral basis for the universally experienced but radically idiosyncratic desire that fuels the sexual revolution. The most varied sexual repertoire, the most abandoned promiscuity takes on a positive moral significance, however loath we are to admit it, in a culture in which the desire of the masses is as important as their labor.

Sexualization, then, is the newest phase of individualism. But we have seen that systems of natural law have come to exist in a kind of opposition to the very fields of individualism they open up; they are, in other words, partial reterritorializations, imposing an immanent law in those areas in which transcendence has been banished. In the West, natural law has implied a type of self-regulation apparently compatible with individual freedom. In this context, sexology takes on a particularly titanic significance because it appears as the last line of defense against a universal democratization and dissolution of the social order. Sexology, itself symbolic of the dissolution of holism, presents itself as the final barrier against the disintegration of the last remnant of holism embodied in the family. No wonder the whole 'sexual question' is discussed in an increasingly charged atmosphere.

Against this background, the work begun by Darwin and elaborated by Krafft-Ebing, Havelock Ellis, and Freud more or less centered on the formulation of a natural law of sex. If classical political economy argued that the self-determination of the possessive individual was compatible with a self-renewing (masculine) productive order, the sexual science that emerged after Darwin implied that the self-determination of the genderless consuming individual was compatible with a self-renewing reproductive order that embraces both sexes. In general, by postulating that desire, in the healthy individual, inevitably leads to reproduction, sexology argued that the reproductive order was a self-regulating system. In other words, as transcendence was ejected from the sexual sphere, sexology elaborated an increasingly complex immanent law of sex to replace that vanishing transcendence.

It is not surprising that the sexologists sensed the strategic importance of their enterprise. If the slogan of the political economists had been 'let the economy alone,' the slogan of the sexual scientists might just as well have been 'let the sexonomy alone.' From the end of the nineteenth century, sexologists sought to subject a wide area of jurisprudence to the natural law of desire, thus emancipating the immanent law of sex from a legal system ultimately grounded in the assumption of transcendence. Havelock Ellis thus wrote of Krafft-Ebing that he was endowed 'with the firm conviction that he was conquering a great neglected field of morbid psychology, which rightly belonged to the physician.'[1] As sexology developed, it contrived to decontrol large areas of sexual life. Yet, in so far as it withdrew from the overt regulation of sexuality, the state transferred its power to the plethora of psychiatrists, psychologists, sex therapists, and social workers who, armed with the new doctrines of sexual science, became the engineers of the autonomous 'realm of sex.' Thus Foucault was right in arguing that sexual science was a new discourse of control. But sexology also furthered the very individualism that it attempted to limit.

[*Consuming Desire: Sexual Science and the Emergence of a Culture of Abundance, 1871–1914*
(Ithaca, NY: Cornell University Press, 1988), 12–14.]

HAVELOCK ELLIS

67   Biological Foundations

In this particular field the evil of ignorance is magnified by our efforts to suppress that which never can be suppressed, though in the effort of suppression it may become perverted. I have at least tried to find out what are the facts, among normal people as well as among abnormal people; for, while it seems to me that the physician's training is necessary in order to ascertain the facts, the physician for the most part only obtains the abnormal facts, which alone bring little light. I have tried to get at the facts, and, having got at the facts, to look them simply and squarely in the face. If I cannot perhaps turn the lock myself, I bring the key which can alone in the end rightly open the door: the key of sincerity. That is my one panacea: sincerity.

I know that many of my friends, people on whose side I, too, am to be found, retort with another word: reticence. It is a mistake, they say, to try to uncover these things; leave the sexual instincts alone, to grow up and develop in the shy solitude they love, and they will be sure to grow up and develop wholesomely.

But, as a matter of fact, that is precisely what we can not and will not ever allow them to do. There are very few middle-aged men and women who can clearly recall the facts of their lives and tell you in all honesty that their sexual instincts have developed easily and wholesomely throughout. And it should not be difficult to see why this is so. Let my friends try to transfer their feelings and theories from the reproductive region to, let us say, the nutritive region, the only other which can be compared to it for importance. Suppose that eating and drinking was never spoken of openly, save in veiled or poetic language, and that no one ever ate food publicly, because it was considered immoral and immodest to reveal the mysteries of this natural function. We know what would occur. A considerable proportion of the community, more especially the more youthful members, possessed by an instinctive and legitimate curiosity, would concentrate their thoughts on the subject. They would have so many problems to puzzle over: How often ought I to eat? What ought I to eat? Is it wrong to eat fruit, which I like? Ought I to eat grass, which I don't like? Instinct notwithstanding, we may be quite sure that only a small minority would succeed in eating reasonably and whole- somely. The sexual secrecy of life is even more disastrous than such a nutritive secrecy would be; partly because we expend such a wealth of moral energy in directing or misdirecting it, partly because the sexual impulse normally develops at the same time as the intellectual impulse, not in the early years of life, when wholesome instinctive habits might be formed. And there is always some ignor- ant and foolish friend who is prepared still further to muddle things: Eat a meal every other day! Eat twelve meals a day! Never eat fruit! Always eat grass! The advice emphatically given in sexual matters is usually not less absurd than this. When, however, the matter is fully open, the problems of food are not indeed wholly solved, but everyone is enabled by the experience of his fellows to reach some sort of situation suited to his own case. And when the rigid secrecy is once swept away a sane and natural reticence becomes for the first time possible.

[*Studies in the Psychology of Sex*, i: *The Evolution of Modesty: The Phenomena of Sexual Periodicity, Auto-Erotism* (Philadelphia: F. A. Davis Company, 1919), pp.iii–v. First published in *Sexual Inversion* (1897).]

ARNOLD I. DAVIDSON

68 Pathology and Norm

The *Oxford English Dictionary* reports that the first modern medical use in English of the concept of perversion occurred in 1842 in Dunglison's *Medical Lexicon*: ' "Perversion", one of the four modifications of function in disease; the three others being augmentation, diminution, and abolition.' The notions of perversion and function are inextricably intertwined. Once one offers a functional character- ization of the sexual instinct, perversions become a natural class of diseases; and without this characterization there is really no conceptual room for this kind of disease. Whatever words of pathological anatomy he and others offered, it is clear that Krafft-Ebing understood the sexual instinct in a functional way. In his *Textbook on Insanity* Krafft-Ebing is unequivocal in his claim that life presents two instincts, those of self-preservation and sexuality; he insists that abnormal life presents no new instincts, although the instincts of self-preservation and sexuality 'may be lessened, increased or manifested with perversion.'[1] The sexual instinct was often compared with the instinct of self-preservation, which manifested itself in appetite. In a section entitled 'Disturbances of the Instincts,' Krafft-Ebing first discusses the anomalies of the appetites, which he divides into three different kinds. There are increases of the appetite (hyperorexia), lessening of the appetite (anorexia), and perversions of the appetite, such as a 'true impulse to eat spiders, toads, worms, human blood, etc.'[2] Such a classification is exactly what one should expect from a functional understanding of the instinct. Anomalies of the sexual instinct are similarly classified as lessened or entirely wanting (anaesthesia), abnormally increased (hyperaesthesia), and perverse expression (paraesthesia); in addition there is a fourth class of anomalies of the sexual instinct, which consists in its manifestation outside of the period of anatomical and physiological processes in the reproductive organs (paradoxia).[3] In both his *Textbook on Insanity* and *Psychopathia Sexualis*, Krafft-Ebing further divides the perversions into sadism, masochism, fetishism, and contrary sexual instinct.[4]

In order to be able to determine precisely what phenomena are functional disturbances or diseases of the sexual instinct, one must also, of course, specify what the normal or natural function of this instinct consists in. Without knowing what the normal function of the instinct is, everything and nothing could count as a functional disturbance. There would be no principled criterion to include or exclude any behavior from the disease category of perversion. So one must first believe that there is a natural function of the sexual instinct and then believe that this function is quite determinate. One might have thought that questions as momentous as these would have received extensive discussion during the nineteenth-century heyday of perversion. But, remarkably enough, no such discussion appears. There is virtually *unargued unanimity* both on the fact that this instinct does have a natural function and on what that function is. Krafft-Ebing's view is representative here:

During the time of the maturation of physiological processes in the reproductive glands, desires arise in the consciousness of the individual, which have for their purpose the perpetuation of the species (sexual instinct).... . With opportunity for the natural satisfaction of the sexual instinct, every expression of it that does not correspond with the purpose of nature—i.e., propagation—must be regarded as perverse.[5]

Nineteen-century psychiatry silently adopted this conception of the function of the sexual instinct, and it was often taken as so natural as not to need explicit statement. It is not at all obvious why sadism, masochism, fetishism, and homosexuality should be treated as species of the same disease, for they appear to have no essential features in common.[6] Yet if one takes the natural function of the sexual instinct to be propagation, it becomes possible to see why they were all classified together as perversions. They all manifest the same kind of perverse expression, the same basic kind of functional deviation. Thus this understanding of the instinct permits a *unified* treatment of perversion, allows one to place an apparently heterogeneous group of phenomena under the same natural disease kind.[7] Had anyone denied either that the sexual instinct has a natural function or that this function is procreation, diseases of perversion, as we understand them, would not have entered psychiatric nosology.

['Closing up the Corpses: Diseases of Sexuality and the Emergence of the Psychiatric Style of Reasoning', in George Boolos (ed.), *Meaning and Method: Essays in Honor of Hilary Putnam* (Cambridge: Cambridge University Press, 1990), 307–9.]

RICHARD VON KRAFFT-EBING

69   Perversity and Perversion

In this condition there is perverse emotional colouring of the sexual ideas. Ideas physiologically and psychologically accompanied by feelings of disgust, give rise to pleasurable sexual feelings; and the abnormal association finds expression in passionate, uncontrollable emotion. The practical results are perverse acts (perversion of the sexual instinct). This is more easily the case if the pleasurable feelings, increased to passionate intensity, inhibit any opposing ideas with corresponding feelings of disgust; or the influence of such opposing conceptions may be rendered impossible on account of the absence or loss of all ideas of morality, aesthetics and law. This loss, however, is only too frequently found where the wellspring of ethical ideas and feelings (a normal sexual instinct) has been poisoned from the beginning.

With opportunity for the natural satisfaction of the sexual instinct, every expression of it that does not correspond with the purpose of nature—i.e., propagation—must be regarded as perverse. The perverse sexual acts resulting from paraesthesia are of the greatest importance clinically, socially, and forensically; and, therefore, they must here receive careful consideration; all aesthetic and moral disgust must be overcome.

Perversion of the sexual instinct, as will be seen farther on, is not to be confounded with *perversity* in the sexual act; since the latter may be induced by conditions other than psycho-pathological. The concrete perverse act, monstrous as it may be, is clinically not decisive. In order to differentiate between disease (*perversion*) and vice (*perversity*), one must investigate the whole personality of the individual and the original motive leading to the perverse act. Therein will be found the key to the diagnosis.

[*Psychopathia sexualis, with Especial Reference to the Antipathic Sexual Instinct*, trans. Franklin S. Klaf (New York: Stein & Day, 1965), 52–3.]

The first of the perversions to be widely discussed among specialists was inversion, though not at first or exclusively under that name. The term was widely used at the end of the nineteenth century, particularly in France, England, and the United States, because it seemed to describe exactly the contemporary perspective on male–male sexual attraction in which the sexual was 'inverted' in its normal expression. The German psychiatrist Karl Westphal had earlier (1869) coined the term 'conträre Sexualemfindung' (contrary sexual feeling), which gives the same sense. Earlier still (1864–5), the German jurist Karl Ulrichs had invented a term for men who loved men, 'urnings', or 'uranists', whom he described as beings who had 'a female soul in a male body', and around the turn of the century the German physician Magnus Hirschfeld wrote about a 'third sex' intermediate between male and female. Though eventually 'homosexuality' (coined by the Hungarian jurist K. M. Benkert in 1869) superseded all these terms, this did not occur uniformly until well into the twentieth century.

Leaving aside the older terminology (sodomy, paedophilia) and the rich linguistic inventions of popular culture, these terms all convey the notion that same-sex love involved an apparent disjunction between anatomy and instinct. 'Contrary' instinct contradicted the anatomical semiotics of the body, particularly the genitalia, which historically had been the first and last resort of sex determination for legal and medical purposes. Medical specialists scrutinized the genitalia and the secondary sexual characteristics of patients and sex criminals with keen interest in these years. Though decisive evidence was lacking that inverts of either sex had gross anatomical aberrations, most experts were convinced that tastes and behaviour so apparently at odds with the norm had to have a biological foundation.

However, while experts were willing to concede that inversion was an inherited biological condition, it was common for most doctors to imagine that a pathogenic social environment or wilful vice could also contribute to the acquisition of the disorder. In an era before the emergence of Mendelian genetics, it was possible for the Chicago physician G. Frank Lydston to argue a theory of inverted sexuality that appreciated both the social *and* biological origins of perversion. The genitals were no longer the most reliable guide to individual sexuality, but it had not yet become a wholly psychological phenomenon either. Lydston's eclectic account illustrates many of the themes discussed above (Extract 70).

Despite the linguistic tribute to 'inversions' of the sex instinct in theories of the perversions, the power of the two-sex model of sexuality was such that the earliest medical accounts undermined it in practice. The German physician Albert Moll, whose *Studies of Sexual Inversion* (1891) was one of the first book-length studies of the phenomenon, was convinced that 'uranists' (also 'inverts', or 'psycho-social hermaphrodites') preferred manly men to men like themselves, who were 'really' women (Extract 71).

The same judgements were made about female inverts, despite relatively less medical interest in the female version. In the following passage about medical diagnoses of female inverts in America, 'inversion' did not refer simply to the reversal of the polarity of sexual attraction, but to the whole being of the female invert herself, whose entire nature provided evidence for the condition (Extract 72).

We have some evidence about what educated homosexual men and women might have thought when they read the work of the early sexologists. John Addington Symonds, a distinguished British man of letters, began writing his memoirs at the age of 50 in 1889, at least partly to account for what he called his secret *vita sexualis*. Symonds had married and was to all outward appearances an upstanding example of high Victorianism, but he had experienced homo-sexual cravings from an early age and had resisted them with only partial success. In the following passages, he describes his youthful sexual experiences in the literary language familiar to a man of his taste and class. The only clinical observation is his reference to himself at the outset as a 'somewhat abnormally constituted individual'. Symonds set his memoirs aside for a number of years, devouring in the interim a number of the contemporary medical texts on inver-sion. He then inserted a 'note' in which he ruminates on what he has learned. He does not conclude by acceding to the medical judgement that he was an irremediably unhealthy man burdened with pathological sexual proclivities; he engages in dialogue with these medical ideas, accepting some, rejecting others. But his language changes perceptibly between the earlier and later passages. It becomes more tinged with medical than with literary terminology, and he expresses some satisfaction at having discovered a scientific account of his sexual nature in the writings of Ulrichs. There is a defensive tone here that illu-minates the situation of many men and women whose sexual desires were not 'normal' by the lights of established medical theories (Extract 73).

It is puzzling to the healthy man and woman, to understand how the practices of the sexual pervert can afford gratification. If considered in the light of reversion of type, however, the subject is much less perplexing. That mal-development, or arrested development, of the sexual organs should be associated with sexual perversion is not at all surprising; and the more nearly the individual approximates the type of foetal development which exists prior to the commencement of sexual differentiation, the more marked is the aberrance of sexuality.

There is one element in the study of sexual perversion that deserves especial attention. It is probable that few bodily attributes are more readily transmitted to posterity than peculiarities of sexual physiology. The offspring of the abnormally carnal individual is likely to be possessed of the same inordinate sexual appetite that characterizes the parent. The child of vice has within it, in many instances, the germ of vicious impulse, and no purifying influence can save it from following its own inherent inclinations. Men and women who seek, from mere satiety, variations of the normal method of sexual gratification, stamp their nervous systems with a malign influence which in the next generation may present itself as true sexual perversion. Acquired sexual perversion in one generation may be a true constitutional and irradicable vice in the next, and this independently of gross physical abberations. Carelessness on the part of parents is responsible for some cases of acquired sexual perversion. Boys who are allowed to associate intimately, are apt to turn their inventive genius to account by inventing novel means of sexual stimulation, with the result of ever after diminishing the natural sexual appetite. Any powerful impression made upon the sexual system at or near puberty, when the sexual apparatus is just maturing and very active, although as yet weak and impressionable, is apt to leave an imprint in the form of sexual peculiarities that will haunt the patient throughout his after life. Sexual congress at an early period, often leaves its impression in a similar manner. Many an individual has had reason to regret the indulgences of his youth because of its moral effect upon his after life. The impression made upon him in the height of his youthful sensibility is never eradicated, but remains in his memory as his ideal of sexual matters; for—if you will pardon the metaphor—there is a physical as well as an intellectual memory. As he grows older and less impressionable, he seeks vainly for an experience similar to that of his youth, and so joins the ranks of the sexual monomaniacs, who vainly chase the Will-o'-the-wisp: sexual gratification, all their lives. Variations of circumstance may determine sexual perversion rather than abnormally powerful desire. Let the physician who has the confidence of his patients inquire into this matter, and he will be surprised at the result. Only a short time since, one of my patients, a man of exceptional intellect, volunteered a similar explanation for his own excesses. Satiety also brings in its train a deterioration of normal sexual sensibility, with an increase, if anything, in the sexual appetite. As a result, the deluded and unfortunate being seeks for new and varied means of gratification, often degrading in the extreme. Add to this condition, intemperance or disease, and the individual may become the lowest type of sexual pervert. As Hammond concisely puts it, regarding one of the most disgusting forms of sexual perversion: 'Pederasty is generally a vice resorted to by debauchees who exhaust the resources of the normal stimulus of the sexual act, and who for a while find in this new procedure the pleasure which they can no longer obtain from intercourse with women.'

When the differentiation of sex is complete from a gross physical standpoint, it is still possible that the receptive and generative centers of sexual sensibility may fail to become perfectly differentiated. The result under such circumstances might be, upon the one hand, sexual apathy, and upon the other, an approximation to the female or male type, as the case may be. Such a failure of development and imperfect differentiation of structure, would necessarily be too occult for discovery by any physical means at our command. It is, however, but too readily recognized by its results.

There exists in every great city so large a number of sexual perverts, that seemingly their depraved tastes have been commercially appreciated by the *demi-monde*. This has resulted in the formation of establishments whose principal business it is to cater to the perverted sexual tastes of a numerous class of patrons. Were the names and social positions of these patrons made public in the case of our own city, society would be regaled with something fully as disgusting, and coming much nearer home, than the *Pall Mall Gazette* exposure.[1]

[*Addresses and Essays*, 2nd ed. rev. and enlarged (Louisville, Ky.: Renz & Henry, 1892), 247–50.]

ALBERT MOLL

71   Hegemony of the Two-Sex Model: Males

The normal man does not love all women in the same manner. If his love is profound he feels himself attracted to some women with whom he has relations, sometimes passing, sometimes durable, as in marriage, for example. The same phenomenon exists in the Uranist who very often feels himself peculiarly attracted by a class of men or by a single individual for whom he preserves his passion for years. It even appears to me that Uranists are much more spirited than normal men. In the normal man the passion for a woman can render him impotent towards all other women; the same phenomenon sometimes exist in the Uranist. However, a great many Uranists are rather polygamous: they have relations sometimes with one man, sometimes with another and do not attach themselves for a long time to the same individual. On the other hand, the monogamous Uranist remains a long time with his 'acquaintance' whom he deceives, however, rather willingly when the occasion presents itself. A great many of them cannot have sexual intercourse with other Uranists. I was told that the Uranists know this quite well so that they are often obliged in order to avoid disgusting the man they love to hide their tendencies from him. Frequently a Uranist has relations with men in whom he does recognize the same tendencies as his own; but the moment he perceives his error, whether he makes the discovery of his own accord or whether the man discloses his character to him, immediately all further sexual contact becomes impossible for him. It must be admitted that it is the idea, the representation of man, which excites the Uranist; so that as soon as he perceives the effeminate nature of the man he loves—and the Uranist is in realty nothing else but a woman—all excitation ceases.

It is my impression that the majority of Uranists prefer to have sexual intercourse with normal men. A Uranist confessed to me that he felt himself attracted to men who make love to women but he never dared to propose to them. We have said that some Uranists cannot have sexual intercourse with their kind. These need normal men, and it is this fact that explains the recent development of the masculine prostitution in large cities. To show to what extent Uranists feel themselves attracted toward virility it suffices to cite the fact that they prefer men who possess large virile members. Krafft-Ebing tells of a Uranist who from the beginning could not have relations with individuals having the same tendencies as himself unless they had erections.

The moral possession of the beloved and purely spiritual love are rarely sought by Uranists. But this occurs. The desire of the Uranist meets with considerable difficulties not only because of social ostracism but also because of the fact that the love of a Uranist for a normal man is not reciprocated. The impossibility of fulfilling their desire is for a great many Uranists a source of torment and despair. An old Uranist told me even when the thing appears impossible Uranists always continue to delude themselves and to hope to be loved some day by a normal man.

[*Perversions of the Sex Instinct: A Study of Sexual Inversion Based on Clinical Data and Official Documents*, trans. Maurice Popkin (Newark, NJ: Julian Press, 1931), 96–8.]

MARGARET GIBSON

72   Hegemony of the Two-Sex Model: Females

Given the wide variety of groups and meanings associated with abnormal, enlarged clitorises, the female invert's assumed enlarged clitoris painted a powerful image of her. However much she was lumped together with other marginalized women, the female invert still had a unique combination of sexual diagnoses; her assigned traits were generally shared with other types of women, but the relative importance of each trait varied between the types. The mental and physical masculinity and the hypersexuality of the invert were more heavily emphasized than with the other degenerate and hypersexual women who also exhibited these traits. The cultural meanings placed on the clitoris and sexuality in nineteenth-century America would predetermine many aspects of this new creature, demonstrating the power of such body metaphors and associations.

According to the nineteenth-century understanding of sexuality and genitalia, the female invert was constructed as masculine for two reasons: first, because she was active in a sexual role with another women, and therefore could not be classified as an asexual, 'normal' woman; second, because her clitoris was larger than the average woman's. An enlarged clitoris, threatening to become or be used as a penis, indicated that the invert could not be considered truly female, and thus underlined her essential masculinity. By placing the female invert outside the world of womanhood, doctors maintained the image of the asexual woman. The medical literature supported these equations by supplying ample evidence of the masculinity of the female invert.

Within the category of 'sexual inversion,' doctors often described women in terms of the degree of their inversion, rather than simply whether they were inverted or not. In determining an individual's placement on the scale of inversion, doctors relied heavily on the assumption that a true invert was in some sense masculine—she might merit the remark: 'such a person "ought to have been a man"'.[1] Ellis identified the final stage in congenital homosexuality as 'androgynia ... in which the general bodily form corresponds in some degree to the abnormal sexual instinct and psychic disposition'.[2] Thus, the progression from less to more inverted culminated in a physical masculinization that would embody the masculinity of the sex drive, possibly through genital abnormalities like clitoral growth.

In their case studies, physicians frequently listed evidence of masculinity in clothing, features, habits, or abilities as relevant facts concerning inversion. Well-developed muscles, a 'masculine type of larynx,' habits such as smoking, and a distaste for feminine tasks were examples of such elements in the invert's masculine gender role.[3] Childhood enjoyment of 'masculine pastimes' was a frequent sign of subsequent inversion.[4] Further evidence of the masculinity of the invert was found in the fact that only feminine men would ever be attracted to her, providing the required 'passive' complement to her 'active' masculinity. This last example demonstrates that 'inversion' was not entirely equivalent to the contemporary meaning of 'homosexuality,' but left room for sexual relations with certain members of the opposite sex. Finally, the patients themselves were often said to view themselves as masculine.[5]

Female inversion was sometimes attributed to sexual excesses, in itself a 'masculine' quality, which had led her to ever increasing levels of perversity in order to gain satisfaction. Homosexuality was the ultimate last resort in this hierarchy, chosen when the sexual sense was too accustomed to other stimulation to be satisfied by anything less depraved: 'sexual perversions ... are sometimes... acquired vices being the result of a continual search for new sexual stimuli on the part of voluptuaries'.⁶ As mentioned above, inversion was frequently linked to nymphomania; in some cases there was no distinction between the two in terms of treatment.

In general, the hypersexuality of the invert was uncontrollable and potentially violent—qualities both attributed to male sexuality. One woman was described as prone to 'periodical attacks of sexual furor'.⁷ Other accounts suggested that the invert was possibly in danger of raping others. In one such case, the patient 'attempted to violate a female relative,' while another subject 'embraced the female attendant [in a hospital ward] ... and came near to overpowering her'.⁸ Implicit in the description of such violent cases was the idea of female inverts possessing greater, masculine, physical strength. Another account of a dangerous and corrupting invert described 'a woman who practices orgies of tribadism with other women after getting them under the influence of drink'.⁹ The female homosexual, as a 'female physically but a male psychically,' was out of control, and unlike a 'normal female,' she 'gave in to that sexual thirst'.¹⁰ Once again, the connection between inversion and inevitable criminality and insanity was fortified through the invert's evident lack of sexual self-control.

Such overt masculinity in the female invert presented in medical accounts was further supported by her enlarged clitoris. Clitoral hypertrophy in an invert was not always attributed to a specific cause, and could be congenital, acquired, or possibly both. On the one hand, it could result from lesbian sexual activity involving clitoral stimulation, since 'most organs grow by manipulation'.¹¹ Another doctor argued that 'sexual perversions may result in pseudohermaphrodism,' as indicated by clitoral growth. Women who were not originally pseudohermaphrodites could become so after 'experiments' with 'pseudohermaphroditic' females.¹² This process demonstrates the feared power of sexual activity to alter the apparent gender of the invert and consequently to disrupt social order as well as swell the ranks of inverts through their contagious encounters with 'experimenting' women. On the other hand, some doctors viewed sexual perversion as attributable to genital abnormalities, rather than the other way around. One doctor believed so strongly that sexual perversion needed to have a somatic cause that he claimed the perversion itself was sufficient to prove the genital abnormality, even it if could not be distinguished by examination: genital abnormality 'would necessarily be too occult for discovery by any physical means at our command. It is however, but too readily recognized by its results'.¹³

['Clitoral Corruption: Body Metaphors and American Doctors' Constructions of Female Homosexuality, 1870–1900', in Vernon A. Rosario (ed.), *Science and Homosexualities* (New York/London: Routledge, 1997), 122–4.]

73   The Medicalization of 'Inverted' Sexuality

Containing material which none but students of psychology and ethics need peruse
The plan of these memoirs, which are intended to describe the evolution of a somewhat abnormally constituted individual, obliges me to interpolate a section here which might otherwise have been omitted with satisfaction to myself. When the whole interest of a life centres, not in action, but in mental development and moral experience, truth becomes imperatively necessary with regard to points of apparent insignificance.

No one, however, can regard the first stirrings of the sexual instinct as a trifling phenomenon in any life. It is only prejudice and false shame which leads people to conceal the facts and phases of the *vita sexualis*, so essentially important is a formation of character and determination of mental qualities.

The earliest idea I gained of sex was caught from a coarse remark made by our head nurse Sarah Jones. We were out walking with the nursery-maid and my sisters, passing through a turnstile which led from George Street through the gravel path round Brandon Hill. The sudden revelation that there is something specific in the private parts, distinguishing them from other portions of the body, made a peculiar and uneasy impression on my sensibility—so strong that an image of the landscape, as it was that morning, remains imprinted on my memory: Bristol below, with its church towers and ships, the freshness of the west wind blowing from the channel, the wavering soft English sunlight.

About the same time, I heard much whispered conversation in our nursery concerning a man who stood and exposed his person before the maids at a spot fronting our back window. I could not understand the indignation mingled with excitement and curiosity expressed by the women.

Among my earliest recollections I must record certain visions, half-dream, half-reverie, which were certainly erotic in their nature, and which recurred frequently just before sleeping. I used to fancy myself crouched upon the floor amid a company of naked adult men: sailors, such as I had seen about the streets of Bristol. The contact of their bodies afforded me a vivid and mysterious pleasure. Singular as it may appear that a mere child could have formed such fancies, and unable as I am to account for their origin, I am positive regarding the truth of this fact. The reverie was so often repeated, so habitual, that there is no doubt about its physical importance.

A handsome lad of a full-blown healthy type once masturbated in my presence during the period of childhood. He wanted me to try the game. But though the sight disturbed me not uncomfortably, I shrank with horror from his touch and managed to escape from the room. The attractions of a dimly divine almost mystic sensuality persisted in my nature, side by side with a marked repugnance to lust in action, throughout my childhood and boyhood down to an advanced stage of manhood.

At the same time, I was unfortunate enough to be thrown into the society of a coarse girl, who liked to expose herself and make me touch her sexual organs. It neither attracted nor repelled me, nor did they rouse my curiosity, only they displeased my sense of smell. Once when I found a male cousin of mine preparing to copulate with her, I felt a strange and powerful disgust.

A dirty-minded schoolfellow, when I was about nine years old, initiated me into the mysteries of sexual duality, coition, impregnation, childbirth. This interested my intelligence, but did not affect my imagination. My reveries still reverted to the naked sailors, whose physical contact seemed so desirable. And in all these early experiences, the sex which drew me with attraction was the male.

Our earliest memories of words, poems, works of art, have great value in the study of psychical development. They indicate decisive points in the growth of personality. The mere sharp recollection we retain of certain images is a sign of their potency. Now the first English poem which affected me deeply—as it has, no doubt, impressed thousands of boys—was Shakespeare's 'Venus and Adonis'. I read it certainly before we left 7 Berkeley Square and, I think, before I was ten years old. It gave form, ideality and beauty to my previous erotic visions. Those adult males, the shaggy and brawny sailors, without entirely disappearing, began to be superseded in my fancy by an adolescent Adonis. The emotion they symbolized blent with a new kind of feeling. In some confused way I identified myself with Adonis; but at the same time I yearned after him as an adorable object of passionate love. Venus only served to intensify the situation. I did not pity her. I did not want her. I did not think that, had I been in the position of Adonis, I should have used his opportunities to better purpose. No: she only expressed my own relation to the desirable male. She brought into relief the overwhelming attraction of masculine adolescence and its proud inaccessibility. Her hot wooing taught me what it was to woo with sexual ardour. I dreamed of falling back like her upon the grass, and folding the quick-panting lad in my embrace.

I cannot of course tell what would have happened if Shakespeare had emphasized the fascination of the female instead of dwelling on the fascination of the male. Probably the poem would have made no more impression on me than did the 'Rape of Lucrece' to which I remained indifferent. As it was, I took 'Venus and Adonis' in the way Shakespeare undoubtedly meant it to be taken. And doing so, it stimulated while it etherealized my inborn craving after persons of my own sex.

Character might be described as the product of inborn proclivities and external circumstance. If we regard temperament as one factor and circumstance as another, we must also bear in mind that temperament takes and rejects, assimilates and discards, the elements of nutrition afforded by circumstance according to an instinct of selection. Boys of more normal sexuality might have preferred the 'Rape of Lucrece' to 'Venus and Adonis'. Or, in the latter, they might have felt the attraction of the female—condemning Adonis for a simpleton, and wishing themselves for ten minutes in his place.

I am glad to close this section, in which, after long reflection, I have set down what I know to be absolutely certain facts about the development of sex in me before the age of eleven.

Note to the foregoing section

When I wrote these recollections of my earliest sexual impressions, I was not aware how important they were for the proper understanding of *vita sexualis*, and how impossible it would have been to omit them from a truthful auto-biography. I had not then studied the works of Moreau, Tarnowski, Krafft-Ebing,[1] who attempt to refer all cases of sexual inversion to a neurotic disorder inherited or acquired. I had not read the extraordinary writings of Ulrichs,[2] who maintains that the persons he calls *Urnings* form a sex apart—having literally a feminine soul included within a male body.

It does not appear to me that either Ulrichs or the school of neuropathical physicians have solved the problem offered by individuals of my type. The 'neuropathic grandmother'[3] is too common an occurrence in modern families to account for what is after all a somewhat rare aberration of sexual proclivities; and the hypothesis of a female soul shut up within a male body savours of bygone scholastic speculation.

The problem being then still one awaiting solution, all facts which throw light upon it, especially upon the origination of abnormal sexual feelings, their spontaneity and probable innate character, are scientifically useful.

It is certain that the medical school of theorists would claim me as a subject of neurotic disease. My mother's family on the paternal side (Sykes) was tainted with pulmonary phthisis, and on the maternal side (Abdy) with extreme nervous excitability, eccentricity, even madness. Of four male children conceived by my mother, two (twins) were still-born into the world, the third died of acute hydrocephalus: I, the last and the survivor, suffered from night terrors, extreme shyness, nervous affections, somnambulism; I shunned the society of masculine boys, disliked physical exercises of a violent kind, preferred solitude and study to games, because subject at the age of puberty to excessive involuntary losses of semen, stammered for a period in my speech; in short I exhibited many of the symptoms which Krafft-Ebing and his school recognize as hereditary neuroticism predisposing its subject to sexual inversion.

Still I do not think that the whole tenor of my life up to the age of fifty, which I have now reached, justifies the opinion that I have been the victim of concep-tual neurotic malady. It is notorious that in literature I have done a very large amount of work, not only brilliant, but solid and laborious, which has placed me in the front rank of English authors. My literary achievement is no doubt due in part at least to a high degree of nervous sensibility; and compared with the average of men, I may be pronounced to have exhibited an abnormal strain of nervous energy. This nervousness has been a condition of my performance. But is it either logical or prudent to diagnose so marked a specimen of the artistic temperament as morbid? I leave that question to psychologists, only remarking that it seems to me dangerous to classify poets, men of letters, painters, almost all of whom exhibit some nervous abnormalities, with the subjects of hereditary disease. Here we approach too near to the paradox that genius is a species of madness. [...]

With regard to Ulrichs, in his peculiar phraseology, I should certainly be tabulated a *Mittel Urning*, holding a mean between the *Mannling* and the *Weibling*; that is to say, one whose emotions are directed to the male sex during the period of adolescence and early manhood; who is not marked either by an effeminate passion for robust adults or by a predilection for young boys; in other words one whose comradely instincts are tinged with a distinct sexual partiality. But in this sufficiently accurate description of my attitude, I do not recognize anything which justifies the theory of a female soul. Morally and intellectually, in character and taste and habits, I am more masculine than many men I know who adore women. I have no feminine feeling for the males who rouse my desire. The anomaly of my position is that I admire the physical beauty of men more than women, derive more pleasure from their contact and society, and am stirred to sexual sensations exclusively by persons of the male sex.

Finally, it appears to me that the abnormality in question is not to be explained either by Ulrichs's theory, or by the presumptions of the pathological psychologists. Its solution must be sought far deeper in the mystery of sex, and in the variety of type exhibited by nature. For this reason, a detailed study of one subject, such as I mean to attempt, may be valuable.

[*The Memoirs of John Addington Symonds*, ed. Phyllis Grosskurth (Chicago: University of Chicago Press, 1984), 61–5.]

II.b.ii. SADISM

Cruelty and violence in sexual relations are as old as humankind. It was only at the end of the nineteenth century, however, that sexual penchants of this kind were given a name and made to figure in the list of sexual perversions. The man who gave his name to this perversion was the Marquis Donatien de Sade. Sade died in 1814, but his reputation as a monster of sexual infamy survived in the many novels he wrote exploring combinations of pain and pleasure in sexual relations. Sade himself had a particular fondness for passive anal intercourse, but in his own age he passed for a libertine of the sort that Mozart sends to hell in his celebrated opera *Don Giovanni* (1786): a man who was prepared to take his victims by force if need be and who was indifferent to their age, station, or appearance.

Michel Foucault has pointed out a certain continuity in the modern history of libertinage with his phrase 'Beneath the libertine the pervert': the classic image of a hypersexual male seducing the 'weaker' sex by ruse and force becomes, in the modern catalogue of the perversions, a sadist. As with inversion, the norm against which sadism was constructed was heterosexual love. Heterosexual couples engaged in genital, intromissive sexual relations and aimed, at least in theory, at procreation. As we shall see, the typical sadist was a male who was both more so and less so than the norm. He was *more* violent and cruel in his sexual behaviour, but he was also *less* virile, that is to say, less potent in his [normal] sexual function.

In the following passages on sadism taken from Richard Von Krafft-Ebing's *Psychopathia sexualis*, these basic themes are developed and explained in his characteristic psychopathological terminology. We see here clear evidence of the continued power of the degenerational model of morbid inheritance, a notion of sexual pathology that depends on excesses and deficits in a functional norm, and the reification of what came to be called heterosexuality into an idealized 'kind'. We see Krafft-Ebing's tolerance for the mild sadism of marital sex play shade into horror at the 'monstrousness' of extreme acts of sexual cruelty (Extract 74).

Sadism, especially in its rudimentary manifestations, seems to be of common occurrence in the domain of sexual perversion. Sadism is the experience of sexual pleasurable sensations (including orgasm) produced by acts of cruelty, bodily punishment afflicted on one's own person or when witnessed in others, be they animals or human beings. It may also consist of an innate desire to humiliate, hurt, wound or even destroy others in order thereby to create sexual pleasure in one's self.

Thus it will happen that one of the consorts in sexual heat will strike, bite or pinch the other, that kissing degenerates into biting. Lovers and young married couples are fond of teasing each other, they wrestle together 'just for fun,' indulge in all sorts of horseplay. The transition from these atavistic manifestations, which no doubt belong to the sphere of physiological sexuality, to the most monstrous acts of destruction of the consort's life can be readily traced.

Where the husband forces the wife by menaces and other violent means to the conjugal act, we can no longer describe such as a normal physiological manifestation, but must ascribe it to sadistic impulses. It seems probable that this sadistic force is developed by the natural shyness and modesty of woman towards the aggressive manners of the male, especially during the earlier periods of married life and particularly where the husband is hypersexual. Woman no doubt derives pleasure from her innate coyness and the final victory of man affords her intense and refined gratification. Hence the frequent recurrence of these little love comedies.

A further development of these sadistic traces may be found in men who demand the sexual act in unusual places, for this seems to offer an opportunity to him to show his superiority over woman, to provoke her defense and delight in her subsequent confusion and abashment.

CASE 14. One of my patients, hereditarily tainted, a crank, married to an extremely handsome woman of very vivacious temperament, became impotent when he saw her beautiful, pure white skin and her elegant toilette, but was quite potent with an ordinary wench, no matter how dirty (*Fetichism*). But it would happen that during a lonely walk with her in the country he would suddenly force her to have coitus in a meadow, or behind a shrub. The stronger she refused the more excited he became with perfect potency. The same would happen in places where there was a risk of being discovered in the act, for instance, in the railway train, in the lavatory of a restaurant. But at home in his own bed he was quite devoid of desire.

In the civilized man of to-day, in so far as he is untainted, associations between lust and cruelty are found, but in a weak and rather rudimentary degree. If such therefore occur and in fact even light atrocious manifestations thereof, they must be attributed to distorted dispositions (sexual and motoric spheres).

They are due to an awakening of latent psychical dispositions occasioned by external circumstances which in no way affect the normal individual. They are not accidental deviations of sentiment or instinct in the sense as given by the modern doctrine of association. Sadistic sensations may often be traced back to early childhood and exist during a period of life when their revival can by no manner of means be attributed to external impressions, much less to sexual temper.

Sadism must, therefore, like Masochism and the antipathic sexual instinct, be counted among the primitive anomalies of the sexual life. It is a disturbance (a deviation) in the evolution of psychosexual processes sprouting from the soil of psychical degeneration. [...]

Through such cases of infliction of pain during the most intense emotion of lust, we approach the cases in which a real injury, wound, or death is inflicted on the victim. In these cases the impulse to cruelty which may accompany the emotion of lust, becomes unbounded in a psychopathic individual; and, at the same time, owing to defect of moral feeling, all normal inhibitory ideas are absent or weakened.

Such monstrous, sadistic acts have, however, in men, in whom they are much more frequent than in women, another source in physiological conditions. In the intercourse of the sexes, the active or aggressive *rôle* belongs to man; woman remains passive, defensive.[1] It affords man great pleasure to win a woman, to conquer her; and in the art of love making, the modesty of woman, who keeps herself on the defensive until the moment of surrender, is an element of great psychological significance and importance. Under normal conditions man meets obstacles which it is his part to overcome, and for which nature has given him an aggressive character. This aggressive character, however, under pathological conditions may likewise be excessively developed, and express itself in an impulse to subdue absolutely the object of desire, even to destroy or kill it.[2]

If both these constituent elements occur together—the abnormally intensified impulse to a violent reaction towards the object of the stimulus, and the abnormally intensified desire to conquer the woman,—then the most violent outbreaks of sadism occur.

Sadism is thus nothing else than an excessive and monstrous pathological intensification of phenomena—possible, too, in normal conditions in rudimental forms—which accompany the psychical sexual life, particularly in males. It is of course not at all necessary, and not even the rule, that the sadistic individual should be conscious of his instinct. What he feels is, as a rule, only the impulse to cruel and violent treatment of the opposite sex, and the colouring of the idea of such acts with lustful feelings. Thus arises a powerful impulse to commit the imagined deeds. In so far as the actual motives of this instinct are not comprehended by the individual, the sadistic acts have the character of impulsive deeds.

When the association of lust and cruelty is present, not only does the lustful emotion awaken the impulse to cruelty, but *vice versâ*; cruel ideas and acts of cruelty cause sexual excitement, and in this way are used by perverse individuals.[3]

A differentiation of original and acquired cases of sadism is scarcely possible. Many individuals, tainted from birth, for a long time do everything to conquer the perverse instinct. If they are potent, they are able for some time to lead a normal sex life, often with the assistance of fanciful ideas of a perverse nature. Later, when the opposing motives of an ethical and aesthetic kind have been gradually overcome, and when oft-repeated experience has proved the natural act to give but incomplete satisfaction, the abnormal instinct suddenly bursts forth. Owing to this late expression, in acts, of an originally perverse disposition, the appearances are those of an acquired perversion. As a rule, it may be safely assumed that this psychopathic state exists from birth.

Sadistic acts vary in monstrousness according to the power exercised by the perverse instinct over the individual thus afflicted, and in accordance with the strength of opposing ideas that may be present, which nearly always are more or less weakened by original ethical defects, hereditary degeneracy, or moral insanity. Thus there arises a long series of forms which begins with capital crime and ends with paltry acts affording merely symbolic satisfaction to the perverse desires of the sadistic individual.

Sadistic acts may be further differentiated according to their nature; either taking place after consummated coitus which leaves the excessive desire unsatisfied; or, with diminished virility, being undertaken to merely stimulate the diminished power; or, finally, where virility is absolutely wanting, as becoming simply an equivalent for impossible coitus, and for the induction of ejaculation. In the last two cases, notwithstanding impotence, there is still intense *libido*; or there was, at least, intense *libido* in the individual at the time when the sadistic acts became a habit. Excessive sexual desire must always be regarded as the basis of sadistic inclinations. The impotence which occurs so frequently in psychopathic and neuropathic individuals here considered, resulting from excesses practiced in early youth, is usually dependent upon spinal weakness. Often, too, there is a kind of psychical impotence, superinduced by concentration of thought on the perverse act with simultaneous fading of the idea of normal satisfaction. No matter what the external form of the act may be, the mentally perverse predisposition and instinct of the individual are essential to an understanding of it.

[*Psychopathia sexualis, With Especial Reference to the Antipathic Sexual Instinct*, trans. Franklin S. Klaf (New York: Stein & Day, 1965), 53–4, 56–7.]

II.b.iii. MASOCHISM

As with the term sadism, Krafft-Ebing coined the term masochism after another literary figure, the German writer Leopold von Sacher-Masoch, whose novel *Venus in Furs* (1870) explored the world of sexual domination. In 1888 Sacher-Masoch explained the origins of his obsession with pain and humiliation in a semi-autobiographical fragment published in a French literary periodical (Extract 75).

Krafft-Ebing and other sexologists of his generation could think of no better way to describe this phenomenon than to ascribe it to a pathological 'effemination' in men, inasmuch as the overwhelming majority of their clinical examples were men who humbled themselves in the presence of women. It was thus the 'feminine' 'counterpart' to sadism, in which the typical 'masculine' urge to dominate assumed an exaggerated form. The appearance of both sadistic and masochistic traits in the same person, which Freud and a later generation of sexologists would call 'sado-masochism', was difficult for Krafft-Ebing to understand. In the two-sexed world in which he lived, one possessed either masculine or feminine sex instincts, even if these were inverted from the norm. Thus, in accounting for the relative absence of masochism in women, Krafft-Ebing explained that it was difficult to discover the juncture between woman's natural passivity and a truly morbid disposition to subordination (Extract 76).

Many sexologists noted the masochistic aspect of religious asceticism, and, as with the other perversions, combed human history for earlier examples of the phenomenon, assuming that it was a more or less fixed 'type' that appeared and reappeared through the ages. This kind of exercise is still taking place, though in terms that are less indebted to biological determinism. As Extract 77 suggests, there are some extraordinary echoes of the modern notion of masochism in the religious asceticism of the fourth and fifth centuries, but such a demonstration only serves to draw attention to the differences between the two.

75   The Origins of Masochism

Whether she is a princess or a peasant girl, whether she is clad in ermine or sheepskin, she is always the same woman: she wears furs, she wields a whip, she treats men as slaves and she is both my creation and the true Sarmatian woman.

I believe that every artistic creation develops in the same way that this Sarmatian woman took shape in my imagination. First there is the innate tendency common to all of us to capture a subject that has eluded most other artists; then the author's own experience intervenes and provides him with the living being whose prototype already exists in his imagination. This figure preoccupies him, seduces him, captivates him, because it corresponds to his innate tendencies and mirrors his particular nature; he then transforms it and gives it body and soul. Finally, in the reality which he has transformed into a work of art, he encounters the problem that is the source of all subsequent images. The inverse path that leads from the problem back to the configuration is not an artistic one.

When I was still a child I showed a predilection for the 'cruel' in fiction; reading this type of story would send shivers through me and produce lustful feelings. And yet I was a compassionate soul who would not have hurt a fly. I would sit in a dark secluded corner of my great-aunt's house, devouring the legends of the Saints; I was plunged into a state of feverish excitement on reading about the torments suffered by the martyrs.

At the age of ten I already had an ideal woman. I yearned for a distant relative of my father's—let us call her Countess Zenobia—the most beautiful and also the most promiscuous woman in the country.

It happened on a Sunday afternoon; I shall never forget it. I had come to play with the children of my aunt-in-law—as we called her—and we were left alone with the maid. Suddenly the countess, proud and resplendent in her great sable cloak, entered the room, greeted us, kissed me (which always sent me into raptures) and then exclaimed: 'Come, Leopold, I want you to help me off with my furs.' She did not have to ask me twice. I followed her into the bedroom, took off the heavy furs that I could barely lift, and helped her into the magnificent green velvet jacket trimmed with squirrel that she wore about the house. I then knelt to put on her gold-embroidered slippers. On feeling her tiny feet in my hands I forgot myself and kissed them passionately. At first my aunt stared at me in surprise, then she burst out laughing and gave me a little kick.

While she was preparing our tea we played hide-and-seek; I do not know what devil prompted me to hide in my aunt's bedroom. As I stood concealed behind a clothes rack, I heard the doorbell and a few moments later my aunt entered the bedroom followed by a handsome young man. She closed the door without locking it and drew her lover into her arms.

I did not understand what they were saying, still less what they were doing, but my heart began to pound, for I was acutely aware of my situation: if they discovered me I would be taken for a spy. Overcome with dread, I closed my eyes and blocked my ears. I was about to betray my presence by sneezing, when suddenly the door was flung open and my aunt's husband rushed into the room accompanied by two friends. His face was crimson and his eyes flashed with anger. But as he hesitated for a moment, wondering no doubt which of the two lovers to strike first, Zenobia anticipated him.

Without a word, she rose, strode up to her husband and gave him an energetic punch on the nose. He staggered; blood was pouring from his nose and mouth. But my aunt was still not satisfied; she picked up a whip and, brandishing it, showed my uncle and his friends the door. The gentlemen were only too glad to slip away, and not last among them, the young admirer. At that moment the wretched clothes rack fell to the ground and all the fury of Madam Zenobia was poured out on me: 'So you were hiding, were you? I shall teach you to play at spying.'

I tried in vain to explain my presence, but in a trice she had seized me by the hair and thrown me on the carpet; she then placed her knee on my shoulder and began to whip me vigorously. I clenched my teeth but could not prevent the tears from springing to my eyes. And yet I must admit that while I writhed under my aunt's cruel blows, I experienced acute pleasure. No doubt her husband had more than once enjoyed a similar sensation, for soon he returned to her room, not as an avenger but as a humble slave; it was he who fell down at the feet of the treacherous woman and begged her pardon, while she pushed him away with her foot. Then they locked the door. This time I was not ashamed, and did not block my ears, but listened attentively at the door—either from spite or childish jealousy—and again I heard the crack of the whip that I had tasted only a moment before.

This event became engraved on my soul as with a red-hot iron; I did not understand at the time how this woman in voluptuous furs could betray her husband and maltreat him afterward, but I both hated and loved the creature who seemed destined, by virtue and her strength and diabolical beauty, to place her foot insolently on the neck of humanity.

Subsequently other strange scenes, other figures, in regal ermine, in bourgeois rabbit fur or in rustic lamb's fleece, produced new impressions on me; until one day this particular type of woman became crystallized in my mind, and took definite shape for the first time in the heroine of *The Emissary*.

Much later I isolated the problem that inspired the novel *Venus in Furs*. I became aware first of the mysterious affinity between cruelty and lust, and then of the natural enmity and hatred between the sexes which is temporarily overcome by love, only to reappear subsequently with elemental force, turning one of the partners into a hammer and the other into an anvil.

['Choses Vécues', in Gilles Deleuze, *Masochism* (New York: Zone Books, 1989), 273–6.]

In woman voluntary subjection to the opposite sex is a physiological phenom-enon. Owing to her passive *rôle* in procreation and long-existent social condi-tions, ideas of subjection are, in woman, normally connected with the idea of sexual relations. They form, so to speak, the harmonics which determine the tone-quality of feminine feeling.

Any one conversant with the history of civilization knows in what a state of absolute subjection woman was always kept until a relatively high degree of civilization was reached,[1] and an attentive observer of life may still easily recog-nize how the custom of unnumbered generations, in connection with the passive *rôle* with which woman has been endowed by Nature, has given her an instinctive inclination to voluntary subordination to man; he will notice that exaggeration of customary gallantry is very distasteful to women, and that a deviation from it in the direction of masterful behaviour, though loudly repre-hended, is often accepted with secret satisfaction.[2] Under the veneer of polite society the instinct of feminine servitude is everywhere discernible.

Thus it is easy to regard masochism in general as a pathological growth of specific feminine mental elements—as an abnormal intensification of certain features of the psycho-sexual character of woman— and to seek its primary origin in the sex. It may, however, be held to be established that, in woman, an inclination to subordination to man (which may be regarded as an acquired, purposeful arrangement, a phenomenon of adaptation to social requirements) is to a certain extent a normal manifestation.

The reason that, under such circumstances, the 'poetry' of the symbolic act of subjection is not reached, lies partly in the fact that man has not the vanity of that weakling who would improve the opportunity by the display of his power (as the ladies of the middle ages did towards the love-serving knights), but prefers to realize solid advantages. The barbarian has his wife plough for him, and the civilized lover speculates about her dowry; she willingly endures both.

Cases of pathological increase of this instinct of subjection, in the sense of feminine masochism, are probably frequent enough, but custom represses their manifestation. Many young women like nothing better than to kneel before their husbands or lovers. Among the lower class of Slavs it is said that the wives feel hurt if they are not beaten by their husbands. A Hungarian official informs me that the peasant women of the Somogyer Comitate do not think they are loved by their husbands until they have received the first box on the ear as a sign of love.

It would probably be difficult for the physician to find cases of feminine masochism.[3] Intrinsic and extraneous restraints—modesty and custom— naturally constitute in woman insurmountable obstacles to the expression of perverse sexual instinct. Thus it happens that, up to the present time, but two cases of masochism in woman have been scientifically established.

[*Psychopathia sexualis, With Especial Reference to the Antipathic Sexual Instinct*, trans. Franklin S. Klaf (Stein & Day: New York, 1965), 130–1.]

VERN L. BULLOUGH, DWIGHT DIXON, AND JOAN DIXON

77 Christian Masochism?

It was in the fourth and fifth centuries that the Christian Church changed from being a barely tolerated and sometimes persecuted minority group to an officially established religion favoured by the state. This new kind of status not only resulted in an influx of new members but brought a change in attitudes to many of the more traditional-minded members of the Church, who felt discouraged and even betrayed by the resulting compromises. One result was the attempt by some to escape the anxieties, pains and turmoils of the world in order to remain pure in heart.[1] There was also a widely prevalent belief that those who had not suffered in this world were condemned to suffer in the next world; similarly, any suffering endured on this earth would result in a corresponding purification of the soul in the next.[2]

The consequence was a deeply embedded inclination for masochism, since by suffering one could rapturously anticipate ultimate salvation and the wonderful pleasures awaiting those who suffered. As a corollary those who inflicted punishment or held others in submission, sadists if you will, could believe that they were also doing this not only for the salvation of the person being punished but for their own salvation as well. Once such a mindset became established in Western thought, it continued to influence Western culture; there is, in effect, a continuing progression from the early martyrs to the Marquis de Sade and Leopold von Sacher-Masoch. [...]

These ascetics could endure almost any kind of earthly suffering by contemplating salvation, thinking of heavenly bliss, anticipating the rapturous joys awaiting them in the next world. The result was that many not only took to inflicting pain and suffering upon themselves but went into ecstatic trances by so doing. A good illustration of such a case is Macarius the Younger (AD 394), who spent forty days every year keeping Lent and practising self-mortification in a dark cell in the ground. Palladius, the source of much of our information about these ascetic Fathers of the Church, described these cells as having no 'opening but a hole through which one could creep, for they were made in the inner desert to which no visitors were admitted'. Space was so restricted, he continued, 'that it was impossible even to straighten out one's legs in them'. Even this extreme of ascetic mortification, however, was not enough. Palladius reported that one day when Macarius was sitting in his cell, a gnat stung him on the foot. Feeling the pain he killed it with his hands, and it was gorged with his blood. He accused himself of acting out of revenge [thus killing one of God's creatures] and condemned himself to sit naked in the marsh of Skete out in the great desert for six months. Here the mosquitoes lacerate even the hides of wild swine just as wasps do. Soon he was bitten all over his body, and he became so swollen that some thought he had elephantiasis. When he returned to his cell after six months he was recognized as Marcarius only by his voice.[3]

Accompanying this suffering were ecstatic visions which involved a 'high' similar to what some participants in sado-masochistic activities of today recount. For example, a sado-masochist in 1979, responding to a question as to why anyone would want to be dominated and punished by others given the risks inherent in such procedures, answered: 'Because it is a healing process ... the old wounds and unappeased hunger I nourish, I cleanse and close the wound. I devise and mete out appropriate punishments for old, irrational sins ... A good scene doesn't end with orgasm—it ends with catharsis.'[4]

Similarly, the idea of the Christian ascetics was to rid themselves of their old-style body, transforming their flesh through fasting and maceration until they arrived at a new psychological consciousness which they associated with a deified body and a near-miraculous state. The 'new' body was capable of over-coming the problems of space, of treating suffering with contempt, of passing through the centuries of time, and ultimately of having the substance and power of the angels.[5] Macarius himself in one of his *Spiritual Homilies* put the process simply: 'A Man cannot be considered a saint until he has purified the clay of his being.'[6]

St Jerome (AD 420) described the experience more personally:

There I sat, solitary, full of bitterness; my disfigured limbs shuddered away from the sackcloth, my dirty skin taking on the hue of the Ethiopian's flesh; every day tears, every night sighing; and if in spite of my struggles sleep would tower over and sink upon me, my battered body ached on the naked earth ... Yet that same I, who for fear of hell condemned myself to such a prison, I the comrade of scorpions and wild beasts, was there, watching the maidens in their dance; my face haggard with fasting my mind burnt with desire in my frigid body, and the fires of lust alone leaped before a man prematurely dead. So destitute of all aid, I used to lie at the feet of Christ, watering them with my tears, wiping them with my hair, struggling to subdue my rebellious flesh with seven days' fasting ... and, the Lord himself is witness, after many tears, and eyes that clung to heaven, I would sometimes seem to myself to be one with the angelic hosts.[7]

Masochistic reaction in the Christian ascetics often aroused erotic feeling. Ammonius, for example, who had cut off his left ear rather than leave his desert retreat, was reported never to have pampered his flesh. Yet when desires of the flesh 'rose up in revolt', the good saint 'heated an iron in the fire and applied it to his limbs, so that he became ulcerated all over'.[8] Palladius, the recorder of the lives of these early ascetics, wrote that he himself was often bothered by concu-piscence. He finally consulted with a devoted monk by the name of Pachon who told him that the fight with one's passions was an almost never-ending one and that it was important not to relax or the earthly passions would win out. Ultimately, however, God would help those who persevered and suffered enough over their passions.[9] The faithful came, in fact, to believe that these tinglings of the flesh were put there by God to remind the sufferers that they were not yet quite exalted and to encourage them to continue to strive through suffering to achieve exaltation.[10]

['Sadism, Masochism and History, or When is Behaviour Sado-masochistic?', in Roy Porter and Mikuáš Teich (eds.), *Sexual Knowledge, Sexual Science: The History of Attitudes to Sexuality* (Cambridge: Cambridge University Press, 1994), 52–3, 53–5.]

Perhaps none of the perversions discovered at the end of the nineteenth century so perfectly illustrates the cultural and social influences on the formation of modern sexuality as well as fetishism, which Michel Foucault called the 'master perversion' in his *The History of Sexuality* (1980).[1] The first medical discussions of the subject appeared in France of the *belle époque*, a time and place when unprecedented wealth and a multifaceted cultural life embracing both 'high' and popular entertainments provoked a wave of moralistic musings about decadence.

The neurologist Jean-Martin Charcot and the psychiatrist Valentin Magnan co-authored a paper in 1882 in which they equated an invert's passion for an inappropriate sexual object with the passion some individuals manifested for night bonnets, aprons, or shoes. They theorized that deflections (or inversions) of the sex instinct of this kind were a product of a weakened drive that allowed imagination to intervene and substitute other objects for sexual satisfaction.[2] This weakening, they believed, was a product of the advance of civilization with its hyper-refinement and multiplying sources of stimulation and pleasure. The medical psychologist Alfred Binet was the first to give this perversion its name (Extract 78).

The greatest body of case studies on fetishism was compiled by the German psychoanalyst Wilhelm Stekel. As with Binet, Stekel regarded the evasions of fetishism as a sign of masculine failure, a deficit in the courage required to make 'normal' love to a woman. The notion that masculinity was undergoing some kind of 'crisis' around the turn of the century was widespread in Europe, at least partly in response to the appearance of feminism and the 'new' independent woman. In passages such as the following, Stekel endorses this view in his characterization of the fetishist as a modern Don Juan who by implication lacks the male force and conviction of his eighteenth-century namesake (Extract 79).

At around the same time (1912), Sigmund Freud offered an explanation for what he called the most 'prevalent' form of degradation in erotic life, namely impotence in the presence of the 'normal' love object. Freud has deepened the explanation for such behaviour in males by linking such 'substitute' paraphilias to unconscious impulses to avoid incest with female family members who raised them as children. The 'degraded' object of desire is different from that of Stekel's rose fetishist, but the ultimate cause for the evasive impulse was similar in both cases. This is Freud's accounting for the 'madonna' and 'whore' phenomenon we noted earlier. Freud then goes on to explain how the cultural impulse of 'civilization' to idealize women has given rise to a host of unpleasant sexual disorders (Extract 80).

[1] Michel Foucault, *The History of Sexuality*, vol. i (New York: Vintage, 1980, 154.

[2] Jean-Martin Charcot and Valentin Magnan, 'Inversion du sens génitale', *Archives de neurologie*, 3 (Jan. 1882), 53–60; 4 (Nov. 1882), 296–322.

It was not until 1887 that Charcot's student Alfred Binet finally gave a name to this strange phenomenon. Binet published 'Fetishism in Love' not in an obscure medical journal but in the prestigious *Revue philosophique*, thereby ensuring a broad audience for his synthesis. He set the whole problem of fetishism against the background of cultural crisis and exhaustion. The very appearance of these multiple attachments, he wrote, is the consequence of the unique need, 'so frequent in our epoch, to augment the causes of excitation and pleasure. Both history and physiology teach us that these are the marks of enfeeblement and decadence. The individual does not look for strong excitations with such avidity but when his power of reaction is already in a weakened state.'[1]

Binet admitted that all love was to some extent fetishistic, but he maintained that a kind of 'psychic impotence' was invariably associated with the obsessive attention fetishists paid to a particular feature of the loved one or an article of clothing or, worse still, an unrelated object. Binet agreed with Charcot and Magnan that a 'perverse predisposition' was the 'characteristic fact' of fetishism, no matter what form it took, but he insisted that heredity itself could not explain the particular attachment each fetishist displayed, for the origins of an individual fetish harkened back to some accident in the victim's psychic past.[2] As Charcot and Magnan had done, Binet treated inversion as a fetish, arguing that the only difference between an invert and a boot fetishist was a variation in life experience.[3]

Binet left little doubt that his essay was also a critique of contemporary culture. He cited recent novels where some variety of fetishistic love figured prominently.[4] He scorned the modern fascination for makeup, where the lover fixes his attention on the artificial rather than the real, on the actress rather than the woman who hides behind the mask. True love, he argued, is a kind of symphony, an emotional 'polytheism,' which celebrates all the glories of the beloved, not an impoverished 'monotheism,' which focuses impotently on a single unworthy object. 'Normal love,' he wrote, 'leads always to the deification of the whole individual, a natural enough consideration *given its aim of repro-duction.*'[5]

Other medical commentators amplified these themes. Nearly all the books written on perversions in this era treated homosexuality as a fetish.[6] They also regularly distinguished between the fetishistic and the sadomasochistic perversions as a difference between a *monstrum par excessum* (sadism, masochism) and a *monstrum par defectum* (fetishism).[7] Fetishists and inverts were not truly potent, because their orgasms were dependent on 'abnormal' sexual stratagems and were marked by 'hyperesthesia' or 'irritable weakness.'[8] The criticism doctors leveled at their culture reads like Old Testament prophecy with a twist. Men admired clothes and refinements, avidly sought riches, intellectual emancipation, sensual pleasures, and excessive amounts of food and drink; but they did so not out of sheer unregulated vitality or powerful penchants for evil—the standard Judeo-Christian point of view—but from a kind of weakness in which 'cerebral' stimuli had overridden depleted natural instincts. As the sexologist Charles Féré summed up this outlook, 'The sexual preoccupations [of individuals] are often in inverse ratio to their sexual powers. Nations that perish through sterility are remarkable for licentiousness.'⁹

In spite of the stern tone of some of these medical jeremiads, many of the texts on fetishism reveal an ambivalence toward male sexual aberration that seems somehow more in the worldly spirit of the *belle époque*.¹⁰ Many of them freely admit the fetishistic elements in normal love, and some even suggest the utility of creating fetishes in individuals as a form of sexual therapy.¹¹ Since the line between the normal and the pathological was only one of degree, as we have seen, a passage such as the following on buttock fetishism does not stand as a refutation of the grimmer views on such matters:

Have you ever contemplated at the National Museum of Naples the Venus Callipyge, that divine piece of marble which throws of sparks of life, grace, and love? Is it not the most beautiful, the most lifelike, the most voluptuous, the most desirable of antique Venuses? In the presence of that incomparable spectacle the fetishism of buttocks is self-explanatory, for it is highly unlikely that all the admirers of the Venus Callipyge are sick.¹²

A male point of view is obvious here. It was somehow inconceivable for this generation of doctors to imagine that women might somehow be able to transcend their roles as 'natural' sexual objects and have a subjective orientation toward love (as opposed to mere 'subjectivity').¹³ It is also clear here that the medical theory of sexual fetishism was in a certain sense also an aesthetic psychology. The 'search for beauty' cannot, Binet admitted, be satisfied in the same way as the 'material' instincts (genital, hunger, thirst); it springs from the same kind of cerebral and imaginative condition that drives the fetishist and causes him to exaggerate and overvalue the object of his love.¹⁴ That this thirst for beauty sprang from weakness and decline rather than a healthy vigor is an irony that was not lost on the psychiatrists or the partisans of the decadent movement in literature, with the difference, perhaps, that the latter aficionados of decay relished rather than feared its ultimate consequences.

['The Medical Origins of Sexual Fetishism,' in Emily Apter and William Pietz (eds.), *Fetishism as Cultural Discourse* (Ithaca, NY: Cornell University Press, 1993), 21–4.]

If we study various cases of fetishism we will ever find that the tendency to flee from the female is of the utmost importance. I recall the well-known case of Moll, who exhibited a case of rose fetishism. The man lived in absolute abstinence. He never had intercourse with women and even declared that he was a misogynist. One evening he saw a woman who was wearing a beautiful rose upon her breast and promptly fell in love—with the woman, but primarily with the rose. Secretly he soon engaged himself to this woman, but his desire was solely directed to her roses. He never rested until the roses she wore became his property. He would then take them home, smell them over and over again and thereby sense the deepest raptures. He finally collected quite a museum of roses with a great deal of industry. I wish also to point out that this is a characteristic which we will observe time and again. This collecting of the symbolic objects is what I have called the harem cult of the fetishist. It never is absent in any case of genuine fetishism. It is a characteristic sign of the true bent and is at bottom the symbolic representation of the individual's latent Don Juan strivings. The fetish lover is a Don Juan type or has, at least, secret appetites of this kind. But they are at war with his inner morality. Instead of collecting women,[1] however, he collects fetishes.

Every fetish adept has his harem of handkerchiefs, drawers, shoes, braids, photographs, hair, corsets, garters, etc., etc. Each single fetish soon loses its enchanting qualities as a fetish and the devotee quickly and hungrily finds himself another sample only to drag forth the old one again after a while; all just like a pasha in his harem. There is always a favorite for the moment.

But to get back to our rose fetish. Did he marry the woman whose roses he had learned to love so well that he had become engaged to their possessor? By no means. He did as all fetishists do. He gave some lame excuse for breaking off the engagement, gave up the woman and remained true to his roses. The fetish has fulfilled its duty. It kept the man from the woman and took the latter's place.

But behind this apparent paraphilia there is a secret anxiety.

This man hides between Scylla and Charybdis, between satanical desires and puritanical tendencies. He is a Don Juan without the nerve to commit sin. The female appears to him devoid of any fascination because the seductive qualities have been violently passed on to a small object, the rose. It's no sin to kiss roses. Nor can the rose put his potency to the test. The rose as companion will never force him into the struggle of the sexes, the battle which the fetish lover always avoids.

Now, this also explains to us a form of fetishism which turns out not to be fetishism at all in the sense in which we here use the word. I mean the preference some men have for small, old, crippled, ugly, bent and short women who are cross-eyed and limp; for misshapen creatures, in a word. The famous case of the philosopher Descartes, who was attracted only by cross-eyed women, belongs in this group. I would like at this point also to point out that there are men who choose women who have one leg amputated or who wear crutches. In addition to the well-known and understandable infantile source of these cases (memory of an infantile sexual object), the majority of them probably have another motivation. The man feels sympathetic towards these deformed women. They are not accepted at the full female value. One of Merzbach's cases, of which I shall speak later, corroborates this supposition fully. Destiny had branded them and they are underrated. With such women, it is easier for the man to feel the full importance of his personality, a circumstance which plays a deciding rôle in the business of wooing and wedding a woman. Compared with such half-women, the man feels himself whole. This also gives us insight into the reason why some men are so potent when with prostitutes and such failures with decent women. This type of man so over-estimates the decent female that he feels inferior in her presence and this circumstance often precludes the possibility of any sexual aggression because potency and the feeling of superiority are intimately related feelings. In such cases, then, the man drops to the level of the 'branded' woman, he makes her happy with his favor, whereas *he* is otherwise the one who is favored.[2]

[*Sexual Aberrations: The Phenomena of Fetishism in Relation to Sex*, trans. S. Parker, (New York: Liveright Publishing, 1952), 21–2.]

SIGMUND FREUD

80   Impotence and the Idealization of Women

In only very few people of culture are the two strains of tenderness and sensuality duly fused into one; the man always feels his sexual activity hampered by his respect for the woman and only develops full sexual potency when he finds himself in the presence of a lower type of sexual object; and this again is partly conditioned by the circumstance that his sexual aims include those of perverse sexual components, which he does not like to gratify with a woman he respects. Full sexual satisfaction only comes when he can give himself up wholeheartedly to enjoyment, which with his well-brought-up wife, for instance, he does not venture to do. Hence comes his need for a less exalted sexual object, a woman ethically inferior, to whom he need ascribe no aesthetic misgivings, and who does not know the rest of his life and cannot criticize him. It is to such a woman that he prefers to devote his sexual potency, even when all the tenderness in him belongs to one of a higher type. It is possible too, that the tendency so often observed in men of the highest rank in society to take a woman of a low class as a permanent mistress, or even as a wife, is nothing but a consequence of the need for a lower type of sexual object on which, psychologically, the possibility of complete gratification depends.

I do not hesitate to lay the responsibility also for this very common condition in the erotic life of civilized men on the two factors operative in absolute psychical impotence, namely, the very strong incestuous fixation of childhood and the frustration by reality suffered during adolescence. It has an ugly sound and a paradoxical as well, but nevertheless it must be said that whoever is to be really free and happy in love must have overcome his deference for women and come to terms with the idea of incest with mother or sister. Anyone who in the face of this test subjects himself to serious self-examination will indubitably find that at the bottom of his heart he too regards the sexual act as something degrading, which soils and contaminates not only the body. And he will only be able to look for the origin of this attitude, which he will certainly not willingly acknowledge, in that period of his youth in which his sexual passions were already strongly developed but in which gratification of them with an object outside the family was almost as completely prohibited as with an incestuous one.

The women of our civilized world are similarly affected by their up-bringing and further, too, by the reaction upon them of this attitude in men. Naturally the effect upon a woman is just as unfavourable if the man comes to her without his full potency as if, after overestimating her in the early stages of falling in love, he then, having successfully possessed himself of her, sets her at naught. Women show little need to degrade the sexual object; no doubt this has some connection with the circumstance that as a rule they develop little of the sexual overestimation natural to men. The long abstinence from sexuality to which they are forced and the lingering of their sensuality in phantasy have in them, however, another important consequence. It is often not impossible for them later on to undo the connection thus formed in their minds between sensual activities and something forbidden, and they turn out to be psychically impotent, i.e. frigid, when at last such activities do become permissible. This is the source of the desire in so many women to keep even legitimate relations secret for a time; and of the appearance of the capacity for normal sensation in others as soon as the condition of prohibition is restored by a secret intrigue—untrue to the husband, they can keep a second order of faith with the lover.

In my opinion the necessary condition for forbiddenness in the erotic life of women holds the same place as the man's need to lower his sexual object. Both are the consequence of the long period of delay between sexual maturity and sexual activity which is demanded by education for social reasons. The aim of both is to overcome the psychical impotence resulting from the lack of union between tenderness and sensuality. That the effect of the same causes differs so greatly in men and in women is perhaps due to another difference in the behaviour of the two sexes. Women belonging to the higher levels of civilization do not usually transgress the prohibition against sexual activities during the period of waiting, and thus they acquire this close association between the forbidden and the sexual. Men usually overstep the prohibition under the condition of lowering the standard of object they require, and so carry this condition on into their subsequent erotic life.

['The Most Prevalent Form of Degradation in Erotic Life', in *Collected Papers*, vol iv, authorized translation under the supervision of Joan Riviere (London: Hogarth Press, 1953), 210–12.]

II.b.v. EXHIBITIONISM

Exhibitionism was another of the perversions that was judged to be a largely male disease. Throughout much of Western history not much was made of nudity in general or male nudity in particular. Men and women bathed together in public until plague epidemics forced greater caution upon all, and there was generally little prudishness about semi-public performances of washing, dressing, and excretion. Upper-class male fashions such as the codpiece were devised to draw attention to the genitals and exaggerate their size, and the riotousness of carnival time produced displays of genitalia intended to shock, insult, or amuse. However, the change in male fashions around 1800 from tight breeches to baggy trousers foretold a heightening of the sense of shame attached to male nudity, as did the disappearance of naked male bodies from highbrow painting. By the end of the century, male genitalia were described by Sigmund Freud as the ugliest part of the anatomy, and their exhibition became a pathological act. In the following extract Angus McLaren traces the emergence of the exhibitionism diagnosis and explains why it might have been so widely practised and condemned at this time (Extract 81).

This idea that a certain sort of otherwise sane man—the exhibitionist—might have an overwhelming need to expose himself, which was only taken up in England at the turn of the century, had been first advanced by French psychiatrists. According to Paul Garnier, a medical expert attached to the Paris prefecture of police, cases of such men exposing themselves became so common on the continent in the last third of the nineteenth century that magistrates finally turned for help to the doctors. The result was the elaboration by French physicians of a new psychiatric syndrome. A typical case was that of D——, a forty-five-year-old typographer arrested in 1893. Since 1877 D—— had been arrested five times for exposing himself. He was a dreamer whose unspecified hereditary weakness, which surfaced in childhood, led to his being released from the army. He claimed to have no knowledge of his acts, but little girls told their parents, 'Cet homme m'a montré son devant.' As he suffered on occasions from a mysterious 'mal,' something like epilepsy, the court agreed with the medical expert that D—— was sick and sent him to the asile of Sainte-Anne.[1]

A similar case requiring treatment was that of a young, married worker previously arrested twice for masturbating in front of a girls school. The doctors attributed the man's pernicious habit to his 'bad heredity,' his addiction to onanism, and his having been led astray at an early age by a young woman. Though married this small, weak, naive individual experienced the need to 'se déboutonner et d'étaler ses organes génitales.' It was clearly an obsession. He knew others did not do it, and he struggled against it.[2] A final example was that of E——, a timid thirty-two-year-old knife-grinder, who though illiterate and burdened with an asymmetrical head, had proven himself a good worker and soldier. An orphan, he had been first caught at the age of thirteen masturbating near some women. As an adult he exposed himself to women and children. Occasionally he paid the latter a few sous to touch his penis. The idea of exposing himself, sometimes inspired by the presence of little girls, would come to him while working. His wife could notice the change in his expression. He claimed not to know what he was doing but afterward experienced feelings of fear and guilt. Usually he did not have an erection and was always repentant. His punishments, which escalated from a twenty-five-franc fine to eight days in jail to three months in prison, had no effect. In 1895 he was condemned to four months in prison for having shown his 'verge' to some little girls on the main street of P——, a town of two thousand inhabitants. It was his fourth offense. He left prison on 14 January 1896; on 3 February he again exposed himself and was re-arrested.[3] Such manias argued the doctors, proved the impotency of attempting to deal with perverts via the Criminal Code. These men were not criminals; they were victims of an exhibitionistic obsession.[4]

What did the experts mean by the term *exhibitionisme*? Paul Garnier defined it as 'a sexual pervert obsession and impulse characterized by an irresistible tendency to exhibit in public, generally with a sort of fixity of hours and place, the genitalia in a state of flaccidity without any lascivious provocation; an act in which the sexual appetite expresses itself, and the accomplishment of which, closing the agonizing struggle, finishes the attack'.[5] Dr Charles Lasègue (who in 1873 had also created the concept of the hysterical syndrome of anorexia nervosa) coined the term *exhibitioniste* in 1877.[6] The concept was quickly picked up.[7] Valentin Magnan stressed the importance to the patient of the particular time and place of the act, his struggle to fight against it, and his limited goal.[8]

Who was an exhibitionist? The first point that the doctors stressed was that only men were exhibitionists, an issue to which we will return. The second point was that the 'true' exhibitionist could not help himself.[9] Krafft-Ebing, the leading German sexologist, labeled exhibitionists psychopaths, the majority of whom he claimed were senile, epileptic, and impotent. Modesty and decency were expected of the normal. He who violated decency was either an idiot incapable of moral feelings or a neurotic suffering a loss of consciousness.[10] On the contrary, most experts came to exclude the weak-minded and imbeciles including some who whistled to draw attention to themselves. Also excluded were general paralytics, the senile, and epileptics.[11] The doctors stressed that those who felt a compulsion to expose themselves and achieved sexual pleasure thereby were not just the old and the debauched, the drunk and the mad; they included the married and others who were otherwise 'normal.' The true exhibitionist was silent and repetitive. He was conscious and struggled against his desires but knew he would succumb despite his best intentions. [...]

Sexologists and psychologists advanced their professions' fortunes by medicalizing variations in sexual practices. It would be wrong, however, to imagine that nineteenth-century experts were free, for the purposes of increasing their professional power, to 'invent' perversions at will. The experts, we might paraphrase, made the pervert but not under conditions of their own choosing. These conditions in the nineteenth century were dominated by shifting gender relationships that focused the attention of all members of society on relatively new notions of sexual incommensurability. It is possible, though we can never really know, that this new stress on males being biologically the 'opposite' of females led to an actual rise in the number of men who exposed themselves. At the very least, the new range of 'body techniques' employed by some men in the last century to cloak their physicality in a decent way presumably incited and taught others how to expose theirs in an indecent fashion.[12] In addition, worries about lower-class sexual predators, greater concerns about juvenile sexuality, and a fear of actions that in an urban milieu were not given the innocent gloss they might have been awarded in a rural setting forced a timeless practice on to the attention of legal and medical authorities. Our chief interest has been in the demonstrable increase in the 'reportage' of exhibitionism. Males had no doubt long exposed themselves, but doctors in discovering and diagnosing such acts as psychotic compulsions granted them an unprecedented significance.[13]

The notion that the surveillance of sexuality should be entrusted to doctors benefited the medical profession; what of the exhibitionists? Typically shy, impulsive, and obsessional, they were 'eccentric' rather than psychopathic. They represented a broad cross-section of the population by age and profession, though they were more timid and inhibited than most. One commentator has likened their vice to stammering, not communicating but making oneself conspicuous.[14] Though they were rarely violent or otherwise criminal, exhibitionists were treated severely. In the twentieth century, more men were jailed for exhibitionism than any other crime. Why was their form of erotic enjoyment regarded as so dangerous? A common argument was that exhibitionists might go on to rape their victims. This on occasion did happen, but it was most unusual for a minor offense to progress to a more serious one. In any event the rapist was regarded by doctors as being a more healthy heterosexual than the exhibitionist. The actions of the former made sense; those of the latter did not. Indeed the fact that such men did not seek complete intercourse called all men's virility into question and was what led the experts to label exhibitionism a 'silly' act. Accordingly the man who exposed himself was labeled a pervert; the rapist was not. In England exhibitionists, along with pimps and transvestites, were flogged as being less than men. Those who sexually assaulted women, though they were subjected to longer jail terms, were spared such humiliating punishments.

Which brings us finally to the gender question raised by the doctors' discussion of exhibitionism, an issue that Foucault in his insistence on the innocence of 'bucolic pleasures' completely overlooks. Doctors and magistrates asserted that only men could be legitimately labeled exhibitionists. Erich Wulffen, the German expert in sex crimes, stated in the 1930s that he had never found a case of a woman being tried for such a crime.[15] But this did not mean that the experts believed that women were inherently more modest than men. On the contrary, as Alfred Swain Taylor complained in his recounting of the English law on indecent exposure, the legislation only targeted males. 'It is strange that the law should have confined the offense to persons of the male sex only, for there are plenty of women so depraved that they could easily be capable of committing this offense.'[16] Some doctors also grumbled that it was not fair that only men were labeled as voyeurs and exhibitionists. Émile Laurent asserted that it was well known that menopausal women pursued priests and bachelor doctors.[17] Maids and other female domestics, reported Hôpital, traditionally tried to excite young boys.[18] Voisin informed his colleagues that he even had a patient, a 'dame du meilleur monde,' who in epileptic fits showed her breasts to passersby.[19] [...]

When it came to apply the term exhibitionism in the pathological sense, doctors reserved the label for men. Exhibitionism by a man was viewed by sexologists as a perversion inasmuch as the man—who was supposed to be sexually active—was thereby rendering himself a passive spectacle for the female gaze. Women's exhibitionism, however, posed no challenge to gender norms. They were supposed to be sexually passive and make themselves accessible to the male gaze. Like children they were 'naturally' but not perversely exhibitionistic. For example, in revealing their breasts, argued Paul, women were being true to their role of innocently offering themselves to males. Such exposure was not perverse since it was what women were supposed to do.[20] Ironically this gendering of the perversions resulted in doctors declaring that a man who exposed his penis— presumably the most masculine of acts—was behaving like a woman. In citing the case of the exhibitionism of an American minister suffering from mental decay, a consulting physician could accordingly conclude with a straight face that the vice was to be taken as evidence of the man's 'feminine morbid erotism.'[21] What such commentators were unconsciously admitting was that the purpose of clothing was to accentuate rather than hide sexual differentiation. As Balzac noted, in relating a story of children who could not tell the sex of the characters in a painting because they had no clothes on, nudity could blur rather than clarify gender boundaries.

[*The Trials of Masculinity: Policing Sexual Boundaries, 1870–1930* (Chicago: University of Chicago Press, 1997), 195–7, 203–4, 205.]

Sigmund Freud is best known as the founder of psychoanalysis, certainly the most influential body of clinical theory and practice for the treatment of the neuroses in the twentieth century. It is well known that Freudian theory postulates the existence in persons of a sexual libido that, depending on the experiences of childhood and maturity, could become fixed on 'inappropriate' sexual objects or be expressed in 'inappropriate' ways. The attempt to resist or repress these libidinal attachments could result, in Freud's view, in neurosis, sometimes of a crippling kind. Freud's work and speculations ranged over an astonishing variety of topics, but in the early twentieth century he was best known as a sexologist of roughly the same generation as Moll, Krafft-Ebing, Ellis, Hirschfeld, and others. Though he was not a vociferous campaigner for the legal reform of laws repressing sexual deviance, Freud was perhaps the most revolutionary and progressive theorist among his contemporaries and the one most responsible for helping direct sexology away from its origins in theories of biological degeneration.

The text in which Freud elaborates his most important ideas on the perversions is *Three Essays on the Theory of Sexuality* (1905), a relatively early work in which many of the excrescences of older concepts are still visible. It is worth extracting a large chunk of this text to gain a solid sense of Freud's general theoretical perspective, his style of reasoning, and his powerful critique of the degeneration model. Freud engages here with the work of many of the sexologists of his era, accepting some ideas and rejecting others. Most of the section included here deals with inversion, a common enough preoccupation with early twentieth-century sexology, as we have seen. It is clear that, though Freud is not willing to dispense with the dominant distinction between pathology and norm in sexual matters, he is far more flexible, one might say tolerant, in how he defines it and in the conclusions he draws from it (Extract 82).

In the concluding extract, Arnold Davidson comments on this important text and argues in favour of Freud's revolutionary break with the older form of psychiatric reasoning. Instead of assuming that sexual aim and object were grounded firmly in biological sex, Freud imagined libido as a force shaped by the psychodynamics of childhood. He regarded the genitals to be more important as symbols than as markers of sex; by detaching aim and object from anatomy in this way, he helped invent modern sexuality as a natural category. As we shall see, however, by arguing that one became an invert (or other kind of pervert) rather than being born that way, Freud helped to sow the seeds of a later controversy about the ethics and the possibility of therapeutic 'cure'. Freud was a force for enlightenment and tolerance in his own times, but some of his heirs have run afoul of our contemporary sexual politics (Extract 83).

The fact of the existence of sexual needs in human beings and animals is expressed in biology by the assumption of a 'sexual instinct', on the analogy of the instinct of nutrition, that is of hunger. Everyday language possesses no counterpart to the word 'hunger', but science makes use of the word 'libido' for that purpose.

Popular opinion has quite definite ideas about the nature and characteristics of this sexual instinct. It is generally understood to be absent in childhood, to set in at the time of puberty in connection with the process of coming to maturity and to be revealed in the manifestations of an irresistible attraction exercised by one sex upon the other; while its aim is presumed to be sexual union, or at all events leading in that direction. We have every reason to believe, however, that these views give a very false picture of the true situation. If we look into them more closely we shall find that they contain a number of errors, inaccuracies and hasty conclusions.

I shall at this point introduce two technical terms. Let us call the person from whom sexual attraction proceeds the *sexual object* and the act towards which the instinct tends the *sexual aim*. Scientifically sifted observation, then, shows that numerous deviations occur in respect of both of these—the sexual object and the sexual aim. The relation between these deviations and what is assumed to be normal requires thorough investigation.

Deviations in respect of the sexual object

The popular view of the sexual instinct is beautifully reflected in the poetic fable which tells how the original human beings were cut up into two halves—man and woman—and how these are always striving to unite again in love. It comes as a great surprise therefore to learn that there are men whose sexual object is a man and not a woman, and women whose sexual object is a woman and not a man. People of this kind are described as having 'contrary sexual feelings', or better, as being 'inverts', and the fact is described as 'inversion'. The number of such people is very considerable, though there are difficulties in establishing it precisely.

Inversion
Behaviour of inverts
Such people vary greatly in their behaviour in several respects.

(*a*) They may be *absolute* inverts. In that case their sexual objects are exclusively of their own sex. Persons of the opposite sex are never the object of their sexual desire, but leave them cold, or even arouse sexual aversion in them. As a consequence of this aversion, they are incapable, if they are men, of carrying out the sexual act, or else they derive no enjoyment from it.

(b) They may be *amphigenic* inverts, that is psychosexual hermaphrodites. In that case their sexual objects may equally well be of their own or of the opposite sex. This kind of inversion thus lacks the characteristic of exclusiveness.

(c) They may be *contingent* inverts. In that case, under certain external conditions—of which inaccessibility of any normal sexual object and imitation are the chief—they are capable of taking as their sexual object someone of their own sex and of deriving satisfaction from sexual intercourse with him.

Again, inverts vary in their views as to the peculiarity of their sexual instinct. Some of them accept their inversion as something in the natural course of things, just as a normal person accepts the direction of *his* libido, and insist energetically that inversion is as legitimate as the normal attitude; others rebel against their inversion and feel it as a pathological compulsion.

Other variations occur which relate to questions of time. The trait of inversion may either date back to the very beginning, as far back as the subject's memory reaches, or it may not have become noticeable till some particular time before or after puberty. It may either persist throughout life, or it may go into temporary abeyance, or again it may constitute an episode on the way to a normal development. It may even make its first appearance late in life after a long period of normal sexual activity. A periodic oscillation between a normal and an inverted sexual object has also sometimes been observed. Those cases are of particular interest in which the libido changes over to an inverted sexual object after a distressing experience with a normal one.

As a rule these different kinds of variations are found side by side independently of one another. It is, however, safe to assume that the most extreme form of inversion will have been present from a very early age and that the person concerned will feel at one with his peculiarity.

Many authorities would be unwilling to class together all the various cases which I have enumerated and would prefer to lay stress upon their differences rather than their resemblances, in accordance with their own preferred view of inversion. Nevertheless, though the distinctions cannot be disputed, it is impossible to overlook the existence of numerous intermediate examples of every type, so that we are driven to conclude that we are dealing with a connected series.

Nature of inversion
The earliest assessments regarded inversion as an innate indication of nervous degeneracy. This corresponded to the fact that medical observers first came across it in persons suffering, or appearing to suffer, from nervous diseases. This characterization of inversion involves two suppositions, which must be considered separately: that it is innate and that it is degenerate.

Degeneracy

The attribution of degeneracy in this connection is open to the objections which can be raised against the indiscriminate use of the word in general. It has become the fashion to regard any symptom which is not obviously due to trauma or infection as a sign of degeneracy. Magnan's classification of degenerates is indeed of such a kind as not to exclude the possibility of the concept of degeneracy being applied to a nervous system whose general functioning is excellent. This being so, it may well be asked whether an attribution of 'degeneracy' is of any value or adds anything to our knowledge. It seems wiser only to speak of it where

(1) several serious deviations from the normal are found together, and

(2) the capacity for efficient functioning and survival seem to be severely impaired.

Several facts go to show that in this legitimate sense of the word inverts cannot be regarded as degenerate:

(1) Inversion is found in people who exhibit no other serious deviations from the normal.

(2) It is similarly found in people whose efficiency is unimpaired, and who are indeed distinguished by specially high intellectual development and ethical culture.

(3) If we disregard the patients we come across in our medical practice, and cast our eyes round a wider horizon, we shall come in two directions upon facts which make it impossible to regard inversion as a sign of degeneracy.

(a) Account must be taken of the fact that inversion was a frequent phenomenon—one might almost say an institution charged with important functions—among the peoples of antiquity at the height of their civilization.

(b) It is remarkably widespread among many savage and primitive races, whereas the concept of degeneracy is usually restricted to states of high civilization (cf. Bloch); and, even amongst the civilized peoples of Europe, climate and race exercise the most powerful influence on the prevalence of inversion and upon the attitude adopted towards it.

Innate character

As may be supposed, innateness is only attributed to the first, most extreme, class of inverts, and the evidence for it rests upon assurances given by them that at no time in their lives has their sexual instinct shown any sign of taking another course. The very existence of the two other classes, and especially the third [the 'contingent' inverts], is difficult to reconcile with the hypothesis of the innateness of inversion. This explains why those who support this view tend to separate out the group of absolute inverts from all the rest, thus abandoning any attempt at giving an account of inversion which shall have universal application. In the view of these authorities inversion is innate in one group of cases, while in others it may have come about in other ways.

The reverse of this view is represented by the alternative one that inversion is an acquired character of the sexual instinct. This second view is based on the following considerations:

(1) In the case of many inverts, even absolute ones, it is possible to show that very early in their lives a sexual impression occurred which left a permanent after-effect in the shape of a tendency to homosexuality.

(2) In the case of many others, it is possible to point to external influences in their lives, whether of a favourable or inhibiting character, which have led sooner or later to a fixation of their inversion. (Such influences are exclusive relations with persons of their own sex, comradeship in war, detection in prison, the dangers of heterosexual intercourse, celibacy, sexual weakness, etc.)

(3) Inversion can be removed by hypnotic suggestion, which would be astonishing in an innate characteristic.

In view of these considerations it is even possible to doubt the very existence of such a thing as innate inversion. It can be argued that, if the cases of allegedly innate inversion were more closely examined, some experience of their early childhood would probably come to light which had a determining effect upon the direction taken by their libido. This experience would simply have passed out of the subject's conscious recollection, but could be recalled to his memory under appropriate influence. In the opinion of these writers inversion can only be described as a frequent variation of the sexual instinct, which can be determined by a number of external circumstances in the subject's life.

The apparent certainty of this conclusion is, however, completely countered by the reflection that many people are subjected to the same sexual influences (e.g. to seduction or mutual masturbation, which may occur in early youth) without becoming inverted or without remaining so permanently. We are therefore forced to a suspicion that the choice between 'innate' and 'acquired' is not an exclusive one or that it does not cover all the issues involved in inversion.

Explanation of inversion
The nature of inversion is explained neither by the hypothesis that it is innate nor by the alternative hypothesis that it is acquired. In the former case we must ask in what respect it is innate, unless we are to accept the crude explanation that everyone is born with his sexual instinct attached to a particular sexual object. In the latter case it may be questioned whether the various accidental influences would be sufficient to explain the acquisition of inversion without the co-operation of something in the subject himself. As we have already shown, the existence of this last factor is not to be denied. [...]

Sexual object of inverts
The theory of psychical hermaphroditism presupposes that the sexual object of an invert is the opposite of that of a normal person. An inverted man, it holds, is like a woman in being subject to the charm that proceeds from masculine attributes both physical and mental: he feels he is a woman in search of a man.

But however well this applies to quite a number of inverts, it is, nevertheless, far from revealing a universal characteristic of inversion. There can be no doubt that a large proportion of male inverts retain the mental quality of masculinity, that they possess relatively few of the secondary characters of the opposite sex and that what they look for in their sexual object are in fact feminine mental traits. If this were not so, how would it be possible to explain the fact that male prostitutes who offer themselves to inverts—to-day just as they did in ancient times—imitate women in all the externals of their clothing and behaviour? Such imitation would otherwise inevitably clash with the ideal of the inverts. It is clear that in Greece, where the most masculine men were numbered among the inverts, what excited a man's love was not the *masculine* character of a boy, but his physical resemblance to a woman as well as his feminine mental qual-ities—his shyness, his modesty and his need for instruction and assistance. As soon as the boy became a man he ceased to be a sexual object for men and himself, perhaps, became a lover of boys. In this instance, therefore, as in many others, the sexual object is not someone of the same sex but someone who combines the charac-ters of both sexes; there is, as it were, a compromise between an impulse that seeks for a man and one that seeks for a woman, while it remains a paramount condition that the object's body (i.e. genitals) shall be masculine. Thus the sexual object is a kind of reflection of the subject's own bisexual nature.

The position in the case of women is less ambiguous; for among them the active inverts exhibit masculine characteristics, both physical and mental, with peculiar frequency and look for feminity in their sexual objects—though here again a closer knowledge of the facts might reveal greater variety.

Sexual aim of inverts

The important fact to bear in mind is that no one single aim can be laid down as applying in cases of inversion. Among men, intercourse *per anum* by no means coincides with inversion; masturbation is quite as frequently their exclusive aim, and it is even true that restrictions of sexual aim—to the point of its being limited to simple outpourings of emotion—are commoner among them than among heterosexual lovers. Among women, too, the sexual aims of inverts are various: there seems to be a special preference for contact with the mucous membrane of the mouth.

Conclusion

It will be seen that we are not in a position to base a satisfactory explanation of the origin of inversion upon the material at present before us. Nevertheless our investigation has put us in possession of a piece of know-ledge which may turn out to be of greater importance to us than the solution of that problem. It has been brought to our notice that we have been in the habit of regarding the connection between the sexual instinct and the sexual object as more inti-mate than it in fact is. Experience of the cases that are considered abnormal has shown us that in them the sexual instinct and the sexual object are merely soldered together—a fact which we have been in danger of overlooking in consequence of the uniformity of the normal picture, where the object appears to form part and parcel of the instinct. We are thus warned to loosen the bond that exists in our thoughts between instinct and object. It seems probable that the sexual instinct is in the first instance independent of its object; nor is its origin likely to be due to its object's attractions. [...]

The normal sexual aim is regarded as being the union of the genitals in the act known as copulation, which leads to a release of the sexual tension and a temporary extinction of the sexual instinct—a satisfaction analogous to the sating of hunger. But even in the most normal sexual process we may detect rudiments which, if they had developed, would have led to the deviations described as 'perversions'. For there are certain intermediate relations to the sexual object, such as touching and looking at it, which lie on the road towards copulation and are recognized as being preliminary sexual aims. On the one hand these activities are themselves accompanied by pleasure, and on the other hand they intensify the excitation, which should persist until the final sexual aim is attained. Moreover, the kiss, one particular contact of this kind, between the mucous membrane of the lips of the two people concerned, is held in high sexual esteem among many nations (including the most highly civilized ones), in spite of the fact that the parts of the body involved do not form part of the sexual apparatus but constitute the entrance to the digestive tract. Here, then, are factors which provide a point of contact between the perversions and normal sexual life and which can also serve as a basis for their classification. Perversions are sexual activities which either (a) extend, in an anatomical sense, beyond the regions of the body that are designed for sexual union, or (b) linger over the intermediate relations to the sexual object which should normally be traversed rapidly on the path towards the final sexual aim. [...]

The Perversions in General

Variation and disease

It is natural that medical men, who first studied perversions in outstanding examples and under special conditions, should have been inclined to regard them, like inversion, as indications of degeneracy or disease. Nevertheless, it is even easier to dispose of that view in this case than in that of inversion. Everyday experience has shown that most of these extensions, or at any rate the less severe of them, are constituents which are rarely absent from the sexual life of healthy people, and are judged by them no differently from other intimate events. If circumstances favour such an occurrence, normal people can substitute a perversion of this kind for the normal sexual aim for quite a time, or can find place for the one alongside the other. No healthy person, it appears, can fail to make some addition that might be called perverse to the normal sexual aim;

and the universality of this finding is in itself enough to show how inappropriate it is to use the word perversion as a term of reproach. In the sphere of sexual life we are brought up against peculiar and, indeed, insoluble difficulties as soon as we try to draw a sharp line to distinguish mere variations within the range of what is physiological from pathological symptoms.

Nevertheless, in some of these perversions the quality of the new sexual aim is of a kind to demand special examination. Certain of them are so far removed from the normal in their content that we cannot avoid pronouncing them 'pathological'. This is especially so where (as, for instance, in cases of licking excrement or of intercourse with dead bodies) the sexual instinct goes to astonishing lengths in successfully overriding the resistances of shame, disgust, horror or pain. But even in such cases we should not be too ready to assume that people who act in this way will necessarily turn out to be insane or subject to grave abnormalities of other kinds. Here again we cannot escape from the fact that people whose behaviour is in other respects normal can, under the domination of the most unruly of all the instincts, put themselves in the category of sick persons in the single sphere of sexual life. On the other hand, manifest abnormality in the other relations of life can invariably be shown to have a background of abnormal sexual conduct.

In the majority of instances the pathological character in a perversion is found to lie not in the *content* of the new sexual aim but in its relation to the normal. If a perversion, instead of appearing merely *alongside* the normal sexual aim and object, and only when circumstances are unfavourable to *them* and favourable to it—if, instead of this, it ousts them completely and takes their place in *all* circumstances—if, in short, a perversion has the characteristics of exclusiveness and fixation—then we shall usually be justified in regarding it as a pathological symptom.

The mental factor in the perversions

It is perhaps in connection precisely with the most repulsive perversions that the mental factor must be regarded as playing its largest part in the transformation of the sexual instinct. It is impossible to deny that in their case a piece of mental work has been performed which, in spite of its horrifying result, is the equivalent of an idealization of the instinct. The omnipotence of love is perhaps never more strongly proved than in such of its aberrations as these. The highest and the lowest are always closest to each other in the sphere of sexuality: 'vom Himmel durch die Welt zur Hölle.'

Two conclusions

Our study of the perversions has shown us that the sexual instinct has to struggle against certain mental forces which act as resistances, and of which shame and disgust are the most prominent. It is permissible to suppose that these forces play a part in restraining that instinct within the limits that are regarded as normal; and if they develop in the individual before the sexual instinct has reached its full strength, it is no doubt they that will determine the course of its development.

In the second place we have found that some of the perversions which we have examined are only made intelligible if we assume the convergence of several motive forces. If such perversions admit of analysis, that is, if they can be taken to pieces, then they must be of a composite nature. This gives us a hint that perhaps the sexual instinct itself may be no simple thing, but put together from components which have come apart again in the perversions. If this is so, the clinical observation of these abnormalities will have drawn our attention to amalgamations which have been lost to view in the uniform behaviour of normal people.

[*Three Essays on the Theory of Sexuality*, trans. and ed. James Strachey (New York: Basic Books, 1962), 1–7, 10–14, 15–16, 26–8.]

ARNOLD I. DAVIDSON

83 A New Style of Psychiatric Reasoning

In describing popular opinion about the sexual instinct, Freud's use of the analogy of hunger indicates, as it did throughout the nineteenth century, the functional conception of this instinct. Moreover, just as we should expect, the natural function of the sexual instinct is expressed by an irresistible attraction of the sexes toward one another, an attraction whose ultimate aim is sexual union. Freud's use of the phrase 'popular opinion' can easily mislead a reader to think that this conception of the sexual instinct defines popular as opposed to learned opinion. But however popular this opinion was, it was exactly the view of those psychiatrists, listed in the first footnote of this first essay, from whom Freud says his information had been derived. If the argument of Freud's first essay is that these views 'give a very false picture of the true situation,' then we can expect Freud's conclusions to place him in opposition to both popular and, more importantly, medical opinion. The problem is how precisely to characterize this opposition.

In the last paragraph of this preliminary section of the first essay, Freud introduces what he calls 'two technical terms.' The *sexual object* is 'the person from whom sexual attraction proceeds,' while the *sexual aim* is 'the act towards which the instinct tends'.[1] Freud's motivation for introducing these terms is not merely, as he explicitly states it, that scientific observation uncovers many deviations in respect of both sexual object and sexual aim. More significantly, these are precisely the two conceptually basic kinds of deviations we should expect of those writers who subscribed to the popular conception of the sexual instinct. Deviations with respect to sexual object are deviations from the natural attraction exercised by one sex upon the other; deviations with respect to sexual aim are deviations from the natural goal of sexual union. The remainder of the first essay is structured around this distinction between sexual object and sexual aim, and the central role of this distinction is itself firmly dependent on the view of the sexual instinct that Freud will argue is false. I emphasize this point because one must recognize that Freud's opposition to the shared opinion concerning the sexual instinct is an opposition from within, that his argument unfolds while taking this shared opinion as given. Freud's opposition, let me say in anticipation, participates in the mentality that it criticizes. This decisive starting point, Freud's immanent criticism, will show itself in his final formulations and conclusions, specifically in their ambiguities and hesitations.

I want to proceed by reminding you of the general outlines of the next two sections of the first essay, in many ways the core of this essay. The next section discusses deviations in respect of the sexual object. Under this category Freud includes the choice of children and animals as sexual objects, but his most detailed discussion is of inversion, the deviation to which nineteenth-century psychiatrists had themselves devoted the most attention. After describing different degrees of inversion, Freud argues that inversion should not be regarded as an innate indication of nervous degeneracy—an assessment which was widespread, even if not universal, in the nineteenth century. The overturning of the theory of degeneracy as the explanation of nervous disorders was of central importance in the history of nineteenth- and early twentieth-century psychiatry, and Freud played a role here, as did many others.[2] Indeed, Freud insisted that the choice between claiming inversion to be innate and claiming it to be acquired is a false one, since neither hypothesis by itself gives an adequate explanation of the nature of inversion. Freud immediately turns, in a section both complicated and problematic, to the role of bisexuality in explaining inversion, and I shall not even attempt to discuss this section now. Despite the recent attention that has been given to the notion of bisexuality in the development of Freud's early psychoanalytic thought, his remarks in this section become more and more puzzling the more carefully they are studied.

Freud next describes the characteristics of the sexual object and sexual aims of inverts and ends this whole section on deviations in respect of the sexual object with an extraordinary conclusion, a conclusion more innovative, even revolutionary, than I suspect he was able to recognize.

It has been brought to our notice that we have been in the habit of regarding the connection between the sexual instinct and the sexual object as more intimate than it in fact is. Experience of the cases that are considered abnormal has shown us that in them the sexual instinct and the sexual object are merely soldered together—a fact which we have been in danger of overlooking in consequence of the uniformity of the normal picture, where the object appears to form part and parcel of the instinct. We are thus warned to loosen the bond that exists in our thought between instinct and object. It seems probable that the sexual instinct is in the first instance independent of its object; nor is its origin likely to be due to its object's attractions.[3]

In the nineteenth-century psychiatric theories that preceded Freud, both a specific object and a specific aim formed part and parcel of the instinct. The nature of the sexual instinct manifested itself, as I have said, in an attraction to members of the opposite sex and in a desire for genital intercourse with them. Thus, inversion was one unnatural functional deviation of the sexual instinct, a deviation in which the natural object of this instinct did not exert its proper attraction. By claiming, in effect, that there is no natural object of the sexual instinct, that the sexual object and sexual instinct are merely soldered together, Freud dealt a conceptually devastating blow to the entire structure of nineteenth-century theories of sexual psychopathology. In order to show that inversion was a real functional deviation and not merely a statistical abnormality without genuine pathological significance, one had to conceive of the 'normal' object of the instinct as part of the very content of the instinct itself. If the object is not internal to the instinct, then there can be no instrinsic clinico-pathological meaning to the fact that the instinct can become attached to an inverted object. The distinction between normal and inverted object will not then coincide with the division between the natural and the unnatural, itself a division between the normal and the pathological. Since the nature of the instinct, according to Freud, has no special bond with any particular kind of object, we seem forced to conclude that the supposed deviation of inversion is no more than a mere difference. Indeed, Freud's language is indicative of the force of this conclusion. He says, 'Experience of the cases that are *considered* abnormal,' thus qualifying 'abnormal' in a rhetorically revealing manner.[4] These cases of inversion are *considered* abnormal because of a certain conception of the sexual instinct in which one kind of object is a natural part of the instinct itself. Unhinged from this conception, these cases cannot be considered pathological, cannot instantiate the concept of abnormality employed by Krafft-Ebing, Moll, and others. I think what we ought to conclude, given the logic of Freud's argument and his radically new conceptualization in this paragraph, is precisely that cases of inversion can no longer be considered pathologically abnormal.

In light of these remarks, I think that we can conclude further that Freud operates with a concept of the sexual instinct different from that of his contemporaries, or, better yet, that he does not employ the concept of the sexual instinct in his theory of sexuality. What is at issue here is not Freud's choice of words. Commentators are forever remarking that English-reading readers of Freud are led astray by the translation of *Trieb* as 'instinct,' since *Trieb* is better translated by 'drive,' reserving 'instinct' for *Instinkt*.[5] However, since many of Freud's contemporaries, among them, Krafft-Ebing, used *Trieb*, Freud's terminology did not constitute a break with previously established terminology. It is not the introduction of a new word that signals Freud's originality but rather the fact that *Sexualtrieb* is not the same concept as that of the sexual instinct. We can see this, to reiterate my main point, by recognizing that Freud's conclusion is explicitly and directly opposed to any conclusion that could be drawn by using the concept of the sexual instinct. The relationship between the concepts of *sexual instinct* and *sexual object* found in nineteenth-century texts, a rule of combination partially constitutive of the concept of the sexual instinct, was completely undermined by Freud, and as a consequence of this cutting away of old foundations, inversion could not be thought of as an unnatural functional deviation of the sexual instinct. That *Sexualtrieb* is not the same as sexual instinct is shown by the fact that the concept of sexual instinct played a very specific role in a highly structured, role-governed, conceptual space, a space within which psychiatric theories of sexuality had operated since about 1870.

['How to Do the History of Psychoanalysis: A Reading of Freud's *Three Essays on the Theory of Sexuality*,' *Critical Inquiry* (Winter 1987), 263–6.]

II.b.vii. HETEROSEXUALITY

This concept also emerged at about the same time that the perversions were being catalogued. Indeed, it might be argued that, initially, heterosexuality was itself a perversion in which individuals of different sexes engaged in non-procreative sex for pleasure alone. Indeed, the term 'heterosexual' first appeared in America in an 1892 article by the psychiatrist James G. Kiernan to characterize those guilty of 'reproductive deviance'. The first American translation of Krafft-Ebing's *Psychopathia sexualis* appeared the following year and introduced Americans to the notion of 'opposite' sex perversion under the rubric of the hyphenated 'hetero-sexual' (Extract 84).

As George Chauncey has argued, also from the American context, it is not sufficient to consider the appearance of a new category of behaviour—any behaviour—as an invention of medical experts alone. There are invariably parallel changes taking place in society itself that prepare the way for these linguistic innovations and serve as their referents when they begin to circulate as discourse. He posits the existence of a reciprocal relationship between social and cultural causation which aligns words and things until they have a kind of visible substantiality. In this case, Chauncey traces the social and the linguistic dialectic that gave rise to the homosexual/heterosexual binary at the beginning of the twentieth century (Extract 85).

In the heat of different-sex lust, declares Krafft-Ebing, men and women are not usually thinking of baby making: 'In sexual love the real purpose of the instinct, the propagation of the species, does not enter into consciousness.'[1] An unconscious procreative 'purpose' informs his idea of 'sexual love.' His sexual instinct is a predisposition with a built-in reproductive aim. That instinct is procreative—whatever the men and women engaged in heterosexual acts are busily desiring. Placing the reproductive aside in the unconscious, Krafft-Ebing created a small, obscure space in which a new pleasure norm began to grow.

Krafft-Ebing's procreative, sex-differentiated, and erotic 'sexual instinct' was present by definition in his term *hetero-sexual*—his book introduced that word to many Americans. A hyphen between Krafft-Ebing's 'hetero' and 'sexual' newly spliced sex-difference and eroticism to constitute a pleasure defined explicitly by the different sexes of its parties. His hetero-sexual, unlike Kiernan's, does not desire two sexes, only one, different, sex.

Krafft-Ebing's term *hetero-sexual* makes no *explicit* reference to reproduction, though it always *implicitly* includes reproductive desire. Always, therefore, his hetero-sexual implicitly signifies erotic normality. His twin term, *homo-sexual*, always signifies a same-sex desire, pathological because non-reproductive.

Contrary to Kiernan's earlier attribution, Krafft-Ebing consistently uses hetero-sexual to mean normal sex. In contrast, for Kiernan, and some other late-nineteenth- and early-twentieth-century sexologists, a simple reproductive standard was absolute: The hetero-sexuals in Krafft-Ebing's test appeared guilty of procreative ambiguity, thus of perversion.

These distinctions between sexual terms and definitions are historically important, but complex, and may be difficult for us to grasp. Our own society's particular, dominant heterosexual norm also helps to cloud our minds to other ways of categorizing.

Readers such as Dr Kiernan might also understand Krafft-Ebing's hetero-sexuals to be perverts by association. For the word *hetero-sexual*, though signifying normality, appears often in the Viennese doctor's book linked with the non-procreative perverse—coupled with 'contrary sexual instinct,' 'psychical hermaphroditism,' 'homo-sexuality,' and 'fetichism.'

For example, Krafft-Ebing's first use of 'hetero-sexual' occurs in a discussion of several case histories of 'hetero- and homo-sexuality' in which 'a certain kind of attire becomes a fetich.'[2] The hetero-sexual premieres, with the homo-sexual as clothes fetishist.

The second hetero-sexual introduced has a 'handkerchief fetich.' Krafft-Ebing quotes a report on 'this impulse in hetero-sexual individuals' by Dr Albert

Moll, another influential early sexologist. The Victorian lady's handkerchief apparently packed an erotic wallop for a number of that era's men. An intense attraction to ladies' hankies might, it seems, even temporarily undermine patriarchal power. A 'passion for [women's] handkerchiefs may go so far that the man is entirely under their [women's] control,' Dr Moll warns his endangered fellows.

This reversal of the customary male–female power relationship might not be displeasing to the Victorian woman who found herself—and her hanky—the object of a male fetishist's interest. Moll quotes such a woman:

'I know a certain gentleman, and when I see him at a distance I only need to draw out my handkerchief so that it peeps out of my pocket, and I am certain that he will follow me as a dog follows its master. Go where I please, this gentleman will follow me. He may be riding in a carriage or engaged in important business, and yet, when he sees my handkerchief he drops everything in order to follow me,—i.e., my handkerchief.'³

In the above examples, the term *hetero-sexual* signifies a normal different-sex eroticism, though associated closely with fetishism and the nonprocreative perverse.

[*The Invention of Heterosexuality* (New York: Dutton Books, 1995), 21–3.]

GEORGE CHAUNCEY
....

85   The Invention of Heterosexuality

As a number of historians have recently shown, young men in the first two-thirds of the nineteenth century frequently slept together and felt free to express their passionate love for each other. 'Warmth [sometimes] turned into tender attachment, and closeness became romance,' writes Anthony Rotundo, who has studied the diaries of dozens of nineteenth-century middle-class men. 'These ardent relationships were common' and 'socially acceptable.' Devoted male friends opened letters to each other with greetings like 'Lovely Boy' and 'Dearly Beloved'; they kissed and caressed one another; and, as in the case of Joshua Stead and the bachelor lawyer Abraham Lincoln, they sometimes shared the same bed for years. Some men explicitly commented that they felt the same sort of love for both men and women. 'All I know,' wrote one man quoted by Rotundo, 'is that there are three persons in this world whom I have loved, and those are, Julia, John, and Anthony. Dear, beloved trio.' It was only in the late nineteenth century that such love for other men became suspect, as men began to worry that it contained an unwholesome, distinctly homosexual element.¹

As Rotundo, Donald Yacovone, and other historians have argued, the men involved in such same-sex relationships should not retrospectively be classified as homosexual, since no concept of the homosexual existed in their culture and they did not organize their emotional lives *as* homosexuals; many of them were also on intimate terms with women and went on to marry. Nonetheless, the same historians persist in calling such men heterosexual, as if that concept *did* exist in the early nineteenth century.[2] In doing so they mistake the fact that men who passionately and physically expressed their love for other men were considered *normal* for their having been considered *heterosexual*, as if it were not the very inconsistency of their emotional lives with contemporary models of heterosexuality that made them seem curious to historians in the first place. If homosexuality did not exist in the early nineteenth century, then neither did heterosexuality, for each category depends for its existence on the other. The very capacity of men to shift between male and female love objects demonstrates that a different sexual regime governed their emotions. 'Normal' men only became 'heterosexual' men in the late nineteenth century, when they began to make their 'normalcy' contingent on their renunciation of such intimacies with men. They became heterosexuals, that is, only when they defined themselves and organized their affective and physical relations to exclude any sentiments or behaviour that might be marked as homosexual.

A second sign of the emergence of heterosexuality in middle-class culture at the turn of the century was its appearance in middle-class medical discourse. Doctors approached the issue of sexual inversion as members of a profession still struggling to secure a measure of cultural authority and power, and one that often sought to do so by claiming special expertise in the management of 'problems' that had been defined by middle-class men as a whole, including the problem of gender. They also approached the issue as members of a professional class whose manliness seemed increasingly in question and for whom such problems were palpable. Although they claimed a unique, dispassionate perspective on the problem of sexual inversion and their thought had a distinct disciplinary cast, they shared the basic presumptions and anxieties of their gender and class. [...]

Women who challenged the sanctity of the male sphere were subject to particular scorn by physicians, who stigmatized them as biological misfits and inverts. In a direct attack on women who sought to curtail male sexual prerogatives, one doctor characterized them in 1916 as lesbian predators. 'The androphobia [fear and hatred of men], so to speak, of the deeply ingrained sex invert has led to her leadership in social purity movements and a failure to recognize inversion,' he warned. 'Such inverts see no harm in [the] seduction of young girls while dilating on the impurity of even marital coitus.'[3] The same doctor's comments on the work of another doctor suggest how frequently a link between sexual inversion and women's activism was proposed. 'As might be expected,' he wrote in 1914, 'Claiborne does not finish his paper [nominally on unusual hair growth in women] without touching upon the influence of defective sexuality in women upon political questions. While, of course, he does not think every suffragist an invert, yet he does believe that the very fact that women in general of today are more and more deeply invading man's sphere is indicative of a certain impelling force within them.'⁴ Other doctors were less restrained in proposing a literally organic relationship between the women's movement and lesbianism. Dr William Lee Howard warned in 1900 that

the female possessed of masculine ideas of independence; the viragint who would sit in the public highways and lift up her pseudo-virile voice, proclaiming her sole right to decide questions of war or religion, or the value of celibacy and the curse of women's impurity, and that disgusting anti-social being, the female sexual pervert, are simply different degrees of the same class—degenerates.

By this account, the woman who 'invaded man's sphere' was likely to want the vote, have excessive, malelike body hair, smoke cigars, be able to whistle, and take female lovers.⁵

Doctors' analysis of the character of men involved in same-sex relations was somewhat more complex. They sought to explain—and at once stigmatize and contain—the unmanly behavior of some men by pointing to biological defects that made those men literally less than men. They were less sure how to deal with manly men who had sex with other men, however. While many of them reproduced the popular distinction between fairies and trade, they also displayed a distinctly middle-class hostility toward men in the trade category. Many doctors writing in the late nineteenth and early twentieth centuries regarded the fairy as an 'intermediate sex' between men and women, but they also believed that many men engaged in homosexual activity without being inverts. A 'fairy,' they thought, like a woman, was 'naturally' attracted to his opposite, a conventionally masculine 'normal' man, and weak-willed 'normal' men were capable of responding to his advances. They frequently distinguished the two participants in such a relationship as 'inverts' (who, as feminine in character, were naturally attracted to men) and 'perverts' (who, as conventionally masculine men, perverted their normal sexual drive when they responded to the advances of someone who appeared anatomically to be another man, even if that person was actually an invert). While working-class sexual ideology tended to regard men who were trade neutrally, middle-class physicians were more likely to condemn the fairy's masculine partner as morally—if not physiologically—deficient, as the very term *pervert* implies.

In 1921, for instance, Dr Perry Lichtenstein drew such distinctions in a report based on his study of hundreds of men segregated in the homosexual ward of the New York City penitentiary, where he worked as a physician. The fairies he dealt with there were 'freak[s] of nature who in every way attempt to imitate woman,' he explained. 'They take feminine names, use perfume and dainty stationery which frequently is scented, and in many instances wear women's apparel.' Lichtenstein implied that the fairies did not solicit sex with other fairies, but instead sought 'normal' men, who responded to their advances not because of congenital need but because of willful perversity. He demeaned the effeminate fairies as 'degenerates,' but also evinced a certain proprietary sympathy for them, urging that treatment, rather than punishment, be attempted, in an effort to cure them of their malady, over which they surely had no control. But he showed no mercy at all toward the 'normal' men with whom the fairies had sex and made no effort to argue that the medical profession should take over their management from the prisons: 'Let us punish most severely the man who yields to the advances of these individuals,' he insisted, 'for such as he are worse than the pervert [the men most doctors called an "invert"] and deserve no sympathy.'[6]

The commentaries written by other doctors point to the emergence of an even more striking class difference in conceptions of male–male sexual relations. A growing number of doctors began to conceive of the inverts' sexual partners not just as morally lax but as tainted by homosexual desire. In 1913, for instance, A. A. Brill, the chief of the Clinic of Psychiatry at Columbia University, argued that homosexuality was not a sign of somatic or psychic hermaphroditism or bisexualism. While 'in a great many cases' the invert 'would feel like a woman and look for the man,' he conceded, this did not 'indicate the general character of inversion,' which, he argued, had to account for *any* man who had sex with another man. In sharp contrast to popular working-class thought, he explicitly classified the 'masculine' men who had sex with transvestite prostitutes and other effeminate men as 'homosexuals,' who 'retain their virility and look for feminine psychic features in their sexual object.' Citing Freud, he even classed men who 'resorted to homosexuality [only] under certain conditions,' such as prisoners with no access to women, as 'occasional inverts' who were a distinct class of men, different from normal men, because of their capacity 'to obtain sexual gratification from a person of the same sex.'[7] Marking a sharp break with both working-class and earlier middle-class thought, Brill's grouping of fairies and trade together in the single category of the homosexual was predicated on the emerging notion that male normality depended not on a man's masculine comportment but on his exclusive heterosexuality. For all its allusions to psychological complexity, Brill's psychoanalytic article ignored the complex symbolic system of power and imaginary gender that governed the meaning of sexual penetration and the classification of sexual actors in working-class culture. It made the sex of the body with whom a man had sex the arbiter of his heterosexual normality or homosexual abnormality. [...]

The writings of doctors help explicate the shifting terms of sexual ideology in the early twentieth century. But such writers did not *create* the social category of the 'invert' or the 'homosexual,' as some recent theories have proposed.[8] As Lichtenstein's description of the men he had encountered in the city jail demonstrates particularly clearly, their writings represent little more than an (often unsuccessful) effort to make sense of the male sexual culture they had observed or of which they were a part. The medical analysis of the different character of 'inverts,' 'perverts,' and 'normal people' reflected a set of classificatory distinctions already widely recognized in the broader culture. The fairy, regarded as a 'third-sexer,' more womanly than manly, was a pivotal cultural figure in the streets of New York before he appeared in the pages of medical journals. The effeminacy doctors ascribed to the invert was emphasized by the common terms people already used for fairies, such as *buttercup*, *nance*, *pansy*, and *sissy*; and the gender-based distinction some doctors drew between 'normal' (that is, conventionally masculine) men and 'inverts' only reproduced the distinction drawn in the vernacular between 'he-men' and 'she-men.'[9] Similarly, the new division of the sexual world by medical discourse into homosexuals and heterosexuals reflected a shift already evident more broadly in middle-class culture. The fairy and the queer, not the medical profession, forced middle-class men to consider the possibility of a sexual element in their relations with other men.

[*Gay New York: Gender, Urban Culture, and the Making of the Gay Male World, 1890–1940* (New York: Basic Books, 1994), 120–1, 121–4, 125.]

Section III

The Twentieth-Century Sexual Body

The body is the foundation of all sexuality. This was the 'discovery' made by the sexologists and experts who undertook at the end of the last century to sort out the varieties of sexuality in nature and correlate them, if they could, with the body's exterior forms and internal structures, including the mind. At the risk of oversimplifying this quest for correlations, we might say that the starting point for all speculation of this kind was the assumption that there was a 1:1 relation between a body and the aims and objects of its desire, so that as the body differed so did the desire. Despite an occasional willingness to consider the existence of a 'third sex', or to entertain notions of bisexuality, in the end most specialists believed that nature produced two sexes—male and female—and tolerated, but did not favour, intermediate variations.

Since that time, we have learned things about sexuality and the body that have both undermined and reinforced this reassuring binary conception of sex; it is in part the very complexity of the picture that has emerged in the twentieth century that makes sexuality such a fascinating subject for scientific, political, and social discussion. In this section of the book we will look at the various ways in which the old two-sex model of sex has managed to persist and even prosper. It has survived despite the emergence of potentially destabilizing scientific developments, and waves of devastating philosophical and social criticism from those who believe the male–female binary has legitimized patriarchy, sexism, and the oppression of sexual minorities.

As we have done to this point, we will investigate these developments historically. This has the advantage of helping to see how new 'discoveries' were incorporated into the existing two-sex doctrine, and how the doctrine itself evolved into a more flexible instrument for reflecting contemporary sexuality. This part of the book will be more concerned with the theory than the practice of sexuality. In Section IV we will return again to sexual practice and consider the impact on sexuality of the extraordinary developments in twentieth-century biology that have threatened to replace the ancient notion of a unified body with a concept of a fragmented conglomeration that is somehow less than its component parts.

The twentieth-century sexual body has been pulverized into genes, hormones, somatic drives, brain structures, race, and a number of other elements. This fragmentation has in turn encouraged the development and application of new technologies that permit more precise observations of sexuality itself and more direct intervention in its processes, particularly in connection with fertility and reproduction, but also on behalf of altering biological sex. This apparent new mastery of sexuality may encourage us to think we have finally solved the riddle of how sexual desire operates to achieve its ends, but, as we shall see, those ends and that desire remain frustratingly opaque.

The point of departure we will use for this part of the reader is suggested by the following passage from Judith Butler's *Gender Trouble: Feminism and the Subversion of Identity* (New York: Routledge, 1990, 7):

Does sex have a history? Does each sex have a different history, or histories? Is there a history of how the duality of sex was established, a genealogy that might expose the binary options as a variable construction? Are the ostensibly natural facts of sex discursively produced by various scientific discourses in the service of other political and social interests? If the immutable character of sex is contested, perhaps this construct called 'sex' is as culturally constructed as gender, indeed, perhaps it was always already gender, with the consequence that the distinction between sex and gender turns out to be no distinction at all.

These are the questions and the outline of an answer that will guide us in Section III. 'Gender' as a word describing male and female difference (not just applying to words in certain languages gendered masculine and feminine) is an invention of the twentieth century. In British and American English it is gradually supplanting 'sex' as a denominator of the difference between the sexes. Gender carries with it a far less deterministic valence than the older term and is generally, though not always, associated with a social constructionist epistemology.

III.a. The Evolution of Sex

There are two principal senses in which we may talk about the evolution of sex. One is the evolution of sex difference: the origin and maintenance of the morphological differences between male and female. The second is the more fundamental matter of the evolution of sexual reproduction in which two separate gametes contribute genetic material to a new being. We will begin with sex difference, which first attracted attention historically. The first effort to explain systematically the evolution of sex difference, and therefore the foundations of sexual attraction, reproduction, and just about everything else, was made by Charles Darwin in his *The Origin of Species* (1859). Darwin named the mechanism that produced and exaggerated sexual difference in many animals 'sexual selection'; he attached great importance to sexual selection as a subsidiary mechanism of natural selection, the process in which certain 'favourable' variations survived to perpetuate themselves in succeeding generations. Darwin applied his theory of evolution to humans in his *The Descent of Man* (1871) where sexual selection played an even larger role than his previous book. In the following passage from his conclusion, Darwin sums up his argument, distinguishes natural from sexual selection, and makes the point that secondary sexual characteristics and the courtship behaviour of individuals are products of selective processes that favoured extreme sexual dimorphism. In updated form, Darwin's theory has become the most prestigious scientific argument for explaining sexual difference, at least in the higher animals (Extract 86).

Darwin's views soon came under criticism, not only from those who doubted the evolutionary selection for sexual difference, but from critics who believed he had not emphasized enough the foundational quality of sexual difference. The British biologists Patrick Geddes and J. Arthur Thomson wrote an enormously influential book in 1889 called *The Evolution of Sex* in which they introduced to evolutionary biology the terms 'katabolic' and 'anabolic', that is, rapid and slow metabolic activity that they believed were associated constitutionally with males and females respectively. In their view, males provided the variation in nature and females the nutritive qualities to propagate and nourish the young; these qualities were primordially embodied in male and female organisms from single-celled protozoa to man, including human sex cells. In the absence of reliable knowledge of the actual mechanisms of inheritance through chromosomal meiosis, these and related arguments provided the standard account of the evolution of sex for the next forty years (Extract 87).

Views about the primordial and constitutional nature of sex were gradually revised around 1900 following the 'rediscovery' of Gregor Mendel's earlier findings about the recurring patterns of inheritance in garden peas. August Weissman had proposed in 1885 that the union of male and female sex cells somehow allowed the elements of both gametes to be preserved in the fertilized ovum. When this insight was combined with a growing body of microscopical knowledge about cell division it was possible to understand better the implications of sexual reproduction for evolution and, inversely, the implications of evolution for sexual reproduction.

First, it became possible after 1900 to understand that sexual reproduction itself produced the variability required for the adaptation of many species to changing environments, a discovery that eventually marginalized other explanations of the process that had depended on various epigenetic (extra-nucleic) or neo-Lamarckian mechanisms (Extract 88).

It has been tempting for evolutionary theorists to make the inverse argument: that if creatures that reproduced sexually had a certain evolutionary advantage over those that replicated asexually, then sexual reproduction was itself an evolutionarily favoured device that gave added significance to male and female sex. This may simply be something that we higher mammals *want* to believe for reasons of species pride and because we typically organize our human societies along gendered lines. However, recent scientific work has complicated this 'common sense' evolutionary truism in a number of ways. As the following passage reveals, the evolutionary history of species suggests that reproduction and sex have not been invariably linked together, and, moreover, that sex difference does not in itself confer evolutionary advantage to the species in which it has developed. It is not possible, therefore, to conclude that human beings are somehow the culmination of a 'superior' reproductive process of which sex difference is an indispensable feature. As we shall see, the separation of sex (the mixing of genes from the two sexes) from reproduction is significant in other ways in our understanding of the modern sexual body (Extract 89).

One of the most productive areas in recent research on the evolution of sex is gamete evolution and its relationship to sexual behaviour. In this work we see that the component parts of the modern sexual body have also been exposed to the pressures of natural selection, with interesting consequences for the organism as a whole. It is important to bear in mind that research questions in any field are often driven by culturally cued questions that tend to support or explain dominant sex and gender systems. Research on human sexuality is particularly likely to reflect such questions.

On the assumption that in the human evolutionary past females were polyandrous, and in the certain knowledge that they were, unlike most mammals, more or less permanently receptive sexually, a theory of 'sperm competition' has emerged that tries to explain, among other things, the fact of the relatively longer penises of human males (in contrast to other primates) and the unusual behaviour of human sperm. In a community of polyandrous women, so the theory goes, the male with the longest penis and/or largest ejaculation will be most successful in impregnating females and thus passing on his genes to similarly endowed male offspring. But the theory also works to explain sperm competition itself (Extract 90).

On this theory, there are related consequences for female sexual behaviour, particularly for the nature and function of the female orgasm. This information has been correlated with data from the behaviour of other animals, particularly birds, to interesting effect. With apologies for the inaccurate description of the 'wealth' of Emma Bovary's husband, Extract 91's summary of the full theory is most pertinent.

Sexual selection depends on the success of certain individuals over others of the same sex, in relation to the propagation of the species; whilst natural selection depends on the success of both sexes, at all ages, in relation to the general conditions of life. The sexual struggle is of two kinds; in the one it is between individuals of the same sex, generally the males, in order to drive away or kill their rivals, the females remaining passive; whilst in the other, the struggle is likewise between the individuals of the same sex, in order to excite or charm those of the opposite sex, generally the females, which no longer remain passive, but select the more agreeable partners. This latter kind of selection is closely analogous to that which man unintentionally, yet effectually, brings to bear on his domesticated productions, when he preserves during a long period the most pleasing or useful individuals, without any wish to modify the breed.

The laws of inheritance determine whether characters gained through sexual selection by either sex shall be transmitted to the same sex, or to both; as well as the age at which they shall be developed. It appears that variations arising late in life are commonly transmitted to one and the same sex. Variability is the necessary basis for the action of selection, and is wholly independent of it. It follows from this, that variations of the same general nature have often been taken advantage of and accumulated through sexual selection in relation to the propagation of the species, as well as through natural selection in relation to the general purposes of life. Hence secondary sexual characters, when equally transmitted to both sexes can be distinguished from ordinary specific characters only by the light of analogy. The modifications acquired through sexual selection are often so strongly pronounced that the two sexes have frequently been ranked as distinct species, or even as distinct genera. Such strongly-marked differences must be in some manner highly important; and we know that they have been acquired in some instances at the cost not only of inconvenience, but of exposure to actual danger.

The belief in the power of sexual selection rests chiefly on the following considerations. Certain characters are confined to one sex; and this alone renders it probable that in most cases they are connected with the act of reproduction. In innumerable instances these characters are fully developed only at maturity, and often during only a part of the year, which is always the breeding-season. The males (passing over a few exceptional cases) are the more active in courtship; they are the better armed, and are rendered the more attractive in various ways. It is to be especially observed that the males display their attractions with elaborate care in the presence of the females; and that they rarely or never display them excepting during the season of love. It is incredible that all this should be purposeless. Lastly we have distinct evidence with some quadrupeds and birds, that the individuals of one sex are capable of feeling a strong antipathy or preference for certain individuals of the other sex.

Bearing in mind these facts, and the marked results of man's unconscious selection, when applied to domesticated animals and cultivated plants, it seems to me almost certain that if the individuals of one sex were during a long series of generations to prefer pairing with certain individuals of the other sex, characterised in some peculiar manner, the offspring would slowly but surely become modified in this same manner. I have not attempted to conceal that, excepting when the males are more numerous than the females, or when polygamy prevails, it is doubtful how the more attractive males succeed in leaving a large number of offspring to inherit their superiority in ornaments or other charms than the less attractive males; but I have shewn that this would probably follow from the females,—especially the more vigorous ones, which would be the first to breed,—preferring not only the more attractive but at the same time the more vigorous and victorious males.

['The Descent of Man,' in *Darwin: A Norton Critical Edition*, ed. Philip Appleman (New York: W. W. Norton, 1970), 272–3.]

PATRICK GEDDES AND J. ARTHUR THOMSON

87 Sexual Difference

The point of view is simple enough. The agility of males is not a special adaptation to enable that sex to exercise its functions with relation to the other, but is a natural characteristic of the constitutional activity of maleness; and the small size of many male fishes is not an advantage at all, but simply again the result of the contrast between the more vegetative growth of the female and the costly activity of the male. So, brilliancy of colour, exuberance of hair and feathers, activity of scent-glands, and even the development of weapons, are not, and cannot be (except teleologically), explained by sexual selection, but in origin and continued development are outcrops of a male as opposed to female constitution. To sum up the position in a paradox, all secondary sexual characters are at bottom primary, and are expressions of the same general habit of body (or to use the medical term, *diathesis*), as that which results in the production of male elements in the one case, or female elements in the other.

Three well-known facts must be recalled to the reader's mind at this point; and firstly, that in a great number of cases the secondary sexual characters make their appearance step by step with sexual maturity itself. When the animal—be it a bird or insect—becomes emphatically masculine, then it is that these minor outcrops are exhibited. Thus the male bird of paradise, eventually so resplendent, is usually in its youth comparatively dull and female-like in its colouring and plumage. Very often too, whether in the wedding-robe of male fishes or in the scent-glands of mammals, the character rises and wanes in the same rhythm as that of the reproductive periods. It is impossible not to regard at least many of the secondary sexual characters as part and parcel of the sexual diathesis, as expressions for the most part of exuberant maleness. Secondly, when the reproductive organs are removed by castration, the secondary sexual characters tend to remain undeveloped. Thus, as Darwin notes, stags never renew their antlers after castration, though normally of course they renew them each breeding season. The reindeer, where the horns occur on the females as well, is an interesting exception to the rule, for after castration the male still renews the growth. This however merely indicates that the originally sexual characters have become organised into the general life of the body. In sheep, antelopes, oxen, &c., castration modifies or reduces the horns; and the same is true of odoriferous glands. The parasitic crustacean *Sacculina* has been shown by Delage to effect a partial castration of the crabs to which it fixes itself, and the same has been observed by Giard in other cases. In two such cases an approximation to the female form of appendage has been observed. Lastly, in aged females, which have ceased to be functional in reproduction, the minor peculiarities of their sex often disappear, and they become like males, both in structure and habits,—witness the familiar case of 'crowing hens.'

From the presupposition, then, of the intimate connection between the sexuality and the secondary characters (which is indeed everywhere allowed), it is possible to advance a step further. Thus in regard to colour, that the male is usually brighter than the female is an acknowledged fact. But pigments of many kinds are physiologically regarded as of the nature of waste products. Such for instance is the guanin, so abundant on the skin of fishes and some other animals. Abundance of such pigments, and richness of variety in related series, point to pre-eminent activity of chemical processes in the animals which possess them. Technically expressed, abundant pigments are expressions in intense metabolism. But predominant activity has been already seen to be characteristic of the male sex; these bright colours, then, are often natural to maleness. In a literal sense animals put on beauty for ashes, and the males more so because they are males, and not primarily for any other reason whatever. We are well aware that, in spite of the researches of Krukenberg, Sorby, MacMunn, and others, our knowledge of the physiology of many of the pigments is still very scanty. Yet in many cases, alike among plants and animals, pigments are expressions of disruptive processes, and are of the nature of waste products; and this general fact is at present sufficient for our contention, that bright colouring or rich pigmenting is commonly a natural expression of the male constitution. For the red pigment so abundant in the female cochineal insect, which appears to be of the nature of a reserve and not a waste product, and for similar occurrences, due exception must be made. [...]

Sexual Selection: its Limit as an Explanation.—We are now in a better position to criticise Mr Darwin's theory. On his view, males are stronger, handsomer, or more emotional, because ancestral forms happened to become so in a slight degree. In other words, the reward of breeding success gradually perpetuated and perfected a casual advantage. According to the present view, males are stronger, handsomer, or more emotional, simply because they are males,—*i.e.*, of more active physiological habit than their mates. In phraseology which will presently become more intelligible and concrete, the males live at a loss, are more *katabolic*,—disruptive changes tending to preponderate in the sum of changes in their living matter or protoplasm. The females, on the other hand, live at a profit, are more *anabolic*,—constructive processes predominating in their life, whence indeed the capacity of bearing offspring.

No one can dispute that the nutritive, vegetative, or self-regarding processes within the plant or animal are opposed to the reproductive, multiplying, or species-regarding processes, as income to expenditure, or as building up to breaking down. But within the ordinary nutritive or vegetative functions of the body, there is necessarily a continuous antithesis between two sets of processes,—constructive and destructive metabolism. The contrast between these two processes is seen throughout nature, whether in the alternating phases of cell life, or of activity and repose, or in the great antithesis between growth and reproduction; and it is this same contrast which we recognise as the fundamental difference between male and female. [. . .]

Our special theory lies, however, in suggesting the parallelism of the two sets of processes,—the male reproduction is associated with preponderating katabolism, and the female with relative anabolism. In terms of this thesis, therefore, both primary and secondary sexual characters express the fundamental physiological bias characteristic of either sex. Sexual selection resembles artificial selection, but the female takes the place of the human breeder; it resembles natural selection, but the selective females and the combative males represent a rôle filled in the larger case by the fostering or eliminating action of the environment. As a special case of natural selection, Darwin's minor theory is open to the objection of being teleological, *i.e.*, of accounting for structures in terms of a final advantage. It is quite open to the logical critic to urge, as a few have done, that the structures to be explained have to be accounted for before, as well as after, the stage when they were developed enough to be useful. The origin, or in other words the fundamental physiological import, of the structures, must be explained before we have a complete or adequate theory of organic evolution. [. . .]

Sexual Attraction.—Mantegazza has written a work entitled 'The Physiology of Love,' in which he expounds the optimistic doctrine that love is the universal dynamic; and from this Büchner quotes the sentence, that 'the whole of nature is one hymn of love.' If the last word be used very widely, this often repeated utterance has more than poetic significance. But even in the most literal sense there is much truth in it, since so many animals are at one in the common habit of serenading their mates. The chirping of insects, the croaking of frogs, the calls of mammals, the song of birds, illustrate both the bathos and glory of the love-chorus. The works of Darwin and others have made us familiar with the numerous ways, both gentle and violent, in which mammals woo one another. The display of decorations in which many male birds indulge, the amatory dances of others, the love lights of glow-insects, the joyous tournaments or furious duels of rival suitors, the deliberate choice which not a few females exhibit, and the like, show how a process, at first crude enough, becomes enhanced by appeals to more than merely sexual appetite. But it is hardly necessary now to argue seriously in support of the thesis that love—in the sense of sexual sympathy, psychical as well as physical—exists among animals in many degrees of evolution. Our comparative psychology too has been too much influenced by our intellectual superiority; but while this, no doubt, has its correspondingly increased possibilities of emotional range, it does not necessarily imply a corresponding emotional intensity; and we have no means of measuring, much less limiting, that glow of organic emotion which so manifestly flushes the organism with colour and floods the world with song. Who knows whether the song-bird be not beside the man what the child-musician is to the ordinary dulness of our daily toil and thought? The fact to be insisted upon is this, that the vague sexual attraction of the lowest organisms has been evolved into a definite reproductive impulse, into a desire often predominating over even that of self-preservation; that this again, enhanced by more and more subtle psychical additions, passes by a gentle gradient into the love of the highest animals and of the average human individual. [. . .]

Intellectual and Emotional Differences between the Sexes.—We have seen that a deep difference in constitution expresses itself in the distinctions between male and female, whether these be physical or mental. The differences may be exaggerated or lessened, but to obliterate them it would be necessary to have all the evolution over again on a new basis. What was decided among the prehistoric Protozoa cannot be annulled by Act of Parliament. In this mere outline we cannot of course do more than indicate the relation of the biological differences between the sexes to the resulting psychological and social differentiations; for more than this neither space nor powers suffice. We must insist upon the biological considerations underlying the relation of the sexes, which have been too much discussed by contemporary writers of all schools, as if the known facts of sex did not exist at all, or almost if these were a mere matter of muscular strength or weight of brain. [. . .]

It is equally certain that the two sexes are complementary and mutually dependent. Virtually asexual organisms, like Bacteria, occupy no high place in Nature's roll of honour; virtually unisexual organisms, like many rotifers, are great rarities. Parthenogenesis may be an organic ideal, but it is one which has failed to realise itself. Males and females, like the sex-elements, are mutually dependent, and that not merely because they are males and females, but also in functions not directly associated with those of sex. But to dispute whether males or females are the higher, is like disputing the relative superiority of animals or plants. Each is higher in its own way, and the two are complementary.

While there are broad general distinctions between the intellectual, and especially the emotional, characteristics of males and females among the higher animals, these not unfrequently tend to become mingled. There is, however, no evidence that they might be gradually obliterated. The sea-horse, the obstetric frog, many male birds, are certainly maternal; while a few females fight for the males, and are stronger, or more passionate than their mates. But these are rarities. It is generally true that the males are more active, energetic, eager, passionate, and variable; the females more passive, conservative, sluggish, and stable. The males, or, to return to the terms of our thesis, the more katabolic organisms, are more variable, and therefore, as Brooks has especially emphasised, are very frequently the leaders in evolutionary progress, while the more anabolic females tend rather to preserve the constancy and integrity of the species; thus, in a word, the general heredity is perpetuated primarily by the female, while variations are introduced by the male. Yet along paths where the reproductive sacrifice was one of the determinants of progress, we shall see later that they must have the credit of leading the way. The more active males, with a consequently wider range of experience, may have bigger brains and more intelligence; but the females, especially as mothers, have indubitably a larger and more habitual share of the altruistic emotions. The males being usually stronger, have greater independence and courage; the females excel in constancy of affection and in sympathy. The spasmodic bursts of activity characteristic of males contrast with the continuous patience of the females, which we take to be an expression of constitutional contrast, and by no means, as some would have us believe, a mere product of masculine bullying. The stronger lust and passion of males is likewise the obverse of predominant katabolism.

That men should have greater cerebral variability and therefore more originality, while women have greater stability and therefore more 'common sense,' are facts both consistent with the general theory of sex and verifiable in common experience. The woman, conserving the effects of past variations, has what may be called the greater integrating intelligence; the man, introducing new variations, is stronger in differentiation. The feminine passivity is expressed in greater patience, more open-mindedness, greater appreciation of subtle details, and consequently what we call more rapid intuition. The masculine activity lends a greater power of maximum effort, of scientific insight, or cerebral experiment with impressions, and is associated with an unobservant or impatient disregard of minute details, but with a stronger grasp of generalities. Man thinks more, women feels more. He discovers more, but remembers less; she is more receptive, and less forgetful.

[*The Evolution of Sex* (New York: Scribner & Welford, 1890), 22–4, 25–6, 27, 266–7, 267, 270–1.]

Although the work of late-nineteenth-century cytologists revealed many of the morphological characteristics of sexual reproduction and showed that it could no longer be dismissed as a minor variation of the normal asexual processes, the details of the process and its biological significance remained obscure, the focus of controversy. By 1905, however, the speculation had ended. By then cytologists were interpreting sexual reproduction as a process without which evolution could not have occurred, a process which introduced variations into a population. Variations arose, they argued, because the gametes produced during maturation division were different from each other and because their chromosomes did not fuse during fecundation—just as Weismann had claimed.

This rapid end to the reduction–division controversy can be traced to two major turn-of-the-century developments. First, the work of Hugo de Vries and the rediscovery of Mendel's work provided cytologists with a theoretical base from which to reinterpret their findings. Mendel's theories were not accepted because they could be fitted into an already established cytological picture; on the contrary, the cytological picture was quickly realigned to fit the new theoretical framework. The absence of such a framework had perpetuated the cytological controversy of the 1890s; the presence of a unified framework solved the problem in the first decade of the twentieth century. Second, the anti-Weismann position was fatally undermined when many of its advocates gave up cytology or changed their opinions. [. . .]

In *Mutationstheorie*, de Vries claimed that new species arise through the appearance of 'progressive mutations,' or new pangenes, while varieties arise through a change in the position of already existing pangenes. Such a change, he argued, comes about as a result of sexual reproduction, which 'can unite characters by exchange of elements in every possible kind of combination.'[1] Elaborating on this claim in his paper 'Befruchtung und Bastardierung,' which was read at the 1903 meeting of the Dutch Society of Science, he stressed what he called the 'principle of duality': that every being is a double being, inheriting one part of its nature from its mother and the other half from its father. He noted, however, that though the bearers of these parental characters are intimately connected, 'they are not, by any means, fused into a new indivisible entity. They form twins, but remain separate for life.'[2] 'Thus, he continued, when two sex nuclei unite at fertilization, very little happens. 'A penetration or fusion of their substance does not take place. They remain separate in spite of the union.'[3] On this basis de Vries argued that the numerical reduction of chromosomes 'means nothing but the separation of two nuclei which had so far worked together for a period. It is like the parting of two parents who have walked along together for a while.'⁴ Before this separation, de Vries explained, the parental chromosomes lay either side by side or end to end, a difference which explained much of the previous confusion over transverse division of the chromosomes. However, de Vries stressed, the separation of chromosomes was not a simple matter; it involved the creation of a lasting 'reciprocal influence.'

Shortly before their separation, their leave taking, they are still the same as before. But now they exchange their individual units, and thus cause the creation of those countless combinations of characters, of which nature is in need to order to make species as plastic as possible, and to empower them to adapt themselves in the highest degree to their ever changing environment. . . . This increase of variability and of the power of individual adaptation is the essential purpose of sexual reproduction.⁵ [. . .]

The real biological significance of sexual reproduction and conjugation lay in the production of variation. Sexual reproduction was not, as previously assumed, simply a method of procreation. Indeed, as Maynard Smith wrote in 1971, 'at the cellular level sex is the opposite of reproduction; in reproduction one cell divides into two, whereas it is the essence of the sexual process that two cells should fuse to form one.'⁶

Although this disassociation of sex from procreation seems somewhat academic in organisms that reproduce only by sexual means, in plants and many lower animals sexual and asexual reproduction exist side by side, playing, presumably, very different roles. In a very different context this disassociation of sex from procreation came to have enormous social repercussions; it provided the biological backcloth for the 'sexual revolution' of the twentieth century.

[*Gametes & Spores: Ideas about Sexual Reproduction, 1750–1914* (Baltimore: Johns Hopkins University Press, 1982), 189, 199–200, 207.]

LYNN MARGULIS AND DORION SAGAN

89   The Origins of Sexual Reproduction

This book is meant to be an evolutionary detective story that unravels the mystery and history of the origin of sex. Different forms of sex are observed in the biological world. We want to know how sex came to be.

Sex in bacteria crosses species boundaries and allows a flow of genetic information that some consider the basis for a worldwide gene pool composed of bacteria.¹ Other organisms, those with nuclei, probably evolved through endosymbiosis: bacteria living inside each other shared each other's foods, metabolites, and eventually genes.² Nonbacterial, meiotic sex, found only in nucleated organisms, has a different origin and history. Although less important as a raw source of variety for natural selection, it is crucial to the development and reproduction of animals and plants. Our hypothesis is that the history of the meiotic sex of animals and plants depended on cannibalism in protists and the differential replication of their former symbionts, some of which became organelles of these protists. The existence of modern-day protists, which show far more variation on the theme of meiotic sex than any other living group, suggests that sex evolved in their ancestors. Studying sexuality in extant organisms has led us to conclude that meiotic sex became coupled to reproduction in animals and plants only because differentiation of their cells was impossible without it.

To reconstruct the events leading to the origin of sexuality is a difficult task, because the essential cellular events at its basis are so ancient and because they occurred in microorganisms that did not preserve well in the fossil record. In evolution, as in criminology, one is never absolutely sure about a given reconstruction. Nonetheless, it is our pleasure here to provide a scenario for the origins of sex that we feel is consistent with the mass of circumstantial evidence so far accumulated.

Everyone is interested in sex. But, from a scientific perspective, the word is all too often associated with reproduction, with sexual intercourse leading to childbirth. As we look over the evolutionary history of life, however, we see that sex is the formation of a genetically new individual. Sex is a genetic mixing process that has nothing necessarily to do with reproduction as we know it in mammals. Throughout evolutionary history a great many organisms offered and exchanged genes sexually without the sex ever leading to the cell or organism copying known as reproduction. Although additional living beings are often reproduced by a contribution of genes from more than a single parent, sex in most organisms is still divorced from growth and reproduction, which are accomplished by nonsexual means.

Biologically, sex is part of the rich repertoire of life. Any specific instance of a sexual event is complex. Each event in a sexual process—for example, fertilization in a plant or animal—has its own specific history. Originally unrelated phenomena, such as genetic exchange (as in DNA recombination) and cell reproduction, often became entangled after having evolved from separate beginnings. The story of sex starts with an account of the earliest life on Earth. The private activities of early cells are involved even today in courtship among human beings. The intimate behavior of single cells has simply been elaborated to include animals and their behaviors and societies. Mammalian sex is a very late and special variation on a far more general theme.

The origin of sex is a problem that has long perplexed. It lends itself to innovative mythmaking (mythopoiesis); many cultures have imagined a primordial unisexual oneness that, under the influence of a celestial personality, was split into light and dark, heaven and earth, male and female, and so on. In the march of knowledge, however, mythical accounts of the origin of sex have been abandoned. We now realize, thanks to the insights of Darwinian evolution, that the sexual differences that loom so large in the daily lives of men and women did not arise at some specific time in the history of the human species. Evolution takes us far beyond the origin of apes and men, who at their first appearance were undoubtedly already fully sexual. Sex itself arose even earlier than the many species of sexual creatures with which we are familiar. It was present on the Earth when microbes, organisms that cannot be seen without a microscope, totally dominated the planetary surface. Sex was here for hundreds of millions of years before the first animals or plants appeared.

What keeps organisms that have sexual differences from devolving into the asexual state is, as we shall show, a completely different matter from how sex came about in the first place. Biologists, although they have tried, have not been able to prove that sexual organisms have an intrinsic advantage over asexual ones. Many have struggled with the question of how sexual organisms can afford to expend the biological 'cost' of mating in every generation. Asexual organisms, since they can have more offspring per unit time, are, in Darwinian terms, more 'fit'. This sort of analysis implies that sexuality should disappear. But in animals sexuality is tenaciously maintained. We show here that this problem of the *maintenance* of sex (that which keeps animals and plants from becoming asexual) must be clearly distinguished from the problem of the *origins* of sex (the ways in which sex first evolved). There has been some confusion between these two aspects of sexual theory. The mix-up between remaining sexual and becoming sexual is one which we will try to steer well clear of throughout this book.

The origin of sex was not a one-time event. Sex is not a singular but a multi-faceted and widespread phenomenon; it has developed several times, at the very least. The two most consequential appearances of sex were in tiny microbes—a half to about five micrometers long. Sex first appeared in bacteria. Later, in larger, more complex microbes called 'protists,' a new and different kind of sex evolved. Sex in bacteria is a biological mixing and matching on the molecular level: the splicing and mending of DNA molecules. Bacterial sexuality is very different from the meiotic sex of protists, fungi, plants, and animals, and it evolved far earlier. Meiosis, or cell division resulting in reduction in the number of chromosomes, and subsequent fertilization, or reunion of cells to reestablish the original chromosomal number, first occurred in protists. Protists, microbes generally from ten to a hundred micrometers long, are ancestral to fungi, animals, and plants. As protists evolved and gave rise to these other groups of organisms, sex was preserved. From a cellular vantage point, human sex is almost identical to that of some of the protistan microbes.

The main thesis of this book may come as a surprise to some. It is that ultimately males and females are different from each other not because sexual species are better equipped to handle the contingencies of a dynamically changing environment but because of a series of historical accidents that took place in and permitted the survival of ancestral protists. From the beginning the cellular events required for the emergence of differentiation—of cells, tissues, organs, and organ systems—were tied to meiotic sexuality. Conjugation and meiosis were intrinsic to the life cycles of differentiated protists, the ancestors of animals, fungi, and plants. We believe, from inferring the events necessary for the formation of the first sexual beings, that biparental sex itself did not immediately confer any great advantage upon those organisms in which it arose. This idea runs against the grain of the most popular rationale for the existence of sex: that sexual organisms, being on the average more diverse because they combine divergent traits, are more adaptable to changing environments. We do not think there is any evidence to justify the claim that sexual organisms are more diverse and therefore better equipped to cope with the vicissitudes of existence, nor that they reproduce in a sexual fashion because this permits them to 'evolve faster.' We think sexual organisms reproduce in this peculiar and 'costly' fashion because, in the first place, they must reproduce and, second, because certain peculiarities of their evolutionary past have linked their reproduction and tissue differentiation with their sexuality. It is true that natural selection has favored many sexual organisms, but not because they were sexual.

It is natural for human beings—who are mammals in which sex and reproduction are always associated—to think that the 'purpose' of sex is reproduction. But in most microbes, organisms from which ultimately we have descended, sex is quite separate from reproduction. Reproduction is obligatory. All organisms reproduce; sex, on the other hand, is optional. Bacteria often engage in sex but they do not reproduce by cell division as a result of the sexual engagement. (Bacterial sex is not a precursor for the act of reproduction itself, but sometimes it supplies genes for survival at a given moment.) Many species of protists, fungi, animals, and plants can reproduce with or without two-parent sex. In some organisms sex, in fact, is lethal. It produces no offspring and destroys all those that participate in the process.

[*Origins of Sex: Three Billion Years of Genetic Recombination* (New Haven: Yale University Press, 1986), 1–4.]

R. ROBIN BAKER AND MARK A. BELLIS

90   Sperm Competition Theory

Sperm competition theory was first developed in a classical series of papers by Parker.[1] This section simply introduces the basic principles and main areas of contention.

The lottery principle
According to Parker, sperm competition is a lottery. The more sperm a male produces, the greater the chances that his sperm will outcompete the sperm from other males and thus have more chance of fertilizing, and/or will fertilize more of, a female's egg(s).

There is some direct evidence for the lottery hypothesis. Artificial insemination studies of chickens (using sperm from males genetically different for plumage) have shown that the more sperm are inseminated from a particular male, the greater his success in sperm competition. However, even here it must be pointed out that males differ in their fertility. Thus, it is true that, for any given male, 50 million sperm will do better than 25 million sperm when competing against 50 million sperm from another male. However, it is not necessarily true that with 50 million sperm from both males each will fertilize the same number of eggs.

Sperm size and competitiveness

Parker argued that the lottery factor in sperm competition favoured the evolutionary maintenance of tiny sperm. The relative sizes of eggs and sperm in most animals are grossly different. Thus, even if a male produced sperm twice the normal size, the sperm would still make very little contribution after fertilization to the size, energy reserves and hence survival and development, of the zygote. Yet such a male would, all else being equal, produce an ejaculate with half the number of sperm and therefore with half the chances of success in sperm competition. Males who produced small sperm would thus be more successful in sperm competition than males who produced larger sperm. In lineages with a high risk of sperm competition, therefore, males who produced more numerous, tiny sperm would have greater reproductive success than males who produced fewer, larger sperm.

In apparent contradiction to Parker's prediction, species of primates and rodents[2] and butterflies with a higher risk of sperm competition have males which produce larger sperm. Gomendio and Roldan suggest that larger sperm swim faster and are therefore more competitive. Even if larger size reduces the number of sperm ejaculated, the larger size could evolve if the advantage of enhanced competitiveness outweighed any 'lottery' disadvantage.

Sperm warfare and the Kamikaze Sperm Hypothesis

The idea that sperm competition may take the form of strategic warfare rather than a lottery was first mooted for insects by Sivinski[3] and for butterflies and moths by Silberglied et al.[4] In elaborating our 'Kamikaze Sperm Hypothesis', we developed the idea of sperm warfare as a general principle for sperm in all animals.[5]

Briefly, the Kamikaze Sperm Hypothesis suggests that animal ejaculates consist of different types of sperm each programmed to carry out a specific function. Some, often very few, are 'egg-getters', programmed to attempt to fertilize the female's eggs. The remainder, often the vast majority, are programmed for a 'kamikaze' role. Instead of attempting to find and fertilize eggs themselves, their role is to reduce the chances that the egg will be fertilized by sperm from any other male.

We envisage two primary categories of kamikaze sperm: 'blockers' and 'seek-and-destroy'. Blockers take up strategic positions en route to the egg, become relatively immotile, and bar passage to any later sperm. Seek-and-destroy sperm roam around appropriate areas of the female tract, seeking out and attempting to incapacitate and/or destroy any sperm from a different male probably using the highly destructive proteolytic enzymes produced by their acrosomal complex.

In species in which the eggs are fertilized outside the female's body (usually in water), blockers can only really take up a position on the outer surface of the egg itself. Similarly, seek-and-destroy sperm are most likely to be effective in the water or other liquid immediately surrounding the egg. This may occur especially when mechanisms are used by external fertilizers to concentrate gametes (e.g. fish such as the European bitterling, *Rhodeus amarus*, laying their eggs within mussels).

In species in which the eggs are fertilized inside the female's body, however, different blockers may take up positions in any suitable constriction in the female tract. Equally, different types of seek-and-destroy sperm may be programmed to locate and patrol any suitable region of the female tract. The more complex the female tract, the more scope for different types of kamikaze sperm, each type programmed to locate and operate within a particular region of the tract.

Restraint in sperm ejaculation

Whether sperm competition is a lottery, a race, or warfare, it is likely that the more sperm a male enters for the competition, the greater his chances of winning.[6] The selective pressures generated by the risk of sperm competition would seem only, therefore, to favour males who ejaculated as many sperm as possible on every occasion. Yet there is now abundant evidence, at both the species and individual levels, that males adjust the number of sperm they ejaculate according to the risk of sperm competition. When the risk of sperm competition is low, males apparently restrain themselves in the number of sperm ejaculated, reserving maximum ejaculation for occasions when the risk of sperm competition is highest.

Such restraint over the number of sperm ejaculated when the risk of sperm competition is low implies that males suffer some disadvantage if they ejaculate too many sperm on any given occasion. Two main disadvantages have been suggested: (1) that the sperm and other constituents in an ejaculate are costly to produce;[7] and (2) that, in the absence of sperm competition, the more sperm a male ejaculates, the lower his chances of fertilizing the egg(s) of the current female.[8]

How many sperm should be ejaculated?

The precise format of sperm competition and the nature of any disadvantage in ejaculating too many sperm are still very much open to discussion and experimentation. Whatever the final conclusion, however, the major predic-tion of sperm competition theory remains the same. The number of sperm a male should ejaculate on any given occasion is the optimum trade-off between two opposing factors: (1) an advantage in ejaculating more sperm to increase the chances of winning any sperm competition that might occur; and (2) an advantage in ejaculating fewer sperm (either because of sperm cost or because of a lower chance of fertilization) if sperm competition does not occur. The result of these opposing pressures should be that more sperm are ejaculated when the risk of sperm competition is high than when it is low.

[*Human Sperm Competition: Copulation, Masturbation and Infidelity* (London: Chapman & Hall, 1995), 22–4.]

MATT RIDLEY

91   **Female Adultery**

Emma Bovary and female swallows

What's in it for the birds? For the males it is obvious enough: Adulterers father more young. But it is not at all clear why the female is so often unfaithful. Birk-head and Møller rejected several suggestions: that she is adulterous because of a genetic side effect of the male adulterous urge, that she is ensuring some of the sperm she gets is fertile, that she is bribed by the philandering males (as seems to be the case in some human and ape societies). None of these fit the exact facts. Nor did it quite work to blame her infidelity on a desire for genetic variety. There seems to be little point in having more varied children than she would have anyway.

Birkhead and Møller were left with the belief that female birds benefit from being promiscuous because it enables them to have their genetic cake and eat it—to follow the Emma Bovary strategy. A female swallow needs a husband who will help look after her young, but by the time she arrives at the breeding site, she might find all the best husbands taken. Her best tactic is therefore to mate with a mediocre husband or a husband with a good territory and have an affair with a genetically superior neighbor. This theory is supported by the facts: Females always choose more dominant, older, or more 'attractive' (that is, ornamented) lovers than their husbands; they do not have affairs with bachelors (presumably rejects) but with other females' husbands; and they sometimes incite competition between potential lovers and choose the winners. Male swal-lows with artificially lengthened tails acquired a mate ten days sooner, were eight times as likely to have a second brood, and had twice as high a chance of seducing a neighbor's wife as ordinary swallows.[1] (Intriguingly, when female mice choose to mate with males other than those they 'live with,' they usually choose ones whose disease-resistance genes are *different* from their own.[2])

In short, the reason adultery is so common in colonial birds is that it enables a male bird to have more young and enables a female bird to have better young.

One of the most curious results to come out of bird studies in recent years has been the discovery that 'attractive' males make inattentive fathers. Nancy Burley, whose zebra finches consider one another more or less attractive according to the color of their leg bands, first noticed this,[3] and Anders Møller has since found it to be true of swallows as well. When a female mates with an attractive male, he works less hard and she works harder at bringing up the young. It is as if he feels that he has done her a favor by providing superior genes and therefore expects her to repay him with harder work around the nest. This, of course, increases her incentive to find a mediocre but hardworking husband and cuckold him by having an affair with a superstud next door.[4]

In any case, the principle—marry a nice guy but have an affair with your boss or marry a rich but ugly man and take a handsome lover—is not unknown among female human beings. It is called having your cake and eating it, too. Flaubert's Emma Bovary wanted to keep both her handsome lover and her wealthy husband.

The work on birds has been conducted by people who knew little of human anthropology. In just the same way, a pair of British zoologists had been studying human beings in the late 1980s, largely in isolation from the bird work. Robin Baker and Mark Bellis of Liverpool University were curious to know if sperm competition happened inside women, and if it did, whether women had any control over it. Their results have led to a bizarre and astonishing explanation of the female orgasm.

What follows is the only part of this book in which the details of sexual intercourse itself are relevant to an evolutionary argument. Baker and Bellis discovered that the amount of sperm that is retained in a woman's vagina after sex varies according to whether she had an orgasm and when. It also depends on how long it was since she last had sex: The longer the period, the more sperm stays in, unless she has what the scientists call 'a noncopulatory orgasm' in between.

So far none of this contained great surprises; these facts were unknown before Baker and Bellis did their work (which consisted of samples collected by selected couples and of a survey of four thousand people who replied to a questionnaire in a magazine), but they did not necessarily mean very much. But Baker and Bellis also did something rather brave. They asked their subjects about their extramarital affairs. They found that in faithful women about 55 percent of the orgasms were of the high-retention (that is, the most fertile) type. In unfaithful women, only 40 percent of the copulations with the partner were of this kind, but 70 percent of the copulations with the lover were of this fertile type. Moreover, whether deliberately or not, the unfaithful women were having sex with their lovers at times of the month when they were most fertile. These two effects combined meant that an unfaithful woman in their sample could have sex twice as often with her husband as with her lover but was still slightly more likely to conceive a child by the lover than the husband.

Baker and Bellis interpret their results as evidence of an evolutionary arms race between males and females, a Red Queen game, but one in which the female sex is one evolutionary step ahead. The male is trying to increase his chances of being the father in every way. Many of his sperm do not even try to fertilize her eggs but instead either attack other sperm or block their passage.

But the female has evolved a sophisticated set of techniques for preventing conception except on her own terms. Of course, women did not know this before now and therefore did not set out to achieve it, but the astonishing thing is that if the study by Baker and Bellis proves to be right, they are doing it anyway, perhaps quite unconsciously. This, of course, is typical of evolutionary explanations. Why do women have sex at all? Because they consciously want to. But why do they consciously want to? Because sex leads to reproduction, and being the descendants of those who reproduced, they are selected from among those who want things that lead to reproduction. This is merely a form of the same argument: The typical woman's pattern of infidelity and orgasm is exactly what you would expect to find if she were unconsciously trying to get pregnant from a lover while not leaving a husband.

Baker and Bellis do not claim to have found more than a tantalizing hint that this is so, but they have tried to measure the extent of cuckoldry in human beings. In a block of flats in Liverpool, they found by genetic tests that fewer than four in every five people were the sons of their ostensible fathers. In case this had something to do with Liverpool, they did the same tests in southern England and got the same result. We know from their earlier work that a small degree of adultery can lead to a larger degree of cuckoldry through the orgasm effect. Like birds, women may be—quite unconsciously—having it both ways by conducting affairs with genetically more valuable men while not leaving their husbands.

What about the men? Baker and Bellis did an experiment on rats and discovered that a male rat ejaculates twice as much sperm when he knows that the female he is mating with has been near another male recently. The intrepid scientists promptly set out to test whether human beings do the same. Sure enough, they do. Men whose wives have been with them all day ejaculate much smaller amounts than men whose wives have been absent all day. It is as if the males are subconsciously compensating for any opportunities for female infidelity that might be present. But in this particular battle of the sexes, the women have the upper hand because even if a man—again unconsciously—begins to associate his wife's lack of late orgasms with a desire not to conceive his child, she can always respond by faking them.[5]

[*The Red Queen: Sex and the Evolution of Human Nature* (Harmondsworth: Penguin, 1993), 223–6.]

III.b. Hermaphroditism/Intersexuality

It has always been the case that confusions about the sex of individuals could arise from either ambiguous anatomy or from behaviour and desires at apparent odds with the sexed body. The concept of the hermaphrodite arose in Greek times and has continued into modern times, when, as we have seen, sexologists have speculated about a 'third sex' lying somewhere between male and female. Though the varieties of genital and bodily anomalies presented by hermaphroditism were widely noted by the early modern period, it was not until the twentieth century that the statistical occurrence and the developmental causes of such phenomena were fully understood. It was also not until the twentieth century that surgical procedures were developed that could sharpen the sexual lines blurred by imperfect embryological development. The common term for the phenomenon today is intersexuality.

The meaning of this phenomenon has varied historically, depending on the scientific and natural norms that have been used to judge the intersexed individual. The sexually ambiguous person may either confirm or challenge the prevailing order of nature, and thus earn sympathy or scorn from contemporaries. It is useful to reconsider the concepts of the Western medical tradition that have undergirded these different possibilities and their implications for the current situation (Extract 92).

Until the end of the nineteenth century, the fundamental unity of the model of sex, gender role, and sexual desire remained more or less intact. In the *fin de siècle*, the social and cultural changes we have noted, together with the 'discovery' of the perversions, posed a challenge to the coherence of this model. However, despite, or perhaps because of these changes, doctors were all the more anxious to reassert the primacy of the old rules. One hard case of intersexuality dating from 1892 stimulated the experts involved to square identity and desire with what they took to be anatomical sex (Extract 93).

By the 1930s or so, a fairly standard form of classification had been worked out that provided a descriptive anatomical map of the various forms of human hermaphroditism that are presented in nature. Many individuals were found to have the gonads of one sex (testes or ovaries) and more or less complete genitalia of the other. This condition was called pseudohermaphroditism and made up the vast majority of cases. So-called 'true' hermaphrodites are far rarer; these possess both ovarian and testicular tissue in forms that are either 'unilateral' (both forms of tissue only on one side), 'alternate' (ovarian on one side, testicular on the other), or 'bilateral' (both kinds of tissue present on both sides). By 1976 only about 200 such cases had been documented. However, though the descriptive system resembled the anatomical one of the nineteenth century, the emphasis had changed to an analysis of the aetiological origins of these conditions, which could be traced to genetic, hormonal, or other intrauterine causes, or some combination of these. In Extract 94's brief introduction to an ambitious overview of the subject, an analytical approach is suggested by an American physician with an eye for what he calls 'optimum clinical management'.

By the late 1960s, the physician and medical psychologist John Money and his associates had begun to break down the kinds of intersex variations that occurred according to a temporal scheme that identified not only occasions for surgical intervention but situations in which counselling and education can make the 'assigned sex' bestowed on an individual the basis of a satisfactory life experience. Indeed, Money broke with many of his medical colleagues in emphasizing the overwhelming importance of social and cultural experience in establishing a functional gender identity. Money's outlook has dominated the field of intersexuality in recent years. His tone is sympathetic and his point of view incorporates modern gender perspectives, though it is easy to recognize the medical model in operation in this selection (Extract 95).

A critical point of view on these systems of classification and on the clinical and interventionist frame of reference they employ has emerged in recent years to challenge some of the standard assumptions of intersex medicine. Anne Fausto-Sterling, a molecular biologist, has written a brief article in which she illuminates the underlying gender and cultural biases of this interventionist medicine. Her critique has the additional advantage of displaying the extraordinary complexity of the twentieth-century sexual body with which we are concerned in this part of the book (Extract 96).

These traditions differed in a number of important ways, and from them the early modern period inherited two contrasting models of hermaphroditism with radically different sexual, and ultimately social, implications. The oldest, associated with the Hippocratic writers and (in this respect) with Galen, viewed hermaphrodites as beings truly intermediate in sex, neither male nor female, but exactly in between.[1] According to this theory, the sex of the fetus was determined by two important oppositions: between the male and female principles in the maternal and paternal seed and between the left and right sides of the uterus.[2] Depending on which seed from which parent was dominant and the position of the fetus in the womb, the offspring would occupy one of a number of possible points on a sexual spectrum, ranging from unambiguously male (male seed contributed by both mother and father lodged in the right side of the uterus) to wholly female (female seed contributed by both mother and father lodged in the left side of the uterus). Other combinations were thought to produce offspring of intermediate sexual nature: fragile and effeminate males, strong and virile females, and—in the rare event of perfectly balanced male and female factors—the occasional hermaphrodite.[3]

The second model inherited by early modern writers viewed hermaphrodites not as beings of intermediate sex but as beings with doubled or redundant genitalia—a particular and unusual case of twins *manqués*. This model had its roots in the works of Aristotle, most notably the *Generation of Animals*, where he discussed hermaphrodites in the context of multiple births.[4] According to Aristotle, hermaphrodites were produced when the matter contributed by the mother—unlike the Hippocratic writers, he denied the existence of female seed—was more than enough for one fetus but not enough for two. A large amount of extra matter would yield conjoined twins, each almost perfect in form. A small amount would go to make only an extra member, either internal or external, depending on where in the body it happened to be located. On the foot, for example, it would produce a sixth toe; in the groin, a second set of genitals. In this latter case, if the paternal seed had either fully mastered or been mastered by the maternal matter—the basis of Aristotle's general account of sex determination—both sets of genitals would be either male or female; but if the seed mastered the matter in one part but not in the other, the fetus would have one of each. Even in this case, however, the sex of the hermaphrodite was never more than apparently ambiguous, since the sex of the whole fetus was determined by the heat of the heart, which in turn determined the complexion of the body as a whole.[5]

This model expressed the characteristic Aristotelian interpretation of sexual difference, which presented male and female less as points on a spectrum, in the

Hippocratic manner, than as polar opposites admitting no meaningful media-tion.[6] Thus from the Aristotelian point of view, hermaphroditism was a condition only of the genitals—the product of a local excess of matter and imbalance of male and female principles—rather than of the entire organism. There could be no true hermaphrodites in the sense of the Hippocratic model; the animal was either male or female, and the other set of genitals was always inoperative, resembling in that respect a tumor or growth.[7]

Although both the Hippocratic and the Aristotelian accounts were natural-istic, they differed greatly from each other in their implications for sexuality and gender. The Hippocratic model was sexually charged: allowing for a spectrum of intermediate sexual possibilities, it posed a potential challenge to the male–female dichotomy and to the whole social and sexual order based on that dichotomy. The Aristotelian model, on the other hand, had none of those reson-ances; the sexual ambiguity of the hermaphrodite was never more than super-ficial, leaving the bipolar sexual order intact.

Over the course of more than a thousand years, these two contrasting ancient accounts of hermaphroditism were transmitted to medieval and early modern medical theorists in a number of stages, as various key texts were successively translated from Greek into Latin and through the intermediary of Arabic writers such as Avicenna.[8] The result of this piecemeal transmission was a complicated intellectual situation, in which Hippocratic and Aristotelian interpretations wove their way through medieval and early modern medicine and natural philosophy, sometimes in counterpoint, more often in uneasy synthesis. In general, the 'Hippocratic' model dominated writing on the subject in the early Middle Ages.[9] With the Aristotelian revival in the thirteenth century, however, the situation became more complex. Although Aristotle's theory of generation generally gained the upper hand, it was strongly tempered with a distinct admixture of Hippocratic and Galenic elements. The result was a subtle and eclectic body of theory that admitted both debate and difference of opinion on nearly all the central issues raised by the problem of generation.[10] [. . .]

As emblems of sexual ambiguity, hermaphrodites—once consigned to the margins of legal, theological, medical and philosophical treatises—became an urgent topic. The burning questions they raised for early modern writers concerned the authority to judge and the criteria for judgment: who decided the hermaphrodite's sex and on what grounds? When moderns confront these questions, they test the resilience of powerful and contested popularities: male versus female, individual versus society, and nature versus culture. This is certainly one reason why early modern deliberations on sexing hermaphro-dites have attracted so much recent historical attention. It is important to remember, however, that early modern categories were not identical to our own: the opposition between nature and culture—sex versus gender and medi-cine versus law being but special cases of this opposition—would have made little sense to early modern writers on hermaphrodites. Early modern thinkers parsed such phenomena as hermaphrodites in terms of the dichotomies that were meaningful to them: natural versus artificial, natural versus preternatural, and natural versus unnatural. In these dichotomies, and more generally, the natural was usually the normative. In this section, we shall argue that although early modern writers planted hermaphrodites firmly on the natural side of the natural/supernatural divide, their location within the oppositions of natural versus artificial, natural versus preternatural, and natural versus unnatural shifted precariously toward the non-natural pole during this period.

['The Hermaphrodite and the Orders of Nature: Sexual Ambiguity in Early Modern France', *GLQ: A Journal of Gay & Lesbian Studies*, 1/4 (1995), 420–2, 425.]

ALICE D. DREGER
....

93 Gonadal Sex

In the summer of 1892, one not-so-ladylike individual by the name of Louise-Julia-Anna presented herself to Dr François Guermonprez of Lille. She had been referred to him by his colleague, Dr Reumeaux of Dunkirk, with 'no other information than this: "subject interesting from the psychological point of view" '.[1] Though her face had been shaven clean just before their encounter, and though she came wearing a lady's dress, corset, gloves, and hat, Louise-Julia-Anna still stuck Guermonprez as a rather poor specimen of a woman:

Her outfit is rather badly adjusted, lacking in grace and lightness . . . her broach is placed poorly to the side; her girdle goes more to one side than the other; the flowers and the ribbons of her hat are disposed without taste and the entire ensemble bespeaks a sort of negligence, which is not the consequence of bad intentions, but which results mainly from absence of good taste.[2]

Still, Louise's unrefined taste in *dress* was not what made her so 'psychologically interesting' to the doctors. It was, rather, her taste in *lovers*: she desired only men. Indeed, she had had sexual intercourse with more than one man, but never a woman.

What did the doctors find so remarkable about this? Though Louise had been raised as a girl, and though she appeared, and believed herself, to be female, Reumeaux and Guermonprez were convinced that she was really a man. The patient had first come to Reumeaux seeking treatment for an inguinal hernia. But during a preliminary examination, the first doctor had discovered, much to his surprise, testicles, as well as what looked very much like a small penis:

Stupefied, [Reumeaux] interrogated [Louise] with prudence. This person thought herself a woman; she had had relations with men and showed no attraction toward persons of the feminine sex. There was nonetheless no doubt anatomically about the masculine sex of the subject [because she had testicles]; the questions were rephrased in vain: it always resulted in receiving responses which revealed the exclusive penchants of the feminine sex.[3]

If Louise was a man, as the doctors were certain, the doctors wondered why she desired another man, and only men. In Guermonprez's and Reumeaux's eyes, the combination of the subject's 'male' anatomical sex (because of her testicles) and her 'feminine' desires (because directed towards men) constituted a 'bizarre contradiction between the anatomical worth of the subject and the psychic characteristics of her sexual tendencies!'[4] This 'man' had 'womanly' desires, so, the doctors figured, there must be something wrong *psychologically* with Louise. Guermonprez and Reumeaux concluded that their patient was 'truly a teratological being morally as well as physically'.[5]

Guermonprez did not spare Louise the full brunt of his opinion: he told her she was a man, and instructed her to stop pretending otherwise. As might have been expected, 'the revelation of the masculine nature of [her] sex troubled [the patient] profoundly.' Guermonprez triumphantly noted, however, that there was 'not a tear, not a sigh, not the least vestige of an attack of nerves! There was nothing of that profound distress, of a true woman found in the presence of an event which reverses her life all at once'.[6] The fact that Louise took the life-altering news with 'a firmness thoroughly virile' convinced Guermonprez that this diagnosis was right: she must indeed be a 'true male,' a subject of 'pseudo-hermaphroditism.' Her sexual desires for men were therefore, in his eyes, thoroughly inappropriate.

Long before and throughout the nineteenth century, 'hermaphrodite' was the name given to a person who possessed something other than one of the two sets of sexual organs common to most people. That is, a hermaphrodite was a person who appeared to be anatomically something other than a 'typical' man or a woman. People like Louise-Julia-Anna were called more precisely by nineteenth-century medical and scientific men '*pseudo*hermaphrodites' because, as far as the men who studied them were concerned, the subjects did not possess all the organs *essential* to both the male and the female. Interestingly, what has counted as 'essential' to 'true' malehood or 'true' femalehood has changed over time,[7] but for Reumeaux, Guermonprez, and their contemporaries, the gonads (that is, the testes or ovaries) were the markers of true sex. Louise would have to possess both ovaries and testicles to be a 'true' hermaphrodite. Three feminine names, coiffed hair, a dress, a corset, sexual desires for men—all these supposedly 'feminine' traits were not enough to make Louise a woman as far as the doctors were concerned. Her testes defined her as a man, and her doctors thereby demanded 'manhood' from her—bravery in the face of terrifying revelations, and 'masculine' desire for women even after a life of 'mistaken' womanhood.

As is evident in this case, personal and social identity had no role in the medical determination of 'true sex' at the end of the nineteenth century, nor did, for that matter, the external genitalia. 'Truth' was determined by that which was contained inside the body—the gonads—even if that 'truth' were invisible and unsuspected. The label of pseudohermaphroditism, then, could denote one of two general kinds of anatomical situations: (1) when a person had only ovaries or testes, but her/his genitalia displayed elements of both the conventional male and the conventional female anatomy (as when a person had both a 'penis' and a 'vagina'); or (2) when the genitalia looked female while the gonads were male, and vice versa.

A whole range of anatomical hermaphroditism had been documented for centuries before Louise was born and declared a girl (only to have her sex reversed twenty-three years later), but scientific and medical interest in the phenomenon increased greatly in the late nineteenth century. In part, this was because the medical and scientific communities were undergoing tremendous growth, particularly in the area of anatomicopathological research.[8] In the 1860s, the highly publicized sex change and suicide death of the French hermaphrodite Herculine Barbin served to focus medical and lay attention on the bizarre problems of hermaphroditism,[9] and there was no lack of subsequent cases to hold that attention. At the fin de siècle, hermaphrodites attracted the curiosity of many medical and scientific men because it was also then that social tensions surrounding issues of sex and sexuality burgeoned with the growing visibility of people who socially challenged traditional images of two distinct sexes (just as hermaphrodites anatomically challenged them)—people such as feminists, who questioned assumptions about the natures and destinies of men and women, and people such as 'inverts,' who challenged dominant ideas about sexuality by acting on their passionate attractions to people of their own sex. Like feminists and 'inverts,' hermaphrodites posed conceptual and practical problems for those (including members of the scientific and medical communities) who adamantly claimed men and women were naturally, fundamentally, and obviously different, and who also claimed that sexuality (specifically heterosexuality) was the natural result of the evolution of the two distinct sexes.

['Hermaphrodites in Love: The Truth of the Gonads', in Vernon A. Rosario (ed.), *Science and Homosexualities* (New York: Routledge, 1997), 46–8.]

JOE LEIGH SIMPSON

94 The Developmental Etiology of Hermaphroditism

Abnormalities of embryonic development can be delineated in several ways, and the disorders of abnormal sexual differentiation are no exception. I believe that the most logical approach is to categorize abnormalities on the basis of their etiology. Categorization based *exclusively* upon anatomical differences is usually inadequate. That is, individuals with the same disorder need not necessarily show the same spectrum of anomalies, and disorders of completely different etiology may be phenotypically similar. Sometimes delineation based upon anatomical differences is logical and at other times it is the only method available, yet an etiological approach should always be attempted. Although admittedly biased, I believe that delineation of malformations is best approached by a geneticist because geneticists are more accustomed to thinking in etiological terms than investigators in most other disciplines.

Therefore, I believe that a genetically oriented yet clinically relevant volume on abnormal sexual differentiation is in order. In addition, recent advances in genetics and endocrinology have increased our knowledge of abnormal sexual differentiation, and for this reason also I believe that the topic deserves fresh consideration. No other book seems to have emphasized the etiological approach or covered the same areas that this volume does. Some volumes provide practical advice concerning certain common disorders. Other volumes emphasize surgical and clinical management. By contrast, this book surveys the entire field of human abnormal sexual differentiation and tabulates almost all of the disorders that a physician or investigator could encounter, rather than being restricted to the most common disorders. [. . .]

As alluded to above, there is no unanimity concerning categorization of the disorders of sexual differentiation. One intellectually appealing approach is to categorize these disorders on the basis of the presumed site of action for the process that causes an abnormality. That is: Does the process affect the genetic sex, the gonadal sex, or the phenotypic sex?[1] Unfortunately, so few disorders have been studied thoroughly that this approach is not always applicable. Therefore, for both clinical and scientific reasons, I believe there is virtue in retaining several broad clinical categories in which individuals can be grouped on the basis of their chromosomal complement and gonadal status. These categories traditionally have included female pseudohermaphroditism, male pseudohermaphroditism, sex-reversal (XX males and true hermaphrodites), gonadal dysgenesis, and the Klinefelter syndrome. Other categories of abnormal sexual differentiation are hypogonadal states not included in the above categories, disorders of Wolffian and Müllerian ducts, and polysomy X or Y. Within each broad clinical category there are many distinct genetic conditions that must be delineated from one another for optimal clinical management; this delineation should be based upon genetic etiology, so far as possible. I believe that the approach suggested in this volume will not only be practical for the clinician who only occasionally deals with these disorders, but also will provide perspective for the investigator who searches for the cellular etiology.

[*Disorders of Sexual Differentiation: Etiology and Clinical Delineation* (New York: Academic Press, 1976), xi–xii, xii–xiii.]

95 The Kinds of Sex

The ultimate aim of sex education is the development of a child capable of healthy sexual and reproductive functioning in adulthood. Sex education thus fits into a sequence of developmental steps, the orderly progression of which is prerequisite to normal sexual functioning. In normal development, each step follows the other in such logical progression that one does not think of them as possibly being independent of one another. It was only through the study of sexual anomalies in which the sequence of development is not expected (such as I have paid attention to over the past fifteen years), that it became possible to differentiate one step from another and identify the developmental variables of sex which may be independent of one another. One may list these variables as follows:

1. Genetic or chromosomal sex
2. Gonadal sex
3. Fetal hormonal sex
4. Internal morphologic sex
5. External morphologic sex
6. Hypothalamic sex
7. Sex of assignment and rearing
8. Pubertal hormonal sex
9. Gender identity and role
10. Procreative sex impairments

Each of these variables of development has its own probabilities of error or malfunction. Some of the errors overlap from one variable to another. One does not say that an anomaly is caused by a particular variable, because the cause is actually much more complicated than that and usually is a chain of events. Thus, a genetic error may lead to an error in the production of fetal hormones or an error in their use, which in turn leads to an error of sex-organ morphology, and so forth. For this reason, the principle of classification in what follows is a temporal and not a causal one. The different clinical anomalies are arranged according to the time in the developmental sequence of the variables of sex when the most prominent characteristics of the anomaly are set. This arrangement allows for overlap in problems of sex education, such as the issue of predicted sterility, incongruity between gender identity and other variables, transmissible genetic defect, and so on, for these problems are not determined by the origin of an anomaly, per se. [. . .]

For the majority of the human race there is no discrepancy between any of the variables of sex. Gender identity differentiates in agreement with assigned sex and with the somatic variables of sex, all of which agree with one another. In the case of hermaphrodites, where discrepancies may exist between the several variables of sex, there is usually concordance between the assigned sex and the gender identity. This concordance is nowhere better illustrated than when two individuals of the same diagnosis are differently assigned, the gender identity in each case differentiating in accordance with the assignment and rearing.

Concordance between sex of assignment and gender identity is not, however, a universal rule. Psychosexual identity may become established in repudiation, or in partial repudiation, of an assignment which the person interprets as an error. Ambiguity of identity is especially likely to result, in the case of an hermaphrodite, when the parental attitude toward the child's sex is ambivalent, and when the physique and uncorrected genital appearance evoke teasing or remarks of doubt or astonishment, especially from age-mates. An ambiguous gender identity does not necessarily correlate with the chromosomal, gonadal, morphologic, or hormonal sex. Sometimes the correlation exists; sometimes it does not. It is just as likely that a genetic female hermaphrodite with ovaries will have been ostensibly raised as female and want to change to male as vice versa; and correspondingly for a male hermaphrodite.

There are some lucky instances when a definite gender identity does not become established. In such a case, it will be possible to rehabilitate the individual in the other sex, maintaining coital adequacy and reproductive fertility. Thus, it is intellectually and emotionally rather satisfying to most medical specialists if a female hermaphrodite, assigned and partly reared as a boy, wants to change and to live as a girl, rather than if the same individual, raised as a girl, wants to be reassigned as a boy. Nonetheless, there is no point in insisting on the continuance of an unwanted female assignment—or in imposing a female reassignment—when, as a girl, the patient will, irrespective of anatomy and reproductive function, retain a masculine psychosexual identity and fall in love with another girl. The same principle holds true in the corresponding case of a male hermaphrodite.

In male hermaphroditism there are some lucky cases in which the individual rejects a masculine assignment and does not develop a fully masculine psychosexual identity. These are the cases in which the penis will remain forever unfunctional in coitus because of its underdeveloped, clitoral size, whereas, after surgical and hormonal feminization, the individual will function adequately as a female.

The most expeditious rule to follow is that no child after the toddler age should have a sex-reassignment imposed on the basis of an a priori principle. Every case should be individually evaluated and decided upon its own merits.

[*Sex Errors of the Body: Dilemmas, Education, Counseling* (Baltimore: Johns Hopkins Press, 1968), 11–12, 85–6.]

How does one become a man? Although poets, novelists, and playwrights long past answered with discussions of morality and honor, these days scholars deliberate the same question using a metaphor—that of social construction. In the current intellectual fashion, men are made, not born. We construct masculinity through social discourse—that array of happenings that covers everything from the visuals on MTV, rap lyrics, and poetry to sports, beer commercials, and psychotherapy. But underlying all of this clever carpentry is the sneaking suspicion that one must start with a blueprint—or, to stretch the metaphor yet a bit more, that buildings must have foundations. Within the soul of even the most die-hard constructionist lurks a doubt. It is called the body.

In contrast, biological and medical scientists feel quite certain about their world. For them the body tells the truth. (Never mind that postmodern scholarship has questioned the very meaning of the word *truth*.) My task in this essay is to consider the truths that biologists extract from bodies, human and otherwise, to examine scientific accounts—some might even say constructions—of masculinity. To do this, I treat the scientific/medical literature as yet another set of texts open to scholarly analysis and interpretation.

What are little boys made of? While the nursery rhyme suggests 'snips and snails and puppy dog tails,' during the past seventy years medical scientists have built a rather more concrete and certainly less fanciful account. Perhaps the single most influential voice during this period has been that of the psychologist John Money. At least since the 1920s, embryologists have understood that during fetal development a single embryonic primordium, the indifferent fetal gonad, can give rise to either an ovary or a testis. In a similar fashion, both male and female external genitalia arise from a single set of structures. Only the internal sex organs—uteri, fallopian tubes, prostates, sperm transport ducts—arise during embryonic development from separate sets of structures. In the 1950s, John Money extended these embryological understandings into the realm of psychological development.[1] He envisioned that while all humans start on the same road, the path rapidly begins to fork. Potential males take a series of turns in one direction, potential females in another. In real time the road begins at fertilization and ends during late adolescence. If all goes as it should, then there are two and only two possible destinations: male and female.

But of course all does not always go as it should. Money identified the various forks in the road by studying individuals who took one or more wrong turns. From them he came up with a map of the normal. This is, in fact, one of the very interesting things about biological investigators. They use the infrequent to illuminate the common. The former they call abnormal, the latter, normal. Often, as is the case for Money and others in the medical world, the abnormal requires management. In the examples I will discuss, management means conversion to the normal. Thus we have a profound irony. Biologists and physicians use natural biological variation to define normality. Once armed with the description, they then set out to eliminate the natural variation that gave them their definitions in the first place.

How does all this apply to the construction of masculinity? Money lists ten road signs directing a person along the path to male or female. In most cases these indicators are clear, but as in any large city these days, sometimes graffiti makes them hard to read, and the traveler ends up taking a wrong turn. The first sign is *chromosomal sex*: the presence of an X or a Y. The second is *gonadal sex*: when there is no graffiti, the Y or the X instructs the fetal gonad to develop into a testis or an ovary. *Fetal hormonal sex* marks the third fork: the embryonic testis must make hormones that influence events to come—most especially the fourth (*internal morphologic sex*), fifth (*external morphologic sex*), and sixth (*brain sex*) branches in the road. All of these, but most especially external morphologic sex at birth, illuminate the road sign for step number seven: *sex of assignment and rearing*. Finally, to become, in John Money's world, either a true male or a true female, one must produce the right hormones at puberty (*pubertal hormonal sex*), acquire and express a consistent gender identity and role, and, to complete the picture, must be able to reproduce in the appropriate fashion (*procreative sex*).[2]

Many medical texts reproduce this neat little scheme, suggesting that it is a literal account of the scientific truth, but neglecting to point out how, at each step, scientists have woven into the fabric their own deeply social preexisting understandings of what it means to be male or female. Let me illustrate this for several of the branches in the road. Why is it that usually XX babies grow up to be female while XYs become male? Geneticists say that it is because of a specific Y chromosome gene, often abbreviated SDY for 'sex-determining gene on the Y chromosome.' Biologists also refer to the SDY as the Master Sex Determining gene, and say that in its *presence*, a male is formed. Females, on the other hand, are said to be the default sex. In the *absence* of the master gene, they just naturally happen. The story of the SDY begins an account of maleness which continues throughout development. A male embryo must activate its master gene and seize its developmental pathway from the underlying female ground plan.

When the SDY gene starts working, it turns the indifferent gonad into a functional testis. One of the first things the testis does is to induce hormone synthesis. It is these molecules that take control of subsequent developmental steps. The first hormone to hit the decks (MIS or Müllerian Inhibiting Substance) suppresses the development of the internal female organs, which otherwise lie in wait ready to unveil their feminine presence. The next, fetal testosterone, manfully pushes other embryonic primordia to develop both the internal and external trappings of physical masculinity. Again, medical texts offer the presence/absence hypothesis: Maleness requires the presence of special hormones; in their absence, femaleness just happens.[3]

At this point two themes emerge. First, masculinity is an active presence that forces itself onto a feminine foundation. Money calls this 'The Adam Principle—adding something to make a male.'[4] Second, the male is in constant danger. At any point, male development can be derailed: a failure to activate SDY, and the gonad becomes an ovary; a failure to make MIS, and the fetus can end up with fallopian tubes and a uterus superimposed on an otherwise male body; fail to make fetal testosterone, and, despite the presence of a testis, the embryo develops the external trappings of a baby girl. One fascinating contradiction in the scientific literature illustrates my point. Most texts write that femaleness results from the absence of male hormones,[5] at the same time, scientists worry about how male fetuses protect themselves from being feminized by the sea of maternal (female) hormones in which they grow. This fear suggests, of course, that female hormones play an active role after all; but most scientists do not pick up on that bit of logic. Instead they hunt for special proteins the male embryo makes in order to protect itself from maternally induced feminization. (It seems that mother is to blame even before birth.)

Consider now the birth of a boy-child. He is perfect—Y chromosomes, testes descended into their sweet little scrotal sacs, a beautifully formed penis. He is perfect—except that the penis is very tiny. What happens next? Some medical texts refer to a situation such as this as a social emergency; others, as a surgical one. The parents want to tell everyone about the birth of their baby boy; the physicians fear he cannot continue developing along the road to masculinity. They decide that creating a female is best. Females are imperfect by nature, and if this child cannot be a perfect or near-perfect male, then being an imperfect female is the best choice. What do physicians' criteria for making such choices tell us about the construction of masculinity?

Medical managers use the following rule of thumb: 'Genetic females should always be raised as females, preserving reproductive potential, regardless of how severely the patients are virilized. In the genetic male, however, the gender of assignment is based on the infant's anatomy, predominantly the size of the phallus'.[6] Only a few reports on penile size at birth exist in the scientific literature, and it seems that birth size, in and of itself, is not a particularly good indicator of size and function at puberty. The average phallus at birth measures 3.5 cm (1–1.5 in.) long. A baby boy born with a penis measuring only 0.9 inches raises some eyebrows, while medical practitioners do not permit one born with a penis less than 0.6 inches long to remain as a male. (The medical name for this condition is 'micropenis.') Despite the fact that the intact organ may provide orgasmic pleasure to the future adult, it is surgically removed (along with the testes), and replaced by a much smaller clitoris, which may or may not retain orgasmic function. When surgeons turn 'Sammy' into 'Suzanna,' they also build her a vagina. Her primary sexual activity is to be the recipient of a penis during heterosexual intercourse. As one surgeon recently commented, 'It's easier to poke a hole than build a pole.'

All this surgical activity goes on to ensure a congruous and certain sex of assignment and sex of rearing. During childhood, the medical literature insists, boys must have a phallus large enough to permit them to pee standing up, thus allowing them to 'feel normal' when they play in little boys' peeing contests. In adulthood the penis must become large enough for vaginal penetration during sexual intercourse. By and large, physicians use the standard of reproductive potential for making females and phallus size for making males, although Kessler reports one case of a physician choosing to reassign as male a potentially reproductive genetic female infant rather than remove a well-formed penis.[7]

At birth, then, masculinity becomes a social phenomenon. For proper masculine socialization to occur, the little boy must have a sufficiently large penis. There must be in no doubt in the boy's mind, in the minds of his parents and other adult relatives, or in the minds of his male peers about the legitimacy of male identification. In childhood all that is required is that he be able to pee in a standing position. In adulthood he must engage in vaginal heterosexual intercourse. The discourse of sexual pleasure, even for males, is totally absent from this medical literature. In fact, male infants who receive extensive penile surgery often end up with badly scarred and thus physically insensitive members. While no surgeon considers this to be a desirable outcome, in assigning sex to an intersexual infant or to a boy with micropenis, sexual pleasure clearly takes a back seat to ensuring heterosexual conventions. Penetration in the absence of pleasure takes precedence over pleasure in the absence of penetration.

In the world of John Money and other managers of intersexuality, men are made, not born. Proper socialization becomes more important than genetics. Hence, Money and Ehrhardt have a simple solution to accidents as terrible as accidental penile amputation following infant circumcision: raise the boy as a girl.[8] If both the parents and child remain confident of his new-found identity, all will be well. But what counts as good mental health for boys and girls? Here Money and coworkers focus primarily on female development, which becomes the mirror from which we can reflect the truth about males. Money has published extensively on observations of XX infants born with masculinized genitalia.[9] Usually such children are raised as girls, and receive surgery and hormonal treatments to feminize their genitalia and ensure a feminine puberty. He notes that frequently such children have a harder time than usual achieving clarity about their femininity. The signs of trouble include: engaging in rough-and-tumble play, and hitting more often than other toddler girls; thinking more about having a career, and fantasizing less about marriage than other adolescent girls; and having lesbian relationships as an adolescent and young adult.

The homologue to these developmental variations can be found in Richard Green's description of the 'Sissy Boy Syndrome'.[10] Green studied little boys who develop feminine interests—playing with dolls, dressing in girls' clothing, not engaging in enough rough-and-tumble play. These boys, he argued, are at a high risk for becoming homosexuals. Money's and Green's ideas work together to present a picture of normality. And—surprise, surprise—there is no room in the scheme for a normal homosexual. Money makes a remarkable claim. Genetics and even hormones count less in making a man or a woman than does socialization. In sustaining that claim his strongest evidence, his trump card, is that the child born a male but raised a female becomes a heterosexual female. In fact, Milton Diamond has followed up on Money's early case histories and found the outcomes to be far more complex. In their accounts of the power of socialization, Money, Hampson, and Hampson define heterosexual in terms of the sex of rearing. Thus a child raised as a female (even if biologically male) who prefers male lovers is psychologically heterosexual, although genetically she is not.

Again, we can parse out the construction of masculinity. To begin with, normally developing little boys must be active and willing to push one another around; maleness and aggression go together. Eventually little boys become socialized into appropriate adult behavior, which includes heterosexual fantasy and activity. Adolescent boys do not dream of marriage, but of careers and a professional future. A healthy adolescent girl, in contrast, must fantasize about falling in love, marrying, and raising children. Only a masculinized girl dreams of a professional future. Of course, we know already that for men the true mark of heterosexuality involves vaginal penetration with the penis. Other activities, even if they are with a woman, do not really count.

This might be the end of the story, except for one thing: accounts of normal development drawn from the study of intersexuals contain internal inconsistencies. How does Money explain the higher-than-normal percentage of lesbianism or the more frequent aggressive behavior among masculinized children raised as girls? One could imagine elaborating on the socialization theme: parents aware of the uncertain sex of their children subconsciously socialize them in some intermediary fashion. Shockingly for a psychologist, however, Money denies the possibility of subconsciously driven behavior.[11] Instead, he and the many others who interpret the development of intersexual children resort to hormonal explanations. If an XX girl born with a penis, surgically 'corrected' shortly after birth and raised as a girl, subsequently becomes a lesbian, Money and others do not look to socialization. Instead they explain this failure to become heterosexual by appealing to hormones present in the fetal environment. Excess fetal testosterone caused the masculinization of the genitalia; similarly, fetal testosterone must have altered the developing brain, readying it to view females as appropriate sexual objects. Here, then, we have the last bit of the picture painted by biologists. By implication, normal males become sexually attracted to females because testosterone affects their brain during embryonic development. Socialization reinforces this inclination.

Biologists, therefore, write texts about human development. These documents, which take the form of research papers, texts, review articles, and popular books, grow from interpretations of scientific data. Often written in neutral, abstract language, the texts have the ring of authority. Because they represent scientific findings, one might imagine that they contain no preconceptions, no culturally instigated belief systems. But this turns out not to be the case. Although based on evidence, scientific writing can be seen as a particular kind of cultural interpretation—the enculturated scientist interprets nature. In the process, he or she also uses that interpretation to reinforce old or build new sets of social beliefs. Thus scientific work contributes to the construction of masculinity, and masculine constructs are among the building blocks for particular kinds of scientific knowledge. One of the jobs of the science critic is to iluminate this interaction. Once such illumination has occurred, it becomes possible to discuss change.

['How to Build a Man', in Vernon A. Rosario (ed.), *Science and Homosexualities* (New York: Routledge, 1997), 219–25.]

III.c. The Discovery of Hormones

Evidence for the existence and the importance of 'internal secretions' in bodily functions began to accumulate in the mid-nineteenth century. Physiological researchers such as the Frenchman Claude Bernard and the Englishman Thomas Addison found that certain internal organs (eventually, it would be understood, almost all internal organs) secreted substances that played a certain regulatory role in metabolism and general health. The liver and the adrenal glands were among the first to be investigated in this connection. In the course of the twentieth century medical researchers have mapped the extent and function of the endocrine system and explored in great detail the body's production of other chemical substances such as neurotransmitters that enable the nervous system and make sentient life possible.

The discovery of the 'hormonal body' in this century allows us to understand, in short, how important these substances are to the body's health and internal economy. The discovery of the 'sex hormones' was a crucial part of this process of discovery; indeed, one might say it was a necessary part because it was the popular and scientific fascination with their power in the life of the organism that inspired the first efforts to extract and later synthesize them for 'therapeutic' use. One of these synthetic hormones, oestrogen, is the most common prescription drug used in the world.

Research on sex hormones was from the beginning profoundly influenced by an older pharmacological tradition that identified sex—as we have seen above—with the gonads, and by traditional cultural beliefs about sex and sex identity as unitary and indivisible things. The fact that the testes were believed to be the functional and anatomical organs of men and masculinity, and (eventually) the ovaries those of women and femininity, is signified by the importance in ancient and modern pharmacopoeias of extracts made from these organs for a variety of reproductive and health problems. In 1889 Charles-Édouard Brown-Séquard, a distinguished 72-year-old French physiologist, announced to a scientific audience that he had succeeded in 'rejuvenating' himself through injections of an extract derived from guinea pig and dog testicles.

Brown-Séquard did not draw particular attention to improvements in his urinary-reproductive function (though he did call it 'spermatic' liquid) but to an increase in his general vigour; nevertheless, in the generally hostile reception to his findings, the common theme of its impropriety testifies to the underlying concerns such research evoked. In a private letter circulated by a British physician, it was suggested that 'The object of these abominable proceedings is to enable broken-down libertines to pursue with renewed vigour the excesses of youth, to rekindle the dying embers in the debilitated and aged, and to profane the bodies of men which are the temples of God by an elixir drawn from the testicles of dogs and rabbits by a process involving the excruciating torture of the innocent animals, which elixir is then injected by a physician into the veins of his patient whom he has caused to practice a degrading and loathing vice.'[1] Brown-Séquard's findings were not successfully replicated and remained controversial, but the extract method he pioneered was applied within a few years with great success to thyroid and adrenal deficiencies, and the modern science of endocrinology and the medical practice of hormone therapy were under way (Extract 97).

It was a long time, however, before the gonad-centred notion of masculinity and femininity was challenged. This was literally and figuratively true. Following the slaughter of a generation of European and American men in the First World War, fears of population decline and cultural senescence gripped the West. Serious scientists and health quacks alike set to work on nostrums and experiments for improving fertility and sexual vigour. The most famous of these was Serge Voronoff, a Russian physician who emigrated to France before the war and who became famous in 1919 as the inventor of a technique of grafting monkey testes onto human testicles. The endocrine revolution had made great strides by that time and the notion that 'You are only as old as your glands' had made headway in public consciousness. Voronoff wrote a book in 1920 in which he summarized some of his most important findings and techniques. His style combined the mixture of self-promotion and claims for success typical of medical entrepreneurship in any age (Extract 98).

An Austrian researcher, Eugen Steinach, made similarly far-reaching claims for his 'rejuvenation' procedures in the inter-war period. Steinach's great discovery was nothing less (or more) than vasoligation, the operation of tying off the seminal vesicles through which spermatic fluid enters the urethra. Steinach was vague about how his procedure actually worked, but he appears to have simply subscribed to the age-old notion that retained spermatic fluid was somehow recycled back into the body as a source of vigour. In addition, by perfecting techniques for grafting testes and ovaries in animals, Steinach was able to produce a wide range of intersexual conditions, suggesting an infinite sexual malleability in the sexual nature of organisms. He did not conclude in favour of such malleability, however, but subscribed to the idea of 'sex antagonism' between specifically male and female sex hormones, which came, respectively, from the male and female gonads and acted in opposition to one another in the organism. They were thus conceptualized, as the historian Nelly Oudshoorn has pointed out, as 'the chemical messengers of masculinity and femininity'.[2] In a passage from his autobiography *Sex and Life*, Steinach pays

[1] Quoted in Michael J. Aminoff, *Brown-Séquard: A Visionary of Science* (New York: Raven Press, 1993), 165–6.

[2] Nelly Oudshoorn, *Beyond the Natural Body: An Archeology of Sex Hormones* (London: Routledge, 1994), 17.

enthusiastic tribute to the importance of the hormonal revolution and the centrality of sex and sex difference (Extract 99).

By the end of the 1930s, what came to be called 'oestrogens' and 'androgens' had both been successfully extracted from the urine of male and female horses. This discovery, when linked with the findings that the adrenal glands also produced sex hormones, undermined the notion of the sex-specific origin and nature of sex hormones. It was also found that sex hormones were not limited in their chemical function to the body's sexual development, but were also indispensable to a number of other metabolic processes. These discoveries ought to have played havoc with the concept of sex-specific hormones, but, as Nelly Oudshoorn explains, the linkage was maintained in both scientific terminology and in the research agendas of scientists specializing in this branch of endocrine research. What is more, though their findings complicated the traditional concepts of sex, sex difference, and sexuality, endocrinologists most often inscribed their new findings on the archetypal bodies constructed by classical sexology (Extract 100).

97 Testicular Rejuvenation

On the 1st of June last I made at the Société de Biologie of Paris a communication on the above subject, which was published in the *Comptes Rendus* of that Society on June 21st (No. 24). I will give here a summary of the facts and views contained in that paper and in two subsequent ones, adding to them some new points.

There is no need of describing at length the great effects produced on the organisation of man by castration, when it is made before the adult age. It is particularly well known that eunuchs are characterised by their general debility and their lack of intellectual and physical activity. There is no medical man who does not know also how much the mind and body of men (especially before the spermatic glands have acquired their full power, or when that power is declining in consequence of advanced age) are affected by sexual abuse or by masturbation. Besides, it is well known that seminal losses, arising from any cause, produce a mental and physical debility which is in proportion to their frequency. These facts and many others have led to the generally admitted view that in the seminal fluid, as secreted by the testicles, a substance or several substances exist which, entering the blood by resorption, have a most essential use in giving strength to the nervous system and to other parts. But, if what may be called spermatic anaemia leads to that conclusion, the opposite state, which can be named spermatic plethora, gives as strong a testimony in favour of that conclusion. It is known that well-organised men, especially from twenty to thirty-five years of age, who remain absolutely free from sexual intercourse or any other causes of expenditure of seminal fluid, are in a state of excitement, giving them a great, although abnormal, physical and mental activity. These two series of facts contribute to show what great dynamogenic power is possessed by some substance or substances which our blood owes to the testicles.

For a great many years I have believed that the weakness of old men depended on two causes—a natural series of organic changes and the gradually diminishing action of the spermatic glands. In 1860, in a course of lectures at the Paris Faculty of Medicine, discussing the influence possessed by several glands upon the nervous centres, I put forward the idea that if it were possible without danger to inject semen into the blood of old men, we should probably obtain manifestations of increased activity as regards the mental and the various physical powers. Led by this view, I made various experiments on animals at Nahant, near Boston (United States), in 1875. In some of those experiments, made on a dozen male dogs, I tried vainly, except in one case, to engraft certain parts or the whole body of young guinea-pigs. The success obtained in the exceptional case served to give me great hopes that by a less difficult process I should some day

reach my aim. This I have now done. At the end of last year I made on two old
male rabbits experiments which were repeated since on several others, with
results leaving no doubt as regards both the innocuity[1] of the process used and
the good effects produced in all those animals. This having been ascertained, I
resolved to make experiments on myself, which I thought would be far more
decisive on man than on animals. The event has proved the correctness of that
idea.

Leaving aside and for future researches the questions relating to the
substance or substances which, being formed by the testicles, give power to the
nervous centres and other parts, I have made use, in subcutaneous injections, of
a liquid containing a small quantity of water mixed with the three following
parts: first, blood of the testicular veins;[2] secondly, semen; and thirdly, juice
extracted from a testicle, crushed immediately after it has been taken from a
dog or a guinea-pig. Wishing in all the injections made on myself to obtain the
maximum of effects, I have employed as little water as I could. To the three
kinds of substances I have just named, I added distilled water in a quantity
which never exceeded three or four times their volume. The crushing was
always done after the addition of water. When filtered through a paper filter,
the liquid was of a reddish hue and rather opaque, while it was almost perfectly
clear and transparent when Pasteur's filter was employed. For each injection I
have used nearly one cubic centimetre of the filtered liquid. The animals
employed were a strong and, according to all appearances, perfectly healthy
dog (from two to three years old), and a number of very young or adult guinea-
pigs. The experiments, so far, do not allow of a positive conclusion as regards
the relative power of the liquid obtained from a dog and that drawn from
guinea-pigs. All I can assert is that the two kinds of animals have given a liquid
endowed with very great power. I have hitherto made ten subcutaneous injections of such a liquid—two in my left arm, all the others in my lower limbs—
from May 15th to June 4th last. The first five injections were made on three
succeeding days with a liquid obtained from a dog. In all the subsequent injections, made on May 24th, 29th, and 30th, and June 4th, the liquid used came
from guinea-pigs. When I employed liquids having passed through Pasteur's
filter, the pains and other bad effects were somewhat less than when a paper
filter was used.

Coming now to the favourable effects of these injections, I beg to be excused
for speaking so much as I shall do of my own person. I hope it will easily be
understood that, if my demonstration has any value—I will even say any significance—it is owing to the details concerning the state of my health, strength,
and habits previously to my experiments, and to the effects they have produced.

I am seventy-two years old. My general strength, which has been considerable, has notably and gradually diminished during the last ten or twelve years.
Before May 15th last, I was so weak that I was always compelled to sit down after
half an hour's work in the laboratory. Even when I remained seated all the time,

or almost all the time, in the laboratory, I used to come out of it quite exhausted after three or four hours' experimental labour, and sometimes after only two hours. For many years, on returning home in a carriage by six o'clock after several hours passed in the laboratory, I was so extremely tired that I invariably had to go to bed after having hastily taken a very small amount of food. Very frequently the exhaustion was so great that, although extremely sleepy, I could not for hours go to sleep, and I only slept very little, waking up exceedingly tired.[3]

The day after the first subcutaneous injection, and still more after the two succeeding ones, a radical change took place in me, and I had ample reason to say and to write that I had regained at least all the strength I possessed a good many years ago. Considerable laboratory work hardly tired me. To the great astonishment of my two principal assistants, Drs D'Arsonval and Hénocque, and other persons, I was able to make experiments for several hours while standing up, feeling no need whatever to sit down. Still more: one day (the 23rd of May), after three hours and a quarter of hard experimental labour in the standing attitude, I went home so little tired that after dinner I was able to go to work and to write for an hour and a half a part of a paper on a difficult subject. For more than twenty years I had never been able to do as much.[4] From a natural impetuosity, and also to avoid losing time, I had, till I was sixty years old, the habit of ascending and descending stairs so rapidly that my movements were rather those of running than of walking. This had gradually changed, and I had come to move slowly up and down stairs, having to hold the banister in difficult staircases. After the second injection I found that I had fully regained my old powers, and returned to my previous habits in that respect.

My limbs, tested with a dynamometer, for a week before my trial and during the month following the first injection, showed a decided gain of strength. The average number of kilogrammes moved by the flexors of the right forearm, before the first injection was about 34½ (from 32 to 37), and after that injection 41 (from 39 to 44), the gain being from 6 to 7 kilogrammes. In that respect the forearm flexors re-acquired, in a great measure, the strength they had when I was living in London (more than twenty-six years ago). The average number of kilogrammes moved by those muscles in London in 1863[5] was 43 (40 to 46 kilogrammes).

I have measured comparatively, before and after the first injection, the jet of urine in similar circumstances—i.e., after a meal in which I had taken food and drink of the same kind in similar quantity. The average length of the jet during the ten days that preceded the first injection was inferior by at least one quarter of what it came to be during the twenty following days. It is therefore quite evident that the power of the spinal cord over the bladder was considerably increased.

One of the most troublesome miseries of advanced life consists in the diminution of the power of defecation. To avoid repeating the details I have elsewhere given in that respect, I will simply say that after the first days of my experiments I have had a greater improvement with regard to the expulsion of fecal matters than in any other function. In fact a radical change took place, and even on days of great constipation the power I long ago possessed had returned.

With regard to the facility of intellectual labour, which had diminished within the last few years, a return to my previous ordinary condition became quite manifest during and after the first two or three days of my experiments.

It is evident from these facts and from some others that all the functions depending on the power of action of the nervous centres, and especially of the spinal cord, were notably and rapidly improved by the injections I have used. The last of these injections was made on June 4th, about five weeks and a half ago. I ceased making use of them for the purpose of ascertaining how long their good effects would last. For four weeks no marked change occurred, but gradually, although rapidly, from the 3rd of this month (July) I have witnessed almost a complete return of the state of weakness which existed before the first injection. This loss of strength is an excellent counter-proof as regards the demonstration of the influence exerted on me by the subcutaneous injections of a spermatic fluid.

My first communication to the Paris Biological Society was made with the wish that other medical men advanced in life would make on themselves experiments similar to mine, so as to ascertain, as I then stated, if the effects I had observed depended or not on any special idiosyncrasy or on a kind of auto-suggestion without hypnotisation, due to the conviction which I had before experimenting that I should surely obtain a great part at least of these effects. This last supposition found some ground in many of the facts contained in the valuable and learned work of Dr Hack Tuke on the 'Influence of the Mind over the Body.' Ready as I was to make on my own person experiments which, if they were not dangerous, were at least exceedingly painful, I refused absolutely to yield to the wishes of many people anxious to obtain the effects I had observed on myself. But, without asking my advice, Dr Variot, a physician who believed that the subcutaneous injections of considerably diluted spermatic fluid[6] could do no harm, has made a trial of that method on three old men—one fifty-four, another fifty-six, and the third sixty-eight years old.[7] On each of them the effects have been found to be very nearly the same as those I have obtained on myself. Dr Variot made use of the testicles of rabbits and guinea-pigs.

These facts clearly show that it was not to a peculiar idosyncrasy of mine that the effects I have pointed out were due. As regards the explanation of those effects by an auto-suggestion, it is hardly possible to accept it in the case of the patients treated by Dr Variot. They had no idea of what was being done; they knew nothing of my experiments, and were only told that they were receiving *fortifying* injections. To find out if this qualification had anything to do with the effects produced, Dr Variot, since the publication of his paper, has employed similar words of encouragement, whilst making subcutaneous injections of pure water on two other patients, who obtained thereby no strengthening effect whatever.[8]

['The Effects Produced on Man by Subcutaneous Injections of a Liquid Obtained from the Testicles of Animals, *Lancet* (20 July 1889), 105–6.]

DAVID HAMILTON
....

98   The Monkey Gland Affair

[Voronoff's] book was called *Life*, and the English version was translated from the French by his wife. It was well reviewed, and may have sold well. Its publication was important to Voronoff. He had been late into this field, and had done only a small number of experimental grafts, but to publish a book on gland grafts, and a well-written one, placed him at the forefront of public and even professional attention. It was a remarkable coup. In the book he used an argument which was to recur in his writings. Carrel's work had shown, he said, that cells grown outside the body are immortal. Therefore old age is due to poisons or a deficiency. The obvious deficiency is the atrophy of the testis, *ergo* testis grafting will cure old age. Voronoff mounted a plausible array of evidence for this thesis. He begins by saying that castration is associated with premature ageing and loss of vitality, not only in gelded horses but also in human eunuchs and in patients with loss of both testicles. Voronoff used classical allusions, quoting the story according to which the poet Abelard never wrote again after his castration. He also credulously cited the cases of Goethe, whose long life he credited to well-preserved genitals, and Thomas Parr. In explaining his use of the monkey as a donor, he said that his choice was initially forced on him by the lack of human donor glands. However, he found that not only did the monkey glands succeed, but they survived better than human glands, because of their 'virility'. The monkey (a chimpanzee in his early work, and baboon later) was chosen simply because it was so close to man, and Voronoff pointed out that this species shared many of the blood groups of man. [. . .]

On his return to Paris, Voronoff had the melancholy job of re-operating on his first two human testis transplant cases and removing the infected, dead monkey grafts. But by the end of the year he had done four more gland transplants. As before, he failed to obtain a supply of human glands. Though he turned to monkey donors instead, he hinted that pressure had been put on him by potential patients to find human donor glands. He made it known that human donors prepared to give one gland for transplantation would be welcome. Two men volunteered, but their fee was too high, so he continued to use grafts from the monkey. [. . .]

The four cases carried out in late 1920 were much more successful. His patients are described in later publications as 'a civil servant' aged fifty-nine, a French 'man of letters' aged sixty-four, an American 'man of letters' aged thirty-three, and a Spanish engineer aged sixty-six. In none of these patients was there any pre-existing active local disease in the testis area. The patients' complaints were of premature senility or general debility: sexual decline or impotence was also complained of in all cases. These operations went well, with the exception of infection and necrosis in one graft, on one side of one patient, but the patient's remaining graft on the other side survived. Voronoff must have been delighted that there was no major technical complications. Moreover, all patients, he claimed, showed improved intellectual and physical powers, and three of the four reported increased sexual activity. One of them returned three years later for a second graft, when he felt the benefit of the first had worn off. So 1920 ended well for Voronoff. The secret, embarrassing failures with his first two cases were now behind him, and his American visit and his book had been successful.

[*The Monkey Gland Affair* (London: Chatto & Windus, 1986), 40–1, 41, 42.]

EUGEN STEINACH

99 Hormones and Sex Difference

Sexuality is an integrating component of the life concept. Just as all animal existence is linked to sex, so also does sex rule life's shape and course. Sex is at once the root and the crown of every higher form of life. Without it there can be no animal life and, concomitantly, life devoid of sex can be neither real nor complete. The most elemental differentiation in all nature, that between the masculine and the feminine, is an expression of sex—an expression which is, curiously enough, just as obvious in the part as in the whole. Even the separate organs of an individual, with their tissues and cells, may bear an emphasis either masculine or feminine, depending upon the degree of development they have reached in a particular man or woman. This may be observed, in the female, in the way the mammary gland develops into the bosom and in the luxuriant growth of the long hair of her head; while in the male it may be noted in the larger and more powerful bones, joints, and muscles, together with the wider larynx and consequent deeper voice. [. . .]

Research revealed that some organs of glandular structure secrete chemical substances of extraordinary nature. Because these glands are not furnished with ducts through which their secretions can be distributed to the outside or to the other internal organs of the body, they are called glands of 'internal' secretion, or ductless glands, in distinction to those which are equipped with ducts, and those which have both ducts and an internal secretion. In the case of the ductless glands the important substances secreted, called hormones or endocrine substances, must be transported by some other means. Such a transporting agent was found in the blood, which takes up these substances as it circulates through the glands, and carries them to other parts of the body. [. . .] The ductless glands constitute, in fact, a mutually interacting system—the endocrine system—in which, though each member has its predestined function, all are combined in the task of regulating our growth, body type or 'habitus', psychic makeup, emotions, instincts, and desires—in a word, our personalities.

This practically omnipotent co-ordinating association also embraces the gonads, not indeed as leaders, but as co-equal partners; not as superiors, as has been suggested, but as coordinate associates. This role of the sex glands was determined by the discovery that the gonads fulfill the function not only of *external secretion*, for purposes of reproduction and race propagation, but also of *internal secretion*, producing a hormone which is taken up by the blood in exactly the same manner as are the secretions of the thyroid and pituitary and other glands. In other words, the sex glands exercise a dual function: the function that is all-important for the preservation of the species, and the scarcely less important one of fashioning and maintaining the individual. It was only after this revelation of the dual function of the gonads that the full significance of 'sex' began to emerge. It was picturesquely suggested that just as the sex glands are situated in the middle of the body, so too are they at the hub of life itself. In any case, the understanding of the hormonal character of the connection between the gonads and life led to a complete revolution of thought concerning the relationship between sex and life. This relationship was proved by an experiment which served as a negative control upon the known results of castration and thus acquired a fundamental importance. In the original layman's castration, the sex glands were removed from the body; by the new, the scientist's operation, the sex glands were placed in a body that was without them. Thus was returned with one hand what the other had previously abstracted; that is, testicles and ovaries were first removed from mammals, and then after a lapse of time were reintroduced into a different site in the same body from which they had been taken. [. . .]

It soon became obvious that these implantation experiments were destined to furnish the foundation for still more extensive revelations. They afforded proof that it is indeed the sex hormone that causes the excitability of the brain and brings about the 'erotization' (as I called it) of the individual, giving him that inner impulse through which the complete erotic makeup of the mature individual is determined; further, that this hormone releases all the other psychic hallmarks of masculinity and femininity. They showed that the sex hormones cause the appearance of physical characteristics, not by originating them, but by stimulating the development of latent predispositions in young animals and by enabling older animals, in whom these characteristics are already developed, to maintain them.

Such considerations, based on my transplantation experiments, led to my work on the experimental transformation of sex character. The first purpose was to determine whether the hormones of the male and female gonads were identical in effect, or whether they differed. If their effect was identical, it would make no difference whether, for example, a testicle or an ovary were implanted into a young male castrate. In either case masculinity would develop. But if the effects were not identical, then it should be possible to induce femininity by implantation of an ovary into an animal originally male but rendered neuter through castration. And on the same principle, by implantation of a testicle to induce masculinity in an animal originally female but similarly rendered neuter by spaying. In actual fact, it was found possible to achieve both: to develop feminism in male (feminization) and masculism in female mammals (masculization).

These successes are attributable to the capacity of the gonadal hormones not only to promote the peculiarities of a given sex but also to retard and even to inhibit the development of latent predispositions toward the opposite sex. The sex hormone is therefore not only sex-specific, but it is also counter-specific, on the one hand fostering the efflorescence of sexual characters of like sex, while on the other operating as a barrier to those of the other sex, thus assuring, as nature intended, the principle of normal differentiation between male and female.

This feature of the developmental mechanics of the sex glands explains how it is possible, by interchange of gonads, to thrust newborn males into female form and, vice versa, females into male, bringing them to complete or partially complete development as male and female just as these occur in nature. For even in nature the line of demarcation between the sexes is not as sharp as is generally taken for granted. Absolute masculinity or absolute femininity in any individual represents an imaginary ideal. A one hundred percent man is as non-existent as a one hundred percent woman, though individuals made up of equal parts of both sexes, the so-called hermaphrodites, are met with. The latter I have also made an object of my research, and I have studied this phenomenon, as it is possible to do with exactness only in animal experimentation, by an artificial creation of 'experimental hermaphroditism.' The simultaneous implantation of both an ovary and a testicle into an animal previously rendered neuter by castration resulted in the manifestation of both male and female attributes. This sexual duality was not only physical (technically known as androgyny), but it also manifested itself in the simultaneous occurrence of inclinations typical of both sexes, so that the experimental animal exhibited both homosexuality (inclination toward the like sex) and heterosexuality (inclination toward the opposite sex). This experiment formed an interesting complement to all preceding investigations.

[*Sex and Life: Forty Years of Biological and Medical Experiments* (New York: Viking Press, 1940), 1, 4–5, 6–8.]

The debate about the terminology and classification of sex hormones makes it clear how the different professional backgrounds of the disciplines involved in hormonal research led to a different conceptualization of sex hormones. Biochemists assigned meanings to their objects of study that were different from those of biologists. The hormone of the biochemist is in many respects quite different from the hormone of the biologists. From the chemical perspective, hormones were conceptualized as catalysts: chemical substances, sexually unspecific in origin and function, exerting manifold activities in the organism, instead of being primarily sex agents. From the biological perspective, hormones were conceptualized as sexually specific agents, controlling sexual characteristics.

What exactly happened to these different interpretations? Which interpretation of hormones became accepted as the dominant conceptualization of sex hormones? Although the chemical interpretation—emphasizing the resemblance of male and female sex hormones and the possibility of conversion from one to the other—did provoke confusion in the field of sex endocrinology, the prediction of the Amsterdam School was not fulfilled: the biological concept of sex hormones did not disappear. In the 1930s, we see the frequent use of a more specialized, technical terminology for sex hormones. Female sex hormones became known as estrin and estrogen (as a collective noun). For the male sex hormone the names androsterone and testosterone as specialized terms, and androgens as a collective term, became more frequently used. This new terminology did not, however, replace the old terms of female and male sex hormones.[1] Although scientists abandoned the concept of sexual specificity, the terminology was not adjusted to this change in conceptualization. The concept of sex hormones thus showed its robustness under major changes in theory, allowing talk of sex hormones to continue unabated, even though new properties were being ascribed to the hormones. From the 1930s until recently, the names male and female sex hormones have been kept in current use, both inside and outside the scientific community.[2] In this respect the biological perspective overruled the chemical perspective.

This outcome illustrates the strength of the tradition of biologists in the young field of sex endocrinology. The biologists had established a much longer tradition in the field than the biochemists, who were after all newcomers in the field. This does not mean that biologists can be portrayed as the 'winners' of the debate. Both biochemists and biologists adjusted their interpretations of the concept of sex hormones: biologists adjusted their original interpretation of sex hormones as substances sexually specific in origin and function; while biochemists dropped their interpretation of hormones as catalysts. The interpretation that finally came to dominate the field may thus be considered as the result of a compromise between biologists and biochemists. [. . .]

The introduction of the concept of sex hormones not only meant a shift in the study of sex away from an anatomical identification of the body to a causal explanation of sexual differentiation, but also entailed another major change in the study of sex. Instead of locating the essence of femininity or masculinity in specific organs, as the anatomists had done, sex endocrinologists introduced a quantitative theory of sex and the body. The idea that each sex could be characterized by its own sex hormone was transformed into the idea of relative sexual specificity. Sex endocrinologists suggested that, although female sex hormones were more important for women (especially during pregnancy) than for men, their potency was the same in both sexes. Male sex hormones were thought to be of greater importance for the internal and external phenotype of men, but this was regarded as only a difference of degree. In *The Annual Review of Physiology* published in 1939, the American physiologist Herbert Evans postulated this theory as follows:

It would appear that maleness or femaleness cannot be looked upon as implying the presence of one hormone and the absence of the other, but that differences in the absolute and especially relative amounts of these two kinds of substances may be expected to characterize each sex and, though much has been learned, it is only fair to state that these differences are still incompletely known.[3]

Or as Robert Frank suggested:

The explanation naturally suggesting itself is in favor of the theory of a quantitative and fluid transition from male to female.[4]

With this quantitative theory, the endocrinologists introduced a new conceptualization of sex. In the earlier anatomical definition of sex individuals could be classified into two, or actually three, categories: on the basis of the type of sexual organs an individual was categorized as male or female, and in cases where an individual possessed the sexual organs of both sexes, as a hermaphrodite. However, with the new concept of relative sexual specificity endocrinologists constructed a biological foundation for a definition of sex in which an individual could be classified in many categories varying from 'a virile to effeminate male' or from 'a masculine to a feminine female,' as Robert Frank described it. Laqueur's group described this conceptualization of sex in 1928 as follows:

The occurrence of the female hormone in the male body gives rise to many fantastic reflections. . . . It is now proved that in each man there is something present that is inherent in the female sex. Whether we will succeed in determining the individual ratio of each man, in terms of a given percentage of femininity, we don't know.[5]

Other scientists joked, privately, that the new biochemistry meant the end of sex differences: 'there but for one hydroxyl group go I'.[6]

The new model of sex in which sex differences are ascribed to hormones as chemical messengers of masculinity and femininity, agents that are present in female as well as male bodies, made possible a revolutionary change in the biological definition of sex. The model suggested that, chemically speaking, all organisms are both male and female. Sex could now be conceptualized in terms of male / masculine and female / feminine, with the elements of these two pairs no longer considered *a priori* as exclusive. In this model, an anatomical male could possess feminine characteristics controlled by female sex hormones, while an anatomical female could have masculine characteristics regulated by male sex hormones.

This hormonal model of sex provided the life sciences with a model to explain the 'masculine characteristics' in the female body and vice versa. In obstetric science, for example, the hormonal model was used in the 1930s to substantiate the classification of female pelves into 'masculine' and 'feminine' types.[7] Physicians and clinicians used the quantitative model of sex to account for the purportedly feminine character of homosexual men.

[*Beyond the Natural Body: An Archeology of Sex Hormones* (London: Routledge, 1994), 36–7, 38–9.]

III.d. Developmental Biology and Psychology

Knowledge about the cycle of sexual maturation is as old as the Greeks. However, each age has mixed its scientific knowledge with its cultural preoccupations to produce a particular understanding of the process of sexual development. At the high-water mark of Victorianism, the innocence of children had become a cultural shibboleth of the highest order, especially among the middle classes. At the turn of the century, the new sexology and the first research on hormones deepened contemporary knowledge of sexual development in important ways. Puberty was increasingly understood as a biological event that was programmed into the organism by an underlying genetic and evolutionary design and guided by the hormones of growth and development. However, far from being regarded as an autonomous natural event, puberty was for the first time integrated into adolescence, a new conceptual category that acknowledged the importance of cultural expectations for pubescent youth. The years 11–16 were no longer regarded as late childhood or as uneventful years on the road to adulthood but as a self-contained and tumultuous stage of life through which all children must pass and which deserved the attention of educators, parents, and medical experts. As exemplified in turn-of-the-century literary and artistic modernism, the concept of adolescence was an excellent heuristic for the contemplation of the rebelliousness, the tortured idealism, and the sexual exoticism of the age.

The myth of the non-sexual child was shaken if not exploded by the first generation of sexologists, who found abundant evidence of sensuality, erotic attachments, and even orgasms in children. If he was not the first to speculate in this way, Freud none the less became the exemplar of such views, as well as the most eloquent proponent of the view that children should be taught the elementary facts about sexuality. In Extract 101 he briefly summarizes his views on the subject.

One consequence of the amalgamation of puberty and adolescence in this era is that we moderns are unable to think about social or psychological aspects of adolescence outside a sexualized frame of reference. Another is our eternal problematizing of adolescence as a period of life whose primitive energies require domestication or control. In this amalgamation of puberty and adolescence, changing notions of adolescence are characteristically mapped on the bodies of pubescent youths. This was true of the first major work on adolescence in the West by the Harvard professor G. Stanley Hall, whose pioneering study of 1904 drew upon the biological science of his day. Hall firmly places the crises of pubescent youth in a context of contemporary American anxieties about urbanization and social disorganization. He then distinguishes between boys, whom he believes are tormented principally by problems arising from their maturing genitalia, concern for 'normalcy', and the temptations of masturbation, and girls, whose adolescent crises are subsumed within the biological cycle of periodicity, but who are thus also slaves of their sex organs (Extract 102).

In the fifty years or so after Hall published his influential study, the literal analogies between the sexual organs of adolescents and the passages to adult sexual life have been loosened but not broken. The notion that a woman's life is wholly governed by her menstrual cycle is no longer taken seriously amongst experts or in popular culture. Menarche is thus no longer simply a rite of biological and family passage for American and European girls, but increasingly a hygienic and cosmetic event manipulated in part by the sanitary products industry and by social expectations (Extract 103).

Finally, psychoanalysts in the Freudian tradition have emphasized in their work with adolescents that the years of puberty are crucial in the development of gender identity. Analysts like Erik Erikson, for instance, have laid great stress on the power of culture to shape the moral outlook and self-concept of adolescents, breaking more or less decisively with the biological determinism of Freud's generation. In his work, however, the 'normal' forms that identity takes are still built upon the underlying plan of the genitals. This commitment in turn reinforced traditional notions of gender roles that had been unsettled or reversed during the upheavals of the Second World War. In Erikson's important *Childhood and Society* (1950), he studied play in pubescent boys and girls, looking for patterns that would illuminate this stage of human development. He found strong associations between play activity, character, and gender, which he linked ultimately to the child's sexual anatomy and peculiarities of physical development (Extract 104).

101   The Sexual Enlightenment of Children

It is commonly believed that the sexual instinct is lacking in children, and only begins to arise in them when the sexual organs mature. This is a grave error, equally serious from the point of view both of theory and of actual practice. It is so easy to correct it by observation that one can only wonder how it can ever have arisen. As a matter of fact, the new-born infant brings sexuality with it into the world; certain sexual sensations attend its development while at the breast and during early childhood, and only very few children would seem to escape some kind of sexual activity and sexual experiences before puberty. A more complete exposition of this statement can be found in my *Drei Abhandlungen zur Sexualtheorie*. The reader will learn that the specific organs of reproduction are not the only portions of the body which are a source of pleasurable sensation, and that Nature has stringently ordained that even stimulation of the genitals cannot be avoided during infancy. This period of life, during which a certain degree of directly sexual pleasure is produced by the stimulation of various cutaneous areas (erotogenic zones), by the activity of certain biological impulses and as an a accompanying excitation during many affective states, is designated by an expression introduced by Havelock Ellis as the period of auto-erotism. Puberty merely brings about attainment of the stage at which the genitals acquire supremacy among all the zones and sources of pleasure, and in this way presses erotism into the service of reproduction, a process which naturally can undergo certain inhibitions; in the case of those persons who later on become perverts and neurotics this process is only incompletely accomplished. On the other hand, the child is capable long before puberty of most of the mental manifestations of love, for example, tenderness, devotion, and jealousy. Often enough the connection between these mental manifestations and the physical sensation of sexual excitation is so close that the child cannot be in doubt about the relation between the two. To put it briefly, the child is long before puberty a being capable of mature love, lacking only the ability for reproduction; and it may be definitely asserted that the mystery which is set up withholds him only from intellectual comprehension of achievements for which he is psychically and physically prepared.

[*The Sexual Enlightenment of Children*, ed. Philip Rieff (New York: Collier Books, 1963), 19–20.]

Among the chief external causes of the diseases of this age are all those influences which tend to precocity, e.g., city life with its earlier puberty, higher death rate, wider range and greater superficiality of knowledge, observations of vice and enhanced temptation, lessened repose, incessant distraction, more impure air, greater liability to contagion, and absence of the sanctifying influences and repose of nature in country life. At its best, metropolitan life is hard on childhood and especially so on pubescents, and children who can not pass these years in the country are robbed of a right of childhood that should be inalienable, and are exposed to many deleterious influences which jeopardize both health and morals. Civilization with all its accumulated mass of cultures and skills, its artifacts, its necessity of longer and severer apprenticeship and specialization, is even harder on adolescents, and even in a republic the submerged fraction of the population not adequate to achieve success in its ever fiercer competitions, who drop limp and exhausted in body and soul to a condition acknowledged by many anthropologists to be essentially inferior to that of most of the lowest savages, increases, and institutions for defectives and those who live on charities multiply. Modern industrialism makes poverty ever more unendurable. When we add to these predisposing causes the small and decreasing families, the later marriages, so that more and more are born of post-mature parents and thus physiologically tend to precocity; the over-nurture of only children who are so prone to be spoiled and ripened still earlier by unwise fondness; the mixture of distinct ethnic stocks that increase the ferments of adolescence by multiplying the factors of heredity and so increasing its instability, we no longer wonder that many in these most vulnerable years make more or less complete shipwrecks at every stage of these hothouse demands, which in the entire life of our race are so recent.

Under these provocations, some instincts spring into activity with a suddenness that is almost explosive, and so prematurely, that as, e.g., with sex and drink, the strong and complex psychic mechanism of control has no time to develop and forbidden pleasures are tasted to satiety, till the soul has sometimes not only lost its innocence before it understood what purity and virtue really mean, but life is blasé, a burnt-out cinder, admiration, enthusiasm, and high ambitions are weakened or gone, and the soul is tainted with indifference or discouragement. [. . .]

Whatever the analyses and localizations of the factors of this instinct, if not before, certainly and at the latest at early puberty, when the changes normal to that period supervene with attendant new sensations, these parts for a time, and especially in boys, play a great and hitherto not adequately recognized rôle in consciousness. Owing in part to the great variability of form, size, or function, or all together, very many boys suffer from the fear that they are abnormal in form and not infrequently life is for years overcast by apprehensions. Incidental comparisons with others made, for instance, in bathing, are very apt to suggest, as variability is so great, individual abnormality. Cases are given where several boys recently developed, on seeing others, have thought themselves deformed, and suffered acutely with manifold forebodings for the future. These fears often deepen into phobias when connected with the new activities normal to this period, and every variation is ascribed by a hypersensitive consciousness of abnormality of function to sin. From cases which might fill a small volume, I select here as typical one only, viz., that of a doctor of philosophy, prominent in his profession and a father of several healthful children, who writes in substance:

The one greatest fear of all my boyhood was connected with my sexual organs; the big boys would expose us little ones, and said mine were too small. I began to brood over this, age eight; felt disgraced, and haunted with forebodings; one day there seemed a very slight inflammation, age twelve; I thought I had done a nameless sin, and prayed God to let me get well, which I soon did, but a morbid association between it and a hen's neck long persisted; I read literature on lost manhood, self-abuse, etc.; fancied I had all the diseases, and had committed the unpardonable sin; the first spontaneous emission nearly paralyzed me, but although I found myself still alive, felt that my days were numbered; I corresponded with a quack, and later began to study my urine with great alarm, and found plenty of marks of disease; there were reddish and whitish settlings, lack of color and overcolor, strong smell and no smell, it was too clear, too thick, too copious, too scanty, or, worst of all, had an iridescent scum; when fourteen I gradually settled to the fact that I was sexually abnormal, might possibly live seven years, till twenty-one, and then find what I had heard was a sure cure in marriage; I found encouragement from quack advertisements, which said the wretched beings sometimes held out for years; I lived on, and people said I was in robust health, but it was years before I realized that I was perfectly normal; Bible passages greatly aggravated my fears, such as one in Deut. xxiii, and others; as I look back, my entire youth from six to eighteen was made miserable from lack of knowledge that any one who knew anything of the nature of puberty might have given; this long sense of defect, dread of operations, shame and worry has left an indelible mark.

Dr Seerley tells me he sees one hundred cases a year of young men who deem their case hopeless. One typical youth of good heredity and otherwise normal decided that he would not go to college, was ruined, and must soon inevitably become insane. Another bought a revolver and planned, after a farewell visit to his mother in a distant town, to shoot himself in despair. Another selected a spot at the river where he would drown himself, which he prepared to do, but almost by accident met a physician who persuaded him after two hours that he was all right, when he went to work with renewed courage, and now seems entering upon a promising career. Another young man selected a cord, which he carried in his pocket for a long time, trying to muster courage to hang himself, because he could only disgrace his friends and his parents, who had made so many sacrifices for him. Another gave up a promising career and shipped on a long voyage, hoping to find this a cure. Another turned on the gas at night, but was discovered and saved in time, etc.

Perhaps masturbation is the most perfect type of individual vice and sin. Where practised, not by the old or by defectives as mitigations of the dangers of procreation for those unfit for it, but by the young, it is perhaps the purest illustration of mere sense pleasure bought at the cost of the higher life. It is destructive of that perhaps most important thing in the world, the potency of good heredity; it is the acme of selfishness; it is the violation of the restraint perhaps most of all imperative, and yet all we know points to the conclusion that it is far more common among civilized than among savage races, owing in part to the postponement of marriage. The ideals of chastity are perhaps the very highest that can be held up to youth during this ever lengthening probationary period. This is the hard price that man must pay for full maturity. Idleness and the protected life of students increase temptation, so does overfeeding, which also increases sterility, so that enjoyment and the power of effective parenthood with God and nature united part company and at a certain variable period become inversely as each other. Although the facts in this chapter may lessen respect for our race and make us less hopeful of its future, the saving fact remains that the outburst of adolescent growth still precedes that of sexual maturity. If this interval were to lessen instead of to increase, so that the race tended, as do abnormal individuals in it, toward a development of the sexual function so premature and intense as to interfere with or obviate the increased rate of growth now normal, this would mean sure ethnic devolution. [. . .]

Ever since Hippocrates the period of first menstruation has been thought to be very critical for the development of the nervous system. The entire genital organism is congested; the volume of the uterus and ovaries increases; the Fallopian tubes grow turgescent; the breasts are enlarged and tender; the thyroid gland swells; the nerves are tense and irritable; from 250 to 500 grams of venous and often clotted blood are lost normally, and this of itself in girls not properly instructed may cause great alarm, aggravated, as it often is, by idiopathic horror of blood, which indeed it may cause, and which may still more prompt unhygienic and even dangerous modes of concealment, removal, stanching, etc. It may thus lay deep in the nervous system, the foundation of psychic perturbations at every period. Few more pitiable objects exist in nature than a girl, especially if nervous or overworked, who must encounter this experience for the first time, uninstructed or alone. The quality of motherhood has nowhere a more crucial test than in meeting the needs of this epoch. The individual variations are so very wide that every girl should be a special case by herself, and all reasoning from one person to another is apt to be fallacious. All of the physical and psychic phenomena are peculiarly prone to abnormal defect or perversion, and for a considerable time everything that in the least degree jeopardizes the harmony and balance of the many factors involved in the settled establishment of regularity and normality should give way. Now begins a great and ineradicable difference between the physical and psychic life of woman and that of man. [. . .]

To understand a woman's body and soul is a larger problem than to understand a man's. It is true of her more than of him, that to know a part we must know the whole; first, because her nature is more generic and less specific, and, second, because reproduction, the deepest secret of animate nature, plays a larger rôle in her life. Illness constitutes a greater element of her existence and is in a sense more a part of her. Each woman is a more adequate representative of her sex than a man is of his, so that to know one well more involves knowing all; hence experts and specialists, apparatus and particular processes, while often helpful, are more liable to be an insult to the deeper laws of her being. Our medical science, our psychology, and our philosophy are still inadequate to answer the questions her nature propounds. [. . .]

In fine, puberty for a girl is like floating down a broadening river into an open sea. Landmarks recede, the water deepens and changes in its nature, there are new and strange forms of life, the currents are more complex, and the phenomena of tides make new conditions and new dangers. The bark is frail, liable to be tossed by storms of feeling, at the mercy of wind and wave, and if without chart and compass and simple rules of navigation, aimless drifting in the darkness of ignorance, amidst both rocks and shoals, may make of the weak or unadvised wrecks or castaways. The change itself is exciting, and half knowledge of popular and perhaps prurescent fallacies only augment instead of allaying the strain. Four or five days a month for some thirty years the girl's system will be depleted, and there will be lassitude with peculiar susceptibility to physical or mental shock, and complex problems of regimen that even with the best instruction must receive a large residuary personal solution. Shall she withdraw, and make or accept excuses which seem to her a kind of implicit confession which is so hard even to those nearest her? Does she show or can she conceal her state at least from strangers, or will they suspect, or must she make an effort to be natural?

[*Adolescence: Its Psychology and its Relations to Physiology, Anthropology, Sociology, Sex, Crime, Religion and Education* (New York: D. Appleton & Co., 1908), 321–2, 451–3, 503–4, 505, 507–9.]

JOAN JACOBS BRUMBERG

103   **Changing Meanings of Menarche**

Although the industry's educational efforts undoubtedly were part of the important demystification of menstruation, the long-term consequences for girls at puberty may not be so benign. In fact, surrendering menarche to Walt

Disney probably contributed in some measure to the difficulties we face today in the realm of female adolescent sexuality. As the industry became an ever-present third party in mother–daughter, doctor–patient, and teacher–student discussions, personal experience and testimony from older women became even less authoritative. There was more information available but it was increasingly abstracted from real-life experience; in the Disney case, menstruation was reduced to a cartoon shown primarily in school or in girls' groups. The oral histories also suggest that the availability of free, corporate-sponsored materials meant that many mothers and teachers simply gave out pamphlets and free samples rather than provide personal advice and counsel about growing up female. We know from personal reports that this was not a satisfying substitute and that young women wanted (and continue to want) meaningful exchanges about female sexuality and womanhood in addition to the best techniques for keeping their clothes and their genitals clean. Unfortunately, however, American girls in the twentieth century have grown up equating the experience of menarche and menstruation with a hygiene product. To wit: a woman who spent her childhood in Pittsburgh in the 1940s recalled that before any of her friends had gotten their periods, one of their fellow fifth-graders suddenly declared one day that she could not slide down a snowy hill. When asked why, this prepubertal girl said laughingly, 'I can't, I'm practicing Kotex.'[1]

This childish remark captures the extent to which the sanitary products industry was implicated in the long-term transformation of menarche from a maturational event into a hygienic crisis. But it was also a perceptive piece of cultural logic on the part of a young girl coming of age in a society where identity, particularly adult female identity, was inextricably linked to purchases in the marketplace.[2] In harnessing adolescent angst over menstruation to capitalist imperatives, the sanitary products industry paved the way for the commercialization of other areas of the body that were of great concern to developing girls—namely, their skin, their hair, and their 'figures.' By the late 1940s and 1950s, menstruation was owned by neither mothers nor doctors; in fact, the rites of passage for American girls were clearly in the commercial realm, where they centered on consumer activities such as the purchase of sanitary products, high heels, lipsticks, and 'training bras.' Never before, with adult approval, had so many girls become followers and interpreters of 'the fashion system.'[3] As a result, mothers and their teenage daughters became absorbed in a discussion (or tug-of-war) about 'good grooming,' a dialogue that ultimately contributed little to the adolescent girl's understanding of her body and her sexuality. This state of affairs, combined with the fact that young women were menstruating earlier than ever before, left girls unprepared and unprotected for the new sexual liberalism that characterized American life in the 1960s and 1970s.

['"Something Happens to Girls": Menarche and the Emergence of the Modern American Hygienic Imperative', *Journal of the History of Sexuality*, 4/1 (1993), 126–7.]

I set up a play table and a random selection of toys and invited the boys and girls of the study, one at a time, to come in and to imagine that the table was a movie studio, and the toys actors and sets. I then asked them to 'construct on the table an exciting scene out of an imaginary moving picture'. This instruction was given to spare these children, the majority of whom were eleven years old, the indignity of having to play at 'kids' stuff'; at the same time it was thought to be a sufficiently impersonal 'stimulus' for an unselfconscious use of the imagination. But here was the first surprise: although, for over a year and a half, about 150 children constructed about 450 scenes, not more than a half dozen of these were movie scenes, and only a few dolls were named after a particular actor. Instead, after a moment of thoughtfulness, the children arranged their scenes as if guided by an inner design, told me a brief story with more or less exciting content, and left me with the task of finding out what (if anything) these constructions 'meant'. [. . .]

In order to convey a measure of my surprise at finding organ modes among what (in contrast to *unique* elements) I came to call the *common* elements in these children's constructions, it is necessary to claim what is probably hard to believe, namely, that I tried not to expect anything in particular, and was, in fact, determined to enjoy the freshness of the experience of working with so many children, and healthy ones. To be ready to be surprised belongs to the discipline of a clinician; for without it clinical 'findings' would soon lose the instructive quality of new (or truly confirming) finds.

As one child after another concentrated with a craftsman's conscientiousness on configurations which had to be 'just right' before he would announce that his task was done, I gradually became aware of the fact that I was learning to expect different configurations from boys than from girls. To give an example which brings us immediately to the mode of female inclusion, girls much more often than boys would arrange a room in the form of a circle of furniture, without walls. Sometimes a circular configuration of furniture was presented as being intruded upon by something threatening, even if funny, such as a pig or 'father coming home riding on a lion'. One day, a boy arranged such a 'feminine' scene, with wild animals as intruders, and I felt that uneasiness which I assume often betrays to an experimenter what his innermost expectations are. And, indeed, on departure and already at the door, the boy exclaimed, 'There is something wrong here', came back, and with an air of relief arranged the animals along a tangent to the circle of furniture. Only one boy built and left such a configuration, and this twice. He was of obese and effeminate build. As thyroid treatment began to take effect, he built, in his third construction (a year and a half after the first) the highest and most slender of all towers—as was to be expected of a boy.

That this boy's tower, now that he himself had at last become slimmer, was the slenderest, was one of those 'unique' elements which suggested that some sense of one's physical self influenced the spatial modalities of these constructions. From here it was only one step to the assumption that the modalities *common* to either sex may express something of the sense of being male or female. It was then that I felt grateful for the kind of investigation which we had embarked on. For building blocks provide a wordless medium quite easily counted, measured, and compared in regard to spatial arrangement. At the same time, they seem so impersonally geometric as to be least compromised by cultural connotations and individual meanings. A block is *almost* nothing but a block. It seemed striking, then (unless one considered it a mere function of the difference in themes), that boys and girls differed in the *number* of blocks used as well as in the *configurations* constructed.

So I set out to define these configurations in the simplest terms, such as towers, buildings, streets, lanes, elaborate enclosures, simple enclosures, interiors with walls and interiors without walls. I then gave photographs of the play scenes to two objective observers to see whether they could agree on the presence or the absence of such configurations (and of combinations of them). They did agree 'significantly', whereupon it could be determined how often these configurations were said by these observers (who did not know of my expectations) to have occurred in the constructions of boys and of girls. I will abstract their conclusions here in general terms. The reader may assume that each item mentioned occurs more (and often considerably more) than two thirds of the time in the constructions of the sex specified and that in the remaining one third special conditions prevail which often can be shown to 'prove the rule'.

The most significant sex difference was the tendency of boys to erect structures, buildings, towers, or streets; the girls tended to use the play table as the interior of a house, with simple, little, or no use of blocks.

High structures, then, were prevalent in the configurations of the boys. But the opposite of elevation, i.e. *downfall*, was equally typical for them: ruins or fallen-down structures were exclusively found among boys. (I quoted the one exception.) In connexion with the very highest towers, something in the nature of a downward trend appears regularly, but in such diverse forms that only 'unique' elements can illustrate it: one boy, after much indecision, took his extraordinarily high and well-built tower down in order to build a final configuration of a simple and low structure without any 'exciting' content; another balanced his tower very precariously and pointed out that the immediate danger of collapse was the 'exciting' element in his story: in fact, *was* his story. One boy who built an especially high tower laid a boy doll at the foot of it and explained that this boy had fallen from the top of the tower; another boy left the boy doll sitting high on one of several elaborate towers but said that the boy had had a mental breakdown. The very highest tower was built by the very smallest boy; and, as pointed out, a coloured boy built his *under* the table. All these variations make it apparent that *the variable high–low* is a *masculine variable*. Having studied a number of the histories of these children I would add the clinical judgement that extreme height (in its combination with an element of breakdown or fall) reflects a need to overcompensate a doubt in, or a fear for, one's masculinity.

The boys' structures enclosed fewer people and animals inside a house. Rather, they channelled the traffic of motor-cars, animals, and Indians. And they blocked traffic: the single policeman was the doll used most often by boys!

Girls rarely built towers. When they did, they made them lean against, or stay close to, the background. The highest tower built by any girl was not on the table at all but on a shelf in a niche behind the table.

If 'high' and 'low' are masculine variables, 'open' and 'closed' are feminine modalities. Interiors of houses without walls were built by a majority of girls. In many cases the interiors were expressly peaceful. Where it was a home rather than a school, a little girl often played the piano: a remarkably tame 'exciting movie scene' for girls of that age. In a number of cases, however, a disturbance occurred. An intruding pig throws the family in an uproar and forces the girl to hide behind the piano; a teacher has jumped on a desk because a tiger has entered the room. While the persons thus frightened are mostly women, the intruding element is always a man, a boy, or an animal. If it is a dog, it is expressly a boy's dog. Strangely enough, however, this idea of an intruding creature does not lead to the defensive erection of walls or to the closing of doors. Rather, the majority of these intrusions have an element of humour and of pleasurable excitement.

Simple enclosures with low walls and without ornaments were the largest item among the configurations built by girls. However, these enclosures often had an elaborate gate: the only configuration which girls cared to construct and to ornament richly. A blocking of the entrance or a thickening of the walls could on further study be shown to reflect acute anxiety over the feminine role.

The most significant sex differences in the use of the play space, then, added up to the following modalities: in the boys, the outstanding variables were height and downfall and strong motion (Indians, animals, motor cars) and its channelization or arrest (policemen); in girls, static interiors, which are open, simply enclosed, and peaceful or intruded upon. Boys adorned high structures; girls, gates.

It is clear by now that the spatial tendencies governing these constructions are reminiscent of the *genital modes* discussed in this chapter, and that they, in fact, closely parallel the morphology of the sex organs: in the male, *external* organs, *erectable* and *intrusive* in character, *conducting* highly *mobile* sperm cells; *internal* organs in the female, with a vestibular *access* leading to *statically expectant* ova.

Does this reflect an acute and temporary emphasis on the modalities of the sexual organs owing to the experience of oncoming sexual maturation? My clinical judgement (and the brief study of the 'dramatic productions' of college students) incline me to think that the dominance of genital modes over the modalities of spatial organization reflects a profound difference in the sense of space in the two sexes, even as sexual differentiation obviously provides the most decisive difference in the ground plan of the human body which, in turn, co-determines biological experience and social roles.

[*Childhood and Society* (Harmondsworth: Penguin Books, 1970), 92, 93–100.]

III.e. The Physiology of Sexual Function

An important part of the discovery of the modern sexual body has been the penetration by the clinical-scientific gaze of genital anatomy to the level of underlying physiological processes. Because of the crowd of scientific and ethical problems associated with a detailed study of human sexual function, empirical research was almost non-existent until the 1960s. However, the growth of treatment facilities for sex therapy and dysfunction encouraged two medical pioneers in this field to devise a set of experimental techniques that would allow them to study human sexual response in a volunteer population in a controlled and scientifically persuasive way. When William Masters and Virginia Johnson's *Human Sexual Response* appeared in 1966 it was received with some of the same excitement as Alfred Kinsey's epochal *Sexuality in the Human Male* in 1948 (see Section IV). For the first time, it was thought, the biological story behind human sexual function had been dispassionately investigated.

Masters and Johnson were particularly interested in producing scientifically useful results and in exploding some of the hoary myths about sexuality, in particular those concerning the supposed differences between male and female orgasm, the so-called difference between clitoral/vaginal orgasms in women, and the effects on sexual response of ageing. They therefore postulated the existence of a 'human sexual response cycle' for which analogous anatomico-physiological processes could be found in both men and women, at one stroke equalizing sexual experience and producing scientific results that were both universal and materially measurable. They famously identified four phases of the HSRC: (1) the excitement phase; (2) the plateau phase; (3) the orgasmic phase; (4) the resolution phase. One could select passages from a number of different parts of the study to illustrate the tone and content of their findings, but Extract 105 on *the* female orgasm will suffice, including some comment on the male experience.

Critics of this work have pointed out that the materialistic and reductionistic research programme required to align this work with mainstream science produced some distorting and alienating effects. The historian Paul Robinson has argued, for instance, that the sections on the 'psychology' of orgasm scarcely rise above the level of description presented previously as a sequence of discrete physiological events (Extract 106).

Even more telling, perhaps, is the fact that a version of the HSRC of Masters and Johnson has since been assimilated into the American Psychiatric Association's official manual of mental illness as the 'normal' template for evaluating sexual disorders, a development that will recall the spectrum of pathology and norm in classical sexology. In addition, as Leonore Tiefer points out, the 'fragmentation' of body parts characteristic of the HSRC model conceals a continued emphasis on the genitals and on genital sexuality that simply reinforces the traditional ideal of reproductive sexuality in the same way as we have seen with sex at the level of chromosomes and hormones (Extract 107).

105 **The Female Orgasm**

Female orgasmic experience can be visually identified as well as recorded by acceptable physiologic techniques. The primary requirement in objective identification of female orgasm is the knowledge that it is a total-body response with marked variation in reactive intensity and timing sequence. Previously, other observers have recognized and interpreted much of the reactive physiology of female orgasm. However, definition and correlation of these reactions into an identifying pattern of orgasm per se has not been established.

At orgasm, the grimace and contortion of a woman's face graphically express the increment of myotonic tension throughout her entire body. The muscles of the neck and the long muscles of the arms and legs usually contract into involuntary spasm. During coition in supine position the female's hands and feet voluntarily may be grasping her sexual partner. With absence of clutching interest or opportunity during coition or in solitary response to automanipulative techniques, the extremities may reflect involuntary carpopedal spasm. The striated muscles of the abdomen and the buttocks frequently are contracted voluntarily by women in conscious effort to elevate sexual tensions, particularly in an effort to break through from high plateau to orgasmic attainment.

The physiologic onset of orgasm is signaled by contractions of the target organs, starting with the orgasmic platform in the outer third of the vagina. This platform, created involuntarily by localized vasocongestion and myotonia, contracts with recordable rhythmicity as the tension increment is released. The intercontractile intervals recur at 0.8 second for the first three to six contractions, corresponding in timing sequence to the first few ejaculatory contractions (male orgasm) of the penis. The longer contractions continue, the more extended the intercontractile intervals. The number and intensity of orgasmic-platform contractions are direct measures of subjective severity and objective duration of the particular orgasmic experience. The correlation between platform contractions and subjective experience at orgasm has been corroborated by study subjects during thousands of cycles. Vaginal spasm and penile grasping reactions have been described many times in the clinical and nonprofessional literature. Orgasmic-platform contractility provides an adequate physiologic explanation for these subjective concepts.

Contractions of the orgasmic platform provide visible manifestation of female orgasmic experience. To date, the precise mechanism whereby cortical, hormonal, or any unidentified influence may activate this and other orgasmic reactions has not been determined (perhaps by creating a trigger-point level of vasocongestive and myotonic increment).

Orgasmic contractions of the uterus have been recorded by both intrauterine and abdominally placed electrodes. Both techniques indicate that uterine contractions may have onset almost simultaneously with those of the orgasmic platform, but the contractive intensity of the uterine musculature is accumulated slowly and contractions are too irregular in recurrence and duration to allow pattern definition. Uterine contractions start in the fundus and work through the midzone to terminate in the lower uterine segment. With the exception of the factor of contractile excursion (indication of intensity), physiologic tracings of uterine orgasmic contractions resemble the patterns of first-stage labor contractions. Uterine contractile intensity and duration vary widely from orgasm to orgasm. However, there is some early indication that both factors have a positive relation to the parity of the individual and the prior extent of her orgasmic experience, both incidental and cumulative.

Involuntary contractions of the external rectal sphincter also may develop during orgasm, although many women experience orgasm without evidencing sphincter contraction. When the contractions do occur, they parallel in timing sequence the initial intercontractile intervals of the orgasmic platform. The rectal-sphincter contractions usually terminate before those of the orgasmic platform.

The external urethral sphincter also may contract two or three times in an involuntary expression of orgasmic tension release. The contractions are without recordable rhythmicity and usually are confined to nulliparous premenopausal women.

The breasts evidence no specific response to the immediacy of orgasm. However, detumescence of the areolae immediately subsequent to orgasm is so rapid that its arbitrary assignment purely as a resolution-phase reaction has been cause for investigative concern. Often areolar detumescence is evident shortly after subjective report of orgasmic onset and usually develops simultaneously with the terminal contractions of the orgasmic platform. As a final stage of the rapid detumescent reaction, the areolae constrict into a corrugated state. The nipples remain erect and are turgid and quite rigid (the false-erection reaction).

Rapid detumescence of the vasocongested areolae, resulting in a constricted, corrugated appearance, occurs only with orgasm and is an obvious physical manifestation that provides for visual identification of female orgasmic experience. If orgasm does not occur areolar detumescence is a much slower process, corrugation does not develop, and the false-erection reaction of the nipples usually is reduced in intensity.

The sex flush, a maculopapular rash distributed superficially over the body surfaces, achieves its greatest intensity and its widest distribution at the moment of orgasmic expression. Subsequent to orgasmic experience, the sex flush disappears more rapidly than when resolving from plateau-phase levels of erotic tension.

From a cardiorespiratory point of view, orgasm is reflected by hyperventilation, with respiratory rates occasionally over 40 per minute. Tachycardia is a constant accompaniment of orgasmic experience, with cardiac rates running from 110 to beyond 180 beats per minute. Hypertension also is a constant finding. The systolic pressures are elevated by 30–80 mm. and diastolic pressures by 20–40 mm. Hg.

The clitoris, Bartholin's glands, and the major and minor labia are target organs for which no specific physiologic reactions to orgasmic-phase levels of sexual tension have been established.

Aside from ejaculation, there are two major areas of physiologic difference between female and male orgasmic expression. First, the female is capable of rapid return to orgasm immediately following an orgasmic experience, if restimulated before tensions have dropped below plateau-phase response levels. Second, the female is capable of maintaining an orgasmic experience for a relatively long period of time.

[*Human Sexual Response* (Boston: Little, Brown & Co., 1966), 128–31.]

PAUL ROBINSON

 Psychology *is* Physiology

Having completed their detailed account of the physiological aspects of sexual arousal (including, as noted, the precise timing of the orgasmic contractions of the penis and the vaginal platform), they turn their attention to the 'subjective' side of the same process. If, however, the reader anticipates here some discussion of the ecstasy, the sense of transcendence, and the loss of self that accompany orgasm, or of the psychological 'meaning' of sexual experience, he will be sorely disappointed. The 'psychology' of orgasm turns out to be nothing more than the individual's conscious perception of the physiological changes that Masters and Johnson have observed and measured. In other words, it is body psychology, the mental representation of physical occurrences. Their account of the 'psychology' of female orgasm runs as follows:

Orgasm has its onset with a sensation of suspension or stoppage. Lasting only an instant, the sensation is accompanied or followed immediately by an isolated thrust of intense sensual awareness, clitorally oriented, but radiated upward into the pelvis. . . . The sensation of intense clitoral-pelvic awareness has been described by a number of women as occurring concomitantly with a sense of bearing down or expelling. Often a feeling of receptive opening was expressed. . . .

As a second state of subjective progression through orgasm, a sensation of 'suffusion of warmth,' specifically pervading the pelvic area first and then spreading progressively throughout the body, was described by almost every woman with orgasmic experience.

Finally, as the third stage of subjective progression, a feeling of involuntary contraction with a specific focus in the vagina or lower pelvis was mentioned consistently.[1]

The male's 'subjective' experience is also described as a sequence of body perceptions. In this instance Masters and Johnson's account is even more literal (there is nothing so metaphorical as 'sensation of suspension' or 'a suffusion of warmth'), and it is also surprisingly inadequate purely as a description of what orgasm feels like:

In the human male a sensation of ejaculatory inevitability develops for an instant immediately prior to, and then parallels in timing sequence, the first stage of the ejaculatory process (accessory-organ contractions). This subjective experience has been described by many males as the sensation of 'feeling the ejaculation coming.' From onset of this specific sensation, there is a brief interval (2 to 3 seconds) during which the male feels the ejaculation coming and no longer can constrain, delay, or in any way control the process. This subjective experience of inevitability develops as seminal plasma is collecting in the prostatic urethra but before the actual emission of seminal fluid begins. The two- to threefold distention of the urethral bulb developing in the terminal portions of the plateau phase also may contribute proprioceptively to the sensation of ejaculatory inevitability.

During the second stage of the ejaculatory process (propulsion of seminal-fluid content from prostatic urethra to the urethral meatus), the male subjectively progresses through two phases: First, a contractile sensation is stimulated by regularly recurring contractions of the sphincter urethrae. Second, a specific appreciation of fluid volume develops as the seminal plasma is expelled under pressure along the lengthened and distended penile urethra.[2]

This seems a satisfactory rendering of the preface and conclusion of male orgasm, but it hardly does justice to the main event—that 'brief interval' of two to three seconds between the sense of inevitability and the perception of contractions. My point, however, is not that the description is inaccurate but that it assumes an extremely narrow, and fundamentally materialistic, conception of psychology. Even when it addresses itself to supposedly psychological questions, *Human Sexual Response* never strays far from the realm of 'physiologic fact.'

[*The Modernization of Sex* (New York: Harper & Row, 1976), 175–7.]

LEONORE TIEFER

107   The Human Sexual Response Cycle

The cycle metaphor indicates that Masters and Johnson envisioned sexual response from the start as a built-in, orderly sequence of events that would tend to repeat itself. The idea of a four-stage cycle brings to mind examples such as the four seasons of the annual calendar or the four-stroke internal combustion engine. Whether the cycle is designed by human agency or 'nature,' once begun it cycles independently of its origins, perhaps with some variability, but without reorganization or added stages, and the same cycle applies to everyone. [. . .]

By omitting the concept of drive from their model, Masters and Johnson eliminated an element of sexuality that is notoriously variable within populations and succeeded in proposing a universal model seemingly without much variability. In what I think is the only reference to sexual drive in their text, Masters and Johnson indicated their belief that the sexual response cycle was actually an inborn drive to orgasm: 'The cycle of sexual response, with orgasm as the ultimate point in progression, generally is believed to develop from a drive of biologic origin deeply integrated into the condition of human existence'.[1] The cycle of sexual response, then, reflects the operation of an inborn program, like the workings of a mechanical clock. As long as the 'effective sexual stimulation' (i.e., energy source) continues, the cycle proceeds through its set sequence. [. . .]

I have elsewhere detailed the development of sexual dysfunction nosology in the four sequential editions of the American Psychiatric Association's *Diagnostic and Statistical Manual of Mental Disorders (DSM)*.[2] Over a period of thirty-five years, the nosology evolved from not listing sexual dysfunctions at all[3] to listing them as symptoms of psychosomatic disorders,[4] as a subcategory of psychosexual disorders,[5] and as a subcategory of sexual disorders.[6]

The relation of this nosology to the HSRC language can be seen in the introduction to the section on sexual dysfunctions (identical in both *DSM-III* and *DSM-III-R*):

The *essential feature* is inhibition in the appetitive or psychophysiological changes that characterize the *complete sexual response cycle*. The complete sexual response cycle can be divided into the following phases: 1. Appetitive. This consists of fantasies about sexual activity and a desire to have sexual activity. 2. Excitement. This consists of a subjective sense of sexual pleasure and accompanying physiological changes. . . . 3. Orgasm. This consists of a peaking of sexual pleasure, with release of sexual tension and rhythmic contraction of the perineal muscles and pelvic reproductive organs. . . . 4. Resolution. This consists of a sense of general relaxation, well-being, and muscular relaxation.[7]

In fact, this cycle is not identical to Masters and Johnson's HSRC (although it, too, uses the universalizing language of 'the' sexual response cycle). The first, or appetitive, phase was added when sexologists confronted clinical problems having to do with sexual disinterest. In their second book,[8] Masters and Johnson loosely used their HSRC physiological research to generate a list of sexual dysfunctions: premature ejaculation, ejaculatory incompetence, orgasmic dysfunction (women's), vaginismus, and dyspareunia (men's and women's). These were put forth as deviations from the HSRC that research had revealed as the norm. By the late 1970s, however, clinicians were describing a syndrome of sexual disinterest that did not fit into the accepted response cycle. Helen Singer Kaplan argued that a 'separate phase [sexual desire] which had previously been neglected must be added for conceptual completeness and clinical effectiveness'.[9] *DSM-III* and *DSM-III-R* then merged the original HSRC with the norm of sexual desire to generate 'the complete response cycle' presented above.

Clearly, the idea and much of the language of the nosology derived from Masters and Johnson's work, and in fact they are cited in the *DSM* footnotes as the primary source. Is it appropriate to use the HSRC to generate a clinical standard of normality? Is it appropriate to enshrine the HSRC as the standard of human sexuality such that deviations from it become the essential feature of abnormality?

Let us briefly examine how sexual problems are linked to mental disorders in the *DSM* and how the HSRC was used in the sexuality section. The definition of mental disorder offered in *DSM-III* specifies:

In *DSM-III* each of the mental disorders is conceptualized as a clinically significant behavioral or psychological syndrome or pattern that occurs in an individual and that is typically associated with either a painful symptom (distress) or impairment in one or more areas of function (disability). In addition, there is an inference that there is a behavioral, psychological or biological dysfunction.[10]

In an article introducing the new classification scheme to the psychiatric profession, the APA task force explained their decisions. With regard to sexual dysfunctions, the task force members had concluded that 'inability to experience the *normative sexual response cycle* [emphasis added] represented a disability in the important area of sexual functioning, whether or not the individual was distressed by the symptom'.[11] That is, deviation from the now-normative sexual response cycle was to be considered a disorder even if the person had no complaints.

The diagnostic classification system clearly assumed that the HSRC was a universal bedrock of sexuality. Yet I have shown that it was a self-fulfilling result of Masters and Johnson's methodological decisions rather than a scientific discovery. It was the result of a priori assumptions rather than empirical research. Arguably, a clinical standard requires a greater demonstration of health impact and universal applicability than that offered by Masters and Johnson's research.

In fact, it is likely the case that the *DSM* authors adopted the HSRC model because it was useful and convenient. Professional and political factors that probably facilitated the adoption include professional needs within psychiatry to move away from a neurosis disorder model to a more concrete and empirical model, legitimacy needs within the new specialty of sex therapy, and the interests of feminists in progressive sexual standards for women.[12] Thus, the enshrinement of the HSRC and its upgraded versions as the centerpiece of sexual dysfunction nomenclature in *DSM-III* and *DSM-II-R* is not scientifically reliable and represents a triumph of politics and professionalism.

Sexuality as the Performances of Fragmented Body Parts

One deleterious clinical consequence of the utilization of the HSRC model as the sexual norm has been increased focus on segmented psychophysiological functioning. Just for example, consider the following disorder descriptions, which appear in *DSM-III-R*:

1. 'partial or complete failure to attain or maintain the lubrication-swelling response of sexual excitement [Female Arousal Disorder]'
2. 'involuntary spasm of the musculature of the outer third of the vagina that interferes with coitus [Vaginismus]'
3. 'inability to reach orgasm in the vagina [Inhibited Male Orgasm]'

In the current nosology, the body as a whole is never mentioned but instead has become a fragmented collection of parts that pop in and out at different points in the performance sequence. This compartmentalization lends itself to mechanical imagery, to framing sexuality as the smooth operation and integration of complex machines, and to seeing problems of sexuality as 'machines in disrepair' that need to be evaluated by high-technology part-healers.[13] If there is a sexual problem, check each component systematically to detect the component out of commission. Overall satisfaction (which is mentioned nowhere in the nosology) is assumed to be a result of perfect parts-functioning. Recall that subjective distress is not even required for diagnosis, just objective indication of deviation from the HSRC.

This model promotes the idea that sexual disorder can be defined as deviation from 'normal' as indicated by medical test results. A bit of thought, however, will show that identifying proper norms for these types of measurements in a tricky matter. How rigid is rigid? How quick is premature? How delayed is delayed? The answers to these questions are more a product of expectations, cultural standards, and particular partner than they are of objective measurement. And yet a series of complex and often invasive genital measurements are already being routinely used in evaluations of erectile dysfunction. Norms for many of the tests are more often provided by medical technology manufacturers than by scientific research, and measurements on nonpatient samples are often lacking. Despite calls for caution in use and interpretation, the use of sexuality measurement technology continues to escalate.

This example illustrates a general medical trend: While reliance on tests and technology for objective information is increasing, reliance on patients' individualized standards and subjective reports of illness is decreasing. The end result may be, as Lionel Trilling worried in a review of the first Kinsey report, that 'the sexuality that is measured is taken to be the definition of sexuality itself'.[14] Although it seems only common sense and good clinical practice to want to 'rule out' medical causes prior to initiating a course of psychothera-peutic or couple treatment for sexual complaints, such 'ruling out' has become a growth industry rather than an adjunct to psychological and couple-oriented history-taking. Moreover, there is a growing risk of iatrogenic disorders being induced during the extensive 'ruling out' procedures.

The HSRC has contributed significantly to the idea of sexuality as proper parts-functioning. Masters and Johnson's original research can hardly be faulted for studying individual physiological components to answer the question, 'What physical reactions develop as the human male and female respond to effective sexual stimulation?' But once the physiological aspects became solidi-fied into a universal, normative sequence known as 'the' HSRC, the stage was set for clinical preoccupation with parts-functioning. Despite Masters and Johnson's avowed interest in sexuality as communication, intimacy, self-expres-sion, and mutual pleasuring, their clinical ideas were ultimately mechanical.[15]

Exclusive Genital (i.e., Reproductive) Focus for Sexuality

'Hypoactive sexual desire' is the only sexual dysfunction in the DSM-III-R defined without regard to the genital organs. 'Sexual aversion,' for example, is specifically identified as aversion *to the genitals*. The other sexual dysfunctions are defined in terms of *genital* pain, spasm, dryness, deflation, uncontrolled responses, delayed responses, too-brief responses, or absent responses. The DSM locates the boundary between normal and abnormal (or between healthy and unhealthy) sexual function exclusively on genital performances.

'Genitals' are those organs involved in acts of generation, or biological repro-duction. Although the DSM does not explicitly endorse reproduction as the primary purpose of sexual activity, the genital focus of the sexual dysfunction nosology implies such a priority. The only sexual acts mentioned are coitus, [vaginal] penetration, sexual intercourse, and noncoital clitoral stimulation. Only one is not a heterosexual coital act. Masturbation is only mentioned as a 'form of stimulation.' Full *genital performance during heterosexual intercourse is the essence of sexual functioning*, which excludes and demotes nongenital possibil-ities for pleasure and expression. Involvement or noninvolvement of the nongenital body becomes incidental, of interest only as it impacts on genital responses identified in the nosology.

Actually, the HSRC is a whole-body response, and Masters and Johnson were as interested in the physiology of 'extragenital' responses as genital ones. Yet the stages of the HSRC as reflected in heart rate or breast changes did not make it into the DSMs. As Masters and Johnson transformed their physiological cycle into a clinical cycle, they privileged a reproductive purpose for sexuality by focusing on the genitals. It would seem that once they turned their interest to sexual problems rather than sexual process, their focus shifted to sexuality as outcome.

There is no section on diagnosis in Masters and Johnson's second, clinical, book, no definition of normal sexuality, and no hint of how the particular list of erectile, orgasmic, and other genitally focused disorders was derived. The authors merely described their treatments of 'the specific varieties of sexual dysfunction that serve as presenting complaints of patients referred'.[16] But surely this explanation cannot be the whole story. Why did they exclude problems like 'inability to relax, . . . attraction to partner other than mate, . . . partner chooses inconvenient time, . . . too little tenderness' or others of the sort later labeled 'sexual difficulties'?[17] Why did they exclude problems like 'partner is only interested in orgasm, . . . partner can't kiss, . . . partner is too hasty, . . . partner has no sense of romance,' or others of the sort identified in surveys of women?[18]

In fact, the list of disorders proposed by Masters and Johnson seems like a list devised by Freudians who, based on their developmental stage theory of sexuality, define genital sexuality as the sine qua non of sexual maturity. Despite the whole-body focus of the HSRC physiology research, the clinical interest of its authors in proper genital performance as the essence of normal sexuality indicates their adherence to an earlier tradition. The vast spectrum of sexual possibility is narrowed to genital, that is, to reproductive performance.

[*Sex is Not a Natural Act and Other Essays* (Boulder, Colo.: Westview Press, 1995), 41–2, 43, 49–53.]

III.f. Transsexuality

The possibility of changing sexes (as opposed to surgical intervention on inter-sexual individuals that aligns them with one sex or the other) is largely a product of new technologies and surgical practices. Before the middle of the twentieth century there is no example of anyone who successfully changed sexes, nor, more to the point, of anyone who wanted to change sexes. There were theories, as we have seen, about male souls trapped in female bodies, and vice versa, but these were attempts to explain homosexual tastes and behaviour. Even those who advanced such theories did not accompany them with a demand to alter anatomical sex to conform to an internal disposition. The endocrine revolution, however, by demonstrating the powerful role of the sex hormones in shaping physical development and sexual drives, made it at least conceivable that adults could influence their sexual natures by appropriate dosages of the 'correct' sex hormones. This was the era, remember, when the 'hormonal body' was believed to be the most important influence on sexual life in animals and in humans.

In 1948 George Jorgensen was an ex-GI who had feelings of being in a 'sexual mix-up'. He was attracted to some men but was repelled by the idea of homo-sexual sexual contact. Seeking information on his condition he first consulted a psychiatrist and, as he tells the story, came across a book in the library that seemed relevant to his condition. In consultation with American and Danish doctors, Jorgensen embarked on a course of oestrogen treatment. His breasts grew in size, muscle was slowly replaced with softer tissue, and his body approached a womanly ideal he had only dreamed about. As he explained it to his anxious parents five years later, sex was all more or less a matter of hormones. Eventually George had his penis excised and a rudimentary vagina constructed, changed his name to Christine, and 'came out' as a woman to sensational press attention (Extract 108).

When the Jorgensen case became front-page news in 1952 a young American newspaperman found himself convinced something of the kind would work for him. He married, unhappily, and in the 1970s decided to begin oestrogen treatments. By that time surgical procedures had been refined to the point that vaginas could be surgically constructed to accommodate a penis, and produce pleasure and even orgasm for the recipient. Even with this knowledge, 'Nancy' Hunt was at first perfectly satisfied with the startling mental and physical effects of the oestrogen treatments. 'Nancy' began dressing as a woman at work and was accepted by many co-workers as a woman. It was a sexual encounter with a male co-worker, however, that convinced her to proceed with 'sex reassign-ment' surgery (Extract 109).

Once again the genitals assert their priority. Even for transsexuals living as women (the overwhelming majority of transsexual surgery is male to female), and feeling themselves to be female, the final step of genital alteration becomes an inescapable rite of passage. The period of sexual confusion in which they possess 'female' desire but still possess a non-erectile penis (the effect of oestrogen treatments) is a torment for many transsexuals who yearn for anatomical completeness and the possibility of 'normal' sexual encounters. Researchers have noted the centrality of this rite of incorporation as a social incorporation (Extract 110).

It is important to understand the fact that none of this would have been possible without the endocrinal revolution in biology and the development of techniques of cosmetic surgery that can reconstruct functional genitalia. This realization presents us with the most dramatic illustration possible of sex and sexuality as constructed entities, but entities that are still patterned on nature. In the 1960s the notion of gender as the core underlying identity to which aberrant sex must be adjusted produced the term 'gender dysphoria'. This development coincided loosely with a 'gender revolution' in society and with an increasing use of the term 'gender' as an alternative to the older term 'sex'. As Bernice L. Hausman points out, this inversion of the usual hierarchy (sex as the biological substratum of identity; gender as social role) has encouraged the idea that our sexual bodies are infinitely malleable and our 'core' identity is an internal and invisible gender identity (Extract 111).

The First Sex Change Operation

While browsing through the endless rows of books in the local library one day, a title suddenly caught my attention. *The Male Hormone* by Paul de Kruif. I had remembered reading the same author's *Microbe Hunters* with complete absorption a few years before. I slipped the narrow volume from its place on the shelves, flipped open the cover, and on the title page, I read a quotation that was to stay with me for all time. 'Remember, Paul, people are very open-minded about new things—so long as they are exactly like the old ones.'

I walked to the nearest library table, sat down, and slowly began to read. For a time on that wintry afternoon, there was no other world but the fascinating, incredible one created by Paul de Kruif. Unfamiliar words and new ideas exploded in my mind from almost every page. 'Manhood is chemical, manhood is testosterone. Over and beyond testosterone, manhood seems to be partly a state of mind.' Also, I struggled with the term 'clinical endocrinology,' which dealt with the various glands of the body and their relationship to health and mental outlook. As I read on, my mind raced with this new knowledge, for throughout the narrative, there was woven a tiny thread of recognition pulled from my own private theories.

The book stated that at the time the author was doing his research in preparation for writing it, matters pertaining to glands were considered dangerous and somewhat unsavory, and the men who dared reach into this field had risked their scientific reputations. I read on eagerly, no doubt oblivious to everything but the printed pages before me.

'There is an uncanny ability in one of the pure female hormones, to alter the lives and fate of man, and the pure male hormone—testosterone—to bring about deep changes in the sex lives of women.' These facts, Dr de Kruif stated, had been discovered by a surgeon in his search for hormone controls over certain urological diseases.

'Chemically, all of us are both man and woman because our bodies make both male and female hormones, and primarily it's an excess of testosterone that makes us men, or an excess of female hormones that makes us women; and the chemical difference between testosterone and estradiol is merely a matter of four atoms of hydrogen and one atom of carbon.'

I didn't know how my own case might be related to these ideas but at that moment it seemed possible to me that I was holding salvation in my hands: the science of body chemistry. Even then, I think I knew that Providence had intervened again and opened a door on a new and shining vista.

On what was to me a fateful day in December of 1948, I left the library in a state of excitement and with a deep feeling of gratitude. I remember walking through the falling snow, passing shop windows ablaze with Christmas lights and decorations. That day, I bought myself a Christmas present—a copy of *The Male Hormone*, which was to become thoroughly worn and dog-eared before I took the next vital step toward a solution.

My total preoccupation with these new chemical theories was interrupted by the Christmas holidays, which I spent at home in the Bronx. After the holiday intermission, I returned to school and the all-consuming study of the principles of body chemistry, contained in Dr de Kruif's book. If, I wondered, hormones were to be a possible answer, which way should I turn? Should I follow the course already suggested and try to become more masculine by developing the outward physical signs of manhood? However, I reasoned, if that was possible, would I then have a man's desires, attitudes, and emotions? I felt certain, even then, that the answer to that would be 'No.' Then what of the more drastic measure of trying to become more feminine? Could the transition to womanhood be accomplished through the magic of chemistry? At that point, I feared the answer to that question was 'No,' also. [. . .]

Mine is an unusual case, although the condition is not so rare as the average person would think. It is more a problem of social taboos and the desire not to speak of the subject, because it deals with the great 'hush-hush,' namely, Sex. It was for this reason that I came to Europe to one of the greatest gland and hormone specialists in the world. This doctor was very willing to take my case, because he doesn't have the chance very often of finding a patient who can give such complete cooperation as I have. This cooperation meant months of daily tests and examinations. I do not know if you know that both men and women have hormones of both sexes in their bodies. Regardless of many outward appearances, it is the quantity of those hormones which determines a person's sex. All sex characteristics are a result of those hormones. Sometimes, a child is born and, to all outward appearances, seems to be of a certain sex. During childhood, nothing is noticed, but at the time of puberty, when the sex hormones come into action, the chemistry of the body seems to take an opposite turn and, chemically, the child is not of the supposed sex, but the opposite one. This may sound rather fantastic and unbelievable, but I think the doctor's words fit: 'The body and life itself is the world's strangest thing. Why then, should we be shocked or even surprised by anything that this strange mechanism does?' And how true those words are.

[*A Personal Autobiography* (New York: Paul S. Eriksson, Inc. 1967), 78–80, 124–5.]

NANCY HUNT

109   The Truth of Sexual Desire

I could not reconcile myself to sex-reassignment surgery. My health was blooming under the estrogens, my mood was euphoric. Why let some hack surgeon have at me with a knife and ruin everything? Moreover, I couldn't see that I had any practical need for a vagina. Though I had been elated to discover that I could arouse a man, had even felt some physical response in myself, my abhorrence of homosexuality curtailed any wish to be able to perform as a woman.

So a vagina seemed somehow superfluous. I had no dread of the operation; neither did I have any late compunction about shedding my male genitalia. But I did feel that I should have a compelling and rational argument for stretching myself supine on the operating table.

Society provided enough such reasons, heaven knows. If I continued to dress as a woman while retaining my male anatomy, I would be living outside the law, subject to arrest and disgrace on half a dozen counts. But if I joined the select company of 'postsurgical transsexuals,' I could change my birth certificate and my driver's licence and live free of any legal sanctions. The operation might wreck me physically and emotionally, but for society's purposes I would be saved. Somehow this prospect lacked the power to move me toward the table.

Still, even as I pondered and agonized, I expected that I would undergo surgery later if not sooner. I could plot the events of my transition on a graph and establish a line of progress like the the parabolic curve in a calculus problem. By a combination of metaphysical computations and guesswork, I could project that curve until it crossed the anatomical x axis. If the solution to this equation failed to reach me in the marrow of my bones, my mind's eye could still see that graph. I had not progressed far enough to cross the axis, but I knew I would. [. . .]

The possibility of Tony being discreet was at that point something that I could not easily imagine. 'The living room lights are on,' I protested. 'My room-mate is still up. This just isn't going to work.' (The household arrangements weren't the only thing that wasn't going to work, I thought balefully. What on earth did he expect to do to me?)

Tony told the taxi driver to wait and slipped him some money to make sure that he did. Then he escorted me upstairs, where, as I had predicted, Ellen was not only awake but fully clothed and happy to see me. She did not at first see Tony, breathing hard in the doorway behind me, but as soon as she did, she tact-fully withdrew into the bedroom, leaving me to deal with events as best I could.

Tony drew me roughly out onto the landing, pulled off my coat and flung it across the banister. Then with one hand he clasped me to him while with the other he unzipped his fly and lowered his trousers far enough to present a potent omen of his intentions, but not so far as to impede his progress should circumstances suggest a hasty retreat.

Despite our precarious situation, I was beginning to enjoy the proceedings, so I did what little I could for Tony, which was a good deal more than I had ever supposed I would do for a man. Somehow that failed to bring him relief. Tony then proposed to assault me from the rear, but a decent respect for convention prompted me to decline. It was only with great difficulty, however, that I dissuaded him. At length, reluctantly, like a disappointed little boy, Tony zipped up his pants and descended to his waiting taxi. I went inside to bed, elated. I was still terribly excited, but I was also triumphant and relieved. I had liked it. Liked it? Hell, I had loved it! It was going to be all right! My sexual orientation conformed with my gender, or at least was askew in the same direction. Now I knew what I was going to do with my new vagina, and given half a chance, I was going to do it often.

[*Mirror Image* (New York: Holt, Rinehart & Winston, 1978), 144–5, 176–7.]

ANNE BOLIN

110   The Truth of Anatomy

The surgical procedure and the resulting genitalia are symbols of transsexuals' incorporation into society, the culmination of a long and arduous passage. They finally achieve the status of full-fledged women by fulfilling the cultural prerequisites of gender: people who claim the label female must a priori have vaginas. For transsexuals, the vagina presents them with possibilities denied them as women with penises. Several pre- and postoperative transsexuals described what the surgery meant to them. Their comments, presented below, all pointed to the perceived options inherent in the status of genital women.

I want the surgery because it will permit me to express my sexuality in the manner appropriate to a woman.

I want to look more like a woman. My life won't change much at all. All surgery will do for me is make me more happy that I can undress completely in a health spa, etc.

It will allow me to have sex as a female and totally be a female.

A long-term monogamous relationship is important to me. I don't think I can really settle down as a normal person until after the surgery. With the final exception of intimate relationships, it won't change much.

Surgery will make me whole like any other woman.

I want my life to be complete. I am functioning about 95 percent of the time in the female role. The other 5 percent involves things that involve my sex organ, like not being able to join a health spa or having normal sex with a man.

I want surgery so my body conforms to my spirit. It is discomforting to see yourself in a mirror with male genitalia and know it isn't right. Surgery will complete my external image.

Being able to have relationships or even brief sexual encounters is one component of transsexuals' bid for membership in normal society. Whether they choose to explore that option is not as important as having the option as women rather than people who are regarded as deviant males, transvestites, or homosexuals. [. . .]

The rite of transition concludes with the rite of incorporation, in which transsexuals are vested with symbolic keys to the full range of women's options. The gradual process of preparation for full incorporation has thrust them into life crises produced by their social and personal identity as women that is contradicted by the ever-present symbol of masculinity. These crises are ritually ameliorated by the medical profession.[1] The rite of incorporation resolves the genital disconformity and alleviates the somatic source of stigma. They can now confront a new system of social relations.

The surgery is much more than just a 'technical affirmation'.[2] It is a ritual rebirth: the birth of a woman. This symbolic birth follows a transition. It will be recalled that the term transition refers to transsexuals' real life test. It is also a medical term for the period of cervical expansion in the pregnant woman prior to the final phase of expulsion: birth of the infant. Semantically, the analogy with birth is inescapable. Transsexuals are like infants, only in their case infancy follows their social puberty and maturity.

After the surgery, doctors provide written verification of the fact that transsexuals have been surgically reassigned. This statement is a metaphor for 'It's a girl!' On the basis of this affidavit, transsexuals can request either a new birth certificate or a modified one in which their sex is declared female. The surgical conversion expresses symbolically the ascription of sex at birth, a legal as well as social assignment. Through the remarkable surgical procedure, transsexuals are symbolically reborn as well as actually reborn. The vagina is a testimonial to their lives as women, as are their new or modified birth certificates.

[*In Search of Eve: Transsexual Rites of Passage* (South Hadley, Mass.: Bergin & Carvey, Inc., 1988), 179–80, 180–1.]

BERNICE L. HAUSMAN

111 The Reassertion of Gender

It is my contention that advances in medical technologies and the discourses that surround and support the use of those technologies make possible new forms of being human. To take transsexualism as a form of being human that emerges in the twentieth century is to suggest that something happened historically to facilitate its emergence and codify its existence. Endocrinology, as the scientific study of the glands of internal secretion, was an essential discipline for the incipient development of what might be called 'transsexual subjectivity'— understood as involving the demand for sex change through hormonal treatment and plastic genital surgery. In order to understand the impact of endocrinology on the emergence of transsexualism, we must examine both medical theories of the endocrine regulation of personality and those discourses produced for 'public' consumption. Distinguishing between these discourses will not be as important for this analysis as demonstrating their points of convergence, since it is the public dissemination of scientific knowledge of the human endocrine system that will help us understand how certain human subjects in the twentieth century came to understand themselves as members of the 'other' sex. [. . .]

Both plastic surgery and endocrinology are medical technologies that some have argued can (and should) be used to regulate human behavior through the production and maintenance of a physical 'normality' that will lead to psychological 'normality' and health. It is precisely the production and instantiation of this discursive network, the overlapping theories that claim the body as the basis for mental and emotional actions and attitudes, that sets the stage for the emergence of transsexualism in the 1950s. To advocate hormonal and surgical sex change as a therapeutic tool for those whose 'gender identifications' are at odds with their anatomical sex, it is necessary to believe that physiological interventions have predictable psychological effects. In order to do this, evidence of the unpredictable psychological effects of plastic surgery must be marginalized, understood as aberrant (neurotic or psychotic) reactions, or controllable through patient selection—and certainly not the norm. It is necessary to believe, further, that patient 'happiness' is a recognizable and realizable goal for surgeries that have no physiological indication. And, in addition, it is necessary to acknowledge a certain autonomy of the psychological realm such that the psyche is understood as the realm of stability and certainty, while the body is deemed mutable.

This last qualification was not entirely established by the ideologies of endocrinology and plastic surgery, although the development of their technologies made the body 'plastic' and the target for medical interventions in significant ways. It was not until the intersex research in the 1950s that 'psychological sex'—or gender, as it was named—gained prominence as a dependable category and the physiological sexes (in particular, secondary sex characteristics and genitalia) were understood as alterable in the face of the fixity of 'gender.' By that time, the technologies of plastic genital surgery had improved to the extent that they could serve as material support for the developing theories concerning the case management of intersexual subjects, which depended heavily on the concept of gender and its stability in the face of uncertain physiological sex.

The semiotic shift from sex to gender, from body to mind, relied on the use of plastic surgical technologies as putative treatments for impaired psychological functioning. The history of plastic surgery and the development of cosmetic surgery services in the early to mid-twentieth century demonstrates that plastic surgeons were actively involved in the delineation of the semiotic field in which they practiced. Unwilling to settle for the patients who would come to them due to accidents, car wrecks, or congenital deformities, cosmetic surgeons decisively rewrote the code of normal appearance to enhance their practices. [. . .]

More significant to this analysis, however, is the fact that cosmetic surgeons also produced surgical 'treatments' for psychological disturbances, as well as a set of discourses defending and espousing the success of such 'treatments.' The practice of plastic surgery for the purpose of psychological health contributed to the elaboration of a semiotics of sex that upheld traditional values under the sign of cultural advancement. Advances in medical technology supported a seemingly progressive distinction between biological sex and cultural or psychological gender. However, one central tenet of plastic ideology held that cultural standards of appearance were irrefutable and immutable, just as a central component of the idea of 'gender' [. . .] was its irrevocable establishment as a core aspect of identity by the age of two years. The body became the target of surgical interventions so that culture could be bracketed off (as 'gender', 'norms of appearance,' etc.) and remain untouched by the semiotic changes effected through transformative medical technologies and physicians' activist appropriations of those technologies.

[*Changing Sex: Transsexualism, Technology, and the Idea of Gender* (Durham, NC: Duke University Press, 1995), 25–6, 62–4.]

III.g. The Gay Gene and the Sexual Brain

One of the most recent trends in research on the sexual body has been the attempt to locate the causes of sexual orientation in general and homosexual orientation in particular. Many of the scientific and professional workers in these fields acknowledge more or less openly the political and social motivations of their work, and popularizations of this research almost invariably discuss the 'implications' of what it means to be born with a genetically determined sexual orientation. The abundant criticism of these perspectives has not deterred those who believe strongly in the existence of solid proof for human sexual 'nature'. In contrast to the way non-Western cultures assure gender roles through cultural rituals, it has been suggested that in modern times Western culture has used biological investigations of sex differences to police these same boundaries.[1] This familiar 'discourse' is deployed when pressing social or political questions are raised about changing sex or gender roles in society at large.

In the recent era, the traditional gender and sex arrangements of business, government, the professions, and the military have been dramatically altered by large influxes of women, gay men, and lesbians. These developments have brought about in turn both open advocacy of further change and equally adamant resistance to it. This advocacy has scrambled the usual relations between nature–nurture arguments and has complicated enormously our usual association of conservative political and social views with biological determinism and progressive ones with a social-constructionist, environmentalist perspective. Fundamentalist Christians opposed to homosexuality reject determinism in favour of a free-will theory stressing the sinfulness of free choice, and advocates of gay 'rights' insist gays and lesbians are 'born' that way and deserve the same legal tolerance as people of colour. There are still plenty of critics of biological explanations in the 'progressive' political camp, and no end of conservative determinists, but the scientific and ideological variations in these issues are perhaps more complex than ever before.

The search for the 'gay' gene was initiated by Dean Hamer, a molecular geneticist at the National Institute of Health, who had previously studied gene regulation in primitive organisms. He began his work in 1991, looking for the sorts of linkages in genetically related individuals that would suggest higher than normal concentrations of individuals with homosexual orientations. Hamer's work was begun amidst a very public debate initiated by the Clinton administration over the place of homosexuals in the military. Though Hamer denies it, there were very real implications for the outcome of this debate by 'proving' that homosexuals are born, not made. By studying the

---

[1] Marianne van den Wijngaard, *Reinventing the Sexes: The Biomedical Construction of Femininity and Masculinity* (Bloomington: Indiana University Press, 1997), 24.

genetic pedigrees of twenty-nine families in which homosexual brothers had appeared, he hoped to find a gene or gene location shared by an unusual number of family members. What he found was a sex-linked connection on one arm of the X-chromosome inherited by males from their mothers. He did not find the gene itself, and there are certain limitations to his study that he freely admits. However, he remains convinced, as we see in Extract 112, that further research will succeed in isolating the gene, or combination of genes that are responsible for gay male orientation.

In the same year Hamer began his search for the 'gay' gene, Simon LeVay, a biological researcher at the Salk Institute, who had studied the structure, function, and development of vision in the cerebral cortex, published an article purporting to have found a structure in the hypothalamus of the brain unique to gay men. LeVay's work is far from the simple anatomical determinism of nineteenth-century advocates of homosexual 'difference'. Because his work follows the hormone revolution, he considers the complex influence of hormones on the structure and function of the brains of developing organisms. Scientists have long understood that the timing and quantity of hormones in the bloodstreams of growing organisms affects a wide range of their physical and behavioural characteristics. LeVay looked particularly at the hypothalamus, which had already been shown to regulate mounting and other sexual behaviour in rats. In Extract 113 LeVay describes his own research on the medial preoptic region of the hypothalamus and some related research.

The criticism of Hamer's and LeVay's work has been widespread, not particularly on the grounds that they are themselves gay men advocating a particular explanation of gay sexuality, but for committing a variety of methodological and logical errors. As William Byne, a brain researcher and psychiatrist argues, the biological research on gay sexual orientation is essentially an extention of the research tradition constructed to investigate male and female sexual difference (Extract 114). The psychologist Michael Gorman argues that, in the same way as much of the research on sex difference, research on homosexual orientation incorporates the gender biases of the surrounding society (Extract 115).

As with any first-time study, our results need to be repeated, by us or another lab, before they can be fully accepted. Had we announced linkage for some common disease, such as manic depressive illness or Alzheimer's, labs around the world would have been repeating our experiments on their own samples the minute our paper was published. But the genetic study of sexual orientation was brand-new, and nobody else in the world had collected DNA from a comparable series of gay brothers and their families. Just as I had hoped, the publication of our paper stimulated new interest in the genetics of sexual orientation. In 1994, at least one group was collecting families, and two more were applying for funding.

In the meantime, our lab continued to seek families to repeat the entire linkage analysis. People sometimes ask if it isn't boring to repeat the same experiment. I just remind them of how Nobel laureate Alfred Hershey, one of the discoverers of the biological role of DNA, defined heaven: 'To find one really good experiment and keep doing it over and over.'

What The Study Did Not Show

Proving that a gene exists is one thing. Isolating or finding the gene, measuring its incidence and effect on people, and understanding how it works is another, and those goals may take many years to achieve. Given the brief history of the genetic study of sexual orientation, we're pleased to have made as much progress as we have, but many things, indeed most things, remain to be explored.

Population Parameters

Our study was not designed to address the role of the Xq28 locus in the population at large or even among all gay men. Mary-Claire King, discoverer of the breast-cancer locus, made this point most succinctly: 'It is impossible to use either the family history or the linkage data to estimate the magnitude of genetic influence on homosexuality in the general population.'

King then outlined some of the questions that remain to be answered. What fraction of all gay men carry an Xq28-linked allele that influenced their sexual orientation? What is the frequency of this allele among heterosexual men? How many different alleles are present at Xq28, and what is the effect of each? What other genes and nongenetic factors influence sexual orientation, and what role does each play?

Our study could not address these questions because we deliberately studied a population enriched for the gene we were searching for—enriched because we only studied those families with two gay brothers, no gay fathers, and no more than one lesbian. This selected population was necessary to determine whether a gene on the X chromosome had any effect on sexual orientation, but it could not show the precise magnitude of that effect.

To estimate the role of Xq28 in the population at large, researchers would have to isolate the gene, determine what parts of the DNA sequence were variable, and then perform a population-based survey on a large number of individuals with various sexual identifications. The results of such an experiment on a particular population, say residents of Washington, D.C., still would be limited and would not necessarily apply to other populations, such as Salt Lake City or Tokyo, where the same genes might express themselves differently because of the different cultural environments. A person with a 'gay gene' growing up in a repressive society, for example, might develop differently than someone with the same gene growing up in a permissive society.

This type of measurement is still a long way from being feasible. In the meantime, we can make only educated guesses about the importance of Xq28 in the population at large. On the high side, the region couldn't possibly influence more than 67 percent of gay men, the proportion 'linked' to this region in our highly selected group of gay siblings. On the low side, if much of homosexuality is caused by environmental factors, or by a large number of interacting genes, Xq28 could account for as little as a few percent of the variation in male sexual orientation. The median range, taken from our linkage data and from the available twin and family studies, suggests that Xq28 plays some role in about 5 to 30 percent of gay men. The broad range of these estimates is proof that much more work remains to be done.

In-betweens

We never did find many bisexual men, so there is no way to speculate on the role of Xq28 in people who identify as bisexual, asexual, or anything outside our simplistic dichotomy of 'gay or straight.' This was not an oversight but deliberate, because our first goal was to determine whether genes had any influence on sexual orientation, which meant it was important to study only those individuals whose orientation was unambiguous. A more systematic approach to this question will be possible after the gene is identified.

Lesbians

Twin and family studies suggest that female sexual orientation is as likely to be inherited as male sexual orientation, but narrowing the role of individual genes will require more effort than did the male project. In general, women display a wider diversity of sexual expressions and developmental patterns than do men. Furthermore, by early 1994 we had not observed any obvious transmission patterns in our ongoing studies of the extended families of lesbians. A complicating factor was that even if the X chromosome were involved in female sexual orientation, the expected patterns would not necessarily show an excess of either paternal or maternal gay relatives, because a woman inherits one X chromosome from her mother and one from her father.

There is no way to be sure yet, but it's unlikely the same version of Xq28 associated with male homosexuality also is associated with lesbianism. If it were, we would have found more families with both gay men and women. If Xq28 influences sexual orientation by directing a person's sexual attraction, it would be unlikely to influence both gay men and lesbians, because the objects of their affection are just the opposite. On the other hand, if Xq28 acts more indirectly, perhaps influencing personality traits, it's conceivable the same region is involved in both men and women. During early 1994, Angela Pattatucci continued collecting families with lesbian sisters and obtaining DNA samples to begin to answer those questions.

A Linkage Is Not a Gene

The most important limitation of our research was that we didn't isolate a 'gay gene'; we only detected its presence through linkage. We narrowed the search to the neighborhood, the X chromosome—and even the block, Xq28—but we didn't find the house.

More precisely, our mapping showed the 'gay gene' is most likely somewhere between the markers GABRA3 and DXYS154, which span a distance of about five million base pairs. That represents less than 0.2 of the three billion base pairs in the human genome, but because the genome includes somewhere around 100,000 different genes, such a small area has enough room for up to 200 or so different genes.

Narrowing a search to two hundred apartments in a big city isn't very helpful if you are looking for one person. The traditional method for localizing a gene is recombinational mapping, which takes advantage of the rule that the number of crossovers between a gene and a marker is proportional to the distance between them. Unfortunately, this method is poorly suited for mapping complex traits such as sexual orientation. It only works well for simple, single-gene traits that follow Mendel's laws. The main problem is not knowing whether a gay man is missing a particular marker because of a recombination event (the mixing of DNA) or if he is gay because of some different gene or a nongenetic reason.

A second method of gene mapping uses something called linkage disequilibrium, which involves searching for patterns of markers among unrelated gay men instead of searching for sharing of markers among brothers. Such patterns would emerge if the 'gay gene' were sitting very close to a distinctive set of richly varied markers.

The third approach is candidate gene analysis, which examines the coding sequences of genes that 'look like' they might have something to do with sexuality. For example, genes that are expressed in regions of the brain thought to control sexual activity, such as the hypothalamus, or that act differently in men and women. Unfortunately, we don't yet know of any such genes in Xq28.

The final approach is brute force; that is, to look for sequence variations in each and every protein coding sequence in Xq28. Right now, we don't have the necessary knowledge, techniques, or people to do that, but thanks to the Human Genome Project, there should be a complete catalog of all the genes in Xq28 available sometime in the next five to fifteen years. DNA sequencing technology is developing so rapidly that we probably will have the necessary methods to screen all these genes for interesting variations. So if there really is a 'gay gene' in Xq28, it will be found.

[*The Science of Desire: The Search For the Gay Gene and the Biology of Behavior* (New York: Simon & Schuster, 1994), 144–8.]

SIMON LeVAY

113   The Sexual Brain

Are there differences in the anatomical or chemical structure of the brain between homosexual and heterosexual individuals? As I stated at the beginning of the chapter, the answer to this question must in principle be yes, because a person's sexual orientation remains unaltered after all brain activity and metabolism have been temporarily halted. So the practical question is: Are the structural differences scattered through a million widely dispersed, anonymous synapses in the cerebral cortex (as the structural differences representing preference for different musical composers presumably are) or are they concentrated at a key location, where they so dominate the cellular landscape as to make themselves evident to an anatomist's inspection?

My own research suggests that there is at least one such key location, the medial preoptic region of the hypothalamus. This region of the brain is believed to be involved in the regulation of male-typical sexual behavior, and it contains at least four small groups of neurons termed the interstitial nuclei of the anterior hypothalamus (INAH). One of these, named INAH 3, is bigger on average in men than women. The others either show no sex differences (INAH 1 and 4) or show equivocal differences that may be limited to certain age ranges (INAH 2). I obtained the brains of gay men (all of whom had died of AIDS) as well as the brains of heterosexual men who had also died of AIDS (these were intravenous drug abusers) and of presumably heterosexual men who had died of a variety of other causes. In addition, I obtained the brains of several women, presumably heterosexual ('presumably' means simply on the basis of the preponderance of heterosexual women in the population: a woman's sexual orientation is rarely if ever noted in her medical records). I was not able to obtain the brains of any women known to have been lesbian.

I processed and analyzed the hypothalamic tissue from these brains 'blind,' that is, not knowing which specimen came from which group of subjects. After decoding the results, I obtained two significant results. First, INAH 3 was on average two- to threefold bigger in the presumed heterosexual men (whether or not they died of AIDS) than in the women. This result confirmed that of Laura Allen and colleagues at UCLA. Second, in the gay men INAH 3 was on average the same size as in the women, and two to three times smaller than in the straight men. It should be emphasized that these differences were in the averages: some of the women and gay men had a large INAH 3, and some of the presumed heterosexual men had a small one. None of the other three nuclei showed any differences between groups.

This finding suggests that gay and straight men may differ in the central neuronal mechanisms that regulate sexual behavior. Although the data described only the size of the nuclei, not the numbers of neurons within each nucleus, it is very likely that there are fewer neurons in INAH 3 of gay men (and women) than in straight men. To put an absurdly facile spin on it, gay men simply don't have the brain cells to be attracted to women.

Several important qualifications have to be made. All the gay men in my sample died of AIDS. Was the disease rather than their sexual orientation responsible for the small size of INAH 3? After all, we know that AIDS and its complications can devastate the brain. My reasons for thinking that the disease was not responsible were fivefold. First, the control group of AIDS patients who were heterosexual had a large INAH 3. Second, none of the other three nuclei showed differences between groups, as they might well have done if the disease was destroying neurons nonselectively in this region of the brain. Third, there was no correlation between the length of the patients' illness, or the complications that occurred, and the size of INAH 3. Fourth, there were no dying cells, inflammatory reactions, or other signs of a pathological process at work. Lastly, after publication of my study I obtained the brain of one gay man who died of a disease other than AIDS (he died of lung cancer). I examined this brain 'blind' along with three other brains from presumably heterosexual men of similar ages. Already during the analysis I correctly guessed which was the hypothalamus of the gay man; INAH 3 was less than half the size of the nucleus in the other three men.

Even if, as I believe, AIDS was not the reason for the difference in the size of INAH 3, the use of brains from AIDS patients does raise other problems. Are gay men who die of AIDS representative of gay men as a whole, or are they atypical, for example in preferring receptive anal intercourse (the major risk factor in homosexual sex) or in having unusually large numbers of sexual partners (another risk factor)? It is difficult to answer these questions decisively. However, HIV infection is now so widespread in the gay community that it is unrealistic to imagine a group to be highly atypical simply because they died of AIDS.

To many people, finding a difference in brain structure between gay and straight men is equivalent to proving that gay men are 'born that way.' Time and again I have been described as someone who 'proved that homosexuality is genetic' or some such thing. I did not. My observations were made only on adults who had been sexually active for a considerable period of time. It is not possible, purely on the basis of my observations, to say whether the structural differences were present at birth, and later influenced the men to become gay or straight, or whether they arose in adult life, perhaps as a result of the men's sexual behavior.

In considering which of these interpretations is more likely, one is thrown back on the animal research discussed in earlier chapters. The sexually dimorphic nucleus of the medial preoptic area in rats (which may or may not correspond to INAH 3 in humans) is highly susceptible to modification during a critical period that lasts for a few days before and after the rat's birth. After this time, it is difficult to change the size of the nucleus by any means. Even castrating adult rats (which removes the rat's source of androgens and greatly impairs the rat's sexual behavior) has at most a very slight effect on the size of the nucleus. If the same is true for INAH 3 in humans, it would seem likely that the structural differences between gay and straight men come about during the initial period of sexual differentiation of the hypothalamus. If this is the case, it is possible that these differences play some role in determining a person's sexual orientation. However, we cannot exclude the possibility that in humans, with their longer lifespan and better developed cerebral cortex, gross changes in the size of INAH 3 might come about as a result of adult behavior.

The ideal experiment would of course be to measure the size of INAH 3 in newborn infants by some scanning technique, to wait twenty years, and then to inquire about their sexual orientation. If the size of the nucleus at birth were to any extent predictive of the person's ultimate sexual orientation, one could argue more strongly that the size of the nucleus might play some kind of causative role. This experiment is not possible, at the moment at least, as scanning techniques capable of imaging INAH 3 in living people do not yet exist.

In the rat research, the major factor influencing the size of the sexually dimorphic nucleus has been shown to be the levels of circulating androgens, which act on the neurons of the nucleus during the critical period to promote their survival. This suggests two possible developmental mechanisms by which the different size of INAH 3 in gay and straight men might come about. One would be that there are differences between 'gay' and 'straight' fetuses in the levels of circulating androgens during the critical period for the development of INAH 3. The other would be that the levels of androgens are the same, but that the cellular mechanisms by which the neurons of INAH 3 respond to the hormones are different.

More recently, another difference in brain structure between gay and straight men has been described, this time by Allen and Gorski at UCLA.[1] They found differences in the anterior commissure, which is an axonal connection between the left and right sides of the cerebral cortex and is generally larger in women than men. Allen and Gorski's finding (which like my work was made on autopsied brains, many from AIDS patients) was that the anterior commissure is on average larger in gay men than in straight men. In fact they found it to be larger in gay men even than in women, but after correction for overall brain size the size of the structure was about the same in gay men and in women. (As in my study, Allen and Gorski were unable to determine the sexual orientation of the women from their medical records; presumably the majority of them were hetereosexual.)

This finding is interesting for several reasons. First, it strengthens the notion that the brains of gay and straight men are indeed different. Second, it may relate to some of the cognitive differences mentioned above: if cerebral functions are less strongly lateralized in gay men than in straight men, there may be greater need to interconnect the two hemispheres. Finally, the very fact that the anterior commissure is not involved in the regulation of sexual behavior makes it highly unlikely that the size differences result from differences in sexual behavior. Much more probably, the size differences came about during the original sexual differentiation of the anterior commissure, either under the direct influence of gonadal steroids or as a consequence of developmental events in the cortical regions that it interconnects. Thus, whatever the functional significance of the size of the commissure may be, it may serve as an independent label for processes that went forward differently in 'gay' and 'straight' fetuses or young children.

Unlike INAH 3, which is far too small to be imaged in a living person's brain by any available scanning technique, the anterior commissure can be seen, although not terribly clearly, in magnetic resonance images (MRI scans). Modest improvements in technique might allow the commissure to be measured accurately in living persons. This would allow the issue of brain structure and sexual orientation to be extended to women, and it would also allow one to obtain a detailed sex history, including details of preferred erotic roles, childhood characteristics, and so on, from the same individuals whose brain structures were measured.

[*The Sexual Brain* (Cambridge, Mass.: MIT Press, 1993), 120–4.]

WILLIAM BYNE

114   The Biological Evidence Challenged

Human-rights activists, religious organizations and all three branches of the U.S. government are debating whether sexual orientation is biological. The discussion has grabbed headlines, but behavioral scientists find it passé. The salient question about biology and sexual orientation is not whether biology is involved but how it is involved. All psychological phenomena are ultimately biological.

Even if the public debate were more precisely framed, it would still be misguided. Most of the links in the chain of reasoning from biology to sexual orientation and social policy do not hold up under scrutiny. At the political level, a requirement that an unconventional trait be inborn or immutable is an inhumane criterion for a society to use in deciding which of its nonconformists it will grant tolerance. Even if homosexuality were entirely a matter of choice, attempts to extirpate it by social and criminal sanctions devalue basic human freedoms and diversity.

Furthermore, the notion that homosexuality must be either inborn and immutable or freely chosen is in turn misinformed. Consider the white-crowned sparrow, a bird that learns its native song during a limited period of development. Most sparrows exposed to a variety of songs, including that of their own species, will learn their species' song, but some do not. After a bird has learned a song, it can neither unlearn that song nor acquire a new one. Although sexual orientation is not a matter of mimicry, it is clear that learned behavior can nonetheless be immutable.

Finally, what evidence exists thus far of innate biological traits underlying homosexuality is flawed. Genetic studies suffer from the inevitable confounding of nature and nurture that plagues attempts to study heritability of psychological traits. Investigations of the brain rely on doubtful hypotheses about differences between the brains of men and women. Biological mechanisms that have been proposed to explain the existence of gay men often cannot be generalized to explain the existence of lesbians (whom studies have largely neglected). And the continuously graded nature of most biological variables is at odds with the paucity of adult bisexuals suggested by most surveys.

To understand how biological factors influence sexual orientation, one must first define orientation. Many researchers, most conspicuously Simon LeVay, treat it as a sexually dimorphic trait: men are generally 'programmed' for attraction to women, and women are generally programmed for attraction to men. Male homosexuals, according to this framework, have female programming, and lesbians have male programming. Some researchers suggest that this programming is accomplished by biological agents, perhaps even before birth; others believe it occurs after birth in response to social factors and subjective experiences. As the function of the brain is undoubtedly linked to its structure and physiology, it follows that homosexuals' brains might exhibit some features typical of the opposite sex.

The validity of this 'intersex' expectation is questionable. For one, sexual orientation is not dimorphic; it has many forms. The conscious and unconscious motivations associated with sexual attraction are diverse even among the people of the same sex and orientation. Myriad experiences (and subjective interpretations of those experiences) could interact to lead different people to the same relative degree of sexual attraction to men or to women. Different people could be sexually attracted to men for different reasons; for example, there is no a priori reason that everyone attracted to men should share some particular brain structure.

Indeed, the notion that gay men are feminized and lesbians masculinized may tell us more about our culture than about the biology of erotic responsiveness. Some Greek myths held that heterosexual rather than homosexual desire had intersex origins: those with predominantly same-sex desires were considered the most manly of men and womanly of women. In contrast, those who desired the opposite sex supposedly mixed masculine and feminine in their being. Classical culture celebrated the homosexual exploits of archetypally masculine heroes such as Zeus, Hercules and Julius Caesar. Until a decade ago (when missionaries repudiated the practice), boys among the Sambia of New Guinea would form attachments to men and fellate them; no one considered that behavior a female trait. Indeed, the Sambia believed ingesting semen to be necessary for attaining strength and virility.

But there is a more tangible problem for this intersex assumption: the traits of which homosexuals ostensibly have opposite-sex versions have not been conclusively shown to differ between men and women. Of the many supposed sex differences in the human brain reported over the past century, only one has proved consistently replicable: brain size varies with body size. Thus, men tend to have slightly larger brains than women. This situation contrasts sharply with that for other animals, where many researchers have consistently demonstrated a variety of sex differences.

If brains are indeed wired or otherwise programmed for sexual orientation, what forces are responsible? Three possibilities come into play. The direct model of biological causation asserts that genes, hormones, or other factors act directly on the developing brain, probably before birth, to wire it for sexual orientation. Alternatively, the social learning model suggests that biology provides a blank slate of neural circuitry on which experience inscribes orientation. In the indirect model, biological factors do not wire the brain for orientation; instead they predispose individuals toward certain personality traits that influence the relationships and experiences that ultimately shape sexuality.

During past decades, much of the speculation about biology and orientation focused on the role of hormones. Workers once thought an adult's androgen and estrogen levels determined orientation, but this hypothesis withered for lack of support. Researchers have since pursued the notion that hormones wire the brain for sexual orientation during the prenatal period.

According to this hypothesis, high prenatal androgen levels during the appropriate critical period cause heterosexuality in men and homosexuality in women. Conversely, low fetal androgen levels lead to homosexuality in men and heterosexuality in women. This hypothesis rests largely on the observation that in rodents early exposure to hormones determines the balance between male and female patterns of mating behaviors displayed by adults. Female rodents that were exposed to androgens early in development show more male-typical mounting behavior than do normal adult females. Males deprived of androgens by castration during the same critical period display a female mating posture called lordosis (bending of the back) when they are mounted.

Many researchers consider the castrated male rat that shows lordosis when mounted by another male to be homosexual (as is the female rat that mounts others). Lordosis, however, is little more than a reflex; the male will take the same posture when a handler strokes its back. Furthermore, the male that mounts another male is considered to be heterosexual, as is the female that displays lordosis when mounted by another female. Applying such logic to humans would imply that of two people of the same sex engaged in intercourse only one is homosexual—and which member of the couple it is depends on the positions they assume.

In addition to determining rodent mating patterns, early hormonal exposure determines whether an animal's brain can regulate normal ovarian function. A male rat's brain cannot respond to estrogen by triggering a chain of events, called positive feedback, that culminates in the abrupt increase of luteinizing hormone in the bloodstream, which in turn triggers ovulation. Some researchers reasoned from this fact to the idea that homosexual men (whose brains they allege to be insufficiently masculinized) might have a stronger posi-tive-feedback reaction than do heterosexual men.

Two laboratories reported that this was the case, but carefully designed and executed studies, most notably those of Luis J. G. Gooren of the Free University in Amsterdam, disproved those findings. Furthermore, the feedback mecha-nism turns out to be irrelevant to human sexual orientation: workers have since found that the positive-feedback mechanism is not sexually dimorphic in primates, including humans. If this mechanism is indistinguishable in men and women, it is illogical to suggest that it should be 'feminized' in gay men.

Moreover, a corollary of the expectation that luteinizing hormone responses should be feminized in homosexual men is that they should be 'masculinized' in lesbians. If that were true, homosexual women would neither menstruate nor bear children. The overwhelming proportion of lesbians with normal menstrual cycles and the growing number of openly lesbian mothers attest to the fallacy of that idea.

If the prenatal hormonal hypothesis were correct, one might expect that a large proportion of men with medical conditions known to involve prenatal androgen deficiency would be homosexual, as would be women exposed prenatally to excess androgens. That is not the case.

Because androgens are necessary for development of normal external geni-tals in males, the sex of affected individuals may not be apparent at birth. Males may be born with female-appearing genitals, and females with male-appearing ones. These individuals often require plastic surgery to construct normal-

appearing genitals, and the decision to raise them as boys or as girls is sometimes based not on genetic sex but on the possibilities for genital reconstruction.

Research into the sexual orientation of such individuals tends to support the
social learning models. Regardless of their genetic sex or the nature of their
prenatal hormonal exposure, they usually become heterosexual with respect to
the sex their parents raise them as, provided the sex assignment is made unambiguously before the age of three.

Nevertheless, some studies report an increase in homosexual fantasies or
behavior among women who were exposed to androgens as fetuses. In accordance with the notion of direct biological effects, these studies are often interpreted as evidence that prenatal androgen exposure wires the brain for sexual
attraction to women. The neurobiologist and feminist scholar Ruth H. Bleier has
offered an alternative interpretation. Rather than reflecting an effect of masculin-
izing hormones on the sexual differentiation of the brain, the adaptations of
prenatally masculinized women may reflect the impact of having been born with
masculinized genitalia or the knowledge that they had been exposed to aberrant
levels of sex hormones during development. 'Gender must seem a fragile and
arbitrary construct,' Bleier concluded, 'if it depends upon plastic surgery.'

Stephen Jay Gould of Harvard University has written of the way that the
search for brain differences related to sex and other social categories was for the
most part discredited during the past century by anatomists who deluded themselves into believing that their brain measurements justified the social preju-
dices of their day. The search for sex differences in the human brain was
revitalized in the late 1970s, when Roger A. Gorski's team at the University of
California at Los Angeles discovered a group of cells in the preoptic part of the
rat hypothalamus that was much larger in males than in females. The
researchers designated this cell group the sexually dimorphic nucleus of the
preoptic area (SDN-POA). The preoptic area has long been implicated in the
regulation of sexual behavior.

Like the sex differences in mating behaviors and luteinizing hormone regulatory mechanisms, the difference in the size of the SDN-POA was found to result
from differences in early exposure to androgens. Shortly thereafter, Bleier and I,
working at the University of Wisconsin at Madison, examined the hypothalamus of several rodent species and found that the SDN-POA is only one part of
a sexual dimorphism involving several additional hypothalamic nuclei.

Three laboratories have recently sought sexually dimorphic nuclei in the
human hypothalamus. Laura S. Allen, working in Gorski's lab, identified four
possible candidates as potential homologues of the rat's SDN-POA and designated them as the interstitial nuclei of the anterior hypothalamus (INAH1-
INAH4). Different laboratories that have measured these nuclei, however, have
produced conflicting results: Dick F. Swaab's group at the Netherlands Institute
for Brain Research in Amsterdam, for example, found INAH1 to be larger in
men than in women, whereas Allen found no difference in that nucleus but

reported that INAH2 and INAH3 were larger in men. Most recently, LeVay found no sex difference in either INAH1 or INAH2 but corroborated Allen's finding of a larger INAH3 in men. LeVay also reported that INAH3 in homosexual men tends to be small, like that of women. (Neurologist Clifford Saper of Harvard and I are in the process of measuring the interstitial nuclei; at present, we have no definitive results.)

LeVay's study has been widely interpreted as strong evidence that biological factors directly wire the brain for sexual orientation. Several considerations militate against that conclusion. First, his work has not been replicated, and human neuroanatomical studies of this kind have a very poor track record for reproducibility. Indeed, procedures similar to those LeVay used to identify the nuclei have previously led researchers astray.

Manfred Gahr, now at the Max Planck Institute for Animal Physiology in Seewiesen, Germany, used a cell-staining technique similar to LeVay's to observe what appeared to be seasonal variations in the size of a nucleus involved in singing in canaries. Two more specific staining methods, however, revealed that the size of the nucleus did not change. Gahr suggested that the less specific method might have been influenced by seasonal hormonal variations that altered the properties of the cells in the nucleus.

Furthermore, in LeVay's published study, all the brains of gay men came from AIDS patients. His inclusion of a few brains from heterosexual men with AIDS did not adequately address the fact that at the time of death virtually all men with AIDS have decreased testosterone levels as the result of the disease itself or the side effects of particular treatments. To date, LeVay has examined the brain of only one gay man who did not die of AIDS. Thus, it is possible that the effects on the size of INAH3 that he attributed to sexual orientation were actually caused by the hormonal abnormalities associated with AIDS. Work by Deborah Commins and Pauline I. Yahr of the University of California at Irvine supports precisely this hypothesis. The two found that the size of a structure in mongolian gerbils apparently comparable to the SDN-POA varies with the amount of testosterone in the bloodstream.

A final problem with the popular interpretation of LeVay's study is that it is founded on an imprecise analysis of the relevant animal research. LeVay has suggested that INAH3, like the rat's SDN-POA, is situated in a region of the hypothalamus known to participate in the generation of male sexual behavior. Yet studies in a variety of species have consistently shown that the precise hypothalamic region involved in male sexual behavior is not the one occupied by these nuclei. Indeed, Gorski and Gary W. Arendash, now at the University of South Florida, found that destroying the SDN-POA on both sides of a male rat's brain did not impair sexual behavior.

Jefferson C. Slimp performed experiments in Robert W. Goy's laboratory at the Wisconsin Regional Primate Research Center (shortly before I joined that group) that suggested that the precise region involved in sexual behavior in male rhesus monkeys is located above the area comparable to that occupied by INAH3 in humans. Males with lesions in that region mounted females less frequently than they did before being operated on, but their frequency of masturbation did not change. Although some have taken these observations to mean that the lesions selectively decreased heterosexual drive, their conclusion is unwarranted; male monkeys pressed a lever for access to females more often after their operations than before. Unfortunately, these males had no opportunity to interact with other males, and so the study tells us nothing about effects on homosexual as opposed to heterosexual motivation or behavior.

Interstitial hypothalamic nuclei are not the only parts of the brain to have come under scrutiny for links to sexual orientation. Neuroanatomists have also reported potentially interesting differences in regions not directly involved in sexual behaviors. Swaab and his co-worker Michel H. Hofman found that another hypothalamic nucleus, the suprachiasmatic nucleus, is larger in homosexual than in heterosexual men. The size of this structure, however, does not vary with sex, and so even if this finding can be replicated it would not support the assumption that homosexuals have intersexed brains.

Allen of U.C.L.A., meanwhile, has reported that the anterior commissure, a structure that participates in relaying information from one side of the brain to the other, is larger in women than in men. More recently, she concluded that the anterior commissure of gay men is feminized—that is, larger than in heterosexual men. Steven Demeter, Robert W. Doty and James L. Ringo of the University of Rochester, however, found just the opposite: anterior commissures larger in men than in women. Furthermore, even if Allen's findings are correct, the size of the anterior commissure alone would say nothing about an individual's sexual orientation. Although she found a statistically significant difference in the average size of the commissures of gay men and heterosexual men, 27 of the 30 homosexual men in her study had anterior commissures within the same size range as the 30 heterosexual men with whom she compared them.

Some researchers have turned to genetics instead of brain structure in the search for a biological link to sexual orientation. Several recent studies suggest that the brothers of homosexual men are more likely to be homosexual than are men without gay brothers. Of these, only the study by J. Michael Bailey of Northwestern University and Richard C. Pillard of Boston University included both nontwin biological brothers and adopted (unrelated) brothers in addition to identical and fraternal twins.

Their investigation yielded paradoxical results: some statistics support a genetic hypothesis, and others refute it. Identical twins were most likely to both be gay; 52 percent were concordant for homosexuality, as compared with 22 percent of fraternal twins. This result would support a genetic interpretation because identical twins share all of their genes, whereas fraternal twins share only half of theirs. Nontwin brothers of homosexuals, however, share the same proportion of genes as fraternal twins; however, only 9 percent of them were concordant for homosexuality. The genetic hypothesis predicts that their rates should be equal.

Moreover, Bailey and Pillard found that the incidence of homosexuality in the adopted brothers of homosexuals (11 percent) was much higher than recent estimates for the rate of homosexuality in the population (1 to 5 percent). In fact, it was equal to the rate for nontwin biological brothers. This study clearly challenges a simple genetic hypothesis and strongly suggests that environment contributes significantly to sexual orientation.

Two of three other recent studies also detected an increased rate of homosexuality among the identical as opposed to fraternal twins of homosexuals. In every case, however, the twins were reared together. Without knowing what developmental experiences contribute to sexual orientation—and whether those experiences are more similar between identical twins than between fraternal twins—the effects of common genes and common environments are difficult to disentangle. Resolving this issue requires studies of twins raised apart.

Indeed, perhaps the major finding of these heritability studies is that despite having all of their genes in common and having prenatal and postnatal environments as close to identical as possible, approximately half of the identical twins were nonetheless discordant for orientation. This finding underscores just how little is known about the origins of sexual orientation.

Dean H. Hamer's team at the National Institutes of Health has found the most direct evidence that sexual orientation may be influenced by specific genes. The team focused on a small part of the X chromosome known as the Xq28 region, which contains hundreds of genes. Women have two X chromosomes and so two Xq28 regions, but they pass a copy of only one to a son (who has a single X chromosome). The theoretical probability of two sons receiving a copy of the same Xq28 from their mother is thus 50 percent. Hamer found that of his 40 pairs of gay siblings, 33 instead of the expected 20 had received the same Xq28 region from their mother.

Hamer's finding is often misinterpreted as showing that all 66 men from these 33 pairs shared the same Xq28 sequence. That is quite different from what the study showed: Each member of the 33 concordant pairs shared his Xq28 region only with his brother—not with any of the other 32 pairs. No single, specific Xq28 sequence (a putative 'gay gene') was identified in all 66 men.

Unfortunately, Hamer's team did not examine the Xq28 region of its gay subjects' heterosexual brothers to see how many shared the same sequence. Hamer suggests that inclusion of heterosexual siblings would have confounded his analysis because the gene associated with homosexuality might be 'incompletely penetrant'—that is to say, heterosexual men could carry the gene without expressing it. In other words, inclusion of heterosexual brothers might have revealed that something other than genes is responsible for sexual orientation.

Finally, Neil J. Risch of Yale University, one of the developers of the statistical techniques that Hamer used, has questioned whether Hamer's results are statistically significant. Risch has argued that until we have more details about the familial clustering of homosexuality, the implications of studies such as Hamer's will remain unclear.

Studies that mark homosexuality as a heritable trait (assuming that they can be replicated) do not say anything about how that heritability might operate. Genes in themselves specify proteins, not behavior or psychological phenomena. Although we know virtually nothing about how complex psychological phenomena are embodied in the brain, it is conceivable that particular DNA sequences might somehow cause the brain to be wired specifically for homosexual orientation. Significantly, however, heritability requires no such mechanism.

Instead particular genes might influence personality traits that could in turn influence the relationships and subjective experiences that contribute to the social learning of sexual orientation. One can imagine many ways in which a temperamental difference could give rise to different orientations in different environments. [. . .]

The possible interaction between genes and environment in the development of sexual orientation can be sketched here only in the most oversimplified of ways. For example, many researchers believe aversion to rough-and-tumble play in boys is moderately predictive of homosexual development. (Direct-model theorists argue this aversion is merely the childhood expression of a brain that has been wired for homosexuality.) Meanwhile psychoanalysts have noted that of those gay men who seek therapy, many report having had poor rapport with their fathers. They thus suggest that an impaired father–son relationship leads to homosexuality.

One could combine these observations to speculate that a genetically based aversion to rough-and-tumble play in boys could impair rapport with fathers who demand that they adhere to rigid sex-role stereotypes. Fathers who made no such demands would maintain a rapport with their sons. As a result, the hypothetical gene in question could affect sexual orientation in some cases but not in others. Even such a reductionist example (based on traits that reflect cultural stereotypes rather than biology) shows how neither temperament nor family environment might be decisive. Studies focusing on either one or the other would yield inconclusive results.

These speculations reemphasize how far researchers must go before they understand the factors—both biological and experiential—that contribute to sexual orientation. Even if the size of certain brain structures does turn out to be correlated with sexual orientation, current understanding of the brain is inadequate to explain how such quantitative differences could generate qualitative differences in a psychological phenomenon as complex as sexual orientation. Similarly, confirmation of genetic research purporting to show that homosexuality is heritable makes clear neither what is inherited nor how it influences sexual orientation. For the foreseeable future, then, interpretation of these results will continue to hinge on assumptions of questionable validity.

While attempts to replicate these preliminary findings continue, researchers and the public must resist the temptation to consider them in any but the most tentative fashion. Perhaps more important, we should also be asking ourselves why we as a society are so emotionally invested in this research. Will it—or should it—make any difference in the way we perceive ourselves and others or how we live our lives and allow others to live theirs? Perhaps the answers to the most salient questions in this debate lie not within the biology of human brains but rather in the cultures those brains have created.

['The Biological Evidence Challenged', *Scientific American* (May 1994), 50–5.]

MICHAEL R. GORMAN
....
115   **Male Homosexual Desire**

The term *homosexuality*, as used here, refers to sexual desire or arousal provoked by stimuli associated with individuals of the same sex. I shall deal exclusively with male homosexuality, as the amount and nature of the evidence differ for lesbians and gay men, precluding a concise treatment of both. A homosexual is considered to be an individual who is primarily aroused by same-sex rather than opposite-sex stimuli, whether or not his sexual behavior reflects this desire or arousal.[1] The term *gay* will refer to the self-identified subpopulation of homosexuals whose sexual behavior we may assume usually reflects their sexual desire. *Sexual orientation* is used to describe the preferred sexual object in terms of a homosexual/heterosexual continuum. *Masculinity* and *femininity* are used nontechnically, except where noted, for the attributes typically associated with male and female gender roles.

Sexual differentiation refers to the processes by which biological and behavioral differences between males and females are established. In the 'sexual differentiation hypothesis,' male homosexuality and female heterosexuality are posited to reflect similar neural organization and developmental causes.[2] To the extent that mechanisms underlying sexual orientation also act to sexually differentiate other traits, similarities between homosexual men and heterosexual women and differences between homosexual and heterosexual men among these traits—e.g., hormones, brain structure, cognitive abilities—would support this hypothesis. In the alternative hypothesis presented here, male homosexuality and female heterosexuality reflect different neural organizations and developmental causes. To the extent that other traits are influenced by mechanisms underlying male sexual orientation, these traits would not show systematic similarities between homosexual men and heterosexual women. Rather, qualitative differences in traits among homosexuals and heterosexuals of both genders support this hypothesis.

Factors such as hormones involved in sexual differentiation clearly have secondary actions which affect traits in ways other than to establish male/female differences. Thus, the argument that homosexuality is independent of sexual differentiation does not preclude a role of hormones or other factors in the development of sexual orientation. Furthermore, evidence for a role of hormones in the development of homosexuality does not imply that female heterosexuality and male homosexuality have similar causes or control structures in the brain. Male homosexuality may have little to do with sexual differentiation and may resemble neither male nor female heterosexuality.

Attitudes towards Homosexuality

Contemporary American society strongly associates male homosexuality with femininity or effeminacy. Many of the terms used to denigrate male homosexuals—*fairy, nelly, pansy, queen, sissy*—as well as previous medical terminology—*hermaphrodite, gynandromorph, invert*—expressly or implicitly attribute stereotypically feminine qualities to male homosexuals. The stereotypical male homosexual is viewed as weak, unathletic, interested in domestic chores, and often transvestite. College students asked to list attributes of homosexual and heterosexual men described the former as having high-pitched voices, wearing jewelry and feminine clothing, and having a feminine walk and mannerisms. Male heterosexuals were described as athletic, strong, and masculine.[3] Similarly, college students viewed independently judged 'feminine' male faces more likely than 'masculine' faces to be those of homosexuals.[4]

The association between male homosexual desire and femininity, while ingrained in American culture, has not been evident in all cultures. Among the ancient Greeks, male homosexuality was commonplace in institutions which fostered masculine ideals, such as the military and wrestling schools.[5] Among Melanesian societies, adolescent homosexual behavior is institutionalized as a necessary aspect of normal masculine development, although adult homosexuality is proscribed.[6] [. . .]

Male Homosexuality and Femininity, an Inapt Metaphor

Leaving aside the problems of detection and researcher bias, does the evidence support the idea that adult male homosexuals differ from heterosexual males and resemble heterosexual females in ways other than the gender of the preferred sexual object? Because 'femininity' and 'masculinity' are extremely ill-defined terms, it is possible only to assess whether on a specific measure gay men differ from straight men, and if so, whether the values for gay men are in the feminine direction. A representative sample of measures follows:

No physiological measures are known to differentiate reliably homosexual and heterosexual male populations. Reports of differences in concentrations of blood testosterone, estrogen, gonadoptropins, prolactin, and androstendione between male homosexuals and heterosexuals were all contraindicated by subsequent research and thus failed the replication test. The neuroendocrine organization of the hypothalamus, as reflected by the luteinizing hormone (LH) feedback response to injected estrogen, was likewise investigated: initial reports indicated that when injected with estrogen, heterosexual women and homosexual men show an initial decrease in LH followed by an increase above and eventual return to baseline levels. In heterosexual men, LH only declined and returned to baseline.[7] As with earlier hormone studies, however, other investigators failed to find differences between heterosexual and homosexual men and provided convincing alternative explanations for the earlier reports.[8]

Assessment of psychological similarity to heterosexual females is more diffi-cult, especially as many scales in use employ sexual attraction to men as a measure of femininity. Weinrich found higher scores on the Femininity scale in gay men than straight men on the California Personality Inventory, the Bem Sex Role Inventory, and the Strong-Campbell Vocational Interest Inventory.[9] He found no differences, however, in Bem Masculinity, which is independent of the Femininity scale. Other researchers, using a variety of measures, report higher femininity scores for homosexual compared to heterosexual men,[10] although there are exceptions. Other evidence, reviewed in Green, suggests that adult homosexuality is more commonly associated with stereotypically feminine behavior in childhood than is adult heterosexuality.[11]

Results from neuropsychological tests of spatial and verbal abilities, which produce reliable sex-differences, are more mixed. In one study, gay and straight men performed equally on three tests and differed on two others, with gay males scoring in the feminine direction on one and in the masculine direction on the other.[12] Other studies found no differences between gay and straight men,[13] differences in accord with the femininity hypothesis,[14] and differences which suggest cognitive abilities unlike both heterosexual males and females.[15] Handedness, itself a reflection of neuropsychological organization, is related to performance on tests of spatial ability: right-handed gay men resembled heterosexual females on one test of spatial ability but were indistinguishable from heterosexual males on two others; non-right-handed gay men resembled heterosexual males on the first test, and heterosexual females on the others.[16]

Given that by definition homosexual men and heterosexual women are alike in terms of the gender of their preferred sexual object, one might expect to find other similarities between them in sexual and courtship behavior, and differ-ences from heterosexual men. In terms of physiological response during sexual activity, males and females show markedly different patterns, whereas homo-sexual and heterosexual men are identical.[17] Among sexual behaviors and desires considered to differ between male and female heterosexuals, homo-sexual men appear to be, if anything, more masculine than heterosexual men. Arousability by visual stimuli, variety-seeking in sexual partners, the develop-mental sequence of romantic relationships, and the importance of physical attractiveness of sex partners are cited as examples of heterosexual male traits which are equally or more salient among homosexual men.[18] At least in terms of sexual behavior, 'homosexual men behave in many ways like heterosexual men, only more so'.[19]

The comparisons just made demand extreme caution, as this exercise may inherently lead to statistical associations of homosexuality and femininity. Suppose the mechanisms which determine male homosexuality influence a given sexually dimorphic trait, but that these mechanisms are distinct from those which determine the sex dimorphism in heterosexuals. On a one-dimensional measure with male and female heterosexuals at opposite poles, e.g., brain nucleus volume or a spatial abilities test score, measures of this trait in male homosexuals might fall on the 'masculine' extreme, the 'feminine' extreme, or in the middle. Two of the three possible outcomes would likely be interpreted as evidence of 'feminization' relative to the male heterosexual norm, even though the mechanisms were presupposed a priori to be independent of those underlying sexual differentiation.

In summary, the similarities between homosexual males and heterosexual females in sexual object choice are not present in physiology or sexual behavior styles. Neuropsychological studies are inconsistent, but where differences appear, they suggest that homosexual males differ qualitatively from both male and female heterosexuals. Gay men often score higher than straight men on indices of psychological femininity. These assessments, however, are made in an environment where most homosexual desire may be hidden, and where male homosexuality is viewed as antithetical to masculinity. The pervasive association of adult male homosexuality and femininity, therefore, may reflect social artifact more than empirical fact.

['Male Homosexual Desire: Neurological Investigations and Scientific Bias', *Perspectives in Biology and Medicine*, 38/1 (Autumn 1994), 63–5, 69–71.]

Section IV

Sexual Revolution?

Perhaps the most useful way to begin this concluding section on the 'Sexual Revolution' is to explain the question mark that appears after the title. Despite the perfect conviction of many who lived through the late 1960s, and 1970s, that they were witnessing a profound and permanent change in the sexual landscape of Western Civilization, it is by no means certain that the events of those years were either revolutionary or particularly deep and long-lasting. When Masters and Johnson 'discovered' women's multiorgasmic capacity through clitoral stimulation in 1966, Enovid, the first widely available birth control pill, had been on the market for six years and was being taken by 6 million women. The promise of a 'liberation' of women (and men) from the fear of unwanted pregnancy and the prospect of endless, worry-free orgasms combined to produce an intoxicating brew for many contemporaries. But did this timely convergence of a 'discovery' and a new technology change anything important, and was it the first time such a 'revolutionary' upheaval had taken place?

There is no denying that the 1960s and 1970s were a time of widespread libertarian experiments. Sexual utopias, 'open' marriages, swinging, and sex clubs famously flourished, spawning a huge literature and contemporary comment. However, the apparent disappearance of many of these phenomena, together with the changes in sexual behaviour occasioned by the global AIDS epidemic, has enabled some observers to argue that sexual behaviour has returned to 'normal'. It seems as unlikely that nothing at all has changed as that everything has been transformed.

The aim of this part of the reader will thus be to explore the ways that the 'sexual revolution' was not particularly revolutionary, but also to acknowledge how the developments of the past fifty years or so have in fact altered our consciousness about sexuality and its place in modern selfhood. As we have learned from the previous material, there is a sense in which sexuality has always been a public phenomenon; public authorities have attempted, so far as possible, to regulate sexual and reproductive behaviour in the general interest. Such efforts continue to this day. What seems new in the late twentieth century is the incorporation of sexual tastes and dispositions into private behaviour that stand as the foundations of a new kind of personal identity. It seems almost as if the relations between public and private sexualities had been reversed. With some notable exceptions, private sexuality once unfolded within the limits of publicly gendered roles decreed by tradition, law, and religion; now initiative rests with individuals, who are increasingly obliged to present to the world a self based in large degree on personal sexual identity. Whereas the public person once subsumed the private individual, the opposite now seems to be the case. There are of course limits to this apparent inversion of the public and the private spheres, and some of these will be explored in this part of the reader.

IV.a Pioneers of Sex Reform

If a regimented and 'public' control of sex and reproduction has begun to fade away in the last few decades, this was by no means the experience of most citizens in the industrialized West during most of the twentieth century. A number of 'sex reform' movements took shape before and after the First World War advocating a variety of causes from birth control to sexual emancipation. The activities of these groups were sharply opposed by governments bent instead on replacing the portions of their populations lost to war and disease. On behalf of the eugenic mission of promoting more numerous and healthier births, many post-war governments banned the sale and advertisement of contraceptives (other than condoms), prosecuted abortion, and outlawed the dissemination of birth control propaganda. More affirmatively, however, governments and their allies in patriotic and natalist organizations actively supported 'abandoned' women and single mothers with children and engaged in informational and hygienic activities that brought about a proliferation of knowledge about sex. The great irony of the struggle between militant sex reformers and their mainstream political and cultural enemies is that both sides contributed to the 'emancipation' of sex from reproduction and reinforced the autonomy of sexual pleasure.

Perhaps the best known of the sex 'radicals' in the first half of the twentieth century was the American feminist Margaret Sanger. Sanger had become acquainted with the sexologist Havelock Ellis before the war and embraced many of his free-thinking ideas on women's sexual freedom and love without jealousy. She endured legal harassment and imprisonment in the United States to establish the first birth control organization (the predecessor to Planned Parenthood) and was instrumental in the furthering of the international movement. For Sanger, access to birth control information was the indispensable condition for women's emancipation generally and their sexual emancipation in particular. As Extract 116 makes clear, though Sanger and her allies met considerable opposition in their struggle to make birth control information available to all women, the social, economic, and cultural changes of the First World War and its aftermath created interest world-wide.

At the same time that Sanger was articulating the material and cultural conditions of greater personal autonomy and sexual fulfilment for women, American men were well on their way to breaking with the 'Victorian' ideals of the Christian gentleman, sexual self-discipline, and suspicion of the lower instincts. New cultural values based on an appreciation rather than a demonization of the 'primitive' in nature and in humans gradually replaced the older code of proper masculine sexual comportment. These changes in the sexual 'system' of early twentieth-century America were a consequence, as Extract 117 indicates, of important changes taking place in the wider economy and society.

In the manner of most radicals, critics of the Victorian sexual system envisaged a society that would be an inverted version of contemporary norms. In place of marriage they would have the free association of free beings; in place of procreative genital sex they would have sexual relations filled with rich, polymorphous pleasure; in place of jealousy and exclusiveness they would have friendship and camaraderie between and among the sexes. While it would be too much to claim that they constituted a 'movement', a large number of like-minded socialist and leftist intellectuals took up the cause of sexual emancipation in a way that anticipated by seventy-five years many of the ideals of the 'sexual revolution' of the 1970s. One of the leading British figures in this group was the famous novelist and science fiction writer H. G. (Herbert George) Wells. Wells married twice, but had numerous sexual liaisons with the more or less full knowledge of his wives. At the end of his life Wells reflected sombrely on his youthful ideal of free love, adding up the debits and credits of breaking with the sexual order. The first passage of Extract 118 states his initial ideas of sexual freedom and his growing discovery of their inherent limitations, and the second discusses how the company of his like-minded male friends produced in him a predatory attitude toward women and sexual conquests that contradicted his high-minded precepts of sexual equality. Both passages grudgingly acknowledge the power of tradition and the persistence of gender inequality in the prevailing cultural system.

The mainstream resistance to the birth control movement and sexual libertarianism took the form of both legal opposition and the implementation of national 'campaigns' to promote marriage, increase the birth rate, and assure the health of newborns. In inter-war Italy, Mussolini's fascist regime gathered demographic data, rigged the tax code to punish bachelors and aid families with numerous offspring, and promoted medical knowledge of sexual and childrearing 'hygiene'. In his study of these developments David G. Horn points out the ironies that emerged from making the 'natural' and 'private' qualities of reproduction into 'social' and 'public' ones. Official efforts to promote births may have encouraged the opposite effect by increasing the awareness of sex and reproduction as deliberate acts subject to control and planning. Fascist interventionism may have contributed to the fact that Italy now has the lowest birth rate in the industrialized world, far short of what is required for population replacement (Extract 119).

In post-First World War France there was, if anything, an even greater concern about the geo-political dangers of stagnant population growth. France had experienced devastating losses of manpower during the war and political leaders did all they could to discourage abortion and birth control and provide incentives for marriage and procreation. Some national leaders favoured a traditional Catholic 'hands-off' approach to sexual matters, particularly female sexuality, but more progressive thinkers favoured a broad dissemination of progressive medical information that would stimulate healthy reproduction without offending Catholic sensibilities. Working with government agencies, a semi-private organization called the French Society for Sanitary and Moral Prophylaxis (SFPSM) created a committee aimed at a modern sexual education for women. In Extract 120 a medically trained activist, Dr Germaine Montreuil-Straus, attempted to carry out the committee's work among single mothers and young single women, with the ambiguous results we have seen for the Italian case.

Until the advent of the Nazi regime in 1933, the inter-war governments of republican Germany permitted birth control movements a considerable measure of freedom to organize, propagate their ideals, and set up clinics and workshops to educate women. There was less overt concern in Germany about stagnant population growth, but there was a widely held conviction, shared by both public authorities and private activists, that births should be intended and healthy. Since abortion was strictly forbidden, the motto of the birth control and hygiene groups was 'Prevent: Don't Abort.' The first and largest of these voluntary organizations came from the political left (National Union for Birth Control and Sexual Hygiene (RV)), which devoted its activities to spreading the gospel among the working classes. It represented itself as strictly concerned with 'rationalizing' sexual activity in light of science and healthy births, but, like interventionist activity elsewhere, also contributed to heightening awareness of sexual pleasure in—and also out—of marriage. Extract 121 reveals that movements like the RV, later suppressed by the Nazis, trafficked in some old-fashioned ideas, but put the emphasis squarely on mutual sexual satisfaction.

If the political prerequisites for a birth control organization were in place, despite the continued reservations of some feminist leaders, so too were the economic conditions for a persuasive argument that women should be offered reliable and cost-effective contraception. Between 1870 and 1930 the number of employed American women increased by tenfold, bringing the total to over 10 million, or one fourth of the eligible female population. And increasingly higher percentages were older, married, and American born. As child labor laws prohibited the employment of young girls, and as immigration laws restricted the entry of foreigners, the numbers of single and foreign women in the work force diminished. By 1930, more than a quarter of the female work force were married, almost three fourths were native born, and studies showed that more than 90 percent of women workers contributed all or part of their incomes to the maintenance of families. No longer was it possible to sustain the traditional image of working women as immigrants gaining an economic foothold, as young girls biding time until they found husbands, or as spinsters who had never found them at all. And if married women were working in greater numbers than ever before, then rationalization and control of their fertility was paramount.

More important, perhaps, women's overall visibility as workers increased, even while the vast majority remained at home or were segregated in low-paying, entry-level jobs, such as personal and domestic services. As the nation's consumer and service economy developed, the numbers of women in clerical and service positions (store clerks, office workers, and telephone operators, for example) surpassed those in manufacturing. With more and more people living in cities, fewer women were left in inconspicuous, family-based agricultural pursuits. At the same time, though professional opportunities for women tended to be limited to teaching and nursing, the few intrepid pioneers who managed to enter the closed sanctums of business, law, medicine, and government achieved greater notoriety. It was widely believed that their opportunities were increasing, even if aggregate statistics did not always bear out this impression.

Whatever the reality, the very perception of change itself provoked another round of vigorous public debate over the fertility of American women, and over the possibilities and practicalities of combining child rearing and career. In circles of progressive, educated women there was no issue more prominent. Even such an established feminist as Charlotte Perkins Gilman broadened her focus to embrace a concern about reconciling marriage and family with work. Margaret [Sanger] herself, though never shy on the subject, responded with special vehemence when queried by a reporter. Branding full-time domesticity 'drab and monotonous,' she claimed that work often disciplines a woman to appreciate her home more. Acknowledging that children need their mothers a great deal, she nonetheless argued that 'young children are by nature selfish, and they will let you indulge them as much as you please.' 'It isn't good for them though,' she concluded on a harsh, if personally revealing note. 'As a matter of fact, they should be taught by example that a mother is not here merely to be their attendant, but that she is a superior human being, a personage as well. They have much more respect for her then.'[1]

Margaret's message was intended to be prowoman, not antifamily, with emphasis on the new style of feminism she espoused, which accommodated and indeed encouraged sex and marriage. Once again, she advertised birth control as bridging the discontinuities of a feminist agenda that offered women a public role at the expense of their private lives. Only with universal availability of contraception could women hope to realize their full potential.

However halting and partial it may have been, the economic and political empowerment of married women during the 1920s forced yet another redefinition of their role within the home. Behavioural psychologists suddenly scorned Freud's developmental imperatives as overly sentimental and instead echoed John Watson's recommendation that women avoid their children's excessive reliance on mother love. At the same time, purveyors of the consumer frenzy driving the nation's economy forward reshaped the housewife into a domestic professional, freed by technology from the responsibility and drudgery that had bound her mother to the hearth. A burgeoning industry in advertising and public relations for electrical gadgets, packaged foods, storebought clothes, and other new commodities of the era encouraged women to be efficient managers of household goods and services. In high schools, colleges, and universities, courses in home economics were consciously designed to offer a reconstituted vision of marriage and family life, one that promoted time and labor-saving devices and emphasized the importance to women of the equality of their relationships in the family, not just of their material obligations and responsibilities as wives and mothers.

This vision of modern womanhood implicitly assumed the voluntary control of childbearing. It also consciously encouraged a more active sexual role for women on the practical grounds that the liberated homemaker and wife had time available for more romance in her life. Once considered scandalous, the ideal of mutuality in the sexual relations of husbands and wives found a large public audience in the 1920s. The most popular and enduring symbol of freedom for women of the decade was explicitly sexual. The youthful, eroticized flapper, her hemline dramatically and provocatively shortened, was emblazoned in national magazines and on billboards. Her figure lean and angular, her hair short and shingled like a man's, or marcelled in the new and somewhat softer style of middecade, she symbolized the assertion by women of social and sexual parity. Gone was the buxom, matronly woman common to advertisements in the past, whose very appearance assumed her primary maternal responsibility. In her place, a slender, stylish woman suddenly turned up, shopping in a department store, riding in an open roadster, or even dancing the night away at a speakeasy. This kind of woman used contraception within marriage and perhaps even outside it.

With hindsight it becomes clear that not all of these developments were positive. Though present in the labor force in greater numbers than ever before, women in the 1920s did not necessarily consolidate and advance their economic power. And the decade's frenzied consumerism only escalated standards of domestic comportment, allowing housework along with affective relationships to continue to absorb female effort and time. What is more, the sexual revolution did not always leave women the equal partners of men, even as it fostered a new heterosexual intimacy. Yet as a gender consciousness and solidarity declined, the collective interests of women were left with no mobilizing agent or vehicle.

The popular journalist Dorothy Dunbar Bromley best expressed this shift in sentiment when she identified 'new-style feminists' in 1928 as 'intensely self-conscious' and professing 'no loyalty to women *en masse.*' Bored with the stridency of suffrage and the narrowly defined objectives of organized efforts on behalf of women's rights, a new generation of women who were coming of age took the struggles of their predecessors for granted. They listened to authorities like John Watson, who also claimed that militancy on women's issues betrayed poor social and psychological adjustment. Indeed, the birth control movement provided one of the few women's causes that thrived in the 1920s, because it wed new personal and sexual interests to the larger set of public concerns that had motivated women in the past. Margaret Sanger wrote to much acclaim in *The Pivot of Civilization:*

Women can attain freedom only by concrete, definite knowledge of themselves, a knowledge based on biology, physiology and psychology. . . . Birth control is no negative philosophy concerned solely with the number of children brought into this world. It is not merely a question of population. Primarily it is the instrument of liberation and human development.[2]

[*Woman of Valor: Margaret Sanger and the Birth Control Movement in America* (New York: Simon & Schuster, 1992), 206–9.]

KEVIN WHITE

117 The Deconstruction of Victorian Sexuality

After 1880, severe stresses appeared in the Victorian system of morality that heralded its demise. Self-control, discipline, delayed gratification, and self-sacrifice, ideal qualities in an economy geared towards production, seemed less appropriate in the late nineteenth century world of the national marketplace and of large bureaucratic corporations that undermined the small business-men and farmers who had held sway in high Victorian America. The Self-Made Man with his firm sense of personal autonomy and independence gave way in-creasingly to the bureaucrat or manager and the salesman, who felt all the more enclosed and confined and limited in the corporations that were growing ever larger as the turn of the century loomed. Further, the closing of the fron-tier, with the concomitant crisis in America's sense of manifest density, only served to aggravate the middle class's sense of being hemmed in and trapped. The crisis of faith brought on by Darwinism and, above all, by the watering down of Protestantism, was significant. Liberal ministers like Henry Beecher and Lyman Abbott preached of a loving God who granted salvation to all. Protestantism degenerated into a vague and wishy-washy deism. Ministers downplayed the existence of hell and of a devil and celebrated material com-fort as the rigorous Calvinist sanctions against sin disappeared.[1] This clouded the moral certainties that were the key to the firm Victorian sense of manhood and to the whole concept of 'character' that held together the Victorian system of morality. In this context, for the middle class the crucial ethical question be-came, what was the point of a lofty Victorian morality when life seemed to lack transcendent meaning? Why accept such rigorous sanctions and maintain 'character' when there was, as historian Jackson Lears memorably put it, 'no place of grace'? Without religious structures, why not then behave badly?

No wonder these developments heralded for men a fundamental 'masculin-ity crisis' as the Progressive era dawned after 1900. What new masculinities and moral systems could replace the Victorian as man's sense of identity became fragmented, and as the need for 'character' became less evident? Faced with the breakdown of religious and moral certainties and faced, perhaps, with a sense of powerlessness in the workplace, where men were now cogs in a bureaucratic machine, commentators noticed an 'American nervousness' afflicting both men and women. Seeking a remedy for such uncertainty, men searched for re-lief in intense experience to break the monotony. The most prominent mani-festation of this was the obsession with the primitive that now openly and publicly swept into the middle class at the turn of the century in American soci-ety—that urge that historian John Higham first identified twenty-five years ago as the desire to be 'young, masculine and adventurous.'[2] [. . .]

The logic of the cult of primitivism developed further as gentility lost ground as a guide to the social relations between the sexes. Work that was hardly respectable but was freely available and widely discussed now revealed the bitter hatreds that lay under the surface between the sexes. Jack London's rugged individualist and independent heroes fled from an effeminizing civiliza-tion, hearing the *Call of the Wild*. In his 1903 novel, London turned primitivism against women, especially with his portrayal of the female character, Mercedes, who having been 'chivalrously treated all her days,' still made the lives of her husband and brothers 'unendurable' as a nag. London commented on this obsessively throughout the text, referring to the way in which she 'interfered' and was 'hysterical.'[3] But London's blatant misogyny was nothing in comparison with that of Frank Norris, whose primitive characters represented a huge break from genteel literary traditions. In *McTeague* the brutal dentist of that name traps his girlfriend Trina on the operating chair. As he feels 'the animal in the man' stirring, he struggles to control himself. On this occasion he succeeds but he wonders why he could not love her purely. After they marry he suffers a series of misfortunes and realizes that he cannot live with her civilization and sophistication. Frustrated, he turns increasingly to violence and eventually beats his wife to death.[4] The ethos of the Victorian underworld was in this way diffused more and more into the middle-class mainstream as men turned to primitivism as remedy and relief from the growing uncertainties of their lives.

This ever more public awareness of underworld primitivism at the turn of the century was of enormous importance for American society. It threatened the precarious balance between the Christian Gentleman and the Underworld Primitive that had driven the Victorian system of morality. Victorians in Great Britain and in the still essentially culturally British United States well understood the centrality of the moral system to men's sense of themselves as men. They strove to rein in the irrational aspects of human society in an unprecedented way. The choices for Victorian males had been clear. A man of 'character,' a Christian Gentleman, controlled his sexuality both publicly and privately. If he could not control his sexual drives, he might visit a prostitute, but such behavior was only tolerated; it was never respectable. He must never admit it for fear that he might lose his 'character'—that is, his very sense of what was best in himself as a man. Yet as late as 1910 the Christian Gentleman still tempered the excesses of primitivism and of the underworld. The single standard still held ascendancy over the double standard. And as late as the end of the first decade of the twentieth century, the Victorian system of morality remained intact, despite the stresses on it.

Yet, after about 1910, this sexual system crumbled. Writer Agnes Repplier declared the 'repeal of reticence.' Editor William Marion Moody announced it was 'Sex O'Clock in America.'[5] Put simply, society became more sexualized. After 1910, a vast corps of experts, be they corporate managers, ministers, doctors, advertisers, or marriage manual writers or dance-hall operators, began to offer new solutions to the nervousness and ethical confusion of Americans and in the process devised a new moral code for American society. This new morality stressed instant gratification and fulfilment through consumption and leisure as a means of assuaging the boredom and aimlessness of twentieth-century life and as a resolution to the seeming irrelevance of the older system and the dullness of corporate life and concomitant decline of personal autonomy. The growing hegemonic role of these experts in American life had enormous implications for the American sexual system.[6] They encouraged sexual expression rather than repression in an ideal that represented the solid begin-nings of a liberation of sexuality from Victorian rigors. The implications of ideology and behavior of this revolutionary shift in sexual mores for American men are the subject of this book.

[*The First Sexual Revolution: The Emergence of Male Heterosexuality in Modern America* (New York: New York University Press, 1993), 9–10, 12–13.]

H. G. WELLS

118   Sexual Radicalism

Between the ages of thirty and forty I devoted a considerable amount of mental energy to the general problem of men and women. And never with any real disin-terestedness. I wanted to live a consistent life, I wanted a life that would stand ex-amination, I hated having to fake a front to the world, and yet not only were my thoughts and fancies uncontrollable, but my conduct remained perplexingly disin-genuous. I did my best to eliminate my sense of that disingenuousness by candid public theorizing. I spoke out for 'Free Love.' I suppose I was going through phases roughly parallel with those through which Shelley had passed eighty years before. Hundreds of thousands have passed that way. I did my best to maintain that love-making was a thing in itself, a thing to thank the gods for, but not to be taken too seriously and carried into the larger constructive interests of life.

The spreading knowledge of birth-control,—Neo-Malthusianism was our name for it in those days—seemed to justify my contention that love was now to be taken more lightly than it had been in the past. It was to be refreshment and invigoration, as I set out quite plainly in my *Modern Utopia* (1905) and I could preach these doctrines with no thought of how I would react if presently my wife were to carry them into effect, since she was so plainly not disposed to carry them into effect, and what is much more remarkable, with my recent storm of weeping in that little farm kitchen at Twyford, very conveniently—but quite honestly—forgotten. This again I think is after the common fashion. We are not naturally aware of our two-phase quality. We can all think in the lib-eral fashion in our phases of dispersal; there is always a Free Love contingent in any community at any time; but its membership varies and at any time any of its members may lapse towards a fixation and towards its attendant exclusive-ness and jealous passion. People drop out of the contingent or return to it. At one time love is the happy worship of Venus, the goddess of human loveliness, the graceful mutual complement of two free bodies and spirits; at another it is the sacred symbol of an intense and mystical personal association, a merging of identities prepared to live and die for one another. It is this variation of phase that plays havoc with every simple dogmatic ruling upon sexual behaviour.

Advocates of free love, in so far as they aim at the liberation of individual sexual conduct from social reproach and from legal controls and penalties, are, I believe, entirely in the right. Nevertheless, with such a liberation, very little is attained. Circumstances are simplified, but the problem itself remains unchanged. We are still confronted with the essential riddle of our own phases of development as we pass from youth to maturity and, as I have already insisted, with this other, more persistent, alternation of phase between dispersal and intensification. The tangle is further complicated by the absolute right of society to intervene directly the existence of children is involved, and by a third mass of difficulties due to the fact that emotionally and physically, and thence to an increasing degree in its secondary associations and implications, love is a different thing for men and women. In a universe of perfect adaptations these differences would reciprocate; in this world they do nothing of the sort.

But here I approach questions and experiences that will be better deferred until I come to that phase of my middle years during which I produced various hesitating yet enterprising love novels. Then, almost in spite of myself, I was forced by my temperament and circumstances to face the possibility that men and women as such, when it comes to planning a greater world order, may be disposed to desire incompatible things. Feminine creativeness and feminine devotion may differ from their masculine parallels and though women radicals and men radicals are members of the same associations and speak to the same meetings, their ends may lie far apart. There may have to be a new treaty of mutual tolerance between the sexes.

But in the early days of my second marriage I did not even suspect the possibility of these fundamental disagreements in the human project. My wife and I had still to win the freedom to think as we liked about our world. What we were then going to think about it, lay some years ahead of us. While we struggled we liked each other personally more and more, we dropped our heroics and laughed and worked together, we made do with our physical and nervous incompatibilities and kept a brave face towards the world.

We dropped our disavowal of the Institution of Marriage and married, as soon as I was free to do so, in 1895. The behaviour of the servants of that period and the landladies and next-door neighbours, forced that upon us anyhow. Directly the unsoundness of our position appeared, servants became impertinent and neighbours rude and strange. How well we came to know the abrupt transition from a friendly greeting 'passing the time of day' to a rigid estrangement. Were they really horrified when they 'heard about it,' or is there a disposition to hate and persecute awaiting release in every homely body? I believe that there has been a great increase in tolerance in the last forty years but in our period, if we had not married, half our energy would have been frittered away in a conflict of garden-wall insults and slights and domestic exactions. We had no disposition for that kind of warfare.

[*Experiment in Autobiography: Discoveries and Conclusions of a Very Ordinary Brain (since 1866)*
(New York: The Macmillan Co., 1934), 362–5.]

Now I have tried to show in my story how the Lover-Shadow had developed in my life, and that it was a very grave and lively complex of desire. This stream of rakish boasting flowed across that gathering drive and had, I realize now, a stronger effect upon it than I perceived at the time. It vulgarized it and made it practical. Inherently, I wanted to meet and love and be loved by the Lover-Shadow, but through suggestion and competitiveness, in a sort of response to the brag and implications of these associates, brag and implications reflected endlessly by the contemporary stage and novel, I wanted, for my own self-respect, to *get* women. The Lover-Shadow was, I began to feel, elusive dream-stuff. The reality of women was something which was glad and happy to be brag-material for such swaggering males as Bowkett, Harris and Bland. All through this 'Postscript to *Experiment in Autobiography*' the sensitive reader will detect the strain of essential vulgarity about sex, coming out in quick response to these codpiece-minded males. I am disposed to blame them for a streak that was in me already. Even now I smirk if anyone suggests that I have been a gay lad in these matters.

So the very lively bent of my mind towards a Shelley-like liberalism of sexual conduct, which I have described in my *Autobiography*, was supplemented by the growth of this coarser, less fastidious disposition to *get* girls and women, and, as my freedom of movement increased and opportunity multiplied about me, I found myself first of all trying to get, and then getting them, on the slightest attraction, with an increasing confidence of method. I think it is straining the word 'love' to call these *amours* 'love affairs.' In all my life I think I have really loved only three women steadfastly; my first wife, my second wife and Moura Budberg, of whom I will presently tell. I do not know if I loved Rebecca West, though I was certainly in love with her towards the latter part of our liaison. I had one great storm of intensely physical sexual passion and desire with Amber Reeves. Beyond that, all these women I have kissed, solicited, embraced and lived with, have never entered intimately and deeply into my emotional life. I have liked them, found them pretty, exciting, amusing, flattering to the secret rakish braggart in my composition. I was jealous of them as one is jealous in a partnership, and jealous about them as one is jealous in a competition—and my impression is that I got nothing better than I gave. I was loved as I loved. Once I raised a storm of crazy love-hatred that I found very repellent and painful, but for the rest the exchanges were fairly equal—two libertines met—and when I *got* a woman, a woman *got* a man.

Yet each affair, cool-hearted though it was, had its individuality. Some at least of these encounters had a loveliness, often a quite accidental loveliness. They could be like flower-shows or walks in springtime or mountain excursions. Few ended bitterly, and most left a residue of friendliness and understanding. I cannot make up my mind that I regret any of them. And yet, unreasonably and illogically, there spreads over all this system of memories a haze of regret. The fundamental love of my life is the Lover-Shadow, and always I have been catching a glimpse of her and losing her in these adventures.

The first wanderings of my desires are very hard to trace. I was disposed to covert Bowkett's wife; and when Dorothy Richardson came to Worcester Park she and I took a special grave interest in each other. (I am Hypo in her 'Miriam' novels.) Such glimpses of errant desire occur in the life of every curate. It was only when Spade House was building, that I found myself trying definitely to *get* anyone.

[*H. G. Wells in Love: Postscript to an Experiment in Autobiography*, ed. G. P. Wells (Boston: Little, Brown & Co., 1984), 60–1.]

DAVID G. HORN

119   The Ironies of State Promotion of Births: The Italian Case

The heterogenous social technologies that composed the 'demographic campaign' encountered varied and local resistance. Efforts to enumerate the population, to penalize bachelorhood, to check the movements of migrants to urban areas, to police 'neo-Malthusian' practices, and to encourage large families came up against the desires and multiple 'ways of making do' of Italian women and men:[1] southerners' evasions of the census taker, middle-class concerns with the 'quality' of offspring, young women's aesthetics of the body, the housing practices of recent immigrants to the metropolis.[2]

Second, constructing social technologies as governmental 'intrusions' risks naturalizing the 'private' spaces of the family and reproduction and may obscure the creation of *social* spaces, which were simultaneously places of knowledge, intervention, and the articulation of duties. I have argued that specific practices designed to reduce mortality, promote marriage, and increase fertility worked to redefine reproduction as a social phenomenon, with specific and predictable social effects, and as a site of particular kinds of contestation. Thus, we might begin to examine women and men's negotiations with this new set of scientific constructions, political rationalities, and governmental practices, including the normalizing practices of urbanism, architecture, social work, and medicine. I want to suggest, in short, that social technologies of reproduction, and the modern forms of knowledge and power on which they have depended, might be analyzed in terms of the modifications they brought to a field of tactical possibilities.

It is in this context that we can ask, for example, to what extent social technologies of reproduction were *successful* at redefining the Italian family, not only as a target of interventions but also as a bearer of social duties. Married women, in particular, were made responsible for the health and welfare of their children—for the hygiene of the home, diet, and child-rearing. Paradoxically, the success of new models of the family in Italy—this new relationship among hygienic spaces, mother, child and society—may have operated to *reduce* fertility. Saraceno suggests that 'the increased value put on child welfare by the offer of health care and maternity education may not have strengthened the desire for many pregnancies so much as enhancing the value . . . of the individual child, thereby justifying the limitation of their numbers'.[3]

In fact, there is much to suggest that social scientific constructions (of health and welfare, of dangers and risks) could be reappropriated or even used to critique the state's inadequate services, the erratic and piecemeal nature of its assistance, and its failures to be 'modern'. De Grazia speaks of the emergence of an 'oppositional familism' in Italy, an antistatist attitude that drew precisely on the new constructions of the family: 'Once family interests became legitimate grounds for demanding government action, they also became grounds to retreat from government impositions'.[4] In other places as well, 'welfare' and 'health' have come to have multiple and contested meanings and have made possible practices at odds with the normalizing interventions of states.

Perhaps the most lasting and ironic consequence of interwar efforts to know and manage procreation has been a thorough denaturalization of reproductive bodies. As late as the 1970s, Italy's legal codes would continue to consider procreation as a natural fact, 'to be defended against any technical or medical artifice'.[5] But by the end of the fascist regime, it was really no longer possible (if indeed it ever had been) to speak of reproduction as innocent or natural, even when it took place in the countryside and resulted in large families. Women could not be counted on to be naturally fertile or to be naturally good mothers. Reproduction was instead marked as (and has remained) an object of social scientific knowledge, social-technical and biomedical intervention, and political debate. And if today many Italians and others—in and outside the West—take it for granted that reproduction can be 'planned' or 'managed,' this is in some measure the result of a modern, social-scientific construction of social bodies as objects of knowledge and government.

This effect has only been heightened in recent years by the appearance of 'new reproductive technologies' that further erode the idea that reproduction is natural. As Marilyn Strathern points out, though 'nature' continues to have considerable rhetorical force, it can no longer be taken for granted: 'Nature becomes a department of human enterprise, and we discover that it was never autonomous'.[6] Nature has not, of course, disappeared from scientific discourses surrounding 'infertility,' but Strathern suggests there has been a 'subtle shift from regarding naturalness as part of the workings of physiology to attributing it to parental desire'.[7]

[*Social Bodies: Science, Reproduction and Italian Modernity* (Princeton: Princeton University Press, 1994), 125–7.]

In arguing for state-institutionalized sex education, social hygienists such as Montreuil-Straus consciously defined their position over and against that of the Catholic moralists. From the late nineteenth century onward, the social hygiene movement had fought a battle against the priest and his traditional power in the French family. Catholic moralists based sexual education on one central idea: 'between the two elements that constitute a human being, between the flesh and the spirit, a struggle is inevitable, and in this struggle, the spirit must assure itself of victory.'[1] Sexual education, Catholics believed, was safe only in the hands of parents and priests, and should be as vague as possible for fear that the young girl 'will be offended, wounded in one of her noble qualities, modesty.' While they acknowledged that 'even for young girls, ignorance is more and more the exception,' Catholics aimed to educate them strictly to encourage 'purity' or self-control.[2]

Montreuil-Straus and her colleagues were anxious not to antagonize more socially conservative audiences, yet they conceived sexual education in opposition to these Catholic moralists.[3] The secular, scientific posture of social hygiene was congruent with the republican, anticlerical educational system where they sought access.[4] If the Catholics understood the aim of sexual education to be purity, Montreuil-Straus defined this goal as biological and social health. Although she agreed that sex education 'must certainly lead to a higher morality,' she also insisted that it 'be above all based on the scientific study of normal phenomena, the anatomy and physiology of genital apparatus and the reproductive function, particularly in the woman.'[5] If the Catholics required that the teaching of sex be a vague and moralistic enterprise, Montreuil-Straus demanded that it should be 'honest,' 'open,' 'neutral,' and 'scientific.' While Catholic moralists were convinced that such an education would 'arm vice with scientific arguments,' Montreuil-Straus and other social hygienists demonstrated a strong faith in the morally cleansing properties of science.[6] Defining their expertise in scientific, value-free terms would, they hoped, sterilize the potential seaminess of their subject matter.[7] 'In every instance that it is treated scientifically, such an education will awaken neither romantic nor sensual images,' assured Montreuil-Straus in 1922. She went on to quote a popular educator: 'Science anesthesizes what it touches.'[8]

But, as in the case of Mauvezin, the rationalizing tendencies in social hygiene also posed problems for Montreuil-Straus, as she attempted to apply the SFPSM's educational mission to the case of women. Once having created a female sexual instinct, Montreuil-Straus had to be careful not to lose control of it. In her own words, did it not demand to be not only recognized but also

'surveyed' and 'directed'? In particular, the positing of a healthy and ennobling female sexual instinct could validate women's sexual need or pleasure
as an end in itself. Such a validation would challenge the sexual double standard that lay at the heart of the SFPSM's ideology of sex, their belief in the
fundamental asexuality of the middle-class woman. In creating a philosophy
of women's sexual education, Montreuil-Straus had to come to terms with
the complex configuration of notions concerning sexual identity that had
grounded the SFPSM's prewar antivenereal policies. In grappling with these
notions, Montreuil-Straus avoided undermining the sexual double standard
so fundamental to the SFPSM's ideology of sex, much as Mauvezin avoided
threatening the sexual division of labor. Both women resolved the conflict in
the same way: by privileging domestic, maternal ideals. [. . .]

In a perfect conflation of sexual and reproductive identities, Montreuil-
Straus summarized 'normal sexual life' in these words: 'love, union, father-
hood, motherhood and family.'[9] She conceived the object of her pedagogical
project as the future mother: 'in order to be prepared for her role as mother and
wife, the young girl should know the composition of her body, the organs of
maternity, their normal functioning . . . the precautions that she must take in
order to stay healthy and bear healthy children.'[10] In *Avant la maternité*, she described female genitals as 'the group of organs destined to carry out the maternal function' and 'the organs of motherhood, still called genital organs or
female sexual organs.'[11] She limited sexual expression to a married, reproductive
context: 'any union in which motherhood intervenes as a surprise, an accident,
or even, let us say the word, a catastrophe, not only represents an error against
social and moral laws, but also denotes a false understanding of happiness and
the profound meaning of life.'[12] Montreuil-Straus saw no contradiction between the traditional moral tone of these statements and her description of the
volume as having a rational, medical, and scientific character. Despite all attempts to distance herself from the Catholic moralists, Montreuil-Straus reaffirmed a traditional Catholic morality of sex as strictly reproductive.

Montreuil-Straus had to change the rationale of prewar sex education in
order not to project an image of single women as promiscuous. In the prewar
era, sex education had been conceived as a form of prevention against venereal
disease and as a project of dissuasion against sexual promiscuity among single
young men, particularly in the military. Montreuil-Straus accepted current
medical opinion that the male was the principal agent of contamination for the
family in 95 percent of all venereal cases, so that justifying sex education for
women on these grounds seemed foolish. In 1923, she admitted the traditional
strategy of the SFPSM in these terms: 'it may be judged superfluous and even
injurious to give adolescent girls lectures on chastity before marriage and on
the harmlessness of abstinence, when for them, these have already been the
rules of a natural morality for centuries.'[13] By defining normative female sexuality as conjugal and reproductive, Montreuil-Straus could validate her project

without producing a notion of female sexual desire. Like her predecessors in the SFPSM, Montreuil-Straus campaigned for the protection of the single woman from the dangers of ignorance in sexual matters. But by these dangers, she meant not sexual seduction or temptation, as had the prewar SFPSM, but unforeseen sterility, miscarriages, and other threats to future motherhood. In this way, Montreuil-Straus justified sex education without disrupting the ideology of the sexual double standard. She did so precisely at a time when social and sexual constraints were breaking down, thanks to the increasing numbers of women of all classes working outside the household context. Under the liberal guise of 'enlightening' women concerning sexual matters, the CEF sought to discipline sexual behavior of all kinds, 'rescuing' sex from the fumbles and whispers of the streets and confining it to the clean rigidities of the conjugal bed.

Compared to notions of female sexuality being formulated by Freudian psychologists and sexologists in Great Britain and America Montreuil-Straus's reproductive sexual morality appears dramatically more conservative. But her affirmation of a Catholic sexual morality diverted attention from the fact that she also produced a notion of female sexuality that was radical and new.[14] 'It is natural, it is just,' she argued, 'that young girls want to know the joys of love and motherhood.'[15] A young *normalienne* in one of the seventeen *écoles normales* that Montreuil-Straus surveyed responded, 'It is a very natural thing to want to be able to taste one day all the happiness and the joys of the wife and mother.'[16] By conceiving female sexuality in strictly reproductive terms, Montreuil-Straus seemed to be merely reinforcing traditional morality, but in fact she was also talking about sex in relatively subversive terms. The affirmation of female sexuality as reproductive and domestic enabled the production of a female sexual identity that was healthy and natural. Although Montreuil-Straus isolated the married woman as alone able to enjoy a sexual identity, one wonders whether such notions of female identity could remain so cleanly categorized. Their very contradictions imply a possibility of subverting boundaries, promising new identities for women, whether married or single.

[*Civilization without Sexes: Reconstructing Gender in Postwar France 1917–1927* (Chicago: University of Chicago Press, 1994), 200–1, 203–5.]

ATINA GROSSMANN

121   More Rational Sex: The German Case

An eclectic coalition of political actors constituted this sex reform movement (*Sexualreformbewegung*). Some came from commercial leagues selling birth control products; others were members of the Communist and Social Democratic parties or smaller working-class political groups. They were joined by representatives of the medical profession, state agencies, and the international birth control movement, embodied by the globe-trotting American birth controller Margaret Sanger. All were united by the conviction that sexuality was better regulated than repressed, and that it was more sensible to manage and steer the birth rate decline than to mourn it. They adhered to a motherhood-eugenics consensus which assumed that motherhood was a natural and desirable instinct in all women, only needing to be properly encouraged, released, and regulated, and which understood the bearing of healthy offspring as a crucial social task. In the search for effective birth control and sexual advice, they both clashed and cooperated in campaigns to limit births and promote sexual hygiene.

Sex reformers undertook the practical work of establishing birth control and sex advice counseling centers that took as their motto, 'better to prevent than to abort.' They also organized mass and parliamentary campaigns for the reform or abolition of paragraph 218 and the legalization of abortion. Across a wide political spectrum, they shared a vision of a 'healthy' modern society in which access to legal abortion, contraception, eugenic sex education, and general social welfare would assure a new 'rational' social order that was both stable and humane and that would promote both collective welfare and individual happiness. [. . .]

The RV's journal, *Sexual-Hygiene* (*SH*), was another important source of advice, a self-proclaimed weapon in the campaign against 'sexual illiteracy.' Attractively printed on glossy paper and nationally distributed, it had by 1932 an official circulation of 21,000, which did not represent all its readers since only one copy was sent to a household and many were handed out for free. *SH* carried simply written educational articles that avoided some of the more melodramatic features of other lay journals. In 1929, for example, issues introduced Freud's ideas of psychoanalysis, explained mechanical and chemical birth control methods, publicized the campaign to abolish paragraph 218, and warned women that since male sperm was crucial to female health and vitality, coitus interruptus was also an undesirable contraceptive method for them (lest they become 'dried out').[1] In keeping with alarmist social hygiene tenets about the dangers of national degeneration, *SH* also carried eugenic horror stories of children conceived in drunken lust who grew up doomed to disease or criminality. More positively, *SH* exhorted:

Our time needs women who know their bodies, who are familiar with the laws of enlightened eroticism—and who in harmony with the ancient ideals of the beauty of body and soul will give life to healthy children.[2] [. . .]

Doctors committed to preventive medicine insisted that good health could best be achieved not by human or animal experimentation, immunization, or the profession's 'injection mania' but by proper hygiene, fitness, nutrition, and decent living conditions.[3] They suggested a diet without meat, low in salt and spices, and rich in whole wheat bread, steamed vegetables, spinach juice, muesli, soft cheese, yogurt, celery, red beets, and chamomile and lavender tea.

Common prescriptions for physical fitness included breathing techniques, and mud baths, massage, and morning exercise to stimulate skin and metabolism. Recommended sports included skiing, skating, water sports, and hiking. Clothes were to be loose and comfortable.

Intent on counterbalancing the perceived physical and psychic deficits of urban life, sex reformers touted the weekend as a time for cultivating body fitness rather than drinking, carousing, or competitive sports. Mass entertainments like cinema, soccer, boxing, and other spectator sports were viewed with great suspicion. Leisure and relaxation were not to be left to chance, any more than were sex and health; they too needed to be organized, rationalized, set up in the most time-effective manner for maximum benefit. Some of the admonitions for abstinence from alcohol and cigarettes, clean, well-ventilated separate bedrooms for parents and children, and 'a pleasant bathroom for every home' must have seemed quite exotic to a working-class audience.[4] Dr Wolf reassured his readers that he had lived 'as a vegetarian for more than twenty years and is still not debilitated or dim-witted.'[5] Women were of course responsible for enforcing unfamiliar regimes of household and sexual hygiene, as well as budgeting for, buying, and preparing in an appetizing manner foods, such as carrots, cabbage, tomatoes, and sauerkraut, which contained the proper balance of vitamins and minerals, while resisting expensive stimulants like coffee and tea.

Sex reform periodicals and films glorified, indeed fetishized, the ancient Greek ideal of the harmony of body and soul and the pure beauty of the naked body in motion.[6] Well-scrubbed physical attractiveness was linked to eugenic health; ugliness to ill health and degeneration. Sexologists tinkering with hormone therapies experimented with 'fountain of youth' cures. The emphasis on healthy motherhood and its new connection to fulfilled female sexuality presupposed a new fascination with the female body as an object of active strength and beauty rather than simply as a static object of ornament. Gymnastic systems especially designed for women, modern dance, and light athletics gained popularity; in general, the stress on sports and outdoor activities served to display especially the female body in novel and unexpected ways. Journals were filled with semipornographic photographs of well-toned unclothed bodies, which were of course always defended as depictions of wholesome nudity.[7] The 'Body School (Körperschule) Adolf Koch' in Berlin, for example, proudly reported that in the six years of its coeducational existence, not a single case of venereal disease had occurred among its 78 percent unmarried membership—a clear sign of the moral and hygienic superiority of its sensible and 'natural' approach to sexuality.

Dr Max Hodann's advice column in SH served as an extension of the counseling center or the doctor's consulting room. It reflected sex reformers' scientifically objective and determinedly matter-of-fact approach, and outlined a body regimen clearly meant to be both disciplinary and emancipatory. Hodann, who was widely known and beloved as the author of sex education booklets for children and youth, defined sexuality as the most natural thing in the world, which would flourish in an atmosphere of openness and good common sense. To the question, 'Is daily intercourse advisable?' the good doctor replied, 'If it feels good, why not.'[8] To the concerned husband who wrote, 'My wife can only come when she's on top. What can I do about this?' Hodann sensibly riposted, 'If one position is more satisfying than another, there's absolutely no reason not to enjoy it.'[9] He reassured readers that masturbation was harmless—in moderation—and admonished them not to marry anyone with whom they had never had sexual relations.[10]

Under the rubric 'Dr Hodann answers,' he gave advice on birth control methods, treatment for vaginal discharge, tight vaginas, and menstrual cramps, and how to avoid exhaustion after intercourse and premature ejaculation. Eclectic in his scientific allegiances, Hodann recommended hormone treatment for vaginal dryness, but suggested Freudian psychoanalysis for a more intractable case of 'frigidity.'[11] In this manner, Hodann specifically intended to translate into accessible didactic language not only Freudian theories on sexuality but also the flowery but highly precise prescriptions for mutual sexual fulfilment contained in Th. van de Velde's sex manual *Ideal Marriage*, which had first appeared—to great press attention and satire—in German translation in 1928. *Sexual-Hygiene* therefore provided valuable sexual and medical advice to working-class readers, especially those in small towns and rural areas who otherwise relied on quacks and traveling salespeople. It also offered clients access to mail-order contraceptives or the opportunity to obtain them in closed meetings without the embarrassment and additional expense of purchasing them at the local pharmacy.

Sexual-Hygiene was not the only sex reform forum in Weimar Germany or the only one to call upon the expertise of Max Hodann and other 'sex doctors' like Hirschfeld, Elkan, or Lehfeldt. The journal *Ideal Lebensbund* (*Ideal Life Union*), for example, contained a mixture of mildly titillating nude photographs, lightly erotic fiction, and a good deal of birth control information. By 1928, it had changed its name several times, from *Kultur-Ehe* to *Ideal-Ehe* to *Ideal-Lebensbund*, presumably both to evade legal prosecution on obscenity charges and to find a title that suggested companionship rather than legal marriage. Max Hodann chose its pages to announce that, 'It is certain that monogamy is a catastrophe. The new path is still not clearly defined.'[12] Over the course of a year, it covered a wide variety of topics: the hereditary nature of criminal characteristics; 'misunderstood' (i.e., frigid) wives; hypnosis, sadism, and masochism (in a special issue on the 'erotic'); advice on how to find a marriageable man; diet; and tips on 'scientific' matchmaking by handwriting analysis.[13]

Wherever the ubiquitous Hodann published, he always used his dual authority as physician and working-class activist to plead for tolerance and run interference for 'people in trouble.'[14] In another typical column, he counseled parents not to punish a daughter whose love letters they had found, and instead to give the young couple time to get to know each other sexually before being forced into marriage:

The pressures of everyday life, the disruptive power of habit can only be overcome through experience, erotic experience, and where would young people get this? They are fed sex propaganda, they are being titillated by shrill advertising of revues and by erotic, lewd publications, but nowhere are they given an inkling of how serious a matter eroticism is.[15]

In their column 'Out of Sexual Misery,' Magnus Hirschfeld and Maria Krische, the editors of the journal *Enlightenment* (*Aufklärung*), offered similarly direct advice, defending single women's right to sexual activity and motherhood, and brusquely informing a jealous husband that his wife's lesbian affair was none of his business so long as she also served him well sexually: 'There is no property right to the body of another. Or do you see your wife as your slave?'[16] In other lay journals, readers could study Van de Velde's graphs charting the path to mutual orgasm, and instructions for how to use a diaphragm diagrammed by Hirschfeld himself.

[*Reforming Sex: The German Movement for Birth Control and Abortion Reform, 1920–1950* (New York: Oxford University Press, 1995), 14–15, 25–6, 27–9.]

IV.b. Second Wave Sexology

By the end of the First World War a number of factors were in place that encouraged the eroticization of marriage. Birth rates, as we have seen, were in decline, both for long-term reasons and on account of the new availability of birth control information and technology. The typical family was becoming more 'nuclear' and more mobile and therefore less likely than before to be part of extended or family clan relationships. And because more women were working in non-rural jobs than ever before, their lives were not as devoted to child care. There was space and time in modern marriage for the expansion of sexual pleasure beyond the model of procreative coupling.

When these changes in the structure of the family were viewed in connection with the alarming rise in requests for divorce—by then legal almost everywhere in the industrial West—it seemed to many that the institution of marriage itself was in jeopardy. The visibility and success of feminist movements and the appearance of the 'new' uncorseted, short-skirted, silk-stockinged woman also fed fears that marital and family life no longer had its traditional appeal. Governments worried about depopulation, churches fretted about the straying of the flock, and moralists voiced doubt about the cultural transmission of decency and sound values.

One very popular answer to this perceived problem was the eroticization of marriage, or, as a recent historian has called it, the 'sexualization of love'.[1] Building on the appropriate aspects of 'first wave' sexology (Freud, Ellis, Hirschfeld, Moll, Krafft-Ebing), a new generation of sexologists produced marriage manuals that were written to educate the general public about the secret delights of marital love. Unlike 'first wave' sexology, which stressed the pathologies and the darker aspects of sexuality, 'second wave' sexology emphasized the positive; indeed, it rescued and rehabilitated some of the sexual behaviour that the first generation had put beyond the pale of 'normalcy', a pattern that would be continued by subsequent practitioners of the *genre*.

The first popular British marriage manual, *Married Love*, was written by Marie Stopes, a palaeobotanist by training, whose first marriage had ended after five years of unconsummated union. It appeared in 1918, just in time to welcome home the troops, and during a confusing period of social readjustment to gender roles inverted in a wartime economy. Stopes emphasized the importance of physical and sexual compatibility to a successful marriage, arguing that a sexually happy union could withstand the wear and tear of marital discord better than one that was physically cold.

Following its publication, Stopes received thousands of letters from male readers, indicating that her message about men's primary responsibilities in

---

[1] Vern Bullough, *Science in the Bedroom* (New York: Basic Books, 1994), 136.

marriage had been clearly received. The correspondence reveals that men were extraordinarily grateful for the knowledge of women's sexual needs the book provided, while revealing the depths of their own ignorance about basic physiology (Extract 122).

However, there is another way to read *Married Love* and similar texts in the inter-war period. They were certainly, in comparison to an earlier generation of such books, enlightened, particularly with respect to the matter of female sexuality and need for reciprocity in sexual relations. However, most of the books, Stopes's included, simply took for granted a patriarchal and traditional notion of gender difference and responsibility that largely perpetuated the ancient practice of *naturalizing* the differences between men and women. The fact that they did so while fighting on behalf of sexual enlightenment and in the face of hostile contemporary criticism probably helped make such views acceptable to progressive readers. Margaret Jackson presents an interpretation of Stopes's work that emphasizes this critical feminist perspective (Extract 123).

The most popular book of the inter-war period was *Ideal Marriage: Its Physiology and Technique*, written by the Dutch physician Theodor van de Velde. First published in 1926, the book was translated into every European language and has had an extraordinary longevity, having enjoyed a new American edition as recently as 1965. Like Stopes, van de Velde also appealed to men on behalf of greater understanding of women's sexual requirements. In Extract 124 van de Velde places the responsibility for successful marital sexual relations squarely with the husband, who must educate and guide his untutored partner to sexual fulfilment. Van de Velde explicitly warns husbands that the consequences of failing to carry out this responsibility are disastrous to love and therefore to marriage. He is thus among the first of the modern sexologists to focus, for good or ill, on a masculine performance principle as the indispensable feature of full sexual enjoyment. As he made clear in his text, simultaneous orgasm through genital penetration was the *summa* of sexual bliss.

The most important of the 'second wave' sexologists was the American Alfred Kinsey, whose two books on male and female sexual behaviour in 1948 and 1952 broke new ground in sexological research and had an enormous, if somewhat delayed, effect on contemporary opinion. The newest and most promising social science technique of Kinsey's day was anonymous polling, but Kinsey was sceptical about the reliability of results gathered in this way about such a sensitive topic. He decided to conduct interviews with volunteer subjects about their sex lives, eventually perfecting an extensive coded questionnaire that would enable the interviewer to probe even the most sensitive or concealed aspects of interviewees' sex lives. He based both his statistical findings and his qualitative observations on 20,000 interviews conducted over nearly ten years, which allowed him to answer the question that he believed all earlier sexologists had ignored: what do people do?

Kinsey was raised in a religious household, trained as a zoologist, had a wife and children, and taught at a university in a conservative midwestern town (Bloomington, Indiana). He seemed an unlikely candidate to author two books that were among the frankest and boldest statements on behalf of human sexual emancipation ever compiled. His findings suggested that premarital sex and adultery were common (50 per cent of married men, 26 per cent of women), oral sex, masturbation, and female orgasm far from rare, and, most shockingly, that homosexuality was a remarkably widespread phenomenon in American life. Kinsey ascertained that about 4 or 5 per cent of the male population was exclusively homosexual; 50 per cent of unmarried 35-year-old men had had overt homosexual contact; and a significant percentage of married men had experienced some homosexual contact at some time before or during marriage.

By inclination and design, Kinsey decked out his study with a broad array of scientific trappings derived from statistics and biology. He discussed all varieties of sexual activity under the heading 'outlet', and employed a rigidly evolutionary schema for explaining the similarities between animal and human sexuality. But beyond Kinsey's apparently objective inquiry into the mysteries of sexual life there existed a more or less overt desire to subvert the fabric of traditional American sexual mores, a motive that may have shaped the presentation and interpretation of much of his data. Kinsey and his research team regarded themselves as sexually liberated individuals, who were not only tolerant of disapproved sexual behaviour, but themselves willing participants in it. Kinsey for his part was a frequent and enthusiastic practitioner of homosexuality and had no qualms about the extra-marital peccadilloes of his colleagues. Indeed, Bloomington, Indiana, in the mid-1940s harboured a remarkably dedicated group of sexual radicals. A new recruit to the team, Paul Gebhard, immediately began an affair with the wife of a colleague, Clyde Martin. As a recent biography argues, this puts a different slant on Kinsey's much-vaunted objectivity (Extract 125).

It is thus possible to read the sections of Kinsey's book on male sexuality that deal with homosexuality as an effort on his part to make out homosexuality to be as frequent and 'normal' a phenomenon as his data would permit. Extract 126 condenses Kinsey's argument about the 'taxonomies' of heterosexuality and homosexuality as varieties of sexual 'outlet' on a spectrum of possibilities, summed up here in his famous seven-point scale for assessing the degree of homo- or heterosexuality. Despite his thoroughgoing biologistic behaviourism, Kinsey was not nearly as 'essentialist' in his outlook on sexual variation as the sexologists who came before and, in many cases, after him.

The Sexual Misery of Modern Man

The popular conception of the marriage market in the 1920s has been that with the deaths of so many men during the war, the surviving women were competing desperately to acquire the ones who were left. However, according to figures given in Martin Pugh's invaluable synthesis, *Women and the Women's Movement in Britain 1914–1959*, the marriage rate was only slightly reduced and in younger age-groups actually increased, with the marriage ratio for men in fact increasing sharply in the early 1920s. Men seem to have been eager to marry, and increasingly entered wedlock at younger ages. Furthermore, premarital sex seems to have become more frequently indulged in as a prelude to marriage rather than as a bachelor venture with a partner who would never be thought of in such respectable terms. In the Mass Observation 'Sex Survey' which took place after the Second World War, questions about premarital intercourse were almost always assumed to refer to 'anticipation in marriage', rather than to young men gaining sexual experience with prostitutes.

The new vision of eroticized marriage put forward by Stopes and other writers in the emerging marriage manual genre demanded of men a major revision of habits previously assumed to be innate. While such advice conceded that it was 'very rare for a man to use force intentionally',[1] nevertheless 'fatal blunders are often committed and irreparable mischief done in the first night.'[2] Once this traumatic beginning had been safely passed, the couple had to establish 'Mutual Adjustment'. Eustace Chesser's remark of the late 1940s that 'Van de Velde on *Ideal Marriage* is still handed to the enquiring husband as confidently as Mrs Beeton on Cookery has been passed to innumerable wives'[3] indicates the different spheres of expertise allocated to each half of the couple. Experts agreed that 'the husband, understanding his wife's nature, has the joy of arousing her gradually, of creating in her an ardour equal to his own.'[4]

The male response to this perhaps rather arduous new vision of marriage can be seen in the letters received by Stopes. Her correspondents came from a remarkably wide social range: working-class as much as middle-class men appreciated her message. In spite of his construction in *Married Love* and other contemporary works in the genre as an unthinking and insensitive oaf blinded to his wife's needs by his own impetuous desires, the male who appears from a study of this correspondence is a far more complex figure. All ranks from the armed forces, members of the Indian Civil Service, clergymen, schoolteachers, doctors, engineers, tea-planters, men of all social classes and a wide variety of occupations praised 'the perfect frankness and the clean wholesome manner of giving intimate details' of her works in glowing terms. Courage, frankness and cleanness were perceived as her books' outstanding attributes:

every decent feeling man must thank you for the frankness and courage with which you have dealt with aspects of life usually most unfortunately kept 'veiled' in a kind of miasmatic haze.

Married Love struck its first readers as with the light of revelation: 'It has opened my eyes and I have been married ten years.' A not uncommon comment was that it should be in the hands of all young couples about to marry, even to the point of saying: 'No marriage certificate should be issued without a copy of your book.' Men even discussed the work between themselves: 'I have lent the book to several married brother officers who are one and all deeply impressed by it.' Very few considered *Married Love* 'a book written by a woman for the benefit of women exclusively ... its gospel is sacrifice by the man'.

Male concern about the conjugal relationship appears to have begun well before the wedding. Numbers of men, young and less young, wrote to Stopes concerning their anxieties about matrimony, not perceived simply as a licensed outlet for their own desires. While some questions concerned actual sexual competence, and others birth control, many of these men displayed concern for their wife to be and idealism about the potential of marriage: 'I'm extremely passionate but do not want to do anything that would hurt her sense of the aesthetic—I want her to be really happy.' Many men took pride in having kept themselves 'clean' for their future wife.

There was an alleged contemporary belief that men found sexual ignorance in women profoundly arousing: in several of his publications Laurence Housman, writer, brother of the poet, and a founder of the British Society for the Study of Sex Psychology, quoted—while deploring—his stepmother's claim that women could or would not give up premarital ignorance—because 'it's too attractive'.[5] Most men who wrote to Stopes had rather different ideas, often condemning the ignorance in which their wives or fiancées had been brought up and themselves enlightening them, frequently with the aid of Stopes's works. However, one young captain in the Indian Army did write that much as he admired Stopes's books he would have hesitations about letting his fiancée read them.

Female sexual satisfaction was discovered to be far from automatic: in some cases the problem had only been revealed through reading *Married Love*. 'I have not realized till now that I haven't given my wife the satisfaction to which she has a right.' Men asked, 'Will you please tell me how to arrive at this perfect state in the accomplishment of which I consider my duty to my wife.' They regretted that 'when we have union she is very rarely satisfied', and declared: 'I would do anything if only I could help her.' Lack of mutual pleasure tormented these men as well as distressing their wives: it made them feel 'such a cad', 'so selfish and mean'. It was a rare husband who fell into the mechanical-adjustment position of 'Can you tell me how to get this remedied?'

Some men wanted 'to receive those kisses and caresses that I am anxious to bestow on her' or even 'the playing of an active part by the woman during the sex act'. But lack of interest was usually far more profound, with wives 'quite incapable of any sexual feeling or desire'. It was not simply deprivation of intercourse which distressed these husbands, but the degraded quality of intercourse itself when 'general attitude is "I am your wife I must submit"'. Wives might offer themselves out of duty but husbands found that 'just a little nauseating'. Nevertheless, few of the current marriages of Stopes's correspondents seem to have reached the stage of outright breakdown.

This widespread lack of female arousal and satisfaction is less surprising given how very inhibited the husbands revealed themselves to be even when not completely ignorant of how to arouse a woman. Even if aware of the role of clitoral stimulation, men might wonder 'are most women not likely to object to this ...?' Although men were supposed to be the sexually knowledgeable partners in the marriage, they were often ignorant of the most basic sexual information. Stopes's phrase in *Married Love* that 'not only her arms should embrace her husband' generated many requests for explication. The line did not even appear in the earliest editions, suggesting that the revelations of ignorance she received led her to add it.⁶ The standard position was sometimes in doubt: 'I have never yet learnt what is considered the natural position to adopt during union.' Others, though aware of the so-called missionary position, had never heard of or thought of other possibilities. There was seldom (at least explicitly) a search for variety and exotic stimulation, more often an attempt to find a position which worked, which was comfortable for both partners and led to reciprocal satisfaction: 'My wife does not assume a position which allows of simple access on my part to her. I do not seem to get full entry.' These difficulties were perhaps not so remarkable when many married couples indulged in intercourse clothed and in the dark. Far from endeavouring to import rampant eroticism into their marriages, men were confused about the basics of sexual practice.

['Impotent Ghosts from No-Man's Land, Flappers' Boyfriends, or Crypto-patriarchs? Men, Sex and Social Change in 1920s Britain', *Social History*, 21 / 1 (Jan. 1996), 61–4.]

MARGARET JACKSON

123 **The Limitations of Sexual Enlightenment in Marriage**

In some respects Stopes' two marriage manuals are typical of the genre of the period, with their emphasis on the importance of mutual sexual adjustment, not merely for its own sake, but in order to preserve the stability of marriage. At the same time, however, Stopes' writings are unique: not merely in terms of their romantic, semi-mystical style, but in terms of the deeply contradictory nature of her model of sexuality, which was, from a feminist perspective, both radical and reactionary. On the one hand, it combined a critique of the ideology and practice of male sexuality, which owed much to contemporary feminism, with a commitment to female sexual autonomy; on the other hand it remained ultimately rooted in the sexological, and hence patriarchal, model of sexuality—a model which assumed the biological necessity and inevitability of male dominance and female submission. Stopes' model thus had built into it fundamental patriarchal values and assumptions which undermined the female sexual autonomy she was asserting. The contradiction was reflected in her writing, which was an idiosyncratic blend of science, religion, mysticism, romanticism, and feminism.

The 'explosively contagious' main theme of this book which, according to Stopes, made Victorian husbands gasp, was 'that woman like man had the same physiological reaction, a reciprocal need for enjoyment and benefit from union in marriage distinct from the exercise of maternal functions'. She dedicated it to young husbands and 'all those who are betrothed in love', and her aim was to increase the joys of marriage and show how much marital unhappiness might be avoided. Echoing Ellis, she emphasized that sexual love could not be safely left to instinct: 'The great majority of people in our country have no glimmering of the supreme human art, the art of love'.[1]

The central subject of the book was sexual incompatibility between husbands and wives, and how to overcome it. Stopes was extremely forthright in blaming men for women's apparent frigidity and revulsion for sexual intercourse, emphasizing the 'horrors' of the wedding night, from which many women never recovered. She also pointed to the masculine bias of most books, including scientific texts, on sex and marriage, which she linked to the politics of male sexuality:

it has suited the general structure of society much better for men to shrug their shoulders and smile at women as irrational and capricious creatures, to be courted when it suited them, not to be studied. ... Moreover, by attributing to mere caprice the coldness which at times comes over the most ardent woman, man was unconsciously justifying himself for at any time coercing her to suit himself. [...]

The roots of the problem of sexual adjustment in marriage lay, for Stopes, in the inherent difference between male and female sexual desire: while female sexual desire waxed and waned according to a recurring monthly rhythm, male sexual desire was always present. It was

ever ready to awake at the lightest call, and often so spontaneously insistent as to require perpetual conscious repression. ... It would go ill with the men of our race had women retained the wild animals' infrequent seasonal rhythm, and with it her inviolable rights in her own body save at the mating season. Woman, too, has acquired a much more frequent rhythm; but, as it does not equal man's, he has tended to ignore and override it, coercing her at all times and seasons, either by force, or by the even more compelling power of 'divine' authority and social tradition.

She recognized that, given this difference in male and female sexual desire, mutual sexual satisfaction might at first sight seem impossible. As one man had said frankly to her: '"As things are it is impossible for both sexes to get what they want. One must be sacrificed. And it is better for society that it should be the woman."' Stopes disagreed. She insisted that the solution to this problem was for the husband to adapt himself to his wife's sexual rhythm, a radical solution which may well have derived from Elizabeth Blackwell's generation of feminist sexual theorists. No other marriage manual in the inter-war period even hinted at the possibility that the husband could, let alone should, adapt to his wife's sexual needs. Indeed, not until the rise of radical feminism in the late 1960s was such an uncompromising stand against the tyranny of male sexual demands again to be taken.[2]

Stopes' attitude towards male sexuality was thus contradictory: on the one hand she accepted the dominant patriarchal and scientific view that the male sexual urge was 'spontaneously insistent', but on the other hand she shared with feminists the belief that this urge was amenable to rational control, that it could be adapted to suit the pattern of female sexual desire. In describing the penis and the process of male sexual arousal, for instance, she argued strongly that erection did not necessarily require relief through ejaculation, but that it could subside naturally and healthily 'when the nerves are soothed either physically or as a result of a sense of mental peace and exaltation'. She also maintained that it was mistaken to imagine that semen must be frequently discharged, arguing, like Frances Swiney, that the energy and chemical substances that went into its production could be better used by being transformed into other creative work. Moreover, the 'soothing of the nerves' necessary for erection to subside could be accomplished by 'a strong will' and the exercise of self-discipline and control. Furthermore, she added:

It should never be forgotten that without the discipline of control there is no lasting delight in erotic feeling. The fullest delight, even in a purely physiological sense, can only be attained by those who curb and direct their natural impulses.

Thus the husband's adaptation to his wife's rhythm was seen as beneficial, not only to the wife, but to the husband himself. Assuming the wife to have a fortnightly potentiality of desire, Stopes' recommendation was for three or four days of repeated 'unions', followed by about ten days without any at all, unless 'some strong external stimulus has stirred a mutual desire'. She added that even if a woman had only one peak of desire per month, most men should still be able to adapt to this, though if a 'strongly sexed' man found this hard to endure he should 'set himself ardently to woo her' about a fortnight after her last peak, which would be when he had the best chance of succeeding.[3]

It is at this point that the contradictions in Stopes' model of sexuality begin to emerge much more sharply. The language of 'wooing and winning', directly echoing Ellis' analysis of courtship, begins to take over from the insistence on female sexual autonomy:

The supreme law for husbands is: Remember that each act of union must be tenderly wooed for and won, and that no union should ever take place unless the woman also desires it and is made physically ready for it.

It did not occur to Stopes to wonder why, if the woman really did desire coitus, she needed to be *made* ready. Nor did she seem aware that the concept of courtship, based on the assumed biological necessity of the conquest of the female by the male, might undermine the notion of female sexual autonomy. She emphasized repeatedly that the husband must woo his wife before every separate act of coitus, 'for each act corresponds to a marriage as other creatures know it', adding that the man would also benefit from the increased intensity of pleasure when the woman was made 'ready'. She also emphasized that making a woman ready for coitus took time: 'So deep-seated, so profound are woman's complex sex-instinct as well as her organs, that in rousing them the man is rousing her whole body and soul. And this takes time'.[4]

The text abounds with references to 'man the hunter' and 'the thrills of the chase', and she even hinted that the wife should pretend to resist, lest 'by her very docility to his perpetual demand, she destroys for him the elation, the palpitating thrills and surprise, of the chase'. Although she had earlier blamed men for marital maladjustment, at this point in the book there was a subtle shift of sympathy in their direction. She accused women of neglecting their beauty, damaging their health through using corsets, and contributing to their husbands' disenchantment by allowing them to observe the 'unlovely' proceedings of the toilet:

In this respect I am inclined to think that man suffers more than woman. For man is still essentially the hunter, the one who experiences the desires and thrills of the chase, and dreams ever of coming unawares upon Diana in the woodlands. [...]

During the inter-war years, when the 'back-to-the-home movement' was in full swing, there was renewed stress on marriage, motherhood, and femininity, and the married woman's right to work was bitterly opposed and in many areas openly and officially denied. In some respects this was reinforced by the 'new feminists''emphasis on the need for family endowments and their attitude towards protective legislation.[5] While most 'old feminists' believed that women should choose between marriage and motherhood on the one hand, and an independent career on the other, many 'new feminists', like Stopes, insisted that women could and should, if they wished, combine marriage and motherhood with work outside the home. Although this was in some respects a radical position, it was often combined, as it was in Stopes' case, with anti-spinster attitudes. Her campaign against the marriage bar on women teachers was based, not only on the right of married women to economic independence, but on the argument that spinster teachers were a dangerous influence on the young because they were sex-starved and sometimes had lesbian tendencies. A major problem with the 'new feminism' was that it was defined in terms of woman's freedom 'to follow her own nature', a 'nature' which was largely male-defined, and which, in the sexologists' version, substituted 'erotic rights' for equal rights. Stopes' model of sexuality was very much in tune with the 'new feminism', which derided spinsterhood and idealized heterosexual relationships. Although initially there were important elements of the 'old feminism' in her thinking, sexology, because of its scientific status, was a far more powerful force in shaping her ideas. *Married Love*, which was published in 1918 at a watershed between the 'old' and the 'new' feminisms, encapsulated the tension and struggle between the two, as well as celebrating and promoting the 'new feminism'.

[*The Real Facts of Life: Feminism and The Politics of Sexuality c1850–1940* (London: Taylor & Francis, 1994), 132–3, 134–6, 146–7.]

T. H. VAN DE VELDE

124   **New Male Responsibilities**

I also address myself to married men, for they are naturally educators and initiators of their wives in sexual matters; and yet they often lack, not only the qualifications of a leader and initiator, but also those necessary for equal mutual partnership!

They have no realisation of their deficiencies. For the average man, of average 'normal' genital potency, who performs his 'conjugal duties' regularly and with physiological satisfaction to himself, still imagines that he has thereby met all the requirements his wife can make. And if she is not satisfied, and remains in a permanent condition of 'suspended gratification,' then, with regret or indignation according to his own type of temperament, he simply puts her down as one of those 'sexually frigid' women (from 20 to 80 per cent. of all women are supposed to be sexually frigid—a conveniently and conspicuously wide margin of error!), laments his bad luck, and drifts further and further apart from her.

If he has been fortunate enough to wed a woman of warmer and more spontaneous temperament, who is obviously not indifferent to the rites of marriage—if those rites take place in the same invariably scheduled manner, with no varieties of local stimulation or sensory adornment—sexual satiety will in a few short years intrude itself into the consciousness of both, and equally imperil their marriage. For monotony can only be relieved by variation, and, to the uninstructed man, the only possible variation seems to be in the *object* of his efforts; and the rift in the lute is there, and widens.

The thought that the defect and the failure might be on *his* side, that he himself might have prevented the alienation which he truly deplores—this enlightening and humbling truth never dawns upon him!

For he does not know that there are numberless delicate differentiations and modifications of sexual pleasure, all lying strictly within the bounds of *normality*, which can banish the mechanical monotony of the two well-known from the marriage-bed, and give new attractions to conjugal intercourse. Or, if he guesses this truth, he thinks it implies degeneracy and debauchery, for he fails to understand that what is physiologically sound may also be considered ethically sound. He thinks his wife is 'far above that sort of thing,' leaves her more and more to herself, seeks the diversity of stimulation he needs outside his home, and often ends in *real* debauchery in consequence!

This average husband does not even know that his wife's sexual sensations develop and culminate to a slower rhythm than his own. He does not know *at all* that he must *awaken* her with delicate consideration and adaptation. [...]

In *union* or *coitus*, prelude and love-play attain their goal, and sexual relationships their culmination.

In its ideal form, husband and wife take a fully equal and reciprocal share in this most intimate merging; their souls meet and touch as do their bodies; they become *one*.

And fortunately this ideal is not unattainable; it may and sometimes does become actual.

This full equivalence and mutuality obtain in Ideal Marriage, even though the man is the transmitter and the woman the receiver. Even though he is certainly, and must be, essentially active, she is quite as certainly not the purely passive instrument which she has been so long considered, and still is considered, far too often. And in any case she *ought not* to be a purely passive instrument! For sexual union only takes place *physiologically* (*i.e.*, according to the laws of Nature), rightly and suitably, if and when both partners fully participate and feel supreme sexual pleasure and complete relaxation or relief. If, anywhere and in any circumstances, the demand for equal rights for both sexes is *incontestable*, it is so in regard to equal consent and equal pleasure in sexual union, and in the interests of *both*. Therefore in Ideal Marriage, the man does not perform the act on a passive woman, but they *both together* achieve *sexual communion*.

Sexual communion (coitus, copulation, the sexual act, or connection, or intercourse) is the third act in the love drama. It begins with the insertion of the male penis (or *phallos* as the Greeks termed the erect and active organ) into the female vagina (*immissio penis*); and reaches culmination in the ejaculation of semen into the vagina, and in the approximately simultaneous orgasm or summit of enjoyment in both partners. Communion ends when the phallos is removed from the vagina. [...]

The stimuli of the penile nerves may differ in degrees of intensity and shades of quality; and there are corresponding diversities in the sensations of pleasure they bestow. It is of much importance in determining these sensations: whether the stimuli are localised mainly in the *frenulum preputii* or the posterior rim of the *glans*; whether the vagina is a trifle wider or narrower; whether it is smooth or delicately folded and crinkled; whether the *introitus vaginæ* fits the shaft of the penis closely, or hardly clasps it at all; whether the tip of the penis touches the *Portio vaginalis* or cannot reach it. Thus it will be readily understood that a certain correspondence or *congruence* of the sexual organs of the partners is essential for ideal communion. A normal penis can no more be perfectly stimulated by (and/or afford perfect stimulation to) an unusually wide vulva and slack vagina than can an abnormally undeveloped or inadequately erected penis attain satisfaction by, or give it to, normal female genitalia. If a strong desire for sexual satisfaction has been aroused, minor stimuli certainly suffice to cause ejaculation and a *relative* culmination of pleasure or, at least, relief. But the glorious consciousness of having tasted the supreme pleasure, and the soothing, complete relaxation are lacking, and with them the psychic effect, at once tender and triumphant, of an ideally successful *coitus*. [...]

Excessive sexual activity is more often expected of a man in a *relative* than an *absolute* degree: and most often in the form of too rapid repetition of coitus.

The *criteria* of 'excess' are about the same in both sexes. We have enumerated them already. In the man the most conspicuous are slight pains across the loins, and more important—diminished clarity and concentration in brain work. This particular deleterious effect should be avoided, as it may quickly become obstinate, and possibly chronic.

On the other hand, it should be recognized that two or—in strong potency—even three successive acts of communion, *can* be—in certain circumstances—of great advantage. After a few days or a longer period of abstinence, the man often has ejaculation so soon that the preceding stimulation is not enough—or only just enough—to gratify the woman. In these cases, coitus will give both partners *relief*, but a minimum degree of specific *pleasure*, and is therefore inadequate as an *expression of their love. But nothing is more fatal to love than disappointment in sexual intercourse!* So the first relative failure may be redeemed by a prompt repetition of communion. Whether this should occur immediately, or after an hour or so of repose, or on the next morning, depends so much on masculine potency, on mutual inclination and on so many other factors besides, that a *system* cannot well be propounded or definite advice given. Nevertheless, if some suggestions are asked, I would say: if the man's potency is adequate, *then the after-glow or epilogue of the first act should be interwoven with the prelude and love-play of the next.* This gives excellent opportunities for prolonged and delicately varied love-play. During its slow summation the male organism will have had time for recuperation and fresh accumulation, and the stimulation will be mutual and harmonious. There will be ample opportunity to taste all the delight of mutual love, and give expression to all fancies and desires; and the woman may appropriately take a more active *rôle* than usual. If after this experience, the man is able to rest thoroughly and especially to sleep, there is little likelihood that he will be unduly fatigued. It is advisable, for this reason, that repeated sexual acts should take place early in the evening. But if he should feel the mental lassitude and lumbar pains mentioned as signs of sexual strain, the next day, instead of the increased vigour, psychic refreshment and mental and physical efficiency which should normally follow coitus, then he should 'put on the brakes,' and postpone the next occasion, for a few days. And this experience can also teach both partners the desirability of greater sexual activity and initiative on the woman's part, in multiple coitus.

Some of my readers may perhaps feel that the greater feminine *aptitude* or *tolerance of excess in coitus* compared to the man's *potency* as just described, is hardly compatible with what has been stressed in earlier chapters, *i.e.*, her less rapid and facile excitability and the frequency of feminine sexual anaesthesia, 'coldness' or frigidity. But any one who is acquainted with the sexual histories of a large number of women, and has been able to observe them throughout changing phases and periods of their lives, will know that this contradiction is only superficial and apparent. And the attentive reader of these pages will not feel any contradiction or confusion. But for the sake of cleanness, we may summarize as follows: the newly married woman *is as a rule*, more or less completely 'cold' or indifferent to and in sexual intercourse. She must be *taught to love*, in the complete sense in which we here use the term. The husband may perhaps not succeed in imparting this erotic education; generally that is because he takes no trouble about it. She then *remains* permanently *frigid*, which explains the heavy percentage of anaesthesia which all authorities confirm; or else the husband's grave omissions are made good by another man. But even if the husband proves a good teacher, the young wife does not generally at first attain to an equal sexual ardour, a delay which should be allowed for and made good in the ways we have suggested. Only gradually does she develop erotic maturity and experience, and when she does reach her zenith, the comparatively slight provocation which will cause ejaculation in the husband after some days of abstinence, may well be insufficient for her. We have also shown how to meet her requirements in such cases. Her *desire* for sexual intercourse, in happy married life, will have become *at least* equal to his. And her *quantitative* sexual efficiency and endurance surpass his.

[*Ideal Marriage: Its Physiology and Technique*, trans. Stella Browne (New York: Random House, 1930), 7–8, 172–3, 173–4, 269–71.]

JAMES H. JONES

125   The Radical Motives of Kinsey's Sex Research

Gebhard was definitely not 'sex shy,' a fact he punctuated by having an affair almost immediately after he moved to Bloomington. He was not interested sexually in Kinsey or the other male staff members, for Gebhard was decidedly 'straight' in his private life. Because his sexual attitudes were liberal, however, he felt drawn to the free and easy sexual atmosphere Kinsey had fostered among his senior staff members and their wives. Explaining that his wife and son were not able to join him until November, leaving him alone for three months, Gebhard later confessed with a chuckle, 'I was ripe for a little extramarital activity if it were available.'[1]

Within days after arriving in Bloomington, Gebhard started an affair with Alice Martin. 'Kinsey had no objection to interstaff sex. In fact, he sort of encouraged it,' revealed Gebhard. The problem in this instance was that the relationship quickly started to heat up, threatening to become serious. 'He [Kinsey] felt that Alice was getting too involved with me because at that particular moment she was having some trouble with Clyde,' continued Gebhard. To prevent things from escalating, Kinsey spoke with Gebhard, telling him 'to cool it' because Clyde and Alice's marriage was being damaged. An apostle of sexual freedom, Kinsey took no joy in ordering the affair ended. According to Gebhard, 'He made some remark about he didn't like to interfere. He put this rather gently, but his eyes were brimming.'[2]

Decades later, Gebhard denied that the affair had damaged his relationship with Martin. Describing Martin as 'a tolerant person' and 'kind of a gentle person, too,' Gebhard declared, 'If it caused any hard feelings toward me he never expressed them.'[3] Gebhard was badly mistaken, because Martin was emotionally crushed. In retrospect, Martin called his wife's affair 'very brief but very intense' and confessed, '[It] was very upsetting to me, and I thought my world was crumbling.'[4] While Martin feared for his marriage, this may not have been his only concern. Given his lowly status on the staff, he must have felt deeply humiliated by the ease with which a fresh recruit who was higher in the pecking order could move in on his wife. Martin had lost face, as sexual prowess counted mightily within Kinsey's inner circle.

By the end of 1946, then, Kinsey had assembled his team—Martin, Pomeroy, and Gebhard, three fiercely loyal men who shared his sexual attitudes, knew his secrets, and supported his plan for using science to reform the sexual mores of American society. At first glance, they appeared to have little in common. One was a lowly factotum, another a covert Don Juan, and the last a free spirit who saw human sexuality as anthropology's next great frontier. Yet in hiring these men, Kinsey knew exactly what he was doing. The survivors of a process of attrition that had seen one interviewer trainee depart for every one who stayed, Martin, Pomeroy, and Gebhard would stick around to the end, providing Kinsey with the 'hands' he needed, and the loyalty he demanded. [...]

Touting numbers was a key component of Kinsey's attempt to inspire confidence in the male volume. His strategy was to shout 'Science!' at every turn; to proclaim the need for caution in attaching too much emphasis to his findings (followed by assurances that his data were both representative and reliable); to assert over and over his objectivity; and to disavow again and again any thought of influencing social policy. 'This is first of all a report on what people do,' he announced near the beginning of the book, 'which raises no question of what

they should do, or what kinds of people do it.' His goal, he explained, was 'to accumulate an objectively determined body of fact about sex which strictly avoids
social or moral interpretations of the fact.' Such matters, he insisted, should be
addressed only by philosophers, theologians, and others who possessed the appropriate special training. His approach to what he delighted in calling 'the
human animal' was 'agnostic.'[5] Despite his claim of cool disinterest, Kinsey was
nothing of the sort. He had definite ideas about how people should behave sexually, and these preferences were only too transparent in his writing. Anything
but a bloodless treatise, the male volume was packed with special pleadings,
thinly disguised opinions, and polemical stances, all designed to challenge conventional morality and to promote a new social ethic.[6]

Decades after the male volume appeared, Gebhard pointed to the essential
paradox that was Kinsey, acknowledging that the man who postured as an objective scientist was actually a passionate reformer. Dismissing the protesta-
tions of disinterest, Gebhard noted that Kinsey turned his prose into a weapon
for combating sexual repression. 'Now, you had to really twist his arm to get
him to admit to this humanitarian impulse,' observed Gebhard, following the
company line, 'because ordinarily he was the objective scientist without any ax
to grind, without any crusade to pursue. But underneath there was this powerful streak of crusading humanitarianism which, despite his attempts to cover it,
show up in between the lines in everything he ever wrote.' Elaborating,
Gebhard repeated, 'Kinsey tried to be completely objective, but he couldn't succeed, because this thing was too much a matter of heart and emotion with him
to keep it out of his writings.'[7]

Gebhard was certain he understood the source of Kinsey's passion. '[Kinsey]
had led such a wretched, sexually inhibited life himself as a young man that he
was determined that he was going to promulgate a more rational approach to
sex so that people would be happier,' explained Gebhard.[8] Undergirding this
'more rational approach' was a new sexual ethic, the essence of which was simple: sex was good. In keeping with this ethic, Kinsey applauded practically every
kind of sexual activity, and he disapproved of sexual abstinence. 'I think he felt
that the human animal, as he would say, was basically pansexual—that everybody would be a mixture of hetero and homosexuality, about a two on his Kinsey scale,' noted Gebhard. 'And he felt that neither male nor female was
inherently monogamous, and he thought sex was a wonderful thing, and it was
just a pity that it had to be constrained and unnecessarily restricted.'[9]

This enthusiasm for sex was a fundamental tenet of Kinsey's thought, and it
rang out loud and clear in his writing. From start to finish, the male volume was
an ode to Eros, a celebration of the 'human animal's' ability to find sexual outlets in a society obsessed with controlling and restricting sexual freedom. In the
broadest terms, Kinsey showed that Americans were awash in sexual activity,
only a small fraction of which was confined to behavior sanctioned by society.
In addition, he identified and evaluated the factors that determined the number

and the kinds of sexual outlets in which Americans engaged, bemoaning those that restrained sexual activity and celebrating those that propelled people to act upon their sexual needs and desires.

If the male volume provided a compendium of sexual behavior, it also offered a prayer for further liberation. Kinsey looked for signs of hope anywhere he could find them, duly reporting the little victories people had achieved in their struggle to loosen the reins of rigid conformity. For example, when he discussed young boys who had somehow found the courage to defy the sexual morality of their parents, Kinsey spoke not of wicked or evil children but of youngsters who 'triumph over the parents.' Elsewhere, he praised members of the lower class for overriding social restrictions against premarital intercourse. Despite their meager education, he noted, 'even they recognize that nature will triumph over morals,' adding, 'They may "know that intercourse is wrong," but "they expect to have it anyway, because it is human and natural to have it." '[10] This was the language of defiance, hope, and redemption.

Yet no book that bore Kinsey's name could ignore the suffering and pain that had cast such a shadow over his life. 'Sexual histories,' he reported from experience as well as from his research, 'often involve a record of things that have hurt, of frustrations, of pain, of unsatisfied longings, of disappointments, of desperately tragic situations, and of complete catastrophe.'[11] Other parts of the book betrayed his private angst as well, particularly those passages that described the lot of sexual minorities forced to live in a society whose sexual mores had been fashioned centuries earlier by religious zealots.

Reflecting on the issue of motivation, Gebhard thought that Kinsey had two overriding goals for his research. 'One was he felt that knowledge would prevent tragedies, upsets, frictions, guilt—bad things of this sort,' revealed Gebhard. 'In other words, it is almost like the biblical saying "The truth will set ye free." If he could only get the facts and the truth to people,' he explained, 'life would be a lot happier and less guilt [ridden]. That was motivation number one.' Motivation number two was that 'he was a great champion for tolerance and liberality.' Kinsey believed 'that it didn't much matter what you did sexually as long as it didn't hurt anyone else and it made you and your partner happy.' Added Gebhard, 'Both of these motivations showed up in his writings despite his efforts to be clinical and objective.'[12]

Tolerance was the central message of the male volume. To show the need for forbearance, Kinsey bombarded his readers with the theme of sexual diversity. 'There is no American pattern of sexual behavior,' he boldly declared, 'but scores of patterns, each of which is confined to a particular segment of our society.' An accomplished debunker, Kinsey delighted in showing that many forms of sexual behavior labeled criminal, immoral, and rare were actually quite common. Indeed, he argued that 'at least 85 per cent of the younger male population could be convicted as sex offenders if law enforcement officials were as efficient as most people expect them to be.'[13] How could a single, rigid moral code accommodate so much variation? For Kinsey the answer was simple: none could. In the face of so much diversity, tolerance was the only sensible and humane response.

[*Alfred C. Kinsey: A Public/Private Life* (New York: W. W. Norton & Co., 1997), 499–500, 518–21.]

ALFRED C. KINSEY ET AL.

126   **Kinsey's Seven-Point Scale of Sexual Identity**

The Heterosexual-Homosexual Balance

Concerning patterns of sexual behavior, a great deal of the thinking done by scientists and laymen alike stems from the assumption that there are persons who are 'heterosexual' and persons who are 'homosexual,' that these two types represent antitheses in the sexual world, and that there is only an insignificant class of 'bisexuals' who occupy an intermediate position between the other groups. It is implied that every individual is innately—inherently—either heterosexual or homosexual. It is further implied that from the time of birth one is fated to be one thing or the other, and that there is little chance for one to change his pattern in the course of a lifetime.

It is quite generally believed that one's preference for a sexual partner of one or the other sex is correlated with various physical and mental qualities, and with the total personality which makes a homosexual male or female physically, psychically, and perhaps spiritually distinct from a heterosexual individual. It is generally thought that these qualities make a homosexual person obvious and recognizable to any one who has a sufficient understanding of such matters. Even psychiatrists discuss 'the homosexual personality' and many of them believe that preferences for sexual partners of a particular sex are merely secondary manifestations of something that lies much deeper in the totality of that intangible which they call the personality. [...]

The histories which have been available in the present study make it apparent that the heterosexuality or homosexuality of many individuals is not an all-or-none proposition. It is true that there are persons in the population whose histories are exclusively heterosexual, both in regard to their overt experience and in regard to their psychic reactions. And there are individuals in the population whose histories are exclusively homosexual, both in experience and in psychic reactions. But the record also shows that there is a considerable portion of the population whose members have combined, within their individual histories, both homosexual and heterosexual experience and/or psychic responses. There are some whose heterosexual experiences predominate, there are some whose homosexual experiences predominate, there are some who have had quite equal amounts of both types of experience.

Some of the males who are involved in one type of relation at one period in their lives, may have only the other type of relation at some later period. There may be considerable fluctuation of patterns from time to time. Some males may be involved in both heterosexual and homosexual activities within the same period of time. For instance, there are some who engage in both heterosexual and homosexual activities in the same year, or in the same month or week, or even in the same day. There are not a few individuals who engage in group activities in which they may make simultaneous contact with partners of both sexes.

Males do not represent two discrete populations, heterosexual and homosexual. The world is not to be divided into sheep and goats. Not all things are black nor all things white. It is a fundamental of taxonomy that nature rarely deals with discrete categories. Only the human mind invents categories and tries to force facts into separated pigeon-holes. The living world is a continuum in each and every one of its aspects. The sooner we learn this concerning human sexual behavior the sooner we shall reach a sound understanding of the realities of sex.

While emphasizing the continuity of the gradations between exclusively heterosexual and exclusively homosexual histories, it has seemed desirable to develop some sort of classification which could be based on the relative amounts of heterosexual and of homosexual experience or response in each history. [...] An individual may be assigned a position on this scale, for each age period in his life, in accordance with the following definitions of the various points on the scale:

0. Individuals are rated as 0's if they make no physical contacts which result in erotic arousal or orgasm, and make no psychic responses to individuals of their own sex. Their socio-sexual contacts and responses are exclusively with individuals of the opposite sex.

1. Individuals are rated as 1's if they have only incidental homosexual contacts which have involved physical or psychic response, or incidental psychic responses without physical contact. The great preponderance of their socio-sexual experience and reactions is directed toward individuals of the opposite sex. Such homosexual experiences as these individuals have may occur only a single time or two, or at least infrequently in comparison to the amount of their heterosexual experience. Their homosexual experiences never involve as specific psychic reactions as they make to heterosexual stimuli. Sometimes the homosexual activities in which they engage may be inspired by curiosity, or may be more or less forced upon them by other individuals, perhaps when they are asleep or when they are drunk, or under some other peculiar circumstance.

2. Individuals are rated as 2's if they have more than incidental homosexual experience, and/or if they respond rather definitely to homosexual stimuli. Their heterosexual experiences and/or reactions still surpass their homosexual

experiences and/or reactions. These individuals may have only a small amount of homosexual experience or they may have a considerable amount of it, but in every case it is surpassed by the amount of heterosexual experience that they have within the same period of time. They usually recognize their quite specific arousal by homosexual stimuli, but their responses to the opposite sex are still stronger. A few of these individuals may even have all of their overt experience in the homosexual, but their psychic reactions to persons of the opposite sex indicate that they are still predominantly heterosexual. This latter situation is most often found among younger males who have not yet ventured to have actual intercourse with girls, while their orientation is definitely heterosexual. On the other hand, there are some males who should be rated as 2's because of their strong reactions to individuals of their own sex, even though they have never had overt relations with them.

3. Individuals who are rated 3's stand midway on the heterosexual–homosexual scale. They are about equally homosexual and heterosexual in their overt experience and/or their psychic reactions. In general, they accept and equally enjoy both types of contacts, and have no strong preferences for one or the other. Some persons are rated 3's, even though they may have a larger amount of experience of one sort, because they respond psychically to partners of both sexes, and it is only a matter of circumstance that brings them into more frequent contact with one of the sexes. Such a situation is not unusual among single males, for male contacts are often more available to them than female contacts. Married males, on the other hand, find it simpler to secure a sexual outlet through intercourse with their wives, even though some of them may be as interested in males as they are in females.

4. Individuals are rated as 4's if they have more overt activity and/or psychic reactions in the homosexual, while still maintaining a fair amount of heterosexual activity and/or responding rather definitely to heterosexual stimuli.

5. Individuals are rated 5's if they are almost entirely homosexual in their overt activities and/or reactions. They do have incidental experience with the opposite sex and sometimes react psychically to individuals of the opposite sex.

6. Individuals are rated as 6's if they are exclusively homosexual, both in regard to their overt experience and in regard to their psychic reactions.

[*Sexual Behavior in the Human Male* (Philadelphia: W.B. Saunders Company, 1948), 636–7, 638–41.]

IV.c Stripping Off

The 'events' of the 'sexual revolution' of the late 1960s and 1970s were made up of many parts: there were sex manuals of unprecedented explicitness for the married; a new sexual libertarianism for the unmarried; a new openness for same-sex sexuality; and, for everyone, more candour about pleasure, less modesty about nudity, and a keener appetite for literary and pictorial representations of sex. While bearing in mind the anticipations of these developments we have already considered, there is no doubting the differences in degree and participation, and especially in publicity, of the self-conscious effort to break with sexual traditions.

For many, especially younger, participants, sexual 'emancipation' was closely linked to social emancipation generally and to a radical, pacifist, and egalitarian agenda. The slogan of the day was 'The personal is the political.' This set of politically high-minded aims was by no means shared by all; the liberation of sexuality was also an opportunity for sexual entrepreneurship, for experiments in cultural and aesthetic innovation, or for solipsistic or drug-induced explorations of the inner self. However, the movement for freer sexual expression coincided with a number of important developments in the West that linked sexual liberty to long-anticipated movements of political liberation. First, the Vietnam War represented the slowing of national liberation movements in former colonial nations. Second, after considerable legal progress in the 1960s, economic and legal inertia stalled the liberation of black Americans from the thrall of second-class citizenship. Third, non-Communist leftists in Europe found themselves caught between a reinvigorated right and an unrepentant Stalinist left, both of which were inordinately suspicious of personal radicalism in any form. Finally, the long-moribund feminist movement sprang back to life with a vengeance in the 1960s, enjoining both new support and fresh resistance.

The existence of a conviction in the 1960s that a link existed between instinctual liberation and radical social transformation may be traced in part to the work of the German philosopher Herbert Marcuse. By combining Freud's perspective on human sexuality with Hegelian and Marxist ideas, Marcuse was able to provide an analysis of the way sexual libido has been shaped by the historical exigencies of productive economic relations. In the modern industrial era, he argued, the portion of the libido that is not sublimated into unrewarding and monotonous work is siphoned off into a variety of harmless and socially sanctioned forms of heterosexual genital sexuality. Masturbation, non-genital sexual practices, and the 'perversions' were condemned in capitalist societies precisely because they threatened the productive work ethic of 'civilized' sublimation by favouring sensual pleasure over puritanical self-denial. As a good Freudian, Marcuse believed that unmediated expressions of sexual instinct would undermine the good as well as the bad aspects of civilization, but by means of his notion of 'non-repressive sublimation' Marcuse hoped that sexual libido could be used to emancipate and transform social and productive relations, turning work into pleasure and suffusing social relations with *eros*. In a passage from his 1955 book *Eros and Civilization*, Marcuse explains how *eros* came to serve capitalism and describes the emancipatory consequences that would flow from de-linking them (Extract 127).

The two common denominators in the sexual component of the liberationist projects of the 1960s were the newly sanctioned female orgasm(s) and the advent of 'the pill'. Science and technology seemed to have brought about overnight a transformation of the 'condition of woman' questions that centuries of agitation and moral reform had not accomplished. They freed women from fear of unwanted pregnancy and presented them with the opportunity to pursue pleasure in the uninhibited way men had (presumably) always done. This combination of security and sensual promise seemed to both strengthen and undermine marriage. It was deemed a formula for marital sexual bliss *and* it permitted unmarried women to have multiple sexual partners, disconnecting sex and motherhood. Were not women now truly just like men; indeed, in the matter of their capacity for pleasure, their superiors? For radical feminists like the Anglo-Australian writer Germaine Greer, this new sexual equality endowed women with a new social and political power that could be used against patriarchy, violence, and a mindless consumer culture. As she argued in the chapter on 'Revolution' in her hugely popular book *The Female Eunuch* (1970), women should use their sexual power as a weapon for social justice (Extract 128).

In a far less political vein, other sexual radicals were inspired by the promise of endless orgasms to aspire to a reordering of society based on sexual pleasure alone. In Extract 129 John Heidenry describes one of the many American experiments in sexual utopia undertaken in the 1970s, concluding with some observations about their limitations and fate.

The strange mixture of sexual, cultural, and entrepreneurial opportunism that characterized the 1970s is displayed in a memoir of those years by the Anglo-Australian writer Richard Neville, who recalls the European scene from his days in the counter-culture. Sexual outrage, he recalls, was meant to be in some sense a challenge and a subversion of establishment views, but he is not able to remember exactly how it was supposed to work. At the time of the events described below he was editing a much-censored and harassed journal called *Oz* which preached different varieties of sexual emancipation (Extract 130).

Second thoughts about the advantages to women of sexual revolution have been plentiful. The British journalist Linda Grant begins her memoir of the 1970s with a ledger-sheet of the accomplishments and the failures of women's sexual emancipation. It is by no means clear which has prevailed (Extract 131).

For the British feminist critic Sheila Jeffreys, the movement for emancipation was a male-inspired and dominated effort to make women into tractable sex objects and willing partners. In Extract 132 Jeffreys discusses the hetero-sexual and male bias in most of the literature and the sex manuals of the 1960s and 1970s, particularly Alex Comfort's best-selling sex guide *The Joy of Sex* (1972). Apart from their more tolerant and experimental attitude toward sex, she is convinced that the sex manuals of the 1970s were not so different from most of their predecessors on issues of gender equality.

127 Eros and Human Emancipation

The processes that create the ego and superego also shape and perpetuate specific societal institutions and relations. Such psychoanalytical concepts as sublimation, identification, and introjection have not only a psychical but also a social content: they terminate in a system of institutions, laws, agencies, things, and customs that confront the individual as objective entities. Within this antagonistic system, the mental conflict between ego and superego, between ego and id, is at one and the same time a conflict between the individual and his society. The latter embodies the rationality of the whole, and the individual's struggle against the repressive forces is a struggle against objective reason. Therefore, the emergence of a non-repressive reality principle involving instinctual liberation would *regress* behind the attained level of civilized rationality. This regression would be psychical as well as social: it would reactivate early stages of the libido which were surpassed in the development of the reality ego, and it would dissolve the institutions of society in which the reality ego exists. In terms of these institutions, instinctual liberation is relapse into barbarism. However, occurring at the height of civilization, as a consequence not of defeat but of victory in the struggle for existence, and supported by a free society, such liberation might have very different results. It would still be a reversal of the process of civilization, a subversion of culture—but *after* culture had done its work and created the mankind and the world that could be free. It would still be 'regression'—but in the light of mature consciousness and guided by a new rationality. Under these conditions, the possibility of a non-repressive civilization is predicated not upon the arrest, but upon the liberation, of progress—so that man would order his life in accordance with his fully developed knowledge, so that he would ask again what is good and what is evil. If the guilt accumulated in the civilized domination of man by man can ever be redeemed by freedom, then the 'original sin' must be committed again: 'We must again eat from the tree of knowledge in order to fall back into the state of innocence.'

The notion of a non-repressive instinctual order must first be tested on the most 'disorderly' of all instincts—namely, sexuality. Non-repressive order is possible only if the sex instincts can, by virtue of their own dynamic and under changed existential and societal conditions, generate lasting erotic relations among mature individuals. We have to ask whether the sex instincts, after the elimination of all surplus-repression, can develop a 'libidinal rationality' which is not only compatible with but even promotes progress toward higher forms of civilized freedom. This possibility will be examined here in Freud's own terms.

We have reiterated Freud's conclusion that any genuine decrease in the societal controls over the sex instincts would, even under optimum conditions, reverse the organization of sexuality toward precivilized stages. Such regression would break through the central fortifications of the performance principle: it would undo the channeling of sexuality into monogamic reproduction and the taboo on perversions. Under the rule of the performance principle, the libidinal cathexis of the individual body and libidinal relations with others are normally confined to leisure time and directed to the preparation and execution of genital intercourse; only in exceptional cases, and with a high degree of sublimation, are libidinal relations allowed to enter into the sphere of work. These constraints, enforced by the need for sustaining a large quantum of energy and time for non-gratifying labor, perpetuate the desexualization of the body in order to make the organism into a subject-object of socially useful performances. Conversely, if the work day and energy are reduced to a minimum, without a corresponding manipulation of the free time, the ground for these constraints would be undermined. Libido would be released and would overflow the institutionalized limits within which it is kept by the reality principle.

Freud repeatedly emphasized that the lasting interpersonal relations on which civilization depends presuppose that the sex instinct is inhibited in its aim.[1] Love, and the enduring and responsible relations which it demands, are founded on a union of sexuality with 'affection,' and this union is the historical result of a long and cruel process of domestication, in which the instinct's legitimate manifestation is made supreme and its component parts are arrested in their development.[2] This cultural refinement of sexuality, its sublimation to love, took place within a civilization which established possessive private relations apart from, and in a decisive aspect conflicting with, the possessive societal relations. While, outside the privacy of the family, men's existence was chiefly determined by the exchange value of their products and performances, their life in home and bed was to be permeated with the spirit of divine and moral law. Mankind was supposed to be an end in itself and never a mere means; but this ideology was effective in the private rather than in the societal functions of the individuals, in the sphere of libidinal satisfaction rather than in that of labor. The full force of civilized morality was mobilized against the use of the body as mere object, means, instrument of pleasure; such reification was tabooed and remained the ill-reputed privilege of whores, degenerates, and perverts. Precisely in his gratification, and especially in his sexual gratification, man was to be a higher being, committed to higher values; sexuality was to be dignified by love. With the emergence of a non-repressive reality principle, with the abolition of the surplus-repression necessitated by the performance principle, this process would be reversed. In the societal relations, reification would be reduced as the division of labor became reoriented on the gratification of freely developing individual needs; whereas, in the libidinal relations, the taboo on the reification of the body would be lessened. No longer used as a full-time instrument of labor, the body would be resexualized. The regression involved in this spread of the libido would first manifest itself in a reactivation of all erotogenic zones and, consequently, in a resurgence of pregenital polymorphous sexuality and in a decline of genital supremacy. The body in its entirety would become an object of cathexis, a thing to be enjoyed—an instrument of pleasure. This change in the value and scope of libidinal relations would lead to a disintegration of the institutions in which the private interpersonal relations have been organized, particularly the monogamic and patriarchal family.

These prospects seem to confirm the expectation that instinctual liberation can lead only to a society of sex maniacs—that is, to no society. However, the process just outlined involves not simply a release but a *transformation* of the libido: from sexuality constrained under genital supremacy to erotization of the entire personality. It is a spread rather than explosion of libido—a spread over private and societal relations which bridges the gap maintained between them by a repressive reality principle. This transformation of the libido would be the result of a societal transformation that released the free play of individual needs and faculties. By virtue of these conditions, the free development of transformed libido *beyond* the institutions of the performance principle differs essentially from the release of constrained sexuality *within* the dominion of these institutions. The latter process explodes *suppressed* sexuality; the libido continues to bear the mark of suppression and manifests itself in the hideous forms so well known in the history of civilization; in the sadistic and masochistic orgies of desperate masses, of 'society elites,' of starved bands of mercenaries, of prison and concentration-camp guards. Such release of sexuality provides a periodically necessary outlet for unbearable frustration; it strengthens rather than weakens the roots of instinctual constraint; consequently, it has been used time and again as a prop for suppressive regimes. In contrast, the free development of transformed libido within transformed institutions, while eroticizing previously tabooed zones, time, and relations, would *minimize* the manifestations of *mere* sexuality by integrating them into a far larger order, including the order of work. In this context, sexuality tends to its own sublimation: the libido would not simply reactivate precivilized and infantile stages, but would also transform the perverted content of these stages.

The term *perversions* covers sexual phenomena of essentially different origin. The same taboo is placed on instinctual manifestations incompatible with civilization and on those incompatible with repressive civilization, especially with monogamic genital supremacy. However, within the historical dynamic of the instinct, for example, coprophilia and homosexuality have a very different place and function. A similar difference prevails within one and the same perversion: the function of sadism is not the same in a free libidinal relation and in the activities of SS Troops. The inhuman, compulsive, coercive, and destructive forms of these perversions seem to be linked with the general perversion of the human existence in a repressive culture, but the perversions have an instinctual substance distinct from these forms; and this substance may well express itself in other forms compatible with normality in high civilization. Not all component parts and stages of the instinct that have been suppressed have suffered this fate because they prevented the evolution of man and mankind. The purity, regularity, cleanliness, and reproduction required by the performance principle are not naturally those of any mature civilization. And the reactivation of prehistoric and childhood wishes and attitudes is not necessarily regression; it may well be the opposite—proximity to a happiness that has always been the repressed promise of a better future. In one of his most advanced formulations, Freud once defined happiness as the 'subsequent fulfillment of a prehistoric wish. That is why wealth brings so little happiness: money was not a wish in childhood.'³

[*Eros and Civilization: A Philosophical Inquiry into Freud* (New York: Vintage Books, 1955), 180–6.]

GERMAINE GREER

128   Women's Sexual Liberation

It would be genuine revolution if women would suddenly stop loving the victors in violent encounters. Why do they admire the image of the brutal man? If they could only see through the brawn and the bravado to the desolation and the misery of the man who is goaded into using his fists (for battered-looking strong men are always called out by less obviously masculine men who need to prove themselves). Why can they not understand the deification of the strong-man, either as soldier, wrestler, footballer or male model, seeing that his fate so closely approximates their own? If women would only offer a genuine alternative to the treadmill of violence, the world might breathe a little longer with less pain. If women were to withdraw from the spectatorship of wrestling matches, the industry would collapse; if soldiers were certainly faced with the withdrawal of all female favors, as Lysistrata observed so long ago, there would suddenly be less glamour in fighting. We are not houris; we will not be the warrior's reward. And yet we read in men's magazines how the whores of American cities give their favors for free to the boys about to embark for Vietnam.

The male perversion of violence is an essential condition of the degradation of women. The penis is conceived as a weapon, and its action upon women is understood to be somehow destructive and hurtful. It has become a gun, and in English slang women cry when they want their mate to ejaculate, 'Shoot me! Shoot me!' Women cannot be liberated from their impotence by the gift of a gun, although they are as capable of firing them as men are. Every time women have been given a gun for the duration of a specific struggle, it has been withdrawn and they have found themselves more impotent than before. The process to be followed is the opposite: women must humanize the penis, take the steel out of it and make it flesh again. What most 'liberated' women do is taunt the penis for its misrepresentation of itself, mock men for their overestimation of their virility, instead of seeing how the mistake originated and what effects it has had upon themselves. Men are tired of having all the responsibility for sex; it is time they were relieved of it. And I do not mean that large-scale lesbianism should be adopted, but simply that the emphasis should be taken off male geniality and replaced upon human sexuality. The cunt must come into its own. The question of the female attitude to violence is inseparable from this problem. Perhaps to begin with women should labor to be genuinely disgusted by violence, and at least to refuse to reward any victor in a violent confrontation, even to the point of casting their lot on principle with the loser. If they were to withdraw their spectatorship absolutely from male competition, much of its motivation would be gone. [...]

It is difficult at this point to suggest what a new sexual regime would be like. We have but one life to live, and the first object is to find a way of salvaging that life from the disabilities already inflicted on it in the service of our civilization. Only by experimentation can we open up new possibilities which will indicate lines of development in which the status quo is a given term. Women's revolution is necessarily situationist: we cannot argue that all will be well when the socialists have succeeded in abolishing private property and restoring public ownership of the means of production. We cannot wait that long. Women's liberation, if it abolishes the patriarchal family, will abolish a necessary substructure of the authoritarian state, and once that withers away Marx will have come true willy-nilly, so let's get on with it. Let the men distribute leaflets in factories where the proletariat have become hire-purchase slaves instead of communists. The existence of hire-purchase slaves is also based upon the function of the wife as a stay-at-home consumer. Statistics show that almost all hire-purchase contracts are entered into by married people. If women revolt, that situation must change too. Women represent the most oppressed class of life-contracted unpaid workers, for whom slaves is not too melodramatic a description. They are the only true proletariat left, and they are by a tiny margin the majority of the population, so what's stopping them? The answer must be made, that their very oppression stands in the way of their combining to form any kind of solid group which can challenge the masters. But man made one grave mistake: in answer to vaguely reformist and humanitarian agitation he admitted women to politics and the professions. The conservatives who saw this as the undermining of our civilization and the end of the state and marriage were right after all; it is time for the demolition to begin. We need not challenge anyone to open battle, for the most effective method is simply to withdraw our cooperation in building up a system which oppresses us, the valid withdrawal of our labor. We may also agitate hither and thither, picket segregated bars and beauty competitions, serve on committees, invade the media, do, in short, what we want, but we must also refuse, not only to do some things, but to want to do them.

[*The Female Eunuch* (New York: Bantam Books, 1971), 337–8, 350–1.]

A Sandstone-like enclave in Robert Park in a tiny Sonoma valley north of San Francisco, the More House commune was an offspring of Jeff Poland's near legendary Sexual Freedom League devoted to free love. Here, by 1975, eighty-five men, women, and children sought to live together in complete, radical sexual freedom, or anarchy. Members believed they were sexual gods, choosing fantasies that other members went out of their way to fulfill. A bulletin board featured erotic want lists. Typical: 'I want: (1) A new Cadillac. (2) A blow job three times a day. (3) A night with Sally and Sue. (4) A gold-plated revolver to wear with my new cowboy suit.'

Beneath the adolescent veneer, however, lurked an alluring hypothesis. The commune's origins went back to the summer of 1968, when Victor Branco, a middle-aged refrigerator salesman turned acid freak, founded an organization called the Institute of Human Abilities, housed in a formerly condemned nine-bedroom Victorian mansion in downtown Oakland. LSD had convinced Branco he was a god. Like Reich, he was also convinced that full orgasmic release was the key to happiness and financial success. He called his philosophy 'more' and taught people how they, too, could become gods, enjoying all the sex they had ever wanted and earning lots of money in the process.

In the loopy, LSD-saturated fringes of the West Coast, this gospel found an instant following. Branco became immensely successful, bought a mansion in the Oakland hills and a Cadillac limousine, surrounded himself with female devotees, and by 1975 had receded like a sultan into semiretirement.

One of his disciples, though, a man named Patty Matlock, expanded Branco's philosophical concept into a way of life. In 1970 he founded More House, which in only five years became one of the most stable and financially successful sex communes in the world—and also, perhaps not so coincidentally, by far the most radical. Reality, in the More House philosophy, was merely a matter of social agreement.

The commune consisted of four main dormitories, each with its own dining room, kitchen, and house parents. It supported itself through sexuality courses that members offered to outsiders and through a salvage business tearing down old barns and reselling the wood and hardware. Most of the adults were married, as More House was not opposed to marriage—only monogamy.

An obese forty-four-year-old who bore a passing resemblance to Colonel Sanders, Matlock himself was married to a fifteen-year-old named Robin. His greatest inspiration was to study the works of Masters and Johnson and work out in practice the most efficient way for a man and woman to have the most intense possible orgasms. Armed with Masters and Johnson's discovery of the clitoral orgasm, and their finding that only the outer third of the vaginal barrel contained erotically responsive nerve endings, he declared intercourse an inefficient method of obtaining pleasure; oral sex was it. The logical More House conclusion: not *we* do, but *you* do, or *you* are done. Sucking, not fucking, was the watchword.

Matlock also took Masters and Johnson's squeeze technique for men and expanded it to a practice called stroking: an alternating sequence of light manual masturbation, licking, and squeezing to defer orgasm and build up tension, until finally climax was permitted. Masters and Johnson had found that the average male orgasm contained four to six contractions; but at More House, by squeezing, the orgasm could be continued indefinitely. One member claimed to have experienced an orgasm lasting up to twenty minutes, with up to four hundred contractions—a record the group was inordinately proud of.

For women the process leading to orgasm began with a light teasing massage of the clitoris called tumescing, followed by gentle licking, with the person performing cunnilingus elongating the orgasm by stopping and changing rhythm at peak points. Girls as young as seven were taught how to masturbate, using plaster models of vaginas to show them just where to touch.

Matlock and his followers taught these and other theories at regular weekend seminars that all members and guests were obliged to attend. Women were encouraged to be the aggressors. Members practiced an art called hexing: forcing a person to face his or her negative self-projection to the breaking point, then revealing how good they were and how worthy of praise. Sex was both bait and reward, withheld until the person being harried projected herself or himself as a god.

Later More House expanded to at least three northern California communes. Basic Sensuality was an explicit course based on Masters and Johnson's explanation of the human sexual response cycle and the personal observations and experimentation of Sue and Victor Branco. Techniques included peaking, pushouts, and pull-ups to expand and intensify orgasms. A pushout was a technique to deepen an orgasm by expanding (as opposed to contracting) pelvic muscles and directing pressure out on the genitals at the moment of orgasm to engender greater bliss. The More House alternative lifestyle experiment officially ended in the mid-seventies. In 1978 More University was founded in the town of Lafayette, California, where the teachings continue in greatly modified form.

The common denominator—and inherent error—of More House, Sandstone, and other California sex communes was their simplistic ideal that an inhibition-free sexuality was the solution to all societal and individual problems. Their doctrines urged sexual overachievement and discouraged contentment, tantalizing people with illusions of perfect orgasms and preaching the paramount importance of sex. Only a very few sexual pioneers were exploring the notion that freedom of sexual expression, while fundamental to a person's growth and identity, was ultimately a search for love.

[*What Wild Ecstasy: The Rise and Fall of the Sexual Revolution* (New York: Simon & Schuster, 1997), 178–80.]

The cigar-chomping producer from Hollywood was 'hiding out' in Mayfair. 'I've just produced a flop,' he said. Until then, Judd Benarr had been flying high with a credit on an Elvis Presley vehicle, *Double Trouble*. 'But then I had a brainwave, Godamnit.' Judd splashed bourbon on to ice and recounted the recent disaster—a Western set in England, with Terence Stamp playing John Wayne. It was called *Blue*. But Judd's latest idea was bluer. Appetite whetted by the reviews of *Playpower*, he had wheedled me to this office-in-exile with the promise of a 'no-holds barred docudrama' based on my book. It was March 1970.

'I've just bought the rights to a sex fair in Denmark,' he said. 'Mix it up with your stuff and we've got a smash. You're my main man.' The sex fair started in a week. So far, he had no cast, no director, no crew, no script.

'Don't you get it, Dick? It's hip, it's hot. A big screen smash about the clash of sexual attitudes between the flower kids of today and the power creeps of yesterday.'

It seemed dubious. But this sex fair was a world first and the one thing he did have was financial backing. 'Give me the number of your agent,' he barked.

Days later I was flying to Copenhagen, 'sex capital of Europe', with the hastily signed director, Tony Palmer, former producer of *How It Is*. Three members of the Living Theatre had joined the cast, as well as a *Penthouse* pet.

The spruced-up inhabitants of this fairytale city showed no visible scars at the plethora of porn, but what lay under the surface? The first day's shoot was in Palmer's hotel suite. I was to interview a leading Danish sociologist, Professor Yurngst, a slight man in a houndstooth suit. The professor sat on a stiff-backed chair and marshalled the usual arguments against censorship, while I played devil's advocate. A woman from the Living Theatre, Jenny, snaked slowly across the carpet to the foot of his chair. I remembered her performance in *Paradise Now* at the Roundhouse, when she was naked and spit-soaked. The cameras rolling, she unbuttoned the fly of the professor, who had not been forewarned. Yurngst continued to unravel the theories of Wilhelm Reich—that sexual repression leads to violence—which he bolstered with statistics showing that sex crimes had declined since the abolition of censorship. Jenny embarked on a vigorous fellatio. Apart from the beads of sweat on his eyelids and the erratic intakes of breath, Yurngst's manner was valiantly professional. His eyes remained camera-glued. Jenny's lips remained fluid. In the midst of a dissertation on Freud and the libido, the prof suddenly jerked in his chair and let out a couple of gasps. 'Cut,' shouted Tony Palmer, immensely pleased.

I was pleased, too. We were the cutting edge of the sex revolution, slashing away at the media, academia, everyday life. This action proved something of vital importance, but, for the life of me, I can't recall what it was.

By chance, we met the British morals campaigner, Mary Whitehouse, in the lobby, after our camera crews collided. She had come to Copenhagen to decry the abolition of censorship. Our encounter was civil, even warm. The single-mindedness of Mrs Whitehouse was impressive, as was her willingness to flout the turning tide, but her agenda was mad and dangerous. In the bar after dinner, a producer from her doco crew, *World in Action*, was asking around for strong sleeping pills.

'Not for me,' he confided, 'it's to spike Mary's Ovaltine.' The boys from ITV were dying to sample the nightlife of Copenhagen, but didn't dare leave the hotel until she was sleeping soundly.

I caught up with Alex Popov, now married to Lin Utzon, with two children and studying architecture; then flew to Odense, the birthplace of Hans Christian Andersen.It was also the site of the fair, Sex-for-Millions, which had been officially opened by a seventy-one-year-old Danish feminist, Fanny Miranda, who described herself as a sexual suffragette. The pre-fab pavilions offered continuous blue movies and a range of the latest sex toys. Inside a cage labelled Marquis de Sade and decorated with instruments of torture, Super 8 scenes of S&M were projected on to a fake TV screen. All around the marquee, mammoth murals depicted close-ups of intercourse, not only among humans. Nude go-go girls gyrated down catwalks, and blue-rinsed ladies passed out creamy pastries and porno magazines. Visitors with enquiries were assisted by uniformed Girl Guides.

In the main arena, two women entered a makeshift stage and took off their clothes. The speakers blared. 'There will now be a demonstration of public fucking.' The women arranged themselves on a heap of mattresses as two men shambled onstage in socks and smoking jackets, like villains from a Victorian music hall. In a leaden rhythm, the couples copulated. On cue, Jenny and her Living Theatre guerrillas threw their clothes into the air and sprang to the mattresses. They caressed the sullen performers, stroked them, kissed them, chanted OM. It was the clash of two kinds of sexual revolution, I realised, one motivated by mammon, the other by spirit. The impresario rushed on stage and bellowed at the hired hands, who disentangled themselves and disappeared. Jenny arose serenely, Venus in a dosshouse. 'When you make a sexual revolution, make it for love,' she told the crowd, quoting D.H. Lawrence. 'If you can't make it for love, make it for fun.' And then, maintaining her perfect poise, she put on her clothes. Sex-for-Millions, as it turned out, was liberation for no one; a trading of human flesh, which borrowed the hippie slogans of freedom and ran like a sweatshop.

[*Hippie Hippie Shake: The Dreams, the Trips, the Trials, the Love-ins, the Screw Ups ... The Sixties* (London: Bloomsbury, 1995), 189–92.]

For two years women have been saying to me, 'I hear you're writing a book. What's it about?' I would reply, 'the sexual revolution.' And then it would come—archly, provocatively, sadly or with a world-weary *moue* of disillusion, 'Really? Has there *been* a sexual revolution?' For the first few months this perplexed me. I could be standing there talking to a 38-year-old lawyer, who had lived with her partner for ten years and was just about to have her first child (with benefit of nanny, cleaning lady and nursery), and she would still say, 'Has there *been* a sexual revolution?'

I had my facts. Did she realize that until the mid-1960s it was virtually impossible for a single woman to furnish herself with birth control? That in some British family planning clinics, where contraception would be prescribed to the engaged, the receipt for the wedding dress was required as proof that the applicant was free from intentions of immorality? That until the licensing of the Pill in 1960, it was men who took charge of contraception? Did she not remember the burden that virginity placed on girls, who had to be permanently vigilant against its accidental loss or theft? That premarital sex led, invariably, to pregnancy? That landlords would not rent to unmarried couples? That abortion and homosexuality were illegal and the divorce laws trapped people in violent or loveless marriage? That there was no sexual persona for the post-nubile single woman? That women married or had a career, but if they did the latter they would be sexless, repressed—spinsters who, by implication, no man wanted or loved?

It was a smug litany and irrefutable. It silenced any listener. And yet, they said. And yet. They had expected more. A sexual revolution which had eroticized women's lives and given them solid (and hard-won) liberties had somehow failed them, none the less. Sexual freedom had once been the shape of their dreams. The idea of the future has been a controlling metaphor for this century, for modernism. For women born in the last fifty years, the sexual revolution had the same meanings as the Russian Revolution held for a generation of socialists. It promised to demolish the old socio-sexual order of women servicing men's physical needs, with little hope or even knowledge that their own could be fulfilled. It would be an egalitarian answer to the old double standard. But the sexual revolution had turned out to be a history of radical ideas repackaged for the mass market, co-opted by the sex industry and tabloid newspapers. For many women there had been only a betrayal. If anyone had benefited, it was men, it was often asserted. Where before there had existed a restraining morality which put wives, mothers, virgins and children off-limits, a double standard which could work in women's favour, now all women were fair game.

If there had been a sexual revolution, why did women still fear rape whenever they stepped outside the house? Where was the totally safe, totally effective birth control we had been promised? How could teenage girls who slept with their boyfriends stop being called sluts by their friends? Why did men still leave skid marks when a woman made the running? Where were all the thirtysomething men for the thirtysomething women to have sex with? Why was abortion still under threat? Why was there a multi-million-dollar silicone breast implant industry—if women and men were sexually equal, why did women feel such anxiety about their attractiveness? And if women were so free, so liberated, so unbuttoned-up about lust, why did the top-shelf magazines with their pneumatic bimbettes make them feel so uncomfortable? Why were they on the side of censorship in this matter and no other? *Why* had female desire not transformed the world?

[*Sexing the Millennium: A Political History of the Sexual Revolution* (London: Harper Collins, 1993), 1–2.]

SHEILA JEFFREYS

132 The Sexual Revolution Was for Men

The sexual revolutionaries of the 1960s set themselves the task of reconstructing western morality. The sex reform movement of the early twentieth century and particularly the 1920s saw itself as sweeping away the fog of Victorian morality which had decreed that sex was shameful and to be hidden. The sex reformers stated that sex was positive and to be enjoyed. The 1960s sexual revolutionaries saw themselves as having pretty much the same mission. The earlier onslaught on Victorianism had clearly not been successful. Who had stood in the way of the progress of sexual enlightenment? Women. As women in the first wave of sex reform were seen as slow to appreciate the joys of sexual intercourse with men, if not mainly frigid, so 1960s woman was seen as the fly in the ointment of sexual progress. [...]

The sexual revolution completed the sexualisation of women. Both married and unmarried women were expected now to become experts in sexually servicing men, and to get over their own tastes and interests in order to become efficient at this task. Where once a large group of single women might have escaped the destiny of servicing men and concentrated upon their own life work, they were now conscripted into compulsory heterosexuality. That group of women who retained primary ties with women and refused their new role were labelled lesbians. The spinster disappeared. The spinster, whether she sexualised her relationships with other women or not, had been able to live a reasonably independent life, free from the scrutiny and management of the sex regulators. Now there were no spinsters. Single women were divided into lesbians and active heterosexuals. Sexual activity was mandatory and backsliding was unforgivable.

The sexual revolution was heterosexual. Even the most progressive of sex-advice writers was unable to conceive of homosexuality in women or men as a reasonable alternative to heterosexuality. Sexual liberals like the Hegelers tried hard to be non-judgmental about homosexuality and devoted a good few pages to the issue in the *ABZ of Love*. They saw homosexuals as worthy of tolerant understanding and as having the right to a sexual life. It would have been difficult to take a different line when they were liberal about everything else from paedophilia to necrophilia. But Alex Comfort, self-proclaimed sex radical, remained unaffected by this liberal urge, though he too waxed enthusiastic about group sex, anal sex and many other activities which carried serious taboos. He claimed to cover all varieties of sexual behavior in *The Joy of Sex* but did not include homosexuality. He has a section on 'bisexuality' which positively warns readers not to treat sex with their own gender as anything other than a way to jazz up their heterosexual relationships. [...]

When we look in detail at the practices described, it becomes clear that women, in particular, have very good reason to be anxious. Women's anxiety is not just some unnecessary vestige of a past morality but a realistic response to most, if not all the practices and ideas about sex in this book. *The Joy of Sex* shows women to be rather unregenerately 'Victorian' in attitude to sex, never quite catching up to what is modern. Women's backwardness was the problem in all sexual-revolution advice literature. In such literature a range of practices was being normalised which women were seen as having particular problems with. Women are instructed on how to find the taste of semen pleasant lest they feel reluctant to let men ejaculate in their mouths, how to delight in being tied up, how to enjoy being spanked and anal intercourse. Not surprisingly it is women, not men, who have resistance to such practices and need reprogramming. This literature instructs women to turn themselves into willing and enthusiastic sexual objects and servicers of male sexuality even to the detriment of their health, pride and self-respect. Women are told in *The Joy of Sex* that they should cheerfully accept every variant form of sexual interest or fantasy that their male partner might suggest and act it out joyfully. The woman should be joyful even though the fantasies consist of degrading and humiliating her. [...]

The section on women's sexuality, then, turns out to be an apology for inadequacy, together with some instructions for men on what not to do and what would be absolutely gross. Men are not instructed in what women's sexuality inevitably is because, fortuitously, women 'can be less rigid and more experimental'. Men are told that women will adapt. They are not told to learn female sexual response. Men are told to help women to please them.

The dramatic difference between these two sections reveals the real purpose of the book. It is a handbook which will teach women their new role in the sexual revolution, the servicing of male sexuality actively and not just passively.

[*Anticlimax: A Feminist Perspective on the Sexual Revolution* (Washington Square, NY: New York University Press, 1990), 94, 110–11, 116–17, 120.]

IV.d Coming Out

There were various ways that the sexually adventuresome 1960s and 1970s encouraged the process by which men and women with homosexual tastes proclaimed themselves lesbian or gay and presented themselves to one another and the world. First, despite loud contemporary resistance to any and all departures from standard heterogenital sexuality, there is no doubting a growing public tolerance for various forms of sexual nonconformity. The enormous publicity given to the music, politics, and dress of the era's boisterous youth culture left little doubt about the challenges it posed to sexual norms. Second, in consonance with efforts to eliminate some of the most egregious legal race discrimination, campaigns for legal reform of sodomy and 'public decency' laws were begun throughout Europe and North America, one of the most dramatic being the British Sexual Offences Act of 1967 that effectively decriminalized consensual male homosexual relations. Third, after suffering years of official and informal harassment, some homosexual activists discovered the virtues of active civil disobedience and adopted some of the organizational techniques of antidiscrimination, free speech, and anti-war protesters. The process of 'coming out' was both long in preparation and sudden, sexual and political, exhilarating and sobering.

In Great Britain, one of the great watersheds in homosexual history had been the trials and condemnation of the great Irish writer Oscar Wilde in 1895. Wilde's jail sentence of two years at hard labour broke him physically, shortened his life, and destroyed his career. This event provided ample proof, if any were needed, that the establishment would not tolerate the sort of flamboyant and contentious behaviour for which Wilde was well known. Homosexuals in both Britain and France (where Wilde had several acquaintances) learned circumspection from this and subsequent convictions. The Criminal Law Amendment Act of 1885 under which Wilde was convicted punished public or private sexual relations between two males as 'gross indecency'. The law was variously enforced but still on the books when a parliamentary committee chaired by Sir John Wolfenden produced a parliamentary report in 1957 recommending decriminalization of private adult homosexuality. A Homosexual Law Reform Society then took up the cause, resulting in the law of 1967. The historian Jeffrey Weeks discusses how the law emboldened homosexuals both to live more publicly and to organize on their own behalf (Extract 133).

'Coming out' occurred more explosively in the USA. Despite the growth of large and diverse homosexual communities in some large American cities, and the occasional outspokenness of some gay literary figures like Gore Vidal, Allen Ginsberg, and James Baldwin, there were no prominent legal reform movements at the state or national levels and no visible discourse of tolerance.

On a hot summer night in June of 1969, a police raid on the Stonewall bar in

New York City provoked resistance from its gay clientele. Violence, and several nights of rioting in the largely gay neighbourhood, followed. 'Stonewall' quickly became a reference point of great importance to gay activists, initiating a number of openly confrontational organizations, 'Gay Pride' marches, and protests during the 1970s. The suddenness of the transition into political activism produced generational fault-lines within homosexual communities. One of the oldest lesbian communities in the USA in the mid-twentieth century was located in Buffalo, New York; from the 1930s into the 1970s lesbians gathered more or less openly in particular bars to meet and socialize with other women. A 'butch–fem' bonding model generally prevailed and lesbian relationships in the period might be characterized as 'serial monogamy'. After 'Stonewall' younger lesbians were radicalized; many joined women's organizations or other activist groups. It left some of the older women feeling a bit estranged and resentful, as Elizabeth Lapovsy Kennedy and Madeline D. Davis explain in a book based on extensive interviews. They explain how the meaning of 'coming out' has changed with the generations (Extract 134).

In a similar way, the anthropologist Gilbert Herdt has studied the different generational meanings of 'coming out' that succeeded one another in the Chicago gay community between 1930 or so and the present. It was in the homosexual bars of that town that Alfred Kinsey gathered data (and personal experience) about homosexuality. As Herdt points out, four different generational cohorts may be identified, each with its own meaning of 'identity' culminating in the most recent, which resembles the ethnographer's classic 'rite of passage'. With this latest development we seem to be at the apogee of the contemporary notion of sexuality as identity, felt by and reaffirmed by a nurturing community (Extract 135).

The sexual life of the pre-AIDS, post-Stonewall gay community might be said to be a more or less self-conscious effort to overturn the hoary stereotypes of gay men as effeminate, timid, and sexually languid. The most extreme example of such behaviour during the liberated 1970s was manifested by the so-called gay 'clone', hyper-masculine young men who revelled in multiple partners, drugs, and exotic sex. A sociological study of the gay community in New York's West Village done between 1977 and 1984 focused on the inversion of the usual stereotypes that occurred in those years. This behaviour was not typical of homosexual sexuality at this or any other time, but it was the most visible behaviour, and became, for good or ill, a kind of synecdoche for gay sex in general (Extract 136).

Despite its reluctance to appeal directly to the homosexual community, the work of the society did, almost despite itself, act as a stimulus to homosexual self-organization. This tendency was accentuated by the changes in the law. Towards the end of the 1960s Michael Schofield was asked:

'Has the law reform here changed much in people's lives?'

'No. It has changed things only a little. But I think it was vital and it opens the door to serious change in the future.'[1] [...]

This fear of public opinion, and the deep internalization of guilt and secrecy, had a corrosive effect on people's lives. The existence of support groups, however conservative and tiny, has therefore had an important impact. As a result of these many found that their sense of identity and self-esteem had been immeasurably strengthened. This was an important first step. It would take the re-emergence of the women's movement and the development of the Gay Liberation Movement in the 1970s to carry the issue further.

For men, at least superficially, there were more obvious signs of a breaking of the ice-pack in the late 1960s. London, in particular, saw the appearance of a new type of gay club, supplementing the older established clubs and pubs which had for a long time acted as sexual market-places as well as social centres. Peter Wildeblood described a typical club of the early 1950s, its contours shaped by the harsh winds outside.

The clubs where they congregated usually consisted of one room, with a bar and a piano. They were extraordinarily quiet and well-behaved. The clubs closed at 11 o'clock, and most of the men did not go there primarily to drink, but to relax in an atmosphere where it was not necessary to keep up pretences.[2]

Discretion, however, was the rule, as clubs could easily be raided and reputations ruined. By the 1960s there was a slightly more relaxed atmosphere, with the growth of discothèque-type clubs with pop music and dancing (as long as the men did not touch each other). There was often a close integration between the swinging scene and the homosexual world. Many of the youths who worked or shopped in the trendy boutiques of Carnaby Street or the King's Road, Chelsea, might be seen, in the height of fashion, at the new gay bars in the evenings.[3] The magazines that began to appear at the very end of the 1960s, such as *Timm*, *Spartacus* or *Jeremy*, reflected this new affluence and a muted openness, though there were subtle differences in emphasis. *Spartacus*, edited from Brighton by John D. Stanford, had a mixture of features on the gay scene, jokey poems, contact ads ('Trading Post'), correspondence about sex problems, a travel service with package tours to Holland and Denmark, helpful articles on the law or venereal disease, and an occasional moralism: 'Soliciting in public lavatories is perhaps the greatest blight on the homophile community.'⁴ But the mainstay was the slightly risqué, discreetly naked pics that were the chief protein of the audience. After a court case in 1971, the magazine collapsed amid much recrimination, and Stanford retired to Amsterdam, where he began a highly successful and lucrative guide to the international gay world.

Jeremy, which folded before *Spartacus*, was trendier (published from the Carnaby Street area) and glossier. The boys in the photographs were younger, and there was more emphasis on high fashion. Articles wove a web of excitement around new clothes, travel and sexual success. There were special offers of flimsy underpants, *Jeremy* 'fundies', and support badges ('Get down to it with Jeremy!'). Stills from 'gay' movies, such as Fellini's *Satyricon* or the film of Gore Vidal's *Myra Breckinridge*, were featured. There was an agony column ('Hangups''), which revealed less than liberated views: a married man who confessed to homosexual feelings was told to consult his doctor. Overwhelmingly, the magazine was, like *Spartacus*, male-orientated and it was geared to a special type of male: young, pretty, fashionable, affluent (or those who fancied the same). Inevitably it ignored the vast majority of homosexuals who were none of these things. It reflected more than anything the initial penetration in the homosexual subculture of the consumer values of the wider society. [...]

The early 1970s mark the turning-point in the evolution of a homosexual consciousness. The homophile organizations that tiptoed through the liberal 1960s were superseded in the 1970s by a new type of movement which stressed openness, defiance, pride, identity—and, above all, self-activity.

Last time it was done by an elite, who did it by stealth. They didn't have demonstrations in Trafalgar Square. This time it has to be done by us, brothers and sisters.⁵

Of this new movement, the Gay Liberation Front (GLF), which sprang up in London in the autumn of 1970, was the most typical and dynamic representative. By the middle of the decade, though the name lingered on, the GLF had become a nostalgic memory for most of its participants, and a bogeyman for its opponents. But for a time it seemed to many homosexuals that a new day was dawning, ushering in an era of spontaneity, openness and liberation: 'There was, I believe, a general belief among the people who made up the gay movement that we were at the beginning of an historic wave; we were on the crest and it was about to surge forward.'⁶

Although the promise was illusory and only a minority of gay people were directly affected even in the early days, the effect of the movement that the GLF triggered off was deep *and* liberating. It extended the vista for homosexuals in such a way that the homosexual identity, and society's attitudes towards homosexuality, could never be quite the same again. Which is why this chapter concentrates on the Gay Liberation Front, short-lived as it was, and in particular the

London grouping, for in its 'rise and fall' is writ in microcosm the history of a particular, and special, type of movement.

The GLF from the first defined itself as a 'revolutionary organization'. What was new about this was the consequential stress on homosexuality as a political issue. With this came a new emphasis on the oppression of gay people, a belief that the taboo against homosexuality was so deeply embodied in Western civilization (the 'Judaeo-Christian culture') that only a revolutionary overthrow of its structures could truly liberate the homosexual. Furthermore, this could not be done by others *for* the homosexual, but only by homosexuals themselves, acting openly and together. The choice of name, Gay Liberation Front, carries in each word the peculiar flavour of the period, its militancy, its millenarian hopes and its radical aspirations. And it carries, too, the movement's inspiration in a particular American political development.

The gay liberation movement developed in the United States out of the cauldron of revolutionary hopes released in and around the nodal year of 1968. For radicalized youth, and for jaded, middle-aged revolutionaries, 1968 lit a beacon of hope that the idea of revolution had not died in the West. The May events in Paris, the Tet offensive of the Vietnamese against American imperialism, the world-wide revulsion against the excesses of American foreign policy, the enforced abdication of President Johnson, the 'Prague Spring' in Czechoslovakia, the new wave of student militancy in universities across the world, from Britain and Western Europe to Japan; all this, and the 'revolution of the spirit', symbolized in the 'youth movement' by rock music, mass open-air concerts (prefiguring, as Richard Gott suggested in a moment of ecstasy, the communalism of the socialist future), the new freedom and openness about sex: for many it seemed as if the structures of capitalism were already crumbling beneath the new music and being consigned to the junk-yard of history.

Even by the end of the year a more sombre assessment had to be made. Russian tanks in Czechoslovakia and the election of Richard Nixon to the US presidency showed that reaction was not dead, and the long post-war boom that was the material basis for the new youth culture was showing signs of acute instability, bringing with it a new conservatism. But a large part of a generation had been radicalized by 1968, and for the next half-decade the amorphous phenomenon known as 'The Movement' was the carrier of radical ideas in the United States. GLF, which crystallized in America in 1969, immediately identified itself as part of the 'The Movement', claiming solidarity with other oppressed groups, and totally rejecting—at least on a verbal level—compromise with bourgeois society. 'Choosing homosexuality is in itself an act of rebellion, a revolutionary stance.'[7] The choice of the name thus represented a conscious association with other self-defined revolutionary struggles, and particularly the struggles of oppressed nationalities in Asia and Africa, and the blacks in America. 'Black power' was the model for 'gay power', however misleading the comparison. In the London GLF the catch-phrase, 'This is a Gay Liberation *Front*' (with the displaced stress somehow symbolic), was sufficient to still all liberal dissenters who might feel the movement to be too radical or confrontationist. The name was the surest touchstone of GLF's radical intent.

But 'The Movement' was not just—or perhaps at this stage was only very little—about external political change. It was supremely about personal liberation. The Women's Liberation movement, which sprang up parallel with 'The Movement', indicated that profound changes in the nature of sex roles and sexual attitudes were on the agenda, and provided an inspiration for the gay movement, both in method ('consciousness raising' became an important part of the gay movement in the United States and Britain) and in ideas. Gays, like ethnic minorities and women, began to reject the stereotypes that society thrust on them: 'Chick equals nigger equals queer.' Militant homosexuals intended to smash the caricatures and to 'become themselves'.

But if the political tone came from the amorphous radical movement, its style and emotional flavour came from an association with the counter-culture.

A major dynamic of rising gay lib sentiment is the hip revolution within the gay community. Emphasis on love, dropping out, being honest, expressing yourself through hair and clothes, and smoking dope are all attributes of this.[8]

[*Coming Out: Homosexual Politics in Britain from the Nineteenth Century to the Present* (London: Quartet Books, 1990), 177–8, 179–81, 185–7.]

ELIZABETH LAPOVSKY KENNEDY AND MADELINE D. DAVIS

134   **Lesbian Generations**

Sandy, whose leadership was undisputed in this period still carries great bitterness with her as the legacy of this struggle to build a lesbian life.

'You know it pisses you off, because like today, everything is so open and accepted and equal. Women, everyone goes to where they wear slacks, and I could just kick myself in the ass, because all the opportunities I had that I had to let go because of my way. That if I was able to dress the way I wanted and everything like that I, Christ, I'd have it made, really. Makes you sick. And you look at the young people today that are gay and they're financially well-off, they got tremendous jobs, something that we couldn't take advantage of, couldn't have it. It leaves you with a lot of bitterness too. I don't go around to the gay bars much any more. It's not jealousy, it's bitterness. And I see these young people, doesn't matter which way they go, whatever the mood suits them, got tremendous jobs, and you just look at them, you know, they're happy kids, no problems. You say "God damn it, why couldn't I have that?" And you actually get bitter, you don't even want to know them. I don't anyway. 'Cause I don't want to hear about it, don't tell me about your success. Like we were talking about archives, you know where mine is, scratched on a shit-house wall, that's where it is. And all the dives in Buffalo that are still standing with my name. That's it, that's all I got to show.'

The complex culture of resistance in the public lesbian communities of the 1950s and early 1960s provided a heritage from which gay liberation could draw. Although in its youth gay liberation did not have a sense of the past, and therefore did not consciously draw on what had existed before, its ideas were likely influenced by the bar communities. In turn the bar communities provided an environment conducive to igniting a mass movement. And in cities such as Buffalo, members of the bar community formed political organizations at about the same time as the Stonewall Rebellion that became active in the gay liberation movement. In fact visibility, standing up for one's rights, and ending the double life were core issues for both the tough lesbians and gay liberation, though they approached them differently.[1] The prepolitical tactics of the tough lesbians were immediate, spontaneous, and personal. They lacked gay liberation's long-term analysis of and strategy for ending the oppression of gays and lesbians in America and changing the world.

The similarities and differences between the politics of these overtly butch–fem communities and that of gay liberation can be seen in the somewhat ambivalent relationship the Black and white tough lesbians had to the founding of the Mattachine Society of the Niagara Frontier (M.S.N.F.) in which many of them participated. Many narrators felt that M.S.N.F. did not have much new to offer them because they had already achieved visibility and had asserted the right to be themselves. Matty joined M.S.N.F., at first thinking it was a good idea, and then withdrew. She remembers going to a picnic at Madeline's house and being offended by a member of Mattachine's comments about people who thought they were too good for Mattachine.

'"It isn't that we think that we're too good, you have nothing to offer us." And so she [a Mattachine member] said, "What do you mean we have nothing to offer?" I said, "Well, you tell me what you really want and what you're really fighting for, and if you're fighting for something that I don't already have I'll gladly pay another year's dues and get in." She said, "We're fighting to be able to work where you want to." I said, "I work where I want to." She said, "To be able to live where you want to without harassment." I said, "I live where I want to without harassment." You know, "To be able to have your neighbors know what you are and not have them," ... I said, "My neighbors know what I am."'

Jodi expresses similar feelings about how little Mattachine had to offer.

'In terms of how I've lived my life it [gay liberation] really did nothing actually, it's almost zip for me because I was never in the closet. And wherever I went I looked like this and every job I ever got I went like this, and I went to school like this. I got my present job looking like this. I go to work now looking like this, I mean there's some compromises I will not make, no matter what.'

Gay liberation took the offensive so that image was no longer the sole expression of lesbianism. Speech became paramount; visibility became more than the individual person's presentation of self. Gay liberation pursued publicity about gays on TV and in newspapers and organized demonstrations and marches. These new elements of visibility made some narrators uncomfort-able. Even though they were used to being known for who they were, they were hesitant about broader publicity. They didn't feel the necessity of pushing bey-ond individual politics to TV appearances or marches. As a result, many narra-tors had mixed feelings about the tactics of M.S.N.F., as was the case of Matty who withdrew from the organization.

'The only thing I could see is every time I picked up the paper they were in trouble. At that time I don't know if they were all affiliated with the Mattachine, but they were all gung ho on the "let's put on a sign I'm a lesbian and if you don't like it you can just," you know, "take it wherever you want to and march down the street." To me that wasn't get-ting the right thing. It isn't that I wasn't interested in what they were trying to do be-cause I was very interested in what they were trying to do.'

A key element in the new forms of visibility was the explicit discussion of les-bianism with the heterosexual world, including the appropriation and transfor-mation of derogatory words like 'dyke' and 'queer.' Narrators of the 1950s asserted their lesbianism through appearance alone. Although they had words to describe their distinct identity, they did not usually talk about who they were to the heterosexual world, especially to the media. The topics of lesbianism and homosexuality, and the words themselves, did not become part of common conversations until gay liberation. 'I get along with people and with neighbors. I don't hide what I am but I don't walk around with a sign on my back. Every-body knows that sign, if they don't know, it doesn't bother me one way or the other. My whole family knows and all our neighbors, mostly everyone knows' (Matty). Bert explains that hostility and oppression kept them from telling people. 'I had never heard the terms [coming out, closets]. No, no. You didn't go around telling people that you preferred women instead of men, 'cause you were afraid of the oppression, how you'd become ostracized.'

Narrators disagree about whether the expression 'coming out' was used in Buffalo before gay liberation. However, those who remember using it indicate that its meaning was significantly different from today. Today it means telling others that you are lesbian or gay, then it meant having a first sexual relationship with a woman, or recognizing in oneself the desire for such a relationship. The narrators who are sure that they did not use 'coming out' focus on the contem-porary political meaning.[2] Several narrators agree with Bert's view, that al-though being seen by straights at the Carousel was like coming out, she never thought of it that way. 'I guess it's sort of like coming out, in a way you're com-ing out to the people that came in [to the Carousel]. And we didn't even know about coming out. We didn't even know about closets in those days. That we felt more comfortable, you know, one more person knew you and accepted you.' In her mind, coming out is about consciously and explicitly sharing one's lesbianism with the heterosexual world. It is a political process in which she did not engage until the 1970s.

'My real coming out probably in my life was [out West] after the civil-rights rally. I was going to … [a] community college, and I became aware that I had gotten caught up in a life of where I associated with nothing but gay people. So of course I was comfortable with my gayness. And in sociology class one day, we were broken up into groups to work on a project, and somehow one of the gay bars … came up, and the people were talking very freely. They didn't say "queer" though, you don't hear people using that word so much any more. And I all of a sudden realized that I was a minority and that they didn't think I was gay. So that human-rights rally made me so angry that I went back to all my classes and said [I was]. And nobody even reacted. I was totally shocked.'

Another key difference between the prepolitical forms of resistance and the politics of gay liberation was that gay liberation worked through organizations to accomplish social change. Although many narrators from the 1940s and 1950s became members of Mattachine, none of the bar-culture leaders became political leaders. Gay liberation captures the imagination of those who entered the community in the late 1950s at a young age. Ten years later, they went on to give their best energy to gay politics.

'I was involved first in the gay movement in '71. I guess I started with the Mattachine Society here in Buffalo. Being involved in gay liberation gave me some positive feelings about being gay, working with other gay people, not being just confined to the bars. We were doing something; we were trying to make some changes in the world, some changes in our immediate environment. We were all working together. It gave us a sense of ourselves as having some power of togetherness. And it wasn't centered around alcohol and partying. And we did, we did bring about some small changes in our very immediate environment, because of the work that we did.' (Toni)

In distinguishing the prepolitical forms of butch–fem culture from the politics of gay liberation, we do not mean to create an absolute division. In the 1950s bar culture there were many indications of different approaches to resistance, but the times did not allow them to coalesce into politics. Bert, for instance, who had decided she was going to relocate to Florida, was arrested during a raid on a bar in 1960, six months after her arrival. She wanted to fight the case but could not interest a lawyer: 'And I remember getting out, and I went to a lawyer … my civil rights were imposed upon, and he said, "Who do you think you're kidding?" He wouldn't even touch it. Which nowadays somebody would have.'

During this same time period, the cultural push to be identified as lesbians— or at least different—all the time was so powerful that it generated a new form of identification among the tough bar lesbians: a star tattoo on the top of the wrist, which was usually covered by a watch. This was the first symbol of community identity that did not rely on butch–fem imagery. We can trace this phenomenon back to an evening of revelry in the late 1950's, when a few butches trooped over to 'Dirty Dick's' tattoo parlor on Chippewa Street and had the tiny blue five-pointed star put on their wrists. Later, some of the fems of this group also got their stars. Bert thinks it was worn as a sign of defiance. Others claim they just got the idea one night and did it. The community views the tattoo as a definite mark of identification. Bert, who did not get the tattoo, experienced it as a dare: 'And they tried to get me to do it but I wouldn't do it, and the main thing that I can think of that held me back was because of the job that I had at the time. There was the pressure, worried about them finding out why.' She adds that one of her friends had told her: 'The Buffalo police knew [that] the people that had the stars on their wrists were lesbians, and they had their names and so forth. That it was an identity type thing with the gay community, with the lesbian community.'

The fact that the star tattoo was created by those who were firmly into roles, in fact, by the group that was considered the butchy butches and their fems, suggests that the force to assert lesbian identity was strong enough to break through the existing traditions of boldness based in butch–fem roles. The stars presage the methods of identity created by gay liberation. In fact, the mark has become something of a tradition in local circles and has seen a revival since the 1970s.

In contrast to the familiarity most narrators felt with the ideas of gay liberation, they thought that feminism offered something new and important. Some were particularly excited by it like Jodi who felt it opened up new ways for her to be in the world and realize her goals.

'Well it made me aware that I didn't have to do or be some ways to live my life how I choose to live my life, as far as being a lesbian. … I mostly changed how I dressed. Some people still think I'm a boy, what can I say? And I changed some attitudes, but I'm still who I am mostly. But those changes were positive changes, and hopefully I'll always be able to change. I'll always be flexible so that good things, I'll be able to incorporate in my life, and change so that I make many more of what I'd like to be.'

Ironically although lesbian feminists judged these traditional, role-defined butches and fems as an anathema to feminism, many butches, from years of claiming male privilege, and many butches and fems, from building their lives without men, were actively poised and ready to learn about feminism.

[*Boots of Leather, Slippers of Gold: The History of a Lesbian Community* (Harmondsworth:
Penguin Books, 1994), 186–90.]

GILBERT HERDT

135   'Coming Out' as a Rite of Passage

Historically, the secret world of the gay bar and covert social networks made homosexuality an individualized sort of puberty rite into a secret oppressed society. There was no manifest gay culture at the time. Today, the political power of the gay and lesbian community suggests that coming out is more of a collective initiation rite, a public coming-of-age status-adjustment transition into the adult gay community. The media accounts in *Time* magazine, for example, have trivialized coming out as an act of political protest, whereas social surveys have depersonalized it as a bundle of diffuse traits and states, the result of which is homosexual 'preference.'[1] Both these accounts do not fully grasp the contemporary context of gay culture. Humanistic and fictional accounts tend toward the opposite direction; they personalize the events as a self-affirmation of the person's desire to find the new identity. The emergence of coming-out groups in America and other Western cities today embodies coming out in real-life 'experience near' situations, affording unprecedented opportunity for ethnographic study.

The most recent and dramatic form of such emergent organizations is the adolescent coming-out group. Such groups meet regularly in major urban centers of the United States, including Chicago, New York, the San Francisco Bay Area, Minneapolis, and Seattle. Thus far, none have been intensively studied ethnographically, though an exploratory profile of the Chicago youth group begins to address the need for ethnography of coming out in the context of a gay community.[2]

This chapter examines these issues in the study of the Horizons coming-out group in Northside Chicago. Our interdisciplinary investigation of two hundred gay and lesbian adolescents (aged fourteen to twenty) is concerned with the construction of social reality and psychosocial adjustment not only in sexual orientation and behavior but also in gender, selfhood, and social relations in the gay and lesbian community. These youths' confrontation with stigma, discrimination, and self-hatred is a heroic feature of their 'unlearning' in American urban settings. Coming out once meant entry into a secret club of a hidden world, with socialization into its 'homosexual' cultural system, and the tavern was a pivotal social context. Today, Horizons permits adolescent entry first into a self-affirming semisecret group, then by collective socialization into a 'gay' cultural system, with new and open social relationships. To understand this change requires in turn a reconceptualization of 'homosexual' and 'gay' cultural systems.

Coming out must be placed in a particular historical and social field. Study of cultural change in the lesbian and gay movement reveals generational differences in coming-out experiences, despite the unfortunate tendency in the psychological literature to treat coming out as a uniform, ahistorical, stage-driven process. Our work in Chicago has pointed up the existence of four overlapping but distinct historical cohorts who have constructed coming out in different pathways of adjustment across cultural epochs.

The first cohort dates from the turn of the century to the 1930s. These persons, now in their late sixties and older, grew into adulthood and discovered their same-sex desires without typically ever having come out. Most of them remain largely invisible.[3]

The second cohort can be bounded roughly from World War II to 1969, the year of the famous Stonewall riot in New York. The members of this cohort, in their forties and older, recall the *communitas* of having been brought together under the turbulent circumstances of World War II, recognizing or fulfilling same-sex desires for the first time while serving in the armed services. As John D'Emilio has written, 'For men and women conscious of a strong attraction to their own sex but constrained by their milieu from acting upon it, the war years eased the coming out processes and facilitated entry into the gay world.'[4] Post-war changes, such as the founding of the Mattachine Society, gave way to heightened social dis-ease and activism in the late 1960s. Especially critical was the emergence of the gay tavern: 'The bars were seedbeds for a collective consciousness that might one day flower politically', a prophecy borne out.[5] Vacha reports many positive recollections among members of this generation.[6] These Chicagoans still experienced their homosexuality in largely negative terms, however; many remained closeted to avoid harassment, legal sanctions, and violence. Their coming out was late in life and difficult if it occurred at all. Many remain closeted today.

The third cohort came out in great numbers amid the activism of the 'sexual revolution' and the Gay Liberation Front, which saw the Stonewall riot as its watershed. The gay rights movement paralleled earlier civil rights movements[7] and found the most support among children of affluent middle-class families. For lesbians and gays now in their thirties and older who became gay identified after Stonewall, this riot is a symbolic marker: it marks the point at which the cloak of oppression was thrust off. The riots, in fact, are celebrated annually throughout the United States in late June as a cultural event—known as the Gay Pride Day Parade. What seems increasingly clear is that the males in this cohort inaugurated a gender role change as well, a new cult of manliness that rejected gender-inversion images of the past. Now people could live more openly as lesbian- or gay-identified adults, and they did so particularly in such urban gay 'ghettos' as Greenwich Village in New York or the Castro District in San Francisco. Social liberation, 'free love' bathhouse sexual intercourse, and its lusty male etiquette are highly associated with this 'golden age' of the third cohort. Social networks facilitated mass coming out. Nevertheless, these persons came out as individuals, their experience reflecting less the influence of self-affirming groups and more the vagaries of particular places and times. In Chicago, they did not generally have supportive coming-out groups, though by the mid- to late 1970s these became visible.

The fourth cohort dates from 1982 and the advent of the AIDS epidemic.[8] By the early 1980s, the major urban centers of America witnessed the onslaught of AIDS and the beginning of radical changes in sexual values and life-styles among gay men. Not only did this alter the sexual revolution of the previous cohort—with its 'rhetoric of the old gay movement'[9]—but it also ushered in a new epoch of coming out for teenagers and young adults, the youths of our Chicago study. For the first time, an institutionalized process of initiating and socializing youths emerged. [...]

By contrast, youths in Chicago today face a unique cultural opportunity. First, they experience a city more open than ever before, an openness distilled in the social institution that facilitates their identity and role development, the Horizons agency gay and lesbian youth group. This group is situated in between their mainstream heterosexual parents and friends, on the one hand, and gay and lesbian adult advisers, role models, and their friends, on the other. Second, they are growing up in the historical context of AIDS and other sexually transmitted diseases, and their conduct—like that of their heterosexual peers—shows heightened awareness of the epidemic. AIDS has plagued the gay and lesbian community, inserting its presence into many social events and intimate encounters, so that the cultural knowledge of being and acting gay today can no more be disentangled from the reaction to AIDS than, say, the effect of the eugenics movement on the acculturative experience of newly arriving immigrants in early twentieth-century Chicago. Where early cohorts lived closeted and in fear, suffering such huge psychosocial costs as the alcohol abuse associated with the bar culture of that generation, and where the third cohort is now besieged frontally with the death and grief of AIDS, today's youths—witness to these preceding life-styles—are in response developing an alternative cultural reality and future life course. Many Horizons' youths, for instance, now assume the possibility of achieving unprecedented gay life goals and open social relationships at home, school, and work.

['"Coming Out" as a Rite of Passage: A Chicago Study', in Gilbert Herdt (ed.), *Gay Culture in America: Essays from the Field* (Boston: Beacon Press, 1992), 31–2, 32–4, 35.]

MARTIN P. LEVINE

136   The Gay Clone

The social changes of the past three decades profoundly affected the forms of gay life. At the opening of the 1960s, American culture stigmatized homosexuality as a type of gender deviance that required strict social control. That is, gay men were regarded as 'failed men,' as men who deviated from masculine norms because they were either mentally or morally disordered. In this way, gay men were relegated to cultural roles of 'nelly queens,' 'hopeless neurotics,' and 'moral degenerates.'[1]

The stigmatization of homosexuality fostered harsh social sanctions designed to isolate, treat, correct, or punish gay men. For example, most states criminalized homosexual contact, which exposed gay men to police harassment, imprisonment, and blackmail. Moreover, psychiatry regarded homosexuality as a treatable form of mental illness, which left gay men open to mandatory psychotherapy or psychiatric hospitalization. Finally, family and friends frequently taunted, ostracized, and even violently attacked gay men.

Stigmatization meant that the gay world of the sixties functioned as a deviant subculture. This symbolic world constituted a relatively 'impoverished cultural unit.'² That is, the threat of sanction effectively limited structural and cultural elaboration within this world to covert sets of socially isolated, self-hating social networks and gathering places, which were primarily designed to facilitate social and sexual contacts and the management of stigma.

Three techniques for neutralizing stigma largely shaped the patterns of life within this world: passing, minstrelization, and capitulation. Passing accounted for the secrecy that characterized this world and included a set of behaviors that was designed to hide a gay identity and world under a heterosexual facade. Minstrelization explained the patterns of cross-gendering associated with 'camp,' a behavioral style entailing the adoption of feminine dress, speech, and demeanor. Finally, capitulation accounted for the feelings of guilt, shame, and self-hatred associated with the damaged sense of self that resulted from believing that homosexuality was a form of gender deviance.

Stigma management also engendered significant impediments to erotic expression during this period. The lack of anticipatory socialization for male homosexuality in our culture signified that men who eventually became gay experienced essentially the same erotic socialization as men who grew up to be straight. Socialization agents taught both prehomosexual and preheterosexual youths the dictates of the male sexual script. Consequently, gay men acquired a recreational erotic code that held that sex was objectified, privatized, and phallocentric and an arena for demonstrating manly prowess.

Passing and capitulation prevented many gay men from engaging in the recreational sex associated with the male sexual script. The threat that recognition and police raids or entrapment posed to heterosexual passing forced some gay men to shun the opportunities for recreational contacts present in the sexual marketplace of bars, bathhouses, and public restrooms. In addition, the belief that same-sex desires constituted gender deviance blocked others from engaging in recreational sexual contacts.

The gay liberation movement of the sixties fundamentally altered forms of gay life. Many early gay rights activists had participated in either countercultural, antiwar, or civil rights movements and were therefore prepared to advocate libertarian values and the destigmatization of homosexuality. For example, they championed an ethic sanctioning self-expression, especially in regard to experimentation with drugs and sex. In addition, they promoted a construction of same-sex love that stripped homosexuality of its discrediting association with gender deviance. That is, they held that same-sex love was a moral, natural, and healthy form of erotic expression among men who typically conformed to cultural expectations for manly demeanor and appearance. Finally, they actively campaigned to reduce the level of criminal, psychiatric, and social sanction and succeeded in forcing some localities either to repeal sodomy statutes or to cease police harassment of gay men, in compelling the mental health professions to remove same-sex love from the official list of psychological disorders, and in provoking a growing acceptance of gay men in the family, media, and workplace. [...]

The weakening of sanction and the destigmatized definition of homosexuality also modified the forms of life associated with stigma neutralization. For example, the decline in sanction removed the grounds for heterosexual passing, which provoked many gay men to become openly gay. Moreover, the redefinition of homosexuality as a normal, healthy, masculine form of male sexuality erased the basis for the cross-dressing connected with minstrelization, prompting a wholesale abandonment of camp attire, demeanor, and activities. In addition, this definition of same-sex love eliminated the reason for perceiving homosexuality as gender deviance and fostered a new pride and sense of validity in being both gay and a man. Finally, along with the libertarian ethos, the decrease in sanction and heightened self-esteem eradicated many of the impediments to recreational sexual contacts, which provoked an increase in anonymous erotic activity.

The social changes of the 1970s and 1980s further strengthened these emergent urban gay patterns. During the 1970s, the self-fulfillment ethic sanctioned gratification of inner needs and desires, and many urban gay men became openly gay, materialistic, and hedonistic. Consequently, the forms of urban gay life came to include consumerism, erotic exploration, recreational drug use, and disclosure of sexual orientation. [...]

Prior to AIDS, the clone social world was structured around a group of socially isolated social networks and gathering places, networks and places segregated from the broader gay as well as the heterosexual world. That is, the participants in these networks and places were mainly clones.

The social networks included 'cliques' and 'crowds.' Cliques functioned as friendship circles and met the men's basic social, emotional, and material needs. In this sense, they were surrogate families. A crowd consisted of a group of cliques that frequented the same meeting spot. For example, the Saint crowd involved the set of cliques that routinely gathered at The Saint disco. In addition, the members of a crowd usually either recognized or knew each other.

The crowds mixed in a round of meeting spots that was known as the 'Circuit.' The gathering places in the circuit were mainly locales for social, recreational, or sexual activities. For example, the men dined in Circuit restaurants, worked out in Circuit gyms, cruised in Circuit bars, and had sex in Circuit bathhouses. In addition, the men attended Circuit meeting spots according to a fixed schedule called 'Circuit hours.' A retail clerk in his mid-twenties explained, 'After work, we go to the gym, either the Y or the Bodycenter; then we stop by One Potato or Trilogy for dinner. On Friday nights, we cruise the Eagle and Spike. On Saturday nights, we go dancing at the Saint, and on Sunday nights, we go to the baths.'

Three distinctive social patterns characterized the clone social world during this period. First, presentational strategies within this world were typically 'butch.'³ For example, these men usually fashioned themselves after such archetypically masculine icons as body builders and blue-collar workers, and commonly wore work boots, flannel shirts, and button-up Levis and had gym bodies, short haircuts, and mustaches or beards.

Moreover, clones dressed in such a way as to highlight male erotic features and availability. For example, these men frequently wore form-fitting T-shirts and levis that outlined their musculature, genitals, and buttocks. To highlight the penis even further, they often wore no underwear. In addition, they usually wore keys and handkerchiefs that signaled preference for sexual acts and positions: 'White vividly describes the effect of eroticized butchness: a strongly marked mouth and swimming soulful eyes (the effect of the mustache); a V shaped torso by metonymy from the open V of the half unbuttoned shirt above the sweaty chest; rounded buttocks squeezed in jeans, swelling out from the cinched-in waist, further emphasized by the charged erotic insignia of colored handkerchiefs and keys; a crotch instantly accessible through the buttons (bottom one already undone) and enlarged by being pressed, along with the scrotum, to one side.'⁴

Furthermore, expressive strategies in Circuit gathering places evinced similar themes. For example, the decor and names of many Circuit meeting spots used western, leather, or high-tech motifs. One popular bar conveyed cowboy imagery through such furnishings as wagon wheels, corral posts, and western paintings, and staff uniforms consisted of cowboy hats, shirts, and boots. Other bars expressed this imagery through such names as Badlands or The Eagle.

The spatial design and names of some gathering places also articulated butchness. For example, many bars set aside specific areas for 'cruising' and 'tricking.'⁵ Some even showed pornographic films in backrooms. Other places manifested butchness in such names as The Cockring or The International Stud.

Second, erotic patterns within this world included cruising and tricking. Typically, clones cruised Circuit gathering places such as bars, bathhouses, and sex clubs for men who were their 'type,' that is, their erotic ideal, usually either good looking or 'hung,' 'built,' and butch. Generally, clones cruised these men by situating themselves in a position to signal sexual interest and negotiate a time and place for tricking. In most cases, they tricked almost immediately after meeting.

A rough, uninhibited, phallocentric form of sexuality characterized tricking among clones. Tricking frequently involved 'deep throating,' 'hard fucking,' and 'heavy tit work.' For example, fellatio often included vigorously jamming the penis completely down the throat (deep throating), which frequently caused gagging or choking. Anal intercourse usually entailed strenuously ramming the penis entirely up the anus while painfully slapping the buttocks (hard fucking). Nipple stimulation commonly involved robustly sucking, pinching, or biting the nipples to the point of pain (heavy tit work).

Clones often used drugs to overcome pain during rough sex and heighten erotic responsiveness. 'Pot,' 'poppers,' and Quaaludes were particularly popular.[6] A thirty-something health professional reported, 'I love to do poppers during sex because they cause the muscles in my ass and throat to relax, which allows me to suck dick and get fucked without gagging or feeling any pain.'

Most tricks consisted of a single erotic encounter. That is, the men had sex once and never again. For example, a waiter in his twenties in a Circuit restaurant remarked, 'I don't know why I give tricks my phone number. No one ever calls. Most of the time you trick with them and they don't even say hello to you the next time you see them.'

Third, 'partying' constituted the main recreational pattern among clones. These men regularly danced the night away in Circuit discos while 'high' on such drugs as MDA, poppers, or cocaine. Typically, the men took drugs at informal clique get-togethers prior to going to the club, usually for the purpose of sensual stimulation for partying. A financial analyst in his early thirties stated, 'MDA gives me the energy to dance all night. When I am stoned on MDA I can really get into the music and lights. My legs feel rubbery, like they can move to every beat.'

Partying largely occurred on weekend nights in Circuit clubs. On party nights, hundreds of drugged, bare-chested clones jammed the dance floor, where they danced feverishly to throbbing rhythms and dazzling lights while snorting poppers and throwing their arms and clenched fists into the air. The following account incisively depicts partying at the legendary Flamingo:

As we entered the club at one in the morning (the doors had opened at midnight) I saw a room full of husky men, many of them shirtless, sipping beer or Coke. ... Everyone in the audience could have been put on professional display, since the crowd was extraordinarily muscular. ... In the inner room people were dancing. ... The light show was adequate but not obtrusive. ... the blending of the records ... the choice of music were superb. ... Along one wall enthusiasts from the floor had leaped up onto a ledge and were grinding in dervish solitude. The mirror panels were frosted over with condensed sweat. One after another all the remaining shirts were peeled off. A stranger, face impassive, nosed up to us and soon was lending us his hanky soaked in ethyl chloride—a quick transit to the icy heart of a minor moon drifting around Saturn. Just as casually he stumbled off.[7]

['The Life and Death of Gay Clones', in Gilbert Herdt (ed.), *Gay Culture in America: Essays from the Field* (Boston: Beacon Press, 1992), 72–4, 74–5, 76–9.]

IV.e. A Golden Age for Pornography?

One of the most visible components of the sexual revolution of the 1960s was the explosion of pornographic literature, films, videos, sex toy emporiums, and live sex shows, in short the commercialization and mass production of items formerly reserved for a few cognoscenti. Community standards of what constituted obscene materials were changing together with changes in music, dress, and public comportment. D.H. Lawrence's erotic novel *Lady Chatterley's Lover*, originally published in a small edition in 1928, only appeared in an unexpurgated version in America in 1959 and in Britain in 1960. However, by the prosperous 1970s, pornography was being produced and consumed in huge quantities.

Like all aspects of the sea change in sexuality of the 1970s, pornography has served as a lightning rod for legal and ideological debates between feminists, legal libertarians, and moral conservatives. From their first appearance in the Renaissance until the present, pornographic texts and images have been for the most part written by men for the delectation of other men. Though they are sometimes endowed with a small measure of agency, women usually have figured only as objects of male lust or cruelty. Indeed, cruelty, or its sexological variant sadism, has been a feature of much modern pornography since the time of the Marquis de Sade. But the trope of cruelty has been even more broadly represented in pornography since the wars of the twentieth century. Freud linked *eros* and *thanatos* (the erotic and death 'instincts') in his psychoanalytic theory in the 1920s, and subsequent theorists continue to explain the appeal of de Sade's pornographic writings in Freudian terms.

In one of the most remarkable of these post-Freudian reflections on erotic cruelty, the French philosopher Georges Bataille's *Erotism: Death and Sensuality* (first published in 1957), de Sade's pornography is filtered through the sensibility of Bataille's post-Holocaust consciousness, from which perspective de Sade's work, if it does not exactly ennoble humankind, confronts it with the truth of its 'double' nature (Extract 137).

It is revealing to juxtapose the solaces of grand theory to the pathetic reality of contemporary 'straight' porn. In the 1980s the psychoanalyst Robert Stoller, whose theorizing on gender identity has informed much of recent sexological writing, carried out an 'ethnography' of contemporary pornographic filmmaking. In the following selection he interviews 'Bill', an actor-director in the genre. After describing the qualities that made him a porn star, though not one of the first magnitude, 'Bill' expatiates on some of his own motives for appearing in porn films and the appeal his 'work' has for the men who watch him. Here grand theory is brought most decidedly down to earth (Extract 138).

Critics of pornography such as Catherine MacKinnon and Andrea Dworkin have argued that because of the portrayals of violence toward women pornography should be strictly censored if not altogether banned, thereby returning porn to the situation of erotic writings and art in the era prior to the legal publication of *Lady Chatterley's Lover*. However, according to some critics of this position, advocates of censorship err by conflating all forms of pornography (and sexual pleasure) with one another in their efforts to focus attention on the degradation of women (Extract 139).

Others argue that the sexual revolution also decriminalized 'sex work', and emancipated gays, lesbians, and bisexuals, all of whom have the same right as heterosexuals to see their own sexuality represented erotically. Anne McClintock, a South African living in New York, argues that there is a complicated role that fantasy and perspective play in sexual representations, and she indicates the possibility that women can produce pornography of a non-violent and affirmative nature (Extract 140).

Finally, it is possible, as one critic has recently done, to argue that in virtually all its forms pornography acts to subvert the form of sexuality that has been historically dominant in Western culture: heterosexual, reproductive sexuality. The non-reproductive forms of sexuality that doctors, and before them theologians, had damned with the epithet 'perversion' or 'vice' are the forms of sexuality exclusively featured in pornography. The celebration of the perversions, argues the American feminist Linda Williams, is the most effective way to continue to undermine sexual orthodoxy (Extract 141).

137 The Cruelty of the Inner Self

When one considers the most striking manifestations of the principles enunciated, one cannot fail to observe mankind's double nature throughout its career. There are two extremes. At one end, existence is basically orderly and decent. Work, concern for the children, kindness and honesty rule men's dealings with their fellows. At the other, violence rages pitilessly. In certain circumstances the same men practice pillage and arson, murder, violence and torture. Excess contrasts with reason.

These extremes are called civilisation and barbarism—or savagery. But the use of these words is misleading, for they imply that there are barbarians on the one hand and civilised men on the other. The distinction is that civilised men speak and barbarians are silent, and the man who speaks is always the civilised man. To put it more precisely, since language is by definition the expression of civilised man, violence is silent. Many consequences result from that bias of language. Not only does 'civilised' usually mean 'us', and barbarous 'them', but also civilisation and language grew as though violence was something outside, foreign not only to civilisation but also to man, man being the same thing as language. Yet observation shows that the same peoples are alternately barbarous and civilised in their attitudes. All savages speak and by speaking they reveal their solidarity with the decency and kindness that are the root of civilisation. Conversely all civilised men are capable of savagery. Lynch law belongs to men who rate themselves as among the most highly civilised of our age. If language is to be extricated from this impasse, we must declare that violence belongs to humanity as a whole and is speechless, and that thus humanity as a whole lies by omission and language itself is founded upon this lie. [. . .]

De Sade's expression of violence changes violence into something else, something necessarily its opposite: into a reflecting and rationalised will to violence.

The philosophical dissertations which interrupt de Sade's narrative at the least excuse make them exhausting reading in the long run. Patience and resignation are needed to get through them. One has to tell oneself that a way of speaking so different from other people's, from everyone else's, makes it worth going on to the bitter end. Moreover, this monstrous utterance has a strength which imposes respect. We face de Sade's books as a terrified traveller might once have faced giddy piles of rocks. We flinch away, and yet . . . The horror before us is not aware of us, yet by simply being there, does it not hold some meaning for us? Mountains are something that can only appeal to man in a roundabout way, and the same with de Sade's books. But humanity has nothing to do with the existence of those lofty peaks. On the contrary, man is completely committed to an undertaking which would not exist without him. Mankind excises his crazy elements . . . But the rejection of folly is nothing but a convenient and unavoidable attitude, which must call for second thoughts. De Sade's philosophy, anyway, is not to be classed as madness. It is simply an excess, an excess to make our heads reel, but the excess of our own extravagance. We cannot ignore this peak without ignoring our own nature. If we fail to come nearer to the peaks, or at least climb the lower slopes, we must live like frightened ghosts—and it is our nature that makes us tremble with fear.

Let me revert to the long disquisitions that punctuate and clutter up the tales of criminal debauchery and prove interminably that the criminal libertine, and he alone, is right. Analyses and ratiocinations, learned references to ancient or savage customs, paradoxes of an aggressive philosophy, they all take us far away from violence for all their unwearying obstinacy and casual incoherence. For violence means being beside oneself, and being beside oneself is the same thing as the sensuous frenzy that violence results in. If we consciously desire to profit from violence, we can no longer reach the heights of frenzy and lose ourselves in it. Violence, the core of eroticism, leaves the weightiest problems unanswered. We have achieved awareness by pursuing a course of regular activity; every element has its place in the chain of consciousness and is distinct and intelligible. But by upsetting the chain through violence we revert to the extravagant and incomprehensible surge of eroticism. So we experience something blinding and overwhelming, more desirable than anything else, which defies the conscious appraisal we bestow on all the other facts of our experience. Human life, therefore, is composed of two heterogeneous parts which never blend. One part is purposeful, given significance by utilitarian and therefore secondary ends; this part is the one we are aware of. The other is primary and sovereign; it may arise when the other is out of gear, it is obscure, or else blindingly clear: either way it evades the grasp of our aware intelligence. Hence the problem has two sides. Conscious understanding wishes to extend its range to include violence, for such an important part of man's make-up must not be neglected any longer. And on the other hand violence reaches beyond itself to lay hold of intelligence, so that its satisfactions, brought to the surface of consciousness, may become profounder, more intense and more compelling. But in being violent we take a step away from awareness, and similarly by striving to grasp the significance of our own violent impulses we move further away from the frenzied raptures violence instigates. [. . .]

The fact is that what de Sade was trying to bring to the surface of the conscious mind was precisely the thing that revolted that mind. For him the most revolting thing was the most powerful means of exciting pleasure. Not only did he reach the most singular revelations by this means, but from the very first he set before the consciousness, things which it could not tolerate. He himself spoke only of 'irregularity'. The rules we obey are usually intended to conserve life; hence irregularity leads towards destruction. It does not always have this fatal meaning, however; nakedness fundamentally is a kind of irregularity, but where pleasure is concerned it does not lead to real destruction. (Observe that naked-ness can also exist within the rules; nakedness in a doctors' surgery or in a nudist camp has no exciting effects.) De Sade's works introduce one scandalous irregu-larity after another. He insists now and then on the irregular aspect of the sim-plest sort of erotic attraction, for example, a novel way of undressing the partner. According to the cruel characters he brings on to the scene, nothing heats the passions more than irregularity. De Sade's essential merit is to have discovered and effectively demonstrated one function of moral irregularity in carnal pleas-ure. This excitement should theoretically lead to sexual activity. But the effect of any irregularity at all is stronger than the immediate manoeuvres. De Sade finds it equally possible to seek satisfaction through murder or torture in the course of a debauch, or by ruining a family or a country, or even just by stealing.

Independently of de Sade, the sexual excitement of burglars has not escaped notice. But no one before him had grasped the general mechanism linking the reflex actions of erection and ejaculation with the transgression of the law. De Sade knew nothing about the basic interrelation of taboo and transgression, op-posite and complementary concepts. But he took the first step. This general mechanism could not be completely comprehended until we finally and tardily arrived at an understanding of the paradox of taboo and transgression. De Sade expounded his doctrine of irregularity in such a way, mingled with such horrors, that no one paid any heed to it. He wanted to revolt our conscious minds, he would also have liked to enlighten them but he could not do both at the same time. It is only today we realise that without de Sade's cruelty we should never have penetrated with such ease the once inaccessible domain where the most painful truths lay hidden. It is not so easy to pass from the knowledge of mankind's curious beliefs and behaviour, in the field of religion, now linked with our knowledge of taboo and transgression, to that of the strangeness of his sexual behaviour. The deep-seated unity of our nature is the last thing to appear. And if today the average man has a profound insight into what transgression means for him, de Sade was the one who made ready the path. Now the average man knows that he must become aware of the things which repel him most vio-lently—those things which repel us most violently are part of our own nature.

[*Erotism: Death & Sensuality*, trans. Mary Dalwood (San Francisco: City Lights Books, 1986), 186, 191–3, 195–6.]

ROBERT J. STOLLER

138   Why Men Like Porn

Bill Margold[1] suggests ideas for, writes, directs, and acts in porn flicks. As you will see, Bill is profoundly self-centered and an endless talker. Depending on the form and degree of your antisocial elements, you will find his attempts at humor appropriate, tasteless, or—worse—unfunny. Whatever—he can bring you closer to the way porn is created than most anyone you will ever meet. And that, for an ethnographic study, is a gift. In addition, his description of his childhood suggests how its traumas and frustrations feed into his occupation; few in the business allow such entrée into their motives.

He enthusiastically sets forth. This is our first meeting, six years ago.

B: You [Dr Stoller] have the opportunity to be a tourist in a very strange land. It's the most misunderstood industry in the world. The last time I was approached to do something like this [to be interviewed], the man wound up analogizing us to having the same kind of death wish that bullfighters, skydivers, and racecar drivers have, which is probably true, because I'm in an antisocial, highly immoral, against-the-grain, ultra-rebellious form of entertainment. We're the last rebels in society. At least we're better than the stupid terrorists who go around blowing up people. No one ever died from an overdose of pornography.

If you want any background on my part, I'm a college graduate. I got into the Industry years ago, to write stories about it. I wanted to live out my fantasies. In a sense, I'm going through my adolescence at this point. You have to have a totally exhibitionistic, narcissistic flair to survive in the Adult Industry, because you're competing against yourself. It's very difficult under the pressure of the lights and the camera and the action.

We're pieces of meat. I have referred to my cohorts as pieces of meat, and they don't like being called pieces of meat, but we are indeed pieces of meat. Because without the appendage, we are of no value whatsoever. Without the ability to manipulate that appendage up, in, out, and off on cue, we're of no value whatsoever. There are about fifty male performers in the world. And about twenty of those work regularly. The other ones are just nickel-and-dime-type people: stagger in and stagger out. I am not a star. I am not a John Holmes, I'm not a John Leslie, I am not a Jamie Gillis, or an Eric Edwards, or a Herschel Savage, or Paul Thomas, or Joey Silvera. And that's about (oh, maybe Harry Reems), that's about it for the stars in our Industry, the male stars.

S: What makes a star?

B: Longevity. A bit of the macho ethic. They have to look pretty good. We can't have weak-looking, unhealthy, unpalatable people on screen. I have survived because I look ordinary. I have this incredible ability to look different to each person who meets me. I can deliver the 'everyman' to them on a silver platter. But I never pursued the stardom aspect of it. It takes, basically, testing yourself more than I want to be tested. Under the gun I have survived, I have not failed to function since I began performing years ago. I can get up, get in, get out, get off on cue, I can give you a cum shot, which is known as the money shot, the male orgasm, on cue, ten seconds, 'pop.' I can do that while

I'm carrying on a conversation, without real metabolic change half the time, which makes me almost automatistic, like a robot. Which is why I'm not that much fun to be with when I'm working, because I'm concentrating on other things than the sex, which, under the pressure, is secondary. The achievement of controlling yourself and then getting off when you're supposed to, that's the ultimate satisfaction. It results in light-headedness and giddiness, and you laugh a lot. A lot of times in my films when I get off on cue and have done my job well, I'll cackle fiendishly. That's my salute to myself. I'm delighted with myself.

This is the 'playpen for the damned.' [This, and lines like it, are prepared phrases, Bill quoting himself.] We are, like I say, one of the last sets of rebels in America, or in the world. I get a big kick out of that. But the stars are the ones who have done four-five hundred films, a thousand films. Holmes has been in about four thousand different situations. I don't want to be bothered doing that. I'm trying to carve my own niche in the Industry. I'm known as the bad boy, because I usually wind up doing things that are foul on screen.

My whole reason for being in the Industry is to satisfy the desire of the men in the world who basically don't much care for women and want to see the men in my Industry getting even with the women they couldn't have when they were growing up. I *strongly* believe this, and the Industry hates me for saying it. But I really believe that even the most satisfied Casanova-Don Juan-satyr has always wanted somebody he couldn't get, and because of that he starts to harbor a revenge. So we come on a woman's face or somewhat brutalize her sexually: we're getting even for their [the men viewers'] lost dreams. I believe this.

I've been told this by people in audiences after I've done horrible things on screen to women. I'm not hurting them. It's only an act, but it looks real—because I can scare people—I have a booming voice and I can become very intimidating. That gets the audience excited. I've heard audiences cheer me when I do something foul on screen. When I've strangled a person or sodomized a person, or brutalized a person, the audience is cheering my action, and then when I've fulfiled my warped desire, the audience applauds. I am not that way in real life. I don't have the time to beat somebody up in bed. I don't have the inclination or the time. It takes a lot of work to be brutal; it takes a whole lot of work. It's much more fun just to roll and hug like a couple of bears and have sex and enjoy yourself. I enjoy sex. I don't want to be bothered in bed putting on a gigantic show, and fist-fucking, and all that kind of stuff, which really doesn't interest me. It's very difficult for me to fist-fuck anyway now, because my hands have been smashed up from playing football. [Cracks his knuckles wildly.]

[*Porn: Myths for the Twentieth Century* (New Haven: Yale University Press, 1991), 29–31.]

The anti-pornography movement and its texts have been the most extensive expression of this discourse.[1] In addition, proponents of this viewpoint have condemned virtually every variant of sexual expression as anti-feminist. Within this framework, monogamous lesbianism that occurs within long-term, intimate relationships and which does not involve playing with polarized roles, has replaced married, procreative heterosexuality at the top of the value hierarchy. Heterosexuality has been demoted to somewhere in the middle. Apart from this change, everything else looks more or less familiar. The lower depths are occupied by the usual groups and behaviors: prostitution, transsexuality, sadomasochism, and cross-generational activities.[2] Most gay male conduct, all casual sex, promiscuity, and lesbian behavior that does involve roles or kink or non-monogamy are also censured.[3] Even sexual fantasy during masturbation is denounced as a phallocentric holdover.[4]

This discourse on sexuality is less a sexology than a demonology. It presents most sexual behavior in the worst possible light. Its descriptions of erotic conduct always use the worst available example as if it were representative. It presents the most disgusting pornography, the most exploited forms of prostitution, and the least palatable or most shocking manifestations of sexual variation. This rhetorical tactic consistently misrepresents human sexuality in all its forms. The picture of human sexuality that emerges from this literature is unremittingly ugly.

In addition, this anti-porn rhetoric is a massive exercise in scapegoating. It criticizes non-routine acts of love rather than routine acts of oppression, exploitation, or violence. This demon sexology directs legitimate anger at women's lack of personal safety against innocent individuals, practices, and communities. Anti-porn propaganda often implies that sexism originates within the commercial sex industry and subsequently infects the rest of society. This is sociologically nonsensical. The sex industry is hardly a feminist utopia. It reflects the sexism that exists in the society as a whole. We need to analyze and oppose the manifestations of gender inequality specific to the sex industry. But this is not the same as attempting to wipe out commercial sex.

Similarly, erotic minorities such as sadomasochists and transsexuals are as likely to exhibit sexist attitudes or behavior as any other politically random social grouping. But to claim that they are inherently anti-feminist is sheer fantasy. A good deal of current feminist literature attributes the oppression of women to graphic representations of sex, prostitution, sex education, sadomasochism, male homosexuality, and transsexualism. Whatever happened to the family, religion, education, child-rearing practices, the media, the state, psychiatry, job discrimination, and unequal pay?

Finally, this so-called feminist discourse recreates a very conservative sexual morality. For over a century, battles have been waged over just how much shame, distress, and punishment should be incurred by sexual activity. The conservative tradition has promoted opposition to pornography, prostitution, homosexuality, all erotic variation, sex education, sex research, abortion, and contraception. The opposing, pro-sex tradition has included individuals like Havelock Ellis, Magnus Hirschfeld, Alfred Kinsey, and Victoria Woodhull, as well as the sex education movement, organizations of militant prostitutes and homosexuals, the reproductive rights movement, and organizations such as the Sexual Reform League of the 1960s. This motley collection of sex reformers, sex educators, and sexual militants has mixed records on both sexual and feminist issues. But surely they are closer to the spirit of modern feminism than are moral crusaders, the social purity movement, and anti-vice organizations. Nevertheless, the current feminist sexual demonology generally elevates the anti-vice crusaders to positions of ancestral honor, while condemning the more liberatory tradition as anti-feminist. In an essay that exemplifies some of these trends, Sheila Jeffereys blames Havelock Ellis, Edward Carpenter, Alexandra Kollantai, 'believers in the joy of sex of every possible political persuasion,' and the 1929 congress of the World League for Sex Reform for making 'a great contribution to the defeat of militant feminism.'⁵

The anti-pornography movement and its avatars have claimed to speak for all feminism. Fortunately, they do not. Sexual liberation has been and continues to be a feminist goal. The women's movement may have produced some of the most retrogressive sexual thinking this side of the Vatican. But it has also produced an exciting, innovative, and articulate defense of sexual pleasure and erotic justice. This 'pro-sex' feminism has been spearheaded by lesbians whose sexuality does not conform to movement standards of purity (primarily lesbian sadomasochists and butch/femme dykes), by unapologetic heterosexuals, and by women who adhere to classic radical feminism rather than to the revisionist celebrations of femininity which have become so common. Although the antiporn forces have attempted to weed anyone who disagrees with them out of the movement, the fact remains that feminist thought about sex is profoundly polarized.⁶

['Thinking Sex: Notes for a Radical Theory of the Politics of Sexuality', in Carole S. Vance (ed.), *Pleasure and Danger: Exploring Female Sexuality* (Boston: Routledge & Kegan Paul, 1984), 301–3.]

ANNE McCLINTOCK

140   Female-Friendly Porn

Feminist film theory has argued widely that the subject of the gaze is male, and that looking is equated with the male position. Yet the double exposure or double vision characteristic of much female consumption of images cannot easily be equated with the sanctioned position of male gazing, nor reduced to a phallic logic. If, until recently, most male porn has been framed for male pleasure, the camera's I-for-an-eye is fluid and mutable. Identitification in porn can be multiple and shifting, bisexual and transsexual, alternately or simultaneously—although context can limit or prohibit the degree of transgression. Lesbians and gays can consume heterosexual porn, and vice versa, by adopting intricate and shifting patterns of identification across gender and orientation. Where in feminist film and porn theory, moreover, are women of colour? In that brave, nowhere space so adroitly captured in the famous title *All the Women Are White, All the Men Are Black, But Some of Us Are Brave*? Analyses of 'the male gaze' have for the most part ignored the different ways in which women and men of colour negotiate their desires around the magisterial forms of the white male imaginary.

The pornographic imagination shifts libidinously: I am the watcher/the watched; I am the pleasurer/the pleasured. The masturbatory imagination is incoherent: bits of memory, trauma, pleasure, anger, recalled for pleasure. Porn is the theatrical performance of sexual risk, ritually staging pleasure and danger under remote control. The pace of porn—the swerves in scene, the switches of persona, the rehearsal of variety within the structure of compulsive repetition—mimics the floating, chaotic structures of masturbatory fantasy, an obscure logic about which we know very little.

Popular myths that porn is produced by sinister, cigar-chewing humanoids who wear nothing but towels round their middles and spend their time groping the talent off-camera are woefully out of date. Most decriminalized porn in Europe is produced by professional camera crews biding their time to get into the mainstream. As one sex worker says: 'Unprofessional attitudes get in the way of making money and would not be tolerated.' Criminalizing porn only drives the business underground, where it remains brutally managed by men.

Arguably, the most damaging aspect of mainstream porn is its jealous exclusion of women as directors and consumers. More men than I care to count have insisted that women are not excited by erotic images. But arguing that a quirk of anatomical design has left women numb to erotic images is both implausible and reactionary. If some women react to male porn with sharp anxiety, it is because they feel disempowered by a sexual world colonized for male desires and bewildered, perhaps, by a momentary gender confusion and secret, uneasy arousal. Now, however, women are beginning to stage and speak pleasure on our own terms. Femme Productions makes sex videos for women and couples, lesbian and bisexual porn continues to proliferate, and a hard-core porn magazine for women is soon to appear in Britain.

Evidence of women's increased power as porn consumers is pouring in. Women have been targeted as the largest growth area for porn; it is estimated that they now account for 40 per cent of all X-rated video rentals, and a *Redbook* magazine survey confirms that nearly half the women surveyed regularly watch porn films. Another poll estimates that two out of three women in Germany and France watch video porn regularly. At the same time, female porn workers need no longer be ventriloquists' dummies for male fantasies about female pleasure. Sex workers are organizing internationally for the decriminalization of sex work, for better working conditions, and for the removal of gender, class and racial inequities.

The arrival of video has turned porn into a sure-fire coin-spinning venture as never before, and with it has come a historic opportunity for women. With the cheaper, potentially less threatening and more private world of home erotic videos, a new era is upon us. But Cindy Patton's question remains to be answered: Can both women's and men's pleasure be represented simultaneously in heterosexual couples' videos? Or will men still hold the remote control in the living-room?

Creating women's commercial sex complicates the notion of porn as a world absolutely colonized for the male gaze. None the less, celebrating women's pleasure does not mean denying or subduing the penis. Rather, it simply means insisting that the penis take a more modest place in a far more generous world of sexual diversity. At the same time, quarrels over the hierarchical primacy of 'proper' female orgasm should make way for recognition of the polymorphous variety of women's multiple pleasures, which are not reducible to a single male phallic economy. Gay men—particularly now, in the era of safe sex—have, moreover, been pioneers in expanding the pornutopia of male pleasures to include anal, oral and other eroticisms into a far greater diversity of sensual delirium than five minutes of gunga-da-gung.

Recently, I watched performance artist and ex-go-go dancer Tornado challenge male spectators at the Harmony, a strip theatre in New York. I watched Annie Sprinkle, post-porn-modernist, stage male voyeurism and female control of sex work at the Kitchen. At the Three Dollar Bill Theater I saw performance after performance of lesbian singers, poets and performers, sex professionals, and members of PONY (Prostitutes of New York) enrapture an aroused and jubilant crowd of women. It's been a long wait, but it's been worth it. If women organize instead of agonize, we can alter the shape of the industry on terms more suitable to our own uncharted pleasures. At last we can expand our historical experimentations in female sexual pleasure, and demand more power to come.

['Gonad the Barbarian and the Venus Flytrap: Portraying the Female and Male Orgasm', in Lynne Segal and Mary McIntosh (eds.), *Sex Exposed: Sexuality and the Pornography Debate* (London: Virago Press, 1992), 125, 130–1.]

Previous defences of pornography have, for obvious reasons, glossed over the role of perversion in pornographic fantasy. Perversion is understandably difficult to defend. This is especially important in an area of film and video analysis where the analytic terms of perversion have been both crucial (normal) and ambivalently condemnatory. It was not so long ago, some of us may remember, that the fundamental pleasures of film viewing were described and condemned under the rubric of a perverse sadistic-voyeuristic-fetishizing 'male gaze'.

Under the banner of the critique of a perverse masculine visual pleasure, feminist film critics once condemned the 'norm' of masculine heterosexual desire as manifested in narrative cinema. Pornography was usually assumed to be the extreme, and grossly explicit, instance of this perverse, voyeuristic, fetishizing pleasure. While it was enormously important for feminists to critique pornography's phallocentric nature as well as its sadistic excesses, the demonizing effects of this condemnation, as well as the oversimplified understanding of the role of perversions as exclusively pathological and harmful to others, has left us with a problematic heritage: the sexual politics of normal and perverse. In the name of what norms do feminists condemn the perversions of dominant masculine heterosexual desires evidenced in art, mass culture and a much-maligned pornography? Where is the enablement of female sexual agency in this condemnation of masculine dominance? Should we even speak in such binary terms of a female (versus a male) sexual agency?

If feminism succeeded in critiquing masculine phallic sexuality, it did so at the price of demonizing it as a perverse 'other' whose eternal victims were women. It is now possible to see how this feminist critique has fed into a larger critique of deviancy now being used by the right to mount new arguments—not only against pornography but also against gays, lesbians and sadomasochists in NEA funding of art deemed obscene. Feminism has rightly set itself up as a critique of sexual desires that seem oppressive to women, but it has not always been sensitive to the complex ways power and pleasure operate in sexuality.

If, therefore, unlike either Jesse Helms or Andrea Dworkin, we do not want to participate in a politics of demonizing the pervert—whether that pervert is defined as heterosexual or homosexual, or as voyeur, sadomasochist or fetishist—then we need to gain some degree of clarity about these difficult issues. I therefore propose to probe the role of perversion and transgression in the proliferating genres of pornography, dominant and non-dominant, that are currently available on the scene. For the simple dichotomy of the perverse (because sexual?) male and the normal (because less sexual?) female has failed: fantasies that make appeal to transgressive pleasures may indeed be perverse, but as fantasies and representations that offer pleasure they are not necessarily pathological. In an era of diverse sexual identities—of proud gays, lesbians, bisexuals and sadomasochists—and of a pervasive commodity fetishism and a society of the spectacle whose visual pleasures depend upon a certain normative fetishism and voyeurism, the very terms 'norm' and 'perverse' cannot be assumed to attach permanently to features that are *a priori* 'good' or 'bad' for women. [. . .]

But amid this wealth of possible numbers there was usually one shot of a sexual act that tried to be the climactic 'it' of ultimate pleasure: this is what the industry calls the 'money shot', male ejaculation of the penis. While the money shot was usually positioned as the climax of most heterosexual pornography, it was a paradoxical confession of the 'ultimate truth' of sexual pleasure. For while it afforded a perfect vision and knowledge of one genital organ's pleasure, the climax and achievement of a final sexual aim, this aim quite literally missed its mark: the genitals of its object. In fact, the genital 'object' of masculine desire and pleasure is often missing altogether as a visual representation in the frame.

As if to make up for this lack, the money shot would throw in a special rhetorical flourish, with slow motion, optical printing or elaborate montages which would attempt to substitute for what the film could not show: the visible, involuntary convulsions that would be proof of the woman's pleasure. External ejaculation, while ideally visible and affording incontrovertible evidence of at least the male's pleasure, thus 'perverts' 'normal' genital aims. It is a substitute for the invisible female orgasm that this stage of the heterosexual pornographic genre especially solicits. This shot, while undoubtedly explicit and to some certainly obscene, is perhaps most importantly described as contradictory in much the same way that a fetish is contradictory. Like the fetish, it attempts to disavow difference—in this case that the female orgasm is any different from the male's—offering up the spectacle of ejaculation as a substitute for what is not there: the invisible female orgasm. The genre's solution of substituting the male orgasm for the female is thus, by definition, perverse in the literal sense of swerved away from an original aim.

Now it is all too easy to condemn, ridicule or demonize these perverse substitutions. What I have tried to suggest in my book and would like to develop further here, however, is that a *perverse dynamic* operates in all forms of sexual fantasy; that it is inevitable both within heterosexual pornography and outside it, in the non-dominant, non-mainstream forms of gay, lesbian, sadomasochistic and bisexual moving-image pornographies.

I borrow the term 'perverse dynamic' from Jonathan Dollimore, who argues that although perversion is regulated by a binary opposition between the natural and the unnatural, it is nevertheless inextricably rooted in the natural: as in de Lauretis's argument that perversion is intrinsic to sexuality, Dollimore argues that perversion originates internally to the very norm it threatens. The perverse dynamic is thus paradoxically both alien to and inherent within the normal. This idea of perversion is important to the agency and empowerment of those non-dominant, minority sexualities frequently condemned as perverse and evident in gay, lesbian, sadomasochistic and bisexual pornography. It is therefore with an awareness of a non-pathological *perverse dynamic* already at work within the heterosexual category of pornography considered the most normal and dominant that we can begin to chart the other commercially available pornographies existing alongside this heterosexual mainstream.

These pornographies are: homosexual (originally mostly gay male, now also lesbian), sadomasochistic and bisexual. While these categories are not absolutely inclusive—I exclude the many new forms of 'amateur' pornography and the occasional, but not systematic, appeal to racial or other body-types—they constitute the broad areas of professionally made hard-core film and video on the market in the USA today. Of course heterosexual films and videos are almost never marketed *as* heterosexual, since heterosexual, as the presumed norm, needs no mark. It is usually up to the other categories to differentiate themselves from this norm, as they sometimes do with images on box covers or key words in titles (*Hot Male Mechanics, Oversize Load* connote gay; *Suburban Dykes* directly speaks its targeted audience; *The Punishment of Anne* and *China de Sade* suggest sadomasochistic themes; and the ubiquitous word 'Bi' indicates bisexual videos). These different categories of pornography are sometimes integrated into rental outlets that specialize in adult, X-rated materials, sometimes available only in special venues (gay and lesbian rental and sales outlets).

[Pornographies on/scene, or Diff'rent Strokes for Diff'rent Folks', in Lynne Segal and Mary McIntosh (eds.), *Sex Exposed: Sexuality and the Pornography Debate* (London: Virago Press, 1992), 235–6, 242–4.]

IV.f. AIDS

In the last twenty years the most widespread and dangerous sexually related disease in human history has spread throughout the world. Acquired Immune Deficiency Syndrome is caused by the transmission of HIV (human immunodeficiency virus). Though HIV can lie dormant for long periods of time, and can now be treated effectively by various combinations of drugs, there is no known cure for the disease. It has long been understood that HIV was transmitted sexually through the transfer of body fluids (semen or blood) carrying the virus, and that sexual contact was a chief means for doing so. The first populations manifesting high rates of HIV infection in the early 1980s were urban homosexuals in North America. By the end of the decade the epidemic had spread to gay men elsewhere in the West, gained a foothold amongst drug addicts sharing needles, and in places with high concentrations of commercial prostitution such as Africa, the Indian subcontinent, and South-East Asia. Today, the vast majority of HIV-infected people are sub-Saharan Africans, victims of changes brought about in patterns of heterosexual sex from social and political upheaval.

Apart from anti-homosexual fanatics and a few critics in the gay community, there was little sympathy for assessing responsibility in the face of the grief and suffering spread by AIDS. But in tracking down the sources of the disease, some early AIDS activists became convinced that gay sexual practices in the 'liberated' 1970s and 1980s had contributed directly to the spread of the disease. The gay journalist Randy Shilts, himself a victim of AIDS, wrote an influential 'docudrama' identifying a French Canadian airline steward, Gaetan Dugas, as one of the first men in North America to develop symptoms of AIDS. Shilts' treatment suggests that Dugas was implicated in the infection of gay men in New York, Los Angeles, and San Francisco before Selma Dritz, the infectious disease specialist in the San Francisco Public Health Department, tracked him down (Extract 142).

Shilts's account of the origins of the HIV epidemic has been challenged by several writers. Douglas Crimp charges here that Shilts's version was not only inaccurate with respect to the facts, but also played into the hands of the mainstream press which was pleased to identify an individual and a community on which they could project their homophobic fears (Extract 143).

In 1989 the French historian of medicine Mirko D. Grmek wrote a book about AIDS in which he asked the question: 'Is AIDS a new disease?'[1] Grmek answered in the negative, arguing that many of our modern diseases have ancient analogues that appear different to us presently because the organic and physical

[1] Mirko Grmek, *History of AIDS: Emergence and Origin of a Modern Pandemic*, trans. Russell C. Maulitz and Jacalyn Duffin (Princeton: Princeton University Press, 1990), 99.

opportunities for their expression have changed. AIDS, he suggested, may be one of those diseases. Taking up this idea, the gay American journalist Gabriel Rotello has developed a concept of 'sexual ecology' to explain how HIV has been spread chiefly within populations of individuals engaged in dangerous sexual practices. Rotello comments on how the politics of sexual identity enabled gay men to fail to discern their own responsibility and then console themselves that 'safe sex' could adequately cope with the further spread of disease (Extract 144).

There seems to be a dynamic interplay between the different gay communities, their conceptions of their political alternatives, and the larger political culture of which they are a part. Whereas American gay communities have favoured identity politics and based their antagonistic and co-operative relations with the state and with health authorities on a basis of gay identity, the situation has differed elsewhere. In 1987 the British journalist Simon Watney argued that the efforts of the British media to relate the spread of AIDS to the 'promiscuity' of gay sexual practices was tantamount to re-ghettoizing and demonizing gay sex. He offers here an account that emphasizes the distinctive nature of British urban gay sexual culture and explains why a statistical and epidemiological approach to the problem is ultimately insufficient (Extract 145).

Gaetan Dugas examined himself closely in the steamy mirror of San Francisco's most popular bathhouse. He had always been looking for someone, he thought. As a child he had searched for his mother, not the woman who had brought him up in Quebec City, but his real mother. As soon as he was old enough to understand that he had been adopted into that rough-hewn life of the French-Canadian working class, he had dreamed of the day he would meet his true mother. He knew he was meant to be born into a better life, far from the brawny bullies who called him a faggot and rubbed snow in his face during those bitter Canadian winters.

He could see the difference in his face; he was meant for something better. He loved his family and adored his older sister, but they were dark and plain looking while he had always had delicate features and light, winsome hair. He was like the prince taken up by the farmers, he thought. When he did finally meet his natural mother, he told friends they fought. She wouldn't say who his father was and she didn't seem like a princess, and suddenly Gaetan had stopped talking about searching for his parents. Anyway, he had found his own niche in the royalty of gay beauty, as a star of the homosexual jet set.

Now, as he searched the mirror, oblivious to the smiles aimed at his still-handsome body, he was thinking about another search. Who had done this to him? Certainly somebody had. They had passed him the virus that meant he was going to die, and he couldn't get over wondering who it was, the way he once could not stop wondering what his real mother looked like.

Gaetan stood back to give his smooth body another appraisal. He was thirty years old, the age he had never thought he would make. But he was triumphing. He was living in San Francisco, where he had always wanted to live. He had outlived all the doctors' predictions and felt quite nice, thank you, two and a half years after he was told that the small purplish spot near his ear was Kaposi's sarcoma. True, he was a bit more tired these days and sometimes breathing came hard. He could win, nevertheless, and enjoy his evening here at the baths.

Of course, those assholes at the CDC might scream at him for being here, but he had told them to fuck off. They were bothering his old boyfriends with phone calls and nosy questions. The other doctors could fuck themselves, too, with all their warnings that he might be spreading this thing. Everybody knew you couldn't catch cancer. He wanted to see proof. Besides, Gaetan had told the doctors defiantly, somebody gave this to him.

Gaetan peered down the long hallway of cubicles, some with their doors open. Inside, men lay on their stomachs, usually with a can of Crisco and a small bottle of poppers at their side. Gaetan surveyed the material and made his choice. He edged into the small cubicle and waited for the ritual nod that indicated he would be welcome. Without a word, the assignation was set. Gaetan pushed the door shut. [. . .]

Gaetan Dugas's eyes flashed, but without their usual charm, when Selma Dritz bluntly told him he must stop going to the bathhouses. The hotline at the Kaposi's Sarcoma Foundation was receiving repeated calls from people complaining of a man with a French accent who was having sex with people at various sex parlors and then calmly telling them he had gay cancer. It was one of the most repulsive things Dritz had heard in her nearly forty years in public health.

'It's none of your goddamn business,' said Gaetan. 'It's my right to do what I want to do with my own body.'

'It's not your right to go out and give other people disease,' Dritz replied, keeping her professional calm. 'Then you're making decisions for their bodies, not yours.'

'It's their duty to protect themselves,' said the airline steward. 'They know what's going on there. They've heard about this disease.'

Dritz tried to reason further but got nowhere.

'I've got it,' Gaetan said angrily. 'They can get it too.'

Gaetan Dugas was not alone among AIDS patients at the bathhouses. Bobbi Campbell, who had made his self-avowed role as a KS Poster Boy into something of a crusade, was also going to bathhouses, although he denied having sex with people. Gay doctors had told Dritz that several other patients still went as well. The situation was intolerable, Dritz thought, and she had no doubt as to what she would like to do. There was only the question of whether it would stand up in court. These people should be locked up, particularly Gaetan. Dritz started talking to city attorneys to see what laws existed to empower such action. [. . .]

When Gaetan Dugas's best friend moved from Toronto back to Vancouver, he felt like he had landed in the middle of Peyton Place. Everybody was talking about Gaetan as 'the Orange County connection,' going out to the bars and having sex with people. It hadn't helped when Gaetan made a scene at the AIDS Vancouver forum, arguing about whether AIDS actually could be spread through sex. Gaetan's sexual prowling had reached near-legendary proportions since then. He made little effort to conceal his medical problems, casually rolling up his sleeves as he quaffed beers at pubs, despite the lesions on his forearms.

According to one story, one tryst of Gaetan's was so furious when he heard that Gaetan had AIDS that he tracked the former airline steward down to confront him. By the time they were done talking, Gaetan had charmed the man back into bed.

The friend from Toronto sat Gaetan down for a talk. They had known each other for years, since they were Air Canada stewards together in Halifax and had escaped to San Francisco for the Gay Freedom Day parades and parties. He genuinely loved Gaetan, knowing him as a kind and caring friend, not just somebody to party with. If a friend were sick, Gaetan could be relentless in his attentions, and there never seemed to be an end to the little considerate gestures Gaetan doled out to the people close to his heart. Still, the friend suspected that the rumors might be true. Asking Gaetan to give up sex, he knew, would be like asking Bruce Springsteen to give up the guitar. Sex wasn't just sex to Gaetan; sex was who Gaetan was—it was the basis of his identity.

Gaetan at first denied he was having sex with anyone. His friend didn't let it end at that. He suggested to Gaetan that anyone with AIDS should stop having sex. Period.

'They can't tell me that having sex is going to transmit it,' said Gaetan. 'They haven't proved it yet.'

'Yes,' his friend countered, 'but if there's even the slightest possibility, then you shouldn't do it.'

'Yes, I suppose you're right,' Gaetan shrugged.

The friend wasn't sure that Gaetan agreed at all. He recalled the conversations they had had years before in Halifax, deciding whether they could hit the bars on the nights after they had shots for gonorrhea. The doctors always said to wait a few days, but Gaetan figured that since somebody gave it to him, he could give it right back.

'This is incurable,' Gaetan's friend pushed. 'You don't just get a shot. It would be so incredibly unfair to give it to someone.'

Yes, Gaetan said, so unfair.

[*And the Band Played On: Politics, People, and the AIDS Epidemic* (Harmondsworth: Penguin, 1988), 196–7, 200, 251–2.]

DOUGLAS CRIMP

143 Shilts's Miserable Failure

The stories that Shilts tells reduce basically to two: the story of irrational fears of AIDS and loathing of those who have it, and the media's sense of the fascination of its audience with 'sexy' stories about AIDS. What Shilts is thus describing are reactions to AIDS that I think we must recognize as unconscious and therefore extremely intractable, incapable of being rectified by what Shilts calls 'the truth' or objective reporting of the facts.

I want to suggest here that it is only by taking account of reactions to AIDS that operate at the level of the unconscious and by unpacking Shilts's unproblematized notion of 'the truth' or 'objectivity' that we can understand why *And the Band Played On* is so deeply flawed.

Many people have written about why Shilts's book is, by his own admission, a miserable failure, or have addressed criticisms directly to Shilts when they encountered him on his celebrity tour. Needless to say, this is an aspect of being a celebrity that Shilts fails to report in his *Esquire* article. In spite of Shilts's own sense of failure, he arrogantly dismisses the questions raised by his critics. He still appears to feel that he has written the perfect book, the book that really tells the *true* story of the epidemic's first five years.

Let me give you just one example, taken from the transcripts of Shilts's book promotion appearance at the Institute of Contemporary Arts in London. Shilts was asked in some detail about his book's most widely criticized passages, those dealing with the story of Patient Zero, in an exchange with the writer Adam Mars-Jones.

'At what stage did you decide to give [the Patient Zero story] so much prominence?' Mars-Jones asked.

'Well, I don't think it is that prominent in the book . . ., but I thought it was a fascinating story . . . I think it represents very good investigative journalism.'

'There are passages describing how [Patient Zero] would have sex with people in bathhouses, then turn the lights on and say, "I'm going to die and so are you." '

'Which he did! At the time he was doing that, I was hearing about it.'

'But those were rumors.'

'No, it wasn't rumors, I talked to people he did this to . . . I mean, he was doing it quite a bit. The fact is it all happened. The facts are not disputed.'

'William Darrow of the CDC [Centers for Disease Control] does repudiate them.'

'No, he does not. The fact is that William Darrow saw every word that was written about him and about the study [the 1982 CDC cluster study involving the so-called Patient Zero], and he approved every word of it. Now we're getting into very fine points of argument, and they're not very substantial.'[1]

This exchange refers, in part, to a review of *And the Band Played On* that had just been published by Duncan Campbell in the *New Statesman*.[2] Campbell reports a telephone conversation with Darrow in which Darrow explained that the CDC cluster study, which sought to determine whether AIDS was caused by sexual transmission of an infectious agent, was based on speculation that the duration between infection and onset of symptoms was nine to eleven months. Having later learned, as all of us, including Shilts, did, that the period probably averages about eight *years*, Darrow claimed that he made it very clear to Shilts that the Patient Zero story was nonsense. He furthermore said that he pleaded with Shilts not to publish the name of Patient Zero, Gaetan Dugas, fearing that Dugas's family would suffer (and indeed the family later faced death threats).

Shilts cancelled an interview with Campbell when he learned what the *New Statesman* review would entail, and later attacked Campbell in an interview with the gay newspaper *Coming Up*, complaining that this was the typical crap I get from certain segments of the gay press . . . I go way back on working on this [epidemic]—and to get it from Campbell, who just came out of his comfortable closet a year ago. . . . I think he has ideological reasons. He's out front, he says it makes gay people look bad. The fact is Patient Zero did exist. . . .. It's a brilliant book, superb. . . .[The review is] more snide than *The Bay Area Reporter.* It's a nasty, vindictive attack. It's the only place I've gotten a bad review; the mainstream press loved my book.[3]

Indeed, the mainstream press did love Shilts's book. What Shilts does not say, but what he nevertheless makes clear, is that he returns their love. Ultimately he dismisses the Campbell review by saying that the *New Statesman* (a British equivalent to the *Nation* in the United States) is insignificant, a marginal publication. Shilts's book is in every way a product of his identification with the dominant media and their claim to objectivity. It is this claim that allows Shilts, along with the *New York Times*, for example, to disregard the demands of people with AIDS that they not be called AIDS victims. To accede to their demands would be to give in to a special interest group, a group with an ideological bias. Other groups with ideological biases meriting Shilt's disdain, for which there is ample evidence in *And the Band Played On*, are gay community leaders and AIDS activists.

'Personally, I'm not an ideological person,' Shilts said at the ICA. 'I don't think you can be a journalist and really have a political ideology, because you tend to see the fallacies in all ideologies.' Speaking from this dangerously naive or cynically disingenuous ideological position that calls itself 'objective,' Shilts explains that

the whole problem of AIDS from the start was that liberals were trying to be sweet and not tell the whole story, the conservatives did not want to tell the whole story, and I felt what I wanted to do was get the whole story out. At some point I just have to say, I think my work has integrity. I think my work is honest.

Shilts's defense of the Patient Zero story hinges entirely on this naive notion of truth, on the fact, simply, that the story actually happened. But truth is never unproblematic, never a simple matter of empirical facts; it is always selective, always a particular construction, and always exists within a specific context. By the time the narrative of *And the Band Played On* ends, officially 6,079 people had died of AIDS in the United States. Shilts might have selected any one of those people's stories to tell. Among the very few he did select was that of Gaeton Dugas, which makes his story about one six-thousandth of the 'truth.'

Shilts selected Dugas's story, as he said at the ICA, because it was 'fascinating.' But what does it mean in the context of AIDS to be *fascinated*? What are the *unconscious* mechanisms that would account for this very selective will to truth? Is this not precisely what Shilts means when he says of the media that they are interested in sexy stories? Is this not, in fact, the recounting of a story we already know, the story of Typhoid Mary, the story of the murderously irresponsible, sexually voracious gay man? Is this not the story of Fabian Bridges, as told on the 1986 *Frontline* special 'AIDS: A National Inquiry,' in which a black homeless gay man with AIDS, who was forced to support himself by hustling, was bribed by the PBS crew in order to get their story and then reported to the authorities? Is it not the story of the bisexual deliberately infecting 'innocent women' in the *Midnight Caller* episode of December 13, 1988, whose producers defended themselves against the protests of the San Francisco gay community by citing the Patient Zero story as proof that such things really do happen?[4] Is it not the story of Rock Hudson, as it was recounted before a jury who would award his ex-lover millions of dollars in damages? Is it not the story of prostitutes and junkies as the media portrays them every day? Is it not ultimately the story of all people with AIDS as they haunt the imaginations of those whose fear and loathing Shilts is so unable to comprehend? Is it not, finally, in the eyes of the INS, the story of Hans Paul Verhoef, the Dutchman they feared would spread AIDS at the Lesbian and Gay Health Conference?

The problem with the Patient Zero story is not whether or not it is true. We now know, in any case, that it is not, at least insofar as we know that Gaeton Dugas had sex with the other men in the CDC cluster study after they had already been infected. Nor is it merely the problem that this story was selected by Shilts's publishers as the story that would sell the book, and that they therefore gave it pride of place in their publicity and had it serialized in *California Magazine*.[5] The real problem with Patient Zero is that he already existed as a phobic fantasy in the minds of Shilts's readers before Shilts ever wrote the story. And, thanks in part to *And the Band Played On*, that fantasy still haunts us—as it still haunts Shilts—today. 'I had written a book to change the world,' Shilts says in *Esquire*.[6] What he forgot was that this is a world in which people's fantasies of homosexuality include gay waiters running into the kitchen to ejaculate in the salad dressing, or of gay foreigners attending health conferences with no other purpose than to infect their fellow conferees with a deadly virus. Patient Zero is just such a fantasy, and it matters not one whit whether his story is true or not.

['Randy Shilts's Miserable Failure', in Martin Duberman (ed.), *A Queer World: The Center for Lesbian and Gay Studies Reader* (New York: New York University Press, 1997, 642–5.]

GABRIEL ROTELLO

144   The Sexual Ecology of HIV

HIV truly strikes us where we live. Its means of transmission—sex—is the very thing that to many of us defines us as gay men, drives our politics and our erotics, gives us our modern identity, provides the mortar of much of our philosophy and community, animates much of our lives. For these reasons we have good cause to shy away from a close examination of how certain key elements of our identity contributed to the disaster that now engulfs us. We have another good cause as well: Gay men have been blamed for AIDS since the disease appeared in mid 1981, and our reflexive response has been to resist being made scapegoats for a scourge that counted us among its primary victims. It has seemed politically wise instead to shift the focus to the substantial failings of government and media and the scientific establishment. Those failings were so egregious, and contributed so seriously to the epidemic in the early years, that it was hardly a stretch of the imagination to believe that AIDS was the result of factors wholly outside the gay world.

Someone has remarked that if you want to tell a really convincing lie, you have to believe it yourself. If so, AIDS activists must sound very convincing when we argue that 'sex does not cause AIDS, a virus does.' Or when we say, 'There are no risk groups, only risky behaviors.' Or when we insist, 'It's not who you have sex with or where you have it that counts, it's what you do.' Fighting the soundbites of blame with our own soundbites of self-defense has seemed essential to the goal of convincing ourselves of the absolute justice of our cause. And once gay men came to believe in the mid eighties that we had largely solved the problem of HIV transmission through the invention of safer sex—an invention, by the way, that society at large did little to encourage and much to hinder—further discussion of our own role seemed not only politically unwise, but pointless, self-loathing, downright mean. And so we have thrown up a fog of half-truths, and in the process we have blinded ourselves.

Such was already the situation in 1987 when Randy Shilts published *And the Band Played On*. In that seminal work he described the epidemic as a result of a series of failures by the government, the health and research establishments, the media, and, importantly, the gay community. Yet he was vilified by many gay and AIDS activists who felt that any discussion of gay men's role was too much discussion. Many felt then, and many still feel, with some justification, that it is better to circle the wagons, fight off the hate mongers, and leave any theoretical discussions of our own possible role in AIDS to the ponderings of future generations. [. . .]

Our reluctance to examine the epidemiology of AIDS has helped perpetuate a number of myths about the epidemic, at least within the gay world, and so the first chapters of this book will attempt to walk the reader through AIDS as it is now understood by researchers, challenging the misconceptions that have become ingrained in the public imagination of the disease.

Myth: The epidemic occurred primarily because HIV is a new disease in humans, one that crossed from simians to people very recently and found a hospitable niche. In fact, while HIV clearly evolved from a simian virus or viruses, it appears to have existed in humans for at least several decades before the epidemic began in the seventies. It may even have occurred, although rarely, for centuries. It now seems likely that the primary reason the epidemic began when it did was not that a microbe jumped from animals to people, but that large-scale changes in human behavior provided HIV with radically new opportunities to spread.

Myth: It was essentially an accident that the epidemic struck gay men. In fact HIV is extremely selective and only produces epidemics when a population's behavior provides it with a niche. Without favorable conditions, HIV cannot spread in a given population. Among gay men in the seventies, our sexual behavior was extraordinarily conducive to the transmission of HIV.

Myth: These kinds of behavioral explanations cannot really explain why AIDS hit gay men when it did, because gay men have always behaved essentially the same. In fact, gay history provides compelling evidence that there were very significant changes in gay male behavior in the years preceding the epidemic, the very kinds of changes needed to facilitate the rapid spread of HIV. These included a sharp increase in anal sex with multiple partners, the appearance of so-called core groups of men who engaged in extraordinary levels of risky sexual behavior, and a rapid increase in the amount of sexual mixing between people in those core groups and the rest of the gay population. Indeed, few groups in history appear to have changed their overall sexual behavior as rapidly and profoundly as homosexual American men in the decades before AIDS.

Myth: It is homophobic to implicate aspects of gay behavior in the epidemic because straight people behave essentially the same. In fact, HIV will soon sweep the heterosexual population in the United States the same way it swept through gay men. In fact, twenty years after HIV began its relentless decimation of the gay population, it remains largely confined to the same heterosexual groups in the developed world that it infected from the start: hemophiliacs, intravenous drug users, and their female sexual partners and children. The only self-sustaining heterosexual HIV epidemic in the United States appears to be among crack cocaine addicts, who share many factors of sexual ecology with gay men.

Myth: While the above might be true here in the developed world, HIV is a heterosexual disease in the rest of the world, proving that gay behaviour is irrelevant. In fact, HIV is spreading in an extremely selective way in the wider world, causing disastrous epidemics in places where heterosexual ecology favors its spread, and causing no epidemic at all in places where heterosexual behavior is less conducive. If anything, the highly selective spread of HIV around the world shows that AIDS is neither a gay nor a straight epidemic, but an ecological epidemic that exploits certain behaviors, chief among them the practice of having large numbers of partners, straight or gay.

Myth: Multiple partners don't matter, because gay men's promotion of condoms created a workable version of safe sex that allows people to continue to have multiple partners safely. In fact, the condom code does not seem ever to have been very successful in containing the epidemic. The drop in new infections in the mid-eighties, for example, probably occurred because most of the susceptible gay men were already infected. Now that a new generation of susceptible young men have entered the gay world, they are getting infected at rates that indicate that about half will eventually get AIDS, which is about the same ratio as in the older generation. The fact is that many people do not seem able to use condoms consistently enough to stem the epidemic.

Condoms are very important in the battle against AIDS, but total reliance on the condom code blinds us to the fact that condoms are just one narrow possibility in the possible arsenal of responses to AIDS. The condom code in the gay world is, in many ways, as much a political as a medical construction. Its dual purpose has been to prevent HIV transmission while preserving the 'sex positivity' of gay male culture, thereby proving that the gay sexual revolution of the seventies can continue during a fatal epidemic of a sexually transmitted disease. But it provides virtually no room for error, and is in many respects anti-ecological, a classic 'technological fix,' because it has never addressed the larger factors in the gay environment that helped spread HIV. Since it is not working to contain the epidemic, we need to explore more holistic possibilities, which involve challenging and changing larger factors of gay life that encourage unsafe behavior.

Finally, we have the most potentially dangerous myth of all:

Myth: If AIDS is cured or contained by drug treatments, gay men can return to the sexual lifestyle of the seventies. Ultimately, to understand sexual ecology is to understand that the gay sexual revolution of the seventies was profoundly anti-ecological. Gay men can never go back.

In the final portion of this volume I will discuss how ecological thinking might help gay men create a new gay culture that could lower overall risk. The goal is a sustainable gay culture that both affirms gay identity and sexuality and, at the same time, provides a built-in measure of safety that would prevent the resurgence of AIDS or the emergence of new epidemics. I will draw parallels between the challenge facing gay men and that of other ecological movements, particularly the quest for population control, which shares many areas of common concern with AIDS prevention. But before we delve into these issues in more detail, it's important first to draw connections among the basic concepts of ecology, disease transmission, and sexual behavior that will appear again and again throughout this book.

[*Sexual Ecology: AIDS and the Destiny of Gay Men* (Harmondsworth: Dutton, 1997), 5–6, 8–10.]

SIMON WATNEY

145 **Media Fabrications**

This is why the representation of Aids seems so starkly anachronistic: gay sex, read as 'promiscuous', is being medically redefined as unsafe. Aids takes us back to the pre-modern world, with disease restored to its ancient theological status as punishment. Therefore it is most important to question the systematic misclassification of Aids as a Sexually Transmitted Disease (henceforth STD). For although the HIV virus is primarily acquired through sex, this does not mean that it is primarily an STD. As Kaye Wellings of the Family Planning Association observes:

'To include in the category those diseases which "can be transmitted" makes the category so large as to be meaningless. If all conditions that could be transmitted sexually were included, then the common cold might well find itself being dealt with in STD clinics'.[1]

The entire representation of Aids hangs upon the ways in which, as she points out, 'medicine has been used to normalise sexual conduct'.[2] This is the perspective from which we read of the 'Aids virus', a phrase which falsely telescopes and concentrates the entire context of the disease into a narrow alignment with specific sexual acts. Hence the plethora of medical explanations which proceeded from the assumption that there must be something about gay sex as such which rendered so many gay men vulnerable to infection. These 'explanations' included the supposedly 'immuno-suppressive nature' of sperm, and the still more obviously homophobic notion that the mere possibility of blood to sperm contact might be responsible. Needless to say, such explanations would find it difficult to account for the survival of a high proportion of people of both sexes enjoying anal sex over the course of human history.

The fact that an incurable virus has invaded our communities cannot be blamed on gay sex as such, though the situation is exacerbated by the fact that we both fuck and get fucked, thus running a high risk of both absorbing infected sperm, and passing it on. Edmund White has used this same observation to argue against explanations of Aids which attribute it to gay 'promiscuity'. But I do not think this is particularly helpful, since it is obvious that gay culture has enabled us to enjoy sex, and not feel guilty about it, and not always to equate love with lifelong sexual fidelity to one person. This has been the strength of our culture, not its weakness. In any case it remains far from clear that gay men talking about sex, and moralists talking about sex, are actually referring to the same thing. For the moralist sex is a thing you do, an act, with a limited duration and a clear performance principle. For most gay men, however, sex involves a far broader degree of general eroticised physical contact, in which fucking and sucking are episodes of intimacy among others. As Robert Glück has written of pre-Aids bath-house sex in San Francisco: 'We watch the pleasure rather than the men, feeling the potential interchangeability'.[3] Gay sex is about maximising the mutual erotic possibilities of the body, and that is why it is taboo. It comes too close to the infant's experience of polymorphous perversity — deriving potential sexual pleasure from every part of itself and its surroundings — which is so violently repressed in the formation of orthodox adult sexualities.

In this manner powerful social *and* psychic factors combine to frame Aids as a product of sexual 'excess', in terms of quantity and quality. Firm statistics showing the distribution of the virus amongst gay men are impossible to come by, since those coming forward for antibody testing are likely to have done so from a perception of risk which already distinguishes them from most men on the gay scene in Britain. For reasons which I have already touched on, there is little or no equivalent in the UK to the American range of gay identities, since homosexuality here is always in competition with other identities, of class, race and regionalism, all competing for ascendancy. Whilst this ensures that homosexuality is more broadly integrated into other areas of social consciousness, by the same token it also means that gay men have a much weaker sense of collective interest than in the United States. The situation of British gay men is far more atomised than that of our American contemporaries, and we are far more closely subject to immediate and direct regulation, ranging from licensing laws, legal prohibitions against bathhouses, and the enforced absence of anything remotely resembling the sex-affirmative cultural institutions which flourish in America. The disco revolution of the early 1970s has now atrophied into a deafening inferno of hi-energy muzak. The majority of gay pubs are still owned by breweries who have no interest in their clientele beyond issues of profitability. Pubs and clubs alike have signally failed to take any initiatives on behalf of the very people who have no choice but to use their services, given the close invigilation of alcohol licences by the police, which effectively forbids the possibility of an autonomous large-scale gay social scene. There are no national publications remotely comparable to the *Advocate* or the *New York Native* in America, or *Gai Pied* in France, or *The Body Politic* in Canada. British gay men are extraordinarily cut off from other national gay cultures, and in the absence of a local gay press of any seriousness, have little access to information about Aids beyond what is available in the national dailies, and on television. This is the baleful situation in which any realistic discussion of safe sex must be set.

By definition, epidemiology is about statistics. The statistical likelihood of contracting the HIV virus from a new sexual partner in New York is now put at fifty-fifty, and up to five per cent for women. Counselling monogamy as an end in itself in such a context is simply putting the cart before the horse, since monogamous sex is no safer than any other kind, especially if you're gay and potentially at risk of contracting the virus from anyone who's had sex in the last seven years. In a purely statistical sense it could be argued that immediate and total punitive fidelity would lead to something less than an exact doubling of HIV infection, since many people with the virus would presumably end up with partners in the same situation. Then, according to this logic, the situation would be contained. But sex is not about statistics, and punitive fidelity would inevitably produce sexual counteraction, even if it could in any way be effectively policed. Besides, sexuality is intrinsically caught up in unconscious circuits of abandon and denial, desire and resistance. Changes in sexual behaviour cannot be forced, they can only be achieved through consent, consent which incorporates change into the very structure of sexual fantasy. Hence the urgent, the desperate need to eroticise information about safe sex, if tens of thousands of more lives are not to be cruelly sacrificed on the twin altars of prudery and homophobia.

[*Policing Desire: Pornography, AIDS and the Media* (Minneapolis: University of Minnesota Press, 1987), 126–9.]

IV.g. Sex Surveys: Have we Returned to Normal?

The social survey as a method of social science research has continued to evolve since Kinsey's day. One may survey people nowadays about their favourite laundry soap or political views with some confidence about the accuracy of the results. However, just as in Kinsey's day, volatile or intimate issues like politics, religion, and sex are likely to produce assertions or silences that make surveys about them particularly inadequate. One can undertake, as Kinsey did, in-depth interviews conducted by individuals trained to spot inconsistencies, but even when combined with written questionnaires this technique is only likely to diminish the magnitude of inaccuracy. International or cross-cultural comparisons are also problematic since survey instruments, like the things they attempt to measure, vary widely.

France, Great Britain, and the United States have conducted extensive randomized national surveys of sexual behaviour and attitudes within the last five years. They are very different in structure and design. The British survey 'reluctantly' excluded questions on masturbation because test respondents had expressed 'distaste and embarrassment' about them. The British survey also excluded questions about orgasmic frequency in men and women, while the French and Americans included them. The French attempted to distinguish themselves from a behaviourist 'Anglo-Saxon' emphasis on perception of health risk and risk comportment by surveying sexual behaviour alone, and only the American survey actually included data derived from extensive interviews.[1] The only two things they shared in common, it appears, were the fact that they were all driven by the AIDS epidemic and all experienced some degree of political harassment.

Since earlier surveys were often notoriously inaccurate, we cannot accurately measure the changes in sexual behaviour and attitudes that have taken place since mid-century. However, these surveys do incorporate a historical component in the form of survey data from older age cohorts whose sexual attitudes were formed many decades earlier. In a passage from the British survey, we find that non-penetrative sex is more important and more frequently practised in younger cohorts. The authors speculate that education and openness may have brought about this important change (Extract 146).

All the surveys addressed found evidence of significant same-sex sexual behaviour. All the surveys agreed that Kinsey's elevated statistics about the prevalence of homosexuality had been skewed by his selection techniques. The French survey found only 4.1 per cent of males and 2.6 per cent of females had had a homosexual experience in their lives (pp. 138–9). The British survey found slightly higher rates of homosexual 'experience' at 6.1 per cent for men and 3.4

---

[1] Alfred Spira, Nathalie Bajos et al., *Les Comportements sexuels en France* (Paris: La Documentation Française, 1993), 30–1; Edward O. Laumann, John H. Gagnon, et al., *The Social Organization of Sexuality: Sexual Practices in the United States* (Chicago: University of Chicago Press, 1994), 57–63.

per cent for women (p. 191). The American survey on this issue, excerpted below, is remarkable for the multi-level approach it took. But, though its results produced higher numbers in some categories than the British and French surveys, they were still far lower than Kinsey's (Extract 147).

It is difficult to know what to make of these figures. If anything, sex surveys are probably more reliable indicators of the ingeniousness and cultural bias of their creators than guides to the 'facts' of sex, particularly in the case of homosexuality. Indeed the surveys themselves are cultural documents that shape responses and categories of sexuality by the questions they ask and the statistical manipulations they perform on them. There is a considerable chasm between the British survey's failure to even gather statistics on orgasmic experience (as opposed to attitudes about its importance in 'sexual satisfaction') and the French sacralization of the 'simultaneous orgasm' by means of vaginal penetration. The French survey determined that 88.8 per cent of men and 74.6 per cent of women had experienced an orgasm in their last sexual encounter, and 52 per cent of men and 42 per cent of women claimed they 'often' had simultaneous orgasms (pp. 157, 198). The American survey, while reporting high rates of orgasmic frequency, made a particular effort to explain the divergences in the reported frequencies between men and women (Extract 148).

It is tempting to conclude that this makes the British appear prudish, the French erotically self-deluded, and the Americans either cynical or too psychologistic. A recent study of the history of sex surveys in Britain since the Second World War reveals how the questions asked and the questions not asked reveal the gradual evolution of the sense of the permissible, and perhaps even of the conceivable, in their findings. Indeed, as Liz Stanley points out, the notion of sexual enlightenment is built into the structure of each new survey in the form of the assumption that 'sex' will have 'progressed' in various ways from the benighted past. But, as she points out, even the recent National Survey makes certain assumptions about what 'sex' is, privileging penetrational sex in particular, though this might simply be the convergence of a traditional preference with our contemporary obsession with infection by means of 'unsafe sex' (Extract 149).

To get another assessment of the effects of the 'sexual revolution' we might examine a qualitative study by the American anthropologist Michael Moffatt. Moffatt carried out an ethnological study of undergraduate sexuality at Rutgers University in New Jersey in the mid-1980s in which he went underground as a (non-traditional age) undergraduate living in the university dormitory. He supplemented his gleanings from late-night discussions with students with questionnaires and descriptive papers written for him anonymously in his classes. What he found is an interesting mixture of the old and the new in sexual values and comportment, expressed, as it happens, altogether in the language of the 'new' frankness in sexual matters. Extract 150 is an excerpt from his section on 'The New Sexual Orthodoxy.'

Analysis of reporting non-penetrative sex by age group also showed age differences in behaviour. For both men and women aged 18–59, the proportion reporting non-penetrative sex in the last year and ever declined with increasing age. Over 75% of men and women aged 18–24 reported this activity in the last year, but this proportion fell to 47.7% of men and 39.0% of women amongst the over 45s. Nevertheless, this was a common activity in all age groups. The data suggest that such activity may also have increased with successive generations, since 68.3% of men and 61.2% of women over 45 reported ever having experience of non-penetrative sex not leading to intercourse, compared with 85.3% of men and 84.8% of women in the youngest age group (18–24). At first sight, these findings may appear surprising, since the group aged 45–59 became sexually active in the era before the availability of reliable contraception. They might be expected to have relied to a greater extent on non-penetrative sex as a means of sexual expression in order to avoid unwanted pregnancy. Balanced against this is the greater discussion, education and openness in sexual matters in late generations, which may have led to greater knowledge and the practice of a wider sexual repertoire. It is possible that the question on non-penetrative sex was less well understood by older respondents than younger respondents, leading to under-reporting, but this in turn would lend support to an explanation involving generational changes in knowledge of possible modes of sexual expression.

It is evident that the proportion reporting only vaginal intercourse in the last year increases with age. These age effects are less marked in the data for patterns of sexual practices ever, the most marked pattern being the large increase in those over 45 reporting only vaginal intercourse in their lifetime. This suggests both ageing and age cohort effects in the data. Both these effects are less evident for the practice of anal intercourse.

The foregoing discussion has commented in some detail on the age effects on both recent and lifetime experience of sexual practices. It is evident from this that, in addition to possible ageing effects in the frequency and variety of sexual practices, there have also been marked secular trends in patterns of behaviour. [. . .] For both men and women, experience of oral and non-penetrative sex appears to have increased through the 1950s and 1960s, reaching a steady level of more than 80% of those who experienced their first sexual intercourse in the 1970s onwards.

By contrast, there is very little in the way of a secular trend in the reporting of anal intercourse, other than a slight tendency for the most recently sexually active to report this in the last year; this may reflect a more sexually adventurous phase in their careers than their older counterparts, rather than a true trend representing increased frequency of anal intercourse over the generations.

> ['Heterosexual Practices', in Anne M. Johnson et al., *Sexual Attitudes and Lifestyles* (Oxford: Blackwell Scientific Publications, 1994), 168–70.]

EDWARD O. LAUMANN, JOHN H. GAGNON, ET AL.

147   Homosexuality in America

For the purpose of this analysis we have divided the questions that relate to homosexual experiences and feelings into three basic dimensions: behavior, desire, and identity. The questions that we asked about behavior always refer to partners or practices in specific time frames. Desire and identity are measured by questions about the respondents' current states of mind. Because of the many ways in which these three aspects of sexuality might be defined, we first explain how we operationalized them in our questionnaire and then compare their reported frequencies, before turning to an investigation of their interrelations.

Two quite different questions were asked to ascertain the presence of same-gender sexual 'desire'. The first asked about the appeal of sex with someone of the same gender, the second about the gender of the people to whom the respondent is sexually attracted. These questions appear toward the end of the interview after the main questions about partners and behavior. The first question was worded, 'On a scale of 1 to 4, where 1 is very appealing and 4 is not at all appealing, how would you rate each of these activities: . . . having sex with someone of the same sex?' For this analysis, the two answers 'very appealing' and 'somewhat appealing' are combined and treated as indicating the presence of homosexual desire. We call this measure *appeal*.

Later in the interview, at the end of a set of questions about early childhood and first sexual experiences, women were asked, 'In general, are you sexually attracted to only men, mostly men, both men and women, mostly women, only women?' Men were asked the same question, except that the order of the answer categories was reversed. Respondents answering with any of the four categories referring to people of the same gender are treated here as expressing some level of homosexual desire. We refer to this variable as *attraction*.

Immediately following the question about attraction, a single question was asked about how respondents think of themselves: 'Do you think of yourself as heterosexual, homosexual, bisexual, or something else?' This question yielded our measure of self-identification.[1] For the purpose of this analysis, we have treated respondents who said either 'homosexual' or 'bisexual' as having some degree of same-gender identity. Altogether, 2.8 percent of the men and

1.4 percent of the women reported some level of homosexual (or bisexual) identity.[2]

We have constructed five different measures of same-gender behaviour. [. . .][3] The rates for women are lower than the rates for men, varying from 1.3 percent of the sexually active women in the past year reporting at least one female partner to 4.1 percent reporting any female partners since turning eighteen. The rates for men vary from 2.7 percent in the past year to 4.9 percent with any male partners since age eighteen. The next two sets of bars labelled *any age* and *any sex* extend the period for same-gender sex back to puberty. Conceptually, they measure the same thing; however, they approach the measurement in different ways and produce different estimates, especially for the men.

Any age is a measure of the proportion of respondents who have had a same-gender partner at any time since puberty. It is constructed by combining responses from the previous three partner/time frame questions (past year, past five years, and since age eighteen) and the response to a question about the first sexual experience after puberty with a person of the same gender.[4] About 3.8 percent of the women and 7.1 percent of the men had had at least one same-gender partner since puberty according to this variable.

Any sex is based on questions asked on a self-administered questionnaire (SAQ) at the very end of the interview. The interviewer does not see the answers to these questions because the SAQ is placed in an envelope and sealed by the respondent before being handed back. These questions ask about ever having engaged in specific sexual activities with a man or woman since puberty. Both male and female respondents were asked about active and receptive oral sex and the question, 'Have you ever done anything else sexual with another (woman/man)?' Male respondents were also asked about active and receptive anal sex with another man. *Any sex* is the proportion of respondents who completed the self-administered questionnaire who answered yes to any of the activities. Over 4 percent of the women and 9 percent of the men reported having engaged in at least one of these sexual practices with a person of their own gender since puberty.

This last measure produced the highest reporting of same-gender sexual behavior. But the differences are slight for the women and dramatic for the men. There are a number of factors that help explain this pattern. Very few women (about 0.3 percent) who report having sex between puberty and age eighteen with a female partner do not also have sex with a woman after eighteen. On the other hand, almost 2 percent of the men (comparing *any age* and *since 18*) report sex before eighteen but not after. However, when we look at *any sex*, the rate of women having a female partner since puberty increases another 0.5 percentage point, from 3.8 to 4.3 percent. But the rate for men increases another 2 percentage points, from 7.1 to 9.1 percent. If this higher number is correct, this implies that almost 4 percent of the men have sex with another male before turning eighteen but not after. These men, who report same-gender sex only before they turned eighteen, not afterward, constitute 42 percent of the total number of men who report ever having a same-gender experience.

But why should one measure be so much higher for the men than another conceptually similar measure? There are several possibilities. The increased privacy of the self-administered form may increase reporting of socially stigmatized behavior. Or the question may be understood somewhat differently by the respondent and may prompt a different answer. *Any sex* is based on questions about specific sexual practices rather than a question about sex partners. Some respondents may not have given an age for a first same-gender sex partner (the major component of *any age*) but might be prompted to remember a specific incident when a sexual act occurred. Some of these acts may not have been considered when reporting about a first same-gender partner. Finally, the questions about *any sex* are asked at the very end of the questionnaire, providing the fullest chance for recall. This measure produces a dramatically higher rate of same-gender partners than the other measures for men. However, it should be pointed out that, while this 9 percent is higher than any figure reported from the other recent surveys, and while it may be an under-report, it is still a far cry from the 37 percent that Kinsey reported.

[*The Social Organization of Sexuality: Sexual Practices in the United States* (Chicago: University of Chicago, 1994), 292–6.]

EDWARD O. LAUMANN, JOHN, H. GAGNON, ET AL.

148   A Gendered Interpretation of Orgasm

An ambiguity concerning orgasm is highlighted by our respondents' reports of their sex partners' experience of orgasm. Recall that these comparisons are between people sharing the same background attributes, not partners in the same relationship. The assumption is that these individuals are likely to have sex partners who have a similar background status and that this correlation is more robust among certain master status variables than among others (e.g., people of the same race are more likely to be married to each other than are people of the same age). While women's estimates of how often their male partners experience orgasm were very close to the reports of our male respondents (78 and 75 percent, respectively), the proportion of men who claimed that their partners always had an orgasm was 15 percentage points higher than women's own reports (44 and 29 percent, respectively). Some groups reported even larger differences, and, in the case of education, these differences were systemic. Among those men whose education ranged from less than high school to entry into college, the difference between men's estimates of women's orgasm and the self-reports of orgasm of women who were at the same education level was 20 percent and higher. This difference falls to 4 percent among those with advanced degrees.

This suggests that better-educated men have more accurate perceptions of how often their partners achieve orgasm. It is also interesting that men in cohabitational relationships substantially overestimate the proportion of partners always having orgasm when compared to reports by women in cohabitational relationships (the difference is 27 percentage points).

A more detailed multivariate analysis would be needed to determine these differences more precisely. However, there are several possible explanations that might be advanced for this discrepancy. Men may be overreporting how often their partners experience orgasm because it is a socially desirable outcome of sexual interaction. Men may also have more difficulty identifying the occurrence of female orgasm. The desirability of orgasm, coupled with the fact that it is not always easily identified, may lead men to misinterpret certain events occurring during sexual interaction as signs of orgasm. Finally, some women may feign the occurrence of orgasm during sex if it is unlikely to happen and the sex partner involved is highly invested in his capacity to induce orgasm.

[*The Social Organization of Sexuality: Sexual Practices in the United States* (Chicago: University of Chicago, 1994), 115–18.]

LIZ STANLEY

149   The Cultural Bias of Sex Surveys

These British sex surveys are apparently entirely empirical and descriptive in approach, but they actually articulate a coherent set of ideas about sexuality and its relationship to other aspects of social life. There are, of course, differences of approach and emphasis between them. None the less, their frameworks of ideas share a number of distinctive features, which bring them considerably closer to the views and understandings of the people who are the objects of their researches than the authors would have been eager to recognise. In particular, and with the apparent exception of the National Survey, such surveys operate in a context characterised by the taken-for-grantedness of what 'sex' is: everyone is assumed to know and agree about the 'what', 'when' and 'who' of sex, to the extent that the basic behaviours with which these surveys are concerned are not looked at in any detail. The gloss of 'sex' defined as 'intercourse' is more often than not used as though there can be no variant behaviour involved beneath this visible and easily investigated tip. This is linked to their additional assumption that 'what people do' is governed, indeed determined, by 'the natural', by some kind of innate biological urge or imperative which is universally experienced and enacted. However, it is clear from the various 'problems' discussed by these studies that what was considered to be 'natural' underwent some fairly wide-reaching changes over the half-century between the 1940s and the 1990s, and also that such changes considerably impinged on the research carried out.

Thus Slater and Woodside note that younger women compared with older not only expected more of marriage but tended to relate marital problems to difficult material circumstances; and they also note that the women interviewed frequently had no idea of what was meant by 'an orgasm', and were equally uncomprehending of some of the other terms used. Similarly, while Chesser fails to look in any detail at what 'intercourse' and 'petting' consist of, his research does pinpoint the changes that had occurred regarding women's increased sexual experience both before and outside marriage. Schofield's investigation of young people's sexual behaviour begins to deconstruct the monolith of 'sex', looking at a range of constituent behaviours, but many of which are then relegated to the glossing term 'petting' and thereby treated as different from 'real' sex. Here, of course, Schofield adopts a commonsensical viewpoint, although his purpose was neither to analyse commonsensical constructions of what 'sex' is, nor to discuss the different constructions of 'sex' held by men and women that Slater and Woodside's research hints at and Gorer's work centres on. For Gorer, the existence of a 'sexual double standard' constitutes the major way of understanding sexual behaviour, with women seen as having different understandings and behaviours from men. There are similarities here with Chesser's research, which at a number of points implies both that women's orgasmic functioning and sexual desire is different from men's, and also that it thereby constitutes a 'difficulty' that needs to be 'overcome'. The National Survey certainly asked people about a much wider variety of behaviours, the vaginal, oral and anal and 'other genital forms of sex', but, interestingly, it still fails to investigate how these genital sexual behaviours interlink with other erotic and sexual but non-genital behaviour, and nor does it investigate whether and in what ways these 'patterns' might differ with a change of partners, or on different occasions. Thus even at the level of describing the behavioural, the National Survey research is surprisingly limited, while it explicitly excludes meaning altogether and unaccountably eschews analysis except at the most basic of levels.

Behind such taken-for-grantedness about what 'sex' is and how its constituent behaviours articulate lies the even more fundamental assumption of heterosexuality as axiomatically 'the norm', as 'what is natural' in sexual terms because seen as entirely innate. In Slater and Woodside's and Chesser's researches there is no mention of any homosexual behaviour or partners at all, and while Schofield notes that a significant proportion of both boys and girls knew others involved in homosexual sexual experiences, with a smaller group being so involved themselves, this is not explored in his research, which focuses instead on 'sex'—that is, heterosex. Gorer's *Exploring English Character* notes that most of those people who were 'not interested in sex' were actually homosexually involved (and thus *were* 'interested in sex', although not of a heterosexual kind), but his later *Sex and Marriage* completely ignores the existence of homosexual behaviour and the overlapping of homosexual and heterosexual experiences and feelings in a large number of people's lives. Only the National Survey does not proceed from the assumption that the 'sex' that is being inquired about is necessarily heterosexual. However, it too ends by relegating everything else to an implicit 'and also' status, through its concern with fixing people to 'lifestyles' which are conceived as heterosexual or, for a supposedly tiny minority, gay male.[1]

The taken-for-grantedness of (heterosexual) sex links to a further related assumption, that of the synonymity of heterosexuality and specifically *penetrational* forms of sex. Thus Slater and Woodside are concerned almost exclusively with 'intercourse', looking at modes of its 'performance' on a weekly basis and people's assumption of a norm in its performance and their own claimed adherence to such a norm. Similarly, Chesser discusses mainly intercourse within marriage; and although women's perception of the absence or insufficiency of 'petting' behaviours—that is, non-penetrational forms of love-making—provides one of the key reasons they give for sexual dissatisfaction, this is ignored by him. In some contrast and perhaps because he was concerned particularly with teenagers, Schofield does note the different behaviours and stages of 'petting' activities, but then still conceptualises these as falling short of 'sex', that is, penetration. Gorer construes the point at which people first 'had sex' as synonymous with first having intercourse, while his discussion of 'rates of intercourse' is precisely that, not rates of sexual behaviour as such but instead rates of penetration. Again, the National Survey asks about a wider range of activities—vaginal, oral and anal sex and other genital contact—although it remains concerned with what is 'high risk', the specifically genital rather than 'sexual experience' or 'sexual contact' defined more widely.

The assumption of a 'natural' sexual division of labour which assigns different 'roles' in sexual encounters between men and women, a division which can be summarised in stereotypical ideas about male sexual 'activity' and female 'passivity', appears widely in these surveys, along with the accompanying supposition that the different sexual responses of men and women to penetrational sex are the product of constitutional differences. Thus Slater and Woodside propose that women are less successful in their adaptation to 'sex' than men, evidenced in their lower rates of orgasm and their generally greater levels of dissatisfaction with sex in marriage; and here Slater and Woodside apparently discern some common unchanging 'it' which both men and women experience (or ought to) which is somehow independent of the particular relationship and the particular ways that each couple do 'it' together. Chesser proposes something similar, seeing any orgasmic failure in women as the product of changing physiological capacity rather than of the specificities of their experience of sex or of their partners' in/abilities and concerns as a lover. Similarly, Schofield's research notes a number of differences between the sexes: that the sexually active girls most often are so within the context of a sustained relationship, while the sexually active boys are more likely to be involved in a variety of casual relationships; and that more girls than boys do not enjoy their first or even repeated sexual experiences. Gorer's research centres on a 'sexual double standard', seeing women as different in sexual behaviour and even more so in attitude from men, and thereby, of course, treating them as different from an assumed norm which is actually set by *male* behaviour and *male* attitude. Again, the National Survey takes a different approach to sexual divisions of labour, in the sense of asking respondents both 'what they did' and also 'what partners did to them'. None the less, the actually reciprocal nature of many heterosexual sexual practices is glossed by use of behavioural terms that conventionally assign 'passivity' to women and 'activity' to men and this is particularly so regarding the range of penetrational activities the National Survey is especially concerned with.

These different surveys refer to changes in expectations concerning sexual behaviour and sexual pleasure occurring over time. The most obvious example is Chesser's discussion of changes across different age cohorts, although Schofield's research is premised on exploring the apparently different behaviour of young people in the 1960s as compared with earlier generations, while Gorer's work notes the increase in the numbers of women thinking that sex is important when evaluating their marital happiness. However, and with the partial exception of Chesser's work, all of these surveys—including, astonishingly, the National Survey, with its central concern with sexual change, transmission and control—*assume* rather than investigate change over time. The surveys see sexual change starting from relatively repressed and anti-pleasure ideas about sex in a relatively 'safe' context, and moving in the direction of more liberated and pleasure-based views, but in a relatively 'unsafe' context, either morally, or with regard to health, or both. However, in spite of their 'eye on the times' stance, the major change that occurred in sexual attitudes and sexual behaviour over the time-period that these surveys were carried out in is hardly recognised by them. This is the change that 'Little Kinsey' and also Mass-Observation's earlier work on the birth-rate both focused upon: changes regarding women's sexual expectations and women's marital behaviours. The earlier surveys all contain either ignored or undertheorised findings in this regard, while the National Survey excludes such information apart from birth control.

For the present-day reader what is perhaps most surprising is the almost complete failure in these surveys to subject to detailed investigation precisely what 'sex' consists of and how and in what kind of sexual/erotic circumstances the genital articulates with the non-genital. It is this failure to research what people were/are doing and not doing and the meanings that this had/has for them which prevents these surveys from coming to grips with social and sexual change.[2] However, while 'Little Kinsey' too fails to problematise 'sex', none the less it highlights in interesting ways Mass-Observation's more general and, by

1949, long-standing perception of a change in women's attitudes and behaviours, a change that encompassed the expectations that women had about their lives, their marriages and children, and of the part to be played by sex and sexual pleasure within this. In this regard 'Little Kinsey' certainly recognises social change and the part played by women's changing ideas within this, although, as I earlier commented, unlike Mass-Observation's work on the birth-rate it assigns an over-causative role to the sexual within social and economic life.

['Mass-Observation's "Little Kinsey" and the British Sex Survey Tradition', in Jeffrey Weeks and Janet Holland (eds.), *Sexual Cultures: Communities, Values and Intimacy* (London: Macmillan, 1996), 108–12.]

MICHAEL MOFFATT

150   Sex and the Single College Student

The first thing these papers tell us is that, sexually speaking, their undergraduate writers were the products of many influences besides college, let alone of Rutgers in particular. Perhaps one-third of the student writers mentioned the distinctive impact of college and college friends on their sexual developments. And about a third mentioned parental values and religious upbringing. But, on the evidence of these papers, *the* major influence on the sexualities of these undergraduates was contemporary American popular culture. The direct sources of the students' sexual ideas were located almost entirely in mass consumer culture: the late-adolescent / young-adult exemplars displayed in movies, popular music, advertising, and on TV; Dr Ruth and sex manuals; *Playboy, Penthouse, Cosmopolitan, Playgirl*, etc.; Harlequins and other pulp romances (females only); the occasional piece of real literature (one Catholic boy mentioned *Catcher in the Rye* with erotic gratitude); sex education and popular psychology as it had filtered through these sources, as well as through public schools, and as it continued to filter through the student-life infrastructure of the college; classic soft-core and hard-core pornographic movies, books, and (recently) home video cassettes. *Deep Throat* was the paradigmatic college hard-core film at Rutgers in the late 1970s. ('Can a guy really last that long?' one of my sophomore roommates asked me as we returned from the annual student ritual viewing in 1978.) *Bad Girls* and *Debbie Does Dallas* were coming on strong in the mid-1980s.[1]

In *The Sexual Fix*, a recent political and literary analysis of 'western capitalist' popular culture, the British critic Stephen Heath suggests the existence of a 'new sexual orthodoxy,' one that is in some ways as coercive as older, rejected western sexual codes. If pre-Victorians associated sex with sin and guilt but nevertheless often enjoyed it quietly as a private pleasure, Heath argues, and if the Victorians discovered sexuality and then repressed it, contemporary Anglo-Americans almost *must* celebrate it. Sexuality almost *must* be central to one's sense of self. And the essence of sexuality itself, in currently established conventions, is a technique-centred act of intercourse to orgasm—Heath calls it 'the big O.' If the archetypal Victorian novel ended in the good marriage, Heath quips, the archetypal contemporary romance ends in the explicitly described perfect orgasm.[2]

Much in these student sexual self-reports was consistent with Heath's somewhat polemic interpretation of the contemporary mass culture of sex. It was virtually impossible, for instance, for any writer of these papers, woman or man, to say, Sex is incidental, or I'm too young to think about such things, or To tell you the truth, I don't like sex very much. Sex *had* to be important, even for the sexually inactive:

I have never had sexual contact of any kind: no intercourse, no petting, no kissing, no anything. And I am not proud of this fact. You see, I am shy . . . [but] I am not a prude; I'm not content with my lifestyle. I believe in pre-marital sex; I just haven't been fortunate enough to have any. I consider sex a basic need in life, comparable to food and shelter.—Junior male

And those few students who tried to move away from the orthodoxy, who tried to say something idiosyncratic, were in the end 'controlled by the discourse.' In the end, pace Foucault, they virtually had to cop out for the centrality of sex and for sexual pleasure as an ideal:

I personally prefer sex not too often. My boyfriend is just the opposite. . . . I think my disinterest might be from the idea that I am not ready to handle being sexually active. (Don't get me wrong. I do enjoy sex and I do need it.)—Sophomore female[3]

The new sexual orthodoxy, as it was written in many of these papers, posited the normality and importance of sex for any postpubertal individual, female or male, unmarried or married. Among these college students, the value of premarital chastity was thus almost as dead as the dodo. Some of the student writers, about one in five of both the women and the men, did admit to being virgins. But almost all these virgins, like the young man above, suggested that their virginity was an embarrassment to them:

By the time I turned 20 I was growing anxious about my virginity. I was ready to get rid of it but nobody wanted the damn thing.—Junior female.

Only 3 of 144 student writers suggested that they were intentional virgins. All 3 were women; all 3 were Catholics; and all 3 were clearly defensive about their archaic sexual stances:

I don't consider myself a prude, but I strongly believe that *for me* sex without commitment (marriage) is wrong. I stress 'for me' because although I feel that my morals are right, I generally don't judge other people.—Senior female

And even the intentional virgins believed in their right to sexual pleasure as unmarried persons, another tenet of the new orthodoxy:

I have strong sexual desires and would definitely consider myself an extremely sexually-oriented person. . . . I truly believe that I have had good sexual experiences with my past boyfriends. My experiences go from kissing to 'everything but' intercourse. I don't think that my relationships have left my partners sexually frustrated because I take much pleasure in giving and receiving oral sex.—Senior female[4]

Perhaps two-thirds of the women and half the men overtly or tacitly promoted some version of the Playboy ethic, the obvious goodness of sexual pleasure for all persons. Only a few, perhaps 10 percent, were unambiguously sure that they experienced it or had experienced it on a regular basis:

I've always been told that sex is like candy: once you're introduced to it, you can never get enough. And boy, is that the truth!!—Sophomore female

Sex is an awesome sport and I have to admit if I had to stop it, I couldn't wouldn't and won't!'—Senior male

Another 5 percent of the writers considered themselves, all-in-all, unsuccessful at sexual pleasure, and they tended to sound depressed about themselves in general for this reason: they were abnormal in their drives; they were being cheated out of their rights.

I don't enjoy sex. . . . Actually, I think I'm afraid of sex. I have performance anxiety which is based on my lack of experience, my not very strong sex drive and the fear that my body might not match up with my partners. I don't have a very masculine physique.—Senior male

I have a boyfriend and I do feel genuine affection for him, but I never feel arousal. Sexually he is only in a slightly better position than I am . . . but at least he has an orgasm once in a while. I never do. So I guess I'm frigid.—Senior female[5]

The rest of these writers gave their varying experiences with actual sexual pleasure as many different mixed reviews as there were sexual autobiographies. (About two-thirds of these students chose to write sexual life histories.)

Women explicitly promoted the value of sexual pleasure more than men in these papers. This might have been partly due to the history of twentieth-century American sexual discourse regarding females; these women writers often seemed to be making a deliberate or scripted late-twentieth-century denial of an outmoded early-twentieth-century belief, of the stereotype, Nice girls don't (or shouldn't) like to do it. Some women simply said, as above, that sex was fun. Other women, especially the younger ones, came closer to older female ambivalences.

I guess I can't explain how I feel because my sexuality is too intricate and varies in every situation depending upon the male. I am basically afraid of what people might think of me if they knew about my sexual experiences.—Sophomore female

Women also discussed sexual pleasure in the negative more often than men, noting their difficulties achieving it in required form under the new orthodoxy—

orgasm through intercourse. About one-third of the sexually experienced women described their problems reaching orgasm:

The first orgasm I had was about a year ago. I was nineteen years old. I did it myself with the jet stream of water from the shower massage fixture in our shower. . . . My tub in my apartment now doesn't have such a fixture and I miss it.

My present boyfriend is the first and only guy with whom I've had an orgasm. This took place last spring. At first I could only relax enough to come when he'd bring me off with his hand. I feel vulnerable when I have an orgasm because it causes such bizarre movements and noises which I can't really control. Soon I was at ease enough to allow him to make me come by oral sex. ... I still have never had an orgasm just from fucking and sometimes this turns me off to anything but oral sex done on me. I feel like what's the point.—Junior female

About half of these women said they were still 'failing.' The other half reported qualified success resulting from more experience, a change of lovers, the greater trust of sex with love, or the greater thrill of experimental sex.

Six women also described the physical pleasures of orgasm in varying metaphoric detail:

[I] had so many great sexual experiences [with my second boyfriend]. . . . [Once] we pretended he was a t.v. repair man and he was fixing my t.v. I came on to him and we slowly peeled each other's clothes off. . . . We finally make love and both came at the same time. This was the first time I had ever had an orgasm. It was FANTASTIC!—Junior female

The climax I like best is the kind that comes over me slowly and last a while. First my stomach will bottom out—it's kind of like the feeling of an elevator going down too fast—and then all the muscles in my body will tense up, even my toes curl up, my back arches and then everything releases.—Senior female

The explosion. It [feels] like a million geese [have] just taken off in the pit of my stomach.—Senior female

Men discussed sexual pleasure less often than women did, either as an actuality or as a problem. The male subtext on sexual pleasure was, in all probability, Of *course* I enjoy sex. I'm a normal guy. It goes without saying! And the distinctive feature of sex, orgasm, evidently came easier to young American men than it did to young American women. Only two men in the sample talked about problems relating to orgasm. Neither was talking about intercourse; both had had problems having any orgasms at all, apparently because of sexual guilt. [. . .]

As has been suggested, another tenet of the new sexual orthodoxy as it was written or assumed in most of these papers was the contemporary meaning of 'real sex':

I was very sexually active with [a high-school girlfriend] but, I never actually had sex with her. In the beginning we made out a lot and even masturbated each other frequently. . . . Eventually we started having oral sex, she performing fellatio on me more often than I performed cunnilingus on her. . . . We also had a great deal of pseudo-sex through the pants. She had the nicest breasts I've ever seen, they weren't very large but, they were by no means small either. I really liked to put my penis between them, I think that is very exciting. Once we almost had sex, we had all our clothes off and I was wearing a condom, we just started to do it and my mother called me to feed the damn dog. I could have screamed. Ah well, we never did have sex but I gained a lot of experience.—Sophomore male

There was 'sex,' in other words, and there was 'real sex.' 'Real sex,' as Heath and many others have noted, was genital-to-genital heterosexual intercourse, preferably to orgasm—the standard definition of mid-twentieth-century American sexological research. And, as in the classic sex research of Kinsey and his followers, as popularized by Hugh Hefner and his followers, your sexual success, in the implicit logic of most of these papers, is determined by your frequency, by your variety, by your technique, and by your emotional mastery of sexual experience.

Not every student writer was, in fact, in search of all of these sexual goodies at the moment of writing; but those who were not almost always sound a little apologetic:

I'm not exactly well stocked in the technique department. I'm basically a traditional missionary girl. I've never tried it with me on top. I'm still a little inhibited about that. 'Doggy-style' isn't bad, except there's no one in front of you to hug or kiss when you do it that way.—Sophomore female

If intercourse was the most 'real' and the most 'meaningful' sex, however, oral sex was not far behind. Loss of virginity was the event described most often in these papers as a whole. The techniques and experiences of subsequent heterosexual intercourse were the next favorite topics. And the third favorite was oral sex. When saying what they liked best for pure erotic pleasure, men cited oral sex much more often than intercourse. Women also regularly noted its pleasures, though not with quite the unflagging enthusiasm of the men.

According to both female and male accounts, in fact, oral sex had become a multipurpose solution to a variety of problems associated with 'real sex'—it was the new sexual fix-it in the new sexual orthodoxy.[6] In many descriptions of loss of virginity, for instance, oral sex was the last 'base' before 'going all the way,' part of the getting-to-know-you process that preceded intercourse, or the most erotic practice tolerated by the modern technical virgin quoted above. Two out of three of the intentional virgins said they practiced it; the third did not date at all. For most couples, oral sex was the central hors d'oeuvre in the foreplay before 'real sex,' the practice most likely to assure that the woman, like the man, got her 'big O.' According to half a dozen female and male accounts of established couples in which the writer also mentioned very strong mutual fears of accidental pregnancy, elaborate oral sex was the chosen heterosexual substitute for intercourse. And oral sex was the most common sexual practice reported, often with especially detailed relish, by the student writers who defined themselves as homosexuals.

Different writers reported different rates of getting used to oral sex, but with remarkable consistency across both the women's and men's accounts, oral sex was said to be an egalitarian, mutual practice for established couples. Perhaps because it was not quite 'real' sex, oral sex did not seem to touch off the alarm bells of guilt in either female or male practitioners as often as did 'going all the way.' Its dilemmas were more often those of hygiene. Men and women worried about learning how to do it and about whether or not their partner enjoyed doing it to them. Men complained occasionally about vaginal cleanliness. Women commented on male cleanliness as well; but for women, the key issue in the practice of oral sex was whether or not to swallow. Almost everyone said the men were for it. Women writers' policies varied widely, as did their opinions of the aesthetics of the process ('you can't taste it if you love him, it's disgusting if you don't'; 'It's o.k.—I've read it's full of protein').

Despite the AIDS epidemic and the developing fear of its threat to heterosexuals, sexual danger was a minor theme in these papers, one that seemed to be almost intentionally ignored by both female and male writers. Only 5 to 10 percent of the student writers of both sexes discussed sex and disease—herpes, VD, fear of getting AIDS from bisexual male partners.

AIDS was equally absent from similar papers written in early spring 1987. But by late spring that year, the threat of AIDS to heterosexuals was being discussed everywhere; one graduating senior even mentioned it in a commencement address in May. It was widely assumed in the popular press that AIDS was going to reverse the sexual revolution among late-adolescent Americans. Is this likely? If there were major outbreaks of AIDS in heterosexual American college-age populations, something like this might take place. Without such visible danger, however, given the pervasiveness of sexuality in late-adolescent culture and in wider American culture and the unlikelihood that old-fashioned adult supervision could be reestablished over late-adolescents in the late twentieth century, the more likely outcome is a somewhat higher reported use of condoms, a possible decrease in the practice of casual sex, but relatively little effect on other attitudes or behaviors of the sort reported here.

Just as they ignored sexual disease, most of the students, women included, also soft-pedalled the realities of contemporary American sexual violence in their sexual self-reports. Ten out of the one hundred women writers described at least one incident of abuse, rape, or incest being inflicted on them by males during their sexual comings-of-age, for instance, but then deemphasized the significance of these attacks in their subsequent accounts.[7] They assessed the psychological impact of these events on themselves, and then usually went on to assert and to describe their sexual normality in spite of these acts of abuse.

The final tenet of the new American sexual orthodoxy, undergraduate version, was the importance of sex with affection. Almost all the student writers of these papers said or implied that there was a difference between sex with someone you love and casual sex. Different writers had different ethics and opinions about whether or not they themselves could or should enjoy both; and different writers had different opinions about how others should act with respect to these two kinds of sex. But almost all these adolescent Americans—females and males, sexual gourmets and gourmands, conventional heterosexuals and sexual radicals—agreed that the preferable or superior sexual practice was sex with affection (with 'love,' with 'caring,' with 'commitment,' with 'strong feelings,' and so on). To adapt a concept from Louis Dumont, sex with affection was the 'encompassing value' in nearly all these undergraduate sexual self-reports.

[*Coming of Age in New Jersey: College and American Culture* (New Brunswick, NJ: Rutgers University Press, 1989), 194–9, 199–202.]

Notes

Extract 1

GWENDOLYN LEICK: *Inanna Rejoicing in her Vulva*

1. B. Alster, 'The Manchester Tammuz', *Acta Sumerologica*, 14 (1992), lines 4, 46–7.
2. B. Alster, 'Sumerian Love Songs', *Revue d'assyriologie*, 79 (1985), 152.
3. Cf. *VAT* 8381 3–4: 'she (Nintur) had the rightful human seed ejaculated in (her) womb, semen ejaculated in her womb, contracted for (by marriage), giving the man a child'; for further quotes see H. Behrens, *Enlil and Ninlil* (= Studia Pohl: Series Major 8) (Rome, 1978), 133 ff.
4. E. Cassin, *Le Semblable et le différent: Symbolismes du pouvoir dans la Proche-Orient ancien* (Paris, 1987), 341.
5. S. N. Kramer, 'The Sumerian Sacred Marriage Texts', *Proceedings of the Society of Biblical Archaeology*, 107 (London, 1963), 505–8.
6. Poems of self-praise were a feature of Sumerian culture, as in many traditional societies; cf. J. A. Black, review of J. Klein's *Three Sulgi Hymns* and *The Royal Hymns of Sulgi, King of Ur, Archiv für Orientforschung*, 29–30 (1983–4), 110 ff.
7. The *gala* formed part of Inanna's temple personnel with special competence in the singing of elegies and lamentations.
8. B. Alster, 'Two Sumerian Short Tales and a Love Song Reconsidered', *Zeitschrift für Assyriologie*, 82 (1993), 186–201, line 21.
9. Ibid., lines 17–24, obv. col., ii.
10. Ibid. 24.
11. Cassin, *Le Semblable et le différent*, 356.
12. L. Abu Lughod, *Veiled Sentiments: Honor and Poetry in a Bedouin Society* (Berkeley, 1986), 107 ff.

Extract 2

DOMINIC MONTSERRAT: *Festivals of Licence*

1. See, for instance, Silius Italicus, *Punic War* 11. 425–31; Statius, *Silvae* 3.2. 111; Ovid, *Amores* 2. 13. 6–7; Athenaeus, *Deipnosophists* 13. 596b: Juvenal 15. 44–6.
2. Egyptian creation myths are discussed by Lesko in B. Shafer (ed.), *Religion in Ancient Egypt* (London, 1991), who stresses their relative coherence and strong relationship with government structure. For Hathor as the divine hand, see G. Pinch, *Votive Offerings to Hathor* (Oxford, 1993), 243–5.
3. Pinch, *Votive Offerings*, 244–5; she discusses other sexual meanings of the Radiant Festival of the Wadi in the Pharonic period on 157. The festival was still going on as late as 117 BCE, and was known to Diodorus Siculus, who mentions the sacred union of Amun and Hathor (2. 97. 9).

Extract 3

HELEN KING: *Sowing the Field*

1. P. DuBois, *Sowing the Body: Psychoanalysis and Ancient Representations of Women* (Chicago, 1988), 67–81; ancient references to earth/woman listed by D. M. Halperin, 'Why is Diotima a Woman? Platonic *Eros* and the Figuration of Gender', in his *One Hundred Years of Homosexuality* (New York, 1990), 283 n. 100. On medical texts, A. E. Hanson, 'Conception, Gestation, and the Origin of Female Nature in the *Corpus hippocraticum*', *Helios*, 19 (1992), 41; J. R. Pinault, 'The Medical Case for Virginity in the Early Second Century C.E.: Soranus of Ephesus, *Gynecology* 1.32', *Helios*, 19 (1992), 129–30.
2. J. J. Winkler, *The Constraints of Desire* (New York, 1990), 124–5.
3. Ovid, *Art of Love* 3. 101–3; P. Green, *Ovid: The Erotic Poems* (London, 1982), 217; on women as soil in relation to foetal growth, H. King, 'Making a Man: Becoming Human in Early Greek Medicine', in G. R. Dunstan (ed.), *The Human Embryo: Aristotle and the Arabic and European Traditions* (Exeter, 1990), 10–19.
4. Manuals listed by Varro 1. 1. 8–11, Cato, *On Agriculture* 34–5 and 3.

Extract 4

DAVID M. HALPERIN: *Active and Passive Sexuality*

1. See, generally, K. J. Dover, *Greek Homosexuality* (London, 1978), 16, 84–106; Michel Foucault, *The Use of Pleasure*, vol. ii of *The History of Sexuality*, trans. Robert Hurley (New York, 1985), 46–7.
2. On the characteristic failure of 'culturally dominant ideologies' actually to dominate all sectors of a society, and for a demonstration of their greater pertinence to the dominant than to the dominated classes, see Nicholas Abercrombie, Stephen Hill, and Bryan S. Turner, *The Dominant Ideology Thesis* (London, 1980), esp. 70–127. For the documentation of a particular instance, see R. M. Smith, 'Marriage Processes in the English Past: Some Continuities', in Lloyd Bonfield, Richard M. Smith, and Keith Wrightson (eds.), *The World We Have Gained: Histories of Population and Social Structure* (Oxford, 1986), 43–99, esp. 46–7.
3. See J. J. Winkler, 'Unnatural Acts: Erotic Protocols in Artemidorus' *Dream Analysis*', in Winkler, *The Constraints of Desire: The Anthropology of Sex and Gender in Ancient Greece* (New York, 1989), 17–44.
4. Artemidorus, *Oneirocritica* 1. 2 (pp. 8. 21–9. 4 Pack).
5. Winkler, 'Unnatural Acts'.
6. I say 'phallus' rather than 'penis' because (1) what qualifies as a phallus in this discursive system does not always turn out to be a penis and (2) even when phallus and penis have the same extension, or reference, they still do not have the same intension, or meaning: 'phallus' betokens not a specific item of the male anatomy *simpliciter* but that same item *taken under the description* of a cultural signifier; (3) hence, the meaning of 'phallus' is ultimately determined by its function in the larger sociosexual discourse: i.e., it is that which penetrates, and that which enables its possessor to play an 'active' sexual role, and so forth: see G. Rubin, 'The Traffic in Women: Notes on the "Political Economy" of Sex', in Rayna R. Reiter (ed.), *Toward an Anthropology of Women* (New York, 1978), 190–2.
7. Foucault, *The Use of Pleasure*, 215, puts it very well: 'sexual relations—always conceived

in terms of the model act of penetration, assuming a polarity that opposed activity and passivity—were seen as being of the same type as the relationship between a superior and a subordinate, an individual who dominates and one who is dominated, one who commands and one who complies, one who vanquishes and one who is vanquished.'

8. In order to avoid misunderstanding, I should emphasize that by calling all persons belonging to these four groups 'statutory minors', I do not wish either to suggest that they enjoyed the *same* status as one another or to obscure the many differences in status that could obtain between members of a single group—e.g., between a wife and a courtesan— differences that may not have been perfectly isomorphic with the legitimate modes of their sexual use. Nonetheless, what is striking about Athenian social usage is the tendency to collapse such distinctions as did indeed obtain between different categories of social subordinates and to create a single opposition between them all, *en masse*, and the class of adult male citizens: on this point, see Mark Golden, '*Pais*, "Child" and "Slave"', *L'Antiquité classique*, 54 (1985), 101 and 102 n. 38.

9. Paul Veyne, 'La Famille et l'amour sous le Haut-Empire romain', *Annales* (ESC), 33 (1978), 55; and Paul Veyne, 'Homosexuality in Ancient Rome', in Philippe Ariès and André Béjin (eds.), *Western Sexuality: Practice and Concept in Past and Present Times*, trans. Anthony Forster (Oxford, 1985).

10. I have borrowed this analogy from Arno Schmitt, who uses it to convey what the modern sexual categories would look like from a traditional Islamic perspective.

11. See Dover, *Greek Homosexuality*, 84; Jeffrey Henderson, 'Greek Attitudes toward Sex', in Michael Grant and Rachel Kitzinger (eds.), *Civilization of the Ancient Mediterranean: Greece and Rome* (New York, 1988), 1251: 'Social status defined one's sexual identity and determined the proper sexual behaviour that one was allowed.'

12. Maurice Godelier, 'The Origins of Male Domination', *New Left Review*, 127 (1981), 17.

13. On this general theme, see Golden, '*Pais*, "Child" and "Slave"'.

14. Robert A. Pagdug, 'Sexual Matters: On Conceptualizing Sexuality in History', *Radical History Review*, 20 (1979), 3–4; Maurice Sartre, 'L'Homosexualité dans la Grèce ancienne', *L'Histoire*, 76 (Mar. 1985), 12–14.

15. See Pagdug, 'Sexual Matters', 3, who mistakenly ascribes Athenaeus's comment to Alexis of Samos (see *FGrHist* 539, fr. 2).

Extract 5

PLATO: *The Speech of Pausanias*

1. Pausanias is mentioned in the *Protagoras* as a student of Prodicus (315d–e); this dialogue too treats Pausanias' love for Agathon as famous in Athens (cf. 198b). Pausanias' passionate defense of homosexuality is criticized in Xenophon's *Symposium* (8. 32–4).

Extract 6

MICHEL FOUCAULT: *Were the Greeks Bisexual?*

1. On this point, cf. C. K. Dover, *Greek Homosexuality* (London, 1978), 60–3.

2. Cf. Xenophon, *Anabasis* 7. 4. 7, ed. and trans. E. C. Marchant, Loeb Classical Library.

Extract 7

DAVID COHEN: *Honourable Sexuality*

1. See for example Xenophon, *Symposium* 8. 34ff. This point marks the great difference which separates Athens from cultures where homosexual intercourse plays a mandatory role in the initiation of young males. Although some scholars (for example, J. Bremmer, 'An Enigmatic Indo-European Rite: Paederasty', *Arethusa* (1980), 279–98, and B. Sergent, *L'Homosexualité dans la mythologie grecque* (Paris, 1984)) wish to trace Athenian paederasty back to such a process of initiation, such public submission to intercourse, as required of Melanesian initiates, could have resulted in the disenfranchisement of young Athenians. On the variety of Melanesian rituals and attitudes, see G. Herdt, *Ritualized Homosexuality in Melanesia* (Berkeley, 1984).

2. Aristotle, *Rhetoric* 1370b, 1378b, 1383b–4b, *Politics* 1311b; Plato, *Symposium* 182, 217, *Phaedrus* 251; Xenophon, *Agesilaus* 5. 7, *Symposium* 4. 52ff., 7. 9ff., 8. 23–35, *Memorabilia* 1. 2. 29, 1. 3. 11; Lysias 3, *passim*; Demosthenes, 61. 1, 3, 5–6, 17–20; Aristophanes, *Clouds* 1085, *Knights*.

3. Aristotle, *Rhetoric* 1315a15–20, 1378b, 1394a; [Demosthenes] 10. 27; *Letter* 4. 10–12; 22. 58.

4. Demosthenes 22. 61.

5. *Ath. Pol.* 18. 2.

6. *Helen* 58. For the same sentiments in a Roman setting, see Cicero, *Pro Milone* 9, *Pro Caelio* 3. 6–8, *Pro Sestio* 8. 18, 17. 39, 54. 16.

7. J. Pitt-Rivers, *The Fate of Schechem or the Politics of Sex* (Cambridge, 1977), 22.

8. Ibid. 23. J. Campbell, *Honour, Family, and Patronage* (Oxford, 1979), 269–70, for example, reports that a man who is *andrismos* (virile) must be *barbatos* (well-endowed with testicles).

9. This, essentially, is Aeschines' argument against Timarchus.

Extract 9

PETER BROWN: *Paul and Christian Marriage*

1. G. Feeley-Harnick, 'Is Historical Anthropology Possible? The Case of the Runaway Slave', in G. Tucker and D. Knight (eds.), *Humanizing America's Iconic Book* (Chico, Calif., 1982), 120–6.

2. Gerd Theissen, *The Social Setting of Pauline Christianity: Essays on Corinth*, ed. and trans. with an intro. by J. H. Schütz (Philadelphia, 1982), 125–32.

3. 1 Corinthians 7: 2.

4. Ibid. 7: 5.

5. Ibid. 7: 9.

6. H. Strack and P. Billerback, *Kommentar zum Neuen Testament aus Talmud und Midrasch*, 3: 369–73, provides the standard collection.

Extract 10

PETER BROWN: *The Earliest Christian Ascetics*

1. Irenaeus, *Against the Heresies*, in A. Roberts and W. H. Rambaut (eds.), *The Anti-Nicene Library: The Writings of Irenaeus*, vol. ii (Edinburgh, 1869), 4. 34. 1.

2. Tertullian, *Adversus Marcionem*, ed. E. Kroymann, *Tertulliani Opera: Corpus Christianorum, Series latina* (Turnhout, 1954), I. 17.

3. Tertullian, *De pudicitia*, 22. 3 (incompl.).

4. Tertullian, *Adversus Marcionem*, I. 24. 6.

5. Artemidorus, *Oneirocritica*, ed. R. A. Pack (Leipzig, 1963), I. 79: and for that reason, it stands for any kind of inescapable necessity, such as debt.

6. *The Testimony of Truth, NHC IX*, 3, 30. 19ff., trans. B. A. Pearson and S. Giversen, in James M. Robinson (ed.), *The Naq Hammadi Library in English* (Leiden, 1977).

7. Clement of Alexandria, *Stromata*, 3. 12. 92, in H. Chadwick (trans.), *Alexandrian Christianity* (Philadelphia, 1954).

Extract 11

DAVID F. NOBLE: *Celibacy vs. the Family*

1. Elizabeth Clark, *Ascetic Piety and Women's Faith* (Lewiston, NY, 1986), 33, 37.

2. JoAnnn McNamara, *A New Song: Celibate Women in the First Three Christian Centuries* (New York, 1983), 89.

Extract 12

ALINE ROUSSELLE: *The Six Degrees of Chastity*

1. John Cassian, *Collationes*, trans. in *A Select Library of Nicene and Post-Nicene Fathers of the Christian Church*, 2nd series, vol. xi (Paris, 1965), 22.

2. Cassian, *De institutis coenobiorum*, trans. in *A Select Library of Nicene and Post-Nicene Fathers*, 3. 5; 6. 10 and 22; *Collationes*, 2. 23; 4. 15–16; 5. 11; 7. 1; 10. 10; 12. 7.

3. St Antony, *Apophtegmata Patrum*: W. Bousset, *Apophtegmata* (Tübingen, 1923), 22.

4. *Historia monachorum in Aegypto*, ed. A. J. Festugière, *Subsidia Hagiograpica*, 34 (Paris, 1961), 20.

5. Cassian, *Collationes*, 7. 1.

6. Cassian, *De institutis*, 6. 20.

7. Cassian, *Collationes*, 2. 23.

8. Ibid. 12. 7.

9. Cassian, *De institutis*, 6. 11.

Extract 13

JOAN CADDEN, *Do Women Produce 'Seed'?*

1. Albertus Magnus, *Quaestiones super* De animalibus, ed. Aphrem Filthaut, vol. xii of Bernhard Geyer (ed.), *Opera omnia* (Münster, 1955), bk. 15, q. 29, p. 271.

2. Thaddeus Florentinus, *In Isagogas Joannitianas exposito*, in *Expositiones in arduum Aphorismorum Ipocratis, in divinuum* Prognosticorum *Ipocratis librum, in preclarum Regiminis acutorum Ipocratis opus, in subtilissime Joannitii Isagogarum libellum*, ed. Joannis Baptista Nicollinus (Venice, 1527), fo. 372rb.

3. Ibid., fo. 372ra.

4. Albert Mitterer catalogues and explicates the connotations of *occasionatus* in Aristotle, Albertus Magnus, and Thomas Aquinas in 'Mas *occasionatus* oder zwei Methoden der Thomasdeutung', *Zeitschrift für katholische Theologie*, 72 (1950), 80–103.

5. Albertus Magnus, *De animalibus libri XXVI*, ed. Herman Stadler, Beiträge zur Geschichte der Philosophie des Mittelalters 15 and 16 (Münster, 1916 and 1920), bk. 16, tr. 1, ch. 14, §§ 72–3, pp. 1099–100.
6. Ibid., bk. 1, tr. 2, ch. 3, §§ 140–1, p. 51.

Extract 14

JOHN W. BALDWIN: *Sex and Pleasure*

1. Enrique Montero Cartelle (ed.), *Liber minor de coitu* (Valladolid, 1987), 98.
2. Brian Lawn (ed.), *The Prose Salernitan Questions*, Auctores Britannici Medii Aevi 5 (Oxford, 1979), 7.

Extract 15

JOAN CADDEN: *Is Female Pleasure Necessary for Conception?*

1. Danielle Jacquart and Claude Thomasset cite Giles of Rome and Averroës to this effect (*Sexuality and Medicine in the Middle Ages*, trans. Matthew Adamson (Princeton, 1988), 66). Cf. Thomas Laqueur, who sees the 'biological possibility of a passionless female' as originating with the dissociation of conception from female orgasm in the eighteenth century (*Making Sex: Body and Gender from the Greeks to Freud* (Cambridge, 1990)).
2. Marian Kurdzialek, 'Anatomische und embryologische Aeusserungen Davids von Dinant', *Sudhoffs Archiv für Geschichte der Medizin und der Naturwissenschaften*, 45 (1961), 10.
3. Albertus Magnus, *De animalibus libri XXVI*, ed. Herman Stadler, Beiträge zur Geschichte der Philosophie des Mittelalters 15 and 16 (Münster, 1916 and 1920), bk. 10, tr. 1, ch. 1, § 1, p. 730.
4. [Johannes] Buridanus, *Questiones super Secreta mulierum*, Wissenschaftliche Bibliothek, Erfurt, MS Amplon, Q 299 (II). fo. 171^{r-v}.

Extract 16

RUTH MAZO KARRAS: *The Dangers of Female Lust*

1. On the sins in general and as they developed in England, see Hanno Fink, *Die sieben Todsünden in der mittelenglischen erbaulichen Literatur* (Hamburg, 1969); Morton W. Bloomfield, *The Seven Deadly Sins: An Introduction to the History of a Religious Concept, with Special Reference to Medieval English Literature* (East Lansing, Mich., 1952). On the sins as organizing principle for preaching aids, see Siegfried Wenzel, 'Vices, Virtues, and Popular Preaching', in Dale B. J. Randall (ed.), *Medieval and Renaissance Studies: Proceedings of the Southern Institute of Medieval and Renaissance Studies, Summer 1974* (Durham, NC, 1976), 28–54.
2. John of Bromyard, *Summa Praedicantium*, 2 vols. (Venice, 1596), s.v. 'abusionis', a. 6. 3, 1: 8.
3. See Ellen Kosmer, 'The "Noyous Humoure of Lecherie"', *Art Bulletin*, 57 (1975), 1–8; Adolf Katzenellenbogen, *Allegories of the Virtues and Vices in Medieval Art* (London, 1939); Anthony Weir and James Jerman, *Images of Lust: Sexual Carvings on Medieval Churches* (London, 1986), 58–79. When sins themselves were personified rather

than represented by examples, of course, all were depicted as female because abstract nouns in Latin all have feminine gender.

4. Ruth Mazo Karras, 'Gendered Sin and Misogyny in John of Bromyard's "Summa
   Predicantium" ', *Traditio*, 47 (1992), 237.

5. See Donald Weinstein and Rudolph M. Bell, *Saints and Society: The Two Worlds of
   Western Christendom* (Chicago, 1982), 88 and 87, for male saints tempted by women
   and for the connection of sexual problems with even saintly women.

Extract 17

PIERRE J. PAYER: *The Manner of Intercourse*

1. 'Nature teaches that the proper manner is that the woman be on her back with the
   man lying on her stomach'. Albert the Great, *Commentarii in IV Sententiarum* (*Dist.
   XXIII-L*), ed. S. C. A. Borgnet, Opera omnia 27 (Paris 1894), 31. 24 (B 30. 263).

2. The penitential literature prior to the twelfth century was far more explicit in its descriptions of oral and anal heterosexual relations. See Pierre J. Payer, 'Early Medieval Relations Concerning Marital Sexual Relations', *Journal of Medieval History*,
   6 (1980), 357–79; J. A. Brundage, 'Let Me Count the Ways: Canonists and Theologians Contemplate Coital Positions', *Journal of Medieval History*, 10 (1984), 81–93;
   Pierre J. Payer, *Sex and the Penitentials: The Development of a Sexual Code*, 550–1150
   (Toronto, 1984), 29–30.

3. 'For while the natural use, when it slips beyond the marriage pact, that is beyond the
   necessity of procreation, is forgiveable in a wife, it is damnable in a prostitute; the
   use that is against nature is cursed in a prostitute, but more cursed in a wife.'
   Augustine, *De bono coniugali*, ed. J. Zycha (Vienna, 1900), 11. 12 (CSEL 41. 203–4).

4. William Peraldus, *Summa aurea de virtutibus et vitiis* (Venice, 1497), 'De luxuria'
   Schlägl 12, fo. 8vb.

5. Albert the Great, *Commentarii*, 31. 24 (B 30. 263).

6. Peraldus, *Summa aurea*. An unedited confessional summa (incipit, 'Cum ad sacer-
   dotem') advises the confessor to take the following approach: 'For he can inquire
   thus: "The natural manner is that, if a man has intercourse with a woman, he always take the superior position, with the woman lying below. Have you acted otherwise? If you have, don't be ashamed to speak up." If he says no, go on to
   something else.' J. Goering and P. Payer have edited this work, based on Dublin,
   Trinity College, MS 326.

7. Albert the Great, *Commentarii*, 31. 24 (B 30. 263). Since departure from the basic form
   is intrinsically evil, there can be no justifying reasons for it and so it must be refused
   in all circumstances. It is certainly not covered by the mutual obligations arising
   from the marital debt.

8. Albert's view is perhaps derived from Roland of Cremona: 'For no spouse can ever
   sin in paying the debt . . . so long as it is paid in the proper manner, which nature itself teaches' (cited in M. Müller, *Die Lehre des hl. Augustinus von der Paradiesesehe und
   ihre Auswirkung in der Sexualethik des 12. und 13. Jahrhunderts bis Thomas von Aquin*
   (Regensburg, 1954), 194 n. 35).

9. Among his objections Albert describes the position from behind in this way: 'And
   they would have properly united if the woman were bent over facing away from
   the man' (*Commentarii*, 31. 24 (1), obj. 3 (B 30. 262)). For the older expression, see

Burchard of Worms: 'Have you had intercourse with your wife from behind, in dog-like fashion? If you have, you should do penance for ten days on bread and water' (Burchard of Worms, *Decretum*, 19. 5 (PL 140. 959D)).

10. Albert envisages the situations of obesity, a tumour on the woman's stomach, and pregnancy. He replies that deviation is allowed in such cases, since otherwise couples would not be able to have sex at all (Albert the Great, *Commentarii*, 31. 24, ad 2 and 3 (B 30. 263)).

11. Peraldus, *Summa aurea*, 'De temperantia' Schlägl 12, fo. 262rb.

12. Peter Comestor, *Historia scholastica* (Genesis) 31 (PL 198. 1081C). Although I know of no author who makes this point, a possible source of the horror of this position may also be that it is a reversal of the natural roles of the active male and the passive female.

13. Thomas Aquinas, *In 4 Sententiarum* (D. 13–50), Opera omnia 7 (Parma, 1858), 31, expositio textus.

Extract 18

GUIDO RUGGIERO: *Fornication and then Marriage*

1. *Avogaria di Comun*, Raspe: Reg. 3641–58 (Archivio di Stato, Venice), Reg. 3647, fo. 203^r–v (1424).

2. Ibid. Such behavior seems to have run in the family. A year earlier Giacomello's brother was involved in a case investigated by the Avogadori. In exile in Mestre because he had been banned from Venice in an earlier murder case, he had promised to marry a certain Elena, but after one night with her rejected the match, claiming she was a common whore. Nonetheless, he kept her prisoner, which brought the matter first to the attention of the Podesta of Mestre and finally to the Avogadori. Eventually the matter was sorted out with a marriage for the couple and a dowry credited to Elena of 300 ducats, which allowed Giacomello's brother to escape a year jail sentence.

3. Ibid., Reg. 3650, fo. 143^r–v (1455).

Extract 19

GUIDO RUGGIERO: *Uncontrollable Love*

1. *Avogaria di Comun*, Raspe: Reg. 3641–658 (Archivio di Stato, Venice), Reg. 3655, fo. 132^r–133^v (1482).

2. Ibid. Perhaps the vagueness regarding Contarini's wild and bestial acts and the emphasis on his insanity were related to the fact that certain heterosexual acts were labeled sodomy. As sodomy was normally punishable by death, this may have been a way to avoid punishing him for his deeds.

3. Ibid.

4. Gratiosa also collected Domenico's hair, which she burned before an image of the Virgin Mary. On a more prosaic level, after intercourse she dried heself with silk cloth with which she made candle shades dedicated to their love. *Avogaria di Comun*, Reg. 3655, fo. 132^r–133^v (1482).

5. Ibid. It is interesting to note that Gratiosa's magic was highly integrated with her society. It took its inspiration from virtually every potentially spiritual source society had to offer; even the Church played a major role.

Extract 20

LYNDAL ROPER: *Protestant Sexual Discipline*

1. *Ains Erbarn Rats | der Stat Augspurg | Zucht vnd Pollicey Ordnung* (Augsburg, 1537).
2. See W. Köhler, *Zürcher Ehegericht und Genfer Konsistorium*, 2 vols., Quellen und Abhandlungen zur schweizerischen Reformationsgeschichte 7, 10 (Leipzig, 1932, 1942); and J. Goody, *The Development of Family and Marriage in Europe* (Cambridge, 1983), esp. 172–81, on the Reformation's redefinition of incest.
3. Stadtarchiv Augsburg, Reichsstadt, Urgichten, 25 July 1542, Appolonia Strobel d. Ä.
4. For examples of this language, see ibid., Strafbücher des Rats I (1509–26). I am not arguing that 'sin' had never been used by the Council in relation to prostitution before the Reformation. But it was used infrequently, and without the consistency, clarity, and association with the concepts of honour and discipline.
5. Ibid., Urgichten, 8 Aug. 1541, Catherine Ziegler.

Extract 21

JAMES R. FARR: *Catholic Sexual Discipline*

1. John Bossy, *Christianity in the West, 1400–1700* (Oxford, 1985), 127, 133, 135.
2. Boileau, *De l'abus des nuditez de gorge* (Paris, 1675), 135–6, 141–2; Antoine Godeau, *Les Tableaux de la penitence* (Paris, 1656), 363. On adultery as social transgression and religious sin, see also De la Primaudaye, *Académie françoise, en laquelle il est traitté de l'institution des moeurs . . .* (Paris, 1580), 240; Olivier, *L'Alphabet de l'imperfection et malice des femmes* (Rouen, 1634), 262, 263.

Extract 22

STEPHEN HALICZER: *Sexuality in the Confessional*

1. James A. Brundage, *Law, Sex, and Christian Society in Medieval Europe* (Chicago, 1987), 90–1.
2. Thomas Tentler, *Sin and Confession on the Eve of the Reformation* (Princeton, 1977), 176.
3. Archivo Histório Nacional, Sección Inquisición, legajos 1952, exp. 4B, 'Relación de la visita quo a hecho el inquisidor Fernando Martínez este año de 1585'.
4. Brundage, *Law, Sex, and Christian Society*, 566–7.
5. Juan Luis Vives, *Libro llamado instrucción de la mujer cristina*, reprint, trans. Juan Justiniano (Madrid, 1936), 118.
6. Pedro de Luxán, *Coloquios matrimoniales* (Madrid, 1943), 21 in Mariló Vigil, *La vida de las mujeres en los siglos XVI y XVII* (Madrid, 1986), 100.
7. Archivo Histório Nacional, Sección Inquisición, 28 Nov. 1713, legajos 230, exp. 10.
8. Archivo Histório Nacional, Sección Inquisición, 29 Nov. 1713, legajos 230, exp. 10.

Extract 24

ALAN BRAY: *Sodomy and its Punishment*

1. There is an extensive example of this in Sir Thomas Herbert's narrative of his journey through Africa and Asia in the early seventeenth century, which repeatedly links homosexuality with non-European races, *A Description of the Persian Monarchy . . . A Relation of Some Yeares Travaile* (London, 1634).

2. Scottish Record Office/JC/1/13, noted in R. Pitcairn (ed.), *Criminal Trials in Scotland*, vol. iii (Edinburgh, 1833), 491.

Extract 26

THEO VAN DER MEER: *Sodomy and Moral Panic in the Low Countries*

1. Gemeente Archief Utrecht (Municipal Archive Utrecht) RA 2236 (1676), between fos. 474–5.
2. Gemeente Archief Utrecht 2236 (1713–27), fo. 920–33.
3. Gemeente Archief Rotterdam (Municipal Archive Rotterdam) Schepen Archief (local court records) 141; Schepen Archief 250, fos. 200^r–203^r; Schepen Archief 251, fos. 15^r–16^r; Schepen Archief 299.
4. Gemeente Archief Rotterdam Schepen Archief 127^v–129^v.
5. Ibid. 177, fos. 55^v–58^r; Schepen Archief 253, fos. 186^r–194^r.
6. The jurist Van Zurck mentioned in *Codex Batavurs* (Delft, 1727) that this penalty was carried out in 1686 in Amsterdam. I have found no court records or verdicts that confirm this. However, in 1730 two men in this city suffered this penalty. It is unlikely that the court did not act on a precedent.
7. Algemeen Rijksarchief (National State Archive) Hof van Holland (Court of Holland) 5374. 18. In these records, there are references to sodomy trials by the local court in the Hague. Obviously, this court destroyed any evidence of sodomy trials before 1730.
8. *Europische Mercurius* (1730), i. 283.
9. *Resolutien Staten van Holland en Westvriesland* (1730), 430–1.
10. Garroting meant that the culprit was put at a stake and strangled from behind with a cord. Gemeente Archief Amsterdam (Municipal Archive Amsterdam) 5029 (1730).

Extract 29

JEAN-JACQUES ROUSSEAU: *Sexuality and Identity*

1. 'Give up the ladies, and study mathematics.'

Extract 30

BARBARA MARIA STAFFORD: *Exception and Norm*

1. Jackson I. Cope, *Dramaturgy of the Daemonic: Studies in Antigeneric Theater from Ruzante to Grimaldi* (Baltimore, 1984), pp. xi, 107–11. See also A. Graeme Mitchell, *Medical Caricature, Proceedings of the California Academy of Medicine*, reprint (1939–40), no pagination.
2. Louis Poinsinet de Sevry, *Traité des causes physiques et morales du rire relativement à l'art de l'exciter* (Amsterdam, 1768), 105; A. F. Sticotti, *Dictionnaire des gens du monde, historique, littéraire, critique, moral, physique, militaire, politique, caractéristique & social*, 3 vols. (Paris, 1771), ii. 41.

Extract 31

LUDMILLA JORDANOVA: *Sex under the Skin*

1. B. Lanza, M. L. Azzaroli Puccetti, M. Poggesi, and A. Martelli, *Le cere anatomiche della specola* (Florence, 1979), 209.
2. I. Veith, *Hysteria: The History of a Disease* (Chicago, 1965), esp. ch. 8.

Extract 32

LONDA SCHIEBINGER: *'Deep Sex' in the Skeleton*

1. Edmond Thomas Moreau, *Quaestio medica: An praeter genitalia sexus inter se discrepent?* (Paris, 1750).

2. Pierre Roussel, *Système physique et moral de la femme, ou tableau philosophique de la constitution, de l'état organique, du tempérament, des mœurs, & des fonctions propres au sexe* (Paris, 1775), 2.

3. Jakob Ackermann, *De discrimine sexuum praeter genitalia* (Mainz, 1788); *Uber die körperliche Verschiedenheit des Mannes vom Weibe ausser Geschlectsheilen*, trans. Joseph Wenzel (Koblenz, 1788), 2–5.

4. Ibid.

5. Bernhard Albinus, 'Account of the Work', in *Table of the Skeleton and Muscles of the Human Body* (London, 1749).

6. D'Arconville (1720–1805) was well known by her contemporaries. She published widely; her works include *Essai pour servir à l'histoire de la putréfaction; Vie de Marie de Médicis, reine de France et de Navarre*; the French translation of Peter Shaw's work on chemistry.

7. Samuel Thomas von Soemmering, *Tabula sceleti feminini juncta descriptione* (Utrecht, 1796).

8. *Journal der Empfindungen: Theorien und Widersprüche in der Natur- und Artzneiwissenschaft*, 6/18 (1797), 17–18.

9. It was thought that a woman did not reach maturity with the onset of menstruation but only with age 18 or 20, after the birth of her first child.

10. Ludwig Choulant, *History and Bibliography of Anatomic Illustrations*, trans. Mortimer Frank (Chicago, 1920), 306–7.

11. John Barclay, *The Anatomy of the Bones of the Human Body, Represented in a Series of Engravings, copied from the Elegant Tables of Sue and Albinus* (Edinburgh, 1829), commentary to plate 32.

12. Ibid.

13. Albinus, 'Account of the Work'.

14. Quoted in Ackermann, *Uber die körperliche Verschiedenheit*, 5–7.

15. Choulant, *History and Bibliography*, 302.

16. Ibid.

17. Soemmering, *Tabula*, commentary to plate.

18. Albinus, 'Account of the Work'.

Extract 33

ROBERT NYE: *Sexual Complementarity*

1. Geneviève Fraisse, *Muse de la raison: La Démocratie exclusive et la différence des sexes* (Paris, 1989), 94.

2. Ibid. 86–9.

Extract 34

ANGUS MCLAREN: *Romantic Marriage, Women, and Fertility*

1. *Mme de Sévigné: lettres*, ed. M. Gerard-Gailly (Paris, 1953).

2. Jean-Louis Flandrin, *Families in Former Times: Kinship, Household and Sexuality* (Cambridge, 1979), 223–34.

3. Roger Schofield, 'Did Mothers Really Die? Three Centuries of Maternal Mortality in the World We have Lost', in Lloyd Bonfield, Richard M. Smith, and Keith Wrightson (eds.), *The World We Have Gained: Histories of Population and Social Structure* (Oxford, 1986), 231–60.

4. J. M. Gouesse, 'Le Refus de l'enfant au tribunal de la pénitence', *Annales de démographie historique* (1973), 238.

5. Ralph Trumbach, *The Rise of the Egalitarian Family* (New York, 1978), 98.

6. Père Féline, *Catéchisme des gens mariés* (Paris, 1880; 1st pub. 1782), 7–8.

Extract 36

LYNN HUNT: *The Sexuality of the Queen*

1. *Vie privée, libertine et scandaleuse*, reprinted in Hector Fleischmann, *Marie Antoinette libertine: Bibliographie critique et analytique des pamphlets politiques, galants, et obscènes contra la reine: Précédé de la réimpression intégrale de quatre libelles rarissimes et d'une histoire des pamphlétaires du règne de Louis XVI* (Paris, 1911), 173–4.

2. *Les Crimes des reines de France, depuis le commencement de la monarchie jusqu'à Marie-Antoinette* (London, 1792), p. vii.

3. *Jugement général de toutes les putains françoises, et de la reine des garces, Par un des envoyés du Père Éternel* (De l'Imprimerie des Séraphins, no pagination, no date).

Extract 37

CAROL PATEMAN: *The Sexual Contract*

1. J.-J. Rousseau, *On the Social Contract and Discourses*, ed. D. A. Cress (Indianapolis, 1983), bk. I, ch. 8, 64.

2. Rousseau, *Emile or on Education*, trans. A. Bloom (New York, 1979), 409.

3. I. Kant, *Anthropology from a Pragmatic Point of View*, trans. M. J. Gregor (The Hague, 1974), 171.

Extract 39

ISABEL V. HULL: *The Middle Class and the State*

1. Anonymous ['Je'], review of Thomas Abbt's *Über innere und äussere Bestimmung des Jünglings zum künftigen nützlichen Mitgliede der menschlichen Gesellschaft. Nebst einer Abhandlung über die Bestimmung des Mädchens* (Halberstadt, 1794), in *Neue Allgemeine Deutsche Bibliothek*, 19/2 (1795), 549.

2. Peter Villaume, *Allgemeine Theorie, wie gute Triebe und Fertigkeiten durch die Erziehung erweckt, gestärkt und gelenkt werden müssen*, in Joachim Heinrich Campe (ed.), *Allgemeine Revision des gesammten schul- und Erziehungswesens von einer Gesellschaft practischer Erzieher*, vol. iv (Hamburg, 1785–92), 556.

3. Anon., ['N'], 'Ueber das Wort und Begrif Liebe', *Hannoversches Magazin*, 18/62 (4 Aug. 1780), col. 991.

4. Anon., 'Nachrichten von einer seltsamen Irrung eines menschlichen Triebes', *Beiträge zur Beruhigung und Aufklärung*, 2 (1789), 329.

5. Anon., 'Gedanken über den Ehestand', *Journal aller Journale*, 11/2 (1788), 101.

6. Anon., 'Vorbereitung zu den künftigen Preisschriften über den Cölibat', *Neuer Teutscher Merkur* (Oct. 1791), 164.

7. See Dieter Hoof, *Pestalozzi und die Sexualität seines Zeitalters: Quellen, Texte und Untersuchungen zur historischen Sexualwissenschaft*, Sexualpädagogische Beiträge 3 (St Augustin, 1987), 442–7, on their efforts to achieve a dichotomy between love and sexual desire.

8. Anon., 'Auch ein Wort über Priesterehe und Cölibat', *Deutsche Monatsschrift* 1 (1792), 82.

9. Karl Gottfried Bauer, *Über die Mittel dem Geschlechtsriebe eine unschädliche Richtung zu geben: Eiene durch die Erziehungsanstalt zu Schnepfenthal gekrönte Preisschrift. Mit einer Vorrede und Anmerkungen von C. G. Salzmann* (Leipzig, 1791), 266, 267, 268.

10. Anon., 'Soll man ihnen Weiber geben? Eine Antwort aus der Erfahrung', *Chronologen*, 8 (1780), 203–4; anon., 'Ehelosigkeit der Geistlichen', *Almanach für Ärzte und Nichtärzte* (1793), 253; anon., 'Eheglück', *Schlesische Provinzial-Blätter*, 11 (1790), 519.

11. Theodor Gottlieb von Hippel, *Ueber die Ehe*, 2nd edn. (Berlin, 1776), 5.

12. Cf. Hoof, *Pestalozzi und die Sexualität seines Zeitalters*, 447, but cf. 449 and 453.

13. Here Bahrdt outlined his latitudinarian understanding of marriage, meaning any regulated, consensual intercouse, including prostitution. This idiosyncratic view would have been highly debatable.

14. Anon., ['Rr'], review of Carl Friedrich Bahrdt, *System der moralischen Religion* (1787), in *Allgemeine Deutsche Bibiothek*, 85/2 (1789), 372–3.

Extract 40

MARTINE SEGALEN: *Peasant Sexuality*

1. Henri Pullès, 'Les Maisons types dans la région de Carcassonne', in Alfred de Foville, *Enquête sur les conditions de l'habitation en France: Les Maisons types* (Paris, 1894), 275.

2. 'Maisons de la région de la Meuse, vallée de l'Ornain (canton de Gondrecourt)', in de Foville, *Enquête*, i. 91.

3. M. Martin, 'Maisons du Drac et du Valgaudemar, Hautes-Alpes', in de Foville, *Enquête*, i. 193.

4. J. Momméja, 'Air de Montauban, Tarn-et-Garonne', in de Foville, *Enquête*, i. 278.

5. Henri Raulin, *L'Architecture rurale française: Le Dauphiné* (Paris, 1977), 63.

6. Émile Guillaumin, *La Vie d'un Simple: Mémoires d'un métayer* (Paris, 1935), 311.

Extract 41

JONAS FRYKMAN AND ORVAR LÖFGREN: *From Peasant to Bourgeois*

1. Herbert Tingsten, *Mitt liv: Ungdomsåren* (Stockholm, 1961), 56ff.

Extract 42

JEFFREY WEEKS: *Middle-Class Views of Working-Class Sexuality*

1. *Hansard*, third series, vol. lxxiii (1844), col. 1100.

2. Peter Gaskell, *Artisans and Machinery: The Moral and Physical Condition of the Manufacturing Population* (London, 1836), 89.

3. T. J. Barnardo in 1889, quoted in Leonore Davidoff, Jean L'Esperance, and Howard Newby, 'Landscape with Figures: Home and Community in English Society', in Juliet Mitchell and Ann Oakley (eds.), *The Rights and Wrongs of Women* (Harmondsworth, 1976), 167.

4. Quoted in Harold Perkin, *The Origins of Modern English Society* (London, 1969), 150.

5. Peter Gaskell, *The Manufacturing Population of England* (London, 1833), 147. The Children's Employment Commission, *First Report of the Commissioners (Mines)* (1842), is a good example of the prurience of investigators as it detailed the use of female labour, often working naked with naked men. For a later worry, about sewing machines inducing female masturbation, see Langdon Down, *British Medical Journal* (12 Jan. 1867).

6. Quoted in Sally Alexander, 'Women's Work in Nineteenth Century London: A Study of the Years 1820–50', in Mitchell and Oakley (eds.), *The Rights and Wrongs of Women*, 62.

Extract 43

FRANK MORT: *Hygiene, Morality, and Class*

1. Evidence of Dr Gilly, Canon of Durham, *Report from the Poor Law Commissioners into the Sanitary Conditions of the Labouring Population of Great Britain*, House of Lords Sessional Papers, XXVI (1942), 124.

2. Evidence of Mr Ridall Wood, ibid. 125.

3. See evidence of Mr Baker, assistant commissioner for Leeds, ibid. 126. For discussion of incest within the working-class family see A. Wohl, 'Sex and the Single Room: Incest among the Victorian Working Classes', in A. Wohl (ed.), *The Victorian Family* (1978).

4. *Report into the Sanitary Conditions of the Labouring Population*, 127.

Extract 44

MICHAEL MASON: *Sexual Respectability in the Working Class*

1. Edwin Chadwick, *The Sanitary Condition of the Labouring Population of Great Britain*, ed. M. W. Flinn (Edinburgh, 1965), 192–3.

2. *Morning Chronicle* (28 Oct. 1850), 5; Françoise Barret-Ducrocq, *Love in the Time of Victoria* (London, 1991), 112; Ellen Ross, '"Fierce Questions and Taunts": Married Life in Working-Class London, 1870–1914', *Feminist Studies*, 8 (1982), 575–602.

3. W. G. Lumley, 'Observations upon the Statistics of Illegitimacy', *JSSL* 25 (1862), 219–74; Dennis R. Mills, *Aspects of Marriage* (Milton Keynes, 1980), 12–14; Barry Reay, 'Sexuality in Nineteenth-Century England: The Social Context of Illegitimacy in Rural Kent', *Rural History*, 1 (1990), 219–47.

4. Enid Gauldie, *Cruel Habitations* (London, 1974), 22.

Extract 45

STEPHEN KERN: *The Ideal of Transcendent Love*

1. Emily Brontë, *Wuthering Heights* (1847; reprinted New York, 1965), 122, 354.

2. Charlotte Brontë, *Jane Eyre* (1847; reprinted New York, 1966), 304.

3. After God took a rib out of Adam and with it made woman, Adam said: 'This *is* now bone of my bones, and flesh of my flesh: she shall be called woman, because she was taken out of Man' (Genesis, 2: 23–4).

4. Brontë, *Jane Eyre*, 476.

5. Denis de Rougemont comments that in Tristan and Isolde 'music alone . . . can harmonize the plaint of the two voices, and make of it a single plaint' and convey 'the transcendental interaction, the wildly contradictory and contrapuntal character of the passion of Darkness.' *Love in the Western World* (1940; reprinted New York, 1974), 229–30.

6. Act II, scene ii.

7. Pseudo-scientific foundation for this apotheosis of fusion was offered by researchers who argued that women became hysterical because their wombs were not regularly bathed with semen and that men and women commingled their selves by having sex, kissing, breathing the same air, or possibly even by the very presence of another person through some 'animal-magnetism'. John S. Haller, Jr., and Robin M. Haller, *The Physician and Sexuality in Victorian America* (Urbana, Ill., 1974), 12–15.

8. Victor Hugo, *Les Misérables* (1862; reprinted New York, 1976), 805, 1139.

9. Gustave Flaubert, *Sentimental Education* (1862; reprinted Penguin, 1964), 269.

Extract 46

JOHN MAYNARD: *Spirituality and Sexual Pleasure*

1. See Arthur J. Engel, 'Immoral Intentions: The University of Oxford and the Problem of Prostitution, 1827–1916', *Victorian Studies*, 23 (1979), 79–107; I am assuming relatively similar conditions held at Cambridge.

2. Quoted, Susan Chitty, *The Beast and the Monk: A Life of Charles Kingsley* (London, 1974), 57. The letter is in the collection of Charles Kingsley's Letters to his Wife at the British Library, at Add. 62552, fo. 177 (henceforward cited as Letters with accession number and folio; the total, important collection is Add. 62552–7).

3. Chitty, *The Beast and the Monk*, 59.

4. Nice Diary, manuscript diary (including time at Nice) kept by Fanny Grenfell from Oct. 1842 to Sept. 1843 as letters to Charles during their enforced separation, with one entry in 1846, private collection of Angela M. K. Covey-Crump: entry for 22 Oct. 1842; Letters, Add. 62552, fos. 71, 46ᵛ; Chitty, *The Beast and the Monk*, 74. They were married in early 1844; Fanny's entry for 4 July 1843 speaks of four years loving Charles 'soul and body'.

5. Letters, Add. 62552, fo. 97.

6. Ibid., fo. 100.

7. Ibid., fo. 65; Charles was bothered because of continual guilt over indulgence in his earlier sexual experience; both he and Fanny admitted shyness about appearing naked before the other and he expressed some fear of the man being 'struck powerless . . . by modest awe, at the holy thing wh is at last his own': fos 181ᵛ–182.

8. Chitty, *The Beast and the Monk*, 159: he claimed to be able to see Ruskin's own sexual failure in his face. He was similarly critical of Carlyle, whom he otherwise revered.

9. Letters, Add. 62552, fos 100, 159ᵛ; Add. 62553, fo. 41.

10. Ibid., Add. 62552, fo. 37ᵛ.

11. James MaHood and Kristine Wenburg (eds.), *The Mosher Survey: Sexual Histories of 45 Victorian Women* (New York, 1980).
12. Letters, Add. 62553, fo. 190.
13. Ibid., Add. 62552, fos 62^v, 587, 69, 43.
14. Ibid., fos 183f. More: the Cambridge Platonist of the seventeenth century.
15. Ibid., fo. 208^v.
16. Ibid., fo. 66. 'My beloved is to me a bag of myrrh, that lies between my breasts.' Interpretation of the sexual matter of the Song of Solomon was a central issue in the Victorian period that continued sexual discussions in Judaism and Christianity that had been going on for thousands of years; it is rather a pleasure to find one where the work was not rationalized as the love of God for Israel or for mankind.

Extract 47

PETER GAY: *Passion amidst Propriety*

1. 24 August 1879, Journal III, box 46, Mary Loomis Todd Papers, Yale Manuscripts and Archives (MLT).
2. 11 Dec. 1881, Journal III. See Mabel Loomis Todd's letter to her mother, 16 Mar. 1879, from her honeymoon: 'As for David—well, he gets up and brings me apples or oranges to eat before breakfast every morning . . .' a somewhat laundered but still highly suggestive acount of her night life (box 31).
3. 12 May, Diary 1879; Mabel Todd to David Todd, 1 Aug. 1879, 18 Dec. 1882, box 12, David Peck Todd Papers, Yale Manuscripts and Archives (DPT); David Todd to Mabel Todd, 20 Aug. 1879, 9 Dec. 1881, box 35, MLT.
4. 10 and 11 Sept., Diary 1879; 19 Aug. and 21 Dec. Diary 1880, box 39, MLT; 3 July, Diary 1881, box 39, MLT; 28 Feb., 21 Mar., Diary 1882, box 39, MLT; David Todd to Mabel Todd, 8 Dec. 1882, box 35, DPT.
5. 7 Aug. 1885, Journal IV.

Extract 48

JOHN R. GILLIS: *Sexual Segregation*

1. Flora Thompson, *Lark Rise to Candleford* (Harmondsworth, 1974), 340.
2. Mrs C5P, fo. 29, Elizabeth Roberts Oral History Collection, Lancaster University.
3. Standish Meacham, *A Life Apart: The English Working Class, 1890–1914* (London, 1977), 66.
4. Reginald Bray, quoted ibid. 160.
5. Elizabeth Roberts, 'Learning and Living: Socialization outside School', *Oral History*, 3/2 (Autumn 1975), 16.
6. Derek Thompson, 'Courtship and Marriage in Preston between the Wars', *Oral History*, 3/2 (Autumn 1975), 39; Meacham, *A Life Apart*, 160–1; Paul Thompson, *The Edwardians: The Remaking of British Society* (Bloomington, Ind., 1975), 64–5.

Extract 49

CARROLL SMITH-ROSENBERG: *Intimacy between Women*

1. For an example of a mother and daughter giving birth literally in the same bed, see *The Memoirs of Gluckel of Hameln*, trans. Marvin Lowenthal (New York: Schocken

Books, 1977). Ann Bradstreet is a good example of a woman who continued to bear children after her own children had married, and whose father had sired a large family after her own marriage and the beginning of her child-bearing career. Her half-sisters were therefore younger than her own children (their nieces and nephews). For a quick sketch of Ann Bradstreet's life, see Ola Elizabeth Winslow's entry in Edward James and Janet James (eds.), *Notable American Women, 1607–1950: A Biographical Dictionary* (Cambridge, Mass.: Belknap Press of Harvard University, 1971).

2. Mary Hallock Foote to Helena DeKay Gilder, n.d. [1890s], Mary Hallock Foote Collection, Manuscript Division, Stanford University. See also quotations in Blanche Cook, 'Female Support Networks and Political Activism: Lillian Wald, Crystal Eastman, Emma Goldman', *Chrysalis*, 3 (1977); and Lillian Faderman, *Surpassing the Love of Men* (New York: William Morrow and Co. 1981), 190–203.

Extract 50

JOHN D'EMILIO AND ESTELLE B. FREEDMAN: *Intimacy between Men*

1. Jonathan Ned Katz (ed.), *Gay/Lesbian Almanac: A New Documentary* (New York, 1983), 39; Vern L. Bullough and Martha Voght, 'Homosexuality and its Confusion with the Secret Sin in Pre-Freudian America', *Journal of the History of Medicine and Allied Sciences*, 28/2 (Apr. 1973), 143–55; Jonathan Katz (ed.), *Gay American History* (New York, 1976), 26; Lillian Faderman, *Surpassing the Love of Men: Romantic Friendship and Love between Women from the Renaissance to the Present* (New York, 1981), 291. On the shift from homosexual acts to the homosexual role, see Mary McIntosh, 'The Homosexual Role', *Social Problems*, 16 (Fall 1968), 182–92.
2. Michael Lynch, 'New York City Sodomy, 1796–1873', paper presented at the Institute for the Humanities, New York University, 1 Feb. 1985, 1–2.
3. Charley Shively (ed.), *Calamus Lovers: Walt Whitman's Working Class Camerados* (San Francisco, 1987), 56–8.
4. Katz, *Gay American History*, 33–4.
5. Lynch, 'New York City Sodomy', 3, 10, 17; John Burnham, 'Early References to Homosexual Communities in American Medical Writings', *Medical Aspects of Human Sexuality*, 7/8 (Aug. 1973), 34, 40–1, 46–9.
6. Shively, *Calamus Lovers*, 99; Katz, *Gay American History*, 655 n. 35, 470, 27-8.

Extract 51

ABRAM DE SWAAN: *Professionalization and Medical Problems*

1. Irving K. Zola, 'Healthism and Disabling Medicalization', in I. Illich (ed.), *Disabling Professions* (London, 1977), 41–68.
2. J. Caplan, 'Lawyers and Litigants: A Cult Reviewed', ibid., 93–110.
3. T. R. Dewar, 'Professionalization of the Client', *Social Policy*, 8/4 (1978), 4–9.

Extract 52

DANIEL PICK: *Degeneration*

1. See B. A. Morel, *Traité des dégénérescences physiques, intellectuelles et morales de l'espèce humaine* (Paris, 1857), 5.

2. Ibid. 335.
3. J. J. Moreau (de Tours), *La Psychologie morbide* (Paris, 1859), 104.
4. Ibid. 99.

Extract 53

JACQUES DONZELOT: *The Priest and the Doctor*

1. See Alex Mayer, *Des rapports conjugaux considérés sous le triple point de vue de la population, de la société et de la morale publique* (1857).

Extract 54

SANDER L. GILMAN: *Degenerate Sexuality*

1. See Burton Pike, *The Image of the City in Modern Literature* (Princeton, 1981).

Extract 56

JANN MATLOCK: *Hysteria and the Prostitute*

1. Alexandre-J. B. Parent-Duchâtelet, *De la prostitution dans la ville de Paris*, vol. i, 3rd edn. (Paris: Baillière, 1857), 280–2.
2. Pierre Briquet, *Traité clinique et thérapeutique de l'hystérie* (Paris: Baillière, 1859), 124–5. Hector Landouzy (*Traité complet de l'hystérie* (Paris: Baillière, 1846)) alone of authors of major studies between 1830 and 1872 believed prostitutes unlikely to be hysterical. Like him, Émile Mathieu (*Études cliniques sur les maladies des femmes* (Paris: Moquet, 1847)) targeted continence as hysteria's source. Depot doctor and Charcot disciple Henri Colin returned to this view, arguing that hysterics are smarter and more sensitive than prostitutes (*Essai sur l'état mental des hystériques* (Paris: Rueff, 1890), 39–41. Jacques-Henri Girard de Cailleux lamented the mixing of *filles inscrites* with other Salpêtrière patients, noting that 'this deplorable confusion is morally revolting and casts a slur upon the poor but honorable families among whom misfortune has most frequently produced madness, whereas the madness of prostitutes is almost the certain result of debauchery and a licentious life' ('Rapport sur les aliénés traités dans les asiles de Bicêtre et de la Salpêtrière', Archives de l'Assistance Publique, Pièce D-141 (manuscript, 1836), 17).
3. Briquet, *Traité clinique*, 125.
4. Ibid. 125–6.

Extract 57

MARK S. MICALE: *Sexual Hysteria*

1. Jules Falret, 'Folie raisonnante ou folie morale' (1866), reprinted in *Études cliniques sur les maladies mentales et nerveuses* (Paris: J.-B. Baillière, 1890), 500–3.
2. Jacques-Joseph Moreau (de Tours), *Traité pratique de la folie névropathique (vulgo hystérique)* (Paris: Germer Baillière, 1869).
3. Ibid. 163–70.
4. Ambroise Tardieu, *Étude médico-légale sur la folie* (Paris: J.-B. Baillière, 1872), 159–74.
5. Ibid. 163.

Extract 58

GEORGE FREDERICK DRINKA: *Prostitute and Saint*

1. Désiré Bourneville and Paul Regnard, *Iconographie photographique de la Salpêtrière* (Paris: Progrès Médical, 1877–80), i. 50–90.
2. Ibid. 51.

Extract 59

JUDITH R. WALKOWITZ: *Stigmatization and the Contagious Diseases Act*

1. *Parliamentary Papers*, 1871, XIX, Q. 8429.
2. *Shield*, 17 Dec. 1870.
3. Ibid. 26 May 1871.
4. Quoted in Josephine Butler, 'The Garrison Towns of Kent', *Shield*, 25 Apr. 1870.
5. J. J. Garth Wilkinson, *The Forcible Introspection of Women for the Army and Navy by the Oligarchy Considered Physically* (London, 1870), 15.
6. *Parliamentary Papers*, 1871, XIX, Q. 20297.
7. Ibid., Q. 7206, 10548.
8. Ibid., Q. 12631.
9. 'Illegal Detention of a Woman at the Royal Albert Hospital', *Abolitionist Flysheets*, Butler Collection, Fawcett Library, London.

Extract 60

LYNDA NEAD: *Stigmatization of Prostitutes*

1. Ralph Wardlaw, *Lectures on Female Prostitution* (Glasgow, 1842), 14–15.
2. William Acton, *Prostitution Considered in its Moral, Social, and Sanitary Aspects in London and Other Large Cities and Garrison Towns; with Proposals for the Mitigation and Prevention of its Attendant Evils*, 2nd edn. (1870), 166.
3. Report of the Select Committee on the Contagious Diseases Act, July 1869, quoted in Acton, *Prostitution*, 2. See also Mr Jacob Wright, MP for Manchester, addressing the House of Commons on the Contagious Diseases Act, 20 July 1870, quoted in William Logan, *The Great Social Evil: Its Causes, Extent, Results and Remedies* (1871), 215: 'The House is aware that the Act professes to be directed against common prostitutes . . . The Act, however, contains no definition of this term. I believe there is a definition in the Police Act. The term there implies women who are seen soliciting in the streets.'

Extract 61

ALAIN CORBIN: *Prostitution and the New Forms of Desire*

1. It was during a train journey that Léon Mirat caught the syphilis that drove him to suicide (Michel Corday, *Vénus ou les deux risques* (Paris: Charpentier, 1901)).
2. See Proust's description of the building of a deluxe brothel on the Normandy coast, near Balbec, in *Sodome et Gomorrhe (Cities Of the Plain)*.
3. A visit by a provincial notable to the local prostitute is described by J. K. Huysmans in *Un dilemme*.
4. See *Contributions à la psychologie de l'amour*, and passages by Jean Borie on this subject in *Le Célibataire français* (Paris: Sagittaire, 1976), 47.

5. L. Fiaux, *La Femme, la mariage et le divorce: Étude de physiologie et de sociologie* (G. Baillière, 1880), 116.
6. Theodore Zeldin, *Ambition, Love, and Politics*, vol. i of *France 1848–1950*, 303.
7. A fictional example of a husband condemned to continence for this reason occurs in Octave Mirbeau's *Journal d'une femme de chambre*.
8. This insistence on a semblance of seduction does not contradict the collapse of the Don Juan myth observed by Jean Borie (*Le Célibataire français*, 52). Insofar as the practices of seduction were intended for prostitutes, they were devalued. Don Juan in the salon of a *maison de rendez-vous* was certainly one of the elements of the psychopathology of the myth. The real contradiction lies at another level: it is at the point where the scientific literature speaks of the satisfaction of the genetic instinct—that is to say, of animality in the individual—that the prostitute's triumph demands more feeling. Is there a time lapse here between discourse and actual behavior? A simpler explanation might be that, frustrated at both poles of his sexuality by marriage, man pursues with the prostitute the satisfaction of a self-contradictory need for unbridled sex with a pure, angelic partner.

Extract 63

CHRISTOPHER LOOBY: *Sexual Self-Observation*

1. Homer Bostwick, *A Treatise on the Nature and Treatment of Seminal Diseases, Impotency, and Other Kindred Affections: With Practical Directions for the Management and Removal of the Cause Producing Them; Together with Hints to Young Men* (Burgess: Stringer & Co.: New York, 1847), 50–5, some ellipses omitted. Philip C. Van Buskirk, a nineteenth-century American seaman, evidently kept a similar diary record of his seminal emissions. From January 1852 (when he resolved to discontinue masturbation) until the end of 1858, according to B. R. Burg, he kept a scrupulous record of his seminal losses, itemizing 'all expenditure of semen by date and by immediate cause, recording whether they were involuntary, induced by a partner, or caused by solitary masturbation' (Burg, *An American Seafarer in the Age of Sail: The Erotic Diaries of Philip C. Van Buskirk, 1851–1870* (New Haven: Yale University Press, 1994), 30).

Extract 64

VERNON A. ROSARIO: *Masturbation and Degeneracy*

1. Claude François Lallemand, *De pertes séminales involontaires*, 3 vols. (Paris: Béchet Jeune, 1836–42), i. 435.
2. See Dora Weiner, 'Le Droit de l'homme à la santé: Une belle idée devant l'Assemblée Constituante: 1790–1791', *Clio Medica*, 5 (1970), 209–23; and *The Citizen-Patient in Revolutionary and Imperial Paris* (Baltimore: Johns Hopkins University Press, 1993) on the rise of socialized medicine and the construction of the 'citizen-patient' in Revolutionary France. See Erwin Ackerknecht, 'Hygiene in France, 1815–1848', *Bulletin of the History of Medicine*, 22 (1948), 117–55, on Napoleonic public hygiene. William Coleman, *Death is a Social Disease: Public Health and Political Economy in Industrial France* (Madison: University of Wisconsin Press, 1982), 21, discusses Restoration hygienists' metaphors of the social body and its pathologies.
3. Julien Joseph Virey, *Hygiène philosophique appliquée à la politique et à la morale*, new edn. (Paris: Crochard, 1831 (1st pub. 1828)), 79.

4. Fournier and Béguin, 'Masturbation', *Dictionnaire des sciences médicales*, 31 (Paris: Panckoucke, 1819), 101–2, emphasis added.

5. Michel Foucault suggests that this preoccupation with heredity represented a shift from the aristocratic cult of 'blood' to the bourgeois cult of 'heredity' (*Histoire de la sexualité*, i: *La Volonté de savoir* (Paris: Gallimard, 1976), 164). But as we see here, the latter was also a concern with blood—a genetic blood that was malleable to environmental and behavioral manipulations, unlike 'blue blood.'

6. See Coleman, *Death is a Social Disease*, 34–5, on French hygienists' concern over fertility. Depopulation anxieties (probably ill-founded) had troubled the country throughout the eighteenth century too as France saw rival nations outstrip it in industrial and military man power.

7. Joseph Henri Reveillé-Parise, review of *Traité d'hygiène appliqué à l'éducation de la jeunesse* by Simon de Metz, *Revue médicale*, 2 (1828), 93.

8. Ibid. 93–4.

9. Debourge, 'De la mastupratiomanie', *Journal de médicine, de chirurgie et de pharmacologie*, 10/15 (Brussels, 1852), 314.

10. Lallemand, *De pertes séminales involontaires*, i. 440.

11. See Hoxie N. Fairchild, *The Noble Savage: A Study in Romantic Naturalism* (New York: Russell & Russell, 1961), on the political uses of the 'noble savage' ideal.

12. See Nye, *The Origins of Crowd Psychology: Gustave Le Bon and the Crisis of Mass Democracy in the Third Republic* (London: Sage, 1975), and Daniel Pick, *Faces of Degeneration: A European Disorder, c.1848–c.1918* (Cambridge: Cambridge University Press, 1989), on the mounting concerns during the late nineteenth century over the urban poor and the working classes.

Extract 66

LAWRENCE BIRKEN: *Individualism and Sexuality*

1. Havelock Ellis and John Addington Symonds, *Sexual Inversion* (London: Macmillan, 1987), 29.

Extract 68

ARNOLD I. DAVIDSON: *Pathology and Norm*

1. Richard von Krafft-Ebing, *Textbook of Insanity* (Philadelphia: F. A. David, 1904), 79. Krafft-Ebing considers abolition to be the extreme case of diminution.

2. Ibid. 77–81.

3. Ibid. 81. This same classification is given in Krafft-Ebing, *Psychopathia sexualis* (New York: Stein & Day, 1965), 34.

4. Krafft-Ebing, *Textbook on Insanity*, 83–6; and *Psychopathia sexualis*, 34–6. I discuss masochism in 'Sex and the Emergence of Sexuality', *Critical Inquiry* (Autumn 1987).

5. Krafft-Ebing, *Psychopathia sexualis*, 16, 52–3. See also *Textbook on Insanity*, 81. For other representative statements see Albert Moll, *Perversions of the Sex Instinct* (Julian Press: Newark, 1931 (1st pub. 1891)), 172, 182; and Dr Laupts (pseudonym of G. Saint-Paul), *L'Homosexualité et les types homosexuels: Nouvelle Édition de Perversion et perversités sexuelles* (Paris: Vigot, 1910).

6. In eighteenth-century medicine, masturbation was considered exclusively as a causal factor, omnipresent of course, in the genesis of disease processes. It was not

considered a distinct and autonomous disease. See S. A. Tissot, *L'Onanisme: Dissertation sur les maladies produites par la masturbation* (Paris: Bechet, 1823). Originally published in Latin in 1758. In the nineteenth century it came to be thought of as both a distinct morbid entity and a significant causal factor in the genesis of other diseases. For the later understanding, see Paul Moreau (de Tours), *Des aberrations du sens génésique* (Paris: Asselin, 1880), 168.

7. It is instructive to compare this conception of perversion with Aquinas' treatment of unnatural vice. St Thomas believed that there was a distinct kind of lustful vice, 'contrary to the natural order of the venereal act as becoming to the human race: and this is called the unnatural vice.' He considered onanism, bestiality, sodomy, and the sin of not observing the right manner of copulation all to be unnatural vices. He thought them to be not only distinct from but also worse than incest, adultery, rape, and seduction. See *Summa theologica*, Question 154, Articles 11 and 12. One must be careful, however, not to assimilate this moral conception of perversion to the nineteenth-century medical conception.

Extract 70

G. FRANK LYDSTON: *Biological and Social Causation*

1. Since the above was written the world has been regaled with the exposure of an establishment in London patronized by the aristocracy, which was devoted to the procurement of young boys for the purpose of passive pederasty. I have also obtained positive knowledge of a physician in this city who has presented disgusting manifestations of sexual perversion to his female patients.

Extract 72

MARGARET GIBSON: *Hegemony of the Two-Sex Model: Females*

1. Havelock Ellis, 'Sexual Inversion in Women', *Alienist and Neurologist*, 16 (1895), 153.
2. Havelock Ellis, 'The Study of Sexual Inversion', *Medico-Legal Journal*, 12 (1894), 154.
3. Ellis, 'Sexual Inversion in Women', 154.
4. Richard von Krafft-Ebing, 'Perversion of the Sexual Instinct: Report of Cases', *Alienist and Neurologist*, 9 (1888), 580.
5. Ibid. 581. Why women might want to embrace masculinity and adopt the role of the 'mannish lesbian' has been the subject of some debate.
6. Charles L. Dana, 'On Certain Sexual Neuroses', *Medical and Surgical Reporter*, 65 (1891), 242.
7. James Kiernan, 'Sexual Perversion, and the Whitechapel Murders', *Medical Standard*, 4 (1888), 171.
8. P. M. Wise, 'Case of Sexual Perversion', *Alienist and Neurologist*, 4 (1883), 89–90.
9. Irving C. Rosse, 'Sexual Hypochondriasis and Perversion of the Genetic Instinct', *Journal of Nervous and Mental Disease*, 17 (1892), 807.
10. James Kiernan, 'Responsibility in Sexual Perversion', *Chicago Medical Recorder*, 8 (1892), 210.
11. Eugene P. Bernardy, 'One of the Causes of Aneroticism in Women', *Proceedings of the Philadelphia County Medical Society*, 15 (1894), 430.
12. Kiernan, 'Sexual Perversion, and the Whitechapel Murders', 130.

13. G. Frank Lydston, 'Sexual Perversion, Satyriasis and Nymphomania', *Medical and Surgical Reporter*, 61 (1889), 256.

Extract 73

JOHN ADDINGTON SYMONDS: *The Medicalization of 'Inverted' Sexuality*

1. Paul Moreau, *Des aberrations du sens génétique* (Paris, 1887); B. Tarnowsky, *Die krankhaften Erscheinungen de Geschlechtssinnes* (1887); Richard von Krafft-Ebing, *Psychopathia sexualis* (1886).
2. Carl Heinrich Ulrichs (1825–95). His specialities were jurisprudence and theology but under the pseudonym 'Numo Numantius' he wrote pamphlets on homosexuality.
3. According to Steven Marcus, 'The word neuropathic was a generic term of the period and referred to anyone who had or had had a psychiatric illness. At the time they thought all such illnesses were literally located in the nerves (i.e. the neurons, etc.)—hence the term neuropathic. It covered everything from hysterics to neurasthenia to psychotic states. In other words, it was a "scientific" term covering vast areas of ignorance, as so many medical terms continue to do.'

Extract 74

RICHARD VON KRAFFT-EBING: *Sadism as an Exaggeration of Heterosexual Love*

1. Among animals it is always the male who pursues the female with proffers of love. Playful or actual flight of the female is not infrequently observed; and then the relation is like that between the beast of prey and the victim.
2. The conquest of woman takes place today in the social form of courting, in seduction and deception, etc. From the history of civilization and anthropology we know that there have been times, as there are savages today that practice it, where brutal force, robbery, or even blows that rendered a woman powerless, were made use of to obtain love's desire. It is possible that tendencies to such outbreaks of sadism are atavistic. In the 'Jahrbücher für Psychologie', ii. 128, Schäfer (Jena) refers to the reports of two cases by A. Payer. In the first case states of great sexual excitement were induced by the sight of battles or of paintings of them; in the second, by cruel torturing of small animals. It is added: 'The pleasure of battle and murder is so predominantly an attribute of the male sex throughout the animal kingdom that there can be no question about the close relation existing between this side of the masculine character and male sexuality. I believe, too, that by unprejudiced observation I can show that, in men who are mentally and physically absolutely normal, the first indefinite and incomprehensible precursors of sexual excitement may be induced by the reading of exciting scenes of the chase and war—i.e., they give rise to unconscious longings for a kind of satisfaction in warlike games (wrestling), in which the fundamental sexual impulse to the most perfect and intense contact with a companion is expressed, with the secondary thought of conquest more or less easily defined.'
3. It sometimes happens that an accidental sight of blood, etc., puts into motion the preformed psychical mechanism of the sadistic individual and awakens the instinct.

Extract 76

RICHARD VON KRAFFT-EBING: *Masochism in Women*

1. The laws of the early middle ages gave the husband the right to kill the wife; those of the later middle ages, the right to beat her. The latter right was used freely, even by those of high standing. Yet, by the side of this, the paradoxical chivalry of the middle ages stands unexplained.
2. Cf. Lady Milford's words in Schiller's 'Kabale und Liebe': 'We women can only choose between ruling and serving; but the highest pleasure power affords us is a miserable substitute, if the greater joy of being the slaves of a man we love is denied us!' (Act II, scene i).
3. Seydel, 'Vierteljahresschr. f. ger. Med.', vol. ii (1893), quotes as an instance of masochism the patient of Dieffenbach, who repeatedly and purposely dislocated her arm in order to experience lustful sensations when it was being reduced, anaesthetics not being known then.

Extract 77

VERN L. BULLOUGH, DWIGHT DIXON, AND JOAN DIXON: *Christian Masochism?*

1. This is not so much my thesis as that of Ferdinand Lot, *The End of the Ancient World* (reprinted, New York: Harper & Row, 1961).
2. Jacques LaCarrière, *The God Possessed*, trans. Roy Monkcom (London: George Allen & Unwin, 1963), 173–4.
3. Palladius, *The Lausiac History*, trans. and annotated by Robert T. Meyer (Westminister, Md.: Newman Press, 1965), 18. 4, p. 59.
4. Thomas S. Weinberg and G. W. Levi Kamel (eds.), *S and M: Studies in Sadomasochism* (Buffalo: Prometheus Books, 1983), 134.
5. LaCarrière, *The God Possessed*, 205.
6. Quoted by LaCarrière, ibid. from the (Psuedo-) Macarius, *Spiritual Homilies*.
7. Jerome, *Ad Eustochium*, EP 22 in J. P. Migne, *Patrologia Latina* (Paris: Garnier Fretres, 1887, vol. xxii).
8. Palladius, *The Lausiac History*, 11. 4, p. 47.
9. Ibid. 23. 1–6, pp. 81–3.
10. Ibid. 47. 15–16, pp. 128–9.

Extract 78

ROBERT A. NYE: *Fetishism and Modern Civilization*

1. Alfred Binet, 'Le Fétichisme dans l'amour: Étude de psychologie morbide', *Revue philosophique*, 24 (1887), 166.
2. Ibid. 164.
3. Ibid. 165.
4. For instance, Adolphe Belot, *La Bouche de Madame X*, cited in Binet, 'Le Fétichisme', 170.
5. Ibid. 164–5, my emphasis.
6. Paul-Émile Garnier, *Les Fétichistes, pervertis, et invertis sexuels: Observations médico-légales* (Paris: Baillière, 1896), 22; Georges Saint-Paul, *Perversion et perversités sexuelles: Une enquête médicale sur l'inversion* (Paris, 1896), 20–31.

7. Émile Laurent, *Fétichistes et érotomanes* (Paris: Vigot, 1905), 7.

8. Henri Legludic, *Notes et observations de médicine légale: Attentats aux mœurs* (Paris: Masson, 1896), 224–5; Dr Louis Reuss, 'Des aberrations du sens génésique chez l'homme', *Annales d'hygiène publique et de médicine légale*, 3rd series, 16 (1886), 311; Garnier, *Les Fétichistes*, 144–5; Julien Chevalier, *L'Inversion Sexuelle: Une maladie de la personnalité* (Lyon: Storck, 1893), 414–15.

9. Charles Féré, *The Evolution and Dissolution of the Sexual Instinct*, 2nd rev. edn. (Paris: Carrington, 1904), 31. For a similar statement, see Reuss, 'Des aberrations', 315–16.

10. For a remarkable account of the Parisian *vie de bohème* which stresses the ambivalence of bohemian and bourgeois attitudes toward each other, see Jerrold Siegel, *Bohemian Paris* (New York: Viking, 1986).

11. Joanny Roux, *Psychologie de l'instinct sexuel* (Paris: Baillière, 1899), 87–90.

12. Laurent, *Fétichistes*, 44. See also Binet, 'Le Fétichisme', *passim*.

13. As Julien Chevalier, *L'Inversion sexuelle*, 414–25) wrote, women are more instinctive, 'and so resemble one another in love, while men, more conscious, more cerebral, love in a particular and personal fashion.'

14. Binet, 'Le Fétichisme', 61.

Extract 79

WILHELM STEKEL: *Fetishism and Impotence*

1. The reader will doubtless have noticed that I always speak of male fetishism. I have observed a case of jewelry fetishism in a woman and other rudiments of fetishism in females. Fetishism is, despite such cases, generally a male disease, but it is natural that the same points of view hold good in these cases as for male fetishism. Howard has described cases of female clothing fetishism, a thirty-nine-year-old woman who stole trousers, a twenty-one-year-old woman who coddled the drawers of her dead husband, a seventeen-year-old girl who possessed a veritable harem of men's garters (*Zeitschrift für Sexualwissenschaft*, 3 (Jan. 1914)).

2. In some cases of this sort, I have been able to observe a secondary psychic mechanism which I have called the principle of the 'finished product'. I borrow this curious title from a well-known joke which I must insert here because of its psychological value in reference to our theme. A match-maker offers the hand of a rich girl to a young man, but the young man reminds the match-maker that the offer suffers by the fact that the girl once broke her leg and now limps. 'What of that!' said the match-maker; 'just imagine that you were already married to the girl. You take your wife for a walk. Along comes an automobile and your wife is run down. You immediately call an ambulance and have to take your wife to the hospital. The professor comes in. You go through a few weeks of the greatest excitement, and finally you have to come through for the big bills. But here you have a finished product!' This principle of the finished product plays a leading role in some cases of pseudo-fetishism, e.g. in the following case. A man meets with the wife of a friend of his. The woman had always left him cold. Now he finds her quite banged up from a beating her husband had given her. At this moment his entire sexuality rose up in a wave of passion and he practically fell upon her. The woman, on the other hand, nursed a rankling desire for revenge against her husband. They both enjoyed a tremendous satisfaction during intercouse, but the enravishment did not

cease with this experience. The man in this case was a sadist who had never permitted his cruel instincts to become conscious. When he met this woman he came upon a 'finished product.' Fetishists who search for women with amputations have also repressed that bit of sadism which calls for the dismemberment of the woman. The amputated arm or the missing leg is then that reality which offers an anchorage for their fantasy. It is the make-believe of red blood for the animation of their colorless schemes. It is also possible to gain new insight into the psychology of sympathy from this point of view. This feeling also operates according to the principle of 'pleasure without guilt.' The cruel deeds have been accomplished by someone else or by destiny, and we derive our enjoyment therefrom in a form compatible with our ethical conscience. The malicious joy which so frequently precedes our sympathy and secretly accompanies it is the conscious expression of the same tendencies.

Extract 81

ANGUS MCLAREN: *Exhibitionism and Deviance*

1. Paul Garnier, 'Rapport médico-légal sur un exhibitioniste', *Annales médico-psychologiques*, 19 (1894), 97–103.
2. A. Rousset, 'Un cas d'exhibitionisme', *Annales médico-psychologiques*, 3 (1906), 394–401.
3. A. Vigoroux, 'Un exhibitioniste condamné par les tribunaux', *Annales médico-psychologiques*, 3 (1896), 213–16.
4. But Trochon warned that every man who exposed himself could not be simply let off as just 'sick.' A. Trochon, 'Un cas d'exhibitionisme', *Archives de l'anthropologie criminelle*, 3 (1888), 256–64.
5. Garnier, cited in David S. Booth, 'Erotomania: A Case of Exhibitionism—A Medico-Legal Study', *Alienist and Neurologist*, 26 (1905), 2.
6. Charles Lasègue, 'Les Exhibitionists', *L'Union médical*, 3rd series, 23 (May 1877), 709.
7. Ambrose Tardieu, *Étude médico-légale sur les attentats aux mœurs* (Paris, 1878), 5; 'Exhibitionists', *Dictionnaire des sciences médicales* (Paris: Lahure, 1887), xxxvi. 427–9; Alfred Binet, 'Le Fétishisme dans l'amour', *Revue philosophique*, 24 (1887), 256.
8. Valentin Magnan, 'Les Exhibitionists', *Archives de l'anthropologie criminelle*, 5 (1890), 436.
9. The author of the *Dictionnaire des sciences médicales* article on the subject also labeled as exhibitionists men who stalked their loved ones and thus 'exhibited' themselves.
10. Richard von Krafft-Ebing, *Psychopathia sexualis* (New York: Stein & Day, 1965), 338–41.
11. On epileptics, who were often played up in the nineteenth century as exhibitionists and vagabonds, see Cesare Lombroso, *L'Homme criminel* (Paris: Alcan, 1895), ii. 96–7. In the twentieth century, Ellis stated that epileptics should be excluded, and W. Norwood East found no cases of epilepsy in his sample. East did believe alcoholism played a role: in 1913 in England and Wales 866 men were convicted of indecent exposure, but in twelve months of 1922–3, after restrictions on sale of drinks were imposed, only 548. East, 'Observations on Exhibitionism', *Lancet*, 2 (1924), 370–5.

12. Marcel Mauss, 'Body Techniques', *Sociology and Psychology* (London: Routledge & Kegan Paul, 1979 (1st pub. 1950)), 95–123.

13. Exhibitionism was first discovered in Europe and North America. At the turn of the century, Bloch argued that perversions spread as a reaction to the constraints placed on the sexuality of civilized man by the forces of social coercion and sexual conventionality. Barrington Moore Jr. states that in 'primitive' societies, where the boundaries between the private and the public are not firm, discretion is employed to prevent noticing that which should not be seen. See Iwan Bloch, *The Sexual Life of our Time* (New York: Allied, 1930), 472; Moore, *Privacy: Studies in Social and Cultural History* (London: M. E. Sharpe, 1984), 78; Graham Rooth, 'Exhibitionism outside Europe and North America', *Archives of Sexual Behavior*, 2 (1973), 351–63.

14. John M. MacDonald, *Indecent Exposure* (Springfield, Ill.: Charles C. Thomas, 1973), 43.

15. Erich Wulffen, *Woman as Sexual Criminal* (New York: American Ethnological Press, 1934), 363.

16. Alfred Swain Taylor, *The Principles and Practices of Medical Jurisprudence* (London: J. A. Churchill, 1905), ii. 367.

17. Émile Laurent, *Fétishistes et érotomanes* (Paris: Vigot, 1903), 247.

18. Dr Hôpital, 'Quelques mots sur les exhibitionistes', *Annales médico-psychologiques*, 21 (1905), 224.

19. Garnier, 'Rapport', 100.

20. Dr Serge Paul, *Le Vice et l'amour* (Paris: Nouvelle librarie médicale, 1905), 268.

21. C. H. Hughes, 'Morbid Exhibitionism', *Alienist and Neurologist*, 25 (1904), 350.

Extract 83

ARNOLD I. DAVIDSON: *A New Style of Psychiatric Reasoning*

1. Sigmund Freud, *Three Essays on the Theory of Sexuality, The Standard Edition of the Complete Works of Sigmund Freud*, ed. and trans. James Strachey, 24 vols. (London, 1953–74), vii. 135–6.

2. For a useful overview, see Frank J. Sulloway, *Freud, Biologist of the Mind* (New York, 1979).

3. Freud, *Three Essays*, 147–8.

4. Sigmund Freud, *Gesammelte Schriften* (Vienna, 1924), v. 20.

5. For one example, see Bruno Bettelheim, *Freud and Man's Soul* (New York, 1982). I have criticized Bettelheim's claims in 'On the Englishing of Freud', *London Review of Books* (Nov. 1983), 3–16.

Extract 84

JONATHAN NED KATZ: *Heterosexuality as a Perversion*

1. R. von Krafft-Ebing, *Psychopathia sexualis, with Especial Reference to Contrary Sexual Instinct: A Medico-Legal Study*, trans. Charles Gilbert Chaddock (Philadelphia: F. A. Davis, 1893), 9.

2. Ibid. 169.

3. Ibid. 174.

Extract 85

GEORGE CHAUNCEY: *The Invention of Heterosexuality*

1. E. Anthony Rotundo, *American Manhood: Transformations in Masculinity from the Revolution to the Modern Era* (New York: Basic Books, 1993), 77, 78, 82, 85, 278.
2. 'The lack of a word for homosexuality is closely tied to the fact that there was no concept for it, no model for sexuality other than heterosexuality', writes Rotundo (ibid. 83) as if there *were* a word for heterosexuality in the nineteenth century. But neither word—nor concept—existed then.
3. James G. Kiernan, 'Increase of American Inversion', *Urologic and Cutaneous Review*, 20 (1916), 46.
4. Kiernan, 'Bisexuality', ibid. 18 (1914), 375, commenting on Herbert J. Claiborne, 'Hypertrichosis in Women: Its Relation to Bisexuality (Hermaphroditism): With Remarks on Bisexuality in Animals, Especially Man', *New York Medical Journal*, 99 (1914), 1178–83.
5. William Lee Howard, 'Effeminate Men and Masculine Women', *New York Medical Journal*, 71 (1900), 687. For a fuller discussion of this point, see my article 'From Sexual Inversion to Homosexuality: Medicine and the Changing Conceptualization of Female Deviance', *Salmagundi*, 58–9 (Fall 1982–Winter 1983), 114–46, and Caroll Smith-Rosenberg, 'The New Woman as Androgyne: Social Disorder and Gender Crisis, 1870–1936', in her *Disorderly Conduct: Visions of Gender in Victorian America* (New York: Knopf, 1985).
6. Perry M. Lichtenstein, 'The "Fairy" and the Lady Lover.', *Medical Review of Reviews*, 27 (1921), 369–74.
7. A. A. Brill, 'The Conception of Homosexuality', *Journal of the American Medical Association*, 61 (1913), 335.
8. See, particularly, the influential work of Lillian Faderman, *Odd Girls and Twilight Lovers: A History of Lesbian Life in Twentieth-Century America* (New York: Columbia University Press, 1991); and 'The Morbidification of Love Between Women by Nineteenth-Century Sexologists', *Journal of Homosexuality*, 4 (1978), 73–90.
9. For the use of some of these terms, see Gershon Legman, 'The Language of Homosexuality: An American Glossary', in George W. Henry, *Sex Variants* (New York: Paul B. Hoeber, 1941), vol. ii, appendix VII, 1159, 1172, 1173; and their frequent appearance in the 1920s and 1930s in New York tabloids. On the distinction between she-men (as queer) and he-men (as normal), see, for example, one gay character's comment in Richard Meeker's novel *Better Angel*, 180: 'nobody ever accused them of being "queer" Oh no! They are normal—he-men'.

Extract 88

JOHN FARLEY: *Variation and Evolution*

1. Hugo de Vries, *The Mutation Theory*, trans. J. B. Farmer and A. D. Darbishire (Chicago, 1910), 645–7.
2. Hugo de Vries, 'Fertilization and hybridization', in *Intracellular Pangenesis, Including a Paper on Fertilization and Hybridization*, trans. C. S. Gager (Chicago, 1910), 224.
3. Ibid. 227.
4. Ibid. 237.
5. Ibid. 263.

6. John Maynard Smith, 'The Origin and Maintenance of Sex', in George C. Williams (ed.), *Group Selection* (Chicago, 1971), 163.

Extract 89

LYNN MARGULIS AND DORION SAGAN: *The Origins of Sexual Reproduction*

1. S. Sonea and P. Panisset, *The New Bacteriology* (Boston, Jones & Bartlett, 1983).
2. L. Margulis, *Symbiosis in Cell Evolution* (San Francisco: W. H. Freeman, 1981).

Extract 90

R. ROBIN BAKER AND MARK A. BELLIS: *Sperm Competition Theory*

1. G. A. Parker, 'Sperm Competition and its Evolutionary Consequences in the Insects', *Biological Review*, 45 (1970), 525–67; 'Why Are There so Many Tiny Sperm? Sperm Competition and the Maintenance of Two Sexes', *J. Theor. Biol.* 96 (1982), 281–94; 'Sperm Competition and the Evolution of Animal Mating Strategies', in R. L. Smith (ed.), *Sperm Competition and the Evolution of Animal Mating Systems* (London: Academic Press, 1984), 1–60; 'Sperm Competition: Games, Raffles and Roles', *Proc. R. Soc. Lond. B.* 242 (1990), 120–6; 'Sperm Competition: Sneaks and Extra-pair Copulations', *Proc. R. Soc. Lond. B.* 242 (1990), 127–33.
2. M. Gomendio and E. R. S. Roldan, 'Sperm Competition Influences Sperm Size in Mammals', *Proc. R. Soc. B.* 243 (1991), 181–5.
3. J. Sivinski, 'Sexual Selection and Insect Sperm', *Florida Entomology*, 63 (1980), 99–111.
4. R. E. Silberglied. J. G. Shepherd, and J. L. Dickinson, 'Eunuchs: The Role of Apyrene Sperm in Lepidoptera?', *American Nat.* 123 (1984), 255–65.
5. R. R. Baker and M. A. Bellis, '"Kamikaze" Sperm in Mammals?', *Animal Behavior*, 36 (1988), 937-80; 'Number of sperm in human ejaculates varies in accordance with sperm competition theory', *Animal Behavior*, 37 (1989), 867–9.
6. Parker, 'Sperm Competition: Sneaks and Extra-pair Copulations'.
7. D. A. Dewsbury, 'Ejaculate Cost and Male Choice', *American Nat.* 119 (1982), 601–10.
8. R. R. Baker and M. A. Bellis, 'Human Sperm Competition: Ejaculate Adjustment by Males and the Function of Masturbation', *Animal Behavior*, 46 (1993), 861–85.

Extract 91

MATT RIDLEY: *Female Adultery*

1. D. F. Westneat, P. W. Sherman, and M. L. Morton, 'The Ecology of Extra-pair Copulations in Birds', *Current Ornithology*, 7 (1990), 31–69; T. R. Birkhead and A. P. Møller, *Sperm Competition in Birds* (London: Academic Press, 1992).
2. W. K. Potts, C. J. Manning, and E. K. Wakeland, 'Mating Patterns in Semi-natural Populations of Mice Influenced by MHC Genotype', *Nature*, 352 (1991), 619–21.
3. N. Burley, 'Sex Ratio Manipulation and Selection for Attractiveness', *Science*, 211 (1981), 721–2.
4. A. P. Møller, 'Intruders and Defenders on Avian Breedings Territories: The Effect of Sperm Competition', *Oikos*, 48 (1987), 47–54.

5. R. R. Baker and M. A. Bellis, 'Number of Sperm in Human Ejaculates Varies in Accordance with Sperm Competition', *Animal Behavior*, 37 (1989), 867–9; 'Human Sperm Competition: Infidelity, the Female Orgasm and "Kamikaze" Sperm', paper delivered to the fourth annual meeting of the Human Behavior and Evolution society, Albuquerque, N. Mex. (22–6 July 1992).

Extract 92

LORRAINE DASTON AND KATHARINE PARK: *Hermaphroditism and the Orders of Nature*

1. The core texts in this tradition were the Hippocratic treatises *On the Seed* and *On the Nature of the Child*, and two works attributed to Galen called *On the Seed*, one authentic and one pseudonymous. See Joan Cadden, *Meanings of Sex Difference in the Middle Ages: Medicine, Science, and Culture* (Cambridge: Cambridge University Press, 1993), 15–21 (on the Hippocratic tradition) and 30–7 (on Galen).

2. Although some Greek writers also emphasized the role of the right and left testicles of the father, this idea seems to have had relatively little influence in the post-classical medical tradition.

3. See, for example, pseudo-Galen, *De spermate*, cited in Danielle Jacquart and Claude Thomasset, *Sexualité et savoir médical au Moyen Âge* (Paris: Presses universitaires de France, 1985), 195. The simplest form of this doctrine is the theory of the seven-celled uterus: the three right-hand cells produce males, the three left-hand cells, females, while the seventh, in the centre, produces a hermaphrodite; see Fridolf Kudlien, 'The Seven Cells of the Uterus: The Doctrine and its Roots', *Bulletin of the History of Medicine*, 39 (1965), 415–23.

4. See Aristotle, *Generations of Animals*, trans. A. L. Peck (Cambridge, Mass.: Harvard University Press, 1953), 371–95 (bk. 4, ch. 1) and 425–43 (bk. 4, ch. 4, esp. 770b27–773a2). See also Cadden, *Meanings of Sex Difference*, 21–6. Aristotle nowhere uses the term 'hermaphrodite', referring only to animals 'having two sets of genitals'.

5. Aristotle, *Generations of Animals*, 391–3 (bk. 4, ch. 1, 766a30–b8).

6. As Cadden notes, although the opposition between hot and cold can be mediated, other polarities fundamental to the Aristotelian interpretation of sex difference—active and passive, perfect and imperfect, ability to produce semen and the corresponding inability—cannot (*Meanings of Sex Difference*) 24–5.

7. Aristotle, *Generations of Animals*, bk. 4, ch. 4, 772b26–35.

8. See Cadden, *Meanings of Sex Difference*, 39–110.

9. Ibid. 53–104; John W. Baldwin, *The Language of Sex: Five Voices from Northern France around 1200* (Chicago: University of Chicago Press, 1994), 94–6.

10. Cadden, *Meanings of Sex Difference*, 197–201.

Extract 93

ALICE D. DREGER: *Gonadal Sex*

1. François Jules Octave Guermonprez, 'Une erreur de sexe, avec ses conséquences', *Journal des sciences médicales de Lille*, 2 (1892), 337.

2. Ibid. 338–9.

3. Ibid. 338.
4. Ibid.
5. Ibid, 370. Teratology is the scientific study of malformations or 'monstrosities.' The term was coined by the French anatomist Isidore Geoffrey Saint-Hilaire (1805–1861), who published a three-volume work on the subject in 1832–1836, entitled *Histoire générale et particulière des anomalies . . . ou, Traité de tératologie.*
6. Guermonprez, 'Une erreur de sexe', 370.
7. See Dreger, 'Doubtful Sex, Doubtful Status: Cases and Concepts of Hermaphroditism in France and Britain, 1868–1915', Ph.D. dissertation, Indiana University (1995).
8. See Erwin H. Ackernecht, *Medicine at the Paris Hospital* (Baltimore: Johns Hopkins University Press, 1967); Michel Foucault, *The Birth of the Clinic: An Archeology of Medical Perception*, trans. A. M. Sheridan Smith (New York: Vintage Books, 1975), ch. 8.
9. See Herculine Barbin, *Herculine Barbin. Being the Recently Discovered Memoirs of a Nineteenth-Century French Hermaphrodite*, introd. Michel Foucault, trans. Richard McDougall (New York: Pantheon, 1980 (1st pub. 1868)).

Extract 94

JOE LEIGH SIMPSON: *The Developmental Etiology of Hermaphroditism*

1. See J. D. Wilson and J. L. Goldstein, 'Classification of Hereditary Disorders of Sexual Development', *Birth Defects, Original Article Series*, 11 / 4 (1975).

Extract 96

ANNE FAUSTO-STERLING: *How to Build a Man*

1. See John Money, 'Hermaphroditism: An Inquiry into the Nature of a Human Paradox', Ph.D. dissertation, Harvard University, Cambridge (1952); *The Psychologic Study of Man* (Springfield, Ill.: Charles C. Thomas, 1975); John Money and J. G. Hampson, 'Idiopathic Sexual Precocity in the Male', *Psychosomatic Medicine*, 17 (1955), 1–15; John Money, J. G. Hampson, and J. L. Hampson, 'An Examination of Some Basic Sexual Concepts: The Evidence of Human Hermaphroditism', *Bulletin of the Johns Hopkins Hospital*, 97 (1955), 301–19.
2. See John Money and Patricia Tucker, *Sexual Signatures: On Being a Man or a Woman* (Boston: Little, Brown & Co., 1975); John Money and Anke A. Ehrhardt, *Man and Woman, Boy and Girl: The Differentiation and Dimorphism of Gender Identity from Conception to Maturity* (Baltimore: Johns Hopkins University Press, 1972).
3. The data do not actually match the presence / absence model, but this seems not to bother most people. For a discussion of this point, see Anne Fausto-Sterling, 'Society Writes Biology / Biology Constructs Gender', *Daedalus*, 116 (1987), 61–76; 'Life in the XY Corral', *Women's Studies International Forum*, 12 (1989), 319–31; *Myths of Gender: Biological Theories about Women and Men* (New York: Basic, 1992).
4. John Money, *The Adam Principle* (Elmhurst, NY: Global Academic Publishers, 1992).
5. I use the phrases 'male hormones' and 'female hormones' as shorthand. There are, in fact, no such categories. Males and females have the same hormones, albeit in different quantities and sometimes with different tissue distributions.

6. Patricia Donahue, David M. Powell, and Mary M. Lee, 'Clinical Management of Intersex Abnormalities', *Current Problems in Surgery*, 28 (1991), 527.

7. Suzanne J. Kessler, 'The Medical Construction of Gender: Case Management of Intersexed Infants', *Signs*, 16 (1990), 3–26.

8. Money and Ehrhardt, *Man and Woman*, 118–23.

9. John Money, M. Schwartz, and V. G. Lewis, 'Adult Erotosexual Status and Fetal Hormonal Masculinization and Demasculinization: 46, XX Congenital Virilizing Hyperplasia and 46, XX Androgen-Insensitivity Syndrome Compared', *Psychoneuroendocrinology*, 9 (1984), 405–14; John Money and J. Daléry, 'Iatrogenic Homosexuality: Gender Identity in Seven 46, XX Chromosomal Females with Hyperadrenocortical Hermaphroditism Born with a Penis', *Journal of Homosexuality*, 1 (1976), 357–71.

10. Richard Green, *The 'Sissy Boy' Syndrome and the Development of Homosexuality* (New Haven: Yale University Press, 1987).

11. John Money, J. G, Hampson, and J. L. Hampson, 'Hermaphroditism: Recommendations Concerning Assignment of Sex, Change of Sex, and Psychological Management', *Bulletin of the Johns Hopkins Hospital*, 97 (1955), 284–300.

Extract 97

CHARLES ÉDOUARD BROWN-SÉQUARD: *Testicular Rejuvenation*

1. This innocuity was also proved on a very old dog by twenty subcutaneous injections of a fluid similar to that I intended to employ on myself. No apparent harm resulted from these trials, which were made by my assistant, Dr D'Arsonval.

2. For reasons I have given in many lectures in 1869 and since, I consider the spermatic as also the principal glands (kidneys, liver, &c) as endowed, besides their secretory power, with an influence over the composition of blood, which is possessed by the spleen, the thyroid, &c. Led by that view, I have already made some trials with the blood returning from the testicles. But what I have seen is not sufficntly decisive to be mentioned here.

3. I ought to say that, notwithstanding that dark picture, my general health is and has been almost always good, and that I had very little to complain of, excepting merycism and muscular rheumatism.

4. My friends know that, owing to certain circumstances and certain habits, I have for thirty or forty years gone to bed very early and done my writing work in the morning, beginning it generally between three and four o'clock. For a great many years I had lost all power of doing any serious mental work after dinner. Since my first subcutaneous injections I have very frequently been able to do such work for two, three, and for one evening for nearly four hours.

5. I have a record of the strength of my forearm, begun in March 1860, when I first established myself in London. From that time to 1862 I occasionally moved as much as 50 kilogrammes. During the last three years the maximum moved was 38 kilogrammes. This year, previously to the first injection, the maximum was 37 kilogrammes. Since the injection it has been 44.

6. In my third communication at the Biological Society, I said that both the intense pain each injection has caused me and the inflammation it has produced would be notably diminished if the liquid employed were more diluted. The three cases of

Dr Variot have proved the exactitude of my statement. He made use of a much larger amount of water, and his patients had to suffer no very great pain and no inflammation.

7. The paper of Dr Variot and my remarks upon it have appeared in the *Comptes rendus de la Société de Biologie*, 26 (5 July 1889), 451, 454.

8. Since writing the above I have received a letter from Dr Variot announcing that, after injecting the liquid drawn from the testicles into these two individuals, he has obtained the same strengthening effects I have myself experienced.

Extract 100

NELLY OUDSHOORN: *Masculine and Feminine Hormones*

1. It is striking that during the three International Conferences on Standardization of Sex Hormones held in London during the 1930s, the very names of male and female sex hormones were never discussed.

2. The terminological practice in the scientific community in the 1920s and 1930s can be derived from the titles of publications indexed in the *Quarterly Cumulative Index Medicus* in the period from 1927 to 1937. The titles show that the names male and female sex hormones began to be questioned from the beginning of the 1930s. In 1931 the first title appeared with the name 'ambosexual hormone' (vol. 9) and in 1933 the first title appeared in which the author referred to the hormone as the 'so-called female sex hormone' (vol. 13). The nomenclature for male sex hormones changes after 1936. In that year the first publication appeared with the name 'male' hormone (vol. 19). In 1937 the terms 'androgens' and 'estrogens' were introduced as subject entries. From the moment of introduction, more publications were indexed under the subject entries androgens and estrogens than under the other subject entries (like sex hormones, ovarian hormones and internal secretions of testicles). In a rather short period the name androgens and estrogens were accepted as general terms for sex hormones.

3. H. M. Evans, 'Endocrine Glands: Gonads, Pituitary and Adrenals', *Annual Review of Physiology* (The Hague: Martinus Nijhoff, 1939), 578.

4. R. T. Frank, *The Female Sex Hormone* (Springfield, Ill.: Charles C. Thomas, 1929), 115.

5. E. Borchardt, E. Dingemanse, S. E. de Jongh, and E. Laqueur, 'Over het vrouwelijk geslachtshormoon Menformon, in het bijzonder over de anti-masculine werking', *Nederlands Tijdschrift Geneeskunde*, 72 (1928), 1,028.

6. D. Long Hall, 'The Social Implications of the Scientific Study of Sex', in *The Scholar and the Feminist*, iv (New York: The Women's Center of Barnard College, 1976), 20.

7. W. E. Caldwell, H. C. Moloy, and D. A. D'Esopo, 'Further Studies on the Pelvic Architecture', *American Journal of Obstetrics and Gynecology*, 28 (1934), 482–97.

Extract 103

JOAN JACOBS BRUMBERG: *Changing Meanings of Menarche*

1. Krause Collection, Historical Society of Western Pennsylvania, J15B.

2. There is a pervasive interdisciplinary feminist literature on past and present connections between adolescent feminine identity and the consumer culture. Some examples are Kathy Peiss, *Cheap Amusements: Working Women and Leisure in*

Turn-of-the-Century New York (Philadelphia, 1986); Erica Carter, 'Alice in the Consumer Wonderland', in Angela McRobbie and Mica Nava (eds.), *Gender and Generation* (London, 1984), 185–214; Leslie G. Roman and Linda Christian-Smith, *Becoming Feminine: The Politics of Popular Culture* (New York, 1988).

3. Bernard Barber and Lyle S. Lobel, 'Fashion in Women's Clothes and the American Social System', in Reinhard Bendix and Seymour Martin Lipset (eds.), *Class, Status and Power: A Reader in Social Stratification* (New York, 1953), 323–32; Roland Barthes, *The Fashion System*, trans. Matthew Ward and Richard Howard (New York, 1983); Joanne Finkelstein, *The Fashioned Self* (Philadelphia, 1991).

Extract 106

PAUL ROBINSON: *Psychology is physiology*

1. William Masters and Virginia Johnson, *Human Sexual Responses* (Boston, 1966), 135–6; see also 127.
2. Ibid. 215.

Extract 107

LEONORE TIEFER: *The Human Sexual Response Cycle*

1. W. H. Masters and V. E. Johnson, *Human Sexual Responses* (Boston: Little, Brown, 1966), 127.
2. L. Tiefer, 'Critique of the DSM-IIIR Nosology of Sexual Dysfunctions', *Psychiatric Medicine*, 10 (1992), 227–45.
3. American Psychiatric Association (APA), *Diagnostic and Statistical Manual of Mental Disorders* (Washington: APA, 1952), or *DSM-I*.
4. APA, *Diagnostic and Statistical Manual of Mental Disorders* (Washington, APA, 1968), or *DSM-II*.
5. APA, *Diagnostic and Statistical Manual of Mental Disorders* (Washington, APA, 1980), or *DSM-III*.
6. APA, *Diagnostic and Statistical Manual of Mental Disorders* (Washington, APA, 1987), or *DSM-III-R*.
7. Ibid. 290–1, emphasis added.
8. W. H. Masters and V. E. Johnson, *Human Sexual Inadequacy* (Boston: Little, Brown, 1970).
9. H. S. Kaplan, *Disorders of Sexual Desire* (New York: Brunner/Mazel, 1979), p. xviii.
10. APA, *DSM-III*, 6.
11. R. L. Spitzer, J. B. W. Williams, and A. E. Skodol, 'DSM-III: The Major Achievements and an Overview', *American Journal of Psychiatry*, 137 (1980), 153–4.
12. Tiefer, 'Critique'.
13. A. Soble, 'Philosophy, Medicine and Healthy Sexuality', in E. E. Shelp (ed.), *Sexuality and Medicine*, i: *Conceptual Roots* (Dordrecht: D. Reidel Publishing Co., 1987).
14. L. Trilling, 'The Kinsey Report', in L. Trilling (ed.), *The Liberal Imagination: Essays on Literature and Society* (Garden City, NY: Doubleday Anchor, 1950), 223.
15. W. H. Masters and V. E. Johnson, *The Pleasure Bond* (Boston: Little, Brown, 1975).
16. Masters and Johnson, *Human Sexual Inadequacy*, 91.

17. E. Frank, C. Anderson, and D. Rubenstein, 'Frequency of Sexual Dysfunction in "Normal" Couples', *New England Journal of Medicine*, 299 (1978), 111–15.
18. S. Hite, *The Hite Report* (New York: Macmillan, 1976).

Extract 110

ANNE BOLIN: *The Truth of Anatomy*

1. Cf. Elliott Chapple, *Culture and Biological Man: Explorations in Behavioral Anthropology* (New York: Holt, 1970), 302.
2. See Deborah H. Feinbloom, *Transvestites and Transsexuals: Mixed Views* (New York: Delacorte Press / Seymour Lawrence Books, 1976), 232.

Extract 113

SIMON LEVAY: *The Sexual Brain*

1. L. S. Allen and R. A. Gorski, 'Sexual Orientation and the Size of the Anterior Commissure in the Human Brain', *Proceedings of the National Academy of Sciences of the USA*, 89 (1992), 7199–202.

Extract 115

MICHAEL R. GORMAN: *Male Homosexual Desire*

1. Sexual desire rather than sexual behavior is used here as the defining criterion of sexual orientation because of the apparently greater plausibility of sexual behavior compared to sexual desire. Where sexual identity, sexual behavior and sexual desire are incongruent—e.g., a married man fantasizes exclusively about men, behaves bisexually, and yet identifies as a heterosexual (see L. S. Doll, L. R. Petersen, C. R. White, et al., 'Homosexually and Nonhomosexually Identified Men who Have Sex with Men: A Behavioral Comparison, *Journal of Sex Research* 29 (1992), 1–14)—the homosexual element is almost invariably present as fantasy or behavior and almost never as identity. Furthermore, among gay men with previously bisexual behavior and heterosexual identity, most report that their previous heterosexual behavior occurred while their desire was predominantly homosexual (A. P. Bell, M. S. Weinberg, and S. K. Hammersmith, *Sexual Preference: Its Development in Men and Women* (Bloomington: Indiana University Press, 1981)). In such cases, heterosexual behavior is commonly viewed as a consequence of social pressure and not as an authentic expression of their sexuality.
2. S. A. LeVay, 'A Difference in Hypothalamic Structure between Heterosexual and Homosexual Men', *Science*, 253 (1991), 1034–7.
3. M. E. Kite and K. Deaux, 'Gender Belief Systems: Homosexuality and the Implicit Inversion Theory', *Psych. Women Quarterly*, 11 (1987), 83–96.
4. J. H. Dunkle and P. L. Francis, 'Role of Facial Masculinity / Femininity in the Attribution of Homosexuality', *Sex Roles*, 23 (1990), 157–67.
5. K. J. Dover, *Greek Homosexuality* (London: Duckworth, 1978).
6. G. H. Herdt, *Guardians of the Flutes: Idioms of Masculinity* (New York: Columbia University Press, 1981).
7. G. Dörner, W. Rohde, F. Stahl, et al., 'A Neuroendocrine Predisposition for Homosexuality in Men', *Archives of Sexual Behavior*, 4 (1975), 1–8; B. A. Gladue, R.

Green, and R. E. Hellman, 'Neuroendocrine Response to Estrogen and Sexual Orientation', *Science*, 225 (1984), 1496–9.

8. S. E. Hendricks, B. Graber, and J. F. Rodriguez-Sierra, 'Neuroendocrine Responses to Exogenous Estrogen: No Differences between Heterosexual and Homosexual Men', *Psychoneuroendocrinology*, 14 (1989), 177–85; L. Gooren, 'Biomedical Theories of Sexual Orientation: A Critical Examination', in D. P. McWhirter, S. A. Sanders, and J. M. Reinisch (eds.), *Homosexuality/Heterosexuality: Concepts of Sexual Orientation* (New York: Oxford University Press, 1990).

9. J. D. Weinrich, *Sexual Landscapes: Why We Are What We Are, Why We Love Whom We Love* (New York: Scribner's, 1987).

10. R. C. Pillard, 'Masculinity and Femininity in Homosexuality: "Inversion" Revisited', in J. C. Gonsiorer and J. D. Weinrich (eds.), *Homosexuality: Research Implications for Public Policy* (Newbury Park, Calif.: Sage, 1991); G. E. Tuttle and R. C. Pillard, 'Sexual Orientation and Cognitive Abilities', *Archives of Sexual Behavior*, 20 (1991), 307–18.

11. R. Green, *The 'Sissy Boy Syndrome' and the Development of Homosexuality* (New Haven: Yale University Press, 1987).

12. Weinrich, *Sexual Landscapes*.

13. Tuttle and Pillard, 'Sexual Orientation'.

14. B. A. Gladue, W. W. Beatty, J. Larson, and R. D. Staton, 'Sexual Orientation and Spatial Ability in Men and Women', *Psychobiology*, 18 (1990), 101–8; C. M. McCormick and S. F. Witelson, 'Cognitive Profile of Homosexual Men Compared to Heterosexual Men and Women', *Psychoneuroendocrinology*, 16 (1991), 459–73.

15. Gladue, Beatty, Larson, and Staton, 'Sexual Orientation'; McCormick and Witelson, 'Cognitive Profile'.

16. McCormick and Witelson, 'Cognitive Profile'.

17. W. H. Masters and V. E. Johnson, *Homosexuality in Perspective* (Boston: Little, Brown, 1979).

18. D. Symons, *Evolution of Human Sexuality* (New York: Oxford University Press, 1979).

19. Ibid. 304.

Extract 116

ELLEN CHESLER: *The Origins of the Birth Control Movement*

1. The employment statistics are from a two-part article by Chase Woodhouse, 'The Status of Women', *American Journal of Sociology*, 35/6 (May 1930), 1091–5, and 36/6 (May 1931), 1011–16. The Sanger quotations are from Hannah Stein, 'Does Marriage Interfere with a Career? Interview Margaret Sanger', *Syracuse Herald*, 5 Apr. 1926, clipping in the Margaret Sanger Papers, Library of Congress.

2. Dorothy Dunbar Bromley, 'Feminist-New Style 1927', *Harper's Monthly*, 155 (1927), 556. John B. Watson, 'The Weakness of Women', *Nation*, 25 (6 July 1927), 9–10. Margaret Sanger, *The Pivot of Civilization* (New York, 1922), 238–9.

Extract 117

KEVIN WHITE: *The Deconstruction of Victorian Sexuality*

1. T. J. Jackson Lears, *No Place of Grace: Antimodernism and the Transformation of American Culture* (New York: Pantheon, 1981); Peter Gardella in his extraordinary *Innocent*

Ecstacy: How Christianity Gave America an Ethic of Sexual Pleasure (New York: Oxford University Press, 1986) shows how religious writers increasingly encouraged orgasmic ecstacy by emphasizing spiritual ecstasy as a goal in marriage.

2. John Higham, 'The Reorientation of American Culture in the 1890's, in J. Higham (ed.), *Writing American History* (Bloomington: Indiana University Press, 1970), 60–103; James McGovern, 'David Graham Phillips and the Virility Impulse of the Progressive Era', *New England Quarterly*, 39 (Sept. 1966), 348; Joe Dubbert, 'Progressivism and the Masculinity Crisis', in Joseph H. Pleck and Elizabeth H. Pleck, *The American Man* (Englewood Cliffs, NJ: Prentice Hall, 1980), 383–420.

3. Jack London, *The Call of the Wild* (New York: Macmillan, 1903), 131, 132, 119, 142.

4. Frank Morris, *McTeague: A Story of San Francisco* (New York: Norton, 1977). See also the scandal caused by Stephen Crane's *Maggie: A Girl of the Streets* and by Theodore Dreiser's *Sister Carrie*. Their sympathetic portrayal of fallen women broke with Victorian morality.

5. Agnes Repplier, 'The Repeal of Reticence', *Atlantic* (Mar. 1914), 297–304; 'Sex O'-Clock in America', *Current Opinion*, 55 (Aug. 1913), 113–14. The author was anonymous, but the phrase is from William Marion Reedy, editor of the *St Louis Mirror*, quoted in John C. Burnham, 'The Progressive Era Revolution in American Attitudes towards Sex', *Journal of American History*, 59 (Mar. 1973), 163.

6. T. J. Jackson Lears, 'The Concept of Cultural Hegemony', *American Historical Review*, 90 (1985), 567–93; A. Gramsci, *The Modern Prince*, in A. Gramsci, *Selections from Prison Notebooks*, trans. Q. Hoare, and G. N. Smith (New York: Basic, 1983).

Extract 119

DAVID G. HORN: *The Ironies of State Promotion of Births: The Italian Case*

1. Michel de Certeau, *The Practice of Everyday Life*, trans. Steven Randall (Berkeley and Los Angeles: University of California Press, 1984; Anthony Galt, 'Rehinking Patron–Client Relationships: The Real System and the Official System in Southern Italy', *Anthropological Quarterly*, 47 (1974), 182–202.

2. We should not assume that proactive tactics were limited to urban areas or a recent innovation. Many demographers between the wars contrasted the control of births with the 'natural rates of reproduction' that prevailed in the countryside.

3. Chiara Saraceno, 'Redefining Maternity and Paternity: Gender, Pronatalism and Social Policies in Fascist Italy', in Gisela Bock and Pat Thane (eds.), *Maternity and Gender Policies: Women and the Rise of the European Welfare States, 1880s–1950s* (New York: Routledge, 1991), 198.

4. Victoria de Grazia, *How Fascism Ruled Women: Italy, 1922–1945* (Berkeley and Los Angeles: University of California Press, 1992), 113.

5. Massimo Livi-Bacci, *A History of Italian Fertility during the Last Two Centuries* (Princeton: Princeton University Press, 1977), 349.

6. Marilyn Strathern, *Reproducing the Future: Essays on Anthropology, Kinship and the New Reproductive Technologies* (New York: Routledge, 1992), 55.

7. Ibid. 56.

Extract 120

MARY LOUISE ROBERTS: *The Ironies of Sex Education: The French Case*

1. Marc Semenoff, 'La Pureté: Point de vue catholique', in Marc Semenoff (ed.), *L'Education sexuelle: Les Écrits pour et contre* (Paris: André Delpeuch, 1924), 37.

2. Association du marriage chrétien, *Les Initiations nécessaires, Deux discours by R. P. de Ganay, S.J., and Dr H. Abrand* (Paris: Association du marriage chrétien, 1922), 2, 5–6, 10.

3. See Avril de Sainte Croix, *L'Éducation sexuelle* (Paris: Librarie Félix Alcan, 1918), 39; Alain Corbin, 'Le Péril vénérien au début au siècle: Prophylaxie sanitaire et prophylaxie morale', in Lion Murard and Patrick Zulberman (eds.), *L'Haleine des faubourgs* (Fontenay-sous-Bois: Recherches, 1978), 261.

4. Both the CEF and the Société français de prophylaxie sanitaire et morale (SFPSM) argued for the teaching of sex education within the natural science curriculum of the state-run schools. By contrast, Catholic opinion, including that of the General Assembly of Cardinals and Archbishops, held that state-sponsored sexual education 'would be collective, neutral from the point of view of religious morality and exclusively anatomical and physiological in kind, which is to say that this education would be disastrous' (Association, *Les Initiations nécessaires*, Ganay, 3).

5. Montreuil-Strauss, 'Exposé de Mme Montreuil-Strauss sur l'enseignement de l'hygiène sexuelle à l'école', 26 Jan. 1922, Dossier Germaine Montreuil-Strauss, Archives Marie-Louise Bouglé, 14. Montreuil-Strauss believed that the moral element of sexual education should be undertaken by the family rather than the school.

6. Association, *Les Initiations nécessaires*, Ganay, 4.

7. In *Hygiène et morale sociales: Néomalthusianisme, maternité, et féminisme, éducation sexuelle* (Paris: Masson et Cie, 1918), 20, J. Doléris and Jean Bouscatel try to distance themselves from what they call the 'Christian moralists' and do so by emphasizing the importance of science in sexual education.

8. Montreuil-Strauss, 'Exposé', 15.

9. Cited in M. L. Chevrel, 'Germaine Montreuil-Strauss éducatrice et novatrice: Histoire du Comité d'éducation féminine', *Femmes médecins*, 6 (Oct. 1970), 245–6.

10. G. Montreuil-Strauss, 'Devons-nous donner un enseignement sexuel à nos filles?', *Rapport au Congrés international de propagande d'hygiène sociale, 23–27 mai 1923* (Paris: Comité nationale de propagande d'hygiène sociale, n.d.), 383.

11. G. Montreuil-Strauss, *Avant la maternité: Précis des connaissances indispensables aux futures mères* (Paris: Stock, 1922), 21, 26.

12. Ibid. 58–9.

13. G. Montreuil-Strauss, 'Devons-nous donner un enseignement?', 282.

14. Corbin, 'Le Péril vénérien', 262, argues that in their drive to control venereal disease before the war, the SFPSM created a highly negative view of sexual activity.

15. G. Montreuil-Strauss, *Tu seras mère: La Fonction maternelle* (Société français de prophylaxie sanitaire et morale, 1928), 4.

16. G. Montreuil-Strauss, *L'Enseignement se rapportant à l'hygiène sexuelle et aux maladies vénériennes est-il actuellement réalisable dans nos écoles normales et d'institutrices?* (Paris: R. Tancrède, 1926), 7. Another young woman noted that she felt better prepared to face a life alone after having listened to Montreuil-Strauss.

Extract 121

ATINA GROSSMAN: *More Rational Sex: The German Case*

1. *SH* 1/5 (Feb. 1929), 37; 6 (Mar. 1929), 46; 7 (Apr. 1929), 51; 12 (Oct. 1929), 1, 6.
2. *SH* 2/12 (Sept. 1930), 90.
3. Report on public health congress of the Verband Volksgesundheit at the International Hygiene Exhibition, 21–4 June 1930, Dresden, in Bundesarchiv Potsdam, Reichministerium des Innern 26235, 225–34.
4. *Ideal Ehe*, 2 (Dec. 1927), 43.
5. Friedrich Wolf, *Herunter mit dem Blutdruk, Schlaganfall, Verlust der Arbeitskraft, Vorzeitiges Altern sind vermeidbar. Lies dieses Buch* (Stuttgart: Süddeutsches Verlagshaus, 1929), 20.
6. See the photographs in journals such as *Ideal Ehe* (*Lebensbund*), *Der Eheberater*, *Liebe und Ehe*, or the film *Wege zu Kraft und Schönheit*, in Bundesarchiv Koblenz film archive.
7. For discussion of the politics of nudism during Weimar, see Wilfried van der Will, 'The Body and the Body Politics as Symptom and Metaphor in the Transition of German Culture to National Socialism', in Brandon Taylor and Wilfried van der Will (eds.), *The Nazification of Art* (Winchester: The Winchester Press, 1990), 14–52.
8. *SH* 4/5 (May 1932), 39.
9. *SH* 4/10 (Oct. 1932), 86.
10. *SH* 4/6 (June 1932), 45.
11. *SH* 3/9 (Sept. 1931), 71.
12. *Ideal Lebensbund*, 3/4 (Apr. 1929), 105.
13. See *Ideal Lebensbund*, 2/1–10 (1928); no. 4 was a special issue on *Erotik des Lebens*; no. 6 on *Ehe-Schulung* (marriage education). Nos. 2 and 6 were confiscated on grounds of obscenity.
14. See Wilhelm Reich, *People in Trouble* (New York: Farrar, Strauss & Giroux, 1976).
15. *Ideal Lebensbund*, 3/4 (Apr. 1929), 104–5.
16. *Die Aufklärung: Monatschrift für Sexual- und Lebensreform*, 5 (June 1929), 59.

Extract 122

LESLEY A. HALL: *The Sexual Misery of Modern Man*

1. I. Hutton, *The Hygiene of Marriage* (London, 1933 (1st pub. 1923)), 49–50.
2. 'Dr' G. C. Beale, *Wise Wedlock: The Whole Truth: A Book of Counsel for All who Seek for Happiness in Marriage* (n.d. (c.1922)), 69.
3. E. Chesser, *Sexual Behaviour: Normal and Abnormal* (n.d. (1949)), 16–17.
4. H. Wright, *The Sex Factor in Marriage: A Book for Those who Are or Are About to Be Married*, 2nd edn. (London, 1937 (1st pub. 1930)), 67–8.
5. L. Housman, *The Unexpected Years* (London, 1937).
6. M. Stopes, *Married Love: A New Contribution to the Solution of Sex Difficulties*, 12th edn. (London, 1923 (1st pub. 1918)), 92: this passage did not appear in the 1918 edition and may well have been inserted following the many revelations of sexual ignorance Stopes received.

Extract 123

MARGARET JACKSON: *The Limitations of Sexual Enlightenment in Marriage*

1. Marie C. Stopes, *Marriage in my Time* (London: Rich & Gowan, 1935), 44; *Married Love: A New Contribution to the Solution of Sex Difficulties* (London: A. C. Fifield, 1918), p. xiii.
2. Stopes, *Married Love*, 38–9.
3. Ibid. 41, 53, 43.
4. Ibid. 45, 48, 50.
5. The most recent and comprehensive study of the 'back-to-the-home-movement' during this period is Deidre Beddoe, *Back to Home and Duty: Women between the Wars 1918–1939* (London: Pandora Press, 1989). The 'new feminism' and its implications have been discussed by Jane Lewis, 'Beyond Suffrage: English Feminism in the 1920s', *Maryland Historian*, 6 (1975), 1–17; for a different interpretation which focuses on the sexual aspects of the 'new feminism', see Sheila Jeffreys, *The Spinster and her Enemies: Feminism and Sexuality 1880–1930* (London: Pandora Press, 1985), especially chs. 7 and 8.

Extract 125

JAMES H. JONES: *The Radical Motives of Kinsey's Sex Research*

1. Author's interview with Paul H. Gebhard, 14 Oct. 1984, 19.
2. Ibid. 6, 18.
3. Ibid. 6.
4. Author's interview with Clyde Martin, 21 Mar. 1986, 21.
5. Alfred C. Kinsey, et al., *Sexual Behavior in the Human Male* (Philadelphia, 1948), 7, 5, 8.
6. Paul Robinson, *The Modernization of Sex: Havelock Ellis, Alfred Kinsey, and William Masters and Virginia Johnson* (New York, 1976), 49–50. Robinson's analysis of what he calls the 'presuppositions, tensions, biases, and implications' of Kinsey's writings can only be described as brilliant. My own discussion draws heavily on his insights and interpretations.
7. Author's interview with Gebhard, 29 Oct. 1971, 44, 78, Indiana University Oral History Project.
8. Ibid. 44.
9. Author's interview with Gebhard, 14 Oct. 1984, 27.
10. Kinsey et al., *Sexual Behavior*, 445, 385.
11. Ibid. 42.
12. Author's interview with Gebhard, 29 Oct. 1971, 79.
13. Kinsey et al., *Sexual Behavior*, 329, 224.

Extract 127

HERBERT MARCUSE: *Eros and Human Emancipation*

1. Sigmund Freud, *Collected Papers* (London: Hogarth Press, 1950), iv. 203ff.; *Group Psychology and the Analysis of the Ego* (Liveright Publishing Corp., 1949), 72, 78.
2. *Collected Papers*, iv. 215.
3. Ernest Jones, *The Life and Work of Sigmund Freud*, vol. 1 (New York: Basic Books, 1953), 330.

Extract 133

JEFFREY WEEKS: *Political Reform in Britain*

1. Quoted in Arno Karlen, *Sexuality and Homosexuality* (London, 1971), 459.
2. Peter Wildeblood, *Against the Law* (Harmondsworth, 1957), 39. Douglas Plummer, *Queer People: The Truth about Homosexuals* (London, 1963), 51ff., describes the discreet 'membership only' gay club.
3. Kenneth Plummer makes this point in *Sexual Stigma* (London, 1975), 226 n. 18.
4. Roger Baker, in *Spartacus*, no. 23, p. 6.
5. Ray Gosling in Trafalgar Square, 23 Nov. 1975.
6. Dennis Altman, 'The Homosexual Movement in America and its Relationship to Other American Movements', *GLP* 5 (Sydney) (Nov.–Dec. 1974), 5.
7. *Fag Rag/Gay Sunshine*, special joint edition (Summer 1974), 3.
8. Carl Wittman, *A Gay Manifesto* (San Francisco, 1970).

Extract 134

ELIZABETH LAPOVSKY KENNEDY AND MADELINE D. DAVIS: *Lesbian Generations*

1. The founding of gay liberation is usually taken as the Stonewall riots, and, as such, glorifies gays' commitment to fight off the police. For a good overview of the roots of gay liberation in the 1960s, see John D'Emilio, *Sexual Politics, Sexual Communities: The Making of a Homosexual Minority in the United States, 1940–1970* (Chicago: University of Chicago Press, 1983), 129–250.
2. It is impossible to know based on this evidence whether 'coming out' was used in Buffalo prior to gay liberation. John D'Emilio indicates that the concept of 'coming out' predates gay liberation, although it had a very different meaning (D'Emilio, *Sexual Politics*, 235). This leads us to suspect that 'coming out' was used in Buffalo in the 1940s and 1950s. That people do not remember it indicates just how radically the meaning of the term has changed. Also, it is likely that 'coming out' was not a central concept to the pregay liberation culture, and therefore was not used frequently, while in contemporary lesbian and gay culture, it is a core concept.

Extract 135

GILBERT HERDT: *'Coming Out' as a Rite of Passage*

1. A. P. Bell, M. S. Weinberg, and S. Hammersmith, *Sexual Preference* (Bloomington: Indiana University Press, 1981).
2. Camille Gerstell, D. Feraios, and Gilbert Herdt, 'Widening Circles: An Ethnographic Profile of a Youth Group', in G. Herdt (ed.), *Adolescence and Homosexuality* (New York: Harrington, 1989), 211–28.
3. I have little data on this cohort from Chicago, but, for an important historical study from the East Coast, see George Chauncey, Jr., 'Christian Brotherhood or Sexual Perversion? Homosexual Identities and the Construction of Sexual Boundaries in the World War One Era', *Journal of Social History*, 19 (1985), 198–211.
4. J. D'Emilio, *Sexual Politics, Sexual Communities* (Chicago: University of Chicago Press, 1983), 31. See also Allan Berube, *Coming Out under Fire* (New York: Free Press, 1990).
5. Monika Kehoe, 'Lesbians over 65: A Triply Invisible Minority', *Journal of Homosexuality*, 14 (1986), 253–76.

6. K. Vacha, *Quiet Fire* (Trumansburg, NY: Crossing, 1985).
7. B. Adam, *The Rise of a Gay and Lesbian Movement* (Boston: Twayne, 1987).
8. R. Shilts, *And the Band Played On* (New York: St Martin's, 1987), 209; D. A. Feldman and T. M. Johnson, introd. to *The Social Dimension of AIDS: Methods and Theory* (New York: Praeger, 1986), 1–12.
9. Shilts, *And the Band Played On*.

Extract 136

MARTIN P. LEVINE: *The Gay Clone*

1. For a discussion of the cultural roles for homosexuality, see the introduction to Martin P. Levine (ed.,), *Gay Men: The Sociology of Male Homosexuality* (New York: Harper & Row, 1979), 1–16.
2. William Simon and John H. Gagnon, 'Homosexuality: The Formulation of a Sociological Perspective', *Journal of Health and Social Behavior*, 8 (1967), 183.
3. 'Butch' refers to manliness.
4. Edmund White, *States of Desire* (New York: Dutton, 1980), 45–6.
5. 'Cruising' refers to the search for sexual partners, and 'tricking' denotes anonymous sex.
6. 'Pot' refers to marijuana, 'poppers' amyl nitrates. Quaaludes are barbiturates.
7. White, *States of Desire*, 278–9.

Extract 138

ROBERT J. STOLLER: *Why Men Like Porn*

1. Bill has insisted that no facts here be disguised (though he and I have deleted some details less pertinent to our work). First, he wants the world to know who is he and what he has accomplished, and second, he says that everyone mentioned in these transcripts has already been described in his published writings.

Extract 139

GAYLE RUBIN: *Feminist Puritanism*

1. See for example Laura Lederer (ed.), *Take Back the Night* (New York: William Morrow, 1980); Andrea Dworkin, *Pornography* (New York: Perigee, 1981).
2. Kathleen Barry, *Female Sexual Slavery* (Englewood Cliffs, NJ: Prentice-Hall, 1979); Janice Raymond, *The Transsexual Empire* (Boston: Beacon, 1979); Barry, 'Sadomasochism: The New Backlash to Feminism', *Trivia*, 1 (Fall 1982); Florence Rush, *The Best Kept Secret* (New York: McGraw-Hill, 1980).
3. Sally Gearheart, 'An Open Letter to the Voters in District 5 and San Francisco's Gay Community' (1979), Adrienne Rich, *On Lies, Secrets, and Silence* (New York: W. W. Norton, 1979), 225. ('On the other hand, there is homosexual patriarchal culture, a culture created by homosexual men, reflecting such male stereotypes as dominance and submission as modes of relationship, and the separation of sex from emotional involvement—a culture tainted by profound hatred for women. The male "gay" culture has offered lesbians the imitation role-stereotypes of "butch" and "femme," "active" and "passive," crusing, sado-masochism, and the violent, self-destructive world of "gay" bars').

4. Julia Penlope, 'And Now For the Really Hard Questions', *Sinister Wisdom*, 15 (Fall 1980), 103.
5. Sheila Jeffreys, 'The Spinster and Her Enemies: Sexuality and the Last Wave of Feminism', *Scarlet Woman*, 13/2 (July 1981), 26; a further elaboration of this tendency can be found in Judith Pasternak, 'The Strangest Bedfellows: Lesbian Feminists and the Sexual Revolution', *WomanNews* (Oct. 1983).
6. Lisa Orlando, 'Lust at Last! Spandex Invades the Academy', *Gay Community News* (15 May 1982); Ellen Willis, 'Who Is a Feminist? An Open Letter to Robin Morgan', *Village Voice*, literary supplement (Dec. 1982).

Extract 143

DOUGLAS CRIMP: *Shilts's Miserable Failure*

1. See Tim Kingston, 'Controversy Follows Shilts and "Zero" to London', *Coming Up* (Apr. 1988), 11.
2. Duncan Campbell, 'An End to the Silence', *New Statesman* (4 Mar. 1988), 22–3.
3. Quoted in Kingston, 'Controversy', 11.
4. 'Mr. DiLello noted that Randy Shilts, in his acclaimed book about AIDS, "And the Band Played On," wrote about Gaetan Dugas, the man who may have brought AIDS to San Francisco and who continued to have a multitude of sexual partners even after learning that he was ill.' Stephen Farber, 'AIDS Groups Protest Series Episode', *New York Times*, C24 (8 Dec. 1988).
5. Oct. 1987 issue.
6. Randy Shilts, 'Talking AIDS to Death', *Esquire* (Mar. 1989), 124.

Extract 145

SIMON WATNEY: *Media Fabrications*

1. Kaye Wellings, 'Sickness and Sin: The Case of Genital Herpes', paper presented to BSA Medical Sociology Group (1983), 10.
2. Ibid. 26.
3. Robert Glück, *Jack the Modernist* (Gay Presses of New York), 54.

Extract 147

EDWARD O. LAUMANN, JOHN H. GAGNON, et al.: *Homosexuality in America*

1. This question posed several problems. First, about five percent of the men and six percent of the women seemed to be uncertain about the meaning of these terms and gave answers that were coded by interviewers as equivalent to 'normal or straight.' In addition, under one percent of the respondents (thirteen men and ten women in the cross section) answered 'something else' and were prompted to explain. A few of these (two men and four women) said 'gay' or 'lesbian' and have been included with those who chose 'homosexual'. Two respondents said they did not distinguish partners on the basis of their sex (gender). They appeared to be defining themselves as bisexual, but we were hesitant to recode them as such until we checked their sexual experience. Since they had both male and female partners, we included them with the bisexuals.

2. It would be interesting to compare and contrast homosexual (and gay/lesbian) identity with bisexual identity, but the numbers in a sample like ours are just too small. Fewer than one percent of the men and women said that they were bisexual.

3. The base *N*'s for these rates include all the people on whom we have information. In particular, they include the sexually inactive, who have no partners in a given time frame. In that sense, these are incidence and prevalence rates for partnering behavior.

4. The exact wording of the question is, 'Now I would like to ask you about sexual experience with (SAME SEX AS R; males/females) after you were 12 or 13, that is, after puberty. How old were you the first time you had sex with a (SAME SEX AS R; male/female)?'.

Extract 149

LIZ STANLEY: *The Cultural Bias of Sex Surveys*

1. A. Johnson, J. Wadsworth, K. Wellings, and J. Fields, *Sexual Attitudes and Lifestyles* (Oxford, Blackwell Scientific, 1993) and K. Wellings, J. Fields, A. Johnson, and J. Wadsworth, *Sexual Behavior in Britain* (Harmondsworth: Penguin, 1993), both continually slide from 'homosexuality' to 'gay men', with the authors apparently not even noticing that they do this.

2. In L. Stanley, *Sex Surveyed, 1949 to 1994: From Mass-Observation's 'Little Kinsey' to the National Survey and the Hite Reports* (London: Taylor & Francis, 1995), I discuss this concern with change and how, methodologically and substantively, these surveys deal with it. I also compare 'Little Kinsey' with the work of Shere Hite with regard to explaining social change.

Extract 150

MICHAEL MOFFATT: *Sex and the Single College Student*

1. The audiences for these movies at Rutgers tended to be about two-thirds men and one-third women. A few couples attended, but more often women and men came to these films in little single-sex gangs.

2. Stephen Heath, *The Sexual Fix* (New York: Schocken, 1982). Heath's argument draws on, or is consistent with, much of the new social history of western sexuality written in the past twenty years. Notable works include Carroll Smith-Rosenberg, 'The Female World of Love and Ritual', *Signs: Journal of Women in Culture and Society*, 1/1: 1–30; Lawrence Stone, *The Family, Sex and Marriage in England, 1500–1800* (New York: Harper & Row, 1977); Michel Foucault, *A History of Sexuality*, i: *An Introduction* (New York: Vintage, 1980); Jeffrey Weeks, *Coming Out: Homosexual Politics in Britain* (New York, Quartet Books, 1977); and Judith R. Walkowitz, 'Science, Feminism and Romance: The Men and Women's Club 1885–1889', *History Workshop*, 21 (Spring 1986).

3. It might be argued that my assignment encouraged the students to write according to the assumptions of the new sexual orthodoxy. In lectures in the course in which this assignment was given, I did try to show that sexuality was often constituted quite differently in other cultures, however: that sex was rarely, as in contemporary American culture, a thing in itself; that it was much more often an integral part of

wider human or cosmological meanings. Even if my assignment was culturally biased, however, what was striking in the papers was the ease and gusto with which
students wrote within the orthodoxy. On the evidence of these papers, I was certainly not asking them to do something that came hard to them or that did not
make a great deal of cultural sense, even if it was an unusual classroom assignment.

4. On a sex questionnaire that 151 students made out in this class in the following year,
the reported virginity rate was slightly lower, and it was somewhat more differentiated by sex. Again, about 1 in 5 females said they were virgins, 18 in all, 2 of them
intentionally. Only 1 in 8 males owned up the same unhappy state, on the other
hand, none of them by intention.

5. Two of the forty-four male writers of these papers sounded worse than depressed:
they sounded sexually disturbed. One wrote a series of sexual fantasies, which all
turned scatalogical at the end. The other said he had mentally transformed all his
classes into private erotic fantasies since the grade school, often with female teachers in dominant roles. At Rutgers, he said, he once exposed himself in front of a faculty member in her office. And he reported that he sometimes followed his
younger female teachers around the campus, fantasizing about them.

6. The rising acceptability of oral sex, like that of premarital sex, was probably also
part of a recent nationwide trend. M. Hildebrand and S. Abramowitz, 'Sexuality of
Campus: Changes in Attitudes and Behavior in the 1970s', *Journal of College Student
Personnel*, 25 (1984), 534–46, say that in 1971, 77 percent of all the sexually active
students in their sample reported practicing oral sex; in 1977, 85 percent; and in
1981, 88 percent. S. F. Newcomer and J. R. Udry, 'Oral Sex in an American Adolescent Population', *Archives of Sexual Behavior*, 14/1 (1985), 41–6, also report the generally high acceptability of oral sex among contemporary adolescents as a way
around some of the dilemmas of 'real' sex.

7. Three said they had been manually or genitally abused as children or as young adolescents by older males—two by relatives (an uncle and an older brother). Three
said they had suffered acquaintance rape, two at Rutgers. One reported being
forced to fellate a date in high school. And two indicated tolerating long-term physical abuse from boyfriends. No male mentioned sexual abuse in the 1986 papers.
The reported abuse rate was somewhat higher on the sex questionnaire returned
in the same course in 1987. Sixteen percent of the women reported abuse of one
kind or another, and 4 percent of the men (two cases: one by an incestuous mother
who handled the subject much too familiarly after puberty, the other by a homosexual neighbor when the subject was eight to ten years old).

Select Bibliography

SECTION I. BEFORE 'SEXUALITY'

BARKER-BENFIELD, G. J., *The Culture of Sensibility: Sex and Society in Eighteenth-Century Britain* (Chicago: University of Chicago Press, 1992).

BLEYS, RUDI C., *The Geography of Perversion: Male to Male Sexual Behavior outside the West and the Ethnographic Imagination, 1750–1918* (New York: New York University Press, 1995).

BOSWELL, JOHN, *Christianity, Social Tolerance and Homosexuality: Gay People in Western Europe from the Beginning of the Christian Era to the Fourteenth Century* (Chicago: University of Chicago Press, 1980).

BROWN, PETER, *The Body and Society: Men, Women, and Sexual Renunciation in Early Christianity* (New York: Columbia University Press, 1988).

CADDEN, JOAN, *Meanings of Sex Difference in the Middle Ages* (Cambridge: Cambridge University Press, 1993).

D'EMILIO, JOHN, and FREEDMAN, ESTELLE B., *Intimate Matters: A History of Sexuality in America* (New York: Harper & Row, 1988).

DOVER, K. J., *Greek Homosexuality* (Oxford: Oxford University Press, 1978).

EDER, FRANZ; HALL, LESLEY, and HEKMA, GERD (eds.), *Sexual Cultures in Europe*, 2 vols. (Manchester: Manchester University Press, 1998).

HALPERIN, DAVID M., *One Hundred Years of Homosexuality and Other Essays on Greek Love* (New York: Routledge, 1990).

HUNT, LYNN, *The Family Romance of the French Revolution* (Berkeley and Los Angles: University of California Press, 1992).

——*The Invention of Pornography: Obscenity and the Origins of Modernity* (Cambridge, Mass.: MIT Press, 1993).

KEULS, EVA C. *The Reign of the Phallus: Sexual Politics in Ancient Athens* (Berkeley and Los Angeles: University of California Press, 1985).

LAQUEUR, THOMAS, *Making Sex: Body and Gender from the Greeks to Freud* (Cambridge, Mass.: Harvard University Press, 1990).

MASON, MICHAEL, *The Making of Victorian Sexuality, The Making of Victorian Sexual Attitudes* (Oxford: Oxford University Press, 1994).

RUGGIERO, GUIDO, *The Boundaries of Eros: Sex Crime and Sexuality in Renaissance Venice* (New York: Oxford University Press, 1985).

RUSSETT, CYNTHIA EAGLE, *Sexual Science and the Victorian Construction of Womanhood* (Cambridge, Mass.: Harvard University Press, 1989).

SINFIELD, ALAN, *The Wilde Century* (London: Cassell, 1994).

SECTION II. THE DISCOVERY OF 'SEXUALITY' AT THE TURN OF THE CENTURY

BAYER, RONALD, *Homosexuality and American Psychiatry* (Princeton: Princeton University Press, 1987).

BULLOUGH, VERN L., *Science in the Bedroom: The History of Sex Research* (New York: Basic Books, 1994).

CHAUNCEY, GEORGE, *Gay New York: Gender, Urban Culture, and the Making of the Gay Male World* (New York: Basic Books, 1994).

GAY, PETER, *Freud: A Life for our Time* (New York: Norton, 1988).

GROSSKURTH, PHYLLIS, *Havelock Ellis: A Biography* (London: Allen Lane, 1980).

IRVINE, JANICE M., *Disorders of Desire: Sex and Gender in Modern American Sexology* (Philadelphia: Temple University Press, 1990).

KENNEDY, HUBERT, *The Life and Works of Karl Heinrich Ulrichs, Pioneer of the Modern Gay Movement* (Boston: Alyson, 1988).

MICALE, MARK, *Approaching Hysteria: Disease and its Interpretations* (Princeton: Princeton University Press, 1995).

NOYES, JOHN K., *The Mastery of Submission: Inventions of Masochism* (Ithaca, NY: Cornell University Press, 1997).

PORTER, ROY, and HALL, LESLEY, *The Facts of Life: The Creation of Sexual Knowledge in Britain, 1650–1950* (New Haven: Yale University Press, 1995).

——and TEICH, MIKULAS, *Sexual Knowledge, Sexual Science: The History of Attitudes to Sexuality* (Cambridge: Cambridge University Press, 1994).

STEELE, VALERIE, *Fetish: Fashion, Sex, and Power* (New York: Oxford University Press, 1996).

YOUNG-BRUEHL, ELIZABETH, *Freud on Women, A Reader* (New York: Norton, 1990).

SECTION III. THE TWENTIETH-CENTURY SEXUAL BODY

BOURKE, JOANNA, *Dismembering the Male: Men's Bodies, Britain and the Great War* (Chicago: University of Chicago Press, 1996).

CALIFA, PAT, *Sexual Changes: The Politics of Transgenderism* (San Francisco: Cleis Press, 1997).

CONNELL, R. W., *Masculinities* (Oxford: Polity Press, 1995).

EPSTEIN, JULIA, *Altered Conditions: Disease, Medicine, and Storytelling* (New York: Routledge, 1995).

——and STRAUB, CHRISTINA (eds.), *Body Guards: The Cultural Politics of Gender Ambiguity* (New York: Routledge, 1991).

FAUSTO-STERLING, ANNE, *Myths of Gender: Biological Theories of Women and Men* (New York: Basic Books, 1985).

Grosz, Elizabeth, *Volatile Bodies: Toward a Corporeal Feminism* (Bloomington: Indiana University Press, 1994).

HAUSMAN, BERNICE L., *Changing Sex: Transsexualism, Technology, and the Idea of Gender* (Durham, NC: Duke University Press, 1995).

KIMMEL, MICHAEL, *Manhood in Amerca: A Cultural History* (New York: Free Press, 1996).

MARGULIS, LYNN, and SAGAN, DORIAN, *Mystery Dance: On the Evolution of Human Sexuality* (New York: Summit, 1991).

MARTIN, EMILY, *The Woman in the Body: A Cultural Analysis of Reproduction* (Boston: Beacon Press, 1992).

MONEY, JOHN, *Love and Love Sickness: The Science of Sex, Gender Difference, and Pair-Bonding* (Baltimore: Johns Hopkins University Press, 1980).

MOSSE, GEORGE L., *The Image of Man: The Creation of Modern Masculinity* (New York: Oxford University Press, 1996).

OUDSHOORN, NELLY, *Beyond the Natural Body: An Archeology of Sex Hormones* (New York: Routledge, 1994).

VAN DEN WIJNGAARD, MARIANNE, *Reinventing the Sexes: The Biomedical Construction of Femininity and Masculinity* (Bloomington: Indiana University Press, 1997).

SECTION IV. SEXUAL REVOLUTION?

BUTLER, JUDITH, *Gender Trouble: Feminism and the Subversion of Identity* (London: Routledge, 1990).

ELLIOTT, LELAND, and BRANTLEY, CYNTHIA, *Sex on Campus* (New York: Random House, 1997).

EPSTEIN, STEVEN, *Impure Science: AIDS, Activism, and the Politics of Knowledge* (Berkeley, Calif.: University of California Press, 1996).

JONES, JAMES H., *Alfred C. Kinsey, A Public/Private Life* (New York: W. W. Norton, 1997).

LAURETIS, TERESA DE, *The Practice of Love: Lesbian Sexuality and Perverse Desire* (Bloomington: Indiana University Press, 1994).

LEVAY, SIMON, and NONAS, ELISABETH, *City of Friends: A Portrait of the Gay and Lesbian Community in America* (Cambridge, Mass.: MIT Press, 1995).

MERRICK, JEFFREY and RAGAN, BRYANT, T., *Homosexuality in Modern France* (New York: Oxford University Press, 1996).

MICHAEL, ROBERT T., GAGNON, JOHN H., LAUMANN, EDWARD O., and KOLATA, GINA, *Sex in America: A Definitive Survey* (New York: Little, Brown, 1994).

MURRAY, STEPHEN O., *American Gay* (Chicago: University of Chicago Press, 1996).

NEWBURN, TIM, *Permission and Regulation: Law and Morals in Post-War Britain* (London: Routledge, 1992).

PATTON, CINDY, *Fatal Advice: How Safe-Sex Education Went Wrong* (Durham, NC: Duke University Press, 1996).

SEGAL, LYNNE, *Straight Sex: Rethinking the Politics of Pleasure* (Berkeley and Los Angeles: University of California Press, 1994).

STANLEY, LIZ, *Sex Surveyed, 1949–1994: From Mass-Observation's 'Little Kinsey' to the National Survey and the Hite Report* (London: Taylor & Francis, 1995).

STEIN, ARLENE, *Lesbianism, Feminism, and Generational Change* (Berkeley and Los Angeles: University of California Press, 1997).

WEEKS, JEFFREY, *Sexuality* (London: Routledge, 1986).

Biographical Notes

R. Robin Baker, a scientist who teaches at the University of Liverpool, has written on evolution and animal migration. His books include *Sperm Wars: The Science of Sex* (1996).

John W. Baldwin is Professor of History at the Johns Hopkins University. He is the author of *Masters, Princes and Merchants: The Social Views of Peter the Chanter* (1970) and *The Government of Philip Augustus: Foundations of French Royal Power in the Middle Ages* (1986).

Georges Bataille (1897–1962) was a French philosopher and man of letters who wrote widely on sexual experience.

Lawrence Birken is Assistant Professor of History at Ball State University. He is the author of *Understanding Western Civilization: A Chaos Approach* (1996).

Anne Bolin is the author of *In Search of Eve: Transsexual Rites of Passage* (1988).

Alan Bray is an independent scholar living in London. He is the author of *Homosexuality in Renaissance England* (1995).

Peter Brown is Professor of History at Princeton University. He is the author of *Authority and the Sacred: Aspects of Christianisation of the Roman World* (1997).

Charles-Édouard Brown-Séquard (1817–1894) was a French physiologist and doctor who did pioneering work on hormones and illnesses of the nervous system. He taught at the Collège de France.

Joan Jacobs Brumberg is Professor of History at Cornell University. One of her recent works is *The Body Project: An Intimate History of American Girls* (1997).

Vern L. Bullough teaches at California State University, Northridge, and the University of Southern California. He is the recipient of the Distinguished Achievement Award from the Society for the Scientific Study of Sex. His books include *Sexual Variance in Society and History* (1976) and *Science in the Bedroom: A History of Sex Research* (1994).

William Byne is the director of the Laboratory of Neuroanatomy in the Department of Psychiatry at the Mount Sinai School of Medicine, New York City, and a practising psychiatrist.

Joan Cadden is Professor of History at the University of California, Davis. She is the author of *Meaning of Sex Difference in the Middle Ages: Medicine, Science and Culture* (1993).

Robert Brudnell Carter (1828–1918) was a British surgeon. He founded the Nottingham Eye Infirmary and the Gloucestershire Eye Institute.

George Chauncey is Professor of History at the University of Chicago. He is the co-editor of *Hidden from History: Reclaiming the Gay and Lesbian Past* (1990).

Ellen Chesler wrote *Woman of Valor: Margaret Sanger and the Birth Control Movement in America* (1992). She is also the Chair of the International Women's Health Coalition.

DAVID COHEN is Professor of Rhetoric at the University of California, Berkeley. He is the author of *Theft in Athenian Law* (1983) and *Law, Violence and Community in Classical Athens* (1995).

PETER COPELAND is a reporter who has covered the Pentagon and foreign affairs for Scripps news service since 1989. He is the co-author (with Dean Hamer) of *Living with our Genes: Why They Matter More Than You Think* (1988).

ALAIN CORBIN teaches at the University of Paris. He is the author of *Les Filles de noce: Misère sexuelle et prostitution, 19e et 20e siècles* (1978) and many other works on cultural history.

DOUGLAS CRIMP is a Professor of Visual and Cultural Studies at the University of Rochester. He is the author of *AIDS: Cultural Analysis/Cultural Activism* (1997), a collection of essays.

PIERRE DARMON is Chargé de recherche at the Centre national de la recherche scientifique. He is the author of *The Myth of Procreation in the Baroque Period* (1981).

CHARLES DARWIN (1809–82) was a British scientist whose research laid the foundations for and popularized the modern theory of evolution. His ideas on natural selection were formulated in his *On the Origin of Species* (1859).

LORRAINE DASTON is Director of the Max Planck Institute for the History of Science in Berlin. She is the author of *Classical Probability in the Enlightenment* (1988).

ARNOLD I. DAVIDSON teaches in the Department of Philosophy at the University of Chicago. He is the editor of *Foucault and his Interlocutors* (1997) and serves as editor for *Critical Inquiry*.

MADELINE D. DAVIS is Chief Conservator and Head of Preservation for the Buffalo and Erie County Public Library System.

JOHN D'EMILIO teaches at the University of North Carolina, Greensboro. He is the author of *Making Trouble: Essays on Gay History, Politics, and the University* (1992).

DWIGHT DIXON and JOAN DIXON are a husband and wife team of sex therapists based in San Diego, California.

JACQUES DONZELOT is Professor of Political Science at the University of Paris-X Nanterre. He is the author of several books on sociology and founded the Prison Information Group with Michel Foucault.

ALICE D. DREGER is Assistant Professor in Science and Technology Studies at Michigan State University.

GEORGE FREDERICK DRINKA is the author of *The Birth of Neurosis: Myth, Malady, and the Victorians* (1984).

NORBERT ELIAS (1897–1990) was a German sociologist who emigrated to Britain and taught at the University of Leicester. His three-volume *The Civilizing Process: The History of Manners and State Formation and Civilization* (1978) was a study of the control of sexual impulses, based on Freud.

HAVELOCK ELLIS (1859–1939) was a founder of modern sex advice literature. His thinking was based on assumptions about the innate biological differences in men's and women's sex drives.

ERIK H. ERIKSON (1902–94) was an American psychoanalyst who studied the link between parental guidance and later personality growth. He was the author of *Childhood and Society* (1950) and many other works.

JOHN FARLEY is Professor in the Department of Biology at Dalhousie University. He is the author of *Bilharzia: A History of Imperial Tropical Medicine* (1991).

JAMES R. FARR is Professor of History at Purdue University; he is the author of *Hands of Honor: Artisans and their World in Dijon, 1550–1650* (1988).

ANNE FAUSTO-STERLING is Professor of Molecular Biology, Cell Biology, and Biochemistry at Brown University. She is the author of *The Myths of Gender: Biological Theories about Women and Men* (1992).

MICHEL FOUCAULT (1926–84) was a French philosopher who wrote on prisons, welfare, gay rights, and mental illness, among other topics. His books include *Discipline and Punish* (1977) and *Madness and Civilization* (1965). He died before completing his acclaimed series on the history of sexuality.

ESTELLE B. FREEDMAN teaches at Stanford University. She is the author of *Maternal Justice: Miriam von Waters and the Female Reform Tradition* (1996).

SIGMUND FREUD (1856–1939), an Austrian neuropathologist and physician, was the founder of modern psychoanalysis. His early studies of hysteria in his female patients helped formulate his theories of the subconscious mind; his writings include *On Dreams* (trans. 1951) and *Civilization and its Discontents* (trans. 1930) among many others.

JONAS FRYKMAN teaches in the Department of European Ethnology at the University of Lund, Sweden.

JOHN H. GAGNON is Professor in the Department of Sociology at the State University in New York, Stony Brook. He is the co-editor of *Conceiving Sexuality: Approaches to Sex Research in a Postmodern World* (1995).

PETER GAY is Historian Emeritus at Yale University. The author of numerous books on the Enlightenment, he is perhaps best known for his four-volume *The Bourgeois Experience* (1984–95).

PATRICK GEDDES (1854–1932) was a Scottish ecologist and natural philosopher. He taught zoology and botany at the University of Edinburgh and was Chair of Botany at the University of Dundee.

MARGARET GIBSON is an independent scholar in the history of medicine.

JOHN R. GILLIS is Professor of History at Rutgers University and an author, most recently of *A World of their Own Making: Myth, Ritual, and the Quest for Family Values* (1996).

SANDER L. GILMAN is Professor of Liberal Arts in Human Biology and Chair of the Department of Germanic Studies at the University of Chicago. He is the author of numerous books, including *Sexuality: An Illustrated History: Representing the Sexual in Medicine and Culture from the Middle Ages to the Age of AIDS* (1989) and *Freud, Race and Gender* (1993).

MICHAEL R. GORMAN is a social anthropologist and an epidemiologist, and is lecturer at the School of Public Health, University of California, Berkeley. He is the author of *The Empress is a Man: Stories from the Life and Times of Jose Sarria* (1998).

LINDA GRANT is a freelance journalist who has contributed to the *Guardian* and *Independent on Sunday.*

GERMAINE GREER is an Australian-born writer, literary scholar, journalist, and lecturer. She is special lecturer and unofficial fellow of Newnham College, Cambridge. One of her recent works is *The Change* (1991), a discussion of women, ageing, and menopause.

ATINA GROSSMANN is Associate Professor of History at Columbia University. She is co-editor of *When Biology Became Destiny: Women in Weimar and Nazi Germany* (1984).

STEPHEN HALICZER teaches at Northern Illinois University. He is the author of *Inquisition and Society in the Kingdom of Valencia, 1478–1834* (1990).

G(RANVILLE) STANLEY HALL (1844–1924) was an American psychologist and educationist. He founded the *American Journal of Psychology* (1887), influenced the development of child psychology in the USA, and became the first president of Clark University (1889–1920), where he also taught.

LESLEY A. HALL is senior assistant archivist in the Contemporary Medical Archives Centre, Wellcome Institute for the History of Medicine, London. She is the author of *Hidden Anxieties: Male Sexuality 1900–1950* (1991).

DAVID M. HALPERIN teaches at the University of New South Wales. Among his many writings on various scholarly subjects are *Before Pastoral: Theocritus and the Ancient Tradition of Bucolic Poetry* (1983) and *Saint Foucault: Towards a Theory of Gay Historiography* (1995).

DEAN HAMER is Chief of the Section on Gene Structure and Regulation in the Department of Biochemistry at the National Cancer Institute at Bethesda, Maryland.

DAVID HAMILTON is the author of *The Monkey Gland Affair* (1986).

BERNICE L.HAUSMAN teaches in the Department of English at the Virginia Polytechnic Institute and State University, Blacksburg. She is the author of *Changing Sex: Transsexualism, Technology, and the Idea of Gender* (1995).

JOHN HEIDENRY was executive editor of *Forum* magazine from 1982 to 1989. He is co-editor with Edward Springer of *The Penthouse Letters: The Sexual State of the Nation* (1994).

GILBERT HERDT is Professor of Human Development and Psychology at the University of Chicago. His writings include *The Sambia: Ritual and Gender in New Guinea* (1987) and as editor, *Gay and Lesbian Youth* (1989).

DAVID G. HORN is Assistant Professor of Comparative Studies at Ohio State University. He is the author of *Social Bodies, Reproduction and Italian Modernity* (1994).

ISABEL V. HULL is Professor of History and Chair of the History Department at Cornell University. She is the author of *The Entourage of Kaiser Wilhelm, 1888–1918* (1982).

LYNN HUNT teaches at the University of Pennsylvania. She is the editor of *Eroticism and the Body Politic* (1991).

NANCY HUNT is a transsexual and the author of *Mirror Image* (1978).

MARGARET JACKSON has taught social science and women's studies, most recently at Goldsmith's College, University of London. She is the author of *The Real Facts of Life: Feminism and the Politics of Sexuality, c1850–1940* (1994).

SHEILA JEFFREYS teaches political science at the University of Melbourne. She is the author of *The Idea of Prostitution* (1998) and *The Spinster and her Enemies* (1985).

ANNE JOHNSON is Senior Lecturer on Epidemiology at the University College Medical School, London.

VIRGINIA E. JOHNSON is an American journalist, researcher, and sexologist. In 1957 she joined Dr William Masters's research group at Washington University School of Medicine and by 1959 she and Masters were founding the Masters and Johnson Institute to investigate the physiology of sexual intercourse. Later she and Masters published (with Robert Kolodny) *On Sex and Human Loving* (1986).

JAMES H. JONES is Professor of History at the University of Houston. He is the author of *Bad Blood: The Tuskeegee Syphilis Experiment* (1992).

LUDMILLA JORDANOVA is the editor of *The Enlightenment and its Shadows* (1990). She teaches at the University of East Anglia.

CHRISTINE JORGENSEN is a transsexual and the author of *A Personal Autobiography* (1967).

RUTH MAZO KARRAS teaches medieval and intellectual history at Temple University. She is the author of *Slavery and Society in Medieval Scandinavia* (1996) and is a member of the Advisory Board of the Museum of Gay and Lesbian History.

JONATHAN NED KATZ is the author of the documentaries *Gay American History: Lesbians and Gay Men in the U.S.A.* (1992) and *Gay/Lesbian Almanac* (1994). He is the author of numerous articles and reviews.

ELIZABETH LAPOVSKY KENNEDY is Associate Professor of American Studies and Women's Studies at SUNY, Buffalo, and co-founder of the Women's Oral History Project. She is the co-author of *Feminist Scholarship: Kindling the Groves of Academe* (1987).

STEPHEN KERN teaches at Northern Illinois University. He is the author of *Eyes of Love: The Gaze in English and French Culture, 1840–1900* (1996).

HELEN KING is Senior Lecturer in History at Liverpool Institute of Higher Education. She is a contributor to *Hysteria beyond Freud* (1993).

ALFRED C. KINSEY (1894–1956) was an American entomologist and sex researcher. In 1942 he founded the Institute for Sex Research and interviewed thousands of subjects about their sexual conduct. The results were published in two best-sellers, *Sexual Behavior in the Human Male* (1948) and *Sexual Behavior in the Human Female* (1953), books which attempted to classify sexual variation in value-neutral, biological terms.

RICHARD VON KRAFFT-EBING (1840–1902) was an Austrian psychiatrist who studied every aspect of mental psychology. At the end of his career he was Professor of Psychiatry at the University of Vienna. He is best known for his work *Psychopathia sexualis* (1886).

MADAME DE LAFAYETTE (1634–93) was a French aristocrat. Her greatest literary work was *La Princesse de Clèves* (1678).

EDWARD O. LAUMANN is Distinguished Service Professor of Sociology at the University of Chicago. He is the co-author of *Sex in America: A Definitive Survey* (1994).

GWENDOLYN LEICK is the author of *A Dictionary of Near Eastern Architecture* (1988) and *A Dictionary of Ancient Near Eastern Mythology* (1996).

SIMON LEVAY, formerly Associate Professor at the Salk Institute, is co-founder of the Institute of Gay and Lesbian Education, West Hollywood. He is the author of *The Sexual Brain* (1993).

MARTIN P. LEVINE is Associate Professor of Sociology at Florida Atlantic University and a research associate at Memorial Sloan Kettering Cancer Center. He is the editor of *Gay Men: The Sociology of Male Homosexuality* (1979).

ORVAR LÖFGREN teaches in the Department of European Ethnology at the University of Lund, Sweden.

CHRISTOPHER LOOBY is Associate Professor of English at the University of Chicago. He is the author of *Voicing America* (1996).

FRANK LYDSTON (1858–1923) was an American physician. He served as Professor of Surgery at the Chicago College of Physicians and Surgeons.

ANNE MCCLINTOCK is the editor of *Social Text 37: Special Section on the Sex Trade* (1993).

ANGUS MCLAREN is Professor of History at the University of Victoria. He is the author of *A Prescription for Murder: The Victorian Serial Killings of Dr Thomas Neill Cream* (1995).

HERBERT MARCUSE (1898–1979) was a German philosopher who taught at Columbia and Harvard Universities. He was author of *Reason and Revolution* (1941).

LYNN MARGULIS is an American biologist who teaches at the University of Massachusetts. She is the author of numerous books and articles on natural science.

MICHAEL MASON is Senior Lecturer in English at University College in London. He is author of *The Making of Victorian Sexual Attitudes* and *The Making of Victorian Sexuality* (1994).

WILLIAM H. MASTERS is an American biologist and sexual therapist. With the psychologist Virginia Johnson, he investigated the physiological responses to sexual stimulation in male and female subjects; their report, *Human Sexual Response* (1966), created a huge controversy. Later works such as *Human Sexual Inadequacy* (1970) and *Homosexuality in Perspective* (1979) proved almost as controversial. In 1964 he founded the Reproductive Biology Research Foundation, renamed the Masters and Johnson Institute.

JANN MATLOCK is the author of *Scenes of Seduction: Prostitution, Hysteria, and Reading Difference in Nineteenth-Century France* (1994). She taught most recently in the Department of Romance Languages, Harvard University.

JOHN MAYNARD is Professor of English at New York University. He is the author of *Charlotte Bronte and Sexuality* (1984).

THEO VAN DER MEER, a fellow of the Foundation for Historical Reseach of the Netherlands Organization of Scientific Research, is the author of *De Wesentlijke Sonde von Sodomie en Andere Vuyligheeden* (1984).

MARK S. MICALE teaches at Manchester University. He is the editor of *Beyond the Unconscious: Essays of Henri F. Ellenberger* (1993) and is the author of several articles on the history of psychology.

MICHAEL MOFFATT teaches in the Department of Anthropology at Rutgers University. He is the author of *An Untouchable Community in South India: Structure and Consensus* (1979).

ALBERT MOLL (1862–1939) was a German physician and a promoter of sexology and hypnotism. In 1913 he founded the International Society for Sex Research. He wrote a number of important books on the subject, including *Investigations Concerning the Libido Sexualis* (1897).

JOHN MONEY is Professor of Psychoendocrinology at Johns Hopkins University and the author of several books on sexual orientation, including *Love and Lovesickness* (1980).

DOMINIC MONTSERRAT is a lecturer in classics and ancient history at the University of Warwick and editor of *Changing Bodies, Changing Meanings: Studies on the Human Body in Antiquity* (1998).

FRANK MORT is reader in Cultural History at the University of Portsmouth. He is the author of *Dangerous Consumption: Masculinities and Social Space in Late Twentieth-Century Britain* (1996).

LYNDA NEAD lectures on the history of art at Birkbeck College, University of London. She is the author of *Myths of Sexuality* (1988).

RICHARD NEVILLE is a columnist and broadcaster, and the author of *Out of my Mind* (1996), a collection of his writings.

DAVID F. NOBLE is Professor of History at York University in Toronto. He is the author of *Forces of Production: A Social History of Industrial Automation* (1986).

ROBERT A. NYE is the Horning Professor of the Humanities and Professor of History at Oregon State University. He is the author of *Crime, Madness and Politics in Modern France: The Medical Concept of National Decline* (1984).

NELLY OUDSHOORN is Assistant Professor in the Department of Science and Technology Dynamics at the University of Amsterdam.

CHRISTABEL PANKHURST (1880–1958) was a member of the North of England Society for Women's Suffrage. She co-founded, with her mother, the women's branch of the Independent Labour Party, and wrote for the *Suffragette*. She campaigned for women's suffrage and was arrested several times.

KATHARINE PARK teaches the history of science at Harvard University. She is the co-author, with Lorraine Daston, of *Wonders and the Order of Nature, 1150–1750* (1998).

CAROLE PATEMAN teaches political theory at the University of Sydney. She is the author of *The Disorder of Women: Democracy, Feminism and Political Theory* (1990).

PIERRE J. PAYER teaches philosophy at Mount St Vincent University of Halifax, Nova

Scotia. He is the translator of *Book of Gomorrah: An Eleventh-Century Treatise against Clerical Homosexual Practice* (1982), and wrote *Sex and the Penitentials: the Development of a Sexual Code* (1984).

DANIEL PICK teaches intellectual and cultural history at Queen Mary and Westfield College, the University of London. He is the author of *War Machine: The Rationalisation of Slaughter in the Modern Age* (1993).

PLATO (428?–347? BC), a Greek philosopher, was one of the most influential thinkers in Western history. He wrote on ethics, politics, and art among other subjects. *The Republic* describes the ideal national state, while his *Symposium* deals with beauty and love.

UTA RANKE-HEINEMANN teaches history at the Universität Gesamthochschule in Essen. She is author of *Putting Away Childish Things: the Virgin Birth, the Empty Tomb, and other Fairy Tales you Don't Need to Believe to have a Living Faith* (1994).

MATT RIDLEY is a journalist and science editor and Washington correspondent for *The Economist*. He is author of *Origins of Virtue* (1996).

MARY LOUISE ROBERTS is Associate Professor of History at Stanford University. She is the author of *Civilization without Sexes: Reconstructing Gender in Postwar France, 1917–1927* (1994).

PAUL ROBINSON is Professor of History at Stanford University. He has written widely on the history of psychoanalysis, music, and culture. He is the author of *Freud and his Critics* (1993).

LYNDAL ROPER is reader in History at Royal Holloway College, University of London. She is the author of *Oedipus and the Devil and Other Essays in Early Modern Culture* (1994).

VERNON A. ROSARIO II MD, Ph.D. is the editor of *Solitary Pleasures: The Historical, Literary, and Artistic Discourses of Autoeroticism* (1995).

GABRIEL ROTELLO is a journalist and the founding editor of *Outlook* magazine. He is the author of *Sexual Ecology: AIDS and the Destiny of Gay Men* (1997).

JEAN-JACQUES ROUSSEAU (1712–78) was a Swiss-born French philosopher, one of the most influential of the Age of Enlightenment, who wrote on social injustice and inequality. His *Social Contract* (1762) defended the popular will against monarchical ideas while his novel *Julie, or the New Eloise* (1760) explored emotional and sensual expression.

ALINE ROUSSELLE is a French academic. She teaches *sciences humaines* at the University of Perpignan and is the author of *Croire et guérir: La Foi en Gaule dans l'Antiquité tardive* (1990).

GAYLE RUBIN is an anthropologist currently in San Francisco. She has published several articles on homosexual and lesbian culture.

GUIDO RUGGIERO is Professor of History at Penn State University. He is the author of several books on the history of Renaissance Italy, including *Blinding Passions: Tales of Magic, Marriage, and Power at the End of the Renaissance* (1993).

LEOPOLD VON SACHER-MASOCH (1835–95) was an Austrian novelist whose *Venus in Furs* (1870; trans. 1928) related the development of masochistic tendencies in the protagonist.

DORION SAGAN, Lynn Margulis's son, is a biologist and co-author with her of several works on evolution and other aspects of natural science.

LONDA SCHIEBINGER is Professor of History and Women's Studies at Pennsylvania State University. She is the author of *The Mind Has No Sex? Women in the Origins of Modern Science* (1989) and *Nature's Body: Gender in the Making of Modern Science* (1993).

MARTINE SEGALEN is a researcher in the Department of Sociology, University of Paris X, Nanterre.

JOE LEIGH SIMPSON, an American physician, teaches in the Department of Obstetrics and Gynecology at the Baylor College of Medicine, Houston, Texas. He is the author of numerous articles on reproductive genetics.

CARROLL SMITH-ROSENBERG teaches at the University of Michigan. She is the author of *Religion and the Rise of the American City* (1991).

RANDY SHILTS, was a journalist for the *San Francisco Chronicle* and covered AIDS stories full-time. He was the author of *Conduct Unbecoming: Gays and Lesbians in the U.S. Military* (1993) and *The Mayor of Castro Street: The Life and Times of Harvey Milk* (1982).

BARBARA MARIA STAFFORD teaches art history at the University of Chicago. Her most recent book is *Good Looking* (1995).

LIZ STANLEY is reader in Sociology at the University of Manchester. She is the author of *Sex Surveyed* (1995).

EUGEN STEINACH (1861–1944) was an Austrian physician and director of the Biological Institute of the Academy of Sciences in Vienna. He is best known for his work on hormone research with rats.

WILHELM STEKEL (1868–1940) was a sexologist and author. He established a branch of the Scientific-Humanitarian Committee in Austria in 1906.

ROBERT J. STOLLER was Professor of Psychiatry at the University of California, Los Angeles. He was author of *Observing the Erotic Imagination*, and *Presentations of Gender* (1992).

ABRAM DE SWAAN is Professor of Sociology at the University of Amsterdam and Dean of the Graduate School for Social Sciences.

JOHN ADDINGTON SYMONDS (1840–93) was a British man of letters who wrote on art history and homosexuality, best known for his monumental seven-volume *Renaissance in Italy* (1888).

J. ARTHUR THOMSON (1861–1933) was a British biologist who taught natural history at the University of Aberdeen. He was the author of several books on evolution and general biology.

LEONORE TIEFER is Associate Professor in the Department of Urology and Psychiatry, Montefiore Medical Center, New York.

T. H. VAN DE VELDE (1873–1937) was a Dutch gynaecologist and the director of the Gynaecological Clinic at Haarlem.

JANE WADSWORTH is Senior Lecturer in Medical Statistics at St Mary's Hospital Medical School, London.

JUDITH R. WALKOWITZ is Professor of History and Director of Women's Studies at the Johns Hopkins University. She is the author of *City of Dreadful Delight: Narratives of Sexual Danger in Late-Victorian London* (1992).

SIMON WATNEY, a British art historian and author, is director of the Red Hot AIDS Charitable Trust. He is a co-founder of the Sussex branch of the Gay Liberation Front and Outrage!

JEFFREY WEEKS is Professor of Sociology and head of the School of Education, Politics, and Social Science at South Bank University, London. He is the author of *Against Nature: Essays on History, Sexuality and Identity* (1991).

H. G. WELLS (1866–1946), a British author and political philosopher, is best remembered for his futuristic 'message' novels such as *The Time Machine* (1895). His other works critique aspects of contemporary society such as rampant capitalism and the lack of women's rights.

KEVIN WHITE is the author of *The First Sexual Revolution* (1993).

LINDA WILLIAMS teaches film studies and women's studies at the University of California at Irvine. She is the author of *Hard Core: Power, Pleasure, and 'the Frenzy of the Visible'* (1990).

Source Acknowledgements

'Aristotle's Last Legacy', in Randolph Trumbach (ed.), *Marriage, Sex and the Family in England 1660-1800* (Garland Publishing: New York and London, 1986), reprinted by permission of Garland Publishing, Inc.

R. Robin Baker and Mark A.. Bellis, *Human Sperm Competition: Copulation, Masturbation and Infidelity* (Chapman & Hall: London, 1995), 22–4, copyright © 1995 R. Robin Baker and Mark A. Bellis, with kind permission from Kluwer Academic Publishers.

John W. Baldwin, *The Language of Sex: Five Voices from Northern France around 1200* (University of Chicago Press: Chicago, 1994), © 1994 by the University of Chicago, reprinted by permission of the University of Chicago Press and the author.

Georges Bataille, *Erotism: Death and Sensuality*, trans. Mary Dalwood (City Lights Books: San Fransisco, *1986*).

Lawrence Birken, *Consuming Desire: Sexual Science and the Emergence of a Culture of Abundance, 1871–1914* (Cornell University Press: Ithaca , NY, 1988), copyright © 1988 by Cornell University, used by permission of Cornell University Press.

Anne Bolin, *In Search of Eve: Transsexual Rites of Passage* (Bergin & Garvey, Inc.: South Hadley, Mass., 1988).

Alan Bray, *Homosexuality in Renaissance England* (Columbia University Press: New York, 1995), © 1995 Columbia University Press, reprinted with permission of the publisher.

Peter Brown, *The Body and Society: Men, Women and Sexual Renunciation in Early Christianity* (Columbia University Press: New York, *1988*), © 1988 Columbia University Press, reprinted with permission of the publisher.

Joan Jacobs Brumberg, ' "Something Happens to Girls": Menarche and the Emergence of the Modern American Hygienic Imperative', *Journal of the History of Sexuality*, 4 / 1, (1993), © 1993 by the University of Chicago, reprinted by permission of the University of Chicago Press and the author.

Vern L. Bullough, Dwight Dixon and Joan Dixon, 'Sadism, Masochism and History, or When is Behaviour Sado-masochistic?', in Roy Porter and Mikuas Teich (eds.), *Sexual Knowledge, Sexual Science: The History of Attitudes to Sexuality* (Cambridge University Press: Cambridge, 1994), reprinted by permission of Cambridge University Press.

William Byne, 'The Biological Evidence Challenged', *Scientific American* (May *1994*). Reprinted with permission. Copyright © 1994 by Scientific American, Inc. All rights reserved.

Joan Cadden, *Meanings of Sex Difference in the Middle Ages* (Cambridge University Press: Cambridge, 1993), reprinted by permission of Cambridge University Press and the author.

Robert Brudenell Carter, 'On the Pathology and Treatment of Hysteria', in Richard Hunter and Ida Macalpine (eds.), *The Hundred Years of Psychiatry 1535–1860: A History Presented in Selected English Texts* (Oxford University Press: London, 1963), reprinted by permission of Mrs T. M. Hunter.

George Chauncey, *Gay New York: Gender, Urban Culture, and the Making of the Gay Male World*, 1890–1940 (Basic Books: New York, 1994).

Ellen Chesler, *Woman of Valor: Margaret Sanger and the Birth Control Movement in America* (Simon & Schuster: New York, 1992), copyright © 1992 Ellen Chesler, reprinted by permission of International Creative Management, Inc.

David Cohen, *Law, Sexuality, and Society: The Enforcement of Morals in Classical Athens* (Cambridge University Press: Cambridge, 1991), reprinted by permission of Cambridge University Press and the author.

Alain Corbin, *Women for Hire: Prostitution and Sexuality in France after 1850*, trans. Alan Sheridan (Harvard University Press: Cambridge, Mass., 1990). Copyright © 1990 by the President and Fellows of Harvard College, reprinted by permission of the publisher.

Douglas Crimp, 'Randy Shilts's Miserable Failure', in Martin Duberman (ed.), *A Queer World: The Center for Lesbian and Gay Studies Reader* (New York University Press: New York, 1997), reprinted with permission of New York University Press and the author.

Pierre Darmon, *Damning the Innocent: A History of the Persecution of the Impotent in Pre-Revolutionary France*, trans. Paul Keegan (Viking: New York, 1986), copyright © 1985 by Chatto & Windus, reprinted by permission of Viking Penguin, a division of Penguin Putnam Inc., and Random House UK Limited.

Lorraine Daston and Katharine Park, 'The Hermaphrodite and the Orders of Nature: Sexual Ambiguity in Early Modern France', *GLQ*, 1/4 (1995), 420–2, 425. Copyright 1995. Reprinted by permission of Duke University Press.

Arnold I. Davidson, 'Closing up the Corpses: Diseases of Sexuality and the Emergence of the Psychiatric Style of Reasoning', in George Boolos (ed.), *Meaning and Method: Essays in Honor of Hilary Putnam* (Cambridge University Press: Cambridge, 1990), reprinted by permission of Cambridge University Press and the author.

Arnold I. Davidson, 'How to do the History of Psychoanalysis: A Reading of Freud's *Three Essays on the Theory of Sexuality*', *Critical Inquiry* (Winter 1987), reprinted by permission of the author.

John D'Emilio and Estelle B. Freedman, *Intimate Matters: A History of Sexuality in America* (Harper & Row: New York, 1988), copyright © 1976 by John d'Emilio and Estelle B. Freedman, reprinted by permission of HarperCollins Publishers, Inc.

Jacques Donzelot, *The Policing of Families*, trans. Robert Hurley (Pantheon Books: New York, 1979), originally published in French as *La police des familles* by Les Éditions de Minuit, Paris. Copyright © 1977 by Les Éditions de Minuit. Reprinted by permission of Georges Borchardt, Inc.

Alice D. Dreger, 'Hermaphrodites in Love: The Truth of the Gonads', in Vernon A. Rosario (ed.), *Science and Homosexualities* (Routledge: New York, 1997).

George Frederick Drinka, *The Birth of Neurosis: Myth, Malady, and the Victorians* (Simon & Schuster, New York, 1984), copyright © 1984 by George Frederick Drinka, reprinted by permission of Simon & Schuster.

Norbert Elias, *The History of Manners: The Civilizing Process: Volume One*, trans. Edmund Jephcott (Pantheon Books: New York, 1978), copyright 1939 by Herbert Elias, English translation © 1978 by Urizen Books, New York, reprinted by permission of Blackwell Publishers.

Havelock Ellis, *Studies in the Psychology of Sex*, i: *The Evolution of Modesty, The Phenomena of Sexual Periodicity, Auto-Erotism* (F. A. Davis Company: Philadelphia, 1919), reprinted by permission of Professor François Lafitte. The quoted extract was first published in *Sexual Inversion* (1897).

Erik H. Erikson, *Childhood and Society* (Hogarth Press), reprinted by permission of Random House UK Limited.

John Farley, *Gametes & Spores: Ideas about Sexual Reproduction, 1750–1914* (Johns Hopkins University Press: Baltimore, 1982), 189, 199–200, 207, reprinted by permission of the Johns Hopkins University Press. Copyright © 1982 by the Johns Hopkins University Press. All rights reserved.

James R. Farr, 'The Pure and Disciplined Body: Hierarchy, Morality and Symbolism in France During the Catholic Reformation', *Journal of Interdisciplinary History*, 21/3 (Winter 1991), 399, 400–1, reprinted by permission of the editors of *Journal of Interdisciplinary History* and MIT Press, Cambridge, Mass. © 1991 by the Massachusetts Institute of Technology and the editors of *Journal of Interdisciplinary History*.

Anne Fausto-Sterling, 'How to Build a Man', in Vernon A. Rosario (ed.), *Science and Homosexualities* (Routledge: New York, 1997), reprinted by permission of the author.

Michel Foucault, *The History of Sexuality*, trans. Robert Hurley (Pantheon Books, Inc.: New York, 1978), originally published in French as *La volonté de savoir* by Éditions Gallimard, reprinted by permission of Georges Borchardt, Inc. and Penguin Books Ltd.

Sigmund Freud, extracts from 'Sexuality in the Aetiology of the Neurosis' (*Collected Papers, Volume I*), 'The Most Prevalent Form of Degradation in Erotic Life' (*Collected Papers, Volume IV*), *Three Essays on the Theory of Sexuality*, and *The Sexual Enlightenment of Children*, in James Strachey (ed.), *The Standard Edition of the Complete Psychological Works of Sigmund Freud*, trans. James Strachey (London: Hogarth Press, 1975), reprinted by permission of Sigmund Freud Copyrights, The Institute of Psychoanalysis, and the Hogarth Press.

Jonas Frykman and Orvar Lofgren, *Culture Builders: A Historical Anthropology of Middle-Class Life*, trans. Alan Crozier (Rutgers University Press: New Brunswick, NJ, 1987). Copyright © 1987 by Rutgers, The State University. Reprinted by permission of Rutgers University Press.

Peter Gay, *The Bourgeois Experience: Victoria to Freud*, i: *Education of the Senses* (Oxford University Press: New York, 1984). Copyright © 1985 by Peter Gay. Used by permission of Oxford University Press, Inc.

Patrick Geddes and J. Arthur Thomson, *The Evolution of Sex* (Scribner & Welford: New York, 1890).

Margaret Gibson, 'Clitoral Corruption: Body Metaphors and America Doctors' Constructions of Female Homosexuality, 1870–1900', in Vernon A. Rosario (ed.), *Science and Homosexualities* (Routledge: New York, 1997).

John R. Gillis, *For Better, For Worse: British Marriages, 1600 to the Present* (Oxford University Press: New York, 1985). Copyright © 1985 by Oxford University Press, Inc. Used by permission of Oxford University Press, Inc.

Sander L. Gilman, *Difference and Pathology: Stereotypes of Sexuality, Race, and Madness* (Cornell University Press: Ithaca, NY, 1985), copyright ©1985 by Cornell University, used by permission of Cornell University Press.

Michael R. Gorman, 'Male Homosexual Desire: Neurological Investigations and Scientific Bias', *Perspectives in Biology and Medicine*, 38/1 (Autumn 1994), reprinted by permission of the University of Chicago Press and the author.

Linda Grant, *Sexing the Millennium: A Political History of the Sexual Revolution* (HarperCollins: London, 1993), reprinted by permission of A. P. Watt Ltd on behalf of Linda Grant.

Germaine Greer, *The Female Eunuch* (Bantam Books: New York, 1971), copyright © 1971 Germaine Greer, reprinted by permission of Gillon Aitken Associates and the author.

Atina Grossmann, *Reforming Sex: The German Movement for Birth Control and Abortion Reform, 1920–1950* (Oxford University Press: New York, 1995). Copyright © 1995 by Oxford University Press, Inc. Used by permission of Oxford University Press, Inc.

Stephen Haliczer, *Sexuality in the Confessional: A Sacrament Profaned* (Oxford University Press: New York, 1996. Copyright © 1996 by Oxford University Press, Inc.. Used by permission of Oxford University Press, Inc.

Lesley A. Hall, 'Impotent Ghosts from No-man's Land, Flappers' Boyfriends, or Cryptopatriarchs? Men, Sex and Social Change in 1920s Britain', *Social History*, 21/1 (Jan. 1996).

David M. Halperin, *One Hundred Years of Homosexuality and Other Essays on Greek Love* (Routledge: New York, 1990), copyright © 1989, reprinted by permission of Routledge, Inc.

Dean Hamer and Peter Copeland, *The Science of Desire: The Search for the Gay Gene and the Biology of Behavior* (Simon & Schuster: New York, 1994), copyright © 1994 by Dean Hamer and Peter Copeland, reprinted by permission of Simon & Schuster.

David Hamilton, *The Monkey Gland Affair* (Chatto & Windus: London, 1986), reprinted by permission of Random House UK Limited.

Bernice L. Hausman, *Changing Sex: Transsexualism, Technology, and the Idea of Gender* (Duke University Press: Durham, 1995), pp. 25–6, 62–4. Copyright 1995, Duke University Press. Reprinted with permission.

John Heidenry, *What Wild Ecstasy: The Rise and Fall of the Sexual Revolution* (Simon & Schuster: New York, 1997), copyright © 1997 by John Heidenry, reprinted by permission of Simon & Schuster and the Wallace Literary Agency Inc.

Gilbert Herdt, ' "Coming Out" as a Rite of Passage: A Chicago Study', in Gilbert Herdt (ed.), *Gay Culture in America: Essays from the Field* (Beacon Press: Boston, 1992).

David G. Horn, *Social Bodies: Science, Reproduction and Italian Modernity* (Princeton University Press: Princeton, 1994). Copyright © 1994 by Princeton University Press. Reprinted by permission of Princeton University Press.

Isabel V. Hull, *Sexuality, State, and Civil Society in Germany, 1700–1815* (Cornell University Press: Ithaca, NY, 1996), copyright © 1996 by Cornell University, used by permission of Cornell University Press.

Lynn Hunt, *The Family Romance of the French Revolution* (University of California Press: Berkeley, 1992), copyright © 1992 The Regents of the University of California, reprinted by permission of the University of California Press.

Nancy Hunt, *Mirror Image* (Holt, Rinehart, and Winston: New York, 1978).

Margaret Jackson, *The 'Real' Facts of Life: Feminism and The Politics of Sexuality c. 1850–1940* (Taylor & Francis: London, 1994).

Sheila Jeffreys, *Anticlimax: A Feminist Perspective on the Sexual Revolution* (New York University Press: New York, 1990), first published 1990 by The Women's Press Ltd., 34 Great Sutton Street, London EC1V 0DX, reprinted by permission of The Women's Press Ltd.

Anne Johnson and Jane Wadsworth, 'Heterosexual Practices', in Anne M. Johnson *et al.*, *Sexual Attitudes and Lifestyles* (Blackwell Scientific Publications: Oxford, 1994), reprinted by permission of Blackwell Science Ltd. and Peters, Fraser & Dunlop on behalf of the authors.

James H. Jones, *Alfred C. Kinsey: A Public/Private Life* (W. W. Norton & Co.: New York,

1997). Copyright © 1997 by James H. Jones. Reprinted by permission of W. W. Norton & Company, Inc.

Ludmilla Jordanova, *Sexual Visions: Images of Gender in Science and Medicine between the Eighteenth and Twentieth Centuries* (University of Wisconsin Press: Madison, 1989), copyright © 1989, reprinted by permission of the University of Wisconsin Press, Prentice-Hall Europe, and the author.

Christine Jorgensen, *A Personal Autobiography* (Paul S. Eriksson, Inc.: New York, 1967), reprinted by permission of Paul S. Eriksson, Publisher.

Ruth Mazo Karras, *Common Women: Prostitution and Sexuality in Medieval England* (Oxford University Press: Oxford, 1996). Copyright © 1996 by Oxford University Press, Inc. Used by permission of Oxford University Press, Inc.

Jonathan Ned Katz, 'The Age of Sodomitical Sin, 1607–1740', condensed from an essay of that name published in his book *Gay/Lesbian Almanac: A New Documentary* (New York: Harper & Row, 1983), 23–65, copyright © 1983 Jonathan Ned Katz, reprinted by permission of the author.

Jonathan Ned Katz, *The Invention of Heterosexuality* (Dutton Books, 1995), copyright © 1995 by Jonathan Ned Katz, reprinted by permission of Dutton, a division of Penguin Putnam Inc.

Elizabeth Lapovsky Kennedy and Madeline D. Davis, *Boots of Leather, Slippers of Gold: The History of a Lesbian Community* (New York: Routledge, Chapman and Hall, 1993), copyright © 1993, reprinted by permission of Routledge, Inc.

Stephen Kern, *The Culture of Love: Victorians to Moderns* (Harvard University Press: Cambridge, Mass., 1992). Copyright © 1992 by the President and Fellows of Harvard College, reprinted by permission of the publisher.

Helen King, 'Sowing the Field: Greek and Roman Sexology', in Roy Porter and Mikulas Teich (eds.), *Sexual Knowledge, Sexual Science: The History of Attitudes to Sexuality* (Cambridge University Press: Cambridge, 1994), reprinted by permission of Cambridge University Press.

Alfred C. Kinsey *et al.*, *Sexual Behavior in the Human Male* (W. B. Saunders Company: Philadelphia, 1948), reprinted by permission of W. B. Saunders Company.

Richard von Krafft-Ebing, *Psychopathia Sexualis. With Especial Reference to the Antipathic Sexual Instinct*, translated by Franklin S. Klaf (Stein and Day: New York, 1965).

Madame de Lafayette, *The Princess of Cleves*, translated by Nancy Mitford (New Directions Press: Binghamton, NY, 1951). Copyright © 1951 by New Directions Publishing Corp., reprinted by permission of New Directions Publishing Corp.

Edward O. Laumann, John H. Gagnon, *et al.*, *The Social Organization of Sexuality: Sexual Practices in the United States* (University of Chicago Press: Chicago, 1994). © 1994 by Edward O. Laumann, Robert T. Michael, CSG Enterprises, Inc., and Stuart Michaels, reprinted by permission of the University of Chicago Press and Edward Laumann.

Gwendolyn Leick, 'Inanna Rejoicing in Her Vulva', in *Sex and Eroticism in Mesopotamian Literature* (Routledge: London and New York, 1994), reprinted by permission of Routledge.

Simon LeVay, *The Sexual Brain* (MIT Press: Cambridge Mass., 1993), copyright © 1993 Massachusetts Institute of Technology, reprinted by permission of MIT Press.

Martin P. Levine, 'The Life and Death of Gay Clones', in Gilbert Herdt (ed.), *Gay Culture in America: Essays from the Field* (Beacon Press: Boston, 1992).

Christopher Looby, ' "The Roots of the Orchis, the Iuli of Chestnuts": The Odor of Male

Solitude', in Paula Bennett and Vernon A. Rosario II (eds.), *Solitary Pleasures: The Historical, Literary, and Artistic Discourses of Autoeroticism* (Routledge: New York, 1995), copyright © 1995, reprinted by permission of Routledge, Inc.

Angus McLaren, *A History of Contraception: From Antiquity to the Present Day* (Basil Blackwell: Oxford, 1990), reprinted by permission of Blackwell Publishers.

Angus McLaren, *The Trials of Masculinity: Policing Sexual Boundaries, 1870-1930* (University of Chicago Press: Chicago, *1997*). © 1997 by the University of Chicago, reprinted by permission of the University of Chicago Press and the author.

Anne McClintock, 'Gonad the Barbarian and the Venus Flytrap: Portraying the Female and Male Orgasm', in Lynne Segal and Mary McIntosh (eds.), *Sex Exposed: Sexuality and the Pornography Debate* (Virago Press: London, 1992), reprinted by permission of Virago Press.

Herbert Marcuse, *Eros and Civilization: A Philosophical Inquiry into Freud* (Vintage Books: New York, 1955).

Lynn Margulis and Dorion Sagan, *Origins of Sex: Three Billion Years of Genetic Recombination* (Yale University Press: New Haven, 1986). Copyright © 1986 by Lynn Margulis and Dorion Sagan, reprinted by permission of Yale University Press.

Michael Mason, *The Making of Victorian Sexuality* (Oxford University Press: New York, 1994), reprinted by permission of Oxford University Press.

William H. Masters and Virginia E. Johnson, *Human Sexual Response* (Little, Brown & Co.: Boston, 1966), reprinted by permission of Lippincott-Raven Publishers.

Jann Matlock, *Scenes of Seduction: Prostitution, Hysteria, and Reading Difference in Nineteenth-Century France* (Columbia University Press: New York, 1994), © 1994 Columbia University Press, reprinted with permission of the publisher.

John Maynard, *Victorian Discourses on Sexuality and Religion* (Cambridge University Press: Cambridge, 1993), reprinted by permission of Cambridge University Press and the author.

Mark S. Micale, *Approaching Hysteria: Disease and Its Interpretations* (Princeton University Press: Princeton, 1995). Copyright © 1995 by Princeton University Press. Reprinted by permission of Princeton University Press.

Michael Moffatt, *Coming of Age in New Jersey: College and American Culture* (Rutgers University Press: New Brunswick, NJ, 1989). Copyright © 1989 by Rutgers, The State University. Reprinted by permission of Rutgers University Press.

Albert Moll, *Perversions of the Sex Instinct: A Study of Sexual Inversion Based on Clinical Data and Official Documents*, translated by Maurice Popkin (Julian Press, Newark, NJ, 1931).

John Money, *Sex Errors of the Body: Dilemmas, Education, Counseling* (Johns Hopkins Press: Baltimore, 1968), 11–12, 85–6. Copyright © 1968 by The Johns Hopkins Press, Baltimore, reprinted by permission of The Johns Hopkins University Press.

Dominic Montserrat, 'Festivals of Licence' in *Sex and Society in Graeco-Roman Egypt* (Kegan Paul International: London and New York, 1996), reprinted by permission of Kegan Paul International.

Frank Mort, *Dangerous Sexualities: Medico-moral Politics in England since 1830* (Routledge & Kegan Paul: London and New York, 1987), reprinted by permission of Routledge.

Lynda Nead, *Myths of Sexuality: Representations of Women in Victorian Britain* (Basil Blackwell: Oxford, 1988), reprinted by permission of Blackwell Publishers.

Richard Neville, *Hippie Hippie Shake: The Dreams, the Trips, the Trials, the Love-ins, the Screw Ups... The Sixties* (Bloomsbury: London, 1995).

David F. Noble, *A World Without Women: The Christian Clerical Culture of Western Science* (New York: Alfred A. Knopf, 1992), copyright © 1992 by David F. Noble, reprinted by permission of Alfred A. Knopf, Inc.

Robert A. Nye, *Masculinity and Male Codes of Honor in Modern France* (Oxford University Press: New York, 1993). Copyright © 1993 by Oxford University Press, Inc. Used by permission of Oxford University Press, Inc.

Robert A. Nye, 'The Medical Origins of Sexual Fetishism', in Emily Apter and William Pietz (eds.), *Fetishism as Cultural Discourse* (Cornell University Press: Ithaca, NY, 1993), copyright 1993 by Cornell University, used by permission of Cornell University Press.

Nelly Oudshoorn, *Beyond the Natural Body: An Archeology of Sex Hormones* (Routledge: New York, 1994), reprinted by permission of Routledge.

Christabel Pankhurst, *The Great Scourge and How to End It*, in Marie M. Roberts and Tamae Mizuta (eds.), *The Campaigners: Women and Sexuality* (Routledge / Thoemmes Press: London, 1994).

Carole Pateman, *The Sexual Contract* (Stanford University Press: Stanford, CA, 1988). Copyright © 1988 Carole Pateman, reprinted by permission of the Stanford University Press and Polity Press (Blackwell Publishers).

Pierre J. Payer, *The Bridling of Desire: Views of Sex in the Later Middle Ages* (University of Toronto Press: Toronto, 1993), reprinted by permission of University of Toronto Press.

Daniel Pick, *Faces of Degeneration: A European Disorder, c.1848–c.1918* (Cambridge University Press: Cambridge, *1989*), reprinted by permission of Cambridge University Press and the author.

Plato, 'The Speech of Pausanias' in *Symposium*, translated by Alexander Nehamas and Paul Woodruff (Hackett: Indianapolis, 1989), reprinted by permission of Hackett Publishing Co. All rights reserved.

Uta Ranke-Heinemann, 'Non-Christian Roots of Christian Sexual Pessimism', in *Eunuchs for the Kingdom of Heaven*, translated by Peter Heinegg (Doubleday: New York, 1990). Copyright © 1990 by Doubleday, a division of Bantam Doubleday Dell Publishing Group, Inc. Used by permission of Doubleday, a division of Bantam Doubleday Dell Publishing Group, Inc. Originally published as *Eunuchen für das Himmelreich*, Katholische Kirche und Sexualität, copyright ©1998 by Hoffmann und Campe Verlag, Hamburg, used by permission of Hoffmann und Campe, Hamburg.

Matt Ridley, *The Red Queen: Sex and the Evolution of Human Nature* (Penguin: Harmondsworth: 1993), copyright © Matt Ridley 1993, reproduced by permission of Felicity Bryan and the author.

Mary Louise Roberts, *Civilization without Sexes: Reconstructing Gender in Postwar France, 1917–1927* (University of Chicago Press: Chicago, 1994). © 1994 by the University of Chicago, reprinted by permission of the University of Chicago Press and the author.

Paul Robinson, *The Modernization of Sex* (Harper & Row: New York, 1976), copyright © 1976 by Paul Robinson, reprinted by permission of HarperCollins Publishers, Inc.

Lyndal Roper, *The Holy Household: Women and Morals, in Reformation Augsburg* (Clarendon: Oxford, 1989), reprinted by permission of Oxford University Press.

Vernon A. Rosario, *The Erotic Imagination: French Histories of Perversity* (Oxford

University Press: New York, 1997). Copyright © 1997 by Vernon Rosario. Used by permission of Oxford University Press, Inc.

Gabriel Rotello, *Sexual Ecology: AIDS and the Destinies of Gay Men* (Dutton: New York, 1997), copyright © 1997 Gabriel Rotello, reprinted by permission of Dutton, a division of Penguin Putnam Inc.

Jean-Jacques Rousseau, *The Confessions*, translated by J. M. Cohen (Penguin Books: Baltimore, 1954), reprinted by permission of Penguin Books Ltd.

Aline Rousselle, *Porneia: On Desire and the Body in Antiquity*, translated by Felicia Pleasant (Basil Blackwell: Oxford, 1988), copyright Basil Blackwell Ltd, 1988, reprinted by permission of Blackwell Publishers.

Gayle Rubin, 'Thinking Sex: Notes for a Radical Theory of the Politics of Sexuality', in Carole S. Vance (ed.), *Pleasure and Danger: Exploring Female Sexuality* (Routledge & Kegan Paul: Boston, 1984), reprinted by permission of Rivers Oram Press, London (Pandora).

Guido Ruggiero, *The Boundaries of Eros: Sex Crime and Sexuality in Renaissance Venice* (Oxford University Press: New York, 1985). Copyright © 1985 by Oxford University Press, Inc. Used by permission of Oxford University Press, Inc.

Leopold von Sacher-Masoch, 'Choses Vecues', in Gilles Deleuze, *Masochism*, translated by Jean McNeill (Zone Books: New York, 1989), reprinted by permission of Zone Books.

Londa Schiebinger, 'Skeletons in the Closet: The First Illustrations of the Female Skeleton in Eighteenth-Century Anatomy', in Catherine Gallagher and Thomas Laqueur (eds.), *The Making of the Modern Body: Sexuality and Society in the Nineteenth Century* (University of California Press: Berkeley, 1987), copyright © 1986 The Regents of the University of California, reprinted by permission of the University of California Press.

Martine Segalen, *Love and Power in the Peasant Family: Rural France in the Nineteenth Century*, translated Sarah Matthews (University of Chicago Press: Chicago, 1983). © 1983 by Basil Blackwell Publisher and the University of Chicago, reprinted by permission of the University of Chicago Press and the author.

Randy Shilts, *And the Band Played On: Politics, People, and the AIDS Epidemic* (Penguin: Harmondsworth, 1988). Copyright © 1987, 1988 by Randy Shilts, reprinted by permission of Penguin Books Ltd. and St. Martin's Press, Inc.

Joe Leigh Simpson, *Disorders of Sexual Differentiation: Etiology and Clinical Delineation* (Academic Press: New York, 1976), reprinted by permission of Academic Press.

Carroll Smith-Rosenberg, *Disorderly Conduct: Visions of Gender in Victorian America* (Oxford University Press: New York, 1986), copyright © 1985 by Carroll Smith-Rosenberg, reprinted by permission of Alfred A. Knopf, Inc.

Barbara Maria Stafford, *Body Criticism: Imaging the Unseen in Enlightenment Art and Medicine* (MIT Press, 1993), reprinted by permission of MIT Press.

Liz Stanley, 'Mass-Observation's "Little Kinsey" and the British Sex Survey Tradition', in Jeffrey Weeks and Janet Holland (eds.), *Sexual Cultures: Communities, Values and Intimacy* (Macmillan, 1996), copyright © British Sociological Association 1996, reprinted by permission of Macmillan Ltd.

Eugen Steinach, *Sex and Life: Forty Years of Biological and Medical Experiments* (Viking Press: New York, 1940).

Wilhelm Stekel, *Sexual Aberrations: The Phenomena of Fetishism in Relation to Sex*, translated by S. Parker (Liveright Publishing: New York, 1952), reprinted by permission of

Liveright Publishing Corporation. Copyright 1930 by Horace Liveright, Inc., renewed © 1958 by Liveright Publishing Corporation.

Robert J. Stoller, *Porn: Myths for the Twentieth Century* (Yale University Press: New Haven, 1991). Copyright © 1991 by Yale University, reprinted by permission of Yale University Press.

Abram de Swaan, *The Management of Normality: Critical Essays in Health and Welfare* (Routledge: London, 1990), reprinted by permission of Routledge.

John Addington Symonds, *The Memoirs of John Addington Symonds*, edited by Phyllis Grosskurth (University of Chicago Press: Chicago, 1984), copyright © 1984 by The London Library. Reprinted by permission of Random House and Random House UK Limited (Hutchinson).

Leonore Tiefer, *Sex is Not a Natural Act and Other Essays* (Westview Press: Boulder, Colo., 1995).

Theo van der Meer, 'Sodomy and the Pursuit of a Third Sex in the Early Modern Period', in Gilbert Herdt (ed.), *Third Sex, Third Gender: Beyond Sexual Dimorphism in Culture and History* (Zone Books: New York, 1994), reprinted by permission of Zone Books.

T. H. van der Velde, *Ideal Marriage: Its Physiology and Technique*, translated Stella Browne (Random House: New York, 1930), copyright 1930, 1965 and renewed 1957, 1993 by Random House, Inc. and William Heinemann Ltd. Reprinted by permission of Random House, Inc.

Judith R. Walkowitz, *Prostitution and Victorian Society: Women, Class, and the State* (Cambridge University Press: Cambridge, 1980), reprinted by permission of Cambridge University Press and the author.

Simon Watney, *Policing Desire: Pornography, AIDS and the Media* (University of Minnesota Press: Minneapolis, 1987). Copyright © 1987 by Simon Watney, reprinted by permission of University of Minnesota Press and Cassell, Wellington House, 125 Strand, London, England WC2R OBB.

Jeffrey Weeks, *Coming Out: Homosexual Politics in Britain from the Nineteenth Century to the Present* (Quartet Books: London, 1990), reprinted by permission of Quartet Books Ltd.

Jeffrey Weeks, *Sex, Politics and Society: The Regulation of Sexuality since 1800* (Longman: London, 1989), reprinted by permission of Addison Wesley Longman Ltd.

H. G. Wells, *Experiment in Autobiography: Discoveries and Conclusions of a Very Ordinary Brain (Since 1866)* (Macmillan: New York, 1934), reprinted by permission of A. P. Watt Ltd on behalf of the Literary Executors of the Estate of H. G. Wells.

H. G. Wells, *H. G. Wells in Love: Postscript to An Experiment in Autobiography* (Little, Brown, & Co.: Boston, 1984) reprinted by permission of A. P. Watt Ltd on behalf of the Literary Executors of the Estate of H. G. Wells.

Kevin White, *The First Sexual Revolution: The Emergence of Male Heterosexuality in Modern America* (New York University Press: New York, 1993), reprinted by permission of New York University Press and the author.

Linda Williams, 'Pornographies on/scene, or Diff'rent Strokes for Diff'rent Folks', in Lynne Segal & Mary McIntosh (eds.), *Sex Exposed: Sexuality and the Pornography Debate* (Virago Press: London, 1992), reprinted by permission of Virago Press.

Index